A NEW RACE OF MEN

A NEW RACE OF MEN

Scotland 1815–1914

Michael Fry

BIRLINN

First published in 2013 by
Birlinn Limited
West Newington House
10 Newington Road
Edinburgh
EH9 1QS

www.birlinn.co.uk

ISBN: 978 1 78027 142 2

The publishers acknowledge investment from Creative Scotland towards the
publication of this volume

British Library Cataloguing-in-Publication Data
A catalogue record for this book is available from the British Library

Typeset by Initial Typesetting Services, Edinburgh
Printed and bound by Gutenberg Press, Malta

Contents

List of Illustrations

Colour plates

Charlotte Square, Edinburgh, by Robert Adam.

Gilmorehill Campus, Glasgow University.

The Rev. Robert Walker, by Sir Henry Raeburn.

Princes Street, Edinburgh, by Alexander Nasmyth.

Loch Ness, by Alexander Nasmyth.

Pitlessie Fair, by Sir David Wilkie.

Home and the Homeless, by Thomas Faed.

The Thin Red Line, by Robert Gibb.

Dinner at Haddo House, by Alfred Edward Emslie.

The Tennis Party, by Sir John Lavery.

A Hind's Daughter, by Sir James Guthrie.

Les Eus, by J.D. Fergusson.

Foreword

In this book I seek to cast my net wider than is usual in Scottish historiography for the period 1815–1914. In particular, I put the nation's culture, indeed high culture, on a par with the mechanised agriculture, steel production, housing problems and other such matters that form the normal pabulum for academic historians of Scotland.

One reason is a desire for completeness that I hope can be nothing but commendable. A second reason is that the traditional dominance of socio-economic material in Scottish historiography is today doing the nation a disservice. In socio-economic terms, our modern history has been a history of steady assimilation to a greater British entity. And in those terms, Scotland has indeed become a region of a larger economy and society. In fact, today the statistical differences within England among its regions (say, between the north-east and the south-east) are greater than the differences between Scotland as a whole and England as a whole. If a man from Mars came down and looked just at the statistics, he would conclude the Union of 1707 was today reaching a triumphant conclusion in at last making one country out of two countries.

The reality is, of course, different. Within eighteen months or so of my writing these words, Scotland may become an independent nation once again. For nearly half a century now the two partners in the Union of 1707 have, not in their economy and in society but in their politics and culture, been drifting apart. In these latter respects their unity is no longer at all obvious and has rather to be desperately asserted by unionists. Where does this growing difference originate? Is it merely the factitious product of modern political disillusion, or is there some deeper connection with the Scottish past that we can trace back through the nineteenth century and beyond? At any rate the drift apart seems unlikely to come to an early halt, whatever may happen at the referendum in 2014.

In the end, this process must also affect Scottish historiography, sluggish as it has in the past been in responding to fresh trends. It will need to stop concentrating on what makes Scotland the same as England, or taking England as the point of reference against which any Scottish deviation has to be explained. It will need instead to start concentrating on what makes Scotland different, on what makes Scotland Scotland, and on what has assured the extraordinary survival of this nation through the three centuries of its Union with another nation. In other words, the traditional historiographical supremacy of socio-economic topics will need to yield to the study on at least an equal basis of politics and culture. This will be all to the good in a second sense, because it will encourage the study of human beings rather than of statistics. The present work is intended to make a start in that direction.

It is a book I owe above all to my publisher, Hugh Andrew of Birlinn, who first suggested it and doggedly kept reminding me of it when I allowed myself to be diverted by other projects. A word of thanks is due also to Catriona Macdonald, whose own excellent study of Scotland in the twentieth century, *Whaur Extremes Meet*, prompted me to resume my own work when I had let it lie too long; in part I was then able to conceive of my book as a parallel to hers and in the notes below I have, where possible, made appropriate references. I should like to dedicate the result of my labours to the memory of the philosopher George Elder Davie. Having in his own life often assailed the forces of academic conformism, he always encouraged me to do battle with them too. His intellectual legacy will give us all food for thought for a long time to come. At the very least it must inspire us to come ever and again with open minds to the matter of Scotland.

Edinburgh, March 2013

Prologue: 'Scotland for ever'

The Battle of Waterloo was fought over two low ridges running athwart the high road which led up from the French frontier towards Brussels, about 15 miles further off. The British and their allies held the more northerly of the ridges, while the French attacked from the more southerly of them. In between, but to the west of the high road, lay the chateau and estate of Hougoumont. Here was one of the places where Scots soldiers won glory on 18 June 1815.[1]

Hours before either side opened fire that day, the British commander, Arthur Wellesley, Duke of Wellington, and the Emperor of the French, Napoleon Bonaparte, had both identified Hougoumont as a key to their coming clash. If the chateau should be left unguarded, Napoleon's legions might move along the shallow depression between the two ridges and round the flank of the allied position. This would then become indefensible. So Wellington had not just to occupy Hougoumont but also to find for its defence a force steadfast enough to hold out against the relentless assaults sure to be launched on it. He chose Scots for the task. In command of the chateau he placed Colonel James MacDonell of Glengarry, sprung from a fierce race of Highland warriors who had never surrendered to anybody. To him were assigned the Scots Guards and the Coldstream Guards, the latter Englishmen as like to Scotsmen as any ever could be, coming as they did from the lower valley of the River Tweed where it formed the border between the two nations.[2]

While the rest of the allied army snatched a little sleep during the night before the battle, these troops went to work under a heavy downpour of rain to fortify Hougoumont. They hacked loopholes through its walls. They erected firing platforms inside them. They blocked every passage between the buildings round the courtyard except for the main gate on the northern side, which they kept open for supplies and communications. In the nearby orchards and woods they felled trees to clear firing lines, then built the timber into their breastworks. Some of these men themselves came under fire, so close did their labours take them to the enemy's forward positions. Early in the morning Wellington rode out to inspect the preparations with one of his officers, who said the place still looked to him untenable. The duke replied: 'Ah, but you do not know MacDonell.'[3]

About half an hour later the French bombardment of Hougoumont began. It was not long before the assault followed, never slackening despite the fire MacDonell's men kept up in reply. They started to suffer casualties and soon all hands were summoned to the defence. While wounded men crawled into barns, sheds and cellars, their officers dismounted, sheathed their swords and picked up the rifles dropped by the casualties. Skulking through the clouds of gunsmoke, the French managed to surround the chateau and penetrate the grounds, orchard and garden. They reached the northern side of the court-yard where the gate stood open. The men guarding it were taken by surprise, exchanged shots but pulled back inside. About 100 Frenchmen pursued them. Was Hougoumont about to fall?

At this point MacDonell was directing the defence of the garden. He heard triumphant cries in French from behind him, where none of the enemy should have been. He rushed back into the courtyard and found men fighting with whatever came to hand, rifle butts, swords, axes. Some Scots had retreated up the steps to hold the door of the chateau while others were firing down from the windows. MacDonell shouted to three of his officers and a sergeant to follow him and force their way to the gate. The five of them put their shoulders to it and pushed it shut against Frenchmen still trying to enter; the sergeant dropped the stout wooden bar that locked it. They heaped up flagstones and debris to make it secure. Now the defenders could hunt down the enemy within, till just one remained alive or unwounded, a drummer boy who had lost his drum. Hougoumont was saved. 'The success of the Battle of Waterloo depended on the closing of the gates,' Wellington later wrote.[4]

The fighting at Hougoumont went on for an hour and a half before anything happened across the rest of the battlefield. To the east, next to the high road to Brussels, amid the fields and hedgerows of the undulating farmland, stood a concentration of Scottish regiments, the Cameron Highlanders, Black Watch, Gordons and Royal Scots. With them was a force of cavalry, 1,200 men of the Union Brigade, so called because it contained one regiment from each of the three kingdoms of the British Isles, Scots Greys, Inniskillings and Royal Dragoons. This position could not be outflanked so long as

Hougoumont was held, so the French had to make a frontal assault on it. They softened it up with another bombardment. They prepared to deploy over terrain that right in front of them seemed undefended, for the Scottish regiments had taken what shelter they could from the barrage. Now the Scots were ordered up to a hedgerow. When they peered through, they saw the enemy's front rank 40 paces away. The order was given to fire, and 3,000 muskets spat out a volley. 'Charge! Charge! Hurrah!' bawled the officers. The soldiers scrambled through the hedge and got to work with their bayonets on the French, who fell back in confusion.[5]

Behind the line of battle the Scots Greys were waiting, mounted on a double rank of their huge horses so close to one another that the stirrups touched. The command came, 'Scots Greys, charge!' They rode at the hedge and cleared it. Everybody cheered. Down the slope of the ridge they galloped, the horses with heads lowered, picking up speed and tearing the earth with their hooves: the immortal scene depicted in the painting *Scotland Forever* by Lady Butler. And 'Scotland for ever!' was what the cavalry shouted as they headed into the smoke and din before them, where they could hear the bagpipes and make out the Highlanders' feathered bonnets. Officers of the infantry sought to wheel troops back by sections to let the horsemen through, but too late. Foot soldiers were knocked over and trodden underfoot. Even so their mates shouted, 'Go at them the Greys!' And again, 'Scotland for ever!' Some tried to grasp the stirrups and run with the horses, to get in among the crumbling French formations. Soon the enemy were throwing down their weapons, crying out for quarter.

Charles Ewart was an ensign of the Greys. A giant of a man and an expert swordsman, he now had in his eye the glint of a berserker as he slashed his way towards half a dozen Frenchmen defending a standard with a golden eagle on top. It was the standard of the 45th Invincibles, on which Napoleon's victories of Austerlitz and Jena stood inscribed. Ewart recalled: 'One made a thrust at my groin. I parried it off and cut him down through the head. A lancer came at me. I threw the lance off by my right side and cut him through the chin and upwards through the teeth. Next, a foot-soldier fired at me and then charged me with his bayonet, which I also had the good luck to parry, and then I cut him down through the head.' Ewart seized the standard. An officer behind him said, 'My brave fellow, take that to the rear.' And off the field Ensign Ewart rode in triumph. His eagle remains on display in Edinburgh Castle, and his name is still remembered in Scotland.[6]

Scenes like these offer mere details of the vast canvas of Waterloo. But they helped to fix an image of Scotland and Scotsmen that endured right through the nineteenth century and beyond – indeed, it has not faded yet. This martial image was at bottom perhaps one of the noble savage whose qualities had been harnessed to causes greater than the feuds of earlier ages. Placed at the service of Union and Empire, those qualities emerged in renewed strength or even purity. This image of Scotland and Scotsmen endured not only by over-awing others but also by proving useful to themselves, inspiring them at home or advertising their qualities to the world. The nation had been changing ever since the Union of 1707, of course, but during the nineteenth century the rate of change would unmistakably speed up. Earlier it had seemed on the whole a benign process, hallowed alike by religion and philosophy: anyway one purpose of the Union had been to generate change. Even war failed to halt such salutary progress. More and more Scots were doing more and more things to their own and their nation's profit, just as the architects of the Union had hoped. But they did so increasingly in a Scotland that would have appeared unrecognisable to former generations, where by the year old ways were erased and new ways were impressed on the nation. Could anything worthy of being called Scottish survive all this?

The nature of the nation started coming under open question as soon as its tremendous martial exertions shuddered to a halt in 1815. With the peace, economic differences and social problems earlier taken for granted suddenly appeared intolerable. The body politic, by and large quiescent ever since the last Jacobite rebellion of 1745, jerked into spasm. Strident voices called for reform, and radical reform at that. The first response from the ruling class was often panic and repression. Yet some also felt their way towards a more positive response. They decided the task of leadership lay in looking to the character of the people and to the mutual obligations within their society: this was how to deal with the radicals.

For example, after the Scots' triumph in a long struggle all could pride themselves on the values of their nation's past. These were, or were supposed to be, values of morality and order, of religion and patriotism. They had been fostered by the close-knit communities of a small country preserving their character through centuries of strife and change, latterly to be cherished by enlightened philosophers as well as by the common people: perhaps those values might be applied to the challenges of the future as well. All the same, they had been fashioned in an agrarian, pre-industrial society, which Scotland was ceasing to be. The hopes placed in them would be contested, therefore, because they did not take full account of newer Scottish realities.

PART I
ECONOMY

1

Agriculture: 'Fare ye well ye barnyards'

The hopes of 1815 were not always fulfilled even for the heroes, the troops who came back from fighting the French. Some old soldiers would for years ahead enthral their families, friends and neighbours with tales of derring-do in faraway places, yet there were others for whom no such honourable retirement to the domestic hearth lay in store. Among the units returning from abroad was the 93rd Regiment of Foot, the Sutherland Highlanders: spirit of the clans made flesh. At its embodiment in 1799 by Elizabeth, Countess of Sutherland, it had been wholly Gaelic-speaking but for three men. It was not, in fact, present at Waterloo. Since 1806 it had served in faraway corners of the Empire. It went out in that year as part of an expeditionary force to seize the Cape of Good Hope from the Dutch and secure the vital sea lanes to India. In 1814 the regiment transferred to America and tasted defeat for the first time at the Battle of New Orleans against the raw recruits of the United States under General Andrew Jackson. Soldiers tend to take these things as they come, however, and the Gaels' pride in their regiment never dimmed. More dispiriting was what awaited those who at length got home.[1]

Their native county was in the throes of a huge programme of economic improvement undertaken by the Countess of Sutherland and her English husband, the Marquis of Stafford. Clearance is the term usually applied to the programme, though its accuracy is questionable. One aim was, after all, to maintain or even increase the population of the county, and for some decades that happened: it continued to rise, if at a modest rate, to a peak of 25,000 in 1861. The counterpart was destruction of the traditional way of life by which the people had eked out a precarious existence on tiny plots of land in the interior glens. Instead, those glens were to be emptied of people and filled with sheep, in order to supply wool and meat to Britain's industrial regions. The people would meanwhile be moved to new homes prepared for them round the coast of Sutherland, where they could take to modern occupations provided under the noble couple's investments. The plan appeared rational, not to say philanthropic, by the standards of the time. In the long run it failed, though hardly for want of exertion on the part of its authors. The result was a wilderness. Still, only in practice could progressive ideas for the Highlands have been tested: no subsequent planning regime in the region has found a better procedure (or greater success). What the final frustration exposed was the personal suffering of the people who had had their world turned upside down, and all for nothing in the end.[2]

❦

The worst incidents in the improvement of Sutherland are linked with the name of Patrick Sellar. He was a sharp-set solicitor from Elgin who took a lease of Strathnaver, right in the middle of the countess's estate, on land running down from the mountains and moors to the northernmost coast of Scotland. The noble couple employed his services to execute one part of their plan in detail by turning the strath over from outworn uses to fresh ones, from peasant tillage to pastoral husbandry. For that he had to remove the population surplus to requirements.[3]

A year almost to the day before the Battle of Waterloo, on 13 June 1814, Sellar had led parties of men to enforce notices of eviction previously served on the people of the strath's townships and telling them to leave by Whitsunday, early in May. Given notice well in advance, they could reflect on what must come, prepare their minds and pack their possessions. Often, to stress the moral as well as the legal rectitude of the proceeding, a minister of the Church of Scotland would go round when the notices were read out in English to threaten the people with hellfire in Gaelic, should they show any disobedience. They were not just being thrown out: a few miles away new homes stood ready for them. All the same, many stayed on to the last moment in inertia or anxiety at what awaited them in the settlement by the sea, a planned village at the mouth of the River Naver named, after the countess, Bettyhill. Now their time was up.[4]

On that Monday morning in the summer of 1814, the men under Sellar moved against people defenceless in law and in fact. From each house they harshly ordered the family out. Any slow to gather their goods could find the roof going up in flames above them, for nothing was to be left here that might permit continued human habitation. Sellar felt especially keen to deal with one William Chisholm, 'a tinker who had taken possession of an extremely wild piece of land in a morass among the mountains, and was accused by the tenantry of bigamy, theft and riotous conduct, and was put down in my instructions as a person to be expelled from the estate'. Sellar later claimed the people supported the chastisement of this unsavoury character, helping to unroof his house and demolish it. Anyway, when the evictors arrived they found nobody but his bedridden mother-in-law, Margaret Mackay, about 100 years of age. Her daughter came up and protested she was too sick to be moved. By one report, Sellar replied: 'Damn her, the old witch. She has lived too long. Let her burn!'

Sellar laid faggots against the timbers of the house himself. As the flames took hold, the old lady was pulled out just in time, her blanket already smouldering. 'God receive my soul! What fire is this about me?' she cried, perhaps imagining that it was the moment of her passing and that she had been damned. Neighbours carried her to a shed, and barely managed to stop this being burned too. She died within five days.

There was yet less excuse for the treatment of Donald MacBeth, who lay on his deathbed, stricken with cancer, in a house nearby. His son had had to go off to another relation's funeral, and appealed for his father to be left in peace till his return. When young MacBeth got back he found just the stones of his house with the sick man lying among them; he too died soon afterwards. Every other native of Strathnaver had vanished, and it remains more or less empty of human inhabitants to this day.[5]

News of these events took time to get out of the county, too slowly to save hapless peasants with few means of articulating their torment. Some sent a pathetic appeal to the Prince Regent in London, but in those days the government, long run by Tories, did not think to interfere with private property, even with misuse of it. While a rising tide of censure was at length to distress the countess herself, she also found support among Scots who shared the radical chic of her outlook. The *Edinburgh Review*, for example, prided itself on being the most progressive organ in Scotland and Britain, if not Europe and the world. It had made its mark since its launch in 1802 as the first of the many reviews that would become a hallmark of Victorian culture, forums where the nineteenth century worked over its worries, not just literary but also scientific, social, political and economic. It was an ancestor of today's quality journalism, clever, irreverent, probing. Its writers vaunted themselves as intellectuals of capitalism, Whigs to a man, and they laughed at the soppy Scots Tories' sentimental scruples about the welfare of rustics.[6]

The *Edinburgh Review* often employed bright young fellows and gave them their start in a public career. One was James Loch, a devilling advocate who made himself the resident expert on the land of Scotland – how to exploit it, how to improve it, how to reform the law and practices governing its use. A devotee of political economy too, he did not think the land any business of the state. The land had its proper place in commercial society 'whose arrangement is only to be preserved by allowing free scope to the master principle of individual interest'.[7] What Loch found to say might rather be of value to a noble family with a lot of land, wondering what to do with it. Here was where the Countess of Sutherland and the Marquis of Stafford came in.

Loch met the noble couple at a dinner-party. He made such an impression on them that they appointed him their commissioner in the county of Sutherland, charged with drawing up a blueprint for its development. In this capacity he was Sellar's superior. He took against the gauche, tense, overeager little solicitor and may have been instrumental in getting him sacked for his actions in Strathnaver, among other failings. Though history has blamed Sellar for what went wrong with the improvement of Sutherland, the project was, in fact, far more Loch's than anybody else's – though of course the countess, or in particular her husband, provided all the money.[8]

The consequences can be seen to this day. The interior of Sutherland remains bare but fishing villages constructed at Golspie, Helmsdale and Portgower, and over on the Atlantic coast at Lochinver, are there yet. The head burgh of Dornoch is still the handsome stone-built place that replaced the previous miserable cluster of huts. Brora almost had the makings of an industrial town, with coal-mine, brickworks, tile-works, limekiln, saltpans, harbour, not to speak of a horse-drawn railway and a distillery at nearby Clynelish – this, at least, producing even now a fine malt whisky. Such testimonies to the master plan should remind us once again that the purpose was never to empty the county, just to move its people over the 500 miles of road and 134 bridges newly built, by no more than about 20 miles at worst, to render them productive rather than unproductive. Everything came to grief, all the same. The improvement flagged. The sacrifices had been in vain.[9]

That was to make the memory all the more bitter for, in a final twist, the rational plans for Sutherland came to be confounded in the minds of future generations with undoubted cases elsewhere in the Highlands where a wicked landlord did simply evict and abandon his helpless tenants. One such case occurred just across the boundary of Sutherland on the estate of Culrain in Easter Ross, the property of Hugh Munro of Novar. His family, with a shrewd but ruthless talent for moneymaking in its genes, had been among the first to introduce sheep to the north. For him this new economy worked, and he wanted to extend it. He had 500 tenants living at Culrain. He gave them notice but offered no resettlement: they would just have to go, and he did not care where. Yet it was hardly as if the estate had run into difficulty. The rental was rising. The tenants owed no money: when they received the notices, they offered to pay more. The sad fact was, though, that Munro could earn three times as much from a single sheep-farmer as from all of them. His law agent arrived in the spring of 1820 with the statutory witnesses to serve writs of removal, warning the people to quit by Whitsunday. A hostile mob saw off him and the other harbingers of their doom.

At this point higher authority had to intervene. The aged sheriff of Ross, Donald Macleod of Geanies, asked military support of the Lord Advocate in Edinburgh (who did not respond) and convened a meeting of local land-owners. As colonel of the county's militia, he called it out. Riding in his carriage, he led a force of 100 northwards from Dingwall to Culrain. There he found the way blocked by a crowd, apparently of more women than men, though he claimed most were men wearing women's clothes. As he got down from his carriage with the writs, they pressed in on him and his escort. Altercation then riot broke out. A woman struck the first blow with a stick. Soon both sides were thrashing at each other. The militia fired one blank volley but could not still the maddened mob. Macleod's force took to their heels and ran, carrying him with them and abandoning his carriage, which was wrecked. They did not stop running for 4 miles, till they reached Ardgay on the Dornoch Firth. Here they barricaded themselves in an inn. The people threw stones at the windows, shouted insults and at last went home in jubilation. Macleod stayed put at Ardgay for a week, unwilling to return to Dingwall but wary of ventur-ing back to Strathoykel. He feared the locals might storm the inn. In fact, their resistance was over and soon they gave in, accepted the writs and prepared to leave. That was as bad as the rural unrest got in post-war Scotland.[10]

Things had turned out better in the north-east of Scotland, setting the example those more remote landowners sought to follow. The original landscape here hardly looked hospitable either, with its granitic mountains, boulder-strewn terrain and storm-battered coasts, slightly civilised by quaint burghs and baronial castles. Almost till the end of the eighteenth century, it was cultivated as it long had been under the system of runrig. The land was corrugated by strips for each peasant to till, fertile infield contrasting with scrubby outfield and common grazings beyond. People lived in fermtouns, clusters of shelters grimy within, ramshackle without, sinking in muck. To the modern eye the prospect would have appeared bleak, open, treeless, almost wild.

As late as 1794 the minister of Alford, the Revd James Birnie, wrote in the *Old Statistical Account* of the country round him that 'all the old-fashioned prejudices of husbandry are still looked upon as sure and infallible rules of good management'.[11] They were actually the causes of backwardness and poverty, something the landowners would soon prove when they started an agricultural revolution. Sir Archibald Grant of Monymusk had figured among its pioneers, after retiring to his estate from a career of debauch in London. The first effect of the fresh scene was to make him feel all the more jaded, so he set out to work off his gloom with energetic improvements. He drained the ground, cleared the stones and enclosed the fields. On the home farm, he developed the practices of fallowing and of rotating crops. Once he had perfected his techniques he sought likely tenants to follow him, encouraging them on his let farms with low rents and long leases. By 1811, George Skene Keith produced a survey of Aberdeenshire that already showed the ancient system of cultivation to be vanishing.[12] Landowners in neighbouring counties noted the success and followed the lead: the Duke of Gordon and the Earl of Findlater, the Barclays of Ury and the Silvers of Netherley. While some still lived on in medieval piles, splendid new mansions – Cairness or Duff or Fasque – arose to outdo them by far in style and elegance. The face of the whole region underwent a transformation at the hands of them and their fellows. Of course the achievement was due in no less measure to the toil of their tenants, who in turn had seen for themselves what a difference the novel techniques would make.

A witness to almost the entire process was the long-lived Revd George Cruden, minister of Logie Buchan. He wrote in 1840:

> Being one of the few whom it has pleased God to spare to assist in drawing up a second Statistical Account of Scotland, I may be allowed,

more than others, to express my satisfaction at the vast improvements in agriculture which have taken place in Buchan since I transmitted to Sir John Sinclair an account of the parish of Old Deer in the year 1794. When I look around me, I seem to live not only among a new race of men, but in a new world. Cultivation, like the gradual spreading of a garment, has changed the external face of the earth, and every locality wears a new appearance. The irregular patches, and various denominations of arable land which were then interspersed amidst the uncultivated waste, are now absorbed in regular enclosures or extensive fields, the dark expanse of moss is greatly diminished, and the sombre herds of our native brown and black cattle are enlivened by a mixture of the white and speckled Tees-water. The low-thatched farm-houses and long continuous rows of barns and byres are now converted into slated dwellings of two stories, and adjoining courts of offices; and, where necessary, the steep and rugged tracks that led to them into smooth roads of easy ascent.[13]

The south of Scotland also housed a progressive landed class, its grandest ornaments the Dukes of Buccleuch. Sir Walter Scott (sharing their surname), showed his devotion to three generations of them: Duke Henry who had also turned his back on London and come to live on his ancestral estates; Duke Charles whom Scott loved the best, though he died young; and finally Duke Walter, just thirteen years old when he succeeded. Scott wrote: 'It delights me to hear this hopeful young nobleman talk with sense and firmness about his plans for improving his estate and employing the poor'.[14]

Scott was right about the potential of the estate, a huge one sprawling across three counties. The Buccleuchs did not lag behind in the conspicuous consumption befitting noblemen, but they were rich enough to act as benign landlords too. Unlike some lesser and poorer ones, they saw no point in screwing up financial demands so far that their people could never meet them. The tenants remained prosperous by the standards of their class, not just from improved agriculture but also from cottage industries. They worked the fields in season, then spun and wove at home during other times of year. So Buccleuch's empire was as much industrial as agricultural, as much urban as rural. Here too the countryside had emptied when people moved to the booming burghs, the Selkirk where Scott was sheriff or the Galashiels where he built his home. He admired the loyal labours of the shepherds but just as much the sturdy independence of the weavers (unless they turned radical).

In the hills these migrants, too, had left behind more sheep than people, yet the shift away from a peasant existence did not always mean their exchanging a pre-industrial for an industrial way of life. In fact, they could often carry on with work they felt used to. The keys to economic advance here were still human and animal muscle, or else wind and water. Energy came from the River Tweed and its tributaries, driving the mills along the banks. The workers were willing and their raw material of high quality: the tweeds and knitwear they made would sustain the industrial prosperity of their region into the twentieth century.[15]

It can be misleading to separate rural and urban development as distinct categories of analysis during the early nineteenth century. There was in essence one astounding process of change and expansion, intertwined and mutually reinforcing, marked by the large shifts of population. The Lowland countryside underwent clearance too, sometimes indeed because landlords removed the people to consolidate their farms, sometimes because the people sought for themselves a better life elsewhere. The best result was what the English journalist and politician William Cobbett discovered when he made a tour of Scotland in 1832. In wonder he compared the great farms of Berwickshire and the Lothians, producing corn and beef with landless labour and the power of steam, to so many outdoor factories. East Lothian was 'the most fruitful province in Great Britain . . . the most fertile and finest farming land' he had ever seen. During the late war, 'the cattle and victual consumed by the troops was the means of farmers, traders and merchants attaining to moderate wealth, and no wonder they sang with zest: Bonaparte's a friend o' mine, I sell my wheat at ninety nine'. But Cobbett also noticed the depopulation that set off the fertility: 'such cornfields, such fields of turnips, such turnips in those fields, such stack-yards, and such a total absence of dwelling-houses, as never, surely, were before seen in any country upon earth.'[16]

Is it too much too surmise that the noble house of Sutherland aimed in vain at achieving in the north of Scotland just what the noble house of Buccleuch did in truth achieve in the south of Scotland? In other words, what in the north came to be called clearance was in the south called improvement. The north had harsher climate and terrain, indeed, though for the county of Sutherland in particular there was also more money available relative to resources and population: still the improvement faltered and failed. It does not appear to have been a matter just of good or bad will in the landlord.

Rather these episodes belonged to the agricultural revolution that in the end spread across the whole of Scotland. Like any revolution it might eat its children, at any rate maul and wound and terrorise them. Much as all this is to be deplored, we must look at the consequences too. In 1815 most Scots still lived a rustic life, but by the 1840s there was already an urban majority in the nation and it steadily increased. At that stage, though, one in three of the people still worked in agriculture, more than worked in the biggest industrial sectors of the time, textiles and mining, put together. And most rural areas had enjoyed a rising population for as long as we can trace it back. Only in the middle of the century did the big decline set in, so that by 1901 the proportion of male workers engaged in farming had halved.[17]

Even so, the result was not a desolation. On the contrary, in some ways a golden age followed: it gave Scotland a smiling countryside (at least when the sun shone) more picturesque and more productive than ever before or since. Dotted around it, small towns and villages flourished, setting a social ideal for the nation on which it still fondly looks back. Nuclear settlements had in earlier times been far from universal, as the extensive agriculture scattered the fermtouns across the countryside. Now nuclear settlements grew, because the people forced out of the fermtouns did not always go straight to the industrial conurbations and they had to live somewhere, for instance, in the planned villages built by landowners. There they could do the little jobs that little places need. The minister of Logie Buchan, conscientiously listed them: five cartwrights, four blacksmiths, one mason, two millers, three brickmakers, four shoemakers, three tailors, one weaver.[18] The last in the list is a reminder that weaving on handlooms remained a common rural occupation – weavers had authentically figured, for example, in the fictional Dalmailing of John Galt's novel about the old Scotland in its last epoch, *Annals of the Parish* (1821). Only later, as vast textile factories arose in the industrial areas, powered by steam rather than by hand, did weaving in a village lose its point. The weavers, in fact, then did better to move. But the departure of them and other tradesmen from the countryside dried up a ready source of additional labour that had supplemented its income from work on the fields in season. Now farmers complained of the shortage of hands, forcing them to offer higher wages and better cottages. One from Lanarkshire remarked in 1881 that he had never had any trouble getting workers to bring in his harvest 'so long as handloom weaving was kept up, but that is done away with now. Our cottages were largely filled with handloom weavers when I began farming but that trade has gone down. These men were always available for a push.'[19]

Instead the farmers substituted capital for labour, that is, invested in machines. In turn the movement of people from rural to urban Scotland quickened. It was not the result of tyranny, but what happened when industrialisation created demand for labour while stimulating production of food. Over most of the countryside there were no hard times. On the contrary, the demand for more products of the land had in the first place to be satisfied by farmers at home rather than by imports from abroad. The ensemble represented a net social gain. While the changes came at the cost of human displacement, the total population increased without social unrest. Instead, Scotland assumed the character it has retained, a cluster of industrial cities and towns surrounded by landscapes looking rather empty: a kind of combination of Belgium and Norway.[20]

But the old intimacy between land and people was broken, and Lowland farming became a matter of production and profit. In that Scots proved themselves apt. The traditional small farms, communally worked, gave way to big farms, arable or pastoral. The farmers enclosed the fields with ditches and hedges, then drained them. This last task was of great importance, in fact, the precondition of any further progress, for land under runrig, unless naturally drained, would get sodden as water ran off the rigs and gathered in between: no advantage in a cool, damp climate. The answer came in laying down clay pipes as underground channels, an immense labour but so effective that the government encouraged it with loans at low rates of interest under an Act of Parliament in 1846. The soil of the Lowlands, once so cold and wet and grudging, now grew cereals in quantities that would have amazed earlier generations, with potato and turnip – staple items of the Scots diet – raised on the margins. Cultivation still had to be coaxed by heavy use of fertilisers, lime or bone-meal, later guano or industrial phosphates. The rotation of crops further increased yields. Yet for the first time Scotland produced an abundance of food, not to mention an abundance of rents for the landlords.[21]

Local diversity did make the pace of progress uneven. If specialised farming was the most profitable, mixed farming remained the norm over large areas of the Lowlands. And elements of the old system of cultivation survived for quite a long time – runrig, for example, which had formed the whole landscape.[22] Among its many drawbacks was that the crop could not be harvested except by hand. Patrick Bell, a theological student at the University of St Andrews, invented a reaper in 1827 while on vacation at his father's farm in Angus. Since runrig at first prevented its being used everywhere else in Scotland, an adapted American version owed to Cyrus McCormick was what at length conquered the world's markets. Bell finished up not as the founder of a multinational corporation but as the minister of Carmyllie, with nothing but a commemorative plate from the Highland Society for his pains. As runrig retreated, the scythe replaced the sickle, before mechanisation took over. First came the horse-drawn hoe and the seed-drill for planting crops, then the reaper for gathering them in, then the thresher and the winnower to separate the grain. Later the power of steam replaced the strain of muscle. Labour remained cheap, but at least the age-old racking toil of the farm-worker was eased. The rise in efficiency proved dramatic: 'In 1820 . . . to cultivate, reap and deliver five different crops . . . would have taken 53 days, while in 1892 the same operations would be performed by those using modern methods in 35 days.'[23]

As for the livestock, selective breeding raised its quality while modern transport transformed its markets too. Once upon a time Scottish cattle doomed to end up as roast beef on English tables had at great trysts been sold lean to drovers who took them south on the hoof. That had been profitable enough to a nation of pastoral peasants, but nowhere near as profitable as the new traffic became to commercial farmers. By 1876 Scotland was home to more than a million cattle. Some would never leave the country: dairy farms flourished on ready access to urban markets in fresh produce and, for instance, allowed the south-west, a region of small or medium-sized farms, to prosper for the first time. But that region also exported its hardy breed of Galloway cattle, either as beef or as livestock, to other regions of the globe with the same sort of soggy climate. A similar pattern of development emerged on a greater scale in the north-east, here with the Aberdeen Angus developed by Hugh Watson of Keillor. His favourite bull was Old Jock, born in 1842 and sired by Grey-Breasted Jock, a beast given the number 1 in the Scottish herd book of 1862. Watson also owned Old Granny, a cow born in 1824 and struck down by lightning in 1859, but not before she had given birth to twenty-nine calves. The pedigrees of the vast majority of Aberdeen Angus cattle alive today all over the world can be traced back to these two animals.[24]

Such developments showed the acumen of Scottish farmers in making the best use of their comparative advantages. But for that they also had sometimes to be hard men, to force change where it might not be welcome. The people occupying the lowest level in the old system of agriculture had been the cottars, working for tenant farmers in return for a smallholding where they could grow vegetables, even keep a sheep or two. All these smallholdings were now consolidated into larger farms. The cottars then had only long and tiring toil for other people as their source of livelihood. Yet it need not be without dignity. The ploughmen, for example, formed a group apart: they started work at four o'clock in the morning to feed, yoke and take the horses to the field for up to ten hours' ploughing, and ended the day with grooming and suppering back at the stables. These and their fellows followed a mode of recruitment which, in the north-east for example, was by the 1830s recast into a pattern set to continue well into the twentieth century.[25] In the feeing markets at Whitsun and Martinmas the labourers dealt face to face with the farmers, the wage being set according to the particular conditions of that place and season. Labourers often had their own reputations as good or bad workers, farmers as good or bad employers, so some keen bargaining went on. The practice was to hire married couples for a year, and they might be given a cottage on the farm. Unmarried men and women were hired for periods of six months, the men being put up in bothies. This Spartan form of communal living yet gave rise to a genre of folksong that the men created for themselves, the bothy ballads with their simple delight in rustic life. Among the best known is 'The Barnyards of Delgaty':

As I go down to church on Sunday, many's the bonnie lass I see
Sitting by her mother's side, winkin' owre the pews at me.

A linten addie toorin addie, linten addie toorin ae
Linten lowrin lowrin lowrin, the barnyards of Delgaty.

Now, I can drink and no be drunken, I can fight and no be slain
I can court with another man's lass and still be welcome to my ain.

A linten, etc.

Ah, now my candle is burnt oot, my snotter's fairly on the wane
Fare ye well ye barnyards, you'll never see me here again.

A linten, etc.[26]

The high efficiency of Scottish agriculture was exacting not only on the farm-worker but also on the farmer. Entry into the sector became harder, unless the entrant was already rich or at least had a head start as member of a farming family. Movements of prices towards the end of the century deepened the difficulty. As first cereal and then animal prices dropped in the face of foreign imports, only a farm with high turnover and low costs could maintain its competitive edge. Especially in upland areas, those most suitable for larger agricultural units, in the southern parishes of Lanarkshire and Ayrshire, the hill country of Angus or the areas bordering the Highlands, arable farming struggled to produce returns.[27]

In the more fertile parts the progressive tenant farmers might make a good living, even though needing to pay a hefty rent as well: by tradition, one-third of the gross product. Till the middle of the century it had been their incomes that varied, against the more constant rental of the landowners or the wages of the labourer, modest, indeed miserly, as these latter were. In general, the tenants' achievement lay in the continuous ability to improve yields in response to the demands of the markets. More permanent testimonies to their prosperity were the fine solid steadings they built, often of some architectural merit, still to be seen all over the Lowlands today. To make their money they had to be entrepreneurs. At their best in families like the Hopes of Fenton Barns in East Lothian, they were model farmers with an international reputation. George Hope rented a farm with sour soil that he needed to drain and fertilise, then to use the rotation of crops to raise its productivity further. So successful did he prove that experts came from as far away as America or Russia to see what he was doing. But in his spare time he took to Liberal politics too and this, for a farmer without security of tenure, proved to be his undoing, at least temporarily. When his lease at Fenton Barns expired in 1875 his Tory landlord refused to renew it. Despite incredulous public outrage, Hope had to find a new farm in Peeblesshire.[28]

Still, if things went well the social tensions kept within bounds. James Wilson, who worked a medium-sized farm in Banffshire, showed himself realistic but quite lacking in grudges about his situation when he read a paper to the Ballindalloch Mutual Improvement Association in January 1886. It set out a story of success. Everywhere improved breeds of cattle had replaced the 'thin scraggy animals that might have been pasturing the fields some forty or fifty years ago'. The large farmers had shown the way in developing the Aberdeen Angus with its beef of higher quality. They had also taken the initiative of forming agricultural societies, introduced 'new and labour-saving implements', raised the quality of the soil and generally benefited their communities by, for example, giving 'more work to local tradesmen'. Wilson still thought he and his fellows could do better, but the key to this was their own effort rather than any benevolence from on high.[29]

One thing the agricultural revolution did not change was the hierarchical nature of rural society. Scotland housed relatively few owner-occupiers and large landowners dominated almost everywhere. Sir John Sinclair, member of the clan that held sway over Caithness, remarked in 1814: 'In no country in Europe are the rights of proprietors so well-defined and so carefully protected.' For the rest of the nineteenth century they if anything enlarged their holdings. The first official survey of landownership in 1872 showed four-fifths of the land to be owned by 659 individuals, half of it by 117 of them.[30] These included the Duke of Sutherland with more than a million acres, the Duke of Buccleuch with 400,000, the Duke of Richmond and Gordon with nearly 300,000 and the Duke of Fife with 250,000 (despite the name, he was another laird of the north-east). In Scotland, ownership remained concentrated to a greater extent than anywhere else in Europe, even England. Though the industrial revolution generated great wealth among the urban Scots who led it, they could never buy up enough land to rival the old aristocracy in rural Scotland.

On a large estate the interests of landlord and tenant usually coalesced, but might not. The countryside also housed animals, on the ground and in the air, which in part lived off the crops. On these the landlord and tenant were unlikely to agree, because Scotland's ancient game laws reserved the right to kill game solely to the landlord, and a tenant who took it into his own hands to do so could be prosecuted. It was only in 1880 – not least because the injustice had attracted the ranting attention of urban radicals – that tenants won the right to kill rabbits and hares they found nibbling at their own crops. This conflict worsened as lairds sought to maximise the sporting potential of their estates. By the 1870s, they were systematically developing their resources of game. On the great estates they demanded and got huge sporting rents out of land little good for anything else. There had already been recreational shooting on the high moors in the eighteenth century, but in 1800 a consortium led by Sir John Maxwell took a ten-year lease of the estate of Abergeldie on Deeside. Over the next four decades the number of advertised deer forests trebled and much of the land above 1,000 feet was given over to sporting. Grouse-shooting grew as popular as deer-stalking. With it came the muirburn, the burning of the heather that assured the grouse its staple diet of young shoots of heather and altered the landscape of the moors with a mosaic of different colours.[31]

It all took off as a business after an English gentleman, Walter Scrope, published a book in 1838 on *The Art of Deerstalking,* illustrated by the artist brothers Landseer, to tell the world of the excellent shooting he had found on the Duke of Atholl's estate. This new sporting literary genre reached a peak in 1863 with Charles St John's *The Wild Sports and Natural History of the Highlands*, demonstrating a fact odd to townees, that a huntsman can love the creatures he kills. Perhaps the artistic achievement extended to abstract sculpture too, if we may judge by a pair of curious monuments in Aberdeenshire. On Duchery Beg, high above the Water of Tanar, stand two pillars, each with a stone ball resting on a pyramid. They are exactly 267 yards apart, commemorating Sir William Cunliffe Brooks's shooting of a stag at that formidable distance on 9 October 1877.[32]

The men transforming the wide moorlands were most of them English, with Scots appearing in their company usually as gamekeepers and beaters. It was one example of how the history of the Highlands had come to be largely propelled from elsewhere, in this case from the huge fortunes created by the industrial revolution in the rest of Britain and then from the fact that the pursuit of aristocratic blood sports had turned into a marker of high social standing. In theory, stalking deer with a rifle might be compatible with farming sheep over the same kind of country. In practice, it was not. Rich men seldom minded if they paid both a grazing and a sporting rent so long as they could get a clear shot. This was what created the deer forests, a kind of forest unique to Scotland, unique also in that it has no trees, or at least no vegetation likely to get in the way of a bullet from a rifle or shotgun. It was on shooting rents that many an ancient noble dynasty now built itself a new stately home or kept an old one in better repair. As for the incomers from elsewhere, they often ran their estates at a loss out of their industrial revenues and provided a straight subsidy to the needy, if not always grateful, Highlanders working for them. By 1900, sporting estates took up about 60 per cent of the area of Scotland.[33]

❋

While the Highland sheep-farms had prospered through the middle of the century, in the long run they proved unsustainable. The sheep, fastidiously selecting the finer grasses to crop, overgrazed pastures and left room for coarse grass and bracken to invade. Meanwhile competition arose from the eastern Lowlands where farmers had started to rotate grasses and turnips nourishing to sheep as well. And wool from the Empire was beginning to reach Scottish markets, followed by mutton from the Empire, both often better in quality and lower in price than the Highland produce. The reign of sheep in the north of Scotland came to an end. The supreme irony followed of a large-scale clearance of sheep and shepherds. It only heralded the appearance of Highland problems in new forms.[34]

Those problems went back a long way, of course, and had never been fully effaced by the more or less full integration of the clan chiefs into respectable society during the eighteenth century (something from their point of view preferable to a rendezvous with the public executioner). Even so up to 1815 most chiefs exerted themselves to keep their people on their lands. This was partly a matter of prestige, for instance to man a regiment if they took a loyal fancy to forming one. But they might also need labour for new economic activities, such as the harvesting of kelp, the common seaweed that could be reduced to the industrially useful sodium carbonate. After 1815 this market, fostered by war, collapsed. What with the returning soldiers as well, labour was suddenly in surplus. Clearances began.[35]

Clearances could not, however, halt a spectacular rise in the Highland population, to nearly 400,000 by 1841, the highest level ever attained. Crises of subsistence resulted, first in 1836–37 with a blight that rotted potatoes in the ground, then with a much more severe one beginning in 1846 and going on into 1847. The Highlands, like Ireland at the same time, lost their staple food. For once Lowlanders cast old grudges aside and hastened to bring relief. The British government, while officially non-interventionist, yet sought agreement on a policy for long-term development with schemes of roads and harbours, aid for the fisheries and the like. But Victorian Britain was just never going to provide public resources on the scale required, even if there had been any certainty (as there was not) of bringing about the desired result of an improved and stable Highland society. Highlanders no longer able to subsist without help had to be cleared and preferably moved on to the Lowlands, to England, to North America and to the Antipodes. The largest ever emigration followed, and within a short time finished its job of putting an end to the inexorable rise in the Highland population.[36]

Were Highland problems being solved after all? In the following phase of social calm and relative prosperity lasting a quarter of a century, sheep-farmers fared well and crofters perhaps better. The harvests, with a few local exceptions, turned out generous. The price of cattle remained buoyant. Rents rose little, at least for smallholdings, and they lagged behind the growth in incomes, which were boosted besides by seasonal emigration to the booming Lowlands. Anyone dissatisfied could still emigrate, sometimes with a subsidy, always to a warm welcome overseas.[37]

It might have seemed the Highlands had at last begun to follow the path to prosperity already traversed by the Lowlands. The apparent realism of the prospect could be attested by the public debate over it among some of the finest minds in Scotland. George Campbell, eighth Duke of Argyll, was a flame-haired intellectual, an authority on evolution and on economics, who also took up a political career and rose to be a member of William Gladstone's cabinets. Not least, he was a great landowner in his ancestral county. From his study of the charters preserved in his own castle at Inveraray, he concluded there was little substance in the currently fashionable notions of some ideal-ists about the old Celtic society practising a communal form of agriculture, which might now, they were implying, be revived in favour of the crofters rather than obliterated by the improvers. If the pressure of population, rather than the survival of historic rights, had lain at the bottom of any rural com-munism, it also led to repeated crises of subsistence. The ultimate way out, Argyll concluded, was a more advanced and a better capitalised agriculture with a smaller population on the land and a higher standard of living. This meant the same system as in the rest of Scotland, a system of landlords and tenants under the discipline of rents and removal.[38]

The duke found a fierce foe in John Stuart Blackie, professor of classics at the University of Edinburgh, but a man with his heart in the Highlands: he was one of the first Lowlanders who habitually wore a kilt. Ignoring the ribaldry that often greeted his colourful appearance on the streets of the capital, he consciously countered the forces of the market with the call of a culture. An Aberdonian by birth, he spent his holidays at Braemar, where the solitude of the hills poignantly reminded him of a vanished way of life. He argued on grounds of both justice and efficiency that there should be smallholdings for all in the free possession of their occupiers (or at least giving these minimal rental and maximal security of tenure): 'ownership in land exists for the people, not the people for the sake of ownership'. He also rejected the Scots Liberals' facile faith in Britishness as a vehicle of pro-gress. He hated imperialism, at home and abroad, for 'obliterating local types and establishing a uniform monotony of superficial polish'. He got close to denouncing the very Union, something almost unheard of in his time, for 'superficiality, mechanism and monotony', compared to the Scots' 'heritage of a distinct nationality, nobly and manfully acquired'. He lived long enough to be inaugural chairman in 1886 of the Scottish Home Rule Association, the ancestor of the Scottish National Party.[39]

Intellectuals were not left long to debate Highland problems in these terms before crisis returned. After briefly better times the dearth of the early 1880s, with a succession of poor harvests and general depression in agriculture, came as all the more of a shock. The winter of 1882–83 turned out the bleakest for a third of a century. The potatoes failed and other crops were lost in autumnal storms, which also sank or smashed fishing boats. Meanwhile the Lowland economy went into recession as well, and so offered Highland migrants no more jobs. Still nothing like the earlier disasters followed. Landowners continued to collect rent as before. If there was default, they ordered eviction. This met with resistance, for local agents of the law proved far too weak to enforce it.[40]

We might usefully follow this fresh crisis by comparing and contrasting how it unfolded in two different places, the Isle of Skye and the Isle of Lewis. On the Isle of Skye, more specifically on the estate of Lord MacDonald of Sleat, a long evolution reached its end. Clan Donald had dominated the West Highlands before its forfeiture in 1495, after which only cadet branches of the extinct line of paramount chiefs survived, including the MacDonalds of Sleat. These steadily cast off their shaggy Highland past, refining themselves so far that they received a peerage in 1776. It made no difference to the fact that they were running up huge debts in the attempted transformation of their clan from a military into an economic unit. The first Lord MacDonald made initial efforts to set his estate on a firmer financial footing, suffering some reprobation from his more old-fashioned and more martial fellows. But his exertions went on the whole for nothing, and he merely bequeathed the problems to future generations. His successors kept their heads above the deep waters of their debts by selling off land. For the fourth one the crunch came when in 1846 he owed £140,000.[41]

In the best spirit of the past this Lord MacDonald counted his people as part of his wealth, yet now he needed without fail to find better uses for it and them. Like many of his Lowland counterparts, he favoured the planned village as a focus for new economic activities. There was to have been one at Kyleakin, though it languished till the West Highland Railway reached Kyle of Lochalsh in 1897, and a ferry between the two places created the main crossing to Skye. Still, the existence of Portree as the island's metropolis is owed to the Lords MacDonald. They equipped it with a harbour designed by Thomas Telford, with superior houses and with public buildings. They brought in fishermen from the east of Scotland to teach their skills to Skyemen; these showed, however, little interest. They hired miners to demonstrate how to work the seams of coal found down the coast from Portree to the Braes, with the same result. Nemesis at length overtook the estate, but it was hardly for want of efforts to erect on it a viable community. The sad sequels followed not from improvement, but from defeat of improvement. The finances of the fourth Lord MacDonald may be faulted, but not his good intentions.[42]

The estate was put under trust. While Lord MacDonald remained the owner, control passed to trustees charged with cutting costs and raising income till his creditors were satisfied and let him resume his patrimony. Time and again, he pleaded for his own misfortune not to be visited on his tenants. But by law the trustees had to earn what they could, and they decided the people must make way for sheep. If MacDonald had got his way, the people would have stayed on the land or, at worst, been conveyed to new homes with his aid and blessing, according to the consistent policy on his estate.[43]

This was the background to the form the crisis of the 1880s took on Skye. A progressive change in the Highland mentality may be marked by the fact that now the crofters made, as it were, a positive refusal to pay their rents, rather than simply being unable to afford them. They turned poverty to a purpose, to claim the restoration of old rights. What with the sheep and the deer, many crofting communities had been confined within small areas, often of inferior land, while near them large tracts were reserved for extensive agriculture or for sport. While to the lairds the landscape might still have seemed overcrowded, the crofters felt they had been corralled into poverty with emigration as the sole way out. If land should be made available to them, on the other hand, they claimed they could work it efficiently and preserve their way of life, not to say better their condition.[44]

Among rights on Skye the crofters said they had lost, and that only recently, was the right to graze stock on the land held by sheep-farmers of Lord MacDonald. The crofters petitioned for the restoration of this right, but the factor brusquely turned them down. So they refused to pay their rents, with the result that they got summonses of eviction. In April 1882, on a track running down the south-eastern coast of the island, 500 crofters intercepted the sheriff officer coming to serve the summonses. They burned his papers before his eyes and saw him off. Ten days later the law returned in the shape of sixty police from Glasgow. A mob faced them: 'men, women and children rushed forward in all stages of attire, most of the females with their hair streaming lovely in the breeze'. In this Battle of the Braes the police did succeed, before they beat a retreat, in subduing the crofters and taking some prisoner, though not before a dozen constables had also been injured by sticks and stones. Those arrested were tried at Inverness and convicted, but sympathisers paid their fines. The whole episode was reckoned a moral victory for the people. Trouble spread round Skye, then to other islands. In 1885 a gunboat and marines were sent to the Minches. Thousands refused to pay their rents and occupied the sheep-farms. Calm only returned to Skye with the stationing on the island of a garrison of 300.[45] Even from the landlords' point of view, there could be little future for the Highlands if this was how law and order had to be maintained there.

Rebellious crofters and intellectuals supporting them had in 1881 formed the Highland Land League, on the model of a counterpart in Ireland. Its very existence dropped a broad hint that these nascent Scottish troubles might develop after the violent example across the North Channel. The British government decided it had to act, though its action did not in the first instance go beyond the procrastinating expedient of a Royal Commission. This sat under the chairmanship of Lord Napier, a Lowland aristocrat who had served in India as Governor of Madras and there carried through a land reform confirming the rights of peasant proprietors. He brought some of the same ideas to the Scottish Highlands, enriched by his own dash of Celtic romanticism. His report, published in 1884, advocated a sort of revived traditional township, a peasant commune but one run by elected officials to administer the arable ground and pasture. Napier's bright ideas pleased nobody, not even all his fellow commissioners, and certainly not Gladstone. The Prime Minister was more given than Napier himself to high-minded waffle, yet often obscured within the clouds of his rhetoric lay a sharp, by no means timid, sense of practicalities. He saw the report was impractical. Yet he had to do something about the Highland unrest. He ignored Napier and imported to Scotland his government's previous Irish Land Act, with its three Fs: fixity of tenure, fair rents, freedom to inherit a holding. These formed the substance of the Crofters' Act (1886). It did not make the crofters the owners of their land, as many had hoped. But, within crofting areas strictly demarcated, it gave them more or less total security of tenure on the plots they occupied. The landlords remained merely nominal owners, their possession signalled by nothing more than a peppercorn rent. Would this solve the Highland problems? The sequel showed it would not.[46]

The Isle of Lewis belonged to the Matheson family, typical of one sort of successor to the old chiefs, Highlanders who had gone out into the world to earn a fortune and brought it back to the land of their fathers. James Matheson made a stupendous fortune from smuggling opium into China as head of the great oriental trading house of Jardine Matheson. Benjamin Disraeli had him appear in the novel *Sybil* (1845): 'Oh, a dreadful man. A Scotchman richer than Croesus, one Mr Macdrug, fresh from Canton, with a million of opium in each pocket, denouncing corruption and bellowing free trade.' On his return, Matheson purchased Lewis from the bankrupt Mackenzie Earls of Seaforth. The island suffered some of the worst Highland conditions, with a population growing by 2 per cent a year, from 17,000 in 1841 to more than 25,000 by 1881. Almost at once Matheson had to reach into his pocket to support his people during the dearth of 1846. Even amid the terrible blight on the potato he had ample means to cope. He imported meal on his own account and sold it to the people at a quarter of the cost. He contributed £100,000 to public works that would create jobs for them. He never forced them out, but moved only those wishing to exchange bad land for better, or else gave free passage in his own boat to any wanting to seek work on the mainland. In 1847 he was elected the Liberal MP for Ross and Cromarty, which included Lewis. In 1851 Queen Victoria made him a baronet for his philanthropy.[47]

During more than thirty years in charge of Lewis, Matheson spent £384,000, the equivalent of many millions in modern money. In some respects he was a stern Highland landlord of the legendary type, who through dictatorial and unpopular factors forced his tenants to stick to his terms. But he was also the only Highland landlord at once immune to financial pressure and uninterested in making people move unless ready to. Lewis therefore offers an acid test of the question how the Highlanders would have behaved if under no pressure to leave. The answer is that, other things being equal, they would have just stayed on the land and continued to multiply.

Yet Lewis was hardly a fertile island. It had been able to expand its resources somewhat out of the sea, for the fisheries also profited from the general improvements of the age in transport and marketing. While Scotland's main fishing ports lay on the east coast, their entrepreneurs reached out to establish bases at Stornoway on Lewis and at Castlebay on Barra. They offered work to the crofters too: the men helped on the boats while the women gutted the catch onshore. Still a higher income did not alter their way of life. They merely made room for the burgeoning population through subdivision of the existing crofts – already small enough – into fragments smaller still.[48]

This was why the Crofters' Act in itself failed to end social conflict on Lewis. The crofters wanted not more rights but more land, such as the land the Mathesons had put under sheep and deer. To the landowner and factor this request was preposterous: the crofters should be glad they were not on Skye, where they would face eviction. These waxed just as indignant: they were poor men who yet kept up with their rents and followed the factor's instructions. Yet they and their fathers had occupied this land for generations, exchanging obedience to its owners for at least some consideration of their own wants. It was oppressive of the Mathesons now to repudiate their side of an implicit bargain.[49]

So the crofters of Lewis resisted their landlords even after the legislation of 1886 had tipped the social and political balance in their favour. Here indeed the main trouble arose in the following years. During the deer raid of Park in 1887, about 100 men armed with rifles took over land that the widowed Lady Mary Matheson had just turned from a sheep-farm into a sporting estate, when it could have been given back to them. They shot deer, cooked them on the spot and, before tucking in to them, prayed for God's blessing on their meal. If they got it, it did not save them from the secular authorities: the ringleaders were arrested and put on trial in Edinburgh, where a sympathetic jury acquitted them. That was the incentive for the next raid on Aignish, where 1,000 crofters with pipes playing and flags flying occupied the land and killed some of the sheep on it before being driven off by a military force. The ringleaders got fifteen months in jail this time. Lady Matheson received threats to her life and had for a while to move out of the Lews Castle her husband had built for her on a hill overlooking the harbour at Stornoway.[50]

In the end, the Crofters' Act did succeed in defusing the disorder, though over the longer run its results have remained dubious. In essence, it froze a pattern of landholding that might have offered a solution to the Highland problems of 1884 but could hardly be suited to the Highland problems of all later times. The great virtue claimed for it was that it kept the indigenous population on the land, yet almost from the moment it came into force this population began to plunge. The decline was not halted till the late twentieth century, when white settlers started to arrive in the region and practise new economic activities often based on traditional crafts but aided by modern technology. Many have been quickly deterred by the climate and the remoteness, but those who stayed the course might prosper more than crofters ever could. Altogether, while the Crofters' Act coincided with the later stages of Scotland's agricultural revolution it is hard to see the Act as part of that revolution. In fact, the Highlands, certainly the remoter parts, remained the only region of Scotland where the revolution failed, leaving the people relatively no more prosperous or productive than before.[51]

Practically everywhere else, though, the agricultural revolution proved a success, if sometimes achieved at high cost. By the turn of the twentieth century only one in eight Scots worked still on farms. The proportion would from then on head steeply downwards. Even so, agriculture retained a somewhat greater importance to the economy of Scotland than to the economy of England, though the differences are not vast. They arise out of facts of nature or history: that two-thirds of the country are mountain, moor and rough grazing; that there is bound for reasons of climate or terrain to be more pastoral than arable production; that farms are therefore likely to be large and private owners to impress by the size of their acreage rather than by the profits out of it.

Victorian Scotland could in general be proud of the countryside it created, however, and the replacement there of grinding poverty by hard-working prosperity. At the end of the era there came an echo of Cobbett at the beginning, when the English agricultural expert, Daniel Hall, travelled the country to research his classic work *A Pilgrimage of British Farming* (1913). He told how, before he visited the Lothians, he 'had not imagined that the management of arable land could reach such perfection', and in Perthshire he was struck by the 'enlightened opportunism' of its mixed farming practices.[52] The expertise hard-won in the nineteenth century would continue to be tested by conditions scarcely less challenging for the rest of the twentieth century.

2

Industry: 'Blazing volcanoes'

It was at New Lanark, 30 miles up the River Clyde from Glasgow, that the rural and urban blend of the early industrial revolution achieved its finest form. The textile mill at this picturesque spot, built by a Glaswegian business-man, David Dale, dated from 1786.[1] He had started adult life as a weaver's apprentice before he went on to make a fortune in banking. Now, in partner-ship with the English inventor of the spinning jenny, Richard Arkwright, Dale set up his pioneering enterprise just below the waterfalls that were to power the machinery. A religious man, he had left the Church of Scotland for an evangelical congregation where he himself preached for four decades, sometimes being taunted in the streets for his pastoral pretensions. But he did practise what he preached, at least in seeking to be a model employer.

Dale limited the workers at New Lanark to shifts of eleven hours (instead of the seventeen demanded by other bosses). He gave them food, clothes and housing in modest but elegant tenements that still stand in woods on the same pretty stretch of river, today designated a World Heritage Site. It is perhaps hard to discern here one of the seedbeds of modern capitalism, so idyllic does the scene appear. But in its time New Lanark employed 2,000 hands, more than any other factory in Europe or America. They were mostly women or else children recruited from local orphanages, as well as exiled Highlanders. A visitor said: 'If I was tempted to envy any of my fellow creatures it would be men such as Mr Dale for the good they have done mankind.'[2]

Another visitor was Robert Owen, a young Welshman in the textile trade who came on business to Glasgow. He got to know Dale and more especially his daughter, whom he at length married. In 1800 Owen took over as man-ager of New Lanark. In running it, he set himself higher ambitions even than his father-in-law, not just to render capitalism benign but even to exhibit a blueprint for modern society. Universal progress was breaking up the small communities where most people had always dwelt, setting them apart from the natural world which ordered their existence with its slow seasonal rhythms. Owen believed that the traditional environment had formed human nature and that a novel environment would reform it. At this crux there was also a chance for visionaries like himself to step in and make human nature better.[3]

Owen therefore regulated not only the working conditions but also the private lives of his employees. The children slept in 'well-aired rooms, three in a bed', on a straw mattress with sheets and blankets, in dormitories scrubbed weekly and lime-washed twice annually. In summer they were given cotton clothes to wear, in winter woollen suits or linen dresses. They had to get up at six o'clock in the morning to work till six o'clock in the evening, a long stretch broken by meals: early and late porridge with milk, at noon soup, potatoes, bread and cheese alternating with seven ounces of beef for each child on different days, sometimes herrings. Those under ten years of age were excused any labour but attended school to learn reading and writing, arithmetic, music and dancing, with sewing for the girls and military exercises for the boys, and finally some geography, history or natural science. As his charges grew to adulthood, Owen fed their minds and bodies with 'rational amusement'. The happy, healthy orphans were to acquire habits of obedience useful both for their own education and for their future employment. Even after they started full-time work they could look forward at the end of their shifts to self-improving social activities, which should dissuade them from going off to get drunk in the usual Scottish manner.[4]

The regime in any event enforced tight rules against intemperance, theft and other misdemeanours. The supervisors kept 'books of character' on each worker; Owen would inspect them in person in efforts to stamp out 'bad and inferior conduct'. This interest could also turn a bit creepy, however. Owen reminded fellow capitalists how they took care to keep their machinery in working order: 'Now, if the care which you bestow upon machinery can give you such excellent results, may you not expect equally good results from care spent upon human beings, with their infinitely superior structure?' The trouble was they might be intractable: 'the great majority of them were idle, intemperate, dishonest, devoid of truth and pretenders to religion which they supposed would excuse their shortcomings and immoral proceedings'. Incentives for good behaviour had, then, to be matched by punishment for bad behaviour. A boy at New Lanark, Duncan McKinlay, would give evidence later to a parliamentary committee that 'a constant system of beatings took place, not a day without someone suffering'. Nor was every visitor impressed. The English Tory poet, Robert Southey, found these Scots workers were under the same 'absolute management as so many negro-slaves'. He decided that 'Owen in reality deceives himself': in fact, he 'keeps out of sight from others, and perhaps from himself, that his system, instead of aiming at perfect freedom, can only be kept in play by absolute power'.[5]

The fame of New Lanark spread all the same. It became a tourist attraction drawing politicians or industrialists from home and abroad to view its blend of philanthropy and profitability. After 1815, Owen also offered himself as a regular witness at official inquiries into the condition of the country, disturbed as it was by economic troubles following the end of the Napoleonic Wars. He published his theories in tracts for wider circulation. Here his attention shifted away from the practical arrangements he had actually enforced at New Lanark to vaguer ideas on 'villages of co-operation'. The poor or unemployed, after suitable training and under proper management, were themselves to own and organise the villages. Once these reached self-sufficiency, the inhabitants would be 'able to create their own subsistence and repay the interest of all capital invested in the outfit of the establishments'. Owen worked on a premise that 'manual labour, properly directed, is the source of all wealth' – an idea close enough to Karl Marx's labour theory of value to have impressed later generations of socialists. They tend to overlook how Owen then went on to say that 'when properly directed, labour is far more value to the community than the expense necessary to maintain the labourer in considerable comfort'. In other words, the boss would still cream off the surplus value. Owen was no enemy of capitalism, only of its irrational and wasteful aspects. He certainly became an arch-bore, forever harping on about his answers to all the world's problems.[6]

Yet Owen had intervened at a crucial point, just when Scotland's potential as a powerhouse of development was starting to show. Over the next century the potential would be realised, and the economy would ascend heights undreamed of at the outset. One thing this did was let the national population triple, from 1.6 million in 1800 to 4.8 million in 1911. The global figures concealed large changes in the composition of the workforce. There was rise and fall in its various employments, or cycles of both. More than half the Scots laboured on the land at the beginning of the period but fewer than one in twelve by the end. As for industry, the number of textile workers reached 370,000 in the middle of the nineteenth century then dropped to 330,000 at the turn of the twentieth century. Meanwhile the number of metal workers grew from 60,000 to 200,000, of workers in other manufactures from 70,000 to 130,000 and of miners from 50,000 to 130,000.[7] Still, mere statistics scarcely allow us to grasp the drama of how this small nation emerged as a linchpin of the global economy to link the primary producers on distant continents with the industrialising regions of Europe. Telling that story in more human terms is the task for the rest of this chapter.

The industrial revolution transformed the lives that most Scots led. Just as in many other industrial revolutions which have followed among the different nations of the earth, and which still go on today, this one began with textiles. They are often fashioned from the agricultural crops of the country, and their fashioning may come fairly easily to a population still with close links to the land, even after moving into the towns. At first, then, total social dislocation can be avoided.[8]

Since the early decades of the Union of 1707 it had besides been a part of British governments' policy to improve the range and quality of Scottish textiles, so that ordinary Scots, too, might feel some benefit from the connection with England. There was, for example, a public subsidy to the cultivation of flax, which yields a strong natural fibre that can be turned into linen. Thousands of part-time workers in the Lowlands took to spinning and weaving linen in the eighteenth century. It was something peasants could do in the winter, and it added to the output of the towns.[9]

Then, especially in the west of Scotland, certain producers of linen, often in partnership with merchants such as Dale, converted to cotton. It presented better prospects. It could exploit the new oceanic trade into and out of the Clyde and offer profitable further deployment of the fortunes being made from that. In addition, it attracted paternalist landowners extending the agenda of improvement and looking for ways to employ the surplus labour displaced by it. Of course, these old and new leaders of Scottish society also made money, in some cases a great deal of money. And for that reward they needed no huge down payment. To begin with, cotton required little more than linen had done in terms of skills, technology and fixed investment; for example, the bleach-fields laid out and the dye works set up for linen could serve also for cotton.[10]

Before long, however, cotton tended to produce complexes of factories, even if production was not confined to them and retained a large domestic component. But it was the factories that began to exert the social effects of the industrial revolution, and to change the Scots' whole inheritance from the past. In the eighteenth century the urban population had belonged to small burghs, at their best offering a quietly prosperous existence in a secure role to its beneficiaries. For the nation's producers that meant becoming an incorporated tradesman, a status earned only by a seven-year apprenticeship though leading to a steady career with enough to support a family; the rest of the family might work too, but they worked at home, sharing the daily round with journeymen and servants. The way of life was so settled and resilient that it could not be just killed off by mass production. Sturdy weavers, working their looms in familiar surroundings, with time to read radical books and think radical thoughts, might continue to prosper till after 1840 by specialising in goods unsuitable for process in a factory. At Paisley, for example, they made fine Paisley shawls based on Indian designs: there were 6,000 weavers producing them in 1837, though only 3,000 by 1843. This decade marked the turning point. The 80,000 weavers still working in Scotland at the start of it had shrunk to 25,000 by the end of it and to only 8,000 by 1880.[11]

✧

The new industrial age meanwhile dawned. For Scotland we might date its start to 1798, when Robert Millar solved an array of mechanical hitches to bring the power-loom into operation at his textile works in Glasgow.[12] New factors of production and new economic structure created new social super-structure, with a downtrodden proletariat trudging into a grim factory at dawn to toil at some tedious operation till the time came to trudge home again at twilight, too tired to do anything but grab a bite to eat and go to bed. There was no respect to sex or age. As many women as men worked in the factories, perhaps more. And the capitalists found special advantage in using children small enough to crawl under the looms and remove fluff which might snarl the mechanism; if their little fingers and hands got caught in it and were maimed, others could at a moment's notice be found to take their place.

The factories demanded submission to discipline of a kind unfamiliar to Scots, whether they arrived from the congested countryside or out of the cosy burghs of old. The employers made ample investments to keep their mills and machines going by perpetual power. They needed a workforce of hundreds to graft in gear with these mechanical motions. If the people could not accept the regime then it was they that had to go, not the machinery. With a glance at teeming and go-ahead Glasgow from relatively tranquil and old-fashioned Galashiels, Sir Walter Scott remarked how 'manufacturers have been transferred to great towns where a master calls together 100 workmen this week and pays them off the next with far less interest in their future fate than in that of as many worn-out shuttles'.[13]

Scots labour was cheaper than English labour, and cotton became a vast employer of it, maybe of 100,000 people at the peak. By 1868 there were 131 mills at work in Scotland. Still, from about this point on they faced more intense competition, from England but especially from foreign industries often protected by a tariff. Scottish factories found themselves forced away from mass production (which went to the newly industrialising countries) towards the top end of the market, where they became prey to fickle consumers' tastes. It was a challenge the big manufacturers struggled to meet, largely because of a failure in technical innovation that they blamed on resistance among their workers. At any rate by 1910 the output of cotton had virtually collapsed in Scotland, with only nine firms surviving.[14]

Yet there were three branches of textiles in which Scotland managed to hold the lead it had taken early on. In the production of sewing thread Coats of Paisley excelled every rival at home or abroad. This was already the largest single firm in British manufacturing, with 6,000 employees, when it joined with Patons in 1896 to form the largest spinner of thread anywhere. It had set up in the United States to get round the American tariff and soon also dominated the market there. Before long, the amalgamated firm accounted for 80 per cent of the industry's global capacity. Eleven members of the Coats family, engaged in textiles at Paisley since early in the century, became millionaires. When theirs turned into a public company in 1890, it was capitalised at over £5 million. 'Such is the result of an enterprise inaugurated by a humble weaver who first saw the light in a humble cottage,'[15] wrote Andrew Coats of his father James, founder of a mill for making thread at Ferguslie in 1826. No doubt the success also helped to attract the first major foreign investment to Scotland, when the American manufacturer of sewing machines, the Singer Company, built a factory at Clydebank, across the river from Paisley. All the world's seamstresses then looked to this one corner of the west of Scotland.

Jute transformed Dundee just as thread transformed Paisley. In the middle of the eighteenth century the breezy burgh on the River Tay had become a whaling port, sending its ships into Arctic waters. The purpose was to extract oil from blubber, mainly for use in domestic lighting. But surely the capital investment and the bloody slaughter could serve some wider purpose? In

1832 James Watt, a local merchant, discovered how jute soaked in a mixture of whale oil and water turned pliable enough to be worked by machine. Out of this serendipity arose one of the world's great textile industries, by the 1870s employing over 40,000 people in 72 mills and factories. It boomed especially in wartime, during the Crimean War, the American Civil War and all the other wars forever going on somewhere. Jute served for sandbags, then for anything else portable in large, cheap sacks. It was of course just as good for commercial use. Competition would in time arise from Calcutta, because the jute was grown in Bengal and Dundonians set up the first mill to process it on the spot as early as 1855. For a long time, even so, Dundee held on to its prime place in global production of jute. Just like cotton in Glasgow this had stark social effects. The owners of the factories formed a local aristocracy, building grand houses on the Tay and erecting within the city industrial monuments to themselves. Cox's Stack, named after a director, towered 280 feet high over the Camperdown Works. Yet James Cox's company employed women (few men) on the lowest pay of any group of industrial workers in Britain. Dundee could well be called a women's city: by the end of the century, the population between the ages of 20 and 45 was two-thirds female, and one in three households had a woman as head.[16]

A third successful textile town was Kirkcaldy, the global centre for manufacture of linoleum. The little port on the Firth of Forth, where the father of economics, Adam Smith, had been born and grew up, early on enjoyed a brisk foreign trade out of which grew local industries based on spinning and weaving. Michael Nairn started a small handloom factory to make heavy canvas in 1828. He expanded in 1847 when he took out a licence for production of floorcloth, a canvas coated with layers of paint, and opened a works to produce it. He was not only an entrepreneur but also an innovator: he pioneered the use of ovens to season the floorcloth and reduce the length of its processing. Then, when the patent for linoleum (invented by a Yorkshireman, Frederick Walton) expired in 1876, Nairn and other local manufacturers of floorcloth, some his former employees, switched to making this new, more versatile and more durable product. Output of both floorcloth and linoleum occupied seven factories in the town by 1883 and employed 1,300 people. Nairn's own firm expanded its capacity so as to become the biggest single manufacturer in the world, a status it held till the Second World War.[17]

In these ways, during an era of ever more intense foreign competition, three Scots towns continued to prosper through specialisation in textiles, constantly improving the technology and exploiting fresh markets. They therefore survived long beyond the first stage of the industrial revolution. Meanwhile the revolution proceeded.

❁

To the history of Scottish textiles we can link the history of Scottish chemicals, the first new industry to spin off from that old one. The earliest chemical product was salt, made in or near mining areas because the original process of production needed coal for the slow evaporation of seawater in salt pans (origin of the place name Prestonpans). While this industry still existed in the early nineteenth century, it had no future. In 1825 the British government abolished its duty on salt. Scotland was invaded by cheaper English salt produced from springs and underground deposits. Within a decade or two, the Scottish salt pans closed down.[18]

In an economy needing a steady increase in its workforce, decline of an old industry was no disaster. On the contrary, it freed resources and men to pursue more profitable purposes for which Scotland was better endowed. One such purpose lay in the production of chemicals for the textile industry, especially its vital bleaching stage. This had originally been carried out using organic substances. Inventive Scots looked for something better.[19]

Among their qualifications to do so was their country's tradition of medical training. It dated back to the days before the Union when young Scots had gone to qualify themselves at Dutch universities, then the most advanced in Europe for medicine. And this medical education could already be counted as a modern one in an important sense, containing as it did an element of chemistry. James Hutton was one student from Edinburgh who went to the University of Leiden to get his medical degree. Though better known as the father of the science of geology, he made the money to pursue that interest through his partnership in a works producing industrial alkali in the form of sal ammoniac, used as a flux in the refinement of metals.[20]

❁

To the Scots' theoretical expertise was now joined a commercial incentive, to find finishing materials for textiles. So the west of Scotland, Glasgow in particular, offered a natural home to chemical manufacture. By the 1820s Port Dundas, on the Forth–Clyde canal just north of the city, housed half a dozen works producing sulphuric acid or vitriol. Bleaching with chlorine had also been developed, but both substances were dangerous to those working with them. It had come at once as an advance and as a relief when in 1799 Charles Tennant patented a dry bleaching powder (actually invented by his partner, Charles Macintosh). Out of its production grew the enormous St Rollox chemical works at Springburn, established by Tennant in 1798. Tennant's father John had been a classmate and later companion in debauch of Robert Burns, who wrote a poetic epistle to him prophetically commending the young 'wabster Charlie . . . I'm tauld he offers very fairly.' The family would stay in charge of St Rollox for over a century.[21]

St Rollox turned science into money. In 1818 it led the way in adopting the Leblanc process, using sea-salt, for the manufacture of soda. A dozen years later it was by that process producing 10,000 tons of alkali a year. This incidentally sealed the doom of Highland kelp, up to that time the main – and expensive – alternative source of alkali. Now its various applications, in the making of soap, glass, paper, plaster and other products, also became much cheaper and more productive. Once St Rollox had grown into the biggest chemical works in the world, it advertised its status with Tennant's Stalk or Stack, a chimney 455 feet and 6 inches tall. Built in 1841–42, the stack towered there till 1922 when lightning struck and it had to be demolished.[22] The reason for the great height was to spread the terrible pollution from the factory downwind on Glasgow's prevailing westerlies. The Royal Infirmary stood almost next door, which at least meant the workers did not have to go far for treatment of gruesome maladies induced by the chemicals. Here is a description of the works from 1847:

> They are, necessarily, black and dirty, and as infernal in appearance as we can well imagine any earthly place to be. The heaps of sulphur, lime, coal and refuse; the intense heat of the scores of furnaces in which the processes are going on; the smoke and thick vapours which dim the air of most of the buildings; the swarthy and heated appearance of the men; the acrid fumes of sulphur and the various acids which worry the eyes, and tickle the nose and choke the throat; the danger which every bit of broad-cloth incurs of being bleached . . . form a series of notabilia not soon to be forgotten.[23]

The factory belched forth its fumes for the rest of the century and beyond, if at length controlled somewhat by national legislation against pollution. Over that time its technology grew outdated: in newer plants, the more efficient Solvay process replaced the Leblanc process. Yet in Glasgow the Tennants did not want to give up the range of by-products they were generating, which might continue to compensate for the lost lead in process. In 1890, forty-five businesses in the city, including St Rollox, combined into the United Alkali Company under the presidency of a Tennant. It engaged in fierce competition with its English rival, Brunner, Mond & Co, till in 1926 the two were among the companies that merged to form Imperial Chemical Industries. This corporation owned St Rollox up to the demolition of the whole complex in 1964. The site was built over, first with high-rise flats and today with a Tesco.[24]

Yet, though at heavy cost, St Rollox had also brought benefits to mankind. Many were owed in particular to Tennant's original partner Macintosh, son of a Highland tanner who had moved to Glasgow. Clannishness helped the younger Macintosh along, but he was a great chemical entrepreneur in his own right. In 1807 he had set up a factory at Hurlet near Paisley to process the local shales for alum, which could be used in a wide range of cosmetic, medicinal and industrial applications. He struck lucky, awakened a huge demand and before long owned the leading alum works in Britain.

Invention ran in Charles Macintosh's genes. His father George had helped to devise the dyes that might be fixed in Scottish textiles. First he provided financial backing for the manufacture of cudbear, the odd name apparently borrowed from his partner Cuthbert Gordon. By the process they hit on, the maceration of marine lichen in ammonia, they produced a yellow dye. They set up a plant at Leith, which for some reason did not do well. Macintosh then found a new partner in Glasgow and moved the operation there, to a factory surrounded by high walls and employing only monoglot Gaels unable to betray to rivals the secrets of the processes being used. He next turned to one of the most popular colours of the age, Adrianople or Turkey red, bright in hue and concocted by a process involving among other substances soda, salt and sheep's dung, all readily available in Scotland. This time Macintosh went into partnership with Dale of New Lanark and opened at Barrowfield the first works in Britain capable of producing the dye, known locally as Dale's red. The only other dyestuff made in Scotland on any scale was the dark, almost black, Prussian blue, first produced in Edinburgh by the oxidation of iron and later one of the substances manufactured by Charles Macintosh. He also invented processes for calico printing and for bleaching with dry chloride of lime: he was a walking textile industry in himself.[25]

Signal as all these services to Scottish chemicals were, probably they would not in themselves have been enough to bring the younger Macintosh immortality. That he won in consequence of some dealings with the Glasgow Gas Company, run by bright young James Neilson, a self-made engineer. From the inaugural works at Townhead, right next to the cathedral, gas lighting was introduced in 1818 to the city, the first place in Scotland to enjoy it (Edinburgh followed the next year). To begin with the by-products from the works, tar and ammonia, went to waste. But Macintosh thought he could find uses for them and began to buy them in from Neilson. During experiments Macintosh discovered that coal-tar naphtha would dissolve India rubber. In that case thin sheets of rubber might be fashioned and introduced between layers of cloth so as to create the world's original waterproof fabric. Macintosh patented it in 1823, though the process took time to perfect. His early trials had been with wool, which made the garments stiff, heavy and uncomfortable. And if it rained in hot weather – admittedly a rare combination in Scotland – the rubber tended to melt. Still, one by one the problems were solved so that a fabric both flexible and impermeable could be provided at low cost for the production of a wide range of everyday goods. By then the public had given the fabric its inventor's name (modified to mackintosh). It is still made at Cumbernauld. Macintosh's commercial career spanned six decades, and he died a wealthy man in 1843.[26]

Meanwhile Macintosh's old partner Charles Tennant had died in 1838, leaving nine children in whose hands his business at first languished. It was a grandson, also Charles, who brought about a revival after he became a director in 1850. He disposed of a wide range of commercial talents of his own, being a skilled negotiator and perhaps the first capitalist to grasp how large-scale modern business also demanded flair in public relations. The star of shareholders' meetings, he found the knack of making them feel involved while never giving much away. He kept control, in other words. He made a legend of himself in Glasgow as the central figure in a circle of businessmen who trusted his judgment and wanted nothing more than to enter into joint ventures with him.[27]

The industries of Victorian Scotland engaged in unceasing search for fresh productive opportunities. One place they turned to in the 1870s was Spain, a nation that had earlier, and for three centuries, exploited the riches of the New World but so far proved incapable of joining the industrial revolution of the Old World. The province of Huelva, in south-western Spain, had been known since remote antiquity for its mineral deposits of copper, silver and gold; the Phoenicians called it Tarshish, the Greeks and Romans Tharsis. In 1862, Tennant founded the Tharsis Company in Scotland to take over the pyrite mines of Huelva from a previously failed French venture, a deal that came at a knockdown price. He wanted above all to obtain for St Rollox the sulphur that was a by-product of the extraction of copper from pyrites. The pyrites further contained tiny components of gold, which Tennant also set about recovering: the Cassel Gold Extraction Company, formed at his behest in 1884, acquired the rights to a process using cyanide and raising the level of gold won to 95 per cent. Once these other minerals had been taken out they left a residue of iron ore nicknamed blue billy; the generation of quantities of this prompted Tennant finally to establish the Steel Company of Scotland in 1872. Meanwhile in Spain the mining village of Rio Tinto was transformed so as to provide a home from home for Scots engineers who came out to run the operation. They could travel by the railway constructed from the port of Huelva, 30 miles away, then settle into a comfortable house that might have been lifted there from the banks of the lower Clyde. For their spiritual needs, they built a Presbyterian kirk. In their spare time, they played football, which the Spanish labourers learned from them and so introduced to their own country. Its first match took place on 18 March 1890, between Recreativo Huelva and a team from Seville manned by British expatriates constructing that city's waterworks. Tharsis was altogether a pregnant venture.[28]

No less so was Nobel's Explosives, a company set up in Scotland to exploit the patents of the Swede, Alfred Nobel, inventor of modern explosives, also an acute businessman who wished to move into the vast market of the British Empire. Tennant became his partner in Glasgow. He called on the services of another of the city's plutocrats, Charles Randolph, a millionaire from his manufacture of the compound marine engine and from shipbuilding in the yard he founded at Fairfield, Govan. In semi-retirement, he was keeping himself busy with plans to improve the navigation of the Clyde, the disposal of Glasgow's sewage, the network of oceanic shipping lines and other objects no less useful, now to include the introduction of dynamite to Britain.

Nobel had first tried to find partners in London but failed and so turned to Glasgow, by this time housing the world's greatest concentration of chemical companies. The men running them understood instantly, as mercantile Londoners had not, the potential of dynamite. Negotiations for a partnership began and reached a successful conclusion in 1871. The deal reflected the novelty of the risks. A joint-stock company was to be formed of which, in return for transferring his rights, Nobel would hold half the capital. The other three directors were Glaswegians under the chairmanship of Randolph. They built a factory at Ardeer, between Stevenston and Irvine in Ayrshire, amid barren dunes to muffle any blast. This would achieve and sustain a position as the Empire's biggest producer of explosives till well into the twentieth century.[29]

The whole of the chemical saga, from salt to explosives, demonstrates what enormous potential had existed for diversification out of the textile and related industries – and demonstrates, what is more, that Scots fulfilled the potential. But this is scarcely even the half of the history of their industrial revolution. The new industries needed energy, of course, and supplied it from local coalfields. Iron ore was another natural resource that might be exploited in close connection with coal, both linked in turn with engineering. Here lay a second productive cluster that transformed Scotland into a manufacturer for the world.

Coal had been dug in Scotland since the Middle Ages. At the turn of the nineteenth century it still came from mines usually serving just their own localities, though the construction of canals had started to give them wider markets. Soon output rose to meet the growing industrial and domestic consumption. By the middle of the century there were about 350 collieries in Scotland, 250 of them in the west, mainly in Lanarkshire and Ayrshire, which had replaced the older coalfield of Fife as the main sources of coal. Altogether they produced 7 million tons in 1854 before a rapid expansion took the output to 39 million tons by 1914. In 1800 there had been probably no more than 8,000 miners in Scotland. By 1870 the workforce rose to more than 40,000 and by 1914 to 150,000.[30]

The performance was not the sequel to any astounding progress in technology. For much of the Victorian era Scots miners still worked as their forefathers had done, hacking by hand at the coalface in conditions never less than tough and often dangerous. The mining boom worsened these conditions: here the human degradation of the industrial revolution reached its nadir. A Royal Commission mounted an inquiry in 1840. Its report led to an Act of Parliament banning employment underground of women and girls, and of boys below the age of ten; up to the age of thirteen, these must no longer work more than twelve hours a day.[31] The average age of a miner at death was 34, compared to 50 for hands in factories, so to fulfil their productive potential children had had to start work as early as possible, sometimes at five or six years of age. At least that now ended but regulations on safety, even then rather feeble ones, did not come into force till 1861. Life for the men in many mines would not be greatly changed before 1914.

The mining villages, lying in the shadow of the bings and the winding gear, remained frightful too. The families lived in sordid miners' rows, in houses without comfort or sanitation. They had little choice: they could afford nothing better and alternative landlords feared their reputation for drunkenness and violence. Another Royal Commission heard in 1892 of the rows built by William Dixon & Co at Auchenraith near Blantyre, which had a population of 492 people. They consisted of 42 single-roomed and 41 double-roomed houses with no wash-houses or coal-cellars (coals were kept under the bed). An open sewer ran behind, with privies where the users had to squat. There were two drinking fountains.[32] No wonder the wretches confined in such places seemed to others almost savages. But out of segregation on the surface and shared danger underground there developed a strong communal life, together with a sturdy trade unionism. Here the first national leadership of Scottish labour appeared, with Alexander MacDonald in the 1860s and Keir Hardie in the 1890s.

At first all the industries of Scotland made prodigal use of the cheap coal under their feet. But as time went on, and capitalism passed through its alarming cycles, the manufacturers economised. That put mining companies under pressure too, especially in the west of Scotland. Industrial relations here were anyway appalling. Coal-masters almost ran their pits in a spirit of antagonism to the workers. It was not even as if they pushed to introduce new technology, often the cause of conflict in other sectors. On the contrary, they made little use of machinery that might have eased the men's toil. Needing a workforce with no more than basic skills, they seldom bothered about apprenticeships or ladders of promotion. Their obsession was with costs. Frequent strikes, in nearly all of which the miners came off the worse, offered the chance for the pits to take on cheap Irish immigrants and displace the prickly Scots. Robert Brown, factor to the Duke of Hamilton, stated at a public inquiry: 'When the masters find that their men are attempting to impose unreasonable terms upon them they are compelled to introduce new men at their pits. These are generally Irish labourers, who in a few weeks learn to hew coals, and in time become tolerably expert colliers.' The country's biggest mining enterprise was Bairds of Gartsherrie, which owned many pits in the district of Monklands round Airdrie and Coatbridge. They reported to the same inquiry: 'We brought in Irish labourers, who had been working the pits as roadsmen. In three weeks we had the output of coal increased. We were obliged to protect them day and night'[33] – that is to say, from violence at the hands of the Scots whose jobs they had taken. By the time of a similar report in 1848 more than two-thirds of miners in Lanarkshire were estimated to be Irish, their number increasing with every successive strike.[34]

In the mining districts of the east of Scotland, not quite such a closed world, conditions eased somewhat.[35] Without the same concentration of heavy industry round them, the coal-masters here had more incentive to export, more opportunity to spread risks and more chance to maintain the stability needed for investment. The Fife Coal Company, founded in 1872 by a group of entrepreneurs from the county itself, from Leith and from Dundee, was floated in a period of buoyant prices amid the industrial boom caused by the Franco-Prussian War, and continued to thrive on its sales to Europe and the United States. In the same county Randolph Wemyss integrated his mining operations with a light railway to Methil and the specialist port he built there. On the other side of the Firth of Forth, James Hood, head of the Lothian Coal Company, pioneered mechanisation with the use of coal-cutting and coal-washing equipment. The colliery at Newtongrange, today the Scottish Mining Museum, was a beacon of technological progress to the rest.

By the end of the First World War, the proportion of coal cut mechanically was nearly half the output in Scotland, compared with less than a fifth in England. But that could not save the Scottish industry from the problems of a new era, from yet more capricious economic cycles and the loss of foreign markets. Scots coal-masters had already exhausted the most profitable of their seams. Still trying to cut costs, usually in vain, they could probably not have halted their industry's decline anyway. Even belated mechanisation did not improve its overall productivity, and the decline went on.[36]

The biggest user of coal was the metal industry. It had grown even more dramatically than mining did, and in the output of ever more versatile products. Modern manufacture of iron in Scotland started with the Carron Company, founded in 1759 on the River Carron near Falkirk. It made among other things the carronade, a gun of deadly effect at short range, as Admiral Horatio Nelson succeeded in showing at the Battle of Trafalgar (1805). The company continued to thrive and remained independent till 1982.[37]

But in the early nineteenth century Carron suffered eclipse from rivals working the blackband ironstone of Lanarkshire. They produced vast quantities of cheap pig iron, so named from the shape of the containers into which the molten metal was run to cool. The Bairds of Gartsherrie stood as the titans among these ironmasters. Gartsherrie was their original farm near Coatbridge: they launched a vertiginous ascent out of the old steading through exploitation of the ore they happened to find under their fields. At their height they became probably the world's greatest producers of pig.[38]

In 1828 Alexander Baird leased rights to mine ironstone at Gartsherrie and began to build blast furnaces there. He at once applied the hot blast technique just invented by James Neilson, the resourceful manager of Glasgow's gasworks. It involved blowing preheated air into the furnace, so greatly reducing the amount of fuel consumed in production. Baird himself further refined the process, and succeeded in raising his output from 60 to 250 tons of iron a week. When he retired in 1842, four of his sons formed a partnership, named after William Baird but actually run by James Baird. It expanded further to build ironworks and acquire coalfields all over the west of Scotland. By 1870, it produced a quarter of Scotland's pig, around 300,000 tons a year, from a workforce of 10,000 men and boys. And in that year it made a profit of £3 million. Thomas Tancred, compiling an official report on conditions in the mining districts, described the Monklands in graphic terms:

> The groups of blast furnaces on all sides might be imagined to be blazing volcanoes at most of which smelting is continued Sunday and weekdays, by day and night without intermission. By day a perpetual steam arises form the whole length of the canal where it receives waste water from the blast engines on both sides of it and railroads traversed by long trains of wagons drawn by locomotive engines intersect the country in all directions.[39]

In Scotland production of all types of iron reached its highest level at 2.5 million tons by 1857 but then fell steadily as the blackband ore became exhausted. Production of pig by itself did not follow the same pattern because it could use imported ore. Output rose from 800,000 tons in 1854 to peak at 1.2 million tons in 1869; after severe contraction in the 1880s it was at about the same level in 1914.

Those figures at any rate show how pig remained a big item in Scotland's industrial output. Cheap as it was, it yet earned profits to a level that might limit the ironmasters' interest in more advanced products. So Scotland had less incentive than other countries to keep itself at the technological cutting edge. Modern steel, using the Bessemer process, became available elsewhere from the 1850s. At this period the Scots ironmasters, so far from integrating forwards into steel, were integrating backwards into coal, with the Bairds becoming the employers of two out of three Scots miners. If other local industrialists needed some special iron product of their own, they were well advised to make it themselves: just what the shipbuilding cousins Napier did, in the East End of Glasgow, at Robert Napier's Parkhead forge and, in the West End of Glasgow, at David Napier's Lancefield forge.[40]

Still, domestic customers for pig were never lacking. Railways used up huge volumes of it, in a country where so many rivers and arms of the sea had to be crossed. Sir Thomas Bouch built his Tay Bridge in 1878 but it collapsed the next year. The replacement designed by William Arrol opened in 1887 and remains in use today. He also projected the Forth Bridge, which at its completion in 1890 boasted the longest single cantilever span in the world. The cities installed tramlines, in Edinburgh with horse-drawn trams from 1871 and cable-hauled trams from 1888. Glasgow opened a horse-drawn system in 1872 and an electric one in 1898. Aberdeen had electric trams from 1898, Dundee from 1900. Both Edinburgh and Glasgow set about building suburban railways, Glasgow an underground too. The cities also laid down the modern sanitation now essential to their hundreds of thousands of citizens, provided by waterworks, aqueducts and pipelines bringing water in and by sewers carrying it out again. The most elaborate system was the one supplying Glasgow from Loch Katrine, opened by Queen Victoria in 1859 and able to carry 50 million gallons a day along 26 miles of aqueduct and 13 miles of tunnel.[41] If all this did not satisfy the Scottish ironmasters, they found large markets for exports of pig too.

The age of steel came a little late to Scotland but it came quickly. It came late because blackband ore was phosphoric, and the Bessemer process required ores low in phosphorus in order to make this material so much lighter, stronger and more versatile than existing iron products.[42] The problem could be solved, however, and once that happened Scottish steel-making took off. By 1881 it surpassed output in South Wales, till then the British industry's leading region. Production reached nearly half a million tons in 1895.

The pioneer was the Steel Company of Scotland, founded by Sir Charles Tennant and others. It had started up in 1872, intending to use the blue billy that was a by-product from the pyrites of Huelva. For this project Tennant got in touch with the Anglo-German metallurgist William Siemens, who had a Scots wife, Anne, sister of Lewis Gordon, professor of electrical engineering at the University of Glasgow. Siemens, not only an eminent scientist but also a shrewd entrepreneur, conducted experiments on the possible uses of blue billy. Encouraged by the results, Tennant and his friends decided to build a steelworks that Siemens was to design, using the open hearth process he had developed, superior in several respects to the hot blast. In the event it proved too complicated to work in this way with blue billy. But Siemens's plant at Cambuslang would turn out so successful otherwise that it launched Scotland on its career as a steel-making nation, something sustained for a century. By 1885 there were already ten firms producing almost half of British-made steel.[43]

One was Beardmore's, which went into steel in 1879. It operated from the Parkhead forge it had acquired from Robert Napier who, for all his imagination and resource, got into difficulty contracting for the Royal Navy. It seemed a highly promising prospect when in 1861 he won the commission to build HMS *Black Prince*, one of the new class of ironclads. But he had such a struggle meeting the official specifications out of the technology then available that he felt forced to turn for help to an English expert on naval construction, William Beardmore senior. Beardmore became a partner with Napier, moved to Glasgow and brought with him his son, William junior, who went on to found the public company of William Beardmore & Co. in 1886. By the turn of the century his works at Dalmuir was the biggest in Scotland, an area of 25 acres specialising in the manufacture of steel forgings for the local shipbuilding industry. The company also started to make armour plate. It would diversify further into the guns that boomed for Britain in the First World War. It was by then already building aircraft too. Beardmore's and military munitions became synonymous.[44]

David Colville went into steel in 1880. He had opened his first plant in 1872 at the Dalzell ironworks in Motherwell. When the Tay Bridge collapsed in 1879, the young firm won the contract for the supply of iron bars to a new bridge. Colville's son, David junior, spent some years working for the rival Steel Company of Scotland so as to master the technology of the processes it used. Armed with this experience, he joined his father at Dalzell where they built five Siemens furnaces each of 10 tons' capacity. With a steam hammer, plate mill and shearing plant also installed, they could supply both ship and boiler plates. They soon expanded into America, and the first steel plates rolled in the United States came from slabs supplied by Dalzell. They also sold steel to Germany: the *Kaiser Wilhelm der*

Grosse, which in 1898 won the Blue Riband for crossing the Atlantic Ocean in record time, had been built of plates from Dalzell. By the First World War, this was the biggest employer in Motherwell and the most productive steelworks in Scotland.[45]

The streamlined output of steel made a difference above all to the ship-building industry. The yards of the Clyde needed metal plates ever stronger and lighter. The steelworks of the west of Scotland answered those needs.

It was just on a small, local scale that shipbuilding had enjoyed any older tradition in Scotland. Glasgow hardly figured in it because the Clyde was so narrow and shallow. Larger vessels needed to dock downstream, which was why Port Glasgow had been founded in 1668. Till the end of the eighteenth century, the river upstream from Dumbarton was open only to barges. Then, as far as Bowling, the water ran so low and sluggish that the locals might wade across when the tide was out. The channel would finally deepen itself when a series of breakwaters was built to make a faster-flowing current scour the bed, and the Clyde Navigation Trust, formed in 1809, took on the management of the watercourse. By 1825 the river could still only carry vessels of 300 tons to the Broomielaw in the middle of Glasgow, but by 1857 vessels of 3,600 tons might manage. This meant ships could be built, too, along the upper stretch of the Clyde, with the advantage of direct access to the city's iron-working and engineering shops. It is striking that these clustered early on in parts of Glasgow where cotton was spun, at Tradeston opposite the Broomielaw or Camlachie even further east; here lay a link between the textile cluster and the heavy industrial cluster of the new Scottish economy. But later, as ships continued to grow in size, their construction had to be moved downstream again, to Govan and beyond. There the shipyards created a whole town: Clydebank did not exist in 1861, yet in 1901 was home to 30,000 people.[46]

The ships being built were by that time steamships, product of a long technological evolution in Glasgow. The steam engine devised in 1769 by James Watt, maker of scientific instruments to the university, marked a big step forward from its crude prototypes yet in the early nineteenth century it still had to exert its full economic impact. It was then most visible in the steamboats that plied the Clyde, dinky little vessels built of wood, as iron was not yet freely available in Scotland. They puffed their way, consuming huge amounts of coal for the distances they covered, among the sailing ships that remained the normal means of transport by sea. There was a simple reason: the steamships often broke down. They had been puffing since 1812 when Henry Bell's *Comet* began a service between Glasgow and Greenock. Ten years later there were dozens going as far as Largs, Campbeltown and Inveraray, with another on Loch Lomond. These services amounted to little more than tourist attractions: they stopped off for the passengers to take a break in the hotel Bell owned at Helensburgh. Trippers continued to go 'doon the watter' till the 1960s. Yet the charming scene proved more significant than it seemed. While only a small proportion of all the ships built in Britain was at that time launched on the Clyde, they included more than half the steamboats, 42 of them between 1812 and 1820. Still, an enormous array of technical problems had to be solved before they could be put to any more useful purpose.[47]

A technical challenge never failed to appeal to Victorian Scots, however. The challenge of steamships first appealed to the cousins Napier, from a family of engineers at Dumbarton. David was the great inventor and adaptor, the father of marine engineering as a distinct profession, while Robert was the man of affairs, whether in construction or in finance. David had made the boiler and produced the castings for the engines of the *Comet*. On the strength of that, he decided to set up in production himself at Camlachie. In 1816 he delivered his first marine engine, and the next year began operating a steamship on his own account for the run up and down Loch Lomond. Then he turned to seagoing steamers. He built ferries for the routes from Greenock to Liverpool and from Holyhead to Dublin. For the maiden voyage on this latter passage, he took along Charles Macintosh, who feared the boat would sink. He was wrong, and later Napier's widening experience enabled him to introduce a steady series of improvements in the design of hulls, condensers, paddles, screws and engines.[48]

Robert Napier's career took a somewhat different path. He interested himself in the concept of a regular service of steamships across the Atlantic Ocean. After investing in the enterprise that was to become Cunard, he won contracts for steamers that over the next twenty years grew larger and larger.[49] The Royal Navy arrived as his next lucrative customer. Other British and foreign shipping lines followed. By the 1850s this was big business. Napier's company became a magnet for all the brightest and best young managers and apprentices in the west of Scotland. He showed himself generous in the time, effort and encouragement he devoted to them: many went on to set up their own companies. Through them he left a human rather than a corporate legacy. Scottish capitalism remained clannish, with cousins co-operating and sons following fathers. Napier, so resourceful in most ways, did not manage to perpetuate his own dynasty partly because he carried on too long himself, lost touch and in 1871 went out of business. Still, the Napiers were the true fathers of shipbuilding on the Clyde.

The hallmark of that industry was constant technical innovation. The steamers had originally been paddle steamers, to this day still represented on the Clyde by the *Waverley*. The method of propulsion was not best suited to Scotland's stormy waters, as the *Waverley* has continued to show.[50] The idea of the screw propeller had already occurred to James Watt. But it fell to W.J. Macquorn Rankine, professor of civil engineering at the University of Glasgow, to perfect the technology in 1865 and so render paddle steamers obsolete except for pleasure cruises. For twenty years most new Scottish steamers had had screw propellers anyway, but now they became much more powerful and efficient.

The same period saw development of the compound marine engine, which recycled steam through more than one cylinder so as to exploit all its energy. William McNaught took out the original patent in Glasgow in 1845. In 1853 two of the Napiers' former apprentices, Charles Randolph and John Elder, began with the help of Macquorn Rankine their own experiments on compound engines of two cylinders. Their plan was to raise efficiency by reducing the friction of the moving parts, so as to increase power, cut consumption of coal and improve safety. Where others had failed Elder succeeded, because, according to his professorial mentor, he 'had thoroughly studied and understood the principles of the then almost new science of thermodynamics'. Randolph's contribution came in exacting accuracy for gear-cutting and machining, with the result that these two graduates of the university of life on Clydeside were able to take out the further patent that would transform their industry. The company they now founded was to revolutionise the powering of ships. Their new engine came within a couple of decades to drive three-quarters of the British merchant marine.[51]

The scope for innovation on Clydeside had not been exhausted yet. Wooden sailing ships were being built well into Queen Victoria's reign – twice as many as the steamships launched on the Clyde even in 1860. The final flourish in the history of sail came with the *Cutty Sark*, constructed at Dumbarton in 1879 and in service till 1895: but then an epoch in maritime history finally reached its end, at least in any commercial sense. The new age of building in iron had actually started more than half a century before, in 1837, when David Tod and John Macgregor, two more apprentices of Robert Napier, independently opened the first shipyard for that purpose at Mavisbank (where the pyramids stand by the Kingston Bridge now). Napier, in his unfailing benevolence, continued to work with them to improve the technology, still in its infancy and as yet more or less confined to the west of Scotland. Steamships did not finally triumph over sailing ships till they could be built on a much larger scale, which the technical advances of the 1860s at last allowed. In that decade more than 800,000 tons of iron steamships were launched on the Clyde.[52]

The arrival of steel-making in Scotland crowned the development, for now much stronger and lighter vessels could be constructed from material produced near at hand. By the end of the century, 97 per cent of ships from the Clyde were made of steel. It had been in 1879 that William Denny of Dumbarton launched the world's first ocean-going vessel with a steel hull, the *Rotomahana* due to go on service in Australasia. A liberal employer by local standards, he enlisted the practical experience and ideas of his men in a constant search for higher standards, offering them prizes for the best productive improvements they could suggest. He introduced competition into the trials of his ships too, first with prototypes in a test tank, then in real time for the finished products over a measured mile. Out of these boyish enthusiasms grew his expertise on hulls in particular. Denny published many scientific papers on the subject and on techniques of construction. His versatile range of products extended to squat workaday vessels of shallow draught for use in estuaries, a far cry from the sleek elegance of the *Rotomahana*. Out of the fame he won from her he could embark on a huge extension of his yard with a wet dock, longer berths and heavier cranes. He was a canny commercial networker too: he forged links of one kind and another with 19 shipping lines, and to 15 of them he sold 770 ships, for more than £20 million, between 1880 and 1913.[53]

Right into the twentieth century all seemed well on the Clyde. This region, for some time now the global leader in shipbuilding, was still setting records: the peak came in 1913 when it produced an amazing 23 per cent of the entire world's ships, with one launched for every day of the year. At its heart Glasgow claimed the title of Second City of the Empire, and in an industrial sense the claim might have had almost a modest ring. With the towns round it, Glasgow made one-fifth of the steel, one-half of the horsepower of ships' engines, one-third of the railway locomotives and rolling stock, and most of the sewing machines in Britain. In no other part of the world had such a mutually reinforcing combination of forces come together to ensure jobs for the workers, fortunes for their bosses and goods for the rest of the human race. We must not forget the industrial achievements elsewhere in Scotland, of Dundee selling its sandbags, of Aberdeen gathering gear from its granite, of Edinburgh driving bargains for its beer and books, of the markets netted for the knitwear of the Borders or the appetites whetted for the whisky of the Highlands. But it was the heavy industry of the west of Scotland, shipbuilding above all, that left the deepest mark on the nation, apparent even today in popular myth, in the gaunt remains of the yards and in works of art, such as the vigorous etchings of Muirhead Bone. His friend, the journalist C.E. Montague, put into words the world depicted in them:

> There are some kinds of manual work in which men do not easily take pride – work for which there is nothing to show, or only some trivial or rubbishy thing. It is not so with the building of ships. When the riveter's heater-boy said, 'Whaer wid the *Loocitania* hae been if it hadna been for me heatin' the rivets?' he expressed a feeling that runs through the whole of a shipbuilding yard from the manager down . . . Each man or boy employed in building a steamer or battleship feels himself to be part-owner of something organic, mighty, august, with a kind of personal life of its own and a career of high service, romance and adventure before it. For him it comes to the birth on the day when it ceases to be an inert bulk of metal propped into position with hundreds of struts and dog-shores. At last the helpless rigid mass detaches itself quietly like an iceberg leaving the parent floe, and majestically assumes its prerogative of riding its proper element, serene, assured and dominant. For the builder of ships nothing can stale the thrill of that moment or deaden his triumphant sense of parenthood.[54]

All might have seemed well, yet in reality some things were not so well. Foreign competition grew the whole time. Germany, reunified since 1871, embarked on a deliberate naval expansion that also had a spin-off in the construction of passenger liners convertible to warships if need be, and able to cross the Atlantic as fast as or faster than British vessels. Japan, too, started up the shipbuilding that continues to this day. Its industry proceeded directly out of the expertise of young Japanese sent as apprentices to Glasgow. Yozo Yamao arrived to work for Robert Napier in 1866, and after his return home rose at length to be rector of the Imperial College of Engineering; he introduced 'Auld Lang Syne' to Japan where it is sung as *Hotaru na Hikari*, 'Light of the Fireflies', at graduations.[55] American construction, both naval and commercial, had long been something the British needed to keep a wary eye on. Mounting now into the ranks of the great powers, the United States founded its global fortunes on just the sort of heavy industry Scotland had pioneered. But Scotland was a small country: merely from their population and resources the Germans, the Japanese and the Americans could hardly fail in the end to outdo the Scots.

There were problems closer to home too. Not that they went unrecognised: on the contrary, a good deal of gloom pervaded Clydeside, though perhaps in Calvinist Scotland that is always so. It was disturbing that, for two or three decades now, a certain number of ships had had to be built at a loss, with yards taking their chances against fierce competition in unpredictable trading conditions.[56] Another way of dealing with such pressure was to seek business within Britain rather than from abroad, and from the public rather than the private sector – in other words, to win work from the Royal Navy. In the era of an arms race with the Germans this might have seemed sensible but times did in the end change, if only after a world war. And then it was found that the commercial acumen forged by fierce international competition had been lost too.

Perhaps there was anyway something inherently flawed in Scotland's way of doing business, something inhibiting the consolidation of the early industrial lead. Scottish bosses tended to be self-made men or the offspring of founding figures who had learned the ropes through apprenticeships. Charles Tennant the elder launched his career as apprentice to a weaver at Kilbarchan. The first skills Robert Napier acquired lay in ornamental metalwork. James Neilson started out in adult life as a gig-boy on a winding engine at Govan. Charles Randolph began as a wright in a coachworks in Stirling. William Arrol worked as a bobbin-maker in his father's mill before transferring to a blacksmith's forge. David Colville the younger went as a third-hand melter to the Steel Company of Scotland once he finished his schooling at Glasgow Academy. Even Andrew Carnegie, the richest man on the planet after a career in the United States, seemed unable to formulate for his countrymen just what it took to turn versatile adolescent eagerness into sustainable adult achievement: 'One rule I have often suggested to youth,' he solemnly told students at the University of Aberdeen in 1912, 'remain teetotallers until you have become millionaires.'[57]

Something Scots certainly liked was to keep business in the family, or at most in a partnership of friends from the same place or generation[58] – 'using the safe and small', as George Douglas Brown called it in a searing indictment of late Victorian Scotland's mentalities, his novel *The House with the Green Shutters* (1901).[59] The Scots' every tradition and instinct spoke for working up from a diminutive scale as the foundation of all else. It had served them well in the whole fabric of society, not just in the economy. The leaders of business showed in their patronage and philanthropy an intense commitment to their local communities, working there together where they would otherwise have competed.

The counterpart in the actual conduct of business was that in Scotland, more than in the rest of Britain, formal industrial concentration remained rare before 1914. Scots law had shaped the commercial habits, and it made every partnership a legal personality that could sue or be sued, transfer shares and, to a certain extent, offer limited liability. This was indeed something for family and friends rather than for a wider, more impersonal circle of coldly rational investors. Then, in the running of the companies, there would be little room for professional managers so long as the founders or the inheritors were still around: for example, one reason so many brilliant rising men left the family firm of Robert Napier was that they knew his son James was waiting to follow him in charge of it (though James, in the event, died young).[60] On the other hand, when the proprietor had also been the manager, he grew along with his business into his commercial skills. But by the turn of the twentieth century many companies were already of such a size that most managerial functions needed delegation to a staff of subordinates who had not grown with the business and absorbed all its lessons in the manner of the founders.[61] In neither case did management and enterprise quite come together any more.

The Scottish complex of law and custom induced the aversion to takeover too. Firms built up their defences against it by acquiring equity in their rivals or by entering into cartels with them. In shipbuilding, for all the competition among the yards, they held one another's shares and the shares of their customers. This was in one way a source of strength, an incentive to long series of orders and to savings on overheads through the greater scope for standardised designs. In another way it was a weakness, maintaining over-capacity and reducing the drive to innovate. When in 1856, under a reform assimilating corporate law over the whole of Britain, the English type of joint-stock company had come to Scotland, it proved already too late to eradicate the ingrained habits. In allowing the option of non-executive directors, it even encouraged companies to interlock their interests further. Tennants, Napiers, Bairds and so on could now sit not just on their own but on many other boards. This might have been a path to greater integration of manufacture, trade and finance. Instead, it entrenched Scottish clannishness. Above all, it left some of the vital mechanisms of modern capitalism, especially those that weed out failure and promote renewal, wanting.[62]

From about the turn of the twentieth century a basic disjunction with the emergent global capitalism might have been perceived in Scotland. This global capitalism grew out of the new, dynamic set of commercial relationships connecting the continents by the exchange of food and raw materials for manufactured goods, a movement fed and fashioned by the revolution in transport. One way came meat, wool, timber, cotton and grain to Europe. The other way went ships, locomotives and materials for building bridges or railways to regions of the world just starting along the road to development. It was amazing how a small country like Scotland had managed to dominate some of these sectors, but that proved to be a transient phenomenon. Elsewhere, and starting in the United States, the new era spawned multinational corporations overwhelming in scale any partnership or company that Scots could sustain. The revolution in corporate organisation would remain largely absent from the industrial Scotland of the twentieth century except in the form of branch offices and foreign-owned plants.

Why could Scotland not follow the wider development? It is impossible to pass the failure off merely as a function of being a small country, because other small countries – Holland, Switzerland, Sweden, Finland – did at length become and today remain homes to multinational companies, the main vehicle of modern capitalism.[63] Many of Scottish industry's original private partnerships needed in the end to go public for the sake of limited liability and access to capital markets. Expansion could follow, but it often brought with it a steady divorce of ownership from control. The company then stood exposed to takeover by outsiders wielding superior financial power or commercial expertise. It did not help that Scottish commercial conservatism was by this stage extending from the corporate structure to the range of products, despite declining profits, while international competition forced the formation of yet larger global corporations to gain economies of scale. The consequence was in almost every case the dilution of the Scottish character of Scottish companies, or in the end straight takeover by outsiders. In other words, whenever the founding generations passed away, the industries of Scotland found themselves lacking in both the habits of thought and the practical instruments to meet fresh challenges in the world's ever more complex, not to say implacable, economy.[64]

Scots could probably never have prospered to the extent they did in the nineteenth century without the Union of 1707. Compared to independent nations of similar size in Europe, Scotland had developed far faster. Yet in the long run, when they did develop, they were able to safeguard their gains better. While Holland, Switzerland and the Scandinavian countries today all house major international manufacturing corporations, Scotland houses none and has reverted to being an economy of small and medium enterprises. Those other countries were not rigidly protectionist, but over time some sort of symbiosis between industry and the state did help to preserve a degree of national commercial autonomy. Scotland in the nineteenth century still had in certain respects a distinct economy, with probably greater autonomy overall than is enjoyed by most newly industrialising countries at the present time. But Scotland has without its own state never been able to defend itself against external takeover and against the closure of subsidiaries belonging to outsiders, has not even found itself in a position to weigh up the respective merits of commercial protection and economic efficiency. Ultimately one reason lay in the loss of national independence in 1707 – though indeed to Victorian Scots that loss was easily outweighed by industrial success within Britain and its Empire.[65]

3

Services: 'Many sensible men'

The bravest of the early Scottish railways was the Dundee & Newtyle. Eleven miles long, started in 1826 and opened in 1832, it became the first in the country to carry passengers, conveying them between the bustling port on the River Tay and the fertile farmland of Strathmore. This, a century before, had been one of the last bastions of loyalty to the ancient royal house of Stewart and, just as Jacobites once sallied forth from Glamis or Auchterhouse, so now modern technology clanked and snorted right up to their gates. But first the railway needed to traverse the Sidlaw Hills, low by Scottish standards though all the same rising to 1,500 feet. Scots are anyway seldom deterred by such difficulties and the track took a direct run at the hills up three gradients so steep that on each of them stationary engines had to be installed to pull the horse-drawn wagons and coaches to the top. If that did not suffice, there was a device for hoisting a sail so that the Sidlaws' snell winds could carry the train onwards. A final fail-safe was for the wagons to be mounted on bogies: then they might be lifted off if need be and continue their journey by other means. Huffed and puffed along, passengers and goods would get there somehow. Three trains a day went each way, taking just an hour. Alas, the traffic never justified the rose-tinted investment.[1]

The Dundee & Newtyle proved to be not atypical of its time. Even more innocent was the Innocent Railway, so called because it never killed anybody, unlike several others. Opened in 1831, it ran from Dalkeith to Edinburgh and, being horse-drawn too, appeared better reminiscent of the era of stage-coaches than of the age of steam now dawning. Its main job was to transport coal from the mines of Midlothian into the city, to a terminus at St Leonards, though before long it carried passengers too. It had the 'Scotch gauge', 4 feet 6 inches, instead of the future standard gauge 2½ inches broader. A consortium headed by the Duke of Buccleuch saw the construction through. Their engineer was Robert Stevenson, renowned builder of lighthouses and father of Robert Louis Stevenson. The publisher Robert Chambers described the subsequent experience: 'By the Innocent Railway you never feel in the least jeopardy; your journey is one of incident and adventure; you can examine the crops as you go along; you have time to hear the news from your companions; and the by-play of the officials is a source of never-failing amusement. In the very contemplation of the innocence of the railway you find your heart rejoiced.'[2]

In the west of Scotland railways were, of course, a tougher proposition. There the first in the whole country, the Monkland & Kirkintilloch, had opened in 1826, also operated by horses.[3] But its enabling legislation provided for locomotive working, and by 1832 engines pulled most of the trains. Other railways followed, the busiest being the Glasgow & Garnkirk, inaugurated in 1831 and financed by Charles Tennant, the chemical tycoon. He had it laid from a spot near his works at St Rollox down to the coalfield of Monklands as transport for the fuel he needed. There was already the Monklands Canal, passing right by, but to his chagrin it could not carry enough coal. So he built the railway to compete. An excellent investment, it cut the cost of transport to a third of its former level. By 1836 the line carried 140,000 tons of freight. It, too, had meanwhile been opened to passengers, 145,000 that year. To make his engines Tennant installed a small plant at Springburn, the core of the complex which, from 1903, housed the global leader for manufacturing railway engines and rolling stock, the North British Locomotive Company.[4]

But by then the railways offered Scots more jobs in the service of the travelling public than in the production of locomotives for the world. In Scotland the proportion of employment in transport doubled between 1841 and 1911. In numbers that meant a threefold rise from 50,000 to 160,000. Still, such strong growth in a Victorian service industry was nothing unusual: one fact that has in general escaped the attention of Scottish historians is how this sector of the economy marked up the strongest growth of any in the nineteenth century, to eclipse manufacturing industry by some way. In 1851 total employment in manufacturing reached nearly 420,000, and over 650,000 in 1901. During the same half-century, employment in services soared from 380,000 to 880,000, at that level approaching half the total workforce.[5] The services covered an enormous range of activity, from the highest to the humblest, from financiers to footmen, and included the majority of women workers. No full survey can be attempted here, but it should be possible for us to follow a certain logic in one important aspect of their evolution – a logic that, as often in booming economies, could also be skewed and unpredictable. Just as textiles and chemicals, or coal, iron and shipbuilding, developed clusters of varied manufactures, so the railways developed a cluster of varied services.

In this capacity, the railways catered to both the industrial and the agricultural revolution in Scotland. They represented a facet of modernity itself, in which travel over long distances for the first time became easy and normal. With that, in part because of it, the new Scotland committed itself to a paradigm of accelerating urbanisation, industrialisation and technical progress.

Railways in themselves brought multiple economic gains. Perishable goods reached broader markets. Where tracks connected with feeder roads, differentials between urban and rural prices could be much reduced, if not ended, for cheap, bulky goods. The value of land round the burgeoning towns rose as commuter transport enabled people to live further from their places of employment. Many new jobs were created. The workforce grew more mobile.[6]

The central belt of Scotland had been till the end of the eighteenth century not at all as easy to cross as we might imagine from the numberless means of doing so today. Then the usual road between Edinburgh and Glasgow lay a little south of where either the motorway or the railway now runs, along the line of the A71, which was, in fact, the shortest route between the level ground of the valleys of Forth and Clyde. While this road traversed bleak high moors, they were on balance preferable to the bogs and mosses that might impede a horse or carriage further north and lower down. Newer modes of transport were not to be so constrained by the physical character of the land. Along a more northerly route favoured for its lesser gradients, Edinburgh and Glasgow became linked from 1775 by canal, which did not disturb the rustic peace, and from 1842 by rail, which did. The enabling legislation for this railway indeed specified it should follow the line of existing canals. Of course it was meant to carry more and to carry it faster than a canal ever could, for nothing less would justify the cost of £1.2 million, stupendous by the standards of the time. For that sort of money, tricky problems could be solved. To reach the western terminus at Queen Street, Glasgow, the railway plunged over the Cowlairs bank and tunnelled down a steep gradient beneath the Forth–Clyde Canal; trains returning up the slope had to be hauled by cable till 1909. The eastern terminus presented no problems, however, as witnessed by the original edifice of Haymarket Station still standing there today.

Despite the challenges, nobody needed to worry about the railway. From the start the passenger traffic exceeded expectations. The directors had reckoned on carrying 340,000 people a year at their peak. In 1846 the figure was already a million, paying annual receipts of more than £100,000.[7]

At that point Scotland had just, during the winter of 1845–46, suffered a bout of railway mania, of frantic investment in this revolutionary mode of transport that would lead to rapid coverage of the country by a network still in good part there today. The prices of shares in the new railway companies soared, sucking in ever more money from a gullible public, till the inevitable collapse followed. In the process, railways were projected for every part of the Lowlands, and it should have been obvious to any level-headed investor that not all of them could even be built, let alone make a profit. The merchant princes of Glasgow, if no strangers to speculative bubbles themselves, looked on in alarm. At an open meeting called to urge the British government to calm things down somehow, Sir James Campbell, former lord provost, said 'he thought it would be a very great misfortune to the commercial interests of the country if all the railways were conceded which had been applied for. The country could not spare from its other requirements so large an amount of capital.'[8] But by now the bubble was on the point of bursting anyway. It appeared, in fact, to do no permanent damage, to judge from the sensible pattern of development that the Scottish railways afterwards resumed.

Well before the mania, there had been much cogitation on this matter. A Royal Commission on Anglo-Scottish routes, a sure sign of cluelessness in Whitehall, was appointed in 1841. It pronounced after two years of deliberations that a single route to Scotland would be needed, this provided by a chain of independent railways coming up through Crewe, Lancaster and Carlisle to the border, then by Annandale to Glasgow. That was the route the Caledonian Railway took. It became the first company to cross the border, and it always remained the most profitable because of its greater commercial and industrial traffic out of the west of Scotland. Its chief mechanical engineers, Dugald Drummond and John McIntosh, won fame as designers of the great locomotives that powered over the summit at Beattock.[9]

Strange to say, Edinburgh never fancied the Royal Commission's bright idea. John Learmonth, former lord provost and now chairman of the Edinburgh & Glasgow railway, resolved to prove the planners wrong. He proposed a line, to be called the North British, which would run in the first instance as far as Dunbar, all of 27 miles. Try as he might, he could not find enough even of his most credulous countrymen to invest in this. Nothing daunted, he announced the North British would bash on to Berwick, there to meet English lines already stretching towards the border. The chief mechanical engineers of the North British, William Reid and Walter Chalmers, were no less renowned than its rival's. As chairmen after Learmonth, the company sought figures from the summit of Scottish society, a notch up from the mere businessmen who headed the Caledonian: James Balfour of Whittingehame (father of A.J. Balfour), the Marquis of Tweeddale, the Earl of Dalkeith, William Whitelaw (grandfather of Viscount Whitelaw). By way either of the west coast or of the east coast, the journey to London took 12 hours and 30 minutes. For the time being most people still preferred to travel by sea. An English shareholder blamed the low revenue from the routes on the unwillingness of mean Scots to buy anything better than a third-class ticket even if they could afford it.[10]

By 1849, then, railways ran from both Edinburgh and Glasgow to the border as well as between the two. Now Scotland could extend the network. It soon covered the southern uplands and forged northwards to Perth and Aberdeen – the bare bones of a system that by the end of the century made most of the country accessible by rail, even some remote parts of the Highlands. In general, each main stretch was constructed and owned by a separate company, which then might add branches and links to other lines. The expansion continued to excite both the people who ran the railways and the people who rode them.

In part it was feuds among the railway companies that spurred them on both to the extension of services and to technical progress. The most notorious feud, as bad as any among the Highland clans of old, arose from the rivalry of the North British and the Caledonian Railways. The core of the North British's business remained the eastern route to Edinburgh, the core of the Caledonian's business the western route to Glasgow, but it all got much more complicated than that. One Caledonian ambition was to have a continuous line from Carlisle to Aberdeen, so closing off the whole of the north of Scotland to the *soi-disant* North British. The network, in fact, reached Aberdeen through the efforts of other companies, the Scottish Central Railway that arrived at Perth in 1848, the Scottish Midland Railway that carried on to Forfar and the North Eastern Railway that completed the route. At the same time, the North British sought to gain access to the industrial traffic of Clydeside. It achieved this through amalgamation with the Edinburgh & Glasgow and with the Monkland companies in 1865.[11] On the same day the

Caledonian took over the Scottish Central, so at last setting out for Aberdeen; acquisition of the Scottish Midland and the North Eastern followed.

That left the North British with the problem of how indeed to live up to its name and make its own way northwards, while thwarting the Caledonian's ambitions as far as it could. In 1862 it had absorbed the Edinburgh, Perth and Dundee Railway, which ran a ferry from Granton to Burntisland and another from Wormit to Dundee at either end of its line through Fife. This inspiration of the company's manager and resident engineer, Thomas Bouch, created a route across the county as straight as it ever could be but put the passengers to a great deal of bother as they clambered on and off ferries not just once but twice. The sole way to deal with the problem was to bridge both firths. First, in 1878, a spindly structure of lattice girders, made of malleable iron and mounted on brick columns, reached out across two miles of the Tay as it widened towards the sea before Dundee. Designed by Bouch, it had also a series of high girders in the middle to allow passage for ships. Apart from that, it contained a range of weaknesses in both design and workmanship that caused the central portion to fall down, taking a train and sixty passengers with it, in a great storm on the night of 28 December 1879.[12] The bard of Dundee, William McGonagall, was moved to write a commemorative poem of unbelievable awfulness:

> Beautiful Railway Bridge of the Silv'ry Tay!
> Alas! I am very sorry to say
> That ninety [sic] lives have been taken away
> On the last Sabbath day of 1879,
> Which will be remember'd for a very long time.

However bad the poem, McGonagall did manage with a message to Bouch in the final lines to hit the cause of the disaster right on the head:

> I must now conclude my lay
> By telling the world fearlessly without the least dismay
> That your central girders would not have given way,
> At least many sensible men do say,
> Had they been supported on each side with buttresses,
> At least many sensible men confesses.[13]

The cause being clear, it stopped dead the building of a bridge across the Forth also designed by Bouch. Otherwise the North British would have urged on its completion, as yet another blow at the detested Caledonian. And then the bridge would have fallen down, perhaps even sooner than the one over the Tay. But from now on no chances could be taken: the Forth Rail Bridge designed by John Fowler and Benjamin Baker that opened in 1890 was a massive iron cantilever structure allowing a colossal margin of safety. William Arrol took charge of its construction; he also built the more solid, sober Tay Rail Bridge that opened in 1886.

Further up the line, the region round Aberdeen belonged in terms of transport to a company not large but formidable, the Great North of Scotland Railway. It displayed, shall we say, all the negative side of the Aberdonian character. Peevish, possessive, pugnacious, it indulged in some unbelievable behaviour. It charged the price of an express for trains that went at a hearse's pace. It showed a provocative attitude to connecting lines, whistling its own locomotives on their way just as frantic passengers on a different company's train puffed up within sight of the station where they hoped to change. The Great North had the strategic aim of a further link from Aberdeen to Inverness – a prospect not at all welcomed by Invernesians, who with justice thought their own company, the Highland Railway, would provide it with much more consideration for all. This was indeed a commendable company that at length extended its branches over most of the region, even to the northern and western oceans. How it would connect south remained an open question. One route might be round the Grampian Mountains, but that required the co-operation of the Great North. The Great North did, it is true, start building to Keith, yet so slowly that the Highland Railway had time to reach the town first, to the Aberdonians' fury. Their overreaction ensured that the Highland then constructed a direct link from Inverness to Perth through the Pass of Drumochter rather earlier, by 1863, than it might otherwise have done. In time the Great North mellowed a little, flattered that Queen Victoria liked to use it to get to Balmoral; it then unctuously called itself the Royal Railway.[14]

The Caledonian and the North British competed in the same combative spirit right up to the end of the century. Their 'Race to the North' in the end involved the routes all the way from London to Scotland. The first race to Edinburgh between trains travelling in the daytime started in 1888. The second race between overnight trains to Aberdeen went on from 1895. In the latter case, the effective finishing post was Kinnaber Junction, 38 miles short of Aberdeen, where the Caledonian and the North British tracks joined for the final section: whichever train got there first hogged that line to the end. On the approach to Kinnaber the two routes ran either side of the Montrose

Basin, so that each train could see the other steaming towards the common goal. No doubt it was all a big thrill for the drivers and the firemen, even for the guards, but not always for the passengers. The speed of the journey could, in fact, turn out to be an inconvenience for them: instead of arriving in Aberdeen at seven o'clock in the morning (as they were scheduled to) they got there in the small hours, leaving those with onward connections hanging about on that long, exposed platform in the fresh wind off the North Sea. But a serious derailment finally counselled safety over speed, and the race was abandoned in favour of realistic timetables.[15]

Expansion of the network reached an end only with the physical limits of mainland Scotland. Branches of the Highland Railway went west to Kyle of Lochalsh in 1897, and north to Golspie, where it had already arrived by 1868. Whether it should proceed further lay in doubt, even though Wick and Thurso had developed fisheries bound to benefit from fast transport south. The third Duke of Sutherland resolved the doubt. With his family's habitual benevolence, he either himself built or else helped to finance the building of the rest of the line. It passed through an empty landscape of peat bogs to the two northern ports, which it reached in 1874.[16]

The last great Scottish project was the West Highland Railway, built as far as Fort William by 1894 and Mallaig by 1901. Again the North British sought to break out of the bounds the Caledonian sought to impose on it. The westernmost point so far reached by the North British was Craigendoran on the Clyde just short of Helensburgh. Beyond it a demanding but feasible route stretched away into the Highlands, where the Caledonian had already constructed a line to Oban. Never to be outdone, the North British headed for Fort William, which it reached by laying a line across Rannoch Moor, floating the tracks on the bottomless bogs with a mattress of tree roots, brushwood and thousands of tons of earth and ashes. The moor was quite void of people. One of its stations, Corrour, could not be reached by road. The achievement of getting the railway across would be, however, if anything exceeded by the eventual extension of the line to Mallaig, including the spectacular viaduct at Glenfinnan. The whole project cost £2 million and never made a profit. But the Treasury in London was persuaded to pay a sufficient subsidy on the grounds that otherwise the crofters might revolt again.[17]

One further adornment of Scotland by the railways came in the construction of a good number of station hotels, often the best at any particular destination.

In this, too, the North British and the Caledonian Railways competed. In Edinburgh, the Caledonian Hotel (1899–1903) and the North British, now Balmoral, Hotel (1895) still frown at each other from opposite ends of Princes Street, the first importing Glaswegian red sandstone into the heart of the city, the second retorting with the silver-grey sandstone of the New Town. In architecture, the Caledonian works the better despite the Balmoral's clock tower, Edinburgh's most familiar landmark after the Castle and the Scott Monument. Glasgow, too, had a North British, now the Copthorne, Hotel (1903–05) lining half of George Square's most nondescript side. It does not even begin to compare with the Grand Central Hotel (1882–84), massive and handsome, built by the Caledonian Railway at the junction of Gordon Street and Hope Street.[18] Elsewhere in the country, from Inverness to Dumfries, further examples of the genre might be found, the most opulent being the Turnberry Hotel (1906) in Ayrshire, right next to the golf course; here, however, the station was built for the hotel rather than the other way round.

Scottish railway hotels continued to be opened into the twentieth century, on occasion reaching the height of luxury. They were in any event bound to raise the standard of accommodation for visitors, some of whom had found Scotland a bit grim in this respect. The hotels also raised the standard of Scottish food, a big part of the trouble. Of *haute cuisine* there was as yet little sign, though Scotland had gained some acquaintance with it from the residence of the exiled French royal court, in flight from the Revolution, at Holyrood. Scots were astounded at the gastronomic habits revealed to them. 'Until I had seen these Frenchmen, I thought the power of man was limited', wrote Pryse Lockhart Gordon. He went on to describe how 'one day a salmon three feet long, and not less than 25lb, was put down as the second course and in a trice it disappeared.' Perhaps superior culinary arts did then start penetrating the rest of the country a little, to judge from what Lady Elizabeth Grant of Rothiemurchus found at Blair Atholl on her way north: 'Here we were accustomed to a particularly good pudding, a regular soufflé that would have been no discredit to a first rate French cook, only that he would have been amazed at the quantity of whisky poured over it. The German brandy puddings must be of the same genus, improved, perhaps, by the burning, except to the taste of the highlander.' But the service proved a problem: 'The Atholl lad who waited on us was very awkward, red haired, freckled, in a faded, nearly threadbare tartan jacket.'[19]

Otherwise, Scots at table followed the fashion of earlier ages, not so much of elegant sophistication as of disparate excess. Sir Walter Scott used to repair with friends to constitute the Cleikum Club at the Howgate Inn south of Edinburgh, which served dishes set out in *The Cook and Housewife's Manual* (1826) by Meg Dods. He detailed one meal: 'First came the soup – the hare soup; Meg called it rabbit soup, as this was close season . . . stewed red trout, for which the house was celebrated; a fat, short-legged, thick-rumped pullet, braised and served with rice and mushroom sauce; a Scotch dish of venison collops; and though last, not least . . . one of the young pigs, killed since his adventure on the sty.' The whole was washed down with a fine Burgundy, Château Montrachet, and finally with a novel treat: 'Coffee, four years kept, but only one hour roasted, was prepared by the Nabob's own hands – coffee which he himself had brought from Mocha, and now made in a coffee-pot of Parisian invention patronised by Napoleon.'[20]

Still, the Cleikum Club was an exception and most Scots rested content with humbler fare, the culinary legacy of a poor nation with besides a Calvinist suspicion of the sins of the flesh. James Bertram, editor of the *North Briton*, wrote of what had been available for the breaks in his working day in the Edinburgh of his youth:

> Many a time did I indulge in a boiling hot pennyworth of black pudding, confectioned in a small shop close to Tweeddale Court . . . Another gastronomic treat was to indulge in one of Spence's hot pies in his tavern in Hunter Square, a favourite haunt of apprentices like myself . . . My own allowance for the midday meal was twopence halfpenny *per diem*, and I never asked for more; for in the well-known eating house in the east end of Rose Street kept by kindly Jenny Anderson, it provided a substantial meal – say, excellent sheep's head broth, a savoury trotter and a penny loaf.[21]

Wealthy Glasgow would show a way forward with the invention of the tea room. It was in the 1880s that the catering pioneer, Catherine Cranston, founded this successor to the coffee house, known in the trading city since the seventeenth century. But the coffee house had been monopolised by men, while women always entertained at home. According to the novelist Neil Munro, 'Miss Cranston, clever, far-seeing, artistic to her fingertips, and of a high, adventurous spirit, was the first to discern in Glasgow that her sex was positively yearning for some kind of afternoon distraction that had not yet been invented.'[22] In 1884 she rented a half-shop in a hotel in Argyle Street and soon acquired the whole building, which she refashioned as the

Crown Lunch and Tea Rooms. Then she opened premises in Ingram Street and Buchanan Street.

This was also the heyday of the Glasgow School of painting, and the tea rooms turned into an aesthetic adjunct of it. Cranston showed herself inspired in her employment of two gifted but as yet unknown young artist-architects, George Walton and Charles Rennie Mackintosh, with the latter's wife, Margaret Macdonald, as decorator. The journalist William Power wrote: 'Together the designers produced something which was at once severely simple and strikingly original, a varied harmony which was based on the square and the straight line, with black and white, grey and brown, as the leading shades, relieved by small sections of rose and emerald green, and by fresh flowers chosen by Miss Cranston herself.'[23] To her tea rooms she sent, three times a week, a donkey cart driven by a boy in green livery to deliver the flowers from her own garden with precise instructions for their display. In 1904 she opened the Willow Tea Room in Sauchiehall Street, the sole survivor today of her empire. An eye-catching bow window on the first floor, with mullions and decorative leaded windows, indicates the position inside of the Room de Luxe. Here, for both exterior and interior, Mackintosh was given a free hand. He designed the structure itself and then the furniture, the cutlery, even the menu cards: 'Chicken & Ham Rissole & Sauce 9d, Fried Turkey Egg 6d, Small Cold Roast Lamb 10d . . .'[24]

The Willow Tea Room was besides dedicated to temperance, but for most Scots, male Scots at least, pubs remained the centre of social life all through the Victorian era, indeed right up to the final quarter of the twentieth century. At first nothing but drinking dens, they gave their customers little scope to do more than throw booze down themselves as fast as possible. And the temptation was ubiquitous. By the 1840s Edinburgh had 555 pubs, Glasgow 2,300. Even this level of service was beaten in some small burghs. There might be, for instance, not just a drouthy immediate clientele of miners or fishermen but also a gasping client base in the dry parishes of the surrounding countryside where the landowners refused to permit a pub – so market days offered the sole chance of a swally. Good examples could be found in East Lothian, where Tranent had 52 pubs (one for every 76 inhabitants) and Dunbar 53 (one for every 83).[25]

Trying to ward off the alcoholic tsunami was a temperance movement led by an evangelical publisher, William Collins. An Act of Parliament, passed in

1853 at the behest of a Conservative MP, William Forbes Mackenzie, ordered pubs to close at eleven o' clock in the evening and all day on Sunday – though not hotels, where drink could still be served to *bona fide* travellers. Glasgow's drinkers responded by developing an itinerary – out to Yoker, by ferry to Renfrew, back into town by way of Govan – and bevvying their way in good faith round it. At length the law did make some difference to the nation's hard-drinking habits, though it may be changes in social attitudes achieved more by rendering it less respectable for the middle class and for women to get drunk. Consumption of spirits (nearly all whisky) was by 1910 two-thirds of what it had been in 1830, and in the same period the number of spirit licences per head of population plummeted by 80 per cent: in other words, an awful lot of shebeens were shut down.[26]

Yet Scottish drinking laws remained less severe than English drinking laws and the people more inclined to treat drunkenness as a joke, or rather to admire men who could hold their drink. The number of Scots euphemisms for the resulting state of mind and body remains remarkable to this day.[27] Perhaps, as one visitor suggested, 'the poets of Scotland have thrown round the drinking habits of their country the witching glamour of their genius'.[28] Indeed, the cult of Robert Burns, burgeoning in the middle of the century, tended to sanctify the national conviviality. And it was not just something to pass the hours of leisure or enliven a formal celebration. Heavy drinking accompanied rites of passage at work, too, such as the admission of apprentices to the trade. Craftsmen looking for a job did best to go to a pub, find a foreman and buy him a drink. The early trade unions often met in pubs, though before long, aspiring to respectability, they had thought better of it. There was a good reason: once in the pub, Scots found it hard not to get drunk. The chief constable of Dunbarton explained why: 'The habits of the Scotch labouring classes are unfortunately to enter public houses in companies of two, four or six, as the case may be. Each individual stands his round to the company, and in many cases it is not the love of drink that causes them to do this, but being considered shabby if they do not stand their round.'[29]

Meanwhile the publicans rose to the challenge of temperance by making their premises more attractive. Bright, flashy, golden gin palaces lured in the passing trade. The young were wooed by 'free and easies', in effect small music halls where entertainers vamped it up on the piano with bawdy, comic or sentimental songs. Contrary efforts at refinement led finally to the palace pubs, veritable temples of Bacchus.[30] Still, there was always room for more individualistic howffs, the most famous in Glasgow being the Horse Shoe

Bar, remodelled from a warehouse in 1885–87 by a racing-mad proprietor. The front and the interior with its oval bar remain intact today; horseshoes are everywhere. On the south side of the city the Corona Bar offers an example of the sumptuous type, with its openwork parapet, diminutive corner dome, top-lit interior and etched or stained glass. On the former boundary between Glasgow and Govan, the modern exterior of the Old Toll Bar hides a saloon of 1892–93, decorated with painted and engraved glass or mirrors, and an elaborate display of bottles behind a single long counter.[31] In its turn Edinburgh had, with its good beer, good pubs to match. The oldest date in their present state, not much altered, from the 1890s: the Abbotsford, Barony, Bennet's Bar, Café Royal, Canny Man's, Diggers, Doric Tavern, Ensign Ewart, Guildford Arms, Kenilworth, Leslie's Bar. They no longer tolerate spit and sawdust on the floor, but bear little resemblance to the chintzy kind of hostelry that seems most favoured in England.

Robert Louis Stevenson said, 'A Scot of poetic temperament, and without religious exaltation, drops as if by nature into the public house. The picture may not be pleasing, but what else is a man to do in this dog's weather?'[32] The Medical Officer of Health for Renfrewshire, Dr Archibald Campbell, gave a different impression to a municipal commission of inquiry in 1903:

> The man has finished his day's work and has had his ill-cooked tea . . . His education has stopped short of making reading a pleasure to him. The children are noisy, as children are apt to be. There is little room to move. Perhaps there is washing hanging around to dry . . . He might talk to his wife. Or he might play with the children. But for every day, all the year round, it is impossible. He puts on his hat and goes out . . . The public house is warm and bright – and where else is he to go?[33]

Here was one native service industry that prospered on its own terms, despite the do-gooding legislative interference. But perhaps few visitors venturing north of the border on the railways dared as yet to darken the door of a Scottish pub, with its scary denizens and alien customs.

Otherwise traditional Scottish hospitality adapted to novel demands, especially to organised tourism. Some such traffic was already established in the early nineteenth century, not least because war with France forbade travel in Europe to people formerly able to enjoy it. The English Lake Poets, for example, made the best of things by crossing the border to their north. A nervous Dorothy Wordsworth described the still exotic environment, and how at one lodging

> the good woman had provided, according to her promise, a better fire than we had found in the morning; and indeed when I sate down in the chimney corner of her smoky biggin' I thought I had never been more comfortable in my life. Coleridge had been there long enough to have a pan of coffee boiling for us . . . We caressed our cups of coffee, laughing like children at the strange atmosphere in which we were: the smoke came in gusts, and spread along the walls and above our heads in the chimney, where the hens were roosting like light clouds in the sky. We laughed and laughed again, in spite of the smarting of our eyes, yet had a quieter pleasure in observing the beauty of the beams and rafters gleaming over the clouds of smoke. They had been crusted over and varnished by many winters, till, where the firelight fell on them, they were as glossy as black rocks on a sunny day cased in ice. When we had eaten our supper we sate about half an hour, and I think I had never felt so deeply the blessing of a hospitable welcome and a warm fire.[34]

The traffic developed till Scott could remark that 'every London citizen makes Loch Lomond his washpot and throws his shoe over Ben Nevis'.[35] His own novels gave a huge boost to Highland tourism. It had been confined till his time to the edges of the region, for example, in the fashionable 'short tour' starting at Dunkeld and ending at Luss, with Loch Lomond as the climax. Few visitors penetrated the wild country to the north and west. With the 'Lady of the Lake', Scott pointed them towards the Trossachs:

> The summer dawn's reflected hue
> To purple changed Loch Katrine blue;
> Mildly and soft the western breeze
> Just kiss'd the lake, just stirr'd the trees,
> And the pleased lake, like maiden coy,
> Trembled but dimpled not for joy;
> The mountain-shadows on her breast
> Were neither broken nor at rest;
> In bright uncertainty they lie,
> Like future joys to fancy's eye.[36]

Then Scott's 'Lord of the Isles' put Skye on the traveller's map, the shores of Loch Coruisk in particular, where King Robert Bruce was supposed to have trod:

> No marvel thus the Monarch spake;
> For rarely human eye has known
> A scene so stern as that dread lake,
> With its dark ledge of barren stone.
> Seems that primeval earthquake's sway
> Hath rent a strange and shatter'd way
> Through the rude bosom of the hill,
> And that each naked precipice,
> Sable ravine, and dark abyss,
> Tells of the outrage still.[37]

Improved transport now made it easy for people to reach the Highlands. First the seagoing paddle steamer prompted development of an intricate shipping network out of the Clyde, up the west coast and into the Inner Hebrides. Then railways opened the mainland to exploration too. An Englishman, Thomas Cook, used these opportunities to create the modern tourist industry. Organising excursions for groups at fixed rates, he made Scotland one of his prime destinations. His Tartan Tours began in 1846, the year the potatoes failed all over the Highlands. But, from the comfort of steamer or train, the visitors would have found it hard to notice the difference.[38]

On arrival the visitors might equip themselves, from 1851, with *Black's Picturesque Tourist*, offering the expert knowledge of a native publishing house, A. & C. Black. 'Edinburgh,' it reassured the sightseer, 'possesses many advantages. The climate, although it cannot be called mild or genial, is yet eminently salubrious; and favourable, not only to longevity, but to the development of the mental and physical powers.' As for the metropolis of the west, 'in point of picturesque situation Glasgow must suffer in a comparison with Edinburgh; yet, if the tourist will put himself under our guidance for a short time, we promise to shew him one of the finest cities in the British dominions, which, even in a mere landscape point of view, presents a series of pictures of equal beauty and interest'; still, he should keep clear of King Street, 'inhabited by a numerous and rather turbulent population, of the poorest classes'. In Dundee, on the other hand, the tourist was advised to fix his gaze on the river rather on the city: 'The grandest and most important feature of Dundee is its harbour, with its magnificent wet docks, built and in progress, and a number of spacious quays, patent slip, graving dock, &c., spreading along the margin of the Tay, a mile and a half from east to west.' And the nicest thing about Aberdeen was (despite rumours put about by the malicious) the people: 'The history of Aberdeen exhibits it participating largely in the successive vicissi-tudes of the times; but, under all circumstances, its inhabitants have generally been distinguished for their loyalty, prudence, and enterprise.'[39]

While railways and steamers opened Scotland to the world, they also offered a chance to get to know the country to the Scots themselves, at least to some of them. In practice, resorts such as Largs or Dunoon on the west coast and North Berwick or Elie on the east coast were reserved to profes-sional families, or at most to tradesmen and shopkeepers, just as the Highland grouse-moors belonged to the rich. At least for the working man, wife and weans there was always a trip doon the watter. It was not without its risks: William Macgill, surgeon to the police force of Glasgow, told a parliamen-tary inquiry in 1872 'of cases where men have a holiday, and go out with their wives and families and sweethearts . . . it is quite notorious that in many instances, those excursions, instead of being beneficial, become a curse, from the quantities of whisky consumed, and the acts of violence that follow'. In 1882 an Act of Parliament extended closing on Sundays to passenger vessels plying the rivers and firths of Scotland, in view of the 'great evils' that had arisen on them 'from the sale of intoxicating liquors'.[40] Perhaps it was better after all just to gaze on the fine scenery and breathe in the fresh air. A forge in the Gorbals offered neither.

The railways helped besides to generate and expand a quite different cluster of Scottish services, in all that had to do with money. The emergence of a modern economy created on the one hand greater wealth, on the other hand higher risk. Scotland, always juggling meagre resources, was precocious in meeting the challenges. While the country's financial requirements had remained mod-est till 1707 and for several decades afterwards, it was even at that time home to two banks, the Bank of Scotland founded in 1695 and the Royal Bank of Scotland founded in 1727, both under royal charter. They formed a system that, small as it was, managed to benefit humanity by inventing the overdraft. In time, non-chartered banks were set up, normally for local purposes. By 1815 39 Scottish banks existed, 12 in Edinburgh, four in Glasgow, with a scattering in smaller towns. The thing to mark is that they gave Scotland a system separate from England's, little affected by the Treaty of Union.[41]

After 1707, as the treaty specified, the currency of Scotland was the pound sterling. The old pound Scots maintained a spectral existence as a unit of account used, for example, in the calculation of public imposts dating from before the Union and calculated at a fixed exchange rate of 12:1 against sterling. Yet a common currency did not unite different banking systems, any more than it does in the European Union today. The Scottish one ran on with minimal English interference till 1845. In monetary terms, too, Scotland remained a semi-independent country.

Guided by no models and little legislation, the Scottish banks had by the nineteenth century discovered for themselves the essentials of modern banking.[42] They competed, since the absence of control by the state allowed anyone with the requisite resources to set up a bank. They had sound backing, for they soon learned the need of security, of keeping a large capital subscribed and paid up, with a stock of realisable assets. They were also willing in times of difficulty to hold each other's notes, a principle that in modernised form is applied by central banks on an international scale today. They made good profits, through the active encouragement of deposit banking and the invention of the overdraft. They maintained public confidence, because all notes were payable on demand. Since 1771 the banks had cleared each other's notes twice a week. Overissue by any one of them would have made it unable to settle its balances and subjected it to the embarrassment of needing to draw a bill on London. This was avoided. With interest paid on deposits, nobody had an incentive to hold paper. Notes were on average returned to the issuer for settlement within eleven days in the towns and three weeks in the country – 'in this way it is not possible for the circulation to be more than what is absolutely necessary for the transactions of the country'.[43] The banks offered widespread service, with branches set up almost from the outset, even in the remote Highlands. Dispersal of resources also checked sudden runs. And the system built up long-term stability, at a time when there could still be a differential in the exchange rate between Edinburgh and London, despite the common currency; it once reached 4.5 per cent. The banks established a fund to deal with this.[44]

It appears the Bank of England would have been the lender of last resort in any threatened collapse, though no statute or other document said so. But because of the prudence of the Scottish banks, and of the self-policing mechanisms they enforced among themselves, there was never a chance of any such collapse – not even in the period of greatest economic instability after the Napoleonic Wars. This extraordinary exception in troubled times would strike even Karl Marx as he sat in the British Museum in London composing the *Foundations of the Critique of Political Economy* (1859): 'While indeed its contradictions, its antagonisms, the class contradiction and so on, reached an even higher degree than in any other country of the world [here he means the Highland clearances], all the same Scotland never experienced a real monetary crisis ... no depreciation of notes, no complaints and no inquiries into the sufficiency or insufficiency of the currency in circulation.'[45] In effect, it was a monetary system without a central bank, where instead various automatic mechanisms combined to control the note issue, and so (in the absence of gold) the money supply, and so the rate of inflation.[46]

One criticism that could be and was levelled at the banks lay in their catering for the rich. Most demanded a minimum deposit of £10, which amounted to several months' wages for the working poor.[47] Such condescension sat ill with the prudent virtues urged on these Scots by their moral mentors, sacred and secular. When the country's leading churchman, the Revd Thomas Chalmers, moved from tranquil Fife to teeming Glasgow in 1815 and encountered urban poverty for the first time, he enjoined on its victims the correctives of 'labour, thrift and temperance'. Later the sententious Samuel Smiles of Haddington, guru of self-help, would say that 'every thrifty person may be regarded as a public benefactor, and every thriftless person as a public enemy'.[48] Such was the spirit of the age, but in any case strong practical arguments existed even for small saving. No other means was available of providing for illness, old age or widowhood.

It was to meet those needs that the Revd Henry Duncan founded in 1810 the first savings bank at Ruthwell in Dumfriesshire.[49] From this secluded spot the movement spread all over the country. Savings banks were not commercial banks: they did not lend money to business or issue notes. Their deposits, for the most part, were invested in the British national debt. Still, they made an enormous contribution to the Scottish cult of prudence among the thrifty poor. By 1813 Edinburgh had a savings bank, the official title of which – Society for the Suppression of Beggars – gave perhaps a better clue to its motivation. Glasgow and Aberdeen got their own savings banks in 1815, and by 1818 about 130 existed altogether. One explicit aim was to dissuade the workers from squandering their money on drink. The founder in Edinburgh, John Hay Forbes, thought it might foster sexual continence too: 'The foundation of virtue is laid in the restraint of the passions; while a wasteful expenditure of money, in selfish gratifications, is at once the cause and effect of most of the vices of the poor.'[50] Even so, many of the poor must have still preferred their vices: in 1860 depositors in Scottish savings banks totalled fewer than 140,000 in a population of 3 million. Of these, two out of three had banked no more than £15 and their combined savings amounted to just 16 per cent of total deposits.[51]

While Scots sought to adapt the purposes of their system, the government of Sir Robert Peel cut across them with the Banking (Scotland) Act of 1845. His general economic policy was to free trade and lift regulation. But there needed in his view to be a counterpart in a centralised monetary system for the United Kingdom, which had to be run by the Bank of England. Scottish banks were allowed to carry on in some ways regardless, in particular to continue issuing notes as the ordinary medium of exchange in their own country (which they still do). But in future their operations were to be limited to its territory, so far as possible. Efforts to compete in England had already been stamped on, and would be again. By way of compensation, the English banks could in practice never compete in Scotland because without a note issue of their own they would have had to do so at a competitive disadvantage. The practical consequence was the confinement and cartelisation of the Scottish banks (though many Scottish bankers worked in England or the Empire).[52]

The new order proved to be not quite as secure as the legislators imagined. It failed to stop, for example, the spectacular collapse in 1878 of the City of Glasgow Bank. This had been running a business aimed at small savers, but it made a bad habit of paying lavish dividends. The accounts for 1878 showed deposits of £8 million, while a dividend of 12 per cent was declared – a trifle bold when a little bit of deficit on actual banking operations had appeared the year before. It turned out to be the tip of an iceberg. In October 1878, the directors all of a sudden announced the closure of the bank. For some time they had behind the scenes been trying in desperation to support a house of cards. It now emerged that they were, in fact, sitting on net liabilities of more than £6 million, with a lot of toxic loans to Australian mines, Argentine ranches and American railways. In order to cover all this up on a rigged balance sheet, they reported holdings of gold they did not, in fact, hold. To financial insiders some inkling of the fraud had leaked, so that the directors felt forced to spend more of the money they did not have to prop up the price of their own shares by secret purchases of them. The twenty-first century would have found here nothing to teach the nineteenth. A crash was inevitable – and then 254 of 1,200 shareholders faced ruin, being as yet unprotected by limited liability,[53] while scores of Glaswegian businesses went under. The directors of the bank were arrested, tried and jailed.[54]

The episode had the virtue of teaching the other Scottish banks what not to do. Afterwards their system followed the straight and narrow with a vengeance. Of the 17 banks authorised under the Banking Act, just 8 survived by 1914; the rest had vanished through merger. As a whole, though, the system remained secure enough. Total liabilities had more than doubled over 70 years to nearly £170 million.[55] In such a small market the banks needed to pursue every penny of business, so their service was comprehensive to a degree. They had 375 branches in 1844 but 1,253 by 1914, nearly twice as many per head of population as England.[56] Often several banks would compete in well-to-do suburbs, for example, saving customers the trouble of travel into the centre of town, even though in Aberdeen, Edinburgh and Glasgow that was where head offices could be found. Banks might therefore be an important source of local jobs, by tradition reserved for males – at least till the First World War when, amid the inevitable shortages of manpower, many women were taken on, often in the charming role of 'lady typewriters'. Constrained by the British state, Scottish banking remained in its situation of modest, undemanding prosperity almost till the end of the twentieth century. Once the British state did let go, the system before long set about manic abuse of its new freedom. Not far into the twenty-first century it met its Armageddon: in the light of a circumspect history, a bizarre fate. It remains to be seen if 300 years of careful construction have crumbled into dust.[57]

At least the historical record remained comforting. In Victorian times the management of risk had become an area of particular Scottish expertise. The railways, for example, brought new dangers of fire and accident. While standards of safety were steadily raised, they could not exclude every mishap. In that case, there had to be insurance. A boom in this sector followed. Its origins in Scotland went back to the Friendly Society, founded in Edinburgh as long ago as 1719. Now, as business flourished, so the number of companies multiplied. The North British Insurance Company was set up in 1809, the Scottish Widows Fund in 1815, the Edinburgh Life Assurance Company in 1823, the Union Assurance Company in 1824 and the Standard Life Assurance Company in 1825. They employed eager young agents to recruit customers and ask them the right questions: 'Is he temperate or free? Is he thin? Is he middle-sized? Is he lusty? Is he bloated?'[58]

Standard Life became the biggest of all, for it soon looked far beyond Scotland. Unlike some other companies, it never assumed that foreign business ought to be viewed as suspect or that the high rates of interest in many overseas countries signalled unacceptable risk. In 1866 it took over a firm with existing operations in Canada and India, then grew still more profitable from investments in these imperial territories. It played the markets, while taking care they should be reliable markets, as in the securities of colonial governments. After half a century, it was transacting the largest amount in Britain of new annual life business. Still, the search for good returns on investment was always by its nature uncertain. It could scarcely have succeeded with such panache unless Scottish insurers had been so closely integrated with a secure banking system, itself operating within a flexible legal framework responsive to its needs. And all the insurers, bankers and lawyers, especially in Edinburgh, knew one another. Sometimes indeed they were the same people.[59]

Even so, the first line of defence against risk remained the orderly conduct of corporate or personal finances, and in this Scots also specialised. The census of 1841 showed Edinburgh already housing 95 accountants, mainly to deal with the business of bankruptcy and sequestration that arose in the Court of Session. It was business that boomed with the rapid development of the economy and the cyclical busts following on from this. It might also play its part in the transition, often painful, from an older and less calculating Scotland. The 1840s saw a crisis of subsistence in the Highlands extinguish the old social structure there, as chiefly families finally gave up the unequal struggle against overwhelming financial burdens and then on their lands replaced poor peasants with profitable sheep. Yet those who set this anguished process in motion were often not the chiefs themselves but accountants acting as trustees for insolvent estates, in single-minded pursuit of the debts it was their job to recover. If a traditional society collapsed, that was no concern of the men poring over balance-sheets in Edinburgh.[60]

As their business expanded, it needed to be regulated to the same degree as that of other professions in the capital. In 1854 the Society of Accountants in Edinburgh was incorporated, followed in 1855 by the Institute of Accountants and Actuaries in Glasgow and later in 1867 by the Society of Accountants in Aberdeen. The profession of accountancy was another of Scotland's gifts to the world. In emulation of the law, it assured its status by expensive controls on entry for aspiring practitioners: an initial 100 guineas, indentures of five years at a cost of 50 guineas, meagre remuneration (typically, nothing more than the return of the initial fee) and finally the 'menial and monotonous tasks given to most apprentices'. But once the indentures had been endured, a prosperous career beckoned: in 1856 a new Bankruptcy Act was passed for Scotland exactly fitting the bill of the brand-new profession.[61] Its expansion in the rest of Britain and overseas followed.

For Scots at the upper end of the social scale, risk could also bring reward. Here the railways again acted as a catalyst, becoming an important form of wealth and an ample source of income. As a great economic innovation they went hand in hand with the great financial innovation of stock exchanges, founded in both Edinburgh and Glasgow in 1844. The capital sums invested in Scottish railways reached £27 million by 1850 and £166 million by 1900. With steady expansion of the network, the market in the shares remained buoyant, not to say hectic. In effect, that explained why the Scottish exchanges came into being. Edinburgh was already a financial centre, to be sure, and by 1844 counted four individuals, three partnerships and four companies engaged in broking. By 1846, those totals rose to fifteen individuals, fourteen partnerships and six companies. So there had been a step-change in that short intervening period, corresponding to the appearance of the railway companies on a local stock market.[62]

Far and away the biggest stock exchange lay, of course, in London. To it those in Scotland were at once linked by telegraph. They all quoted some of the same securities and these overlaps grew in time, as did the number of exchanges they covered, so that the differences were eroded. Yet the Scottish exchanges kept going because of the number of new joint-stock companies formed in their own country from 1856, transforming its older preference for private partnership as the basic type of corporate structure.[63] Even in major shares like those of the Caledonian or the North British Railways, held all over Britain, the main markets stayed in Scotland. By the end of the century these markets had matured, and were regulated in such a way as to make them accessible through brokers or their agents in the country. This was not an independent structure; nor was any other in the precocious Victorian globalism. But in Scotland stocks and shares became an important, distinct form of property served by its own intermediaries.[64]

People of quite modest means could begin to acquire such stakes in the booming economy. For example, aggregations of savings tiny in themselves represented an important source of funds for urban improvement, tapped by landowners, developers and builders. A builder might put together finance for a scheme of construction by taking out bonds or loans payable over 15 years and yielding interest at, say, 1 per cent above the current rate on gilt-edged stocks. These were, as the projectors liked to say, 'first-class heritable securities'.[65] In a world of the most marginal returns to capital, but with inflation unknown, they made for quite an attractive investment, and in a local market it was easier to sustain confidence among all involved. Again, the Scottish system of feudalism, the essential basis of the law of property, offered scope to generate a small but regular income because the feudal superiority of real estate could in technical terms be separated from the ownership. Feu-duties then payable from vassal to superior might be combined into a modest annuity.[66]

Scotland seemed to house legions of frugal savers concerned not with spectacular financial coups but rather with regular income built up out of trifling components – concerned, that is, not with the price of equity but with the yield. Their satisfaction required close attention to detail, and solicitors took on the task. In the Scottish cities these had ample experience of investment in everything from stocks and shares to the administration of large estates, but they also showed enough patience to deal with a range of clients, not every one of them wealthy. They became skilled at drawing networks together to make up bundles of capital from diverse sources.

Brother Scots always felt happiest in dealing with one another, as they would not have felt in dealing with some outsider. In the close circles of the law, the solicitors might keep in touch with family and friends from school or college who had gone somewhere exotic to seek a fortune. And once the solicitors accumulated enough resources for investment they could, through these contacts, pursue glamorous opportunities from the comfort and safety of home, at the same time offering small savers the chance of higher returns than they would ever have found otherwise. At the other end of the chain of personal connections were colonial entrepreneurs who often had a hard time raising money from the orthodox Victorian financial institutions. The Australians, for example, enjoyed a reputation as a wild bunch, too high a risk for sensible money; they did indeed overreach themselves and suffer a crash in 1890. Even then they could still raise capital in Scotland when it was far from clear that they might have done so in London.[67]

So in this new industry of financial services the dash of colonial pioneers came together with the caution of stay-at-home Scots, not just the wealthy among them but smaller savers as well: professionals, businessmen, women. In the period up to the First World War, the numbers holding foreign assets reached 80,000. *The Statist*, a chirpy financial magazine, explained:

> There are investors and speculators of a sort in all communities, but as a rule they are exceptional beings. In Scotland, however, they form so large a percentage of the well-to-do class as to be rather the rule than the exception. In Edinburgh, Dundee and Aberdeen it would be perfectly sage to bet on any man you pass in the street with an income of over three hundred a year being familiar with the fluctuation of Grand Turks, and having quite as much as he can afford staked on prairies, or some kindred gamble. A dividend of twenty per cent or more is to a Scotchman of this class a bait which he cannot resist.[68]

The fascination was fed by the fact that, as domestic industry matured, returns on the foreign investment looked by comparison better. *Blackwood's Edinburgh Magazine* pointed out as much in 1884: 'If the question were put, why have Scottish investors become at once too partial to America and the colonies? The answer would be on the tip of every tongue – "Because they pay the higher interest" . . . Borrowed at 4 per cent and lending at 8 to 10 per cent, looks like an industry which should be encouraged in these dull times!'[69] A swing followed away from investment at home to investment abroad. In the late 1880s Scots were for this purpose sending £5 million a year overseas. Almost a third of the increase in national income went into foreign investment during the next quarter-century. Over the same period, it accounted for about half the increase in the nation's capital stock.[70]

It then also became possible to attract funds for investment from outside Scotland, for placement according to the expertise Scots acquired. The word got round – round the world, in fact – that their clannish networks might offer a unique service: music to the ears, for example, of Americans hungry for capital, their republic being a net importer of it right up to the First World War. A Yank seeking funds could do worse than turn up on spec in Edinburgh:

> The moment he was heard of in Princes Street, a bevy of SSCs – *anglice*, Solicitors before the Supreme Courts – would be after him

to hunt him down. Every SSC had his own little syndicate at his back – that is, a group of retired drapers, head clerks, and second-rate accountants, who could club together money enough for the advertising, printing and postages needed to float a company.[71]

These companies were legion. A survey has shown 853 of them being formed in Scotland for investment overseas by 1914, of which 315 then remained active and 40 survive today. Most came in the mining sector, which accounted for 376, with plantations and ranches the next most numerous, though well behind. Up to half the capital was destined for the Empire, in which Scottish investment per head ran at 60 per cent above the British average. Indeed, every discovery of a new colonial resource seemed to spark off a burst of Scottish speculation. The Indian gold mania of 1879–81 prompted the formation of 33 Scottish companies with paid-up capital of £2 million, though most of it went into the pockets of the promoters. The so-called Kaffir boom of 1895, in the companies of the Transvaal, mounted on such a scale that it enabled a separate market in mining shares to be set up in Glasgow. Then in 1909–10 there followed a rage for rubber, caused by shortage of the natural product and the opportunity to assure supply by financing plantations in Malaya: Scotland floated 38 companies for this purpose.[72]

Such opportunities might be pregnant with risks too. It was possible to lose all the money. How could somebody with sums to spare in Edinburgh or Glasgow avoid throwing them away in Ecuador or Guatemala? One answer lay in pooling the risks. Canny Scots developed the investment trust as a vehicle for collective deployment of capital. Under professional management, it managed risk by taking money from many investors and spreading it over many investments, returning a dividend based on the average yield.

Investment trusts were not in strict terms a Scottish innovation, having been pioneered in Belgium. Still, Scotland could network round the globe as Belgium could not. The financial genius who imported the concept of the investment trust to his native country, Robert Fleming, established the principles of operation and must count as the father of this novel financial institution. The son of a shopkeeper in Dundee, he had gone to work aged 13 in the offices of one of its textile dynasties, the Baxters. He rose to be private clerk to the senior partner, proving astute and reliable enough to be entrusted with the management of the family's shareholdings. With this experience, he launched the Scottish American Investment Trust in 1873. It caught on at once and soon he had £500,000 deployed in the railways being built across the United States but also in selected mortgages, official securities and much else besides, with never more than 10 per cent of assets staked on a single enterprise.[73]

A second trailblazer at once saw the importance of the innovation and set out to develop it further. William Menzies established the Scottish American Investment Company, soon known as Saints, to finance projects in the Wild West from railways to ranches, then the Scottish American Mortgage Company to concentrate on real estate. Son of the professor of conveyancing at the University of Edinburgh, Menzies had in his own career first specialised in ecclesiastical law, but by now the litigious Scottish churches were losing a little of their desire to see one another in court. So he found time to seek out wider opportunities, and trips to the United States showed him the huge potential of that rising power. He wrote: 'The immense fertility of the soil and the boundless resources of the country lead to enterprise and speculation such as are quite unknown here . . . The tendency to speculation in America is on a scale to which there is no parallel in this country.'[74] Scotland at length housed 87 investment trusts, and became a global leader in this collective capitalism too. Some of the earlier ones were founded in Aberdeen, and many more in Glasgow, though its decline in the twentieth century meant they did not last. Still, investment trusts in Edinburgh and Dundee have survived all ups and downs, remaining to this day an important part of the financial sector in those two cities.[75]

In Victorian Scotland it is as accurate to speak of a revolution in services as of an agricultural or industrial revolution. Services grew from being incidental to the life of the nation, or of no more than domestic significance, to being one of the most successful sectors of the economy, modernising it at home and extending its links abroad. Again, it is hard to see how such vigorous development could have gone on without the Union of 1707 and the opportunities it opened up, though the benefits had always to be created by the Scots themselves rather than handed over on a plate by the English. These services also played their part in integrating Scotland into the Union, physically in the case of railways, mentally in the case of high finance.[76] Yet the Union's flexibility let Scotland develop specialisms of its own: a store of value, perhaps, against some day when the Union might no longer be there.

PART II
SOCIETY

4

Class: 'Regularity and order'

On the morning of 1 September 1842, the royal yacht carrying Queen Victoria and Albert, the Prince Consort, sailed in to moor at Granton Pier on the Firth of Forth.[1] From there the royal couple would have had a fine view of the seven hills on which Edinburgh stood, just three miles inland, except for the thick fog, a common feature of the local climate at this time of year. Waiting for them was the man who had just finished building the pier to ship coal from his mines in Midlothian, the Duke of Buccleuch, with a cheering crowd of loyal locals. He formally welcomed the queen to her northern capital, where she had never been before. While she and her husband got into their carriage, with the Prime Minister, Sir Robert Peel, in another behind them, the duke mounted his horse and then accompanied the party into town.

It made for a quieter affair than the arrival in Edinburgh a couple of decades earlier by the queen's uncle, King George IV, when the biggest crowds ever seen in Scotland had greeted him. His was, after all, the first visit by a reigning monarch since 1651, and today is still marked by more than one memorial: a statue of the sovereign on George Street, a bridge named after him spanning the chasm between the Old Town and the southern suburbs, above all the perennial tartan cult.[2] On that former occasion, just as now for Queen Victoria, the weather had been so inclement as to delay the disembarkation and throw the arrangements for the welcome into some disarray. The queen found on her actual entrance to the city that nobody was expecting her at this particular hour. 'More regularity and order would have been preserved had there not been some mistake on the part of the Provost about giving due notice of our approach,' a tight-lipped monarch later confided to her journal.

Still, any unfortunate impressions Queen Victoria and Prince Albert might have gained at the outset were more than overcome in their wonder at the scenes unfolding before them: 'The impression Edinburgh has made upon us is very great; it is quite beautiful, totally unlike anything else I have seen; and what is even more, Albert, who has seen so much, says it is unlike anything he ever saw; it is so regular, everything built of massive stone, there is not a brick to be seen anywhere.'[3] Two days later they went down to Leith, and there at last beheld the vista from the Forth that the fog at Granton had obscured:

> The view of Edinburgh from the road before you enter Leith is quite enchanting; it is, as Albert said, 'fairy-like', and what you would only imagine as a thing to dream of, or to see in a picture. There was that beautiful large town, all of stone (no mingled colours of brick to mar it), with the bold Castle on one side, and the Calton Hill on the other, with those high sharp hills of Arthur's Seat and Salisbury Crags towering above all, and making the finest, boldest background imaginable. Albert said he felt sure the Acropolis could not be finer; and I hear they sometimes call Edinburgh 'the modern Athens'.

During the entire visit the queen found the Scots 'very friendly and kind'[4], as she was always to find them. 'The country and the people have a quite different character from England and the English,' she declared. To prove it to herself, the next day she 'tasted the oatmeal porridge, which I think very good, and also some of the Finnan haddies'.[5]

It was the start of a long love affair between Queen Victoria and Scotland, which would outlast both her marriage, for Albert died in 1861, and the subsequent years of devotion by her Scots servant, John Brown, who died in 1883. His attendance on her never robbed him of the plain-spoken qualities of a man of the people, which to Victoria said something about that people, and its ability to bridge gaps among classes as the English could never bring themselves to do. Yet she to all intents and purposes restored the monarchy in Scotland, which must raise questions over a society that acquiesced, if it did not rejoice, in this.

When Queen Victoria and Prince Albert returned to Scotland after their initial foray, there was always a problem where they should stay. They spent little time at their palace of Holyroodhouse in Edinburgh, overlooked as it was by the stinking city under a prevailing wind from the west. They resorted instead to the great mansions of the high aristocracy, the Duke of Buccleuch's Dalkeith, the Marquis of Breadalbane's Taymouth and the Duke of Atholl's

Blair. Still they did not feel at home. In 1847 they ventured further north, to rent Ardverikie on Loch Laggan. Here they found themselves in the untamed Highlands. They decided that somewhere in the region they must discover a retreat they could call their own. But this western side of the country, as they experienced it, also had a disadvantage: it rained all the time. The queen's physician, James Clark, who hailed from Cullen in Banffshire, recommended she should look east. And so she came at length to Balmoral, which she and Albert would transform into the favourite residence that the royal family cherishes yet.[6]

It might be argued a Scottish monarchy had ceased to exist on 6 April 1603, the day King James VI crossed the border on his way to London. He himself returned just once, in 1617, and then dismayed his faithful Scots with the English ways he had meanwhile taken on. Even those of his descendants who came to Scotland – Kings Charles I and II, then James VII only while still heir presumptive, and after him just the Jacobite pretenders – came as foreigners. They never loved Scotland and Scotland never loved them, which was not the least foundation for the Scots' eventual acceptance of the Hanoverian succession after 1714. But no Hanoverian monarch turned up before King George IV. His appearance in 1822 with feathered bonnet cocked as Chief of Chiefs, in Highland dress brilliant with jewelled brooches and burnished weaponry, was delightful to himself and to the organiser of his visit, Sir Walter Scott, as well as to ladies admiring the kingly legs clad in pink tights under a mini-kilt: 'Since he is to be among us for so short a time, the more we see of him the better,' said a roguish Lady Hamilton Dalrymple. But it was not something that endeared him to Edinburgh or the Lowlands in general, marked as they were rather by Presbyterian sobriety. Anyway, he did not come back, and the links between Scotland and monarchy might once again have loosened through sheer neglect. But Queen Victoria would change all that.[7]

Not that she and her husband, after they bought Balmoral in 1852, could be said to have put themselves much in touch with the real Scotland either. It was a varied country, but one where the generation of new wealth in industrial conurbations forced social revolution along. This did not interest the royal couple. The Balmoral they preferred could offer them by contrast an ideal, even an idyll, a simple one innocent in its very isolation from the real Scotland, its way of life resistant to change, its values traditional, its environment unspoiled. Albert liked to compare it to the Saxony of his youth, though that too contained burgeoning commercial cities; but princely Saxony remained a country of turreted castles on forested hills. This was perhaps why the Balmoral he had rebuilt by 1855 somewhat resembled those castles – indeed he ordered more turrets to be added to the original design.[8]

The world Queen Victoria and Prince Albert created for themselves at Balmoral was recorded in her *Leaves from the Journal of our Life in the Highlands*, published in 1865 after his death. In her mourning she found Scots of all classes 'but especially of the humbler, readier in the expression of kindly feelings than English men and English women'. Seeking still greater seclusion in 1868, she took up residence with a few servants in a small house, Glassalt Shiel, built for her on the estate. Like her life here her book was an escape, into a country peopled by picturesque peasants engaged in honest toil amid scenes of beauty: 'Scotch air, Scotch people, Scotch hills, Scottish rivers, Scotch woods are all preferable to those of any other nation in the world.' It was a far cry from St Rollox. Perhaps for just that reason the book became an instant best-seller, finding among many Scots a complicity in the queen's dream. She presented herself to them not as a grand or extravagant, let alone snobbish, figure, but as a plain little woman content with the same simple domestic bliss as might be enjoyed by any bourgeois household, respectable, thrifty and moral. In other words, she shared the purposes and the propriety of her loyal subjects in Scotland.[9]

Monarchy in this mode might not have been too hard to sell to the Scots, but it was sold all the same. Balmoral being quite far from anywhere, the royal family needed to travel through other places to get there. They made sure to stop off along the route, unveiling statues, cutting ribbons, opening public institutions, admiring gardens and fountains. The queen herself spent in Scotland almost one in ten of all the days she lived, about eighty months in total (compared to five weeks in Ireland). Far more Scots saw her than ever saw the politicians representing them at Westminster. The annual round of visits entailed a revival of royal protocol with a Scottish twist. Lords lieutenant, sheriffs, peers and lairds had to dress up to be received, preferably in kilts, while Scottish regiments and the ranks of the volunteer movement paraded past to the sound of bagpipes. The queen gave a new lease of life to the Order of the Thistle and created her second son, Prince Alfred, Duke of Edinburgh in 1866, the first royal dukedom with a Scottish title (he later became Duke of Saxe-Coburg-Gotha too). She bridled if anybody omitted the Scottish numbering from the titles of her forebears, King James VI and I or King James VII and II.

As that indicates, Queen Victoria took a close amateur interest in Scottish history. She loved to visit places where its dark destinies had been worked out, and to find some good in its lost causes. Covenanters and Jacobites had to her alike been admirable; she prized loyalty and saw it in both. While at Balmoral, she worshipped every Sunday at Crathie and engaged in earnest spiritual conversation with ministers of the Church of Scotland, especially her chaplain, the Revd Norman Macleod, who 'gave her more real consolation than any clergyman of the south'.[10] She would have nothing said against the 'simple and truly Protestant faith of the Church of Scotland'. It had suffered schism in 1843, half remaining as the religious establishment and the other half seceding from it into the Free Church, but she was impartial between them. At the same time, she had no sense of irony in professing herself a Jacobite and recalling that the blood of the Stewarts ran in her veins. Mary Queen of Scots was her 'poor ancestress' and at Cambuskenneth Abbey she had the tomb of King James III 'restored by a descendant, Victoria'. On the nearby field of Bannockburn, she declared, two of her forebears had met in battle but in her person their enmities could now be reconciled. She claimed the Highland regiments as her own, drawn as they were from the old clans and fighting with no less fidelity now to a Protestant dynasty than in former times to a Catholic one: 'the people are as devoted to me as they were to that unhappy race'.

By the end of her reign, the queen had given the monarchy in Scotland a national character and reconnected Scots with their royal past. Evidence how far she influenced their perceptions can be seen in the hostility to her heir, Edward, and his opting to use the numeral VII when he ascended the throne in 1901. Patriots pointed out there never had been a King Edward of Scotland and retaliated by omitting the numeral from addresses and inscriptions. Without doubt, Queen Victoria had helped to cement the United Kingdom, but did so through strengthening Scottish identity by every means at her command – teaching a wise lesson not learned by all subsequent defenders of the Union. Today the monarchy is perhaps the strongest pillar of the Union, in marked contrast to the Parliament at Westminster that was its explicit embodiment. If Scotland should become once more an independent country, the monarchy will likely continue – thanks in no small measure to Queen Victoria.[11]

The Scots nobility, in the past looked down on by the English nobility, also found favour. The queen wedded one of her own daughters to the ninth Duke of Argyll, the first non-royal marriage of a member of the royal family for two centuries. In the next generation, the Earl Fife was raised to a duke on his marriage to Princess Louise, daughter of King Edward VII and Alexandra of Denmark. The Duke and Duchess of Fife's daughter, Alexandra, married another of Queen Victoria's many grandchildren, Prince Arthur of Connaught.

Meanwhile, the ducal house of Hamilton, itself of royal descent, made its blood still bluer by marriage between the eleventh duke and Princess Marie of Baden, among other things an adoptive granddaughter of Napoleon Bonaparte. If in 1707 the old Scots Parliament had rejected both the Jacobite and the Hanoverian succession, the house of Hamilton would have been next in line. It remained conscious of its premier rank: Hamilton Palace by the River Clyde was the biggest, most splendid non-royal residence in Europe. Lord Lamington, a neighbour, recalled there 'never was such a magnifico as the 10th duke, the ambassador to the Empress Catherine; when I knew him he was very old, but held himself straight as any grenadier. He was always dressed in a military laced undress coat, tights and Hessian boots.'[12] The Egyptian mummies being brought to Britain in the duke's time caught his imagination, and on his death in 1852 he had himself mummified and placed in an ancient sarcophagus (now in the Kelvingrove Museum). It was intended as the centrepiece of the Hamilton Mausoleum he built, with its 'whispering wa's' and the longest lasting echo of any manmade structure in the world. The mausoleum is today the sole reminder of the palace, demolished in 1921 because of subsidence caused by mines below it. That was where the Hamiltons' wealth came from. In 1874 they enjoyed revenues of over £130,000 a year. The 46,000 acres they owned in Lanarkshire had an annual rental of £38,000, but the minerals underneath yielded £57,000. They were industrialists as much as landowners.[13]

Even the Dukes of Hamilton faced eventual decline, however. The fate of their palace symbolised how, despite the past achievements of the Scots nobility, its position in its own country in the end sank. Earlier the possession of land had been the passport to power of all kinds, but now that no longer held true: it was a new age for a new race of men. The aristocracy did not always understand this. In 1839 the thirteenth Earl of Eglinton spent £30,000 on staging a mock medieval tournament at his castle in Ayrshire. Rain fell on it as only Scottish rain can, while the drenched young bluebloods jousted and broke lances against each other. Benjamin Disraeli, in his novel *Endymion* (1880), took the Eglinton Tournament as a metaphor of how a younger generation of noblemen might still lead modern Britain into an age of social harmony. The recent history of Scotland should already have taught him this was unlikely.[14]

Still, the enormous economic and social changes of the era did take a while to work their full effect on the aristocracy. Most Lowland landowners prospered. Some estates changed hands but not many. Though industrial dynasties such as the Coats, Tennants and Bairds bought into land, their total acquisitions never amounted to much compared with the vast domains of the hereditary proprietors. In the absence of *nouveaux riches*, rural society remained hierarchical and some of the old landed class even enlarged their estates for the sake of both prestige and profit. Of the 117 Scottish landholdings with an annual value of at least £10,000 in one county, the largest concentration came in Perthshire, which had eleven, then in Aberdeenshire and Ayrshire with nine each, then in Berwickshire with eight.[15]

Sutherland does not figure in this ranking because the Duke of Sutherland owned almost all of it, over a million acres or 90 per cent of the county. Yet he had nothing like the income the Duke of Buccleuch got from his lesser total of 250,000 acres, yielding £95,000 a year with an extra £15,000 from minerals and from Granton Harbour.[16] In fact, Sutherland's Highland dominion was a drain on him, subsidised out of his English income from industry in the Midlands. That might have been hard to guess from the palace he in his turn built at Dunrobin, its towers rising high on a cliff above the North Sea, a 'fairytale concoction' with a special suite for Queen Victoria to stay in. There was a similar financial structure to the estate of the Marquis of Bute, another of the richest Scots noblemen. He earned his money from mines in South Wales and the creation of the modern city of Cardiff. From there he brought builders and workmen to construct his own Scottish castle of Mountstuart, a flamboyant example of Gothic revival. In it ancient and modern combined: it housed the world's first heated swimming pool and was on its completion the only country house in Scotland to be lit by electricity.[17] For these two aristocrats the Union worked.

Still, since 1707 (as before) there had also been poor Scottish noblemen: that was why a majority of them supported the Union, hoping it would enrich them. Some remained disappointed after a century. In 1823 Lord Melville, political manager of Scotland, wrote at a time of growing public parsimony about one vacancy on his payroll: 'I find by today's post that Lords Home and Kellie, and half the inefficient peers and commoners of Scotland are candidates for the office, and I admit that if it were to be bestowed on any such persons, or even on the ground of charity to Lord Caithness's family, it had better be abolished.'[18]

Public service soon ceased to be a matter of aristocratic sinecure and instead demanded professional standards. But there were enough Scots peers to meet them. A couple became Prime Ministers, the fourth Earl of Aberdeen and the fifth Earl of Rosebery. Up to the First World War, five served as Scottish Secretaries, the Duke of Richmond and Gordon, the thirteenth Earl of Dalhousie, the ninth Marquis of Lothian, Lord Balfour of Burleigh and the Marquis of Linlithgow. Others found, like many of their countrymen, opportunity in the Empire. In two successive generations the Earls of Elgin supplied Viceroys of India, along with the tenth Earl of Dalhousie and the fourth Earl of Minto. One Scots peer, the ninth Lord Napier, founded a colony, Hong Kong. Many others were appointed governors. Amid all this commendable competence, a single visionary stood out, the eleventh Marquis of Lothian who joined Lord Milner's kindergarten as, after the Boer Wars, it planned the Union of South Africa between British colonies and Afrikaner republics. The idealistic youngsters of the kindergarten hoped this Union would herald an eventual imperial federation making the dominions the equals of the mother country in a rationalised and modernised Empire fitted to endure far into the future. Some hoped Scotland would be a member of that federation on terms equal with the others. Of these notions Lothian was to be disillusioned by his friend Mahatma Gandhi.[19]

Military command offered a further field of noble endeavour. The fourteenth Lord Lovat raised the Lovat Scouts for service in South Africa, training them up in tactics, marksmanship and the ways of living off wild country: they were the first military unit to wear ghillie suits, elaborate camouflage looking like heavy foliage. At the same time they learned how guerrilla warfare was no place for vain heroics: 'He who shoots and runs away, lives to shoot another day.' There were Scots heroes all the same. The eighth Lord Dunmore served on the North-west Frontier of India, acting there also as correspondent for *The Times* of London. Under heavy fire in the district of Swat, he rode out with five others to rescue a wounded officer surrounded by enemy swordsmen, a foray in which two men and four horses were killed. For his gallantry Dunmore received the Victoria Cross, the sole journalist ever so honoured. Scots showed less interest in the Royal Navy, with the notable exception of the tenth Earl of Dundonald (and Marquis of Maranhão in the imperial Brazilian peerage), better known by his courtesy title of Lord Cochrane. But he, feared by the French as *le loup des mers* during the Napoleonic Wars, had to quit the senior service when convicted of financial fraud, then became the liberator of Brazil, Chile and Greece in their respective wars of independence.[20]

Against all this derring-do must be set the peers who responded to the decline of their order by retreat. The twenty-fifth and twenty-sixth Earls of Crawford were so interested in astronomy that they built a private observatory at Dunecht in Aberdeenshire. On hearing of a threat to close down Edinburgh's Royal Observatory on Calton Hill in 1888, the twenty-sixth earl donated the scientific instruments and mathematical books needed for a new one, which was placed on top of Blackford Hill and opened in 1896. Father and son also spent much time and money on rare books, on accumulating the *Bibliotheca Lindesiana*, the most impressive private collection in Britain, with a catalogue 250 pages long.[21] Again, such was the erudition of the fourteenth Earl of Caithness that Queen Victoria appointed him tutor to Edward, Prince of Wales, who turned out not an apt pupil. Caithness was otherwise a respected scientist and an ingenious inventor. On his estate at the Castle of Mey he cultivated the fields with a steam-powered plough. He devised a machine for washing the outside of railway carriages that earned him a fortune in the United States. A universal exposition in Paris awarded him a prize for his invention of an artificial leg.[22] Finally, a peer might shun reality altogether. When the twenty-fourth Earl of Mar died in 1828, his insurers made a routine investigation into the circumstances of his final illness. His housekeeper revealed that for three decades he had been taking fifty grains of solid opium and an ounce of laudanum a day. Because he had never admitted to his habit, the insurers refused to pay out on his policy. A consequent case in the Court of Session vindicated them.

There was much murk, too, in the life of the Marquis of Queensberry, the most versatile Scots nobleman of all. Quite mad really, he yet distinguished himself in three ways. He was a patron of sport, in 1866 one of the founders of the Amateur Athletic Association. It published under his sponsorship a set of twelve rules for the boxing ring, at once known as the Queensberry rules. Then in 1872 he was chosen a Scots representative peer and served for two Parliaments, but in 1880 refused to take the religious oath of allegiance to the sovereign. A declared atheist, he said he would have no more truck with 'Christian tomfoolery'. He accepted the presidency of the British Secular Union, and published a long philosophical poem, *The Spirit of the Matterhorn*, written at Zermatt in an effort to set out his views. Back in London he loudly interrupted the performance of a play, *The Promise of May*, by the poet laureate Lord Tennyson, because it included a villainous atheist in its cast of characters; Queensberry was thrown out of the theatre. Finally in 1895, angered by a homosexual relationship between his son, Lord Alfred Douglas, and

Oscar Wilde, Queensberry left a card at the club of the flamboyant man of letters publicly calling him a 'posing somdomite' (*sic*). Wilde sued for criminal libel, and the marquis was arrested. In court, his lawyers portrayed Wilde as a vicious older man who seduced innocent boys. He dropped the case when the lawyers further announced they would call on the testimony of male prostitutes who had had sex with him. In other words, Queensberry destroyed his adversary. But he himself did not long survive. His obituary in *The Times* considered him representative of 'a type of aristocracy which is less common in our time than it was a century ago – the type which is associated in the public mind with a life of idleness and indulgence'.[23]

Queensberry had never minded upsetting people and he upset his own family when in 1894 he sold its seat at Kinmount in Dumfriesshire. Times started to get hard for Scots noble families. The era of Victorian prosperity was drawing to an end, and radical agitations grew more vocal. They had results too: the same year saw the introduction of estate duty. In England the aristocracy was able to renew itself but in Scotland this never happened. By the end of Queen Victoria's reign, she was admitting successful Englishmen to the peerage however humble their origins. Creations of Scots titles had stopped in 1707 anyway yet the British peerage, too, stayed for now closed to the most vigorous element of contemporary Scottish society, the industrialists – this would not change till the First World War, when they could demand and get a social reward for their patriotic exertions. Meanwhile titles went only to Scots who served the British state or who already had blood blue enough, and blue blood with a good income at that; but a good income did not in itself suffice.

The sole exception to all this was a man of the highest scientific distinction, Lord Kelvin. Born William Thomson in Belfast in 1824, he came of a Scots-Irish family that had maintained close links with the mother country. His own father was a graduate of the University of Glasgow, and after he and his son moved back in 1832 they just regarded themselves as Scots. Young William, already showing signs of mathematical genius, was aged ten when he matriculated at the university. At 17 he proceeded to Cambridge, where he found time to row for his college and win a sculling competition. All his life he loved water and the sea. Even in old age he kept a yacht in the bay off his home at Largs. After a spell researching in Paris, Kelvin was appointed to his chair at Glasgow in 1846. He held it till 1899, refusing all offers to move. Instead he used it as a base for revolutionising instruction in academic physics, extending its range with his own discoveries and tying it to industry and commerce.[24]

Kelvin's sharp, creative mind not only defined basic physical laws but also suggested many fresh lines of research to other scientists. His work in pure theory would by itself have assured his fame. In lectures to the Royal Society of Edinburgh, in 1851 and 1854, he expounded the laws of thermodynamics, those of equivalence and transformation or conservation of energy. The latter states that the earth retains the heat it receives from the sun, transforming it into other forms of energy. Kelvin demonstrated this with examples from all branches of physics. During his life he wrote more than 300 scientific papers.[25]

Yet he believed 'the life and soul of science is its practical application', and acted on that too. He invented the submarine cable and superintended the laying of the first one across the Atlantic Ocean in 1858. In odd moments at sea he amused himself with improving the ships' compass. Realising that the practical application of science depended on the quality of the instruments, he spent much of his life devising new ones. He invented the mirror galvanometer, which overcame the problem thus far dogging the long-distance telegraph (namely, the longer the cable, the slower the transmission). The electric meter was also his work (the electric lights at Mountstuart had been preceded by his own at Largs). He went into business in partnership with James White, a maker of optical instruments. The firm of Kelvin & White manufactured and marketed instruments for electrical and optical measurement, for transmission by telegraph and for aids to navigation. By the 1890s it employed 200 skilled technicians in Britain's biggest and most versatile laboratory. Kelvin also took out patents connected with his submarine cables and formed another company to handle this business. In 1879 the patents earned him £5,500, more than five times his professorial salary.[26]

Rich enough or not, Kelvin merited the peerage Queen Victoria gave him in 1892. Yet it might be argued Scotland anyway had a different kind of aristocracy, if we may take the term in its original sense of rule by the best: today we would say a meritocracy, but the nineteenth century never knew this word. Society was already geared to creating castes of men intent on public distinction in Scottish terms. That structure had been enshrined in the very Union, in the guarantees under the treaty of 1707 for the continued existence of the national institutions, the law, the Church and the universities. We shall come to those national institutions in their proper place below, but the Union could also foster analogous structures elsewhere. This was because it made Scotland richer but did not destroy Scottish civil society. Newer avocations might be organised and formalised on a Scottish rather than British scale. We have already seen the process at work in the case of finance. Another example was medicine.

Modern medical schools were set up at Edinburgh in 1726, at Glasgow in 1751 and at Aberdeen in 1787; St Andrews offered degrees in medicine but did not teach it. Edinburgh forged ahead. By the first quarter of the nineteenth century it was producing more surgeons and doctors than anywhere else in Britain, with 2,000 degrees awarded during this period.[27] But some of its old Scots habits died hard. The inaugural holder of the chair of anatomy had been Alexander Monro *primus*, so called because he sired a dynasty. He stayed in harness up to his death in 1767, when his son Alexander Monro *secundus* succeeded him in the chair, he being followed on his own death in 1817 by his son Alexander Monro *tertius*, who expired only in 1859. Half a dozen more medical chairs had been created by the end of the eighteenth century. Diverse courses could then be offered leading to a comprehensive medical degree and a range of careers from scientific research to general practice. The professors ruled the whole roost. They all seemed to live a long time too, which must have said something for their talents, and most clung to their chairs till the Grim Reaper prised them loose: they wished in clannish Scotland to make sure who would take over from them, for preference one of their own kin. The Monros were just the best example of this veritably Sicilian nepotism.[28]

No less Sicilian was the taste for vendetta. Enlightened Scots lost none of the national love of disputation, and an advancing medical discipline offered ample scope for it. James Gregory, professor of the practice of physic at Edinburgh and scion of an academic dynasty stretching back two centuries, vaunted polemics as part of the country's heritage. It was most obvious in religion, but 'even with the aid of the Holy Scriptures to enlighten their understanding, determine their faith and soften their hardness of heart, theologians have differed rancorously on a thousand points. What better, then, could be expected of physicians and surgeons when left entirely to the faint light of their reason?' Or indeed when left to the darkness of their suspicions. Gregory first gained something more than medical renown after supposing an anonymous pamphlet defamatory of him to have been written by two professorial colleagues, a father and son, Alexander and James Hamilton. Meeting James in the street, he beat him with his walking stick. Hamilton sued and won £100 damages. Gregory paid gladly, saying he would give £100 over again for a second go. He wrote in all seven volumes of attacks on and ripostes to his colleagues, covering 3,000 pages and collected in his *Historical Memoirs of the Medical War in Edinburgh.*[29]

Versatility was another attribute of the medical men. Charles Bell became a professor after service as chief surgeon at the Battle of Waterloo. To a later generation he was more renowned as the 'father of neurology'. He looked forwards but also backwards to an era when anatomy had been conceived as part of the divine plan; he wrote a study of the hand demonstrating its design by God. A sensitive soul, half-scientist and half-artist, he taught the painter David Wilkie how to represent the blush on canvas. A more modern figure was William Pulteney Alison, who from his chair of physiology argued disease had more to do with poverty than with sin, the usual contemporary explanation. If he was right, there could be no argument against better public relief: he foreshadowed a system of collective, universal welfare. James Syme gained fame as an innovator in operative technique, especially for the amputation of joints. He too marked up achievement in another distant field, co-operating with Charles Mackintosh in the chemistry that created impermeable textiles. Syme cut an awesome figure. A colleague said he 'never wastes a word, a drop of ink or a drop of blood'. He played on others' expectations of his aloof and imperious nature. Once he received a patient he had treated for an anal fistula, but gave no sign of recognition. Not till the man bared his bottom for examination did Syme exclaim: 'Ah, now I know who you are.'[30]

Pitiless surgical procedures terrified the suffering and their relations while offering no certainty of success. It seems bizarre that surgeons almost compounded their problems by performing operations in public, weltering in blood while the patients screamed in agony, even after stupefying themselves on whisky. This took place in theatres packed with ghoulish spectators or with young students – though they, of course, had no other way of gaining their first experience of surgery. If those under the knife were not to bleed to death, those wielding it needed steady nerve and fantastic dexterity to complete the operation as quickly as possible. Any mistake and they had a corpse on their hands. Students might first stare in horror but once hardened to the sight they looked on in excitement, thrilled at the speed and skill of their mentors. When in mere minutes or even moments the operation succeeded, the students cheered and went off to celebrate. When it failed, they jeered. No wonder we read how the surgeons, their hands plunged in the wound, broke out in sweat, from time to time glancing at the patient's face in case the sudden pallor of death should sweep over it. The almost greater peril of sepsis, of post-operative infection, as yet occurred to none of them: they wiped their scalpels on the tails of their coats, already filthy and stiff with congealed gore from previous operations. Survivors of the surgery and shock ran a high risk of perishing anyway.

The best pupil Syme ever had was an English Quaker, for that reason excluded from higher education at Oxford or Cambridge. The young Joseph Lister came to Edinburgh in 1853. Gentle and stammering, he yet impressed his formidable mentor – so much so that he was at length to marry Syme's daughter. With his father-in-law's patronage, Lister moved up the ladder of medical promotion but his first chance of a chair came at Glasgow, where he was appointed professor of clinical surgery in 1860. There, on 12 August 1865, an eleven-year-old boy called James Greenlees was admitted to the Royal Infirmary with a compound fracture of the left leg, having been run over by a cart. Lister, after cleansing the wound, dressed it with a mixture of putty and carbolic acid. The putty held the acid so it could not be washed out of the dressing by discharges of blood and lymph. The mixture was also spread over the skin round the wound to stop germs getting in, and further covered by tinfoil to reduce evaporation of the acid. Lister finally splinted and bandaged the leg, then left it for four days, the interval in which hospital infections usually appeared. When he removed the dressing he found the leg still very sore, yet it did not stink or show any other sign of putrefaction. He dressed the leg again and left it for five more days, during which wee Jimmy's temperature remained normal and his appetite – well, boyish. When Lister removed the second dressing, he found the skin burned by the acid. This time he applied a different dressing of gauze soaked with a solution of carbolic acid in olive oil, and left it for four further days. When he removed that, he saw the wound was healing. He judged the danger of suppuration to be over, and applied just a water dressing. Six weeks and two days after his accident, Jimmy left the infirmary with two whole legs. Lister had inaugurated antisepsis.[31]

Few in the Scottish medical professoriate were as able and innovative as Lister, or as nice. They did not need to be. They wielded godlike authority over operating theatre, student classroom and public health in general. Like older gods they often proved capricious. One thing they did was in effect set up a class system in the medical profession. They stood at the top. At the bottom stood the general practitioners. That explained a peculiar course of events after the first great epidemic of Asiatic cholera appeared at Leith in 1832. A local doctor, Thomas Latta, found a remedy for its worst symptoms.

Injection of the sufferer with a saline solution was later adopted universally as the first line of defence against the virulent disease. But at the time the professors of Edinburgh, led by Gregory, refused to credit Latta's success in saving lives. Faced with the horrible symptoms of cholera, Gregory jumped to a conclusion owing more to ancient Aristotelian logic than to modern medical science: if the infected body expelled salt and water in ceaseless diarrhoea, it must have an excess of them. Injection of more would make things worse: 'Gregory, who is a tolerably acute man, but disagreeably dogmatic, seemed at once to settle the matter in his own mind – that the practice referred to was inconsistent with physiological principles – that it was dangerous.' Instead he urged the physician to 'seize nature by the throat' with 'free blood-letting, the cool affusion, brisk purging, frequent blisters and vomits of tartar emetic': vigorous methods indeed but against cholera worse than useless, unless to put the patient out of his misery all the sooner. Nobody else followed Latta's procedures, and thousands died a vile death.[32]

It was not just Latta's novel method but also his lack of social or academic standing that led to his being pooh-poohed. Such obstacles to progress were not to be overcome for another generation, and then by a greater figure who gave the whole world reason to be thankful to him, James Young Simpson. He was a man of the people, born at Bathgate in West Lothian, then just a stage on the turnpike between Glasgow and Edinburgh, a younger child of the humble hamlet's baker. All his life he looked like a peasant, but Scottish education was his birthright too. He went at the age of fourteen to the University of Edinburgh and two years later started his medical training. That at once took him into the operating theatre. He felt appalled at what he saw there, thought of giving up medicine for law but persevered. Once he qualified, he became house-surgeon at the Lying-In Hospital of Leith. His duties often took him out into the stinking tenements of the port where poor, sick or abandoned women had to bear their brats. He balked at nothing. Even right at the outset of his career he was asking: 'Cannot something be done to render the patient unconscious while under acute pain, without interfering with the free and healthy play of the natural functions?' For now he had to rely on his own kindness and care. He soon won enough of a reputation to set up in private practice. Genteel ladies flocked to him for their accouchements.[33]

By 1839 Simpson felt ready for a step up in his career. At the University of Edinburgh the professor of midwifery resigned. Simpson applied for the job. By the gerontocratic standards of the existing professoriate he was a novice, and by their nepotistic standards a nobody. The occupant of the chair of midwifery did not need to hold a doctorate of medicine, but from classrooms of the Old College down to drawing rooms of the New Town the professors whispered that anyway Simpson could hardly be considered an enlightened man of letters like themselves. He might know his business, yet so did any number of common midwives, those old crones still called on by most women to help them in childbirth in Scotland and everywhere else. For a chair it was not enough to be an able practitioner; this university needed somebody learned in science and its literature.

In the event Simpson overcame all the professional hostility to him. He would remain Edinburgh's professor of midwifery till his death thirty years later. The whole time, while making many scientific contributions to medicine, he remained a working doctor going out to treat the people of the capital in every station of life: a great man and a good one.[34] From his chair Simpson also stepped up the quest for more humane medicine, in the form of an effective anaesthetic. He did this at his home in Queen Street, using himself and colleagues as guinea pigs. The stuff they sampled often produced unpleasant side effects, till the great day of 19 January 1847 when they tried ether. They sat round a table and drank tumblers of it: 'Immediately an unwonted hilarity seized the party; they became bright-eyed, very happy and very loquacious – expatiating on the delicious aroma of the new fluid. The conversation was of unusual intelligence, and quite charmed the listeners.' The babble grew louder and louder till 'a moment more, then all was quiet, and then – a crash'. The guinea pigs had dropped off into deep sleep before falling under the table. Soon Simpson discovered chloroform made an even better anaesthetic. Still Syme, the haughtiest of the old guard, regarded this upstart as an enemy. He would rend apart Simpson's writings before his classes as he denounced the author's vulgarity. Syme even dismissed chloroform, arguing that efforts to reduce the frequency of operations or simplify their performance would achieve as much as laughing gas ever could. It took Queen Victoria to resolve the dispute in Simpson's favour, when she had herself anaesthetised for the birth of a son in 1853. Scottish medicine at last ceased to be a scene of, among many other things, social strife and class conflict.[35]

At Balmoral the queen always liked to have a medical professor in attendance. A favourite was Robert Christison, who held the chair of materia medica and therapeutics at Edinburgh. He had first won renown in giving the evidence that condemned William Burke and William Hare, the Irish serial murderers. In later life, he often needed to deal with a growing use of drugs in the capital, usually opium from India. He showed a relaxed attitude to them. He said that in the whole town he knew of just ten people who might be defined as addicts. He did not believe even these were going to suffer irreparable damage to their health, let alone death. On the contrary, 'a certain number of opium-eaters may attain a good old age'. Nor was deviant behaviour a necessary result of their habit: 'in many instances, when the opium-eater is under the influence of the drug, no one could suspect the fact'. If problems did arise, then the cold turkey was the right treatment: 'The habit is easily broken, and there is no danger in suddenly breaking it.' Like Simpson, Christison had no hesitation in being his own guinea pig: as Simpson with chloroform, so Christison with cocaine, a new drug from South America. He became the first regular user of it in Britain. A lover of the Scottish hills, he demonstrated its sustaining qualities by chewing it on his more strenuous ascents. While a guest at Balmoral, he may have recommended it to Queen Victoria. And he reportedly passed it on to a fellow guest, a rising young politician called Winston Churchill. Keeping company like this, what did a Scottish professor need with a peerage?[36]

In this social context it is worth recalling that the surgeons had started their history as tradesmen on the same level as, say, the weavers. In all the royal burghs of Scotland the practice of a trade was limited to those who at the end of seven years' apprenticeship joined the corresponding incorporation – not just a long but also an expensive training. The incorporations were represented on the councils of the burghs, which set tables of wages and prices for the different categories of tradesmen and their jobs. In practice, it was rather a tyrannical regime of commercial regulation, penalising the poorer townspeople, if at least offering some protection for members of the incorporations in sickness or old age. Despite the advance of industrial capitalism and the transformation of urban life, the privileges were not abolished till 1846 – though by then, indeed, they were growing somewhat meaningless.

In Edinburgh the weavers had incorporated themselves in 1476, the surgeons and barbers in 1505; for Glasgow the corresponding dates were 1528 and 1599. At first surgeons and barbers could unite because their trades required the same nimble fingers. Both approached customers with sharp instruments in hand to chop bits off, whether long hair or crushed limbs; the difference lay in the fact that customers would survive a meeting with a barber, less often one with a surgeon. In Edinburgh the two callings diverged as the incorporation sought to pass from being a mere trade to being, in its own words, 'a learned society'. So the surgeons wanted rid of an ever more embarrassing bond with the barbers. In 1648 a majority of the incorporation banned further entry into it by barbers. This just caused a shortage of barbers. People complained they had to go to the suburbs to get a haircut, till during the Cromwellian occupation the English officers, roundheads in need of constant croppings, refused to put up with such bull. The surgeons were undeterred: they joined with the more genteel apothecaries, yet still could not shake off the barbers till 1722. Only then did the profession attain the self-esteem to which it felt entitled – just in time for the foundation of medical chairs at the university.[37] The same year Glasgow's surgeons excluded their barbers.

Weavers prospered too, though in a different way. The industrial revolution started in textiles but there were still plenty of specialist jobs for individual tradesmen to carry out on their handlooms. They continued to do so despite the appearance of vast new factories for mass production, which in any case often contracted outwork to them. Weaving had spread beyond the narrow medieval bounds of the royal burghs. In Edinburgh, Dean Village became home to many weavers, in Glasgow a ring of suburbs from Anderston to Camlachie to Gorbals. These weavers were unincorporated, so did not benefit from the privileges and welfare available inside the burghs. They needed rather to rely on self-help and co-operation. They formed friendly societies to provide for sick or disabled members. The societies might also espouse moral purposes. One stipulated that entrants must be 'under the age of forty years, above ten years, free of all known bodily diseases, a Protestant and of an honest character'. When the members convened they could easily go beyond the ordinary business to discuss social and economic questions of the day. It took little more for a friendly society to become the basis for what was then called, with disapproval, a combination – in modern terms, a trade union intent on raising wages and winning other improvements in conditions.[38]

But little could be done to counter the appearance of economic cycles as modern capitalism emerged. War and its aftermath made the cycles all the more violent and disruptive. The Napoleonic Wars produced great inflation too. In Scotland the conjunction brought the system of commercial regulation to the point of collapse. In 1811 the weavers of Glasgow put in a request to the lord provost to convene the magistrates and fix a new, higher table of wages. He said he would rather see the tradesmen and employers sort the problem for themselves, without worrying him or the council. The employers refused to co-operate, however. Getting nowhere with the established procedures, the weavers went to law.[39]

By June 1812 the weavers' case reached the Court of Session. It found they did indeed possess the right they wished to exercise, of getting their wages fixed by the magistrates, and directed that this should happen. When the magistrates of Glasgow duly convened, they accepted the weavers' case for higher wages. But no way could be found of making the employers pay, except through the wearisome and expensive process of pursuing long litigation against each of them. From now on the law ceased to help the weavers. When their patience and money ran out, 40,000 of them struck work in November. The government waited three weeks, then arrested and charged their leaders with planning the strike – though it was not at all clear this even constituted an offence at Scots law. The industrial action went on till February 1813 before it collapsed. The leaders were tried and imprisoned or, if they had fled into England, outlawed.[40]

In court, counsel for the weavers was the Whig advocate (and editor of the *Edinburgh Review*), Francis Jeffrey. He confronted the venerable Tory judge, Lord Boyle, with an opinion handed down by himself some while before. Boyle had ruled that once the magistrates declared a price fair and reasonable and the masters failed to comply, then the journeymen 'had the right to strike in any numbers'. His red-faced lordship could only say now that he had been in error then. Scots law was developing, he explained, not least through the institutional writers, or codifiers of the courts' judgments; one had just given the correct view that combination to strike was illegal. The Parliament at Westminster anyway soon repealed the statutes on wages, in both Scotland and England, dating back to the sixteenth century.[41]

The whole business turned out a disaster for the weavers, vanguard of the Scottish proletariat. They not merely failed to assert their legal rights, but lost them; they were not just beaten, but humiliated. Their desperation even found an outlet in an attempted armed insurrection in 1820, the so-called Radical War, in reality a brief and inglorious episode after which three ringleaders were executed.[42] Such sturdy, independent tradesmen had, in fact, little that was revolutionary about them, but surely represented what any paternalist should have wished for from an educated working class. Yet as these aristocrats of labour began to attain a social and economic standing that might merit translation into a political one, the authorities refused to countenance their claims and treated them as no more than a rabble. Nor was history to vindicate their struggle. They continued to fight in vain against falling prices for their goods and competition from machines. In the end their craft disappeared and the textile sector became fully industrialised. There was nothing the old law, and the old outlook on life it had represented, could do to help. If it would no longer protect the weavers, or let them protect themselves, little hope could be held out to any other group. From now on it became harder and harder to maintain any legal privilege for skilled tradesmen.[43]

The threat of strikes in the factories might yet have set some limit to unbridled capitalism, but a fresh crisis in the spring of 1837 showed this was not going to happen. Amid another sharp recession, the cotton-spinners of Glasgow struck against a cut in wages. They had a trade union to co-ordinate their action. In the grimy suburbs north and east of the city, trouble brewed in the form of 'tumultuous assemblages'. The man charged with quelling them was the sheriff of Lanarkshire, Archibald Alison (brother of William Alison, the liberal professor of physiology at Edinburgh). Archibald was an energetic conservative who gives the impression in his memoirs that he rather enjoyed confrontations. Now he rode over from his house at Possil to Oakbank, an industrial complex by the Forth–Clyde Canal, and found workers occupying a factory. They were armed just with sticks, but had beaten up twenty or thirty 'nobs', or strike-breakers. Of these Alison 'saw several . . . with blood upon their faces and clothes'. While Glasgow had a police force it was unable to act outside the boundaries of the burgh, so the sheriff called up troops from their barracks in Duke Street to cow the strikers. He issued a proclamation 'warning the people of the danger they were in by joining in riotous acts and assemblages, and the determination of the magistrates to punish such acts'. With the military deployment any open defiance ceased, and at the end of three months the spinners were forced back to work on the employers' terms.[44]

But skulduggery went on. After an Irish nob was murdered in July, Alison resolved to arrest the leaders of the cotton-spinners' union, who had gone underground. He consulted the Home Secretary and got permission to enlist the help of certain individuals 'willing to give information if they were protected from danger'. The sheriff 'met the persons in an obscure place in Glasgow, and took their depositions', which included a tip-off 'that another individual named was to be murdered next day'. Alison found out the secret meeting place of the spinners' leaders, the Black Boy pub in the Gallowgate, and arrested the lot of them: five would be tried and imprisoned. With that their union collapsed. The sheriff earned a reputation as scourge of the working class, but he vindicated himself with the claim that 'the stroke against the cotton-spinners' committee told with decisive violence upon all the trades who were out on strike at the time. Violence and intimidation rapidly declined in Glasgow'.[45] Not just that, but the infant Scottish trade unionism was destroyed, in effect for the rest of the century. A rigid stand by the employers with the total support of the state had crushed it.

⚜

This trade unionism had deep defects anyway, bound up with the class structure in which it emerged. A revealing example was to be found at Paisley, a turbulent town that yet produced textiles of high quality. Its weavers wove shawls bearing the Paisley pattern that brother Scots had borne back from the Orient. Here too the craftsmen were respectable and prosperous, at least while things went well, with time and taste to look up from their looms and cultivate letters. The trades of Paisley ran a library and a literary club. Weaver poets such as Robert Tannahill, Alexander Wilson and William Motherwell were urban counterparts to the ploughman poet, Robert Burns, whom they celebrated in the local Burns Club, the oldest in Scotland, founded in 1805. One observer found a 'prominent trait in the character of the Paisley weavers, and that is a pretty general taste for books. If you enter into conversation with them, you will find many of them well-informed on several subjects, particularly general history, natural history, and, of late, politics.'[46]

In Paisley production had been from the start organised in small units, often of just a single weaver and his family, using quite simple technology. It was open to anybody with the little capital needed to set up in it, which meant the weaver might also become an employer if he did well enough to take on journeymen and apprentices. There was in practice little difference between the artisan elite and the small employers: a formula for social mobility and, in the politics of the time, for a united front in favour of reform. But none of this could guarantee economic security. It was because mass production appeared in textile factories all over the region round them that these weavers retreated into the niche market of Paisley shawls, which might earn good money but remained vulnerable to fickle fashion. So it proved in the next recession that followed in 1841–43. The demand for shawls collapsed, and the general economic conditions made it hard for the weavers to switch to another product. More than half the enterprises in Paisley went bust. A quarter of the townspeople were left dependent on poor relief. The council of the burgh had to declare itself insolvent.[47]

This was catastrophic for Paisley but why, given the uninhibited capitalism of the time, could there not be faster adjustment to economic change? One commentator sharply distinguished the independent, educated weavers from the wretched, illiterate hands in the factories:

> The cotton spinning trade now established in this part of the country is highly valuable, on account of such numbers of poor children and women as are employed in its various operations, but it appears to have no tendency to improve the morals of the country. The numbers collected in large cotton mills, from families immersed in ignorance and vice, spread the contagion among such as have been more regularly educated, and profligate conduct is the natural result.[48]

Here was a disreputable underclass, different from the respectable working class that Paisley had earlier bred. Now skilled weavers, schooled, sober and decent, feared a fall into the pit of unskilled ignorance, intemperance and immorality. They just refused to be dragged under, even if they could find nothing else. In their spirit of independence, they felt superior to the pitiable creatures forced into endless hours of soul-destroying grind at power looms, helpless women and children or hapless migrants fresh from the Highlands and Ireland. In other words, the progress of industrialisation, from crafts to factories, weakened and divided the working class.

Yet not everybody was degraded. While Paisley never again escaped the factory system – indeed turned, under the Coats, into a showcase for it – elsewhere the pride of the skilled tradesmen did not get lost. In Edinburgh they catered to the refined taste of the high bourgeoisie. On Clydeside the pride re-emerged from the demands made on the workforce, and successfully met, for the higher standards of heavy industrial production that reached their peak in the shipyards. These were socially interesting places because, as we have seen, the bosses who formed, owned and ran them had risen out of the ranks of the workmates still actually building the ships. In and beyond the shipyards there emerged during the mid-Victorian era what turned out to be quite a robust alliance, one stretching across the economy into politics, between an entrepreneurial class not itself of refined or exalted origins and a class of skilled workers sharing the same values. We might extend the alliance to include the liberal professions carrying out various specialist functions needed by industry, or those members of the lower middle class wearing white collars who worked in the offices of the enterprises. It is easy to stress the great differences in personal incomes at the various levels of this structure.[49]

There has been no lack of Scottish historians to do that.[50] But we should not overlook either the absence of any vast social distance at the extremes of the range, which made upward (and sometimes downward) mobility both possible and practicable. There was never going to be equality of incomes, but social mobility might make up for that. Jock was as good as his maister.

Across that core of mid-Victorian society, most men accepted respectable bourgeois ideals. Even workers without much money could practise self-improvement and thrift, helped along by their religion and their literacy, while the sight of peers risen to high degree demonstrated that the common ideals might benefit them too. The political triumph of the bourgeoisie in the Reform Act of 1832, and the continued exclusion from the franchise of most skilled workers, did raise tensions between the two classes, but their links were never severed. On the whole, the skilled workers assented to the bourgeois argument that the aristocracy's corrupt monopoly of power was the reason for economic distress and social injustice. This formed the basis, as we shall see in a later chapter, of popular Scottish Victorian Liberalism.

It was a new social order that emerged spontaneously out of different forces at work in Scotland.[51] It contradicted the social theories of Robert Owen, a critic of competitive capitalism and advocate of co-operation who did not live long enough to see the new social order achieved within competitive capitalism and without co-operation in any formal structure. That new social order robbed the old Tory aristocracy of its power. Yet it never became inclusive of tens of thousands of unskilled poor people breaking stones, toiling in factories, laying railway lines, labouring on building sites, cleaning the streets or sweeping the chimneys, driving the wagons or running the messages, or else dashing away with a smoothing iron – few of them in stable jobs and most of them therefore inevitably faced with bouts of unemployment as a fact of life.

Such workers left no record; we know of them only as objects of bourgeois investigation. Most poignant are the voices of children sent down the mines, some called to give evidence to the Royal Commission appointed in 1840 to look into their plight: it would recommend a ban on their employment. Here is William Marshall '10 or 11 years old', of the Townhead colliery, Kilsyth: 'I draw father's coals: have done so 12 months. Wrought three years before with father at handloom weaving but it was no good, as father said the loom would na get us oatmeal. Coal work is more sore, but no so confining. I pull in harness, and little brother pushes. Cannot read, and never goes to church, as have no clothes, and mother has nine of us.' Here is Agnes Reid, aged fourteen, of Liberton in Midlothian, now a leafy suburb, then a mining village: 'I bear coal on my back. I do not know the exact weight, but it is something more than a hundredweight. It is very sore work and often makes us cry. Few lassies like it. I would much prefer to work out by or in service but suppose father needs me.'[52]

The history of classes set out in this chapter has been especially illuminated by the experience of two traditional trades, surgeons and weavers. They started off at the same level in an older Scotland but finished up at opposite ends of the Victorian social scale, the surgeons in the high bourgeoisie, the weavers in decline and eventual extinction. This stark divergence came about through the industrial revolution, which held in store for some a flourishing future, for others no future at all. One general consequence for Scotland might have been polarisation, with sections of the nation driven apart, perhaps to the peril of the nation itself. That is what, for example, happened in neighbouring Ireland during the nineteenth century: the landowning aristocracy, the industrial proletariat of Ulster and the population of the poverty-stricken rural regions never found any common cause, but instead drifted into alienation from one another. Ireland has not been able to unite since, in the sense of class or in any other sense.[53]

Yet the Scots sustained themselves as a nation. Queen Victoria thought they had 'a quite different character' from the English. She might not herself have been the one to put her finger accurately on it, but could leave that job to Alexander Sellar, son of Patrick Sellar of Sutherland, Liberal MP for the Haddington Burghs and then for Partick. He painted this picture of the relations of social classes in Scotland:

> While the landed aristocracy and the wealthier professional classes still keep aloof from the people, and have in a great measure adopted English tastes and habits, and Episcopalian forms of worship, and English ideas on education, the middle and lower classes have remained staunch to Scottish traditions and influences. These two classes have become in a manner blended together into one class without any very distinct line of demarcation between them. They attend the Presbyterian churches, send their children to the parochial or other schools, and to the universities, where they sit together on the same benches; they associate together afterwards, and live their own lives, influenced to an almost inappreciable extent by the vexatious restrictions and annoyances of caste which are so noticeable in the middle classes south of the Tweed.[54]

5

Institution:
'I'm proud of my country'

On Sunday 14 May 1843, the Revd Henry Duncan of Ruthwell in Dumfriesshire made his way from his manse to the church where he had been minister since 1799. He knew it was the last time he would do so. Parishioners walked with him, and one recorded the conversation:

> As we crossed the grounds, rendered so beautiful by his taste and skill, on our way to the church ... to our astonishment we found the sun-dial overturned. No part of it was broken but the stile. 'You will never more point your people to the Sun of Righteousness,' remarked one by his side. 'Very likely,' was his quiet reply. Farther on in the lawn we found a flourishing evergreen torn up by the roots, and saw our neighbour's herd of cattle before us, which had broken into the garden. 'Will you say next that old James is not to work again in this garden,' asked another. 'Most likely,' was the answer. We entered the dear old church with solemn thoughts, and heard him preach a sermon on Christ a Priest on His throne, in which he bore his last testimony in that place to the priestly and kingly offices of his Divine Redeemer.[1]

During his long ministry Duncan had expended an extraordinary amount of energy and ingenuity on the cure of the 1,000 or so souls at Ruthwell. The same eyewitness wrote of how, as the minister saw his life's service there coming to an end, he would sit in the parish hall and – looking back on all he had done, right to the era of the Napoleonic Wars – weep:

For forty years he had wedded his affections to his people. That room he had procured for the male and female friendly societies, and there were carried on many of his useful operations. There he had helped them about their ballots for the militia in war time. There, in time of threatened invasion, he had aroused his volunteers. There, in time of scarcity, he had planned with them bringing of ship-loads of Indian corn and potatoes, and there the stores had been distributed. There he had first unfolded his opening scheme of a savings bank for his own parish. There he had many times examined the village Sabbath school; and there, times uncounted, he had met with them of an evening to worship God.[2]

Duncan's ministry at Ruthwell was to end four days after his last sermon from the familiar pulpit because he had decided to leave the Church of Scotland at its coming Disruption (or schism). On that 18 May the General Assembly was due to open in Edinburgh at St Andrew's Church on George Street. While a huge crowd waited outside, the retiring moderator, the Revd Dr David Welsh, professor of ecclesiastical history at the capital's univer-sity, led a prayer to open proceedings. A roll call should have followed. But Welsh stayed on his feet and, to a breathless hush, said: 'There has been an infringement on the constitution of the Church, an infringement so great that we cannot constitute its General Assembly.' He went on to read out a long protest against attacks on the Kirk mounted over the last ten years by the Parliament at Westminster. Redress had been sought in vain, so he and all who held to the spiritual independence of the Church now had no choice but to depart from it. What he meant was, among other things, its right to determine how to appoint ministers: the Kirk said their congregations should elect them, but the law said patrons of parishes could nominate them. Regardless of the detail, the Church of Scotland maintained that it should decide this and other religious questions for itself, as a spiritual corporation with Jesus Christ as its head. By contrast, Parliament maintained that the Church of Scotland, not to say Jesus Christ, must be subject to its own absolute sovereignty. So at will it might overrule the General Assembly, and had done so.[3]

Welsh laid his protest on the table, turned and bowed to the Royal Commissioner, the Earl of Bute, then stepped down from the chair and walked to the door. As he went, other ministers and elders got up to follow him, row after row of them. Outside, when they emerged, the crowd first cheered but then fell solemnly silent. Many more who had pledged to leave the Kirk were waiting in the street. Though no plan for a procession had been made, the crush grew so great that they were all forced to walk in column, three or four abreast. They marched to a meeting place prepared for them at Canonmills, a couple of miles away down the hill. There they constituted themselves the Free Church of Scotland. The Revd Thomas Chalmers was elected its first moderator. About 450 ministers, 40 per cent of the Kirk's clergy, signed a deed of demission giving up their charges, manses and incomes. Nearly half the laity all over Scotland would join them in their secession.[4]

'Well, what do you think of it?' a friend asked Francis Jeffrey, now a judge, who was spending the day at home in Moray Place. He replied, 'I'm proud of my country. There is not another country on earth where such a deed could have been done.'[5]

The issues behind this caesura in national life are so remote from today's concerns as to be scarcely explicable to modern Scots, let alone anybody else. They turned on much more than technicalities of the law or relations of Church and state. Ever since the Reformation of 1560 a continuum had in most respects been sustained in Scottish life, with even the Union of 1707 making little difference. The state looked after temporal concerns and the Church looked after spiritual concerns, widely defined to include education, care of the poor and curbs on the Scots' sins of drunkenness and fornication. In the controversies leading up to the Disruption, the Kirk often spoke about its spiritual independence, which was a reasonably accurate description of its status. There had been collisions before when the state interfered in its government, but the two sides gradually came to terms and in the late eighteenth century reached an equilibrium. It was centred in a circle round the Revd William Robertson, principal of the University of Edinburgh during the high Enlightenment. He organised his clerical colleagues well enough that they could regard themselves, and be regarded, as a party in the General Assembly, with the winsome name of Moderate party. Several, Robertson himself, the Revds Hugh Blair, Adam Ferguson, John Home and Thomas Reid, were themselves leading enlightened intellectuals. Under their guidance the Kirk behaved itself as a polite member of civil society and in return got its constitutional privileges respected.[6]

The Free Church was in part a popular, evangelical revolt against all this. There had been steady dissent and secession from Robertson's kind of Kirk. Drops of its life's blood drained away into each new independent congregation: slow death beckoned. The danger appeared dire to Chalmers by the time he arrived, after ministries in Fife and Glasgow, as professor of divinity at the University of Edinburgh in 1828. For him, preserving the Church of Scotland meant preserving its role not as a mere support but as the saviour of society, guardian of its morals, teacher of its children, protector of its poor. In particular, the religious establishment needed to extend its presence into the burgeoning cities and build many more places of worship to reach the submerged proletariat. Where would the money come from? Chalmers's bright idea was the British state, which turned him down. While demanding money, he refused to submit to any kind of supervision: the Kirk needed freedom of action to meet its challenges. The conflict inherent in his analysis led to the great crisis. The state would not concede control, and the Disruption followed as an act of defiance.[7]

Chalmers claimed victory, yet fooled himself. His vision for Scotland depended on the maintenance of established religion. In fact, he caused its collapse. For the four years of life left to him, he strove rather to prove the Church was better off without the state. So it might have been in worship or discipline, yet the key lay in the social role he always stressed. In person he sought to run in Edinburgh's slums, at the West Port, an experiment in welfare on the voluntary principle: that is, one financed not by taxes but by free contributions from the rich, and giving the poor not handouts but means to help themselves. The experiment failed.[8]

The actual achievement had been to smash the equilibrium of Church and state. On one side of the scales established religion dropped away, now unable to perform its appointed social tasks. The balance then fell down on the opposite side, the side of the British state, the only other entity equal to those tasks. Its influence proved to be an anglicising one. Scotland, with a vital element of its identity gone, had to adjust to a less autonomous position in the United Kingdom. It began to feel more like a province than a nation. We might read into the Disruption a presage of later Scottish nationalism, in the rejection of the absolute sovereignty of Parliament. But the ancestry was indirect, and the Disruption's leaders took care to play down any patriotic aspect. Rather, it was the social evolution of a more British Scotland, which few Scots wanted but all found inevitable, that sowed the seeds of later discord.[9]

Scotland as a Presbyterian community had now to be recast anyway. The Disruption created overnight a fresh force, the Free Church, which at once set out to match the Church of Scotland with a place of worship and a school in every parish. Where did the energy, and again the money, come from? The

Free Church vaunted itself as the Church of the people, though its actual numbers did not quite bear the claim out. They would soon start to complain at being endlessly dunned for this pious project and that. But the resourceful vigour of the enterprise and the contrast with past failings were beyond doubt, as expressed in a jingle:

> The wee kirk, the Free Kirk,
> The Kirk wi'out the steeple;
> The auld Kirk, the cauld Kirk,
> The Kirk wi'out the people.

Soon a second fresh force appeared when earlier dissenting churches, dating from the eighteenth century, felt prompted to band together. They completed their merger into the United Presbyterian Church in 1847. Now Scotland had three main forms of Presbyterianism. According to a religious census of 1851, 32 per cent of the churchgoing population went to the Auld Kirk, 32 per cent to the Free Church and 19 per cent to the United Presbyterian Church.[10] The Auld Kirk, while still represented everywhere, tended to be strongest in the countryside and among the bourgeoisie. The Free Church was most active in the cities but in the Highlands too. The United Presbyterians drew above all on the respectable artisan class. Still, each made strenuous efforts to expand and secure support. Sectarian rivalry was matched by architectural rivalry, with each trying to build bigger and better churches than the others. That is why Scottish towns still have so many religious structures, most today redundant.[11]

It would be easy to dwell on the damage all this did to the inherited fabric of Scottish society, with few obvious gains to compensate. Indeed it was no small thing for a nation of the nineteenth century to lose its Established Church. But if we look inside the subsequent history of the successor churches, the picture may not be quite so bleak.

At first it seemed as if the Auld Kirk might shrivel into a mere sect. In particular, the loss of leadership was grievous: a disproportionate number of the most able and active, and especially younger, ministers seceded. As for the laity, more worldly motives often pushed people into the Free Church, whence they tarred those they left behind with the brushes of cowardice, lack of principle, servility to the lairds and to the British government. We find such views in Christian Watt, a fisherwoman from Broadsea near Fraserburgh, and in the autobiography she wrote. She explained how the Disruption swept through her community because 'the Kirk had become an organisation to suppress the working class. Several folk had been evicted from crofts on the side of Benachie [*sic*]. The Aberdeenshire folk banded together right away, – it must stop forthwith. Ministers preached that it was God's will to go if told so, but folk had had enough. If you had no profession you were of no consequence to a minister, save only to fill the kirk on Sundays.' For her it was, then, a social as well as religious rupture: 'They preached on Broadsea boat shore, the whole natural arena of the braes black with people . . . It was an awful smack in the face to the would-be's [in the Established Church] who were left with nobody to look down on.'[12]

But the Auld Kirk was not ruined. The new leader who stepped out from the wreckage of the Disruption, the Revd James Robertson, professor of ecclesiastical history at the University of Edinburgh, was, if often embroiled in controversy, never a rancorous man. In fact, he revered Chalmers, whose efforts at carrying religion to the masses he sought to emulate.[13] He found an ally in Queen Victoria's chaplain, the Revd Norman Macleod, who held a parish in the middle of Glasgow, the Barony. He, too, saw it as his calling to bring God to the poor and vice versa. He had new schoolhouses built and then a mission church to which only people in working clothes might be admitted (it was a common complaint that many felt unwelcome at regular divine service because they had no Sunday best). He challenged the rigid Scottish sabbatarianism that shut parks and museums on the one day the workers had off. He edited a popular religious magazine, *Good Words,* and wrote couthy books, *Cracks about the Kirk for Kintra Folk* and *Peeps at the Far East,* a record of his tour of oriental missions. Altogether, he helped to make the Kirk more open-minded and tolerant.[14] After Macleod died in 1872, the Revd John Tulloch became its public face. A sober and intellectual figure, he was yet just as good at presentation. This liberal theologian published *Movements of Religious Thought in the Nineteenth Century* (1885), setting out the broad-minded view that, since man was fallen, no church's claims could be absolute. Yet the three leaders sought to show that only an Established Church might be truly national and care for the whole people.[15]

Their work paid off: by the 1860s membership of the Church of Scotland was rising again. The appearance could have been deceptive, for it remained to many the church of default: they might declare adherence to it even if they never darkened the door of any place of worship. That seemed confirmed by its own inquiries in 1874, which found just 175,000 of 680,000 nominal adherents had taken communion during the year. Still, the upward trend alarmed its rivals. The government in London then got rid of the biggest bone of contention back in 1843 by abolishing lay patronage. Where now was the sticking point between Auld Kirk and Free Church? The Scots' love of hair-splitting soon found one. Sure enough, the Free Church started calling for disestablishment of the Church of Scotland, with support from the United Presbyterians. The two rival churches deplored the existence of a religious establishment embracing only a minority of the population: it was a 'corruption of Christian polity' and 'destructive of spiritual interests'.[16] This altercation dragged on for the rest of the century and embittered Presbyterian relations, but brought no change at all.[17]

The call for disestablishment came naturally to United Presbyterians because theirs was a voluntary church, one neither enjoying nor requesting support from the state but sustaining itself by the commitment of its members. That made it also more responsive to their wishes than to clerical quibbles. It was at heart a church of industrious artisans bettering themselves, though some degree of internal tension might result when they did better themselves. From their place of worship at Cambridge Street in central Glasgow, the wealthier members of the congregation, together with the minister, the Revd John Eadie, moved out and built themselves a posher kirk in the suburbs. The day it opened, a wag chalked on its door:

This church is not built for the poor and the needy
But for the rich and for Dr Eadie.
The rich may come in and take their seat,
But the poor must go to Cambridge Street.[18]

In other ways the United Presbyterians were more obviously progressive. At mid-century the three main Scottish churches, while organisationally divided, yet remained at one in their conservative Calvinist theology, as set out in the Westminster Confession of 1647 depicting human nature as totally depraved by the original sin of Adam. Over time, this view became harder for the average United Presbyterian to take, he often being a busy tradesman trying to do his best on meagre earnings by his family and community. If he reproved weakness, irreligion and immorality in neighbours and workmates, he could hardly accept he was in the eyes of God no better than them. The first concession to a less rigid outlook came in 1876 when the United Presbyterians eased the terms on which new ministers were required to subscribe the Westminster

Confession. Now at their ordinations they could declare they viewed it as a general statement of the faith without needing to get into the detail of which dogmas they personally accepted (the Free Church followed this move in 1879, the Auld Kirk only in 1910). Liberal theology made deeper inroads with its claim that the kingdom of God should, to whatever extent possible, be achieved on earth as well as in heaven. A United Presbyterian minister, the Revd Scott Matheson, wrote of this as an imperative of God's will, for 'part of that will is to grapple with social wrongs, abolish poverty and join in all lawful efforts to obtain for labour its due reward, and for the toilers a large degree of amenity in their lot.'[19] It amounted to much the same as political radicalism, or even as early socialism in Scotland; indeed Scots socialists of the day liked to compare the historical struggles of Covenanters and kings with the current struggles of labour and capital.

Vigorous as the other two churches were, or became again, it would be hard to deny the Free Church remained the most vigorous. The drama and sacrifice of its birth in 1843 inspired it for the rest of the century. It maintained its claim to be the true Church of Scotland that would return to establishment one of these days, once its conditions had been fulfilled. Within a decade it built 730 places of worship and 400 manses. It was supporting 500 schoolmasters to teach 44,000 children and, to train its ministers, founded New College in Edinburgh. It set up a home mission to evangelise the urban poor, while most foreign missionaries had adhered to it too. This was a tremendous tribute to the spiritual and material exertions of its members, who saw themselves as the vanguard of Victorian Scotland. They entertained no doubt, for example, that wealth could be a good thing. Their founding father Chalmers had always extolled the classical economics of Adam Smith, which he came close to identifying with the will of God: hence the unfailing trust in individual initiative and voluntary effort rather than in collective action or intervention by the state. In the next generation, Chalmers's disciples brought the same principles and zeal to bear on new social problems as they arose: the Revd James Begg who campaigned for better workers' housing, the Revd Thomas Guthrie who sought to save vagrant children on the streets.[20]

Spiritually militant and socially active, the Free Church also became an intellectual force. Just as it combatted compromise with secular authority or resignation in the face of poverty, so it took its stand against the rising tide of religious scepticism resulting from the progress of science. Scottish geologists,

James Hutton and Charles Lyell, had found in the record of the rocks evidence of evolution contradicting the account of Creation in Genesis. This controversy was diffused at large, on the sceptical side by Robert Chambers, publisher in Edinburgh of a range of works on popular science, and on the orthodox side by Hugh Miller, stonemason and journalist. His best-selling book *The Old Red Sandstone* (1841) reflected his personal experience of hewing in the quarries of Easter Ross. Examining the fossils he unearthed, he decided that 'if fish rose into reptiles, it must have been by sudden transformation' – in other words, by the hand of God. In the end, however, Miller could not reconcile his scientific discoveries with his Presbyterian faith, and he committed suicide.[21]

It was a legacy of the Enlightenment that Scotland remained intellectually close to Europe. Scottish theologians went to study at German universities where the higher criticism had been developed, the technique of analysing the Bible like any other text. A master of this philology was the Revd William Robertson Smith, who had excelled in mathematics at the universities of Aberdeen and Edinburgh before he went to study theology at Tübingen. Later, as professor of Hebrew in the Free Church College of Aberdeen, he started writing articles, generally concerning subjects from the Old Testament, for the *Encyclopaedia Britannica*. They demonstrated the kinship of the religion of ancient Israel with the cults of its heathen neighbours. To him that illustrated how God spoke to man in many ways, but to his clerical colleagues it appeared merely impious. He was arraigned of heresy before the presbytery of Aberdeen and then before the General Assembly. There, in 1881, he suffered condemnation and deposition from his chair – this despite efforts at compromise by the Revd Robert Rainy, *éminence grise* of the Free Church, who in his preference for politics over theology might have felt equally at home in the Church of Scotland. But at least, unlike its rivals, the Free Church confronted the deepest religious dilemmas of the age, even if it could not resolve them.[22]

Not in energy or intellect but certainly in numbers, all three main Scottish churches were ceasing to grow by the turn of the twentieth century; they keenly felt their failure among the working class. Compared to this, the controversies of the Disruption now seemed distant and dated to many Scots. If schism had alienated them, one answer was to seek reunion. In 1900 the Free and the United Presbyterian Churches came together in the United Free Church. It seemed an obvious move to make and of no disadvantage to anybody, yet there were a lot of hair-splitting Highlanders who could not bring themselves to accept it. A number of their congregations, promptly known as the Wee Frees, declined to join in the reunion and continued defending the principles of 1843. They also claimed the entire property (places of worship, manses, colleges and foreign missions) that the Free Church wanted to take with it into the merger. They went to law to secure that property and, to general amazement, at length persuaded the House of Lords to uphold their claim. A Royal Commission and parliamentary legislation were in the end needed to produce a more equal division of the spoils.[23]

While sorting this little local difficulty, the United Free Church held out an olive branch to the Church of Scotland. There were hindrances to reconciliation beyond half a century of sectarian squabbling. The United Free Church wanted to maintain spiritual independence. The Church of Scotland wanted to stay established. The culmination of the debates came in 1921 with recognition of the spiritual independence of the established Church of Scotland in an Act of Security passed at Westminster. Parliament in effect conceded the point on which it had made so many Presbyterians secede from the Auld Kirk in 1843.[24] That led straight on to full reunion of all (or nearly all) Presbyterians in 1929 with the re-establishment of one church for the whole nation. It hoped reunion would inspire the spiritual regeneration of Scotland, though the hope proved vain. Even less could its original guarantee in the Treaty of Union do anything for this central national institution.[25]

The effects of the Disruption were therefore felt not just in the churches but all through Scottish society. The Auld Kirk had been a pillar of it since the Reformation, not least in constructing the system of education, by the eighteenth century one of the best in Europe. Under a law of 1696 every parish had a school with schoolmaster nominated by the minister and the local heritors. Its task was to give a basic education to as many children as possible and to prepare the brightest to go on to university. Scotland housed five universities, three dating from the Middle Ages – St Andrews (1410), Glasgow (1451) and King's College, Aberdeen (1495) – the others from the era of the Reformation – Edinburgh (1583) and Marischal College, Aberdeen (1596). The Treaty of Union guaranteed their status too, one purpose of the relevant provision being to assure a supply of men qualified for the Presbyterian ministry.

But study of divinity had become rather dangerous in an age of religious strife, as likely to lead to banishment and destitution, even to the scaffold, as to a comfortable living in a pleasant parish. Other disciplines flourished: science, mathematics, medicine. And the broader education of students proceeded not so much through theology as through moral philosophy, which Principal Robertson of Edinburgh made compulsory for all taking courses in arts. It was this open approach, coupled with the presence of enlightened thinkers, that raised the universities' standing so high. They were public national institutions, too, not exclusive private corporations, offering access to all who could profit from it: the whole nation had an interest in them just as they served the whole nation. Indeed, they served more than one nation. They educated not only Scots but also Englishmen, religious dissenters excluded from Oxford and Cambridge along with Whigs uneasy at the High Tory ethos of the colleges: of Liberal Prime Ministers in the nineteenth century, Lord Melbourne, Lord John Russell and Viscount Palmerston had all been to the Scottish universities. Otherwise, their catchment areas extended as far as America and Russia. Only with the rise of the German universities did their pre-eminence wane.[26]

The prime feature of Scottish higher education was generalism. When Lord Kelvin went to the University of Glasgow at the age of ten, the next youngest students were just a couple of years older. They would have started with work at what came later to be regarded as a senior secondary level. Not till near the end of the century did it prove possible to set a starting age of seventeen. Except for moral philosophy, no formal curriculum existed, so the professors taught what they liked. The sole pressure on them was to attract enough students to their classes, since in a frugal nation the academic salaries remained meagre and they could only make a decent living from fees they charged. Nor was there even any obligation on students to meet a defined standard. They could drop in and out of classes according to need or taste, at the end of the session collecting a ticket to say they had joined in the bouts of question-and-answer that gave trained Scots minds of this era their verve. Many studied for just a year or two and only one in five or six took a degree, graduation being a mere option.[27]

Professors might succeed in different ways. Joseph Black had introduced the subject of chemistry to the University of Edinburgh at the end of the eighteenth century after making fundamental discoveries himself, and students flocked to learn at his feet. His successor, handsome and debonair Tommy Hope, followed a different tack so long as he held the chair till 1844, with, according to Lord Cockburn, 'amusing and brilliant experiments'. He hit the jackpot when he let his students bring their girlfriends. Then he was lecturing to 300 at a time: 'the ladies declare there was never anything so delightful as these chemical flirtations. The Doctor is in absolute ecstasy with his audience of veils and feathers . . . I wish some of his experiments would blow him up. Each female student would get a bit of him.'[28]

There was a more austere kind of learning experience for the great explorer David Livingstone. In 1836 he had walked from his home at Blantyre to start at Anderson's Institution, an offshoot from the University of Glasgow offering vocational education in practical subjects to part-time students: nothing amusing here, just hard graft under earnest, exigent instructors. Aiming to become a medical missionary, he set himself a broad curriculum. He learned theology and Greek with a fierce foe of slavery, Ralph Wardlaw. He took classes in chemistry from, and became a friend of, James Young, who later made a fortune when he discovered how to extract paraffin from shale. Still young Livingstone felt lonely, and escaped every weekend to Blantyre. There, however, his sisters were delighted to find he had grown 'so genial and pleasant'. In the vacations he went straight back to work as a cotton-spinner.[29]

At Aberdeen's colleges, the usual poverty and ambition went together with some sense of fun; their boisterous lads thought it a hoot when the first English students arrived among them in the 1860s and answered questions with 'yah'. This was also the classic locus of the legendary poor boys from the country living in bare garrets, as described by Neil Maclean in 1872: 'A bag of meal, in which some eggs have been carefully packed, with a small kit of salt herrings, form their staple articles of food, on which they will be contented to live for the whole winter, provided they can drink in the words of knowledge that fall from their professors' lips.' The journalist Robertson Nicoll, who came to Aberdeen in 1866, claimed to 'know of at least once case where a student was practically starved to death with a huge empty oatmeal barrel beside him in his little garret'.[30]

Walter Elliot, a Secretary of State for Scotland in the twentieth century, summed up the old system under the rubric of the 'democratic intellect'.[31] A less succinct but more colourful formulation came from Lyon Playfair, who had both a commercial and an academic career before being elected MP for the Scottish Universities in 1868. He told Parliament: 'The great Napoleon used to say that every soldier carried his Marshal's baton in his knapsack;

so every Scotch peasant, when he goes to school, carried in his satchel a minister's gown, or other emblem of a learned profession, and it is his own fault if he lose it.'[32]

🌣

There was some hope the universities might assume the moral and intellectual leadership that the Church of Scotland had perforce given up. Yet they, in their turn, were to get torn apart by the Disruption. One point at issue in 1843 had been the religious test: the letter of the law required principals and professors to be members of the Kirk. Since a good number already belonged to other denominations or to none, it was a rule observed more in the breach than in the observance. But now certain figures in the Church of Scotland, resolved to salvage for it what they could, tried to revive the test and exclude Free Churchmen from academic appointments.[33]

Their target was David Brewster, principal of the University of St Andrews. He had found success and security only late in life: that post, to which he won appointment in 1838 at the age of 57, was the first academic job he had ever had. His career was so slow to take off because of his terror of public speaking: he once fainted at a dinner-party when invited to say grace. Unable therefore to fulfil his youthful ambition of a career in the preaching Kirk, he had to join the straggling band of Scotland's freelance writers, many but poor. Then as now, there was a floating population of indigent literary men who could never find enough lucrative or congenial employment, perhaps did not want to. They had at least nothing to lose from trying to get into print, in anything from poetry to legal texts. Brewster, too, wrote for a rag-taggle of publications, but became more and more interested in science. He worked for years on the earliest scholarly biography of Sir Isaac Newton (1855) and meanwhile made himself an authority on optics; in fact, he invented the stethoscope and kaleidoscope. He sought also to bring the fruits of scientific discovery to a wider public, for which purpose he founded the British Association for the Advancement of Science in 1831.

So Brewster was a person of some distinction by the time the diehards of the Church of Scotland picked on him. From the start at St Andrews, it counted against him that he was not a clergyman, as every one of his predecessors had been and most of his professors still were. The university cultivated a character of its own, venerable and comfortable. In fact, it was corrupt and sleepy. Brewster burst in on it not only as an evangelical layman but also as a brash reformer. He wanted to clean it up and turn it into a dynamic college of science. He was soon on the worst of terms with the old guard. Wrangling in the common rooms broke out into the open at the time of the Disruption, after the students elected Chalmers as their rector. They did so by an irregular procedure, however, and the senate disciplined them. But Brewster took their side. That provoked the senate to turn on him and try to depose him as a dissenter, in other words because he had joined the Free Church. The attempt failed, establishing in law that men already in academic office could not be so deposed. But the Kirk continued to bar new professors who did not belong to it. It threatened to turn the universities into sectarian seminaries. This nonsense was stopped by the British government, which abolished the test, except for chairs in divinity, in 1853.[34]

Meanwhile the one university where the Free Church might gain a foothold was Edinburgh, a municipal college for which the town council chose the professors – and the Free Church commanded a large faction in that council. In 1850 the chair of moral philosophy fell vacant. There was an obvious candidate in James Ferrier, who held the same chair at St Andrews. Scion of a leading legal and literary family in the capital, he would at any earlier point have been elected without question – and on merit too, as the great white hope of the Scottish intellect, ready to carry its work forward into the second half of the century, initially by coming to terms with German idealist philosophy. But Ferrier was a member of the Kirk and had weighed into the polemics over the Disruption, enough to set the Free Churchmen and United Presbyterians against him. And there might already have been a question mark over his moral conduct as well as over his moral philosophy. He would later catch syphilis from a prostitute, so putting an end to any serious intellectual activity on his part.[35]

The Free Churchmen and United Presbyterians anyway decided Ferrier had to be stopped, yet faced the problem of finding a plausible alternative. The best they could do was Patrick MacDougall, professor of moral philosophy at New College. He was a nonentity, however – a hack and bootlicker to his backers with nothing to say for himself. Candidates for a chair often brought out a quick publication to impress the electors; all he could manage was a slim volume of book reviews written for house organs of the Free Church. Yet in the town council MacDougall beat Ferrier. It was a sensation, but more than that a catastrophic break in the tradition of Scottish philosophy, served in its academic chairs by men of the highest ability for over a century. Now, in this mess of mediocrity, the succession came to an end.[36]

There was in any event mounting criticism of the standards at Scottish universities, thought too low to enable their graduates to compete, at least outside Scotland, with the products of Oxford and Cambridge. These still offered a specialised classical or mathematical curriculum reckoned to develop powers of mind not to be attained through the generalism of Scotland. People of this opinion seemed untroubled by the fact that, for example, France – not exactly a backward nation – had universities fairly like the Scottish ones. The old system did still find staunch defenders in Scotland. But it made all the difference that the Disruption rendered so many dissensions among disputatious Scots quite irresolvable. As in the case of religious tests, the only thing might be for the Parliament at Westminster to step in and reform the universities from the outside. This could, however, also bring anglicisation in its train.

The first example came in the Universities (Scotland) Act of 1858. It did indeed start to introduce into Scottish higher education something of the specialisation of the English system. As it started operating, the ideal of the democratic intellect took a further dent by the discovery that it was anyway a bit of a myth. A Royal Commission on Scottish education, set up under the Duke of Argyll in 1864, cast an eye over the whole system, including recruitment to it.[37] Inquiry revealed that the universities catered for a wide range of the professional and skilled classes in Scotland, but few of the unskilled and poor. About one-third of entrants arrived from professional homes. The offspring of ministers, at one in ten of the whole student body, looked over-represented. A son of the manse had a hundred times better chance of getting to university than the son of a miner.[38]

Glasgow seemed to be where the democratic intellect kept going best. A quarter of its students were drawn from the working class, many to study part-time after they had embarked on industrial or commercial careers. On the principle of open access, they dropped in and out of courses as it suited: of 3,000 students at Glasgow between 1871 and 1876, 36 per cent went for one session, 17 per cent for two and only 47 per cent for more than two.[39] In the old system this would have been regarded not as a defect but as a virtue. Kelvin held practical training should not take place in a university: 'There is a limit to the functions of a university, which is to impart and to certify the scientific knowledge, but not to certify the practical skill, of the candidates.'[40] In fact, the proportion of working-class students remained similar till 1910, with more then coming from shipyards and engineering shops than ever before. All this could have been defined as the survival of a different system, rather than as the mark of an inferior system that theorists and historians in the twentieth century would take it to be.

A general conclusion might be that the universities, starting within the traditional framework, were adapting to the evolution of the class system as we observed it in the last chapter. In Scotland there existed no sharp social division between bourgeoisie and skilled working class. The outlook and interests of both coincided not in every detail but over a broad range. The range excluded the aristocracy at one extreme. At the other extreme it excluded the unskilled working class, toilers in fields and factories and mines, marked not only by poverty but also by attitude and habit. But it was the middle range of Scots, from entrepreneurs to skilled tradesmen, sharing interests, outlook and education, that dominated late Victorian Scotland: no surprise, then, if the universities answered to their interests. In this sense, the sobriquet of democratic intellect was still merited.

Even so, equilibrium would prove hard to maintain, in higher education as elsewhere. A second reform, the Universities (Scotland) Act of 1889, brought further compromise between the Scottish and English systems. A general curriculum survived, but only as an alternative to the shiny novelty of specialisation. After 1892, honours degrees became specialist, with the qualifications for entry raised. Scotland was now on the road to a system quite different from the general philosophical education it had earlier wanted to preserve.[41]

Right till the end of the twentieth century the old system had a doughty defender in the philosopher George Davie, still recalling its glory days. But we should not leave the matter without acknowledging there was some virtue on the other side of the argument. Scotland, like all modern societies, needed greater scientific and technical expertise. The unreformed system of higher education provided it only with difficulty. The reformed one was not an unqualified success either, but can at least be seen as a considered, sympathetic compromise between traditional Scottish values and the imperatives of modernity. The whole evolution issued in higher education more professional, more productive of research, more exacting in standards and more useful for graduates competing in Britain and the Empire.

Progress could then come also in the integration of universities and schools. This was one main aim of that pedagogic milestone, the Education (Scotland) Act of 1872. It rationalised the system established in 1696, which for all its precocity left many gaps, in part filled by an arresting array of private educational enterprise. The scene had been cheerfully chaotic; the Disruption made it more chaotic but less cheerful. The new Act built on existing elements, discarding some while promoting others. Overall, Scottish education was now to be controlled by the state, through local boards elected to supervise the existing parish and burgh schools. The boards could levy a rate or borrow to build new schools. Private schools might stay that way but then would get no help. The Act excluded religious instruction in the classroom, as an answer to the Scots' endless glee in sectarian strife, but that created a problem for minorities, for Roman Catholics and Episcopalians; their schools remained outside the system. The Act was successful, the basis for future educational achievement by the Scots. But it sent a message that the British state had to solve their problems for them.

Still, it would be an error to assume that the Act of 1872 represented an educational revolution, as England's corresponding Act of 1870 did. Scottish education before 1872 had not been quite universal, but certainly general and amazingly diverse, as Argyll's commission found. The basic fault he uncovered was not so much deficiency of provision as malfunction in putting resources where they were needed most. Some parts of the system did work well. At the secondary level, the burgh schools looked back on a long history of preparing pupils from all backgrounds for further studies or careers. In Edinburgh, the High School took in, beside boys from the burgh, scions of noble families coming to spend the social season in the capital. In Glasgow, the High School recruited from the wealthiest families as from the sons of tradesmen. There was room for many other educational initiatives, from more specialist schools in the burghs to private schools in remote counties where a single master catered for all the local children. And the system had continuously expanded. After 1833 the government made capital grants available for new schools. From 1846 schools became eligible for annual awards if they accepted inspection, followed an approved curriculum and engaged teachers who had been certified: this was the origin of the independent Scottish inspectorate. The state gave support to efforts to improve the supply and training of teachers after the opening of a Normal Seminary in Glasgow in 1837, of a further one in Edinburgh a little later, then of others established by the Free Church. So, with subsidies to induce greater compliance with official aims, there had been intervention in Scottish education well before the Act of 1872. It coincided with the ethos of the Scottish system, however: though beyond the bigger burghs the coverage by the secondary system remained patchy, all over the country the public purpose of schools was to serve their local communities (which could not be said everywhere in the British Isles).[42]

After the Act of 1872 the Scottish system continued to develop along its own lines. It did so in response to pressure above all from the middle class – not in itself anglicising pressure, rather a desire for pupils to attain higher intellectual standards and formal qualifications so that they could embark on careers outside Scotland if they wanted to.[43] Scottish debates came closer to those in Europe than to those in England, which seemed satisfied with its emerging class-based system of public, grammar and elementary schools. In France the *lois Ferry* of 1879–83 meanwhile made education compulsory, free and non-denominational. Reunited Germany had by 1900 a system on three levels distinguished not by social class of pupils but by type of subject studied. In both countries the aim was to mould the citizens of a modern nation-state. The Scottish desire for imperial participation might have been somewhat different, yet George Ramsay, professor of Latin at the University of Glasgow, similarly argued that any country's future depended on 'the disciplined intelligence of the great bulk of the community'. He continued:

> We cannot trust only to the intellect of our well-to-do classes, we cannot afford to allow the humbly-born ability to take its chance of being able, by rare good fortune, to struggle out into usefulness and recognition; we must go to meet it wherever it is to be found, and, by a carefully organised system of graded education, placed within the reach of all such as are able to profit by it, do everything that is possible to swell the bulk and improve the quality of the national intelligence.[44]

Even after 1872 it would take time to fulfil this ideal. The best-educated city was Edinburgh, with not only the High School but also rich endowments in the private schools of the Merchant Company and Heriot's Trust, usually known as hospitals. If anything the place had educational charities in excess. Most of their income came from urban property, so in the late nineteenth century soared. Since national frugality here blended with local philanthropy, the question again followed whether available resources were really being put to the best use. Many pupils in the hospitals boarded, yet nearly all were sons or daughters of Edinburgh – as they had to be under the terms of the relevant bequests. Was this the most effective way to spend money on them?[45]

The Merchant Company decided not. In 1879 it resolved to change the nature of its hospitals. It formed five big day schools, fee-paying on a modest scale and with charitable free places still. They flourished. Soon they had 4,000 pupils and 213 teachers, compared to the previous 400 and 26 in all the hospitals combined; the expansion benefited girls especially. Heriot's Trust had to decide whether to follow suit. This was a matter of hot dispute because, among the educational institutions of Edinburgh, Heriot's School most clearly prepared its boys for entry to the trades, where nearly every one ended up. The trust was by now so wealthy it had also built 13 free, elementary 'outdoor schools' in the city. Upwardly mobile members of the working class felt the trust was there for them and did a great job in meeting their needs. As Edinburgh trades council put it, the successful aim had been 'to raise up a respectable, thinking, able class of artisans or citizens'. So there was fierce resistance to any idea Heriot's Trust might ape the Merchant Company and make its main school fee-paying. Yet that was what happened, after a long struggle, in 1885.[46]

Glasgow saw a similar process at the venerable Hutchesons' Grammar School, but did not face the same overall problem because its range of schools was otherwise newer. Here, then, the urban bourgeoisie had less chance to carry out a grab of existing resources. But it did supplement those resources with fresh private foundations. On the day Kelvinside Academy opened in 1878, Glasgow Academy moved from its original site at Charing Cross to Kelvinbridge, and in 1885 Hillhead High School opened its doors. The burgeoning bourgeois suburbs of the West End became almost over-supplied with education. The result was much the same as in Edinburgh: expanded facilities for the middle class, but a middle class understood to comprehend trades as well as professions.[47] Elsewhere the local boards concentrated on the construction of schools charging lower fees than the high schools while offering as full a range of secondary subjects; from here most pupils left at fifteen for commercial careers, but a good number got to university too. The sum of all these parts was not indeed perfectly democratic. Nor, however, did it amount to a rigid class-based system, rather one with access to higher education more open than in most countries.

Finally, the Act of 1872 established universal elementary education. Some features of it were again already in place, but the legislation did make a big difference. Its central principle was compulsion: all children aged five to 13 had to attend school. Scottish education at the end of the century looked different from how it had looked at the beginning. One force at work was anglicisation, which did not overwhelm internal impulses for reform, however, nor yet influence from other countries in Europe. The whole system was no longer so Scottish, though dissimilar from any other country's system. To that extent it still fulfilled an intention of the Treaty of Union, if in forms the framers of the treaty could hardly have imagined.

On the third great national institution, Scots law, the Disruption also exerted its effects, not least because at a basic level it was Scots law that brought the Disruption about. As already mentioned, the big issue driving it was patronage, the legal right of local landowners to present ministers to parishes of the Church of Scotland. But patronage offended Presbyterian principle, which held that congregations should elect their ministers. Since 1712 the Kirk had all the same submitted under protest to the Act of the Parliament, at Westminster, the Patronage Act, imposing the alien practice. In a new age of evangelical revival and political reform, however, such meekness seemed unnecessary. The General Assembly of 1834 passed its own Veto Act. This did not as such seek to abolish patronage, but stated that if the congregation of a parish objected to a minister presented to it, then the responsible presbytery was bound to accept the objection and seek a new candidate.[48]

The Veto Act on the whole worked well enough but did cause some little local difficulties, notably at Auchterarder.[49] The patron here was the Earl of Kinnoul, who at the end of 1834 presented to the parish a certain Robert Young. Well qualified, Young would after all the subsequent troubles be for many years an admirable minister there. But he was the nephew of the earl's factor – and that proved enough in this part of rural Scotland to set the congregation against him. Almost unanimously they objected to his appointment, and the presbytery, following the terms of the Veto Act, turned him down also. A convoluted legal action followed, which by the end of 1837 reached the Court of Session.

The Dean of Faculty, John Hope – 'screaming and sweating' as Cockburn described him – led for the pursuers, claiming the Church of Scotland was bound just like any other subject to obey the will of Parliament: if the Veto Act offended against the Patronage Act, the latter must be decisive. The Lord Advocate, Andrew Rutherfurd, defending, argued for the co-equality of Church and state; many of the Kirk's laws and institutions predated any parliamentary regulation and Scots law had always assumed for it an absolute power over its own doctrine and discipline.

The case carried on for three months before a full bench of 13 judges robed in their scarlet-and-white magnificence. The Lord President was Charles Hope, Lord Granton, a Tory who had held political office 30 years before, but whose 'integrity, candour, kindness and gentlemanlike manners and feelings gained him an almost unanimous esteem', according to Cockburn. However that might have been, he did not, in his judgment on 27 February 1838, beat about the bush: 'My opinion is that the Act of the General Assembly in 1834, now before us, is illegal, and not more contrary to the statute law of the land than it is to the law of the Church itself . . . the Act of Assembly 1834 was quite uncalled for, in the circumstances of the Church and country, and most inexpedient.'[50]

Delivery of the verdicts went on for a week. Six other judges followed straight on in concurrence with the Lord President, so that the Kirk had already lost the case by the time the proceedings were half over. Only then did the tide of condemnation turn, with the judgment of James, Lord Moncrieff, from a family that had long championed reform in the Church of Scotland. He was, in fact, the man who, as a member of the General Assembly, had moved the Veto Act in 1834. He reminded his fellow judges 'that one of the constitutional and most essential safeguards against the undue use of the right [of patronage], though maintained and constantly observed in form, had been reduced by practical operations to nearly a dead letter, that many evils had in consequences been brought upon the Church'. Now 'it ought to be revived in its full spirit, and brought into a state of definite and active efficiency'. But only four other judges agreed. The votes in the court finally stood at eight to five against the Kirk.[51]

The judgment in the Auchterarder case is a point as good as any to mark the end of an epoch in the history of the Court of Session, indeed of Scots law in general. Since 1707 Scots law had on the whole worked in harmony with the other institutions guaranteed under the Treaty of Union. It was basic to the healthy functioning of the nation. As Sir Walter Scott had written, 'Were it not for the difference of the religion and laws poor Scotland could hardly keep a man that is worth having.'[52] Now the institutions were set at odds, internally and externally, so that the fabric originally intended to preserve Scottish society against assimilation to English society just fell apart. The consequences were not hard to predict.

The harmony of the three institutions had been the happier because over the same period Scots law enjoyed its golden age. The Union, so far from damaging it, brought it rapidly to maturity. Only in 1681, James Dalrymple, Lord Stair, had synthesised the nation's historic legal traditions in his *Institutions of the Law of Scotland*. This work achieved much, including the setting of its subject in a universal context. The existence of the *Institutions*, newly minted and of unimpeachable authority, was really what allowed the Scots to preserve their law at the Union, since they could show it off to the English as a complete, self-consistent system simply not to be impugned for some political purpose, however expedient.

But now it was the job of the Parliament at Westminster to legislate for Scotland. In fact, it seldom did so, except to punish the Scots for Jacobite misdemeanour or, in due course, to regulate private matters such as the building of canals and railways. This was all to the good because Scots law could continue to develop along its own lines, not towards English law but in important respects away from it. Existing principles of the civil law were extensively worked out by a succession of institutional writers, by Andrew MacDouall, Lord Bankton, by Henry Home, Lord Kames, by John Erskine of Carnock and by George Joseph Bell. The accolade of institutional writer comes from the fact that they are still recognised as formal sources of the law, to this day cited in the Scottish courts. Their development of the civil law found a parallel in work on the criminal law by David Hume, usually called Baron Hume (one of his judicial offices was baron of exchequer) to distinguish him from his philosopher uncle, also David Hume.

In this era, besides, the Faculty of Advocates could count as a matrix of the Scottish Enlightenment. Much the nicest of all the Enlightenments, it was at its most agreeable in its social life, with good drink and good crack in the howffs along the High Street of Edinburgh round Parliament House, seat of the central courts. That was conducive also to the formation of an intellectual community. The fashion long continued for talented, ambitious men to join the Faculty of Advocates even if they had no professional interest in the law, to find congenial company or to mark up status. There were examples even late on in the nineteenth century such as James Clerk Maxwell or Robert Louis Stevenson. They all made the profession of law in Scotland intelligent and civilised, an essential component of the culture of the country, itself part of the family of European cultures rather than of any narrower insular one.

❦

Still, by the nineteenth century the golden age of Scots law was passing. The business of the central courts had vastly increased since the Union. One general reason was the quickening social and economic change of the time. A more particular reason was that civil appeals could now go to the House of Lords in London where, however, they often had to wait years for a verdict from the English judges. Legal systems tend to be conservative and the Scots one proved sluggish in its adaptation to the changed conditions, especially in its reluctance to reform procedure. So long backlogs of litigation built up in Edinburgh too. By 1823 nearly 3,000 cases a year were coming into the Court of Session, with more than 1,000 appeals going on to the Lords. To a mere handful did this recourse make any difference. Most were deserted for one reason and another before coming to judgment, but only after taking up on average two days of their lordships' time.[53]

The congestion defied the fact that the Scottish judiciary was now larger than ever before. The tally of judges, the 'Auld Fifteen', had been fixed at the foundation of the system in 1532. The Court of Session, for civil cases, had a Lord President appointed from among that number, while the High Court of Justiciary, for criminal cases, had a nominal head, the Lord Justice General, whose post was a sinecure. Then five judges sat in the exchequer, originally established to deal with the fiscal consequences of the Union, plus four each in two older tribunals, the commissary court, dating from the Reformation and dealing with the law of the family, then the Court of Admiralty, which heard a range of maritime cases from piracy to slaving. Finally there was a jury court, set up only in 1819, to deal with selected civil causes – seduction and the like – thought too delicate to be left to crusty old Scots judges sitting alone. Lord Melville wrote: 'As the Scotch bar has to supply sixteen judges for the Courts of Session, Justiciary and Jury trials, who ought to be, and always are if possible, advocates of eminence and considerable practice, I assert that the supplying of sixteen proper persons for those judicial situations is very difficult and scarcely practicable.'[54] His comment referred to a familiar problem in Scotland, arising from the mean salaries paid to public servants, that advocates in successful practice had little incentive to go on the bench.

Reform proceeded crabwise, till its progress reached some sort of an end in 1830 with legislation meant to increase the capacity of the Court of Session for appeals. It then had an inner house of two divisions, each with four judges, taking disputed decisions from an outer house of five permanent lords ordinary, which gave it more or less its modern shape. That might have brought clearer benefits if the judicial establishment had not soon been savagely pruned. Eighteen offices vanished in all. The bench in the Court of Session suffered a reduction of two from the Auld Fifteen. But then the jury court (an unsuccessful experiment) was merged into it. The Court of Admiralty had already been deprived of jurisdiction in prize, in what a Lord President of the twentieth century, Lord Cooper of Culross, called 'a particularly offensive example of the tendency of certain influential interests to regard the English courts as important and the Scottish as local and limited'; this court too was now eliminated. The powers of the commissary court were drastically curtailed. Excepting the last, which survived till 1856, all the other tribunals would be abolished once the Whigs, fanatics for public economy, came to power with the first Reform Act. By 1836 there were only 13 judicial posts altogether in Scotland, half the figure of 1819.[55]

It was also a pity that the long debate over those reforms took on such a partisan tinge. The Tory rulers of Scotland wanted to defend the existing order of things, while the Whig opposition pressed reform as the only way forward. The judicial system was dragged in because it was used by the Tories to suppress unrest. In retort leading Whigs such as Jeffrey and Cockburn developed a critique of it as the fountainhead of Scottish authoritarianism. Cockburn raved on about the alleged dictatorship of successive Lord Advocates: 'There is no one man armed with so great a power in any government professing to be free in Europe.'[56] He defamed the whole structure as uniquely reactionary and oppressive, compared to an English judiciary defending Englishmen's liberties as the Scottish judiciary never deigned to do for Scots: odd he should have said this after three decades of radical turmoil when England had executed 1,400 people, many merely petty criminals, while Scotland had executed 18.[57] After Jeffrey and Cockburn got on to the bench, they represented at the heart of the Scottish judiciary a view of the essential superiority of English law; for them it followed that reform at home should copy the example of the neighbour nation.

The rest of the legal profession could not by then be relied on to resist. Its outlook had narrowed since the eighteenth century, when it was closely connected with a cosmopolitan landed class. For young gentlemen a grand tour of Europe might be combined with study, especially of law, at Dutch, French or German universities. When they got back, they would be put to the law at home, as advocates with an implicit brief to plead if necessary for their kin in the Court of Session: useful ornaments to any family as the Union worked its effects on older social and economic structures. At times, one in three of the advocates came from titled families, far in excess of their proportion in the population as a whole.[58] The legal links they kept up between Scotland and Europe ended with the Napoleonic Wars, never to be restored. If students of law now went to another country, it was to England to be called to the bar. So England became the chief foreign influence on the law of Scotland. The profession was now recruiting from different backgrounds too, though in the end most lawyers turned out to be just the sons of other lawyers, members of a caste reproducing itself. The Faculty of Advocates finished up from all this no longer especially enlightened, rather a professional cartel a bit too inbred. There was little chance of any more civic leadership here.[59]

The pressure of business from an industrial society in any event inhibited cultural pretensions in favour of higher efficiency. Still, the traditions of the Court of Session hardly helped. In the first half of the nineteenth century, the judgments were oral but the pleadings usually written (quite the reverse of modern practice). Not much had changed since James Boswell described his apprenticeship in the 1760s:

> In the first instance a cause is pleaded before the Lord Ordinary . . .
> But no sooner does he give judgment than we give him in replies and
> answers, and replies and duplies and triplies, and he will sometimes
> order memorials to give him a full view of the cause. For it is only
> in causes of great consequence that the Court order a hearing in
> presence. This method of procedure is admirable, for it gives the
> judges a complete state of every question, and by binding up the
> session papers a many may lay up a treasure of law reasoning and a
> collection of extraordinary facts.[60]

These lengthy papers were often adorned with citations from the *Corpus Juris Civilis* of the Emperor Justinian and from the Dutch or German jurists who had revived it for the Holy Roman Empire. But under a reform of the Court of Session in 1850 detailed written pleadings were abandoned. As John Inglis, Lord Glencorse, embarked a little later on his career at the bar, he found the older authorities had already 'vanished into obscurity. When dragged by the erudite from their hiding places they are now greeted with a sneer.'[61] A steady change followed in favour of English authorities, resisted by the hoary old judges but propelled by the trendy young advocates. When Charles Guthrie went to the bar in the early 1870s, 'there was no desire on the part of our judges, but rather the opposite, to have English cases quoted to them'.[62] Things had already changed by 1878 when, in litigation arising from the failure of the City of Glasgow Bank, Inglis, now Lord President, had a blazing row in the courtroom with Patrick Fraser, Dean of Faculty. In the middle of his pleading Fraser flew into a fury at an intervention from the bench founded, he raged, on 'the influence of English law upon our own. I don't know whether it was expected to be better, but I think it has been manifestly for the worse here, – for the worse in a great many respects, in creating calamities without end, that no human being ever anticipated when they undertook these obligations, and which ought not to be imposed if they can be consistently avoided in accordance with our own law'.[63] Yet, as time went on, English law came more and more to be seen as the law of the whole British Empire, and a strong unifying force in that Empire.[64] At the apex of this system stood the House of Lords in its judicial capacity, the final court of civil appeal for Scotland and for every other territory under the crown. By then there was not much room left for the Scots' own institutional writers. In 1907 Guthrie remarked: 'The voices of Craig and Bankton are no more, or seldom, heard in the land.'[65]

As the case just cited suggests, in Scotland commercial law was the unguarded postern gate through which English incursions entered. It was a sensible idea for Britain to have a unified system of commercial law – but whose commercial law might that be? Scotland did not lack commercial law of its own. The prime authority was George Joseph Bell, who stood at the end of the great tradition of institutional writers and occupied the chair of Scots law at the University of Edinburgh from 1822 to 1843. He was a product of the Enlightenment, brother of Charles Bell, the equally eminent professor of surgery, and friend of Scott and Jeffrey, who wrote to him: 'I love and esteem you beyond any man on earth.' Yet when Bell died, Cockburn said: 'His death was not to be regretted – old, blind, poor and getting poorer and never forgetting the disgraceful treatment which excluded him from the bench because he would not be dishonest, life for him had lost most of its attractions. There could not be a better man, and he is the greatest legal writer in Scotland next to Stair.'[66]

Cockburn praised in particular 'the greatest practical book on mercantile jurisprudence that has been produced in modern times'. But the fate of Bell's definitive work on commercial law, as we would now term it, if anything underlines the poignancy of his achievement. He had started his life's labours from what counted at the time as an eccentric interest in bankruptcy. He chose there a novel topic, for the Scotland of old, a feudal, agrarian country, had never needed a law of bankruptcy – not till 1772, when the Bank of Ayr went bust and left a lot of landed investors in it with nothing to show for the money they had put up.[67] 'It was from that time only', Bell wrote, 'that the rise of mercantile law in Scotland is to be dated, and that the attention of our lawyers began to be directed judicially to commercial dealings.'

Though the Scotland of old had tended to settle its financial disputes, like most other disputes, with cold steel, Bell assured his countrymen they need not look far for sources of this novel topic, which were, in fact, all around them: 'The Law Merchant is universal: it is a part of the law of nations, grounded upon the principles of natural equity, as regulating the transactions of men who reside in different countries, and carry on the intercourse of nations, independently of the local customs and municipal laws of particular states.' Before constructing the novel topic, Bell went on, it would be as well to recall that commercial regulation had since 1707 been common to the whole United Kingdom. Yet 'still much caution is to be observed in the adopting of English judgments as authorities in Scotland, and I state this the rather, that I think there has appeared of late some danger lest the purity of this part of jurisprudence, and the integrity of our own system of law, should be impaired by too indiscriminate use of English authorities.'[68] Indeed, though Bell made frequent use of English cases, he was always careful to distinguish them as such and therefore as of interest mainly for their comparative value.

Scottish capitalism had, in fact, developed along its own lines both before and after the Union. There was no reason for it not to, Scotland being one among many trading nations which, while possessed of their own practices, yet needed to traffic with one another, and long before lawyers were taking any interest. For instance, means had to be found of financing foreign commerce in times when no mechanism existed for transfers of funds (except as bars of gold and silver in the ship's hold, handy for the pirates). Instead Scots merchants made friends of correspondents in the ports they shipped to, from Riga to Smyrna, so that each party could carry balances for the other.[69] Maritime and mercantile disputes were of course still bound to arise. They could not be resolved through any defined body of commercial law – because none existed – but only in accord with common practices, borrowed and adapted, accepted on balance by all involved because they knew there had to be rules and usages of some kind. Such a body of common practices often differed from the rest of local law and so needed to be enforced by tribunals outside the normal judicial structure. Scotland's Court of Admiralty was probably one of the best examples, if in operation little different from humbler fair and staple courts that regulated trade in markets and ports right round Europe.[70]

It was this hotchpotch that Bell set out to elevate into a novel topic of the law. A feature of early Scottish capitalism had been that enterprises were generally organised as private partnerships. It was a clannish business: the investors often came from a single extended family, or at least were associated by place of birth or some other personal circumstance. They joined in a partnership because Scots law conferred commercial advantages on it. Every combination of individuals was recognised as a distinct persona, so that the partnership had a legal standing of its own aside from the individuals composing it. Within it, their contract, while renewable, was normally entered into under a definite limit of time, allowing frequent withdrawals of capital and replacement of old by new talents. So, in effect, shares could be transferred, and by holders enjoying limited liability. Altogether, Scots law provided the principal benefits of incorporation in advance of statutory provision for it. It was different from, and superior to, any corresponding English regulation. It was the law under which the Bairds, Napiers, Tennants and other pioneer capitalists had prospered.[71]

All that would be changed with the Joint Stock Companies Act passed at Westminster in 1856. It aimed to provide for the future a common corporate structure over the whole United Kingdom. There was no immediate compulsion on existing enterprises to adopt it. But there would be greater certainty for them following the rest into the system of limited liability (and, by implication, of ready access to capital markets) assured by the new law. Advantageous as it often was for Scottish businesses to enjoy these benefits too, they also, as we saw in a previous chapter, brought about in Scotland's peculiar conditions a steady divorce of ownership from control, which would not have happened before.[72] Bell was by then long dead, and the construction of commercial law for the United Kingdom had in effect been completed on English terms. It drove, this being a commercial age, a coach and horses through the independence and integrity of Scots law.

Indeed the frequent revisions of commercial law demanded during the industrial revolution were always performed in London by English lawyers thinking in English categories and with the English system in mind. Even for the odd Act defined as Scottish that was usually so. Only at the last minute, and with a minimum of alteration, would it be adapted from English to Scottish use. The resulting haphazard legislation on alien principles vexed Andrew Graham Murray, Lord Dunedin, when in 1915 he gave judgment in *Governors of George Heriot's Trust v Caledonian Railway Company*. It arose out of the Lands Clauses Consolidation (Scotland) Act of 1845, a minor measure that all the same seemed on the face of it to introduce a complete new principle into the Scots law of property, in the form of non-feudal tenure. Dunedin was damning: 'The genesis of the 1845 Act is plain enough. It is a copy of the English Act of the same year, the copy being adapted to Scottish needs by a person with a very hazy notion of Scottish real property law. Indications of ignorance crop up all through the statute, in small things as well as great.'[73]

Decisions of the House of Lords in civil appeals opened another channel for anglicisation of Scots law. No judges from Scotland sat in that house till 1876, when the Appellate Jurisdiction Act provided for one Scots Lord of Appeal, still outnumbered by English judges. Since decisions at this level were binding (another concept with no original place in Scots law), whole legal concepts could be imported from England to Scotland. An example came in the speech of Lord Chancellor Cranworth in 1858 on *Bartonshill Coal Company v Reid*. This case decided that the doctrine of common employment, already accepted in English law, was also to be law in Scotland. It stopped a workman, injured at his job through the negligence of his fellow, suing the employer in delict, on the fiction that by getting himself hired in the first place he had accepted the risk that a workmate might be negligent: odd and rather unpleasant law, which yet remained in force in both Scotland and England till repealed by statute in 1947. In *Bartonshill*, Lord Cranworth reviewed previous English cases and then continued, 'I consider . . . that in England the doctrine must be regarded as well settled; but if such be the law of England, on what ground can it be argued not to be the law of Scotland? The law, as established in England, is founded on principles of universal application, not on any peculiarities of English jurisprudence.'[74]

A single judgment did not transform Scots law, and further examples have not transformed Scots law, into just a weird variant of English law. Yet the cumulative effect has been to bring Scots law closer to English law than to any other among its range of European ancestors and relations. For one thing, Scotland has adopted – 'almost unconsciously' as Lord Cooper put it – the English rule of the rigidly binding force of judicial precedents. For another thing, Scotland has left undone, at least up to now, a general codification. This is almost universal outside the Anglo-American tradition, but Scots common law remains law made by judges. In Europe codification had been a project of the Enlightenment, reached an initial consummation in Napoleon's *Code*

Civil of 1804, then achieved a triumph of synthesis in Germany's *Bürgerliches Gesetzbuch* of 1900, legally crowning the process of reunification. Scots law, too, would have been ready for codification, after systematic exposition by institutional writers over a couple of centuries. It never has been codified because of the Union with England, where the law cannot be codified. But this may change before long.

6

Region: 'Confidence and capacity'

Railway mania gathered pace in Scotland right through 1845, though it would take another frenetic year to reach its climax. Symptoms could be observed all over the country, not only in the central belt. They seemed to attain special intensity in Aberdeen, perhaps just because that city was so far away from any other. Several projects competed for public support there, the favourite being the Great North of Scotland Railway.[1] Local businessmen were keen on it, and wholly subscribed the projected capital of more than £1 million. These investors made up a roll call of the richest citizens, as listed in the *Aberdeen Herald*: 'The Bannermans, the Lumsdens, the Haddens, the Blaikies, the Burnetts, the Forbses, the Piries, the Hogarths, the Kilgours, the Jopps, the McCombies, the Davidsons, and, in short, every name of any note in our good city . . . the most enterprising of our moneyed and mercantile men . . . have been equally forward in promoting the undertaking.'[2]

All four Scottish cities could have produced a similar list of local bigwigs, a mix of old and new money if with new money to the fore. Among those Aberdonians, Alexander Bannerman was their Liberal MP, a textile manufacturer who had joined the town council as long ago as 1811 and led its reform from within. He deposed the old leader, James Hadden, also a textile manufacturer and four times lord provost, in some ways a visionary civic leader who had shaped neo-classical Aberdeen, in other ways not; he was finally brought down by his refusal to open up the council to fresh faces and talents, who might have found out things he did not want them to know. Others on the *Herald*'s list – the Blaikies, the Forbes, the Piries, the Jopps, the Davidsons – likewise divided their energies between local politics and local industry. They were altogether typical of the wealthy bourgeoisie that would dominate most aspects of urban life in Victorian Scotland. Few had aristocratic antecedents. Most were self-made men, or at least sons of self-made men. Still, the cause of municipal reform that above all brought them into politics made them paternalists rather than populists.[3]

These elites were more powerful and more rooted in the places they ran than any counterpart today. They arose out of their own localities and did not often look beyond their own localities, being on the whole satisfied with such eminence as their own localities gave them: it remained for the dissatisfied around and below them to seek a remedy in migration, the eternal recourse of the restless Scot. Scotland was by now one nation, yet these features of its regional life remind us the unity had been created only haltingly and out of diverse origins.

In this respect, the making of Scotland turned out to be qualitatively different from the making of England, which early on possessed strong central government, concentration of social authority and intolerance of local deviation from it. The difference has left its mark down to the present on a Scotland which took longer to weld into one nation because it could only ever be formed out of a motley mix of peoples – originally Britons, Gaels, Picts, Angles, later Vikings and Normans, then other minorities. Finally the various elements learned to live together. Ideas of Scotland emerged to which all could subscribe. Scottishness was slow to crystallise but inclusive, rather than sooner formed but exclusive after the English manner.

One consequence, for good or ill, was that Scotland bore marks of its remote origins a millennium after the unifying effort had begun. Names of the petty kingdoms where its indigenous peoples had dwelt – Fife, Galloway, Lothian, Moray and more – survived up to and beyond the Union of 1707; another, Strathclyde, was to be resurrected in the late twentieth century as a monstrous local authority. On several occasions the patchwork might have dissolved. Scotland did manage to maintain its independence into the dawn of the modern era, but it was always a nation more untidy, precarious and provisional than others, than its southern neighbour especially, with never any centralising force durable or determined enough to put off its motley. In the last chapter we saw how even the institutional structure guaranteed by the Treaty of Union was not immune to these contrarieties. Few Scots would want a nation without them. They still have their price.

As for rural Scotland, the transformation in the nineteenth century yet fell some way short of overthrowing the old social hierarchies, as shown in a previous chapter.[4] We need to look at urban Scotland to observe the process in full swing, and the present chapter will deal with the four cities. Many smaller burghs might show similar features in their collective existence and evolution, but limiting the task to the cities makes it manageable. In each case, the nine-teenth century saw transition from an old regime to a new regime, roughly divided by the reform embodied in the Municipal Corporations Act of 1833 – though transition could still be slow rather than abrupt. Urbanisation had occurred later in Scotland than in many European countries, but when it came was much faster and fuller. This country, in fact, notched up about the highest rate of urban growth in Europe between 1750 and 1850, due to massive migration from countryside to town, especially into the central belt. For that very reason, we might start to look at the phenomenon from a standpoint elsewhere.[5]

✿

Aberdeen's status as a royal burgh had been recognised by King David I in the twelfth century. It emerged as the natural centre of a regional economy, living off its hinterland and off the sea. The city was peopled out of its region; it received few immigrants from elsewhere. It counted 50,000 citizens by 1831, a figure that rose to 150,000 at the end of the century. It could rely on none of the natural resources of coal and iron that stoked up industry in the central belt. But it had the advantage of being a seaport with no rival close at hand. It needed to import the raw materials it lacked itself, and it required the outlet for the products of its hinterland. In the period of Hadden and Bannerman, resources were being lavished on expansion of the harbour at the mouth of the River Dee, which had once been a delta with an almost land-locked lagoon (a little like Montrose to this day). The harbour was the big bone of conten-tion between reformers and reactionaries in Aberdeen. The old town council schemed to siphon off the higher revenues expected from the improvements, but Bannerman wrested control away to a separate elected trust that would work for the good of the city rather than of its rulers. Once that issue was resolved, rapid modernisation could proceed. Regular services by steamship started out of the harbour in 1827. Round it the processing of food, among other industries, flourished in readiness for distribution to wider markets.[6]

There was already a large local fleet of ships and a long shipbuilding trad-ition. In 1839 the yard of Alexander Hall launched Aberdeen's first clipper, the *Scottish Maid*, designed for oceanic traffic. At a workaday level many fishing vessels were built along the Dee, usually open boats of less than 5 tons; more than 100 of them fished inshore with baited lines. This fishery underwent a revolution once trawlers started sailing from Aberdeen in 1882. They were steam trawlers, too, able to venture far out on the high seas. They voyaged into Faroese and Icelandic waters to catch cod and haddock. With Aberdeen's speedy connection by rail to distant markets, it became the biggest fishing port in Scotland. By 1912 it had more than 200 steam trawlers.[7]

The harbour not only carried Aberdeen's products away but also brought in imports. Without imports, indeed, the city's textile industry, its biggest during the first half of the nineteenth century, could hardly have existed. Development here followed the same sort of pattern as elsewhere in Scotland. In 1800 production was still domestic, carried out by weavers in their own homes. Before long it would be overtaken by production from factories – eight big ones, three for cotton, three for wool and two for linen, in the end employing about a quarter of the workforce. Still there was nothing special about Aberdeen to save the textile industry from the eventual decline it suffered in Scotland as a whole, and only a couple of these factories survived the 1850s. An offshoot came in production of paper, along the River Don and at Inverurie. It was paper of high quality using rags as the main raw material: at one stage a single mill employed 400 women just to sort rags. This output proved hard to sustain, too, so far from its main markets. But the proximity of the port of Aberdeen allowed transition to use of esparto grass and wood-pulp as raw materials, so production of paper lasted longer.[8]

With shipping facilities on the scale Aberdeen had, the very rock it stood on could be turned to account. By 1817 it was already sending 22,000 tons of granite a year from its quarries to London, which had never built with this type of stone before: it would go into Waterloo Bridge and the terrace of the Houses of Parliament, among other structures. Aberdeen made its own transition to granite, having earlier built in freestone. It became indeed the Granite City, and achieved architectural distinction at the hands of Archibald Simpson. He found how to use this unyielding material in compositions of the greatest elegance, as in the entrance to the Castlegate, which is framed by the Athenaeum with its fine Ionic pillars and by the North of Scotland Bank curving with Corinthian sinuosity round the corner to King Street. Bon Accord Square and Crescent showed he could deploy his talents to equal effect on domestic architecture. Nor should we forget the contribution to the city's unique appearance by Alexander Macdonald. He invented steam-powered machinery to turn and polish the granite, giving it the finish that lends the townscape a spectacular glitter when seen from afar in sunshine after rain. The invention earned him a fortune, which he invested in a collection of 150 paintings, most by contemporary artists. He bequeathed it to form the core of the city's art gallery, founded in 1885, to which he also left a third of his estate, with instructions that only works created within 25 years of the date of purchase were to be acquired. Today this is one of the finest municipal galleries, made so through the quality of its modern art. Infused with local patriotism, Aberdeen's economic structure here generated cultural superstructure in a most precise sense.[9]

Aberdeen took good care of its wealth. By the turn of the nineteenth century it already housed two commercial banks, supplemented in 1815 by a savings bank for the money of ordinary folk that might otherwise 'be squandered away, unsafely deposited, or lost altogether; and to encourage thrift among the poorer members of society'.[10] A more sophisticated financial sector started to emerge with the foundation of the Scottish Australian Company in 1840 to invest in the natural resources of a continent just being opened up. The company was lost to London a dozen years later as the scale of its operations exceeded the financial resources of a provincial city.[11] But later Aberdeen's investment trusts offered a home for the surplus capital that continued to accumulate in the region and cannily sought higher returns outside it than its own economic activities could yield. The trusts pumped money into the United States, Canada and Australia.

At home, the prosperity permitted the refashioning of the townscape counselled by a rising population. As in other cities a grand scheme of improvement was drawn up, here projected on two axes extending out of the ancient burgh by the Dee. One axis crossed the Denburn to the west, on to level ground where layouts resembling the New Town of Edinburgh could arise, with 'solid houses of the more prosperous Aberdonians, of grey or pink granite, set well back in their gardens'.[12] The second axis ran north towards the academic exclave of Old Aberdeen. This was how Union Street and King Street came into being. Still, unlike in Edinburgh and Glasgow, the core of the city did not get abandoned to dereliction, but at least preserved its commercial functions. Aberdeen had poor and squalid quarters, of course, yet none too far from the better parts and on nothing like the scale of the central belt anyway. It remained a compact, self-contained city without a vast sprawl of suburbs, except for the retreats some wealthy families built in the villages of Deeside.

All this took place under an urban government that had been oligarchical from the start and far into the nineteenth century remained so. Right through, those running the city came from three groups, manufacturers, merchants and lawyers. Early on, the bounds of the oligarchy had been drawn tighter still. During the first eighteen terms of lord provostship from the turn of the century, nine individuals held the office. Two of them, the brothers Gavin and James Hadden, served four terms each. Two others, Thomas Leys and James Young, with three terms between them, held partnerships in the Haddens' enterprises. Alexander Brebner, twice provost, was a partner in business with Leys. Just four of the nine provosts came from outside this magic circle, and the outsiders served for only five of the eighteen terms. Most provosts inherited, or acquired by marriage, their entry into the elite, rather than rising into it on merit.[13]

The network of blood and business was so close as to astound a select committee of MPs investigating the state of the Scots royal burghs in 1819:

> The old council elect their successors; by which means it is not only possible, but almost invariably happens, that by alternate election of each other, the same party maintain possession of the council, to the entire exclusion of the rest of the burgesses ... it appears that by the return of members of the council for the last twenty years ... that the majority of the council have been the same individuals during that time and chiefly either relations or connections in business of Provost Hadden, who has been considered the leader of the town council for the last twenty years, and this whether he was in or out of the council at that time.[14]

The committee found evidence of rampant abuse by this clique. They raided public coffers for private gain. They sold off land and rights to friends. They altered the council's minutes after approving them. They produced no accounts, and in public misrepresented the financial position. In 1812 they estimated civic debts at £7,000 when the actual figure was £140,000.[15]

The truth soon came out. In 1817 the treasurer of the city announced he could no longer pay the interest on the debts: bankruptcy loomed. There followed a couple of years of bitter acrimony between the ruling clique and its critics, which also alerted the people of Aberdeen that the politics even of an oligarchy might concern them too. Bannerman emerged as the popular head of the reformers, giving himself the start to a longer and more versatile political career. The city had indeed every reason to be grateful to him for his subsequent work in the matter of the harbour and in other good causes. It was but a short step for this easy-going, well-liked figure (or perhaps rather for his clever and ambitious wife) to become Liberal parliamentary candidate for the city after the Reform Act of 1832. Far from radical, he did not need to be when up against his prospective Conservative opponent, none other than James Hadden. Bannerman could make hay with the sins of the old regime. Finally Hadden did not so much as go to the poll (public in those days), and Bannerman was returned unopposed. He served as MP till 1847, when he took up a new career as a colonial governor.[16]

Hadden failed even to get back on the reformed town council at its first election in 1833. Meanwhile for Scotland as a whole municipal reform had achieved one main aim: from now on householders would have the right of electing their own councils. It still did not make as much difference as reformers hoped. In Aberdeen several members of the old regime held on to a place in municipal life. Electoral manipulation continued, as did cosy commercial deals. Anyway, Aberdonians hardly responded to novel political agitations elsewhere in Scotland. A few Chartists raised their voices but campaigns against the Corn Laws remained muted by Aberdeen's strong agricultural links. The foremost radical was a man outside conventional politics, James Adam, editor of the *Herald*. Portly and prickly, fortifying himself with frequent drams, he attracted round him a circle that would meet in the Lemon Tree Tavern to talk the night away and plot the overthrow of Bannerman. Aberdonians at large had more interest in religious controversy: the ministers of every one of the city's 15 congregations, together with most of their flocks, went into the Free Church at the Disruption of 1843.[17]

Aberdeen's relative political quiescence should not be taken as indicating a lack of social problems, though they were no better and no worse than in any salty but sleazy seaport of the time. The people's dedication to drink could reach the point where at New Year 'old and middle-aged men and women and boys and girls [were] falling about in a state of intoxication at two o'clock in the day'. The visitor might tune in here, it was said, to 'the foulest wealth of anatomical and physiological words known to the British vocabulary'. The language sounded perhaps less offensive for being cast in impenetrable Doric; the poet George Gordon, Lord Byron, who spent his childhood in Aberdeen, remembered that locals pronounced school as squeal. His own upbringing gave him both the taste for the exotic and the precocious experience of sex that impressed themselves on his art.[18]

In Edwin Chadwick's wide-ranging social investigations, the English reformer gathered information on Aberdeen from two local doctors in 1842:

> Aberdeen, like most other towns, had at one time been very closely built; and hence not only the old streets and lanes ... are comparatively narrow, but there are courts and closes ... of which the average breadth is not above seven feet. As nearly all families of the better classes have left the courts for more airy residences, the character of the courts and closes has much fallen. They are occupied by a much inferior description of tenantry than they were some years ago, and much less attention is given to keeping them clean. They are not only ill ventilated but they have an open kennel running along them which is the receptacle for all sorts of filth.[19]

The sanitary problem was not confined to the squalid older quarters either: 'All the sewers and drains of the town terminate in the basin of the harbour. The consequence of this is that the harbour is covered with a thick fetid mud, from which, at nearly low water, the surface becomes covered with bubbles of a fetid noxious gas, which, bursting, gives forth a most intolerable stench that is perceived at a considerable distance in the town.'[20]

The most strenuous effort at bettering the urban conditions came from Sheriff William Watson. He set up the Aberdeen House of Industry and Refuge, more popularly known as the ragged school, to take in waifs and strays and teach them to be useful citizens once they had 'enjoyed, more or less, the food and shelter and discipline of the House'.[21] It then found the younger inmates positions in service in town and country. For instance, no. 818, an orphan girl of 13 was brought in after being charged with petty theft. She learned to read and write, if just a little, and then went into service 'where she has continued ten months, and give satisfaction to her master'. No. 1098 was a female aged 30 rescued from attempts at 'self-destruction' and 'extreme destitution'. She was placed in employment 'in which she has continued six months'. Aberdeen also became 'more celebrated for Industrial Schools than for anything else she possesses'. Watson had first tried to send working-class children to the burgh school, but the teachers were unwelcoming. After establishing Aberdeen's first industrial school for boys in 1841, he helped to create a school for girls in 1843 and a mixed school in 1845. Among the cities of Victorian Scotland, or indeed Britain, this was altogether not a bad record.[22]

A contrast, then: in 1844 Lord Cockburn described Dundee as 'the palace of Scottish blackguardism'.[23] The economy of the city has already been described in a previous chapter,[24] something easy to do because from the middle of the century it was so dominated by jute. It had not a great deal else going for it – though jam and journalism also fixed themselves in popular memory. In size Dundee outdistanced Paisley at the census of 1841, when it had a population of 60,000, then for the rest of the century ran neck-and-neck with Aberdeen as Scotland's third largest city, with more than 160,000 people in 1901; it is smaller today.

Having, at first, an industrial economy of textiles not dissimilar to Aberdeen's, Dundee developed the same sort of politics. The unreformed town council was, as in other royal burghs, a self-electing, self-perpetuating, unrepresentative body. At its head stood the urbane but rascally Alexander Riddoch, who either filled or controlled the office of lord provost from 1787 to 1819. Under his regime the seats the Dundonian merchants held by right on the council proved of little use to them, for his cronies kept hold of the finances. Yet it was the merchants that had been building up Dundee into the commercial centre of its region (in place of Perth). In his novel, *The Antiquary*, Sir Walter Scott celebrates the success, and political loyalty, of the breezy little burgh in fictional guise as Fairport.[25]

Successful and loyal or not, Dundee's merchants could never rely on their town council to serve their interests. They had to exert themselves, when in 1815 plans were afoot for improvements to the harbour, to establish a commission for it that would represent them. Riddoch and his gang otherwise aimed to raise duties on an expected increase in trade so as to service debts they had acquired for different purposes. It was during this struggle that Robert Rintoul, radical editor of the *Dundee, Perth and Cupar Advertiser*, enlisted the support of a local laird, George Kinloch of Kinloch, and then of William Maule, MP for Angus. The last was the man who got through the legislation establishing the commission for Dundee Harbour. Kinloch meanwhile had to flee the country to avoid a charge of sedition but he returned in 1822, was pardoned and lived to serve as Dundee's Liberal MP from 1832 till his death the next year. He left a monument in the works at the harbour that marked the start of the city's modernisation. Its broader rebuilding began with construction of Reform Street and a few neo-classical terraces as places of business and residences for the wealthy. Later came the Kinnaird Hall, Albert Institute, Royal Exchange and High Street. None, however, added architectural distinction to the city's superb natural site.[26]

From the 1830s it is no longer so useful to compare Dundee with Aberdeen, despite the continued importance of textiles to the economy of both. Whereas Aberdeen diversified, Dundee narrowed its specialisations. The range of coarse textiles it had earlier produced gave way to the processing of flax imported from Germany and Russia for linen, sailcloth and sackings. Then jute rose in importance after the local discovery of how the raw material could best be prepared for processing. The economy now took off. By 1850, the Cox brothers had erected the Camperdown Works, the biggest textile factory in the world, though others in Dundee were scarcely smaller.[27] A somewhat erratic long boom followed, not without interludes when the industry seemed to teeter on the brink of terminal crisis. The long boom certainly passed its peak in the 1880s, as Calcutta grew capable of competing with Dundee. Those Dundonian capitalists who had already financed factories on the banks of the River Hooghly did not mind so much; in fact, they welcomed the opportunity to cut wages at home.[28] The long decline only set in about 1914, by which time it was without doubt cheaper to rely on imports of the finished product from India.[29] This had been a fraught economic evolution, yet not more fraught than its social effects.

Elsewhere in these pages it has already been remarked that sharp conflicts of class in Victorian Scotland could be averted because entrepreneurs and skilled workers sprang from the same origins in the bosom of the people, their joint interest in successful industries being reinforced by common education, common language, common religion, common values. Dundee slightly contradicts this thesis, though many of its new leadership of jute barons did, in classic fashion, emerge from humbler backgrounds in the textile trades. William Baxter was from the fourth generation of a family of weavers risen to be merchants. James Cox was from the fourth generation of a family of bleachers and manufacturers at Lochee, who at his outset still bought in cloth from a network of handloom-weavers built by his father and grandfather. The Browns of East Mill were sons of James Brown who had established a rural flax-spinning business. Given Dundee's history as port and market for a region with textiles as its main manufacture, it comes as no surprise to find such backgrounds commonly figuring.[30]

But from now on, in contrast to the intimacy of the old burgh and its hinterland, jute barons lived a world away from their workers. Or at least they lived at Broughty Ferry, three miles out of the centre of the city, a fishing village they turned into something rather different once the railway reached it in 1839. Inside Dundee sanitary problems and pollution of air and water

146

were already appalling, so the exodus of all who could afford it followed, into a suburb of mansions set in verdant grounds looking out on the Tay. It was a place where, to the jute, could be added the jam, or rather the marmalade of Dundee taken at teatime in the blossoming, fragrant garden. The city owed this refinement to Janet Keiller, who had invented it in 1797 in order to make use of a cargo of bitter Seville oranges acquired from a Spanish ship by her husband. Their son Alexander industrialised the production and started selling marmalade from shops in Dundee. It was never a major sector of the city's industry, employing about 300 people at most. But it added a little sweetness to the prevailing bitterness of local life. Today traditional production has become the preserve of larger businesses, but distinctive white jars of Keiller's marmalade can still be bought.[31]

While jute barons were not much given to introspection, one of their progeny, Jo Grimond, a leader of the British Liberals in the twentieth century, recorded what memories of their Dundee had been handed down to him (he himself was born in 1913 at the safe distance of St Andrews). He thought his own family atypical of them, his father being 'not suited to the life of a Dundee businessman. He drank almost nothing, played no card games and took little part in either public life or the more boisterous male social life around him.' Grimond does not venture far into the question what more general result his father's difference in personality might have had: 'When nineteenth-century capitalists are criticised I think of the concern which my father showed for his work people and for the good name of the Grimond business.' But he acknowledges jute barons lived on the other side of a social gulf from their workers:

> They built themselves Scots baronial houses in Broughty Ferry or further afield and vied with each other over their carriages, shrubberies and greenhouses ... They were a tough lot. They achieved much. But let no one be taken in by nostalgia when considering Scottish cities. They had confidence and capacity but under their reign Dundee was ridden with slums and poverty. I can remember as a boy the tenements and the cobbled streets around which semi-naked children played.[32]

One of the few bridges across the gulf was Dundee's journalism, as published by D. C. Thomson & Co. It might be said to have reflected the values of the jute barons but the interests of their workers. Founded in 1905 by David Coupar Thomson and today still owned and managed by his family, the firm publishes a variety of newspapers, magazines and children's comics, including the *Sunday Post, Courier, People's Friend, Beano* and *Dandy*. The *Sunday Post* is the most typical of the stable, a weekly national newspaper with a folksy mix of news, short features and sentimental stories. It was launched in 1914 and still enjoys a wide circulation across Scotland, Ulster and the north of England, if nowadays down from its peak of three million readers. In the Dundee of the twenty-first century jute and jam have gone, but journalism soldiers on, with D.C. Thomson as one of the city's largest employers.[33]

Otherwise jute barons and their workers had little in common. The former made, for example, no contribution to the housing of the latter in the tenements of the grimy inner city, standing in the shadow of the smoky, smelly factories. It would have been unprofitable to build homes for such ill-paid workers, and jute barons felt no 'moral obligation . . . to see that their workers have as good accommodation as their horses'.[34] Wages being so low, the standard of housing remained constrained by the meagre rents that could be paid. In 1901, one in five houses in Dundee consisted of a single room only, about half of two rooms.[35] The sanitary standard remained wretched, with usually one toilet for every six houses – and there was a tenement, sheltering 215 people, that had a single privy for the whole lot.[36] Taking in lodgers was common even among families living in a single room; some lodgers paid rent for a bed in the room, and others paid for a 'share of a bed'. Overcrowding was therefore rife, with cases of six people living in one small room, or ten people in two rooms, and with six to eight people sleeping in one bed while some had no beds at all, just sacking on the floor.[37]

Scenes like these could be found in other Scottish cities too, but Dundee had a unique feature in the dominance of women among the workforce. By 1911, well over 20,000 of 30,000 people employed in jute were women.[38] The most active cohort of the population, aged from 20 to 45, contained three female workers to every two males. Many were married women therefore, with homes to run as well as tedious toil to perform in the factories.[39] There conditions looked bad enough, yet they could be worse for those reliant on casual labour outside: it was 'a familiar sight in Dundee to see a string of ill-nourished and ill-clad women and children waiting at the door of a factory for a bundle of sacks . . . [and then walking] slowly homeward, bent double, and often leaning against a wall to rest or to readjust their burdens'.[40] These women lived from sewing the sacks together; each bundle of sacks weighed between 56lb and 70lb and required 84 yards of stitches.

Dundee's children were not spared. Infant mortality rose higher than in other Scottish cities.[41] Of those who survived their first years, more were put to work than in the rest of Scotland, 18 per cent of boys and 16 per cent of girls between the ages of ten and fourteen.[42] In jute mills, children under 13 could be employed as 'half-timers', attending schools outside on every other day. Or else they could go to special schools inside the factories of the largest employers where their activity would be divided in a different way, working half the day as 'shifters' in the mill and spending the other half in the classroom; this alternative regime was recommended by doctors as less exhausting for children. Once they reached the age of 13, they might work five days a week whole-time from six o'clock in the morning to six o'clock at night (with two hours free for meals), then have lessons for two hours in the evening till they finished, on their 14th birthday, with as much education as they were ever going to get. By 1900, there were 5,000 children both working and learning under one or other of these regimes. An inspector pointed out that making boys and girls of 13 do a 12-hour day appeared to be legal in Scotland, 'while for such children in India a working day above seven hours is forbidden by law'. It was easy to blame Dundee's school board for grant-ing far more exemptions and permissions for half-time work than any other in Scotland, but it came under pressure from poor parents unable to make ends meet without a mite from their own children. Small wonder to find one of those factory inspectors, who knew conditions all over Britain, saying in 1904: 'Personally, the poorest specimens of humanity I have ever seen, both men and women, are working in the preparing and spinning departments of certain Dundee jute mills.'[43]

It may be, then, surprising to learn that one jute baron, William Baxter, also MP for the Montrose Burghs, came from a family with a strong philanthropic tradition. He gave his own expression to it in support, out of funds from the family, for the establishment in 1881 of University College Dundee; till this point there had been no higher education in the city. It was to be a progres-sive institution, open to women and forbidding religious tests. It attracted also a progressive faculty, Patrick Geddes in the chair of botany and D'Arcy Thompson in the chair of zoology. The latter remembered how he found the place on his arrival:

> Dundee was terribly poor. When I first came here the Greenmarket was full of idle men, walking to and fro, hungry and in rags. Of all those young professors who had just come to the town, I doubt if there was one who was not shocked and saddened by the poverty which Dundee openly displayed.[44]

Out of these academic circles arose the Dundee Social Union, which embarked on systematic investigation of the city's problems in housing, health and so on, with a view to finding practical solutions. It was a forward-looking initiative but would take long to bear fruit.

❋

If Dundee showed Scottish urban living at its worst, Edinburgh showed it at its best. Unlike other cities in Scotland or Britain, it never suffered the ravages of the industrial revolution. It still grew fast. During the nineteenth century the population rose fourfold, to pass 400,000 by the census of 1911 (then the pattern changed, the growth slowed and the figure has never quite reached half a million). Meanwhile seven extensions of the boundaries trebled the municipal area. This was not just a matter of the annexation of inner suburbs spilling over from the crowded centre. Large open spaces were swallowed up too: the Braid Hills, Blackford Hill, Corstorphine Hill, the Craiglockhart Hills, even part of the Pentland Hills. Once railways came, development sometimes jumped the open spaces to create a ring of outer suburbs at Barnton, Colinton or Corstorphine. Edinburgh's territorial demands foresaw future urbanisation far beyond the Old Town and New Town. Yet a lot of the greenery within the extensions remains unspoiled to this day, or at worst turned into golf courses.[45]

To the end of the century the capital preserved features it had shown at the start, as a city of the intellect, and of the liberal professions generally, where the landed gentry came to do business or spend money. The rest of the people earned their bread meeting the needs of these elites. There were craftsmen to supply every material want, shopkeepers to sell the goods, legions of diligent clerks, armies of faithful servants, labourers hewing wood or drawing water, finally an underclass eking out its existence from the leavings of the rest.

Apart from the dominance of classes distinguished by trained minds there was little to explain why printing and publishing became a keystone of the economy. James Gibson Lockhart remarked that now English authors sent their works to Edinburgh, whereas once Scots authors had needed to send theirs to London. In the Scottish capital Adam & Charles Black, William Blackwood, William & Robert Chambers, Archibald Constable and Thomas Nelson were all big British publishers of the nineteenth century; some survived the twentieth century, too, till gobbled up by today's multinationals. Growth in the city's other big business, brewing, seems equally unaccountable. Households had once brewed their own beer, but now industrial production supplied it. Apart from the citizens' hard drinking, abundant crops and good water in the hinterland might have been reason enough for this development. Brewers kept in touch with the countryside, for many of their tasks were akin to a farmer's. Their output remained seasonal, affected by the harvest and price of grain – and for transport they used wagons and dray-horses till after the Second World War. At the height more than 40 breweries existed in Edinburgh, standing out from the townscape with brewhouse on three storeys and yard with cellars, cooperage, counting house, maltings and stables. The model was the Holyrood Brewery founded by William Younger in 1749, and closed only in 1986; today the Scottish Parliament stands on the site. Younger's business had grown till, halfway through its history, it dominated the Scottish trade (together with Tennent's in Glasgow).[46]

Publishing and brewing were, then, the sum of Edinburgh's industrial revolution. Cockburn thought it 'merciful' that the city lacked manufactures,

> that is, tall brick chimneys, black smoke, a population precariously fed, pauperism, disease and crime, all in excess. Some strong efforts have occasionally been made to coax these things to us; but a thanks-deserving providence has hitherto been always pleased to defeat them. For though manufactures be indispensable, they need not be everywhere . . . There should be Cities of Refuge.[47]

Still, that positive assessment left out of account the Old Town, which by the end of the eighteenth century the middle class had already abandoned for the New Town. The ancient core of the city did trail along in the wake of the general economic expansion, to the extent of somehow finding room for more and more people to crowd in. They were packed into subdivided flats where the better off had once lived. This population totalled 30,000 by its peak at the census of 1861. The returns then showed the Old Town contained 1,530 flats of one room occupied by six to fifteen people; they needed to sleep in shifts. Middle Mealmarket Stair in the Cowgate had 59 flats with 248 occupants and no toilet. On such a stair, access to each floor was gained by a dark, narrow flight of stone steps with passages off to the flats. Tenants groped about in what natural light there was, and since the tenements had been built so near one another the sun could not reach every window. Anyway there were 120 flats in the Old Town with no window, while another 900 lay in cellars, dark and damp. Ill-paved closes outside remained mired in muck. There was no main drainage. All water for domestic use still had to be lugged up stairs and thrown out the windows when no longer needed; then it gathered in cesspools. The channels for carrying the ooze right out of town were 'foul burns', open sewers leading to some natural watercourse and so at last to the Firth of Forth – though the burns would also be tapped along the way to irrigate market gardens and meadows. Their stench round Holyrood grew so vile that Queen Victoria refused to stay there when she visited her Scottish capital, and descended on the Duke of Buccleuch at Dalkeith.[48]

The stuff of municipal politics lay in expansion of the New Town or its later appendages, in elimination of the squalor left behind in the Old Town, but also, as in Aberdeen and Dundee, in links between the city and the world. Edinburgh was not at the turn of the nineteenth century well equipped to deal with its challenges either. Wanting to paint a picture of municipal affairs about that time, Cockburn started with the seat of the town council,

> a low, dark, blackguard-looking room, entering from a covered passage which connected the south-west corner of the Parliament Square with the Lawnmarket. At its Lawnmarket end this covered passage opened out on the south side of the 'Heart of Midlothian' ... The Council Chamber entered directly from this passage, and, if it had remained, would have been in the east end of the Writers' [Signet] Library. The chamber was a low-roofed room, very dark, and very dirty, with some small dens off it for clerks.
>
> Within this Pandemonium sat the town council, omnipotent, corrupt, impenetrable. Nothing was beyond its grasp; no variety of opinion disturbed its unanimity ... Reporters, the fruit of free discussion, did not exist; and though they had existed, would not have dared to disclose the proceedings. Silent, powerful, submissive, mysterious and irresponsible, they might have been sitting in Venice.[49]

For effect Cockburn overdid the omnipotence; in fact, the council had lost power during the eighteenth century. Finally it became an object of disdain to the landed classes coming here from outside. The family of Lady Elizabeth Grant of Rothiemurchus, whose estate lay in the north of Scotland, owned a townhouse in Charlotte Square. Earlier the Grants had been a gutless clan, swithering between Stewarts and Hanoverians, above all keeping their heads down. Who was she to scorn the lord provost's political coyness? Yet she dismissed him as 'a tradesman of repute among his equals, and in their society he was content to abide'.[50]

In fact, the political manager of Scotland, Lord Melville, felt appalled at the state of the town council and 'the public inconvenience, to say nothing of the personal and constant plague arising from an inefficient and unsafe magistracy'. He was right to worry: bankruptcy threatened after Edinburgh spent £300,000 on improvements to the harbour at Leith. Leith needed a better harbour if it was to entertain any hope of regaining the oceanic trade it had lost to Glasgow since the Union of 1707. Its quays at the mouth of the Water of Leith could not take many ships and no big ships at all. The approaches were shallow and encroached on from the east by a shifting sandbar. When, in 1822, King George IV arrived in his royal yacht, not a huge vessel, he had to anchor a couple of miles out and clamber into a lighter to come ashore – with difficulty, seeing how fat he was.

There had been a plan to deal with all this since 1799. Its author, the engineer John Rennie, proposed to block the progress of the sandbar by a pier to the east and to form a fresh approach through three connected wet docks to the west, stretching over a mile to the greater depth of water at Newhaven. Some work was carried out – though at staggering cost, largely borrowed from the British government on the security of Edinburgh's rates. Still the plan remained unfulfilled. In 1824 William Chapman updated and extended it. He had the pier on the east lengthened by 500 yards and an outer harbour formed on the west. This scheme did, in fact, offer a permanent solution to the problem of the docks; the trouble was it also brought about the bankruptcy of the city of Edinburgh in 1833.

The councillors had seen it coming. That was why they piled on the duties at Leith. Captains entering the port had to pay anchorage, beaconage, berthage, flaggage, pilotage and dock dues, even before officers of HM Customs arrived to charge them on the hold's contents. It hardly encouraged greater use of the harbour, the point of the exercise. Trade stagnated and in some years fell, to the profit of Grangemouth and Dundee. The council had no choice but to go back to the government, which for a final loan in 1826 took security of all the town's property, including the docks. The last resort was a scheme for a joint-stock company to own and run the port from dues charged at a rate enabling its debts to be serviced. This rate, local merchants could see, would ruin them. And who should be shareholders of the company? Why, the councillors of Edinburgh, after flogging its property to themselves.

Melville sought compromise. He vested control of the harbour in commissioners drawn equally from capital and port. But the result was deadlock broken only when Edinburgh did go bankrupt, overwhelmed by its deficit and unable to borrow more. Some debt was cancelled and some rescheduled. The government made the commission for the harbour tripartite, with its own delegates to hold the balance between the two sides. And it liberated Leith from long thraldom by turning it into a separate burgh.[51] This was crushing defeat for Edinburgh. Its independence of five centuries under royal charter shortly came to an end too. The Municipal Corporations Act of 1833 put it on a par with any other burgh – every one now a creature of the absolute sovereignty of the British Parliament. But all the people rejoiced.

<hr />

The reform brought in a different kind of councillor from the nonentities who had run the place before. This was no longer a closed clique but a body of men chosen democratically, if on a suffrage extremely restricted by today's standards. The qualification, for male occupiers and owners of buildings worth £10 a year, enfranchised 5,000 of Edinburgh's 137,000 citizens. Prosperous tradesmen, often radical in politics, made up a large proportion.

Edinburgh had already obtained its first Improvement Act from Parliament in 1827. It provided for opening up new streets to let light and air into the most fetid quarters, even to bypass them overhead, as George IV Bridge did. A second Improvement Act in 1867 created ten more new streets lined with model tenements. These were built in Scottish Baronial style, imitating the medieval castles of Glamis and Craigievar with quaint round turrets and steep conical roofs. It became a national style, one for high and low: Queen Victoria used it at Balmoral in the shadow of the Grampian Mountains just as a local architect, James Lessels, did when he put up tenements surveying the tracks into Waverley Station. Such was the city's mix of architecture that Scottish Baronial could fit in with ease – in fact, extremely well – yet it made a pastiche of much of the Royal Mile. A prime aim was to have buildings appear more venerable than they are. It does seem to take in the tourists.

Under the Act of 1867 one big clearance covered the area south of the Cowgate up to the Flodden Wall, or what remained of it, land that had come to contain some of the worst slums. Through the middle of the reconstructed zone, Chambers Street was built. Today, halfway along, in between the National Museum of Scotland and the original buildings of Heriot-Watt College, stands a statue of the man the street is named after, author of the Act and greatest lord provost of the century, William Chambers. His goal, common among city fathers of his time, lay in fostering civic pride. Unique was his wish to do so in and from the Old Town.[52]

Chambers took over at a crux on becoming lord provost in 1865. Under a separate Act of Parliament of 1848 the town council had also acquired sweeping sanitary powers, but was not using them. Demolition of slums would be fine, yet where were the people to go? Cockburn twittered on about the capital's prettiness being spoiled by all these proles, but a fiery fundamentalist, the Revd James Begg, minister of the Free Church at Newington, roared a retort: 'It is a cruel mockery to speak to the torpid and festering masses of Taste and the beauties of Edinburgh.' Begg was rare in his time in arguing that bad buildings caused bad people, rather than the other way about: 'You will never get the unclean heart of Edinburgh gutted out until you plant it all round with new houses.' His aim was for workers to own their own homes, and he quoted a popular song:

> I hae a hoose o' my ain
> I'll tak dunts frae naebody.[53]

There was a response from the people Begg wanted to reach. Craftsmen formed a co-operative building company in 1860. At Stockbridge they laid out a 'colony', with houses 'two stories high and containing three to six moderately sized rooms, with every convenience, the best sanitary arrangements and a plot of ground 20 foot square' – they are there still, a few occupied by descendants of the original owners. The same followed at Fountainbridge and Merchiston. The labour aristocracy of Edinburgh showed itself well capable of self-help: the different trades engaged in the construction proudly left their armorial bearings at the gable-ends. But what of those lower down the scale? Chambers saw the difficulty of creating a new class of owner-occupiers when most workers lived on a slim margin at best. His idea was rather that the wealthy should sponsor homes built for rent. In 1849 he had helped to launch the Pilrig Model Dwellings Company; its prime development of an H-block, even graced by classical detail, still stands in Pilrig Street down Leith Walk.

Housing controversy in Edinburgh was interrupted on 24 November 1861, when a tenement in the High Street collapsed; 35 people died and many more were injured. A boy trapped in the rubble won the heart of the city by urging on his rescuers: 'Heave awa, lads, I'm no deid yet!' But now the talking had to stop. Horrified public reaction led within a year to the appointment of the country's first Medical Officer of Health, Dr Henry Littlejohn, with broad responsibilities for the urban environment. He first did a statistical survey exposing its huge contrasts, with the death-rate in the worst parishes running twice as high as in the best.

When Chambers entered on his office, he had the ammunition he needed to make himself a great reforming lord provost. As his basis of policy he drew a contrast not between bourgeoisie and proletariat but between respectable and unrespectable working class. While artisans could now live well enough and so move on and up in the world, 'the dwellings from which the honestly industrious have fled are occupied for the most part by classes utterly abject – something at which the upper world would shudder to approach . . . The vacating of dwellings has only rendered our Old Town closes a convenient receptacle for those who in due time furnish occupation to the inspectors of the poor, the police and the criminal tribunals.' Yet Chambers's main pro-ject, of cutting streets through the Old Town, was not meant to turn it into another New Town: 'I think the tenements should be mainly designed for the trading and working classes, with shops or places of business on the ground storeys.' Enlightened improvement at last spread its blessings down the social scale, but in respect for the individualism of people and places rather than in pursuit of a bloodless universal ideal. Chambers felt sure of giving 'a new character to the Old Town without injuring its picturesque appearance'. Industry and decency were to be rewarded within the milieu that generated them – something as unlike public housing policies of the next century as could be imagined.[54]

Those later policies were owed above all to the experience of Glasgow, which already in the nineteenth century had in certain respects little in common with the rest of Scotland. It moved far ahead of a country otherwise of gracious, old-fashioned cities, small burghs and thinly peopled uplands. Its connections with America and Europe were closer than those with London, or even with Edinburgh. It had cast off parochialism and liked to think big.

The population of Glasgow in 1801 was 77,000. Within 20 years it almost doubled, overtaking Edinburgh's, and by end of the century was ten times as large, thanks also to extensions of the boundaries. By the same means it would pass a million during the First World War. The industrial history of the city and its region has been recounted in a previous chapter, so the present one will concentrate on the social and political effects.[55]

Travellers had always found the old Glasgow the most charming of Scots burghs. Perhaps no cleaner than the rest, it was redeemed by its magnificent Gothic cathedral, by its quaint buildings along the banks of the babbling Molendinar Burn or the crystalline River Clyde, then by flowering orchards all around and rugged Highland hills as a backdrop. Change first came with the commercial opportunities of the Union of 1707, especially in the English colonies opened then to Scots. Glasgow turned itself into a centre for transatlantic trade in tobacco and for its re-export to European markets. The traffic reached a peak just before the Americans revolted in 1776, then ground to a halt. It says much for the enterprise of Glaswegians that, with scarce a blink, they redeployed their capital. Instead of tobacco from Virginia they imported cotton or sugar from the West Indies – in fact, trade with the United States would also start up again as soon as the war was over. The Glaswegian merchants' already great wealth then waxed fabulous through blockade-busting in Napoleonic Europe.

Under the control of these merchants the town council was progressive. In 1800 it obtained at Westminster a Police Act creating an independent authority in charge of public order, the first in Scotland – even though the mere 123 policemen employed spent much of their time on such tasks as clearing snow or repairing smashed street-lights; before many years passed, troops would have to be called in to keep the peace. At least the council's intentions were good. It also encouraged the first municipal utilities, the Glasgow Water Company of 1806 and Glasgow Gaslight Company of 1817.[56]

Wealth ruled Glasgow. The merchants were only kept out of the British Parliament by the antique arrangement under which they shared a seat there with three small neighbouring burghs. In 1812, however, the popular Kirkman Finlay won election for the district – the first native Glaswegian MP in 70 years. The breaking of the East India Company's monopoly on trade to the Orient was the city's most devout wish. In a coup Finlay secured Parliament's agreement to it in 1813: one of his ships at once set off for Calcutta. But his liberalism was erratic. He supported the Corn Laws, getting his house attacked by the mob in return, and helped to set up a network of spies to infiltrate radical groups. The Glaswegians' intellectual was James Ewing, richest man in the city and generous with benefactions. In pamphlets and lobbying he may have done more even than Finlay to open up the Indian trade. He and a further member of the circle, James Oswald, represented Glasgow in Parliament after 1832. Oswald can still be seen today, at least as a statue, with the tallest lum hat on George Square.[57]

The political ascendancy of these plutocrats remained little affected by reform. They supported it anyway, and their wealth waxed so that mere legislation could not dislodge them from leadership in urban life. Most now called themselves Liberals, if by no means all; perhaps labels mattered little when they shared the opinions and outlook of their common high mercantile background. Competition with Conservatives gave less trouble than rumpus with radicals, allies in reform though now disillusioned by its limited results.

In Glasgow as elsewhere, their agitations continued. Chartism turned out the most popular, even if in Scotland it never attained the same strength or fervour as in England. Its Glaswegian leader was James Moir, not a proletarian but himself a successful merchant. While not lacking in progressive zeal, and capable of provoking demonstrations, even violence, he was in the end a man with whom the city fathers could do business, political as well as commercial. The reforming impulse, frustrated at the national level, found a local outlet.[58]

Together with a long economic boom in the city came severe social problems. In a certain respect they showed an analogy with Edinburgh's. To the west of the original burgh of Glasgow the richer citizens built themselves a suburb of solid mansions set out on a neat grid of streets rising towards salubrious heights with views over the River Clyde and the surrounding hills. In other words, the well-to-do abandoned the old High Street with the wynds and closes running off it. The tenements there fell into decay. The back-courts had not even the open, stinking drains common in other Scottish towns. Rubbish and excrement just got heaped up in huge middens in the middle till some private contractor thought them worth carting away. This was where the poor lived that the rich left behind.

Despite the flitting of the bourgeoisie, overcrowding in the old burgh remained horrendous. Chadwick was amazed to find in 1841 that in the central parish of Blackfriars the population had grown by 40 per cent in the last ten years but the number of dwellings not at all. A fellow investigator, J.C. Symons, waxed eloquent over the horrors of the High Street: 'I have seen human degradation in some of its worst phases, both in England and abroad, but I can advisedly say, that I did not believe, until I visited the wynds of Glasgow, that so large an amount of filth, crime, misery and disease existed on one spot in any civilised country.' Not that Glaswegians themselves underestimated the physical squalor and its human consequences. Charles Baird, a lawyer who helped Chadwick with his expert local knowledge, put it all down to drink: 'In London, the proportion of public houses to other houses is as 1 to 56; in Glasgow it is as 1 to 10; every tenth house in Glasgow is a spirit shop; I should say, as far as my statistical researches have gone, that the proportion of whisky drunk in Glasgow is twice or thrice as much as in any similar population upon the face of the globe.'[59] The chief constable, David Miller, agreed that in 'the very centre of the city there is an accumulated mass of squalid wretchedness which is probably unequalled in any town of the British dominions'.[60] Overall conditions turned if anything still worse when the boundaries were extended in 1846 to take in the ring of grimy suburbs grown up round the edge of the old burgh. The death-rate in urban Scotland actually rose during this decade, with terrible epidemics of cholera or other infectious diseases. And mortality in Glasgow was highest of all. By 1900 there even came a visitation of plague, unknown for a quarter of a millennium, which killed 16 people.

Yet over and above the degradation at the bottom of the social heap stretched a broad stratum of working-class Glaswegians who, if far from rich, maintained their standards and felt proud of them. Baird wrote: 'That many of the operatives in Glasgow live in comfort and are able to clothe themselves and their families, and to educate their children, is well known to all who know anything of them, and must be evident even to the passing stranger who sees their thousands pouring along the streets on the sabbath-day, apparently well fed and well clad, to their respective places of worship.'[61] The sturdy working-class values especially of the weaving trade became diffused even as that particular trade headed towards extinction. Such values could enjoin political action. A weaver witness to a parliamentary inquiry boasted 'there have been more persons risen to wealth and eminence of handloom weavers than of all other trades put together in Scotland; I could name forty or fifty people who were handloom weavers who are now men of capital and character filling high situations. Two late lord provosts of Glasgow were handloom weavers in my remembrance.'[62] Robert Craig, 'an excellent specimen of an intelligent Glasgow weaver',[63] was active in local reforming politics from 1820. He preached co-operation among the classes and got a response: at one meeting 'after a strong appeal on the necessity of all the middling and lower ranks of society uniting to call for a thorough reform, he concluded amidst cheers and applause'.

These values naturally favoured the city's improvement. More than that, they formed the foundation for a municipal philosophy that prompted the corporation to pioneer public utilities and services. The regime was still not especially democratic: it cared little for the interests of private property in pursuit of its ends, and on the populace it enforced its regulations with rigour and zeal. The first big project came as early as 1854, when the problem of supplying clean water to the city was solved by the scheme to tap Loch Katrine. At length the corporation's policy would go as far as municipal trading. In 1869 it took over the city's gas companies and in 1892 began to generate electricity. From 1894 it operated the tramways and in 1901 set up a telephone network. Nor did it stop at material wants: it also provided high and low culture, in public concerts and the excellent art gallery, or at the People's Palace.

It was in 1856 that the lord provost, Andrew Orr, proclaimed the new aim of the rulers of Glasgow – to make it a 'model municipality'.[64] The aim found its first general fulfilment in 1866 when the city got its own Improvement Act passed at Westminster. The legislation set up a trust to raze the oldest, meanest and foulest parts of the burgh, then replace them with modern streets and buildings. That task was carried out with a vengeance: no other British city had ever before done what Glasgow now did in a few years. On 88 acres of the central area, 39 new streets were formed and 12 old ones reconstructed. Demolition went on so fast that by 1874 the homes of 15,000 people had been knocked down.[65] The Glasgow of Adam Smith and James Watt vanished. In 1889 there arose in triumph on part of its ruins a symbol of the new city, the flamboyant City Chambers in George Square.

Yet the intense building activity formed merely a matrix for a still more comprehensive policy of imposing on the people of Glasgow exemplary sanitary standards. The corporation appointed a Medical Officer of Health and an inspectorate with powers to cleanse the streets, the closes and the middens, to disinfect the houses and to control the number of people living in them. A limit was laid down for flats of up to three rooms. Inspectors went to measure up each flat and calculate the numbers it could legally contain according to cubic capacity. To the door they fixed a metal disc or ticket stating this number, which it would be an offence to remove. At the peak there were 85,500 people in more than 20,000 'ticketed houses'. These became then subject to unannounced raids in the middle of the night by inspectors who had the power to prosecute anybody resident there without authorisation: 'each pair of sanitary inspectors is expected to make one hundred visits per night on all four nights of the week. They have a complete list of all the ticketed houses in the area. These houses they usually visit after midnight, continuing their systematic inspection generally from midnight to four o'clock in the morning.'[66] Archibald Chalmers, Medical Officer of Health from 1900, was candid about such

> extraordinary powers, this right of entry and night inspection, but no one who knows anything of the habits of the people affected by them – the unskilled labourer and the class lower still, our criminal classes – can have any doubt of this necessity nor as to their efficacy and usefulness. If you relaxed your repressive efforts, the old state

of affairs would return in a few weeks. We must not be restrained by any squeamishness about ticketing new property and giving it a bad name, if we find that overcrowding has been transferred with the old tenants of your demolished property. If a landlord finds that such a process deteriorates the value of his property, then he must prevent the overcrowding, otherwise ticketed it must be.[67]

The kind of city being created here formed, of course, part of a wider municipal movement in Britain, originated by Joseph Chamberlain in Birmingham; English historians of the period do not normally bother to look at Scotland but, if they do, concede that in Glasgow the experiment went further and did better.[68] The corporation's principles might well have derived from its special situation in a stateless nation, where the sovereign political authority resident in another country was asked only to provide the statutory wherewithal to local institutions that, in pursuit of the general welfare, acted in the freedom they chose for themselves. As a matter of fact, Victorian Glasgow organised itself at least as well as the British state. One citizen noted in awe that 'our municipality is a microcosm of our state . . . our imitation of imperial housekeeping is very faithful'.[69]

This government of Glasgow rested on two principles: strict economy in finance and the welfare of the people. To the first a council composed of businessmen attended, proud of the profitable enterprise and efficiency that kept consumer prices down. But the second principle of promoting welfare they were reluctant to entrust to the mechanics of capitalism. With the vision and ambition to create an ideal industrial society, they sought to bring the energy of the capitalists and the morals of the citizens into harmony through strict regulation. It gave social control to the bourgeoisie, but also offered much to the workers. These could be kept tranquil at a time when labour was rising as a political force elsewhere. The corporation's policies reinforced their assent to a system where clashes of capital and labour got deliberately defused. Though different parties were represented in the City Chambers, they acted in a non-partisan manner and removed divisive issues from politics. A new public spirit was being born in Glasgow, collectivist and interventionist. It looked alien to the libertarian radicalism of most Scots, and found its critics too. One called the corporation 'the oppressor of the West', using the Parliament at Westminster merely as a 'means of registering its decrees'.[70]

Housing was really the key to the social experiment. So how should housing be provided in Glasgow, especially for the workers? Nobody seemed to
favour a free market – itself remarkable in Victorian Scotland. Or at least the
authorities planning and supervising redevelopment looked to no such solution, not even if supplemented by philanthropy or public regulation. Given
this, there seemed in principle little reason why the corporation should not
go on to build dwellings along with everything else it built, that is to say, just
as an extension of its general range of public services. By 1902 it had, in fact,
constructed about 2,000 flats for rent, though this was only one-tenth of the
number it had demolished.[71] They looked nothing like modern tower blocks
but came in the style of the rest of the city, tenements of four storeys with
shops on the ground floor. The tenants were the respectable working class:
clerks, policemen, mechanics, shopkeepers and other people with regular
wages of between 24 shillings and 30 shillings a week.[72] Every landlord in
Glasgow preferred that type of tenant. In particular, the corporation liked to
house its own employees. But the harder question was where the feckless, the
vicious and the criminal would go. If the corporation could deal with them,
even private landlords and builders might accept this form of municipal
socialism.

Still, nothing stopped private landlords setting as strict rules for their tenants as the corporation did. There was, corresponding to similar bodies in
Edinburgh, a Glasgow Workmen's Dwellings Company that built homes for
rent, again to respectable working people, the 'industrious poor' as opposed to
the 'dirty, destructive, depraved' of the ticketed houses. It meant to educate its
tenants in the advantages of social improvement, so installed in each tenement
a resident caretaker 'to supervise the people generally and press steadily upon
the habits of filth and disorder'. Would-be tenants were tested as to character
and income, and nobody needed to apply who did not have a month's rent
already saved up.

This private but regulated approach seemed preferable to critics prophetically fearing the corporation might create homes for an army of employees
who, when casting votes, would use them to support cheap, subsidised rents
because of their own occupation of public housing, at the expense of all the
other citizens. William Smart, professor of political economy at the University
of Glasgow, thought that, while in the abstract 'cheap rents are as desirable
as cheap food', housing supplied by the corporation added up to 'nothing
more nor less than the municipality offering a bounty to come and dwell in
Glasgow'.[73] As early as 1888 the city's first Medical Office of Health, James

162

Russell, had complained that 'the public of Glasgow already trust too much to authorities and officials for the solution of their social difficulties – more, I think, than any other community.'[74]

The scene was set for future housing action, yet in one respect it had already become the least satisfactory part of Glasgow's social experiment. Old property continued to decay, and as soon as the worst slums were cleared the next worst appeared in their turn intolerable. The city was no closer to abolishing slums in 1902 than in 1866. Then, 15,000 had been scheduled for demolition but, when the scheme reached completion, another 20,000 were somehow there.[75] Glasgow had set itself on a path from which it proved hard to turn aside. At the peak in the twentieth century the corporation owned 63 per cent of the city's housing yet this still included some of the worst in Europe, much of it of recent construction.

Scottish Victorian cities had high hopes of their future, even if they could not precisely foresee it. One thing they wanted was to shape it for themselves: they refused to rely on the British government but set off on the expensive path of private legislation. At Westminster and elsewhere, the reason they gave for tackling matters in their own way was that they could then attend to specific regional needs – which in truth did even within the small compass of Scotland vary widely, making the value of national legislation questionable and its fulfilment arguably impracticable. Still, beneath that rationalisation we might perceive a familiar, indeed historic, Scottish aversion to letting central authority mix in and dictate local affairs. It was a matter of pride, though in this instance the pride came before a fall.

PART III
MARGINS

7

Poverty: 'The worst of any'

In January 1846 William Smythe, secretary to the Board of Supervision in Edinburgh, set out on a tour of duty that would take him right up to Thurso in Caithness, with halts at various places along the way. What his board supervised was the new Scots Poor Law passed at Westminster the year before. It was an important reform, modern Scotland's first attempt at welfare for the people. It represented also a more general step forward for a nation that ever since the Union of 1707 had lacked distinct political institutions, making do instead with mere relics of the old Scottish state. So a civil service in the sense of a central body of officials administering uniform law over the whole country did not exist. Its creation in a modest form now for the particular problem of the poor acknowledged this to be the most pressing question of the moment, one that could be dealt with neither at a local level nor by remote British authorities. An advocate by profession, Smythe needed to build from scratch a novel, intermediate level of Scottish government. His expedition to the north would be a test of him and his ideas.

This was because up to 1845 there had been next to no system of relief operating in that region for its scattered and needy population. The new Poor Law made it for the first time obligatory that every parish in the country should make some provision for paupers in the form of a 'parochial allowance', paid out to them as a dole. It also gave the beneficiaries a right of appeal to the board in Edinburgh if they thought they were not getting enough, and numbers of them had already exercised that right. But without established mechanisms in the more distant parts of the country, the secretary could only go to see for himself what was happening before he decided on a response.

When Smythe reached Urquhart in Moray, for example, he interviewed in person a woman who told him she and her mother could live for two months off a boll (74lb) of potatoes, so that the couple of bolls the pair raised from their own patch of ground every year would see them through a winter. At Dingwall the wife of a labourer with four children said a boll of potatoes with a boll of meal could keep the whole family going for six weeks. This did not sound much to Smythe, 'yet the father and the mother were both able-bodied, and employed at hard work, and the children were not of a very tender age'. When he got at last to Thurso, he came across an old man 'who ate nothing but wheaten bread'; a 4lb loaf a week was enough for him. Finding all such people more or less able to look after themselves, Smythe formed an impression they would not require much money by way of relief. There could perhaps be a sum 'sufficient to provide fish, salt and other small items' or to 'procure any little articles of clothing which may be required'; otherwise, 'as in almost all cases in the rural districts, the paupers sit rent free, and . . . fuel, either peat or wood, is obtained at scarcely any cost'.[1]

After Smythe returned to Edinburgh he wrote up a report summarising his conclusions from the trip: 'The Board will, I am sure, see the expediency both in moral and political view of not increasing the parochial allowances. It would be a moral evil if the poor are suffered to give way to habits of indolence, by the stimulus to their exertion on their own behalf being rendered less urgent than heretofore, while the actual loss arising from there being so much less productive labour will be considerable.'[2] In other words, the poor people of Scotland could not expect much from the secretary to the Board of Supervision.

***

This book has so far looked at the successful sides of Scotland in the nineteenth century. Our attention has focused on the tremendous economic development that spread huge benefits over a wide spectrum of society, if with collateral damage to the historic national institutions that many Scots would rather have preserved (though not, to be sure, at any price). It still all added up to something they could be proud of, perhaps to the extent of feeling they stood at the forefront of modern industrial society. In this third part of the book we will look instead at some ways in which Scots fell short of their highest aspirations and failed to meet the challenges they faced, in whole or in part, or at least are now judged to have failed. This may not mean Victorian triumphalism was unjustified, merely less justified. An overall estimate must be borne in mind when, later still, we come on to Scottish politics and Scottish culture.

In particular, Victorian Scots felt acutely aware of the poverty in their midst, and of their inability to cure it even by their own lights. We have not solved the problem in the twenty-first century either, despite our change of attitude towards it. Whereas we tend to ascribe it to vague social causes, seldom analysed in any convincing rigour, Victorians found it hard to get away from the idea that people were at bottom responsible for their own condition. To escape it, then, the poor had first to rely on personal effort. Just as our laws reflect our attitude, so the Victorians' laws reflected theirs. The nineteenth century can in this respect be divided at the year 1845, when the old Scots Poor Law came to an end and the new Scots Poor Law replaced it.

The old Scots Poor Law dated back to 1574. It was an outcome of the Reformation. Before 1560 the poor had been a charge on the monasteries, but now the monasteries no longer existed. The Reformer John Knox himself pinpointed the need for a novel system to be run by the Reformed Church of Scotland, though even in his own parish of St Giles in Edinburgh this was easier said than done – and a tall order if he expected the capital's canny burgesses to pay for something of no direct benefit to themselves. Here lay a conundrum of Calvinism: those instilled with its godly sense of personal responsibility could take an unforgiving view of those without. Proper objects of charity they might be, but charity would be wasted on them if their poverty were their own fault – better for them to get off their backsides and fend for themselves. Knox himself endorsed this view: 'We are not patrons for stubborn and idle beggars who, running from place to place, make a craft of their begging ... but for the widow and fatherless, the aged, impotent and lamed ... that they may feel some benefit of Christ Jesus now preached to them.'[3]

Right till 1845, Knox's attitude still prevailed. Under the Presbyterian order erected by his followers, legal assessments, or local rates, might be imposed in each parish for support of the poor, yet they were not obligatory. In the countryside, the heritors, or landowners, and the kirk sessions took charge of the arrangements. In the burghs, the municipal and parochial boundaries often coincided, which meant the authority of the magistrates reinforced that of the kirk sessions in poor relief as in all else. Worthy citizens sitting in these seats of petty power preferred to avoid local taxes and for provision of relief to rely on collections from congregations, on charitable bequests and on other forms of giving. Annan in Dumfriesshire raised money for the poor from public drinking bouts, but this was not an option commending itself elsewhere in a Presbyterian nation. The overall level of resources for relief remained limited. During a couple of centuries it still seems to have sufficed, more or less. In Sir John Sinclair's *Old Statistical Account*, compiled during the 1790s out of reports from ministers, there was little complaint about any shortfalls of relief.[4]

The huge surge of migrants into the towns during the industrial revolution changed all that. The era of the Reformation had known nothing of modern trade-cycles, throwing thousands out of work at once, which were now the main cause of unemployment and overwhelmed the existing arrangements to deal with it. The parsimony of the Poor Law tended to intensify pressure for people to move out from the countryside into the towns, as if there were not enough forces working to that end anyway. In the burghs the ministers, like their rural brethren, again bore the burden of distributing such resources as the law provided. They often did it in an uncoordinated and inconsistent fashion, there being no central authority to impose anything else. Still they could never legally hand over money to non-natives of the parish, therefore not to the economic migrants. In particular, they were supposed to leave all the able-bodied unemployed to their own devices. For these, in the circumstances, the hopeful move to the towns might turn out to have been not such a good idea, given the difficulties of ever making their way back.[5]

❁

The operations of the Poor Law had rather been retreating before the realities of a new age. In rural Scotland a series of legal decisions in the eighteenth century transferred control of relief altogether out of the hands of the kirk sessions and into the hands of the lairds, who in turn engineered a tighter redefinition of the law. Once they finished with it there could be no relief in any circumstances except for the aged or disabled, little general resort to poor rates and, with or without poor rates, no contribution whatever by non-resident landlords. In effect it was often the poor that supported the poor, sometimes amid smug reflections from their betters on the virtues of thrift and independence.[6]

Still, in a decentralised system, with good practice left to the judgment of individual parishes, national standards could not be thought of, not even in the most trivial detail. For example, while the minister of Penninghame in Wigtownshire considered spending by the poor on tea, tobacco or snuff to be 'unreasonable', the minister of Dornoch in Sutherland found the poor needed snuff more than anything else and the minister of Snizort on Skye thought the same of tobacco. There was no chance of getting general change in the system except through some elusive evolution of sentiment among the landowning class. Beneath the fragmentation of the structure it was yet over time possible to perceive an increase in poverty. In the 1830s the number of parishes raising assessments on proprietors rose to more than 200, about 10 per cent up on the previous decade, during which this level had risen by 5 per cent. With poverty not just worsening but worsening faster, a number of big urban parishes got into difficulty by the 1840s and no longer had the cash to pay allowances they had agreed.[7]

That did not reflect any loosening of the Poor Law's tight fist. Most of its beneficiaries were women: spinsters or widows rather defenceless in male-chauvinist Scotland. At Aberlady in East Lothian, a widow with five children was struck off the poor roll when her youngest daughter reached the age of two, the tiny tot being apparently now expected to earn something. Oban abandoned its local tax in 1842 and, with less coming in, made deep cuts in payments. Within a few months three-quarters of the town's sick poor died. At Campbeltown in Argyll the usual allowance to the poor amounted to a shilling a week but, at a meeting of the kirk session in 1842, 48 people on the roll, most of them widows with children, were struck off. Instead they received badges authorising them to beg on the streets. Many parishes in any event refused to support a woman with an illegitimate child, or did so only with deep reluctance. The minister of Dolphington in Lanarkshire regarded such support as 'one of the most painful points ... We are obliged to do it but we do it with a grudge, giving a premium to vice.' Oban again went one better: it struck from the roll a woman whose daughter had had an illegitimate child.[8]

The system came under greatest strain in the areas of economic boom, for in these times boom was bound also to bring bust at some point. When recession had struck Paisley once again in 1820, the workers decided they needed something more than desperate, temporary measures to face such recurring bouts of instability. Over 800 of them – much more than a pauper residue – sought to establish their legal entitlement to poor relief. They made a claim to the parish and, when it was refused, to the sheriff, who granted it. The parish appealed to the Court of Session. The court decided for the parish, confirming that even in the new industrial economy there could in Scotland be no such thing as general legal entitlement to relief on grounds of unemployment. Each parish would therefore remain free to give what help to the jobless it wanted – and if it gave nothing that must be the end of the matter. Change in society did not mean change in the Poor Law, then; so long as each parish retained authority over its own relief, there could be no uniform national regulation and no liberalising reform at that level either.[9]

Older burghs at least could often look back on some local usage adaptable to evolving conditions, rather than needing to build up everything from scratch. Aberdeen had since 1768 had a united fund for the poor to co-ordinate income and expenditure from voluntary charities as well as the collections from churches. In effect, the town council ran the fund, if through a committee with delegates from other interested parties and with elaborate respect paid to the kirk sessions in particular. Following a convention that religious dissenters should try to look after their own poor too, congregations from Catholics to Methodists made additional donations to the fund. So here was in effect a unified urban initiative to tackle poverty. It ran without a hitch till 1818 when, amid the post-war depression, the managers decided they needed more money and called for a voluntary local levy. They repeated this call in every year following, though some citizens chose – as was their right – not to pay. Yet the expenditure rose too, and faster than the income. By 1838 it became necessary to impose a compulsory assessment. In the new order of reformed and accountable urban politics, this at once caused problems. Ratepayers wanted some control over money raised from them, while the kirk sessions were unwilling to concede any. The dispute rumbled on till in 1840 the churches withheld the share they owed to the united fund. Now the town council had no choice but to raise a local tax. The next year it published a report on the finances of the system pointing out that every burgh of any size in Scotland relied on a poor rate.[10] In Aberdeen relief had turned secular and municipal.

In Edinburgh some transfer of responsibility from churches to town council happened earlier, in 1740, but never worked so well. The pooled resources did finance a poorhouse, put up on a site near the Bristo Port (a wing of the building survives in a cul-de-sac). It became a dump for undesirables. Even by the local standards of filth it was 'extremely nauseous'. It held 700 inmates, still with strict criteria for admission: first 'the begging poor entitled to the town's charity', as of old; then those who could bring their own blankets or furniture, always in short supply; then orphans; then burgesses and their families who had fallen on hard times; then anybody else that room could be found for. The welcome was not warm. Inmates had to wear drab blue uniforms. They were fed on porridge, broth and bread. The managers of this spartan regime still felt overwhelmed. Paupers were bad enough but patients discharged as incurable from the Royal Infirmary tended to end up here too, having nowhere else to go. A large ward was allocated to people labelled 'depraved'. And the bedlam for the insane lay in the cellars, out of sight, out of mind. Nothing here fostered charity.[11] Sir Walter Scott in *The Heart of Midlothian* hints rather at routine brutality: his character Madge Wildfire often tells the truth in her madness, and she sings of her time in the workhouse:

> I had hempen bracelets strong
> And merry whips ding-dong
> And prayer and fasting plenty.[12]

Otherwise there was a little outdoor relief, that is to say, allowances paid to poor people still staying in their own homes. In the early nineteenth century about 1,000 individuals claimed it. Again, they needed to be citizens of the capital, and show they had been born there. The rule therefore excluded the incoming population from the countryside. Those looking for a better life would not find it if they ended up, as many did, in the Old Town. By now this had been emptied of all but an underclass, people with no choice where to live.[13]

The Revd John Lee, minister of St Giles in the 1830s, was himself the son of a weaver in Midlothian and painted a picture of the urban conditions so harrowing as to catch the attention of Friedrich Engels, who in 1844 quoted him in *The Condition of the Working Classes in England* (*sic*): 'I have seen much wretchedness in my time, but never such a scene of misery as in this parish.' Many poor people had nothing by way of personal possessions, even though some got the maximum support the Church could offer. Lee could name 'seventy-eight houses where there was no bed, in some of them not even straw'. He recalled a case 'of two Scotch families living in a miserable kind of cellar, who had come from the country within a few months, in search of work'; some of their children were already dead. They lived the whole time in darkness, and 'there was a little bundle of dirty straw in one corner, for one family, and in another for the other. An ass stood in one corner, which was as well accommodated as these human creatures. It would almost make a heart of adamant bleed to see such an accumulation of misery in a country like this.'[14] While Lee had legal responsibility for parishioners in this condition, he stressed that relief would be ineffective even if the Poor Law made greater resources available. The world had just changed since 1579: then there had been the steady rhythm of traditional agriculture, now there was the volatility of modern commerce. Both might lurch into crisis, but at least rural society had been sustained by resilient structures, while in the city the poor led lives too unstable to form anything that might be called a community.

If that was Edinburgh, what of Glasgow? Here, yet again, the problems proliferated. Since 1773 there had been a poorhouse, called the Town's Hospital, as inadequate to the scale of distress as its counterparts elsewhere. Glaswegians in need were supposed otherwise to fend for themselves. The reforming lawyer Charles Baird noted that no amount of prudence might save them from penury in consequence of 'the sudden convulsions and fluctuations of trade, the high price of provisions ... and above all their liability to diseases'.[15] Added to these difficulties were huge inflows of migrants during the booms, not just from the surrounding countryside but rather from the Highlands and from Ireland, where many had been destitute even before they left. Should they find themselves starving when the busts arrived there was little chance of their returning home again. If they had got a first foot on the urban ladder it was often in a job where they did not earn enough to feed, house and clothe themselves, let alone a family. The English social reformer Edwin Chadwick and his investigators saw the consequences during their national survey just at the onset of another recession, perhaps the worst of the century, in 1841. Baird showed them round Glasgow, quite possibly to this scene, which he had recorded after calling on three women in the centre of the city:

> They were all actually in a state of nudity, not having clothes sufficient to cover their nakedness. Before I could speak to them they were obliged to cover themselves in something like old torn bed coverlets. The house was completely destitute of beds or other furniture – positively nothing. The inmates were starving, having no food whatever in the house, and it appears they had shut themselves up for the purpose of dying; their modesty having prevented them from making their circumstances known.[16]

Chadwick's team were no strangers to life in the slums: all British cities housed their share of filth, disease, starvation, wretchedness and overcrowding. Yet, in his words, 'the condition of the population in Glasgow was the worst of any we had seen in any part of Great Britain.'[17]

Here there had come, however, one novel response. In 1819 the Revd Thomas Chalmers arrived at the church of St John's in the Gallowgate, a new proletarian parish with a place of worship custom-built for it (demolished in 1956). It was a world away from the fishing haven of Anstruther where he had grown up and from the bucolic Kilmany where he had found his first charge in the tranquil hinterland of Fife. In both those communities, needy parishioners were able to rely on mutual support under the minister's benevolent eye. Chalmers believed the same outlook could and should be carried over from traditional rural Scotland into its soulless industrial society. The purpose of his ministry at St John's was to exemplify this.[18]

Chalmers came to St John's during the post-war crisis that prompted questioning all over Britain of how to deal with the distress. The English already believed their own Poor Law cost them too much, though it offered nothing to those it defined as the undeserving poor. Chalmers never thought much of the English: 'In all parts of England the shameless and abandoned profligacy of the lower orders is most deplorable.' His own ideas, however, tended towards the strictest reading of the stingy Scots Poor Law. For preference he wanted nobody taxed to support the needy. On the contrary, all aid should come out of voluntary contributions by the charitable. But would they produce enough money? Chalmers had no wish to penalise actual incapacity, to cut off destitute people unable to look after themselves. Still, those destitute people able to look after themselves must do so – and that, he judged, would be most of them. It may sound harsh, but for him it was part of his vision of a godly commonwealth in Scotland. It would prompt people to help one another because they believed in Jesus Christ, who blessed the poor. Modern society had grown complex, indeed, but the complexity might meet its match if Christ's commandments created a combination of personal responsibility, ties of blood, love of neighbours and a sense of local community to give the poor as much care as they needed – though no more. He wrote at the outset of his ministry in the East End of Glasgow:

> Out of the ruins of the present system we should see another system emerge, under which pauperism would be stifled in the infancy of its elements; and a reaching application be brought into effectual contact with the very root and principle of the disease; and another generation should not elapse, ere, by the vigorous effect

of Christian education of the young, we should have to do with a race of men, who would spurn all its worthlessness and all its degradation away from them.[19]

One of Chalmers's first moves at St John's was to appoint deacons to visit parishioners claiming relief and see whether they merited it. There was no simple benchmark, but the deacons would suggest to their charges how they might start fending for themselves, if necessary with help from family, friends or neighbours. Not till other possibilities of support were exhausted would aid from the parish be confirmed and continued. The implied overall reduction in relief was not itself the object of this exercise, however, which lay rather in the reformation of individuals who, through self-help, could lessen their own degree of dependency. At the same time the rich were called on for greater charity. From both sides, a more moral and independent community might be created. The available money could then be turned to better uses than poor relief, to building the churches and schools that new urban areas needed.[20]

The charismatic Chalmers blended high hopes with good intentions, and at St John's his scheme seemed to work well enough: while the population of the parish rose during his ministry, the quantum of pauperism dropped. But dispute over his achievement, or otherwise, continues down to the present. Historians brought up in the Scottish socialism of the late twentieth century have taken the sniffiest possible attitude to Chalmers's exertions as being at bottom motivated by dogmatic callousness;[21] little of the revisionism of English historiography on the Poor Law has so far crossed the border.[22] It is a valid critique that not every parish would or could find a Chalmers. Yet in his own time he was much admired for his depth of commitment to his work and his decision to go and live among the poor (as few modern academics would care to do). Even in the Scotland of the twenty-first century we may yet develop a more open attitude to the idea that poverty will be best treated by engagement of local communities and fellow human beings rather than by impersonal handouts from the bureaucracy of a state washing its hands of further consequence.[23]

After four years Chalmers returned to academic life, to a chair of divinity at the University of St Andrews. His system carried on at St John's till 1832, and was tried in one other parish in Glasgow, St George's (now St George's Tron Church in Nelson Mandela Place). Beyond, it was taken up at Dirleton in East Lothian. There a hard-working minister, the Revd William Stark, showed he could at once put an end to assessments yet increase the size of the poor fund through voluntary contributions. And he cut calls on it by persuading more of his poor to fend for themselves, 'so promoting in some measure the revival of that wholesome spirit of independence which an assessment never fails to destroy'.[24] The concept also appealed to the Revd Henry Duncan at Ruthwell in Dumfriesshire, as one of the range of schemes he kept trying out to better the lives of his parishioners. He urged local landowners to top up his poor fund in private so that the question of compulsory assessment would never even arise, a notion threatening 'nothing but danger and overthrow to that salutary spirit of independence which has hitherto so honourably distinguished the Scottish poor'.[25]

Outside the Church, this way of thinking found favour with reforming, progressive Whigs. But their motivation was secular rather than religious. While Chalmers wanted to salvage Presbyterian self-reliance as a social principle, they wanted to enforce the impersonal maxims of the free market. While he felt appalled at the damage done by economic cycles, they felt still more appalled at the idleness resulting. While he called on every local community for moral and material help to its less fortunate members, they just told the unemployed to look for a job. Before 1832 there was never more than a handful of Scots Whigs at Westminster but one, Thomas Kennedy of Dunure, MP for the Ayr Burghs, busied himself with trying to water the Poor Law down to nothing. For a start he wanted to make it impossible for any individual to appeal against refusal by his parish to grant relief. While a Bill to that effect got nowhere, a judicial ruling of 1821 did most of its work for it, stipulating that such appeals must go straight to the Court of Session, that is to say, not by way of the sheriff. On grounds of cost alone, that made legal recourse prohibitive for the poor. In 1824, Kennedy tried to widen this breach in the law with a Bill allowing the heritors in any parish to cease paying a rate provided they themselves took on the relief of existing paupers. After they had arrived at such a decision, no new assessment and no appeals were to be allowed: in time, then, all relief might become voluntary. Kennedy's friend Henry Cockburn was cheerleader for the scheme, crowing that nobody but 'the fools of the kingdom' had come out against it; he added that, when he was taxed to help the poor, it felt like getting his pocket picked.[26]

The fools of the kingdom happened to include the entire Tory establishment, the political manager, Lord Melville, Melville's deputy in the House of

Commons, William Dundas, the Lord President of the Court of Session, Lord Granton, and the Lord Advocate, Sir William Rae. They defeated Kennedy's Bill, but the Whigs came up with a fresh wheeze in 1828 when Lord Rosebery proposed that the period of residence in a parish required of any individual to qualify for relief should be raised from three to seven years. Melville saw through him: 'The sole object of this Bill is to prevent the influx of the poor Irish into Scotland. This mode of legislating is contrary to the spirit of the Act of Union [with Ireland, 1801], and is unfair and invidious.' He objected 'because it is the first attempt to introduce a different species of legislation for different classes of His Majesty's subjects. I contend that the natives of England and Ireland have a right to enter Scotland.'[27] We should not take it, however, that Tories were exactly soft on poverty. So long as they remained in power, the old Poor Law operated on a principle stated by Granton in a judgment of 1828: 'We must decide cases of this kind according to the rules of law, and must not be influenced by feelings of compassion.'[28] At least, unlike the Whigs, he wanted to maintain the rules of law.

The political tables were turned after the Reform Act of 1832, but the victorious Whigs did not at once unleash their designs on the poor of Scotland. The new government in London felt much more concerned about the English Poor Law, which it considered far too lax. At this stage, indeed, it regarded the Scots Poor Law as rather exemplary and saw no need for its amendment. But general economic conditions worsened during this decade, if in an unstable and erratic fashion. Steady, sustained growth in Britain would not resume before the middle of the century. The west of Scotland suffered worse than most regions. Already in 1837 soup-kitchens were feeding 20,000 of Glasgow's poor, one in ten of the population.[29]

This crisis proved a stubborn one. It lifted a little for a year or two before plunging the country into the Hungry Forties, a decade of privation and misery that exposed beyond doubt the deficiency of the old Scots Poor Law. Another member of Chadwick's investigative team in Glasgow had been William Pulteney Alison, professor of physiology at the University of Edinburgh. Like Chalmers, he showed in his professional life deep sympathy towards the poor, but for his part he recognised 'the utter inadequacy of private benevolence'.[30] In 1840 he published a pamphlet of over 100 pages, *Observations on the Management of the Poor in Scotland.* It was a fierce attack on the lack of provision: 'The upper ranks in Scotland do much less (and what they do they do less systematically and therefore less effectively) for the relief of poverty and of sufferings resulting from it than those of any other country in Europe which is really well regulated, and much less than experience shows to be necessary.'[31] Alison demonstrated how Scotland, in fact, just cast many of the unemployed adrift, above all the economic migrants among them. It was cruel to them and it let the rich escape a proper responsibility to society. Alison got carried away in his unfavourable comparisons with the reformed English Poor Law, passed in 1834 after the report of a Royal Commission to which Chadwick had been secretary. The new regime in England did raise and spend much more on the poor than the old regime in Scotland. But that was because it built workhouses, the great innovation of this reform. Here people unable to support themselves could live and labour, if in surroundings made so unpleasant that they would not want to stay unless they had to. The system covered the whole country, with better areas subsidising worse ones inside regional unions of workhouses, all under the control of a central board in London.

Alison unleashed a debate, in part across the border with his friend Chadwick, developed from their peering down dingy wynds and closes at starving, verminous Glaswegians. They both knew poverty and disease went together. Alison, the medical man, believed poverty caused disease. It created an environment through which germs could spread: cure poverty and disease would be cured too. Chadwick believed disease caused poverty. The first concern had rather to be with sanitation, so as to get rid of the filth and stench in which the cycle of deprivation started up. Of course both were in their way right, and in any event did not disagree about the need for some sanitary policy. By now they were knocking at an open door of public opinion. Alison might attack bourgeois indifference, yet nobody snug in a big house could ignore how epidemics spread outwards from the teeming tenements. While Chadwick's measures limited the extent of the contagions, they did not ward off other pitiless companions of poverty, the harrowing infant mortality or the mysterious consumption (tuberculosis had yet to be identified as an infectious disease). Even so, there was common ground between the two reformers.

The same could not be said of a second debate Alison had going, inside Scotland, with Chalmers and on a different plane, as much about social philosophy as about practical measures. While Chalmers proposed his moral and religious ideal, Alison said it just freed the rich of responsibility. The debate moved from abstract to concrete when in 1840 both men accepted an invitation to present their views to the British Association for the Advancement of Science at its meeting that year in Glasgow.

Their encounter filled Blackfriars Church, just off the High Street. In his opening speech Chalmers went back to the days, 20 years before, of his ministry in the East End. People had criticised it, yet they could not deny the results: poverty and crime were reduced by the example set at St John's. If those results had still not turned out quite conclusive, that was because the corporation of Glasgow never co-operated in extending the system. Turning to his adversary, Chalmers addressed their opposing views. Alison believed the urban environment had to be improved before individuals could improve themselves. Chalmers believed the reverse. For him, the first step was the Christian awakening of personal morality, after which better social conditions would 'necessarily follow'. The spirit retained its saving power even in the most degraded surroundings, and the preaching of the Word with the practice of charity could break the cycle of despair. Firm in that belief, Chalmers offered to return from his comfortable academic chair to the hard graft of the parochial ministry and conduct another experiment like the one at St John's, provided this time the corporation co-operated with him. Money? There was no shortage of money, Chalmers thundered. Why, every year the working class of Glasgow spent more than a million on drink. Here was money that, with religious and moral instruction, they would want to use for self-help and communal benevolence. In his response Alison made the mistake, still made by Scottish academics today, of trying to persuade his audience with a barrage of statistics. He proved no match for the practised eloquence of one of the best preachers of the time, by turns poignant and witty. Still, this was an argument not to be won by a single confrontation.[32] For the rest of the nineteenth century the history of Scottish poor relief became in many ways an inconclusive battle between Chalmers's principle of voluntary effort and Alison's call for statutory action.

The Conservatives regained power at Westminster in 1841. An acute crisis arose almost immediately at Paisley when its textile industry collapsed. None of the thousands of weavers thrown out of work had any clear entitlement to relief. Victorian politicians always felt wary of intervening in a local economy, but in this case were alarmed at the scale of the problem. A delegation from the stricken town, led by its treasurer, David Murray, and by one of its ministers, the Revd Robert Burns, went down to lobby in London. They may have felt surprised and gratified to be invited to No. 10 Downing Street to meet three of the most powerful men in Britain, the Prime Minister, Sir Robert Peel, his Colonial Secretary, Lord Stanley (as Earl of Derby a later Prime Minister himself), and the Home Secretary, Sir James Graham, who by reason of his residence in Cumberland knew something about conditions on the other side of the border.[33]

It turned out to be in its way a classic confrontation of Scotland and England. Peel was an ice-cold character with, according to Benjamin Disraeli, a smile like a silver plate on a coffin. Stanley represented the aristocrat in politics, who thought a chap might jog along on £40,000 a year. Graham was another austere administrator, but did most of the talking. He, according to Murray, 'threw off a great deal of official reserve and was not only quite prepared to listen to our statement but start the question of our pound notes, and too great banking facilities, as the cause of our distress, by promoting and encouraging over-trading'. With one gratuitous jibe at the Scots, he changed the subject to deliver another: 'He said that people in the large towns of Scotland drank too much whisky.'[34] This was to wave red rags across the table at Scots moral and earnest though anything but deferential or reticent. The zealous Burns worked himself up into a fury, denouncing the Corn Laws which he argued were the main cause of distress – but which this Tory government, so far anyway, had committed itself to keeping. Peel decided it was time to bring matters to a close. He said that, while his government could do nothing itself, it would support any charitable appeal. The Scots, ushered out the big black door of No. 10, were being brushed off.

Or so it seemed. Yet Peel did not forget the scene or the passion it had provoked. He asked the provost of Paisley and the sheriff of Renfrewshire to send in regular reports on how the local crisis was unfolding. On the strength of them, he dispatched north in the spring of 1842 a senior civil servant, Edward Twistleton, assistant commissioner for the Poor Law in England. Twistleton arrived at Paisley on 7 March. The next day he met the town's relief committee and disclosed he had a large sum in his keeping subscribed by Queen Victoria in person and by the Marquess of Abercorn (each of whom gave £500), then by members of the government – Peel, Stanley and Graham again – who each gave £225, but acting as private individuals. Paisley could have this money provided its able-bodied male applicants for relief were made to work under supervision for at least ten hours a day, and provided relief was changed from cash to kind, that is to say, was made available in the shape of foodstuffs from stores the committee itself would need to run. Twistleton stressed that, while great personages of the British state were intervening in Paisley, the state itself was not intervening. The Prime Minister and Home Secretary had laid down how the relief should be administered (in fact, according to the English Poor Law) but they were not committing the government as such to any action or to any aid.

The men struggling to save Paisley little liked the tidings from Twistleton, but what could they do? He at least promised the government would not let the people starve. His conditions were accepted. He became temporary dictator of the town, distributing supplies through the stores to the unemployed who in return had to work for them. Graham saw all this as a short-term expedient, however, and recalled Twistleton as soon as the worst was over. He feared it might be noticed elsewhere if his commissioner stayed too long on the spot, what with the government proclaiming the virtues of non-intervention. Twistleton left at the end of June 1842. Graham wrote to express 'satisfaction with the prudence which marked his conduct of a very difficult and painful duty'.[35]

At any rate on the political level it was by now no longer possible to pretend nothing needed done in Scotland. The Disruption of 1843 besides crippled the Kirk, custodian of the old Poor Law. Peel set up a Royal Commission under the chairmanship of Melville. The cheerful old Tory was chuffed at being asked to come out of retirement and carry out one more duty for his country. He reported within a year, allowing the Poor Law Amendment (Scotland) Act to be passed in 1845. It would remain in force till 1948.

In preparation for the earlier reform in England a Royal Commission of 1832 had mounted a stinging attack on the old system of relief, but in Scotland the counterpart of 1844 answered to a conservative brief, 'to consider in what way the present law may be made to work most efficiently, without making any very material changes'.[36] Still, changes there had to be, and the effective choice lay between those of Chalmers and those of Alison, with the English programme of Chadwick hovering in the background. Melville tried in his benign manner to see the best on all sides. He said after finishing his work that 'it was very desirable . . . if possible, to let the country feel that they must make adequate provision for those who are legally entitled to it, but also to take the country along with us, by allowing them to do it in their own way, provided they do it effectively.'[37] What he meant by the first point was establishment of a national Board of

Supervision to oversee the workings of fresh legislation. What he meant by the second point was preservation of the parish as the unit through which the poor would be aided. The Act of 1845 that followed his report rested on these principles.

Some of the poor took Melville at his word that a new era was dawning. In consequence, the first few weeks of the Act's operation could be chaotic. One official in charge of it, Henry Hunter, a disciple of Chalmers, described a scene he now witnessed:

> In Glasgow, the advent of the Act caused a great upheaval. Poor people of all kinds thought they were now provided for life. One thousand to thirteen hundred individuals besieged the office each day of the week, demanding relief, hundreds of them waiting till midnight before their cases could be examined. The sight of such a multitude was deplorable, consisting as it did of all kinds of characters – the aged, the infirm, the drunkard and the idler, children in arms and at the feet, all mixed up in one motley multitude. Pauperism in the city increased at the rate of 10,000 a year, and this at a time when employment was good, provisions cheap and the general health quite ordinary. This lapse from the principle of independence and self-reliance was greatly augmented by a rush of people from Ireland, who thought the new poor rate had turned Glasgow into an Eldorado.[38]

They would soon find out.

Nothing momentous seems to have been expected of the Board of Supervision with its limited personnel and resources, especially financial resources. Smythe as its secretary could only recommend that 'in many cases of partial disability an addition of sixpence or ninepence a week is often of the greatest benefit to the pauper, and sufficient to meet those wants which he is unable to supply by his own industry'.[39] On the other hand, he issued warnings against relief to single mothers, deserted wives, people with grown-up families, with rich relations, with imprisoned spouses and 'in general, all persons of idle, immoral or dissipated habits'. Above everything else, 'the funds raised for the relief of the poor are not [to be] perverted to the maintenance of idleness or vice'.[40] But the board's routine lay rather in arbitration of disputes between individuals and parishes that had turned them down for relief, or had not offered them as much as they wanted. These individuals then enjoyed a right of appeal to the board (a right that did not exist in England). This led to somewhat more intervention as it formulated rules and regulations, opinion and advice.

❁

As for Melville's wish to preserve the role of the parishes, it faced the problem that by 1845 Scottish parishes were being duplicated through ecclesiastical schism. The Act solved the problem by creating in effect a new species of secular parish for behoof of the poor. It set up parochial boards – in the end 866 of them – to be chosen every year by ratepayers under a complicated electoral system that favoured owners of property and excluded most of the poor themselves.[41] These boards dealt with the ordinary business of the new dispensation.

First, to pay a regular and adequate allowance to the poor the parochial boards needed money. The law left to their discretion the method of finding it. Soon, though, the flow of regulation from Edinburgh began to force them to abandon their initial preference for voluntary contributions. In 1845 a quarter of the boards raised a poor rate but by 1894 the proportion had gone up to 95 per cent. An intractable residue lay still in the Highlands, where most people had no cash to pay taxes. Nor in the cities, however, was collection of the money always straightforward: in Glasgow in 1867, about one in three ratepayers, over 20,000 individuals in all, failed to pay the rate and so forfeited their parliamentary franchise (this being the penalty).[42]

Next, the parochial boards had to decide who should get relief and who should not. These could be thorny questions, for the poor people of Scotland turned out to be a litigious lot. Possessing a right of appeal, they made full use of it: in half a century of operation after 1845, the Board of Supervision dealt with 20,000 cases. In the first decade the main point at issue was whether the existing ban on relief of the able-bodied unemployed would hold. William Lindsay, a cotton-spinner out of work and starving, a widower also with four children under the age of ten, brought a test case. He 'had nothing to give them [and] had applied, on these grounds, to the inspector of the parish of Gorbals, in which he had his settlement, for relief, but was distinctly refused'. An appeal went to the sheriff of Lanarkshire, Archibald Alison, the Tory scourge of trade unions but in the matter of the poor more lenient; he was the brother, after all, of William Pulteney Alison. Sheriff Alison again turned Lindsay himself down, yet ordered the parochial board to pay relief for the children, they being destitute by reason of their father's destitution and able to do nothing for their own support. Here was a big potential breach in the existing law. The parochial board appealed to the Court of Session. The importance of the case was recognised, and it went before the full bench of 13 judges. In February 1849 they held by a majority 'that an able-bodied man, who is out of employment, and destitute of the means of subsistence, has no legal right to demand parochial relief for relief to his children in pupillarity'.

A parallel test case proceeded further to the House of Lords, where another paragon of Scottish Whiggery, Henry, Lord Brougham, heard it. His judgment noted that 'the universal opinion of the country, and all the text writers, had, for upwards of two centuries, been in favour of the construction which the Court [of Session] had sanctioned'. He did not propose to change matters. An English colleague on the bench concurred that 'no able-bodied person should have any right under the Act to be included in the list of persons entitled to participate in the [poor] rate.' So that was that: the new Scots Poor Law would remain just as mean as the old one.[43]

To put it another way, the new Poor Law did no more than modify the national tradition. By today's standards the tradition might seem harsh, but in its own time it continued to find wide acceptance. It never needed to spend that much because it did not rely on workhouses, those institutions for the English poor with a punitive regime forcing them, as the name suggests, to work for their keep, at picking oakum and the like. One aim here was to bring home to the able-bodied unemployed their moral failing. But since in Scotland such people enjoyed no entitlement to relief anyway, the concept seemed irrelevant.[44]

Yet the frugality of the system meant basic facilities were skimped. Glasgow had a poor house (not the same as a workhouse). It was a big place with 1500 beds. In one of the buildings two washtubs for 290 inmates – which meant that on their bathing days it took twelve hours for them all to take their turn. And then, 'for the daily ablutions of both sexes of this class [ordinary inmates] there is no provision under shelter. In summer and winter they must go to taps and basins in the open air in the back yard.' Again, inspectors 'were constantly shocked at the use of the water-closets as sculleries and pantries'.[45] Yet, here and elsewhere, the inmates did enjoy the protection of the law. After a complaint in 1847 from the poorhouse of St Cuthbert's, Edinburgh, where 'a refractory female' had been tied up, the Board of Supervision ruled that the governor of the house 'was bound to provide a place of safe custody such as would have left no pretext for having recourse to any measure so objectionable as that which was employed'.[46] In a case of 1870 at Cambusnethan in Lanarkshire, the board issued strict guidance that 'no corporal punishment of any description can be inflicted on any child' except under a few clear rules. The same document stated that 'the punishments inflicted on the cripple William M'Ilroy and the paralytic Thomas Beaton were not only without warrant in the rules, but in themselves highly improper. The rules do not authorise a cold bath as a punishment in any case, nor do they sanction the infliction of corporal punishment upon any adult. It cannot be permitted that the governor should strike an inmate of any age with his hand.' Finally this governor was sacked.[47] In Scotland altogether the poor could answer back. The governor of Glasgow's poorhouse introduced a scheme of employing a select group of inmates on the menial task of manufacturing fire-lighters: 'When a few days' trial had perfected the details, the governor intimated to his gang of forty that in future a full day's work must be performed; ten men instantly gave notice of their intention to quit the house and removed themselves from the roll.'[48]

Scottish poorhouses were not English workhouses. Their model lay in the charitable foundations that some big burghs had inherited from an earlier era, therefore not owed to the Poor Law as such and now not intended to force the inmates to work. They sheltered primarily the sick, insane, handicapped and disabled. Some poorhouses did stretch their concept of charity. Aberdeen, for example, acquired a set of lodgings where old people could live in reasonable comfort and independence. On the other hand, one or two larger poorhouses sought to separate deserving from undeserving cases, but most were not big enough to allow for this even if a satisfactory distinction could have been established. Smaller towns and prosperous rural parishes might manage to build themselves a modest poorhouse with a few paid staff. Parishes could combine to share the cost, and this became quite frequent practice in landward areas. In 1850 21 poorhouses existed with room for 6,000 people. By 1900 there were 65 poorhouses with room for 16,000 people.[49] Even then, with numbers higher than ever before, the proportion of paupers relieved by this means amounted to one in seven, compared to one in three on indoor relief in England.[50]

Scots in need preferred to stay away from the poorhouse and rely on outdoor relief: of those 16,000 places available by 1906, just half were taken up. To be sure the poorhouses, if not bent on retribution, remained far from cosy places, imposing a regime of discipline and abstinence, often restricting contact with the outside world; in less populated parts, inmates might anyway have to live far away from friends and relations. In fact, most parochial boards disliked the idea of a poorhouse too, for it did not come cheap. They seldom bothered to take up vacancies in a neighbouring parish because it was more economical to hand out small doles to the destitute. Others rented local lodgings, again on grounds of cost. For the orphans, it was anyway better to pay their keep in a family than to institutionalise them. Some did the same with the lunatics, presumably the harmless lunatics.[51]

The parsimony of the Scots Poor Law was bound up with the fact that most paupers remained to some degree integrated with their local communities. Burdens were hard to share across the boundaries of the parishes anyway, and the Board of Supervision lacked powers to equalise the burdens otherwise. Yet this outcome had advantages. In their local communities the circumstances of the poor would be known and their merits could be weighed. It was then easier to combine relief with charity and with help from the family. The small scale of these operations might also be a virtue in itself, even if they left gaps to fill. In many ways this was Chalmers in practice, though run under the kind of tutelage Alison preferred, not of the Church but of an agency of the state. Of course, in the absence of the English unions of workhouses, certain parochial boards could cope better than others. One response might have been to merge some of them. But in 1872 the chairman of the Board of Supervision, William Walker, nipped in the bud a parliamentary attempt to do just that, taking the opportunity to praise the system as it stood:

> The experience of the board ... is that the administration of the law is most efficient when the area and population are not so large as to make it beyond the power of one executive body to overlook it, and where all the paupers are within the knowledge, and under the constant oversight, of one inspector. As a general rule, it may be said that the smaller the area and population the better is the administration of the law, provided that the parochial board and the inspector know their duty, and are anxious to perform it.[52]

The Scots Poor Law was frugal but not inhuman: the reverse of the modern system of social security. It did not want to chastise the poor, but it would not coddle them either. For a range of particular problems, from deafness to desertion by a spouse, many more specialised charities existed to help the poor along with richer fellow citizens similarly afflicted. These voluntary bodies were as a rule financed through subscription and run by leading donors, then by delegates from local government and by representatives of other civic institutions.[53] They met one aspiration of the Scottish bourgeoisie, for communal leadership that also smoothed social relations and defused political tensions, not least through co-operation with a skilled working class itself committed to self-help and voluntary initiative. It was part of that wider social order in Scotland where respect between worker and employer together with shared pride in the success of an industrial society raised everybody's sights – and made things possible that would otherwise have been improbable.

This social order posited besides that workers in need did not have to be just passive recipients of aid from on high but could also take an active part in mutual aid. Their friendly societies covered the costs of social insurance, sickness and funerals. Their co-operative societies sold cheap and healthy food, while encouraging thrift through payment of dividends. Their savings banks offered safe havens for small funds. More informal types of support within the working class helped people to make ends meet in everyday life. Family and friends lent money to one another, took in washing and cared for children, boarded lodgers and kept an eye on the stair. In the neighbourhood, supplies might be bought on tick and problems of cash flow could be met at the pawnshop or moneylenders. It was better than the poorhouse anyway. If the statutory system of relief seemed miserly, incapable in itself of meeting all the needs of the poor, that did not signify that the needs were never met, rather that they were met by other means – for preference still 'using the safe and small'.[54]

❋

Health is a good test of this proposition. Scots perhaps suffer a genetic weakness, or at least have too many bad habits, that make them rather unhealthy people, something as true for the nineteenth century as for the twenty-first.[55] In 1901 Scottish babies were expected at birth to live just 40 years (compared with 45 for boys and 49 for girls in England, figures about the same as in France and Germany); the equivalents today are 74 for boys and 79 for girls in Scotland, 75 for boys and 80 for girls in England. Yet again, then and now, poor health went together with excellent medical provision in Scotland. By the turn of the twentieth century, nine Royal Infirmaries existed – one each in the four cities, then in Dumfries, Falkirk, Greenock, Perth and Stirling. Here treatment was free. Most of the finance came from private donations, first raised among the prosperous middle class but then also among the workers, who organised schemes within their places of employment to meet members' medical needs. Meanwhile the administration of the infirmaries benefited from the complimentary (and complementary) expertise of businessmen and professionals serving on the boards of management. Smaller burghs could not match the scale of the big urban infirmaries or provide specialist hospitals, but most had adequate general hospitals also supported by charities.

The charities in Scottish cities mounted on a prodigious scale. Glasgow's Royal Infirmary had opened in 1794, and the vast growth of the conurbation over the next century and more prompted an equivalent increase in facilities for treating the industrial population. Some hospitals were built under the Poor Law, for the East End in Duke Street, for the South Side in Eglinton Street, for the north of the city at Stobhill and for the west at Oakbank, with buildings often crowded and sordid however hard anybody tried. There was a far better performance from voluntary institutions, of which the biggest was the Victoria Infirmary founded in 1890. The university had established a lying-in hospital in 1834 and then the Western Infirmary, erected to accompany the move to Gilmorehill in 1874. There were specialist hospitals for 'fevers' or infectious diseases at Belvidere and Ruchill, for women at Redlands (this also staffed by women) and the Royal Samaritan Hospital. There was a lunatic asylum from 1804, eye hospital from 1824, dental hospital from 1879, cancer hospital from 1890, ear, nose and throat hospital from 1905. The poor might be targeted: an ophthalmic institution opened in 1868 'for the treatment of diseases and injuries of the eye in the cases of the afflicted poor' while a central dispensary was there from 1889 'to give gratuitous advice to the sick poor'. As the city's boundaries expanded, the corporation of Glasgow became the owner of hospitals, such as Knightswood, belonging to local authorities it absorbed.[56]

Edinburgh had, beside the Royal Infirmary dating from 1729 and rebuilt in 1879, two other general hospitals, a hospital for sick children and eight special hospitals. Several contained outpatient departments. In addition seven general and two special dispensaries handled 45,000 patients a year. One-third of the population got free medical treatment, according to a survey of 1912. The city also housed 30 charities providing old-age pensions for 2,000 people. It had 150 further general or special charities giving away an annual £250,000. With what the churches gathered in their collections, and what arose from miscellaneous sources, 'we have a grand total of £365,000 available each year for the help of the poor and afflicted in Edinburgh' – equivalent to £42 million in today's money. On the whole, the same sorts of people (councillors, clergymen, experts, ladies bountiful) ran the charities, whether educational or medical or anything else.[57] The hospitals were the most visible, expensive and impressive form of philanthropy, but charities of all kinds proliferated in Scotland – dispensaries, orphanages, district nursing, with institutions for the handicapped, model lodging houses, ragged schools and homes for fallen women.[58]

In 1909 another Royal Commission on the Poor Laws deliberated, this time for both Scotland and England (though still in different reports). For England the commissioners split, the minority producing a separate document penned by Beatrice Webb as a blueprint of socialist welfare. The Scottish report suffered from no such division of opinion. Its main author was William Smart, professor of political economy at the University of Glasgow. In a memorandum attached to the report proper he endorsed Chalmers's view that relief might destroy independence, so that private charity should be the key to covering any shortfall in legal provision for the poor. Smart in effect stuck up for the Scottish system and ethos, in the sense of Chalmers much more than of Alison – and he saw no virtue in anglicisation.[59]

The body of the report showed that, despite compulsory assessments, the Scots still spent less on the poor than the English. By now there were 22 paupers per 1,000 of population in Scotland, against 24 in England (in both countries the rate had almost halved during four decades). But the annual cost per head of population was just 59 pence in Scotland, against 89 pence in England. What was more, this gap – always wide – seemed to be widening still. The obvious explanation lay in a difference in the number and size of workhouses in England compared to poorhouses in Scotland. The report noted in particular that old people in Scotland tended to be looked after by their families, whereas in England they would be shoved off into care. The overall conclusions still found fault with practical workings of the Act of 1845, which had generated too many anomalies and hardships. It induced people to misrepresent their circumstances for the sake of help. It discouraged single mothers from making honest women of themselves. For their part, the parochial boards often committed technical breaches of the law on humanitarian grounds. The report recommended that the time had come for need no longer to be judged in terms of disability: 'Our proposal would leave destitution as the sole qualification for relief.'[60]

Yet the chance to build on the Scottish system was at once overtaken by political developments. The Royal Commission of 1909 reported to a Liberal government in London of which the budgets, introduced by David Lloyd George, laid the foundations for the modern welfare state. Poor relief from parish and local authority had already become a thing of the past by the time that welfare state was legislated into being in 1948. Though welcomed by Scots, it represented a radical break with their history and traditions. Westminster now made all the policy far away from the Scottish communities it supposed it was serving. Social security instead relied on a centralised system working with absolute uniformity, on Lewis as in Lewisham, and more often in response to the needs of Lewisham than of Lewis. No doubt paying out the same money in both places was important, but this system provided nothing beyond the same money. By contrast, in the National Health Service set up about the same time, Scotland enjoyed administrative devolution: Scottish healthcare had been growing under its own impetus for so long that the imposition of absolute uniformity with England, just for its own sake, would without doubt have done damage. In fact, this Scottish service has proved its worth, not least in closing that gap discovered in 1901 in the nation's life expectancy: it was then far lower than England's, but is almost the same today. This makes for a kind of uniformity worth striving after, as merely paying out the same money is not. Many just criticisms could be and were levelled at the way the Scots poor got treated in the nineteenth century, but remoteness and impersonality did not figure among them.[61]

8

Race: 'Raising a pig'

One day in 1846, as the Revd Thomas Guthrie tells in his autobiography,[1] he and a friend went for a walk on Arthur's Seat in Edinburgh. They reached St Antony's Well and sat down to rest on a boulder beside it. Small boys were hanging about the spot and clamoured round them holding out 'tinnies', tin cans that for a halfpenny they would fill with water and bring for thirsty wanderers to drink. They put Guthrie in mind of another friend, Sheriff William Watson of Aberdeen, and the ragged school he had set up in his native city. Guthrie turned to one of the lads and asked: 'Would you go to school if – besides your learning – you were to get breakfast, dinner and supper there?'

'Aye will I, sir, and bring the haill land [tenement] too.'

Perhaps some expression crossed Guthrie's brow that made the waif believe his response had been a bit too eager. So he hastily added in reassurance: 'I'll come but for my dinner, sir.'

In fact, the boy had set Guthrie thinking. It so happened that the minister, or rather his congregation, had quite a lot of cash in hand. His charge was Free St John's (now St Columba's Free), built after the Disruption from the contributions of those of his flock who followed him out of the established Church of Scotland. He was a popular preacher, and inspired them to great generosity. So plenty of money remained after the erection of a new place of worship, and he was pondering just what to do with it.

Guthrie had come to Edinburgh from his native Angus in 1837. He wrote soon afterwards: 'I had not spent a month in my daily walks in the Cowgate and Grassmarket without seeing that, with worthless drunken and vagabond parents for their only guardians, there were thousands of poor innocent children whose only chance of being saved from a life of ignorance and crime lay in a system of compulsory education.'[2] He always held charges in the Old

Town, among the capital's worst slums; Free St John's stood just where the West Bow plunged from the High Street down to the Grassmarket, along the route once taken by condemned criminals on their last walk from the Tolbooth to the scaffold. Municipal efforts at sanitation in this quarter of the city were already under way, but there remained a long list of social problems to tackle too. One lay in the lack of schooling for the poor, which meant their poverty was bound to continue from generation to generation. Here, it occurred to Guthrie as he now sat on Arthur's Seat, was where he could make a difference. Within a year he gathered enough support to set up Edinburgh's first ragged school, a charity dedicated to the free education of destitute children. The building still stands in Mound Place on Castlehill.[3] A public meeting in April 1847 launched the scheme.

There was no trouble in getting children and their parents to take up the chance Guthrie offered them. But he found soon after opening the ragged school that, as his autobiography coyly puts it, 'about half of the children were of Irish and so, presumably, Roman Catholic parentage'. This no doubt reflected their share in the population of that part of Edinburgh. Guthrie remained a firm believer in religious instruction in schools at a time when sceptics were starting to question its expediency in view of the bitter sectarian strife to which Scots seemed addicted, almost as a pastime. But would Guthrie, and his brethren of the Free Church of Scotland, give Catholic instruction to Catholic children? To ask the question was to answer it.

What happened next convinced Guthrie he was the victim of a campaign of vilification. Anonymous letters appeared in the press to accuse him of excluding Catholic children from the ragged school. In a strict sense this was a false accusation: he never said such children could not come. Still, seeing he insisted on giving religious instruction yet nothing but Protestant religious instruction, the difference was in practice not great. A public row blew up. In the midst of it Guthrie wrote to Fox Maule, Undersecretary for Scottish affairs at the Home Office in London:

> It is a very sad thing that one cannot attempt the salvation of these poor outcasts without interference from parties who were leaving them quietly to perish. People who will do nothing themselves for the education and amelioration of these unhappy children, however slow at giving money, are swift at finding fault. Our schools are on a footing truly Catholic; but because we will not permit them to be made a Popish machinery, the priests oppose them, and because

we will not part with God's Word and banish the Bible from these schools, the falsely so-called Liberal Educationalists throw cold water on the holy fire we seek to kindle . . . The priests are at the bottom of this movement, and using others as their tools.[4]

The result was, though, that some of Guthrie's previous backers deserted him and set up an alternative, called a united industrial school, 'on the principle of joint secular and separate religious instruction'. He lost his Catholic pupils to it. This might have been a blow to his pride but his ragged schools flourished anyway, here and elsewhere. After his death they earned him a statue in Princes Street Gardens, where he stands to the present day with a Bible in his hand and a waif under his wing.[5]

Despite his righteous anger, Guthrie could not really have felt so surprised at being pilloried as a militant Protestant, because he was one. A few years later he took a trip to Rome. He saw the sights but wrote that 'even in the matter of architecture, I am heretic enough to think St Peter's a failure . . . I had no patience for the pictures, marbles or frescoes, with such a loathsome sight before me – such degradation of man, such a practical denial of Jesus Christ and the doctrines of his Cross.' He found food for more lurid thought when he went to the Castel St Angelo and viewed its oubliettes 'where the popes of old confined their victims, who, blindfolded, were carried to the castle and, dropped into one of these dark bottles of places, were never heard of more. We had seen the very caldrons in which they boiled the oil that they applied, boiling, bubbling and seething, to the living flesh of heretics.'[6]

Anti-Catholic aspersions were commonplace in Victorian Scotland and most Presbyterians could see nothing wrong with them. It was curious, though, that the disapproval seldom extended to the native Scottish Catholics living in remote enclaves that had survived the Reformation and the subsequent persecutions of the old faith. The harsh disabilities imposed on its adherents were not finally lifted till 1793: no surprise, then, that by then Catholicism persisted only in fastnesses the persecutors could never reach, some glens of the Grampian Mountains, some peninsulas on the western seaboard, some islands in the Outer Hebrides. In the late nineteenth century the population of all such places fell. The fiercest bigot could scarcely have imagined that the remaining tiny pockets of popery offered any conceivable threat to staunchly Presbyterian Scotland.[7]

Still, Victorian Scots' strongest feelings about religion might at bottom have been just as much about race, or what they defined as race. Many did persuade themselves that there was a real Catholic threat to their Calvinist culture, but that it came from Ireland. Since the turn of the century a swelling flow of Irish immigrants had washed up in Scotland, driven first by the over-population of an agrarian country without the resources to feed its people. The famine of the 1840s solved this aspect of the problem by starving a million of them to death, yet the flow did not flag. It was then sustained by the long Scottish industrial boom that drew across the North Channel those looking for a better life than Irish subsistence agriculture could ever give them and willing to take any job they could find, even the most exhausting and least rewarding.[8]

There had of course always been migration across the North Channel, a mere twenty or so miles wide, but in the seventeenth and early eighteenth centuries rather from Scotland to Ireland. In the nineteenth century the flow reversed in no uncertain terms. The difference in development between the two nations explained the change. Ireland remained a backward peasant country while Scotland became one of the world's industrial leaders. It had a huge demand for labour, especially since many of its own people, educated and skilled, sought even greater opportunities by emigration to distant parts of the globe. As the Scots took off out of the upper levels of their society, the Irish filled in at the bottom.[9]

The farms of south-western Scotland had long seen labourers come over from Ireland to help with the harvest, and new links by steamship made this even easier. The better communications also prompted migrants to spread out into other regions and other activities. Canals and railways required heavy labour by men of no fixed abode but able to move across country, living in makeshift camps, as the construction progressed. The Irish were not the only ones to meet this need: so did Scots, especially Highlanders, and even Englishmen. Inside the camps each group kept itself to itself, and outside the camps they often faced a hostile reaction from locals wanting them to do nothing more than get their work over and go away. Here the different nations of the United Kingdom encountered one another only in brawls fuelled by the drink that was the labourers' sole luxury.[10]

Then as the industrial revolution generated regular waged employment, the opportunist trips from Ireland for seasonal or temporary work turned into permanent migration and settlement in Scotland. They did not make the welcome for the Irish any warmer. As early as 1826, the *Edinburgh Review* wrote that

> at this moment from a fourth to a third part of the labourers in the west of Scotland . . . consist of Irishmen. We are indeed firmly persuaded that nothing so deeply injurious to the character and habits of our people has ever occurred as the late extraordinary influx of Irish labourers; and yet the system may be said to be only in its infancy . . . If we do not interfere to give another bias to the current of emigration, Great Britain will continue to be the outlet for the pauper population of Ireland.[11]

So much for the Union of 1801. Mere disapproval could not, of course, stop the Irish coming. The census of 1841, the first to ask about places of birth, showed 126,000 people living in Scotland who were natives of Ireland, nearly 5 per cent of the total population. The Irish famine then quickened the movement. At its height the *Glasgow Herald* reported that

> the streets of Glasgow are at present literally swarming with vagrants from the sister kingdom, and the misery which many of these poor creatures endure can scarcely be less than what they have fled or been driven from at home. Many of them are absolutely without the means of procuring lodging of even the meanest description, and are obliged consequently to make their bed frequently with a stone for a pillow.[12]

Of these Irish immigrants a certain proportion, varying from decade to decade, were Protestants from Ulster, often recrossing the water their Scots forefathers had crossed a century or two before. They had no trouble assimilating back into the local population. Indeed they brought cultural institutions with them, such as the Orange Order, which struck root in this new home. The cultural institutions might also acquire an economic function as conduits for fresh arrivals to find jobs, or the sons of established settlers to get apprenticeships. With the Irish Catholics it was a different matter. The cultural institutions they brought with them, churches where they practised their religion and schools where they taught it, offered a standing affront to Presbyterian Scots. In industrial terms many first arrived as strike-breakers, which did nothing to endear them to the natives they put out of work. And the community tended over time to retreat into a ghetto, once its growing numbers could sustain the necessary social structures. In other words, the Irish Catholics no longer even sought assimilation, rather the reverse. A medical investigator, Dr James Stark, observed the beginning of the process in the Old Town of Edinburgh:

> The first settlers inhabited the lowest descriptions of houses. Old byres, stables and outhouses, never previously considered habitable, were used by them as places of abode perhaps from the greater facilities such places afforded for raising a pig, which many of them continued to do in their new abodes. In proportion as these Irish increased, the Scottish artisans and labourers were driven from their neighbourhood, as they found it impossible to live with any comfort in the midst of the filth, vermin, quarrelling and fighting which constantly attended the abodes inhabited by these immigrants.[13]

The alien habits of the Irish then became even more offensive to the locals, as this report of a Glasgow Fair shows:

> The brawls appeared chiefly to be caused by hordes of low Irish who, so much accustomed to club law in their own unfortunate country, come over to Scotland and bring along with them all their barbarous customs and uncivilised propensities, which they practise so frequently and in such a way as threatens to ruin the youthful portion of our own intelligent and peaceable population in point of morality, as much as they are undermining and depressing them by lowering their wages . . . A pitched battle took place in the Green, at which several watchmen were disabled by the crowd, amounting to some hundreds, who assaulted them with bricks and stones.[14]

It was far from the only case where ill will between Presbyterian Scots and Catholic Irishmen spilled over into violence. The marching season in the summer always turned out to be the worst time. That was when Gourock saw a week of anti-Catholic riots in 1851. At Airdrie in 1854, the Protestant miners went on strike till all the Catholics in the local pits were sacked; the Catholics took revenge at the races, when they set about the Orangemen in their drinking tent and killed one of them. At Dumbarton in 1855, assaults on Catholics at William Denny's shipyard prompted him to dismiss the Irish working there. At Kelso in 1856, a mob burned down a Catholic chapel just opened. At Coatbridge in 1857 Catholics disrupted an Orange parade and even exchanged gunfire with the marchers till troops came over from Glasgow to restore order. At Paisley in 1859, the police urged Orangemen on to retaliate against Catholic miners who barracked their procession. At Coatbridge in 1863, a Catholic family beat up a Protestant family whose daughter had married their son. Shotts suffered a sectarian 'general riot' in 1865. In 1872 a Catholic miner murdered a Protestant miner during disturbances at Wishaw. At Govan in 1874 another 'general riot' followed an attack by Irish nationalists on an Orange lodge. In 1875 the Catholics of Partick publicly marked the centenary of the birth of Daniel O'Connell, drawing 'a fire of jeers and disparaging comments from a crowd of hostile onlookers'; fights broke out and continued all night, till the Riot Act was read from Partick Cross. Motherwell and Coatbridge witnessed similar events in 1883, with the climax of charges by mounted police into the sectarian mobs. On the emergence of the Old Firm, the two rival football clubs in Glasgow, Rangers founded for Protestants in 1872 and Celtic founded for Catholics in 1888, the occasional outbursts of sectarianism assumed a new and more durable pattern. It first showed itself at the Scottish cup final of 1909 when, after a drawn match, the crowd invaded the pitch, uprooted the goalposts, burned the nets and, outside Hampden Park, fought running battles in the streets well into the evening.[15]

In this form, sectarianism has survived to the present day but, before it became itself a criminal offence in 2011, it could already be prosecuted as a proxy form of racism. Crimes are better named by their names, and this usage of the term racism was sloppy. It would be hard to produce any sort of scientific evidence that people of Scottish or of Irish descent belong to different races; both clearly represent a mixture of races, like most other nationalities on the planet. By contrast, the nineteenth century did seek a scientific basis for racism, even if it never found one. In anticipation of it there was, all the same, a general confidence in the terminology of racism, which could be bandied about with none of the qualms felt today.

It may seem odd this should have arisen in a population composed of such obviously disparate elements, whether red-haired and large-limbed, small and dark or tall and blond. Even so, Scots had since the Wars of Independence or even further back regarded themselves as one nation. The literature of the fourteenth century already shows them elaborating myths about their common origins, not least so as to mark themselves off from the English. Various dubious sources were drawn on, but a myth that established itself as central was the fable of the elopement in the time of Moses of a Greek prince Gathelos with Scota, daughter of the Egyptian Pharaoh, whose descendants migrated by way of Spain and Ireland to Scotland. Among those descendants, Fergus MacFerquhard in 330 BC founded the Scottish monarchy – which, against the odds, had ever since just about held Scotland together. It was supposed to be after Gathelos that the Gaels had named themselves, and after Scota the Scots.[16]

So these were Celtic myths, unlike the Germanic myths of Hengist and Horsa and so on that supplied English equivalents. And they were not Lowland myths but Highland myths at that. Lowlanders, if they came over the centuries to deplore almost everything about Gaelic civilisation, yet had no misgivings in recalling it as the matrix of Scotland. Ordinary, everyday experience did not contradict the implied unity. When men and women married across the Highland line they bred not half-castes or misfits but more Scots. Migration across that line had been going on for ages, and it accelerated in the modern era. Names beginning with Mac would soon be commoner in the Lowlands than in the Highlands. The mingling of different stocks in Scotland produced various effects, yet racial change was hardly a useful definition of them.

This process of fusion went on unconsciously till the Enlightenment began to teach Scots to think in terms of race. The new thinking was to pose an unaccustomed problem for this eternally untidy, precarious and provisional nation. For a start it exploded all the cherished myths about the origins and nature of Scotland. In the seventeenth century intellectuals had still extolled their homeland in terms of those myths, but in the eighteenth century they came to view its entire previous history as barbarous, something it should be glad to have put behind it. After the Jacobite rebellions of 1715 and 1745 few Lowlanders, intellectual or otherwise, felt any regret for the consequent collapse of Gaelic civilisation, and its myths along with it.[17]

Yet soon – as soon as it no longer mattered – interest in Gaelic civilisation revived. The revival started up with the apparent rediscovery by James Macpherson in the 1760s of the works of the ancient bard, Ossian, firing a controversy that spread to the rest of Britain and on to Europe. Soon travellers were finding Highland scenery sublime rather than depressing. The ground was fertilised for the blossoming of tartanry that greeted the visit of King George IV to Edinburgh in 1822.[18] But while, in the course of the nineteenth century, obsession with this sort of Scottishness burgeoned, it never really turned nationalistic.[19] All it did was generate a romantic vision of Scottish culture, its former intellectual muscle turned to flab through glutinous sentimentality. By contrast, in parts of Europe, especially Eastern Europe, folklore did stimulate a nationalism no less romantic but in the end capable of producing political results, the eventual independence of old and new countries. In Scotland the nationalism got hopelessly bogged down in the romanticism. And the romanticism turned out to be quite consistent with British identity and imperial pride, if not affirmative of them. It posed in any event no threat to the Union of 1707.[20]

But with the development of scientific racism the Highland cult raised a new issue, of what race the Scots belonged to. Scientific racism was another of the Scottish Enlightenment's gifts to the world. This great movement of the mind launched intellectual enquiries of every kind, some leading forward to the established disciplines of our own day, others petering out in a dead end. Just as it gave birth to economics and sociology, so it bore such mis-shapen offspring as phrenology and scientific racism. In the latter case, that was because the enlightened philosophers had through European imperial expansion grown aware of the diversity of mankind. They sought to account for it as they sought to account for all the other phenomena they subjected to their intellectual enquiries, by seeking natural explanations and placing them in coherent contexts. The whole was the work of a wide variety of particular individuals, who might contribute to it in greater or lesser rigour. Indeed, the very same individual might contribute to it in greater or lesser rigour.

The philosopher David Hume, for example, once had this to say on the subject of race: 'I am apt to suspect the Negroes to be naturally inferior to the Whites. There scarcely ever was a civilized nation of that complexion, nor even any individual, eminent either in action or speculation. No ingenious manufactures amongst them, no arts, no sciences.'[21] For his incautious statement Hume has attracted the odium of today's politically correct. He put it forward only in a footnote, however, so it can hardly be regarded as the considered position of a profound thinker. In any case, no theory will ever be tested except by proposing hypotheses, all of which will finally be falsified except the right one. If Hume is condemned for proposing a wrong one, we give up hope of further scientific advance.

Another philosopher, Henry Home, Lord Kames, in his turn put forward racial hypotheses that benefited from greater deliberation and coherence but still turned out to be wrong. Kames took his stand as a polygenist: he held mankind was so diverse that God could not possibly have created it in a single act as a single race, after the fashion described by the Book of Genesis. Nor could alternative theories, of the environment or the climate, account in any systematic way for the different stages of development in which various races were to be found. Instead they must have been created, or have otherwise come into existence, in separate regions of the earth.[22]

These ideas did not remain confined in philosophical speculation but over time spread into other contexts. In the nineteenth century we find their literary traces, for example, among the works of Sir Walter Scott. The hybrid character of Scotland was in effect a notion underlying the whole series of Waverley Novels. In the course of it, Scott shows the ethnic, political and religious rough edges being smoothed down into the stable structure of the modern, polite and commercial nation. The contrast is drawn most sharply in *Rob Roy* (1817), set in the years soon after the Union of 1707 when half the country, the Highland half, remains barbaric. But already we see a new type of Scotsman, from one point of view not as admirable as past heroes yet from another point of view much more so, in Bailie Nicol Jarvie of Glasgow. He is a comic, even satirical, creation, a hypocritical Presbyterian decent at heart, at least decent enough to find senseless murder repugnant. The future of Scotland belongs to this prosaic Lowland capitalist, not to the fierce Highland warriors besetting him.[23]

Race then plays an explicit part in *Ivanhoe* (1819). It is Scott's first major work to turn from the relatively recent Scottish past to the remote medieval history that, more than anything, would win him his stellar reputation, at least in England, Europe and America. Still, in an allusive way it is as topically Scottish as a Waverley Novel proper. In it we are shown England a century after the subjugation of the Anglo-Saxons in the Norman Conquest. Their manners, law and language are being pushed aside as an alien force stamps itself on a new, hybrid nation still in the early stages of being formed. There is a folk-memory of what has been lost, but also a fruitful reaction as the conflicts produce a folk-hero, Robin Hood, whose name and fame will outlast all this grief. King Richard the Lionheart, when he at last reveals himself to his subjects, also directs them to the future: 'Before me kneels a nation divided – rise as one man, and that one, for England!'[24] Similarly, the perceptive reader may understand, Scots of the nineteenth century are being robbed of their heritage, yet they too can resist and overcome.

In real life Scott showed no less sympathy with the corresponding pre-
dicaments of the Irish. He went to Ireland in 1824 and felt enchanted: 'I
said their poverty was not exaggerated. Neither is their wit – nor their good
humour – nor their whimsical absurdity – nor their courage.' Here is how he
mused on the differences among the three kingdoms:

> While a Scotchman is thinking about the term day, or if easy on
> that subject about Hell in the next world, while an English man is
> making a little hell of his own in the present because his muffin
> is not well roasted, Pat's mind is always turned to fun and ridicule.
> They are terribly excitable to be sure and will murther you on slight
> suspicion and find out next day that it was all a mistake and that it
> was not yourself they meant to kill at all at all.[25]

Five years later, Scott exposed himself to a different Irish encounter. In
January 1829 he stood at a window in Edinburgh to watch the public hanging
of William Burke, the mass murderer who with his pardoned accomplice,
William Hare, had killed 16 people in the poverty-stricken quarter of the
West Port. Burke and Hare were otherwise typical Irish immigrants. They
had come over to find work and probably met while labouring as navvies
on the Union Canal. They at length fetched up in the capital's slums where
they needed ingenuity as well as strength to survive. They showed both.
Almost within a stone's throw of the West Port stood the university, one
of the world's great centres of medical research, with its constant demand
for corpses to dissect. 'Resurrection men', or body-snatchers, supplied the
demand by digging the dead up fresh from their graves. They were then
flogged to the surgeons, who paid well and asked no questions. Today
older churchyards in Edinburgh still have the watch-houses built to deter
this ghoulish enterprise. Yet it was hard to suppress while the supply met
a demand. It occurred to Burke and Hare that they might exploit the market without going to all the bother of exhumation. Instead they turned
to murder.[26]

The best sales outlet for Burke and Hare was the private medical school run
by Dr Robert Knox. He, the most popular lecturer in the city, attracted hundreds to his classes. With a blasted eye and satanic smile, he made an unlikely
ladies' man or object of devotion to his pupils. Yet he was both: women fell
for him still faster than the male students who found him considerate of
them, eloquent at the rostrum and eager to impart his mastery of medical
advance worldwide. For the sake of his business, he too needed the regular

flow of fresh corpses. When Burke and Hare finally got found out, it was because of one such discovered in Knox's possession. So the whole squalid business came to light. As most of the evidence had vanished, however, the case against Burke and Hare remained far from cast-iron. The prosecution solved the problem by persuading Hare to turn king's evidence in return for his life. Burke could then do nothing but confess. His own body went to the surgeons for dissection, and his skeleton can be viewed today at the University of Edinburgh. Hare fled the country after the trial. People shook their heads at the depravity of these inferior Irish. Despite a huge outcry, and the insults of the mob that smashed the windows of his house at Newington, Knox the Scotsman escaped prosecution.[27]

Scott could not suppress a macabre fascination with all this. But when he went back – in a carriage – to the streets of the Old Town he had trodden carefree as a student, he was filled with horror and shame. The thought struck him that, if people of his sort had stayed on living there, it might never have sunk so low. And he wrote: 'I am no great believer in the extreme degree of improvement to be derived from the advancement of science; for every pursuit of that nature tends, when pushed to a certain extent, to harden the heart, and render the philosopher reckless of everything save the objects of his own pursuit; all equilibrium in the character is destroyed.'[28] Is this the obituary of the Enlightenment?

It would have been natural to abuse the Irish, as many did, but not Scott. On getting home from the execution he recorded: 'The mob which was immense demanded Knox and Hare but though greedy for more victims received with shouts the solitary wretch who found his way to the gallows out of five or six who seem not less guilty than he.' A couple of days later he noted that 'the corpse of the murderer Burke is now lying in state at the College in the anatomical class and all the world flock to see him. Who is he says that we are not ill to please in our objects of curiosity? The strange means by which the wretch made money are scarce more disgusting than the eager curiosity with which the public have licked up all the carrion details of this business.' Three months later Scott felt utterly appalled to get 'a letter from one David Paterson, a fellow who was Dr Knox's jackal for buying murdered bodies, suggesting that I should write on the subject of Burke and Hare and offering me his invaluable collection of anecdotes.' Scott never deigned to reply. But he added in his journal: 'The scoundrel has been the companion and patron of such atrocious murderers and kidnappers and he has the impudence to write to any decent man.'[29] In these passages Knox and Paterson come out as much villains of the piece as Burke and Hare. Or we can say the Scots come out as much villains of the piece as the Irish.

🌸

Anyway there was no chance Knox could continue to practise medicine in Edinburgh; finally his contribution to his age proved to be of a quite different order. Now he earned a living from medical journalism, with supplements to his income from lectures and occasional books: *Fish and Fishing in the Lone Glens of Scotland* (1854) sold best. But his favourite subject was race.[30] His ideas on the subject arose out of a lifetime's activity and reflection, not only in Edinburgh but also in Cape Town, where he had earlier served as a military surgeon, and in Paris, where he had attended the medical schools and learned from the pioneering anatomists who lectured there, especially Georges Cuvier. Cuvier anticipated the theory of evolution in demonstrating the history of physical structure in human beings, from the origins they had in common with other creatures to the particular frame and functions of their own species.

Knox sought to contribute to the idea of order in nature that inspired much of this contemporary scientific work, and to do so in the particular matter of the physical characteristics marking out one race from another. He held that in each case this external form gave clues to the interior nature, as well as being connected to the external environment and its history. Every race should be seen as a unique product of a particular set of influences, apart from which it could not survive: therefore colonialism, for example, was a huge error. At the same time the varying demands on the races and their degree of success in meeting them generated a hierarchy. At the top stood the Saxon (Knox's word). This was the argument he offered in his book, *The Races of Men* (1850). It came to the conclusion that race was 'everything',[31] the decisive factor for all humanity. Its like would not be seen again till the twentieth century.

Wrong as Knox's theories were, he had worked hard at refining and sub-stantiating them before presenting his case to the public supported by wide reference and his own great confidence in them. Brother Scots felt not so sure, for the question where they might be rated in Knox's or any other hierarchy was ticklish. It would be nice to think theirs would be a high position, but how could they be certain? Nobody seems to have posited that the Scots might be superior to the English (not in print, anyway). Still, the English plainly stood somewhere around the top of the tree (at least according to those Englishmen who thought about it), along with some related nationalities.

The Celts, more specifically the Irish, stood just as plainly lower down: their physical differences from Englishmen might be slight, but the most cursory examination would expose their feckless personal habits, their lack of industry, their addiction to drink and merriment, their aversion from order and hygiene, their violence and unreason, their inability to create or sustain political institutions and so on. Again, even within the narrower frame of the British Isles, where did the Scots stand in comparison? At their best, in social discipline and intellectual achievement, they matched not just the English but any nation. At least that was true of the Lowlanders. Yet beyond the Highland line – well, there the Scots bore an unmistakable resemblance to the Irish, and the defeat of Gaelic civilisation in the eighteenth century, followed by its headlong descent towards extinction in the nineteenth century, underlined the inferior nature of this disquieting local variant.[32]

A further problem then arose for brother Scots: if they were one nation, could they be two races? It seemed they might be so, and the immense achievements of Lowland Scotland, coinciding with the onset of terminal decline in Highland Scotland, seemed to confirm the impression. It was nothing new: ever since the Middle Ages, Lowlanders had considered themselves superior to Highlanders. Come to that, Highlanders had considered themselves superior to Lowlanders. But the verdict of history lay now beyond dispute.[33]

The problem struck Knox himself, and he set out in *The Races of Men* to investigate it. He did not, to be sure, venture beyond the Grampian Mountains: 'It was here I first saw the true Celt: time nor circumstances have altered him from the remotest period . . . Civilisation but modifies, education affects little; his religious formula is the result of his race; his morals, actions, feelings, greatnesses and littlenesses flow distinctly and surely from his physical structure; that structure which seems not to have altered since the commencement of recorded time.'[34] So what did Knox think he had found?

> War is the game for which the Celt is made. Herein is the forte of his physical and mental character; in stature and weight, as a race, inferior to the Saxon; limbs muscular and vigorous; torso and arms seldom attaining any very large development – hence the extreme rarity of athletae amongst the race; hands, broad; fingers, squared at the points; step, elastic and springy; in muscular energy and rapidity of action, surpassing all other European races . . . Inventive, imaginative, he leads the fashions all over the civilised world. Most new inventions and discoveries in the arts may be traced to him; they are then appropriated by the Saxon race, who apply them to useful purposes.[35]

It may also be reassuring to the politically correct of today to note that Knox concluded Celts were not racists: 'The Celt has not that antipathy to the dark races which so peculiarly characterises the Saxon.'[36]

In any event Knox entertained no doubt that 'the Caledonian Celt of Scotland appears a race as distinct from the Lowland Saxon of the same country as he can possibly be: as negro from American; Hottentot from Caffre; Esquimaux from Saxon'.[37] If the two types of Scot had now started to mix, it was in defiance of the lessons of the past: 'I cannot find any era in history when the Celtic races occupied the Lowlands of England and of Scotland.'[38] This was a matter not merely of speculation but also of practical importance to Scotland, because 'the Celt does not understand what we Saxons mean by independence'.[39] It might have been objected there was the small matter of 1745, when to all appearances the clans had risen behind Prince Charles Edward Stewart in order to fight for Scottish independence, but in Knox's estimation that amounted only to a 'Celtic rebellion of Scotland', not 'a national rebellion of Scotland against England'.[40] The proper conclusion to draw was that nationalism in a hybrid nation such as Scotland made for a contradiction in terms.

As for the Lowland Scots, Knox believed they, too, formed part of a Saxon race marked by 'inordinate self-esteem ... love of independence, which makes them dislike the proximity of a neighbour [and] hatred for dynasties and governments'. All this produced 'democrats by their nature, the only democrats on the earth, the only race which truly comprehends the meaning of the word liberty'. Notable also were some moral qualities vital for the modern world: 'industrious beyond all other races, a lover of labour for labour's sake ... the Saxon cares not its amount if it be but profitable; large-handed, mechanical, a lover of order, of punctuality in business, of neatness and cleanliness. In these qualities no race approaches him.'[41] Saxons were further distinguished by physique: 'a tall, powerful, athletic race of men; the strongest, as a race, on the face of the earth. They have fair hair, with blue eyes, and so fair a complexion, that they may almost be considered the only absolutely fair race on the face of the earth'. If this comes across as a somewhat oversimplified portrait of the Lowlander, we should note how Knox used the term Saxon almost interchangeably with the term Scandinavian, in reference to a pure Nordic race to be distinguished also from the Germans, who were a mixed race and lived in central Europe, not round the North Sea like the Saxons or Scandinavians. These he again demarcated from the modern English too, for 'South England is mainly occupied by a Belgian race, and were it not for the centralisation of London, it is by no means improbable that much of the true Saxon blood would have disappeared from south Britain, by that physiological law which extinguishes mixed races . . . and causes the originally more numerous one to predominate.'[42]

⊛

It all seems crazy stuff. Yet it may start to fall into place if we see in Knox a man obscurely articulating a sober Lowland identity that was, like the gaudy Highland identity, both cause and effect in the debility of Scottish nationalism. Other nations had no problem of this kind. The classical nationalisms in contemporary Europe formed part of a modern movement: at their core stood longings for liberty, democracy and progress, with the past of each people mainly useful for adding colour and inspiring commitment. Knox's shining Saxon exemplar included the concept of free and responsible government, as supplied by the English. Yet in a United Kingdom other contributions were welcome – and a notable one came from the Lowland Scots in their calm, drive, sense and thrift. These egalitarian, hard-working folk were unionists too, so clearly the rest of the aspirations they might have had in common with European nationalists did not also entail what today we call separatism. Knox's racialist theories made this paradox easier to understand: Scotland, if capable of giving expression to those modern ideals, was still not actually a nation in the way of the Czechs or Poles, just because of the racial division at its heart. In his own words, 'as a Saxon, I abhor all dynasties, monarchies and bayonet governments, but this latter seems to be the only one suitable for the Celtic man.'[43] The Union, it followed, was the sole context in which Scotland's centrifugal forces could be held in bounds.

All things are relative, and in some ways Knox's opinions, however extreme they appear now, could actually sound quite mild by the standards of their time. They were almost liberal when placed alongside, for example, those of Thomas Carlyle, the secular Presbyterian prophet from Ecclefechan in deepest Dumfriesshire. Carlyle had somehow come to fear and loathe the Celts so much that he would not mind if they all starved to death. In his tract on *Chartism* (1840) he grouched that 'crowds of miserable Irish darken all our towns. The wild Milesian features, looking false ingenuity, restlessness, unreason, misery and mockery, salute you on all highways and byways . . . The time has come when the Irish population must either be improved a little, or else exterminated.'[44] To uncover a contrary example of superiority, Carlyle in his turn looked to a kind of community of race round the North Sea:

From the Humber to the Forth, still more from the Tyne to the Forth, I find no real distinction at all, – except what John Knox introduced: it is all Scotland Scotch in features of face, in character, in dialect of speech ... They are all Danes, these people, stalwart Normans: terrible Sea-Kings are now terrible Drainers of Morasses, terrible spinners of yarn, coal-borers, removers of mountains; 'a people terrible from the beginning'. The windy Celts of Galloway meet us, not many miles from this, on the edge of Nithsdale: is it not a considerable blessing to have escaped being born a Celt?[45]

Who would ever have guessed that neat Nithsdale nurtured such fizzing frictions? But evidently it had been a crucible for the current global achievements of 'our widely diffused Teutonic clay'.[46]

❁

So relatively measured could Knox's views appear that they soon found some place even in the thinking of official Scotland. The registrar-general, William Pitt Dundas, scion of the family that had ruled the country right through the Enlightenment, did not hesitate to use explicit racialist language when he drew up his official report on the Scottish census of 1871. He set off: 'All the portion of Scotland which we have described as the Lowlands, with the single exception of the county of Caithness, may be described as being inhabited by that mixed race to which the term Anglo-Saxon is now generally applied. This is an energetic race, springing from a mixture of all the various nations which have invaded the country and settled among its original inhabitants.' In Dundas's estimation not only the Germanic tribes that had come over during the barbarian invasions but also the descendants of the Romans and of the Normans should be counted among the Anglo-Saxons so defined. But then there was a second element: 'The whole of what we have described as the Highland portion of Scotland, on the other hand, has as its leading inhabitants a nearly pure Celtic race, still retaining their ancient language, and showing in their configuration and general character the peculiarities of that race.' That did not exhaust the riches of the Scottish racial stocks: 'A race, however, of nearly pure Norsemen, originally from Norway and Sweden, now constitute the majority of the inhabitants of the islands of Orkney and Shetland, of the county of Caithness, and of a great many of the fishing villages on the northern and eastern coasts of Scotland, down even to the fishing villages of Buckie and Newhaven in the Firth of Forth.'

The fertile racial mixture had been to the benefit of Scotland in all past ages, Dundas reckoned, but of late there had come an undesirable change:

Till the year 1820 these were the three main races in Scotland, but during that year an invasion or immigration of the Irish race began, which slowly increased till it attained enormous dimensions after 1840, when the railways began to be constructed over the country. This invasion of Irish is likely to produce far more serious effects on the population of Scotland than even the invasions of the warlike hordes of Saxons, Danes or Norsemen. Already, in many of our towns, do the persons born in Ireland constitute from 5 to 13 per cent of the population; and if we include their children, born in this country, from 10 to 30 per cent of the population of these towns consist of the Irish Celtic race. The immigration of such a body of labourers of the lowest class, with scarcely any education, cannot but have the most prejudicial effect on the population. As yet the great body of these Irish do not seem to have improved by their residence among us; and it is quite certain that the native Scot who has associated with them has most certainly deteriorated. It is painful to contemplate what may be the ultimate effect of this immigration on the morals and habits of the people, and on the future prospects of this country.[47]

Racialist ideas about Scotland proved durable. Halford Mackinder, academic geographer and MP for Glasgow Camlachie from 1910, restated them in fresh form for a new century. We need not doubt which section of his electorate gave him his majority at Camlachie. He told the House of Commons in 1912 that there were 'only two courses open with regard to Ireland. We can pass legislation which will give prosperity and peace to Ireland, or we can hand Ireland over to the Irish.'[48] He had in 1902 published *Britain and the British Seas,* conceived as the inaugural work of a novel discipline of geomorphology, which aimed 'to present a picture of the physical features and conditions of a very definite natural region, and to trace their influence upon the human societies dwelling within it'.[49] In this Atlantic archipelago the main distinction was not between north and south but between east and west, with one littoral populated from Caithness to Kent by blond Teutons and the other littoral from Kintail to Cornwall by swarthy Celts. The proper test should be 'nigrescence' (by which Mackinder meant colour of hair). So the Lowland Scots stood closer to the English than to the Highland Scots. Indeed on either side of the River Tweed, the line along which the old Northumbria had been partitioned in 1018, the physical type and language of the people remained the same even yet. In the course of the twentieth century the sort of racialist theories propounded by Mackinder would be tested to destruction.[50]

❋

Still, the Lowland identity those theories posited, though today largely lost from view, in its time exerted more effect on Scottish political and intellectual culture than the phoney Highland tradition. In politics, it allowed Scots a share in England's Anglo-Saxon constitutionalism. If Lowlanders had started off as Saxons, then back at the beginning they must have possessed the ancient constitution and the common law too (it was convenient that all the records of the Northumbrian kingdom had been lost). In that case the independence of Scotland, vindicated in 1314 and defended right till 1707, should be seen as admittedly heroic yet in the end a big mistake. Now, in the politics and economics of the Victorian Union, the manifest destiny of two kindred peoples, the Lowland Scots and the English, would be realised. They could rediscover their common racial roots and mark out their difference from the wanton, workshy, worthless Celts.[51] This Lowland identity looked rather to its place in Britain and the Empire. Let Celts, Highland or Irish, fill the fetid emigrant ships and go to hew wood or draw water in the colonies. Meanwhile, at the centre or on high, it was for Lowland Scots to make this a British rather than merely an English Empire.

In the matter of race the Scottish Enlightenment had in the end fouled its own nest. Here in the nation that invented racialism, it brought the bizarre result of theorising nationhood away: Scotland was deconstructed so as to take out the nation and leave the races. Of course, other nations of the United Kingdom could be subjected to the same procedure. The right way forward was to integrate them all in Union and Empire, ready for a greater mission to the world. Inside Scotland, however, it left a legacy of confusion, in particular a sense that the Highland expression of Scottish identity made a laughable caricature of the Lowland reality. This was not soil in which nationalism could grow and thrive, at least not for a long time.

❋

Even at this stage it might still have been possible to celebrate the alternative of Scotland as racial mixture, since little could be done to bridge the gap between Lowlands and Highlands. If anything, Celtic reaction and revival

211

widened it. Despite their retreating language, embattled culture and gloomy religion, the Gaels now came through the long era of contempt that to others had justified their persecution or even extermination. But the change of attitude needed to start elsewhere, in Germany rather than in Scotland. The great philologists Franz Bopp, August Schleicher and Karl Brugmann were successfully elaborating the theory of the Indo-European languages, namely that they all – Germanic, Romance, Slavic, Baltic, Iranian and Indian along with Celtic – belonged to one linguistic family, the Indo-European or Aryan family, with roots in prehistoric Central Asia. It was again Germans, Kuno Meyer and Ludwig Christian Stern, that founded in 1897 the first learned journal of Celtic studies, the *Zeitschrift für celtische Philologie*, still going strong today. Given this novel academic status it became hard to insist, in the contemporary intellectual paradigm tending to identify language, race and culture, that there was anything inherently inferior about the Celtic branch of the linguistic family. It was after all kin to others of supreme achievement, notably the Latin and the Greek branches. Classical literature contained many references to the Celts: Plato said they were drunks, Aristotle said they were brave, if senselessly so; Livy found them moved by violent passions, Tacitus thought, of the Caledonians in particular, they were in their love of liberty superior to the corrupt Romans.[52]

This was all grist to the mill of John Stuart Blackie, professor of Greek at the University of Aberdeen and then at the University of Edinburgh. Kilts already enlivened military parades and other ceremonial occasions, but he brightened the mean Lowland streets by wearing the garb of old Gaul every day as he strode on his way to instruct the nation's youth. The ribaldry he met did not bother him, for in his own mind he was demonstrating the difference between 'Celtic fire and Saxon solidity'. In the past the 'Saxo-Norman elements were . . . happily infused into the original Celtic blood of the Scottish people'.[53] But now it was his part to proclaim the proud pedigree of the Gael: 'The Gaelic language is one of the oldest and least mongrel types of the great Aryan family of speech, which has entered so largely into history as the organ of the highest forms of human civilisation both in the East and West.'[54] Blackie was an early Scottish nationalist, the inaugural chairman of the Scottish Home Rule Association and a critic of the anglicised centralism now 'obliterating local types and establishing a uniform monotony of superficial polish'. He championed the crofters, and he led the campaign for endowment of a chair of Celtic at Edinburgh.[55] In this, his great coup was to get a subscription from Queen Victoria herself. The appeal triumphantly succeeded and, at the foundation of the chair in 1882, it was the best endowed in the university.

First to occupy the Celtic chair was Donald Mackinnon, who originally came from Colonsay but had spent much of his career as clerk to the school board of Edinburgh. This prosaic post stifled the poetic side of his character, which from the chair could at last take wing. In his inaugural lecture he paused to commend the Celts as 'a branch of the great Indo-European race', but then went on in fulsome praise of the Gael in particular 'as the child of music and song' who, for all his faults and handicaps 'has attempted, not unsuccessfully, to live not the day and the hour alone but, in a true sense, to live the life of the spirit!' Celts should never be underestimated just because they had been pushed to the edge of Europe, for 'even in those countries from which the language and name have disappeared, their blood and genius remain, shaping the destiny and civilisation of these nations in a thousand ways.'[56] The establishment of the chair was the prelude to a notable era of Gaelic scholarship, bearing fruit also in Alexander Cameron's *Reliquiae Celticae* (1892–94), Alexander Carmichael's *Carmina Gadelica* (1900) and William Sharp's *Lyra Celtica* (1896). In the introduction to this collection of song, Sharp insisted that

> the apparition of this passing race is no more than the fulfilment of a glorious resurrection before our very eyes. For the genius of the Celtic race stands out now with averted torch, and the light of it is a glory before the eyes, and the flame of it is blown into the hearts of a mightier conquering people. The Celt falls, but his spirit rises in the heart and the brain of the Anglo-Celtic peoples, with whom are the destinies of the generations to come.[57]

These were all brave words, but in practice it would remain difficult to transmit the genuine achievements of the new Gaelic scholarship into the wider culture of Scotland – not, at least, without sacrificing it to the vulgarities of the Highland cult. Still, there were people who did try to bridge the gap, usually because they already straddled the two cultures. John Francis Campbell of Islay, Iain Òg Ile, was schooled like much of the Campbell aristocracy at Eton College and then enjoyed an agreeable career as secretary to the Commissioners for Northern Lighthouses, one of his duties being to organise the cruises they took in an official yacht every summer round their watery domain. The trips also served his own scholarly passion for collecting examples of Gaelic oral culture, which he published in the four volumes of

Popular Tales of the West Highlands (1860–62). Many were Fenian tales, derived from the poetic lays of Finn MacCool, Deirdre and Ossian (so vindicating James Macpherson's claims for their authenticity 100 years too late). Campbell was struck by the many survivals among them of motifs found in oral cultures elsewhere. He felt convinced these examples would be of use 'in striving to trace out the origins of races, as philologists use words to trace language, as geologists class rocks by shells and bones which they contain, and as natural philosophers use fairy-eggs in tracing the Gulf Stream'.[58]

Fairies formed indeed one of the familiar motifs, and the most fascinating of all to Andrew Lang, a man of many cultural talents who somehow never used them to the full. Poet, novelist, critic and anthropologist, he also devoted enormous energy to publishing a dozen hefty tomes of fairy tales between 1889 and 1910. He collected them from all over the world and included Scottish examples such as 'The Rider of Grianaig', recorded from a lame carrier of Bowmore on Islay, or 'Ian Direach and the Blue Falcon', recorded from a quarryman at Roseneath on Gare Loch.[59] Lang added also to the scientific literature in this field. In his *Myth, Ritual and Religion* (1887) he explained the irrational elements of mythology as survivals from more primitive narratives. His *Making of Religion* (1898) dwelt on the existence of spiritual ideas among races conventionally defined as savage, research that he continued in his *Social Origins* (1903). He was an incredibly prolific writer who, however, spread himself a little too thin for definitive achievement in any particular topic. And so he remains best remembered for his work on fairies.

Fairies finally featured in another rich scholarly career, that of William Craigie, who published a collection of popular tales about them in 1914. But it was just a brief digression from his lifelong devotion to linguistic science, which gave him a mastery of most Germanic tongues, especially the Scandinavian ones, of the classics and of Gaelic. To the inaugural number in 1897 of the *Zeitschrift für celtische Philologie* he contributed an article on Gaelic loan-words in Icelandic.[60] His untiring researches in the language and history of Iceland made him a revered figure there, but his own nation owes him the deepest debt as originator of one of its great works of modern scholarship, the *Dictionary of the Older Scottish Tongue* (1937–2002). His pupil, collaborator and successor as editor, A.J. Aitken, paid tribute to the 'quietly dignified, rather reserved, yet unfailingly kindly and companionable personality of this tiny Scotsman, with his modest tastes and tidy habits, and his fellow-feeling for simple folk and small nations'.[61] It is worth recalling, too, that without quarrying in that dictionary Hugh MacDiarmid would never have become the Lallans makar he was. And so a meandering tributary of Gaelic culture at last entered the carrying stream of the modern Scottish literary renaissance, to help in determining much that has happened since and perhaps much that may yet happen to Scotland in the twenty-first century.

The interest in race aroused by the Enlightenment led down to the deepest levels of European civilisation and to the springs of its religion and philosophy. One spring, it turned out, lay in Celtic literary and artistic sensibility. But for the workaday world of Victorian Scotland all this reinforced Lowland prejudice against the mystical, emotional Gael fallen out of step with the march of progress, disconnected from modern industrial and imperial realities.[62] Well-meant political action for the Highlands only intensified the prejudice: the Crofters' Act of 1886 confined the Gaels in a native reservation where time stood still, confirming the racist slur that they were unfit for anything but planting potatoes and shearing sheep.

As the Highland identity turned also into the Highland problem (a new problem of inertia rather than the old one of anarchy), it exaggerated the disunity that made Scots such lukewarm or confused nationalists. Elsewhere in Europe, leaders like the Czech, Tomáš Masaryk, or the Pole, Józef Piłsudski, never needed to worry about the united patriotic consciousness of the peoples they led to freedom.[63] It had been shaped out of a century and more not only of struggle but also of intellectual endeavour directed towards national rebirth. This potent brew of folklore, linguistic particularism and tenacious popular memory (embellished by scholarship as the need arose) had brought cultural redress of political subordination. It could just not be done in Scotland.

Scottish national feeling never vanished. But it failed to overcome the perplexity or ambivalence about who and what the Scots were, and what they should do about who they were. Without convincing groundwork, whether in science, history or politics, no robust popular nationalism could be created, only a puzzled, even embarrassed, intellectual and emotional patchwork. It was rather Britain – or at least its heartland of England and Lowland Scotland – that supplied communal loyalties more coherent and so, in the real world, more important to Scots. They made the Lowlanders equals of the English and they identified Scotland with a greater imperial destiny. Yet inevitably they undermined the common nationhood of Lowlander and Gael, to leave a country unsure of its identity and of its destiny.[64]

9

Sex: 'The walls of prejudice'

On 8 August 1848, Frédéric Chopin woke up in unfamiliar surroundings at Calder House, a stately home a dozen miles west of Edinburgh. He was in poor health – in fact, he would be dead little more than a year later – but now, two days after an exhausting journey of twelve hours by train from London, a good night's sleep had refreshed him. A Broadwood piano stood in his bedroom, and perhaps he tinkled an Étude or two while waiting for his breakfast to be brought up (that was how they did things at Calder House). If not, he could look out the window: 'It is an old manor enclosed by an enormous park of ancient trees; you can see only lawns, trees, mountains and sky. The walls are eight feet thick; there are galleries on all sides, dark corridors with endless numbers of ancestral portraits, of various colours, some Scottish, some in armour, some in robes; nothing lacking for the imagination.'[1]

Calder House was the seat of James Sandilands, Lord Torphichen, an old salt who had spent most of his life as a sea captain in the East India Company. Now he dwelt in prosperous, sociable retirement amid the rolling Lothian countryside. He had a much younger sister-in-law, Jane Stirling, who was a pupil of Chopin in Paris: hence the composer's invitation to Scotland. 'In the evenings', he wrote to his family in Poland, 'I play Scottish songs for the old lord, who hums the tune with me, poor fellow, and expresses his feelings to me in French as best he can. Though everyone in high society speaks French, especially the ladies, the general conversation is mostly in English, and I then regret that I don't know the language.' It became more of a trial when, after dinner each night, the household followed the custom of having the ladies withdraw and leave the gentlemen to their whisky and cigars: 'One has to sit two hours at table with the men, look at them talking and listen to them drinking. I am bored to death. I am thinking of one thing and they of another, in spite of all their courtesy and French remarks at the table.'[2]

The talk could get pretty tedious otherwise too: 'Here it's nothing but cousins of great families and great names that no one on the continent has ever heard of. Conversation is always entirely genealogical, like the gospels; who begat whom, and he begat, and he begat, and he begat, and so on for two pages till you come to Jesus.' Chopin knew his hosts were doing their best, but they found little in common with a lonely, homesick invalid: 'They are dear people, kind and very considerate of me. There are a whole lot of ladies, seventy- to eighty-year old lords, but no young folk; they are all out shooting. One can't get out of doors, because it has been raining and blowing for several days.' Chopin at least got to know the vagaries of a Scottish summer.[3]

Jane Stirling returned with Chopin to Paris in November. A wealthy woman, she could do much more for him than pay for the lessons he gave her on the piano. She had already helped him to assemble seven bound volumes of the French editions of his works. She became in effect his secretary, agent and manager. Chopin felt so grateful that he dedicated to her his two Nocturnes, opus 55. While he never married, he needed a woman in his life. For ten years he had been the lover of one of France's *grandes horizontales*, George Sand, a trouser-suited, cigar-smoking novelist who also numbered among her conquests the politician Louis Blanc, the writers Prosper Mérimée and Alfred de Musset, not to mention the actress Marie Dorval. Yet in the end George Sand walked out on Chopin. So it had been Jane Stirling that arranged all the details of the last concert he ever gave in Paris in February 1848. The concluding piece in the programme was his Barcarole in F-sharp major, but he felt too exhausted to complete the final section. After managing to stagger unaided to his dressing room, he collapsed in Jane Stirling's arms. Five days later, yet another French revolution broke out. So long as it lasted – and it lasted most of the year – there could be no more work or income in Paris for composers, pianists or even music teachers. This was why Jane Stirling suggested the visit to Britain, to Scotland in particular. Once they got back to France, she tended him faithfully during his final months, at the end taking charge of his funeral and effects. It was all very touching, yet it seems unlikely they ever became lovers. He told others she bored him; as for her, a noble Scots lady had her standards.[4]

❈

New woman as she became familiar in the twentieth century might already have made her presence felt in the Paris of the 1840s, but not in contemporary

Scotland.[5] Of course there, as in practically all countries in practically all ages, it had been possible for a daughter of the aristocracy to break through the conventional barriers holding the second sex in subjection to the first. But she needed to be flamboyant; there was little point otherwise.

One Scottish example about the turn of the nineteenth century had been Elizabeth, Countess of Sutherland. Orphaned as a baby, she secured her ancient feudal inheritance, with its million bleak acres, only after a long legal dispute about the validity of female succession, finally resolved in the House of Lords. She was then a good match for her English husband, the Marquess of Stafford, who in 1833 would be granted the dukedom of Sutherland in his own right in recognition of his standing as the richest British subject of his day. 'For that he was dull I think there can be little doubt,' wrote a relation, and it was his wife's beauty and vivacity that made her the driving force in the marriage. The same held true of their social and economic schemes that sought, for good or ill, to enhance the united patrimony by applying revenues from the English half to development of the Scottish half.[6]

The early marriage of this heir and heiress had turned them into celebrities in London. But it still came as a surprise when in 1790 the husband, aged only 32, was appointed ambassador to a Paris racked by revolution, a sensitive posting for a man with no diplomatic experience. He and his wife never hid their sympathies. The countess befriended Queen Marie Antoinette, and her son played with the Dauphin; she sent them clothes after they were imprisoned. The embassy had to be withdrawn as war between Britain and France loomed. The ambassador and his lady returned to a round of pleasures, till in 1803 he came into his title and properties. Now they had the capital they needed for their plans in the north.[7]

The countess returned as a stranger to Sutherland. It was an 'object of curiosity' to her, 'quite a wild corner inhabited by an infinite multitude roaming at large in the old way, despising all barriers and regulations, and firmly believing in witchcraft so much so that the porters durst not send away two old women who were plaguing us one day, believing them to be witches.' But the economic possibilities roused even her husband from his habitual torpor: 'We travelled in wind and snow through the Highlands and met Lord Stafford highly pleased with his journey and the improvements he saw in every part of Scotland, for he is seized as much as I am with the rage of improvements.' He was to spend £250,000 on her lands, £100 million at today's prices: a hefty dose of regional aid by any standards.[8]

Yet it all led to the clearances in Sutherland. Patrick Sellar, a lawyer from Moray engaged by the estate, carried out the most notorious of them. The countess never liked him, and his conduct confirmed her dislike: 'The more I hear and see of Sellar the more I am convinced he is not fit to be trusted further than he is at present. He is so exceedingly greedy and harsh with the people, there are very heavy complaints against him from Strathnaver.' When hostile reports appeared in the press, she sent out to her peers a woebegone apology:

> We have lately been much attacked in the newspapers by a few malicious writers who have long assailed us on every occasion. What it states is most perfectly unjust and unfounded, as I am convinced from the facts I am acquainted with, and I venture to trouble you with the enclosed . . . If you meet with discussions on the subject in society, I shall be glad if you will show this statement to anyone who may interest him or herself on the subject.[9]

While some of the countess's contemporaries did listen with a reasonable degree of sympathy to her plea, history has stopped its ears.

Here was an example of *noblesse oblige* gone wrong, but examples did exist of its going right. One lay in the life and work of Ishbel Hamilton-Gordon, Lady Aberdeen. She was by the standards of her day a feminist and became the inaugural president of the International Council of Women founded in Washington DC in 1893. She held this office till 1936, while the council greatly expanded its work yet remained cautious on such contentious issues as the electoral franchise. Meanwhile Lord Aberdeen followed a typical great nobleman's official career, notably as Governor General of Canada. His wife organised his state dinners, which for entertainment featured *tableaux vivants* illustrating the history of the country – Leif Ericsson's arrival with the Vikings, John Cabot's voyage of exploration, Jacques Cartier's discovery of the St Lawrence River, the British capture of Quebec and so on. Members of the Aberdeen family, their staff and their guests, clad in period costume, would pose in striking postures to the thunderous applause of the assembled company, some of whom might have killed for an invitation to these high-lights of the winter's social season in snowy Ottawa.

While the Aberdeens loved travel, they kept in touch with home. In retire-ment, they settled back into domestic bliss at their seat of Haddo House, where she passed the time writing couthy books, *We Twa*, (1925), and *More Cracks with We Twa* (1929 – the title is, alas, ungrammatical in Scots), finally *The Musings of a Scottish Granny* (1936).[10] Another enthusiasm was Onward and Upward, an association she founded to bring out the best in girls working on the land in the north-east. They always had an alternative in the bright lights of Aberdeen, where many went into domestic service. This both deprived agriculture of part of its workforce and exposed the lassies to nameless dangers. Onward and Upward was meant to develop their range of rustic interests so they would not want to quit the byres and bothies. It somewhat misread the local social situation. The region's rate of illegitimate births had long been high because its people took premarital sex for granted, often in the form of 'bundling' in a barn, to the alarm of those who worried about such things. So the girls would not necessarily have maintained Victorian morality even by staying down on the farm.[11] One real peril in the city was that, if things did not work out for them there, they might fall back on an age-old resort for needy single Scotswomen of the lower orders and take to prostitution. Lady Aberdeen targeted this too, not only in Aberdeen but also in London where, to the horror of her family, she aided William Gladstone in his personal forays to save fallen women.

On a different plane, women's suffrage also lay close to Lady Aberdeen's heart, though she remained too conscious of her dignity to condone the suffragettes' stunts. Of greater prominence in their movement was Lady Frances Balfour, daughter of the Liberal magnate, the ninth Duke of Argyll, and also granddaughter of the Countess of Sutherland. Lady Frances herself married Eustace Balfour, the alcoholic, ne'er-do-well nephew of the Marquess of Salisbury, the Conservative who was Queen Victoria's last Prime Minister, as well as the elder brother of Arthur Balfour, who succeeded his uncle at No. 10 Downing Street. Lady Frances did not lack high connections, then. Like many young ladies of her class she never went to school. Instead she educated herself by conversations over dinner with statesmen, whose company she preferred to that of lesser mortals.

Lady Frances Balfour did not, however, grow up to be an especially nice person. A devout Christian, and regular attender at the General Assembly of the Church of Scotland, she was puritanical even by its standards. She refused to go to the theatre or so much as read a play, rejecting William Shakespeare in particular for his moral ambivalence. She loathed Scottish vices like gambling and drinking, in the latter case with good reason because of her own husband's habit. But that did not explain why, as a member of the Royal Commission on divorce in 1910, she refused to accept excessive drunkenness as grounds for wives to separate from their husbands. Along with these other foibles she was a terrible snob, looking down on most people she met and given to acid comments about friend and foe alike.

No doubt, as is often the case, the snobbery arose from an inferiority complex. In a social world of tall, stately ladies Lady Frances Balfour was short and had a limp. At those dinners where she had learned so much in her youth, in her adulthood she bored the guests rigid by harping on and on about women's suffrage. From 1896 she was president of a national society to promote the cause by non-violent means (so in opposition to the militant suffragettes). She spent endless hours going on marches, making speeches at public and private meetings, writing articles for the press and lobbying at the House of Commons – where her contacts were useful to the movement, even if no more than a handful of MPs could be prevailed on to support it. Her being a Liberal married unhappily into a leading Tory family proved symbolic. Despite her impressive social pedigree and her political connections, she never felt quite at ease in her surroundings. Even her presence on the platform at rallies of the suffragettes might have been of doubtful benefit: on the one hand, it gave the protests a certain air of respectability yet, on the other hand, it confirmed in the minds of many working men and women that this struggle was at bottom concerned with votes for rich ladies, that is to say, with a further privilege for those already privileged enough.[12] To her credit, though, when enfranchisement for women over 30 years of age at last came in 1918, she considered her job only half done.

⁂

A noblewoman might in practice enjoy relative freedom, but women in general were relegated to an inferior status by the common law of Scotland. In itself marriage put severe restrictions on them and their rights to property. The husband became the wife's curator, and her movable property passed under his control; this was the *jus mariti*. The wife might own heritable estate but could do nothing with it unless her husband consented; this was the *jus administrationis*. The *jus mariti* came to an end in 1881 (for marriages contracted thereafter), the *jus administrationis* not till 1920.[13] Between those two dates, the wife could still not dispose freely of income out of her heritable estate, even if paid directly to her: on it the *jus administrationis* remained intact. The Lord

Advocate in charge of the legislation of 1881, John McLaren, explained: 'It has not been thought desirable that the control of the husband should be entirely withdrawn or that such a measure of independence shall be conceded as would be likely to cause dissensions or variance between husband and wife, and it is accordingly provided that the husband's consent shall be necessary to any sale or assignment of the wife's property. In this way his legitimate authority is preserved.'[14]

Those bare bones of the Scots law of husband and wife had been fleshed out by particular cases, seldom to the wife's advantage. In 1866 John Inglis, Lord Glencorse, expounded her duty to her husband: 'to love, honour and obey him, to live with him, and to give him the advantage and solace of her society'.[15] In 1868 James Craufurd, Lord Ardmillan, held, for the other part, that 'it is a husband's duty to practise self-restraint, to rule his household prudently, and to guide and regulate his wife's conduct, and set her an example'.[16] The curatorial powers in the marriage rested with him because (by a circular argument) 'it is the mutual intention of the parties that the husband as the natural head of the family should have these powers'.[17] At the same time, 'there is an obligation, both natural and legal, on a husband to provide for his wife'.[18]

The principles of the law were clear enough but in practice sometimes of unexpected, not to say devastating, effect. In 1845 Catherine Menzies, meaning to marry Captain J.H. Murray, drew up an ante-nuptial contract placing her estate of £9,000 in the hands of trustees. Later she sought to end the contract but the Court of Session would not allow her to, on the grounds that the rights secured by it had to last as long as the marriage lasted. The argument was that married women needed protection from taking steps (perhaps under duress) of possible disadvantage to themselves. George, Lord Deas, said: 'The object and effect of the law is not to lay a restraint on the wife to her prejudice, but throw around her a protection for her benefit . . . a wide and equitable protection, not unknown in other relations of society . . . for instance, in the case of persons under age, weak and facile individuals, persons who have voluntarily interdicted themselves and so on.' Marriage required a woman 'to merge her wishes and interests in those of her husband, to change her character and to be, in short, no longer mistress of herself . . . It appears to me that it is founded in nature that the admirable subjugation of the will of one sex to the pleasure of the other for the mutual benefit of both calls for [protection] in return on the ground of humanity.'[19]

James, Lord Moncrieff, noted, however, that for the woman all this went on only so long as the marriage did – 'as what she may do on the dissolution of the marriage is an entirely different matter. She is then a free agent.' To put it another way, a woman's footpath to freedom lay through divorce, desertion or widowhood. Charles, Lord Neaves, confirmed as much, remarking that the irrevocability of a nuptial contract 'never could be effectual if the law looked upon the wife after marriage as a free person . . . in such contracts the law looks upon the condition of the married woman as one requiring protection, even from her own acts . . . a married woman should be protected as if her mind and will were in abeyance'.[20]

A case in 1892 further illustrated the at times twisted logic of the law and its material impact. After her husband went bankrupt, a wife challenged the right of the trustee realising his assets to claim the furniture she had bought. Since they had married before 1881 the furniture fell under the husband's *jus mariti*. George, Lord Young commented that: 'As to the Married Women's Property Act [the statute superseding the *jus mariti*], I think this is a case of entrusting the husband with the furniture in the house. He had a duty to keep a house furnished and habitable for his wife and children. He would not fulfil that duty by providing them with the bare walls of an unfurnished house. The furniture was entrusted to him in order that he should perform this duty. That exposes it to the diligence of the husband's creditors.'[21] In other words, the furniture now had to be sold to pay them.

✿

Clearly these were laws made by men for men, in a world where women expected to marry then confine their interests to home and family. Most did, in fact, do this. Yet times were changing. By the 1870s it became common for wives of professional husbands to concentrate their childbearing in the early years of marriage and not to have any more babies beyond their early 30s. By 1900 the average number of children in families of this class fell to fewer than five. Soon a fair number contented themselves with two, setting the trend for the rest of the twentieth century. As a result, even married women began to discover that, beyond a certain time of life, they became free to make some choices of their own.[22]

There could still be the problem of finding money to do it. Some women were rentiers in their own right. As a rule they might rely on three sources of income: bank deposits, urban property and family trusts. Many such women formed part of the army of small savers handing their funds over to a family solicitor who could use them, through the Scottish investment trusts, to finance anything from railroads across the Rocky Mountains to plantations of oil palms in Polynesia. Bank deposits had the virtues of liquidity and accessibility for the depositrix, for her family and for any businesses the family owned. Independent women, especially spinster sisters, were important sources of capital for family firms, especially in times of crisis. Urban property offered another safe investment. If it was commercial property, it could be leased to entrepreneurs in the family on favourable terms and so generate a return for them all. Women with unearned income generally had much of their wealth under the family's control in trusts or jointures yielding them annuities. In this case the woman enjoyed no rights over the capital, which at her death reverted to the family.[23]

Working women also started, however, to put in a modest appearance among the Scottish bourgeoisie. Many were widows, though more had never been married. The cities attracted increasing numbers of single women surviving either on independent means or by dint of their own efforts. For some it was a necessity because otherwise they might pose a problem for fathers not always able to support adult daughters, whatever the prevailing social mores might expect. If such women did find an entry into the world of work, the usual options were teaching or small business or dressmaking. These occupations tended to get overcrowded, though, with turnover uncertain and income low. Women engaged in them ran the risk of slipping in social status, though this was true in general of entrepreneurs in Victorian society.[24] One change for the better by the end of the century was that efficient, well-spoken women could fill new jobs in offices, at the typewriter or switchboard. In 1881 there were next to no women employed in commerce, but three decades later 30,000 of them had set a trend that in a new era would go much further.[25] In any case, Scotswomen of the middle class won more freedom, legal and practical, than they had ever enjoyed in the past. They looked for ways to exploit that freedom.

The campaign for women's suffrage started up in earnest after Britain's second bout of electoral reform in 1867–68, which gave the vote to most of the urban male working class. Women also got a vote for the first time as ratepayers, that is to say, if they were heads of property-owning households. But it was a vote they could use only in local polls for town councils, school boards and so on. Those without the vote, so long as they were married, could still stand for such bodies. All the same, most women who took up any political activity were single, middle class, well off, in their convictions Liberal and otherwise involved in the philanthropy of the Victorian city. For many, paid work was neither necessary nor acceptable, and charity an outlet for their talents and interests. Despite the stubborn barriers, women did now begin to discover a wider role. It could require the ostentatious piety, application, benevolence and self-sacrifice of the ideal Victorian lady. At least, in practical terms, it trained her in organisation and administration. Typical was Flora Stevenson, chosen to be a member of Edinburgh's school board in 1873, and after a while its chair. An obituary in 1905 would pay her this tribute: 'At a time when public ladies were sneered at as masculine, it required no little courage on the part of Miss Stevenson to break down the walls of prejudice which encircled the causes of women's emancipation. Thanks to ladies of this type no more is heard of the unfitness of women for public life.'[26]

From a modest political base at local level, women started to aim at the parliamentary franchise too. The first Scottish society set up to lobby for it appeared in Edinburgh in 1867, led by Priscilla Bright, wife of one of the capital's MPs, Duncan McLaren, and sister of the English radical politician, John Bright. Other such societies followed. This was never, before the turn of the twentieth century, a vehement campaign, rather one of sedate public meetings and reasoned petitions to Parliament. In 1906 the Scottish societies federated under the leadership of Elsie Inglis. She had trained as a doctor, and it was her experience of low standards in women's care that pushed her into political activity. There were already Scots among the militants in England, notably Flora Drummond, nicknamed the General because she led marches wearing a military uniform and mounted on a horse. She had been radicalised by a personal problem, that she possessed all the qualifications for her chosen career as a postmistress except height: at 5 feet 2 inches, she was judged too short. She decided that this was just an excuse, that it amounted to discrimination on grounds of sex rather than of size. She played on both in her confrontations with politicians.[27]

On the male side the response was never warm, but only after repeated rebuffs did the Scottish suffragettes turn to more telling tactics. They hated Herbert Asquith, MP for East Fife and Prime Minister from 1908, because of his 'Cat and Mouse Act' under which imprisoned women on hunger strike (all in England) were released when their condition became critical but hauled back once they revived. Women protesters attacked Asquith in 1913 while he was on holiday at Lossiemouth, golfing with his daughter. At the seventeenth hole the suffragettes suddenly appeared, rushed at him, knocked his hat off, hit him on the head with a book, 'then proceeded to drag him about . . .

Unimproved agriculture: crofters plant potatoes with the aid of the *caschrom* or foot plough. (Courtesy of the University of St Andrews Library, JV-111832)

Balgay Hill, Lochee, overlooking Dundee. The featureless wastes of unimproved farms gave way over the nineteenth century to a neat and prosperous landscape. (Courtesy of the University of St Andrews Library, JV-1271)

RIGHT. Nitroglycerine operator. Joint ventures between Glaswegian capitalists and Alfred Nobel made Scotland a great producer of explosives, useful for manufacture, mining and war. (© RCAHMS. Licensor www.rcahms.gov.uk)

BELOW. New Lanark. The model agricultural villages built by landowners in the eighteenth century offered a useful example to the industrial pioneers of the nineteenth century. (© RCAHMS (Aerial Photography Collection) Licensor www.rcahms.gov.uk)

ABOVE. The mightiest engineering feat of all was the great bridge that spanned the Firth of Forth with such ease and such elegance.

LEFT. Scotland became for the first time a tourist destination, but the visitors did not always find what they expected. (© www.CartoonStock.com)

CORRECTED.—*Lady Tourist (doing the cathedrals of Scotland).* " This is *Gothic*, isn't it, John ? " *Juvenile Vendor of* " *Guides* " *(severely).* " No, mem, *this* is *Presbyterian.*"

ABOVE. Edinburgh ale: James Ballantine, George Bell and David Octavius Hill, the pioneer of photography, sample the capital's main mass manufacture – beer. (The Metropolitan Museum of Art, The Rubel Collection, Promised Gift of William Robel (L.1997.84.3) © The Metropolitan Museum of Art)

RIGHT. Thomas Chalmers, the greatest leader of the Church of Scotland during the nineteenth century, grew old and weary in his eventually unsuccessful defence of it. (© National Portrait Gallery, London)

The Parliament House, by R.W. Billings. The echoing emptiness of the hall where the nation's fate had once been decided was a constant reminder of the imperfections in Scotland's political system.

The modern South Bridge looms over the ancient Cowgate. The Old Town of Edinburgh, backdrop to so much of Scotland's history, decayed into a slum as the richer citizens moved first to the New Town then to the suburbs. (© City of Edinburgh Council www.capitalcollections.org.uk)

Glasgow, the second city of the Empire, could not, for all its fabulous wealth, deal fast enough with the terrible social problems created by its own expansion.

Robert Knox, the sinister surgical demonstrator who was the best customer for fresh corpses dug up from the cemeteries of Edinburgh later became the global pioneer of scientific racism. (Getty Images)

EXECUTION of the notorious WILLIAM BURKE the murderer, who supplied Dᴿ KNOX with subjects.

William Burke, here being hanged in the High Street, had saved himself the trouble of exhumation and murdered the victims he sold to Knox; his accomplice, Hare, turned king's evidence and escaped the noose. (Getty Images)

LEFT. Robert Dundas stepped into but did not quite fill the shoes of his father, Henry Dundas, in running the Scottish political system till its reform in 1832.(© National Portrait Gallery, London)

BELOW. Henry, Lord Cockburn, urged on the modernisation of Scotland, but for himself preferred rustic bliss at Bonaly, Midlothian. (© National Portrait Gallery, London)

John Galt's novels depicted the charms of the old west of Scotland under the modernising pressures that would lead to their disappearance. (© National Portrait Gallery, London)

The Waverley novels were modern novels, capturing the everyday dilemmas of contemporary Scots, unlike the antiquarian works that won Sir Walter his worldwide fame. (© National Portrait Gallery, London)

James Hogg, the Ettrick Shepherd, was patronised by literary Edinburgh, but his greatest work penetrated to the heart of Scottishness. (© National Portrait Gallery, London)

Robert Louis Stevenson only produced his finest work by leaving the formality of Edinburgh for the wider world. (© National Portrait Gallery, London)

LEFT. Charlotte Square, the grandest of Robert Adam's urban compositions elegantly marked the western boundary of Edinburgh's first New Town. Here the western side with Robert Reid's church in the middle.

BELOW. The original building of the new University of Glasgow on Gilmorehill still dominates the western city, but in its heyday was criticised for betraying Scottish architectural tradition. (University of Glasgow)

RIGHT. The Rev. Robert Walker, by Sir Henry Raeburn (1756–1823) (though the attribution has been disputed), captures clerical serenity on Duddingston Loch. (Scottish National Gallery)

BELOW. Princes Street with the Commencement of the Building of the Royal Institution, by Alexander Nasmyth (1758–1840). Nasmyth shows us, from a central coign of vantage, Edinburgh in the middle of its transformation from a romantic to a classical city. (Scottish National Gallery)

Nasmyth was also Scotland's finest painter of landscapes, and this canvas puts Loch Ness in an Italianate guise. (The Bridgeman Art Library)

Pitlessie Fair, by Sir David Wilkie (1785–1841). No artist depicted the life of the Scots people in such loving detail as Wilkie did, here with an everyday scene near the manse where he grew up. (Scottish National Gallery)

OPPOSITE. Home and the Homeless, by Thomas Faed (1826–1900). Here a single canvas unites images of relative prosperity for some of the Victorian working class and of utter misery for their more unfortunate fellows. (Scottish National Gallery)

BELOW. The Thin Red Line, by Robert Gibb (1845–1932). The Scots' integration into the United Kingdom was forwarded by their military prowess, vaunted in Gibb's picture of the Sutherland Highlanders at the Battle of Balaclava, 1854. (© National Museums of Scotland)

OPPOSITE. Dinner at Haddo House, by Alfred Edward Emslie (1848–1918). The Scottish country house became a regular rendezvous for the British political elite, here with William Gladstone (centre) and Lord Rosebery (left) in the home of the Earl of Aberdeen. (© National Portrait Gallery, London)

BELOW. The Tennis Party, by Sir John Lavery (1856–1941). Lavery's image of leisure in the high bourgeoisie discovers French elegance in a suburban setting from Glasgow. (The Bridgeman Art Library)

RIGHT. A Hind's Daughter, by Sir James Guthrie (1859–1930). Throwing off academic convention, Guthrie found charm and beauty in this humble portrait of rustic life in Berwickshire. (Scottish National Gallery)

BELOW. Les Eus, by J.D. Fergusson (1874–1961). Modernist painters sought to bring out of sober Scotland images of an exuberance not always immediately obvious in its everyday life. (© The Fergusson Gallery, Perth & Kinross Council)

shouting wildly about justice for women'. His detectives came to the rescue and carted them off to the police station at Elgin, where a crowd gathered outside bawling abuse and threatening to throw them in the Moray Firth.[28] They tried again in November, when Asquith went to unveil a statue of his late predecessor at No. 10, Sir Henry Campbell-Bannerman, in the latter's old constituency of Stirling. At Bannockburn a woman crouched down in the road to halt the Prime Minister's car, and as it stopped four others rushed up and lashed at him with dog-whips. Following behind was another car full of police, who again saved the hapless Prime Minister.

By 1914 the women's campaign turned more violent still. A riot ensued when the police tried to arrest the leader of the militant suffragettes, Mrs Emmeline Pankhurst, at a public meeting in Glasgow. Others had meanwhile set light to pillar-boxes, to unoccupied mansions, to a clubhouse at Ayr, to a laboratory at St Andrews and to the railway station at Leuchars. They hoped the insurers required to pay for the damage would bring pressure to bear on the government to grant the vote to women. Yet a different side to the character of the Scottish suffragettes was revealed by the outbreak of the First World War. They at once relapsed into good works. Their societies used their funds to finance hospital units on the eastern front, where Dr Inglis took charge in person. She led a heroic existence and died a moving death.[29]

While spectacular, the campaign for the suffrage should be seen as part of a general assertion of their rights by women, something always more likely among the middle and upper class. Victorian society assigned places and roles for them that not all were prepared to accept: hence, in particular, the demand for access to the universities and to the professions.

The campaign to get women into higher education was run by associations formed in Edinburgh in 1868 and in Glasgow and Aberdeen in 1877.[30] The universities at last threw open their doors in 1892, and female graduates took degrees the next year. Chrystal Macmillan, the first to matriculate at the University of Edinburgh, had been one of the most active in this campaign. Intellectual (with a first in mathematics), respectable (always working within academic channels) and professional (she eventually became a lawyer), she was typical of the Scottish school of feminism.

It is hard to see why the advancement of such worthy ladies should have been offensive. In fact, male attitudes were often confused. Lord Neaves, the judge already quoted on the need for married women to renounce their own will, was yet a supporter of higher education for them. He wrote a poem on the subject in *Blackwood's Edinburgh Magazine*:

> So I wonder a woman, the mistress of hearts
> Should ascend to aspire to be Master of Arts;
> A ministering angel in woman we see,
> And an angel need covet no other degree.
>   – O why should a woman not get a degree?[31]

On this matter lawyers might be liberal, but doctors could be dogmatic. Efforts by women to enter the medical schools as equals started as early as 1870, at a time when they could already receive instruction but not take degrees. A riot at Surgeons' Hall in Edinburgh followed a sustained campaign of harassment and bullying by male students, who swore at the female candidates in public and sent them obscene letters. In an effort to stop them sitting an exam, 200 undergraduates, with the blessing of some members of staff, blocked the entrance to the hall. The leader of the women, Sophia Jex-Blake, described the scene: 'We walked straight up to the gates [which] were slammed in our faces by a number of young men, who stood within, smoking and passing about bottles of whisky, while they abused us in the foulest possible language.'[32] The janitors had to elbow the louts aside and let the women in.

If women of the middle class still had problems in becoming economically active, there was less trouble for women of the working class. On the contrary, the industrial revolution exploited them on a large scale, usually rewarding them miserably too. While technological advance mobilised the resources of society with greater efficiency, wages were left to find their own level.

Yet right through the nineteenth century older prejudices still held, in particular the prejudice that a woman's place was in the home. During the early stages of industrialisation there seems even to have been a touching faith that it would strengthen this domestic role, at least for matriarchs. A medical journal remarked in 1818 that in 'the families in which all the members are so far advanced as to be fit for labour, the aggregate amount of their earnings is very considerable and is in general placed at the disposal of the eldest female, whose sole employment consists in making purchases, and attending to household duties.'[33] According to the occupational census of 1911, things might not have changed that much: it found only one in twenty of women in work to be married. Still, while Scottish historians tend to make a fetish of official statistics, it seems obvious these could not have captured all female economic activity. There was the small matter of housework, infinitely more troublesome and tedious than it is today, quite apart from seasonal labour on farms and casual employment as charwomen and babysitters. Many male labourers had only insecure jobs and low wages, so at intervals needed to send out their wives to seek part-time or temporary work.

What kept the average numbers of women down in the national statistics was that their jobs tended to be concentrated in certain sectors, above all textiles, then agriculture and domestic service. In Dundee seven out of ten working women toiled at producing jute and linen. In Glasgow and Aberdeen, too, textiles came first for female employment, unlike in Edinburgh, where domestic service did. In 1841 those three leading sectors accounted for nine out of ten working women, and by 1911 still seven out of ten. They were also concentrated by age group: two in five women workers had yet to reach their eighteenth birthday and the largest single cohort was of girls aged between thirteen and fourteen.[34] Already in 1833, in evidence to a parliamentary inquiry, a manager from Glasgow had asserted from his experience that 'women do not generally work much in factories once they get married.'[35]

No wonder the women got out if they could, for they also suffered abuse in the factories. Since most were poor, young, single and uneducated, it perhaps came as no surprise to find men set over them in the skilled jobs and supervisory posts. Some factories dismissed women as soon as they got married, while others only let them stay on to teach new girls the ropes. Discipline was harsh and they would be fined for lateness, singing and talking. Overseers did not hesitate to knock them about or kick them. In Dundee the lassies turned the tables with their mocking, irreverent behaviour, so that some men came to fear them rather than the other way round.[36] But in most factories the physical conditions simply did not allow for anything but submission to a regime of racking toil day in, day out. Most unpleasant of all were the cotton mills, where the girls attending wet frames got constantly sprayed with water, while in the hot spinning department the temperature rose to 100°F. In the linen mills the conditions were not quite so awful, yet it could never have been less than utterly exhausting to work the standard week of six days for twelve hours or more each day.[37]

While girls had no chance of apprenticeships, weavers were regarded as skilled and spinners as unskilled, with pay to match. There seems to have been no good reason for this except that the weaving process could more easily go wrong than the spinning process. All the same, women maintained distinctions in the factories as fiercely as craftsmen in the shipyards ever did. In Glasgow, though spinners and weavers both lived the same sort of life in Bridgeton, there was 'a quite remarkable difference in their appearance and habits' and 'little social intercourse between the two'.[38] In Dundee a 'greetin' faced weaver' would not even speak to a 'snuffy spinner'. As one spinner recalled of the rival group, 'They wore a hat, an' they wore gloves . . . we used tae jist rin wi' wir jeckets on – nae hats or gloves.' The broadcaster Billy Kay recorded an old Dundonian joke about the weaver who went to the registrar to make arrangements for her marriage:

> So he says to her, 'Now – you're a spinster?'
> And she says, 'No, look I'm a weaver.'
> And he says, 'Now look lassie, doon on this form put – you're a spinster.'
> She says, 'Dinna ca' me a spinner, because I'm a weaver.'
> So he says to her, 'Look lassie, are you ignorant?'
> She says, 'Aye, fower month.'[39]

Conditions for women were little better outside the regimented urban workforce. In the mining districts (where their employment underground had been banned since 1842) there was next to no work except picking coal at the bings, a dirty and demeaning job in practice only performed by a few poor unmarried girls. The male miner ruled the roost in the pits and in the villages. His work was also exhausting but at least well paid by contemporary standards. When he got home he expected to be looked after. One writer observed the women's 'slavery to the men' at Kelty in Fife:

> Not once can I remember of the women eating their meals with the men . . . There were two big easy chairs in the kitchen . . . and if either of them chanced to be occupied by one of the girls or women when the men arrived it was instantly left . . . I have seen a son of one-or-two-and twenty order his mother across the room to get his pipe which was on a shelf directly above his head a few inches out of his reach from the chair where he was sitting.[40]

A miner who before publication checked through this passage for the author exclaimed indignantly, 'Instead of slavery you should call it devotion'.[41]

In agriculture, the tasks had always been shared between the sexes but mechanisation came more slowly to those the women performed. Reaping with the sickle was traditionally reserved to them. When the heavier scythe came in, reaping turned into a male task and women were confined to gathering sheaves. In the north-east, women could not so much as touch the splendid horses that pulled the ploughs. In general, agricultural employment for them was in decline, and in more rapid decline than for men. The reason, apart from mechanisation, might have been that men's earnings rose far enough to let them spare their wives (and children too) the old backbreaking labour in the fields. Anyway, in the arable areas women were probably only ever called on for half the year. Their work was steadier in the pastoral areas, where dairies kept them busy in every season.[42] In the Highlands the women had their own occupations in the byre and at the spinning wheel. As the nineteenth century went on, more and more Highlanders spent time working elsewhere, not least because they had next to nothing to do on a croft in the winter. Then the women were left in charge. Usually the men had performed the heavier jobs of digging before they left, and would return before the peat needed cut.[43]

Girls in the country might grow up big and strong, capable of doing most things boys could do, yet still they were only paid half as much.[44] But that held true of all employment in all parts of Scotland. Within the female workforce large differentials existed too. They depended on the cleanliness or otherwise of the job, on its requirements for heavy labour or special skills and on its perceived suitability for women. Along those scales, examples could be found of skilled women with relatively high pay, for example, in Edinburgh's important printing and publishing industry. Yet even here the best wage was £1 a week, more or less the same amount as for the lowest-paid unskilled men, the hands in the warehouses.[45] Elsewhere the range went from just about a living wage down to a good deal less. Many working women were young and unmarried, living with their parents, but others, spinsters or widows, needed to rely on their own earnings alone. A quarter of Glaswegian households had women as their heads. While most of them worked from home, this was still sweated labour. For the sector of outwork in the clothing trade, spinsters and widows formed half the numbers employed. A home-based shirt-maker could if fully stretched make 8s a week, but 4s to 5s was more usual. A witness to the Royal Commission of 1909 on the Poor Law said women in Edinburgh earned 'such wages as they could not possibly live on without the parish help'.[46]

Even worse exploited were the many, often elderly, women reliant on washing and charring. Some might find a comfortable niche in a well-to-do home, but others hired by the less wealthy, perhaps as the single maid for an artisan's or shopkeeper's household, felt lucky to get 6d or 9d a day.[47]

After the textile trades, domestic service was the most common occupation for women, accounting by the end of the nineteenth century for one in five of those in employment.[48] It could offer daughters of the respectable working class an easy path from home to work, from childhood to a start in life. Training might begin early, for wee girls were already expected to carry out a share of the household's chores. A stonemason's daughter recalled that the division of labour in her home, in fact, made the girls carry out all the chores: 'They [the boys] didn't have to do anything in the house. We used to have to wash out their white gloves and clean their patent shoes to let them get away to the dancing. They were the apple of my mother's eye. Nothing could go wrong with the boys.' When the time came for marriage, no ordinary Scots girl could bring property with her under the marital roof. What she could bring was a reputation from the well-run home of a steady family, where the mother had given her daughter a thorough training in the numberless skills of a wife.[49]

Before the girl got that far, she might do a stint as a domestic servant. The Victorian middle class often debated the servant problem – how to find and keep respectable, intelligent maids.[50] The bourgeois household with its (by today's standards) primitive amenities could hardly do without staff. The number it employed helped besides to flag up social status. Edinburgh's grandest houses, in Charlotte Square, might have half a dozen servants apiece, but in a lesser home even a single maid signalled that its denizens stood a step up from the masses.[51] Her life was anyway hard. Cleaning and setting the fires before everybody else got up in winter made for a cold and dirty start to the day. Stiff linen needed to be pounded by hand to make it absolutely smooth. Huge expanses of uncarpeted floors had to be polished. With rudimentary technology, it took ages to heat all the water for baths. A good deal of strength was required to put wet washing through the mangle. Agitations by maids for better conditions and wages, as in Edinburgh in 1840 and Dundee in 1872, met public ridicule.[52]

The maid's obligations did not stop with the drudgery. A right-thinking mistress liked to take girls from the working class more generally in hand. In Glasgow she usually found them from agencies recruiting in the Highlands and in Ireland, and she assumed it was for her to instil in them habits of industry, thrift and churchgoing, reinforced by daily prayers and readings from the Bible. They would then be not only introduced to their proper sphere but also instructed in the skills necessary for the comfort of their future husbands and families.[53] They would learn respect for authority too.

Once they left their own homes, their fathers' authority passed to the masters of the employing households, or to their deputies, the wives. When the girls married, the authority then shifted to their husbands. Maids would meanwhile be serving their betters while keeping their place, not to say bearing witness in wider society to the value of respectable manners and morals. It could be seen as a logical progression in an ideal Victorian social order.[54]

Domestic service was therefore often regarded as the best path for a working-class girl, though nothing in economic fact justified that opinion. Certainly the girls themselves might not think so. Many others employed in factories, shops or offices regarded domestic service as demeaning. Especially those in Dundee's mills thought maids were 'skivvies' because, living in their employers' homes, they became subject to rules and regulations in their free time too.[55] From the factories, even after their 12-hour shifts, the girls liked to head into town of a light summer's evening, relax, walk about and have a laugh before going home to bed and bracing themselves in the morning for another 12 hours. The late stroll was their sole pastime, and to hell with anybody who thought it unseemly.[56] In Aberdeen, too, a po-faced report noted that 'much difficulty has been found in inducing girls to go into service' because of their desire for 'liberty'. They would 'labour in shops, in warehouses, in mills, in offices, in places of business of every imaginable kind, rather than go into service, where they would at least be ... prepared for keeping a house of their own'.[57] It was feared these girls, living in lodgings, would be bound to neglect feminine skills.[58] In the end, the family and the community could only suffer. A social investigator uneasily underlined that 'a large proportion of the women in Dundee are artisans, not housekeepers, a circumstance which has a most important bearing on the social and physical conditions of working class life in the city' – and not, presumably, a good one.[59]

Yet the woman emerged as the real strength of the working-class family, always on hand to hold things together while the man went off with his mates to the pub or got into fights at the football. By that same proletarian tradition he would have handed his wages over to his wife after deducting his own pocket money for smokes and drinks. She then needed to deal, usually on her own, with shopkeepers, pawnbrokers and moneylenders. She had to pay the rent, as well as feed and clothe herself and her family while struggling against the odds to keep house and children clean. It was also for her to come to terms with the landlord and his factor, and to haggle over rent and arrears: 'A clean rent book was more than a source of pride, it was a badge of approval, a buffer against control and a possible passport to better housing or employment.'[60] At least in the stairheid parliaments, she had moments to spare and enjoy as she exchanged gossip, opinion and advice with her neighbours.

Within all these tight constraints on their status and activities, women might still fail and fall outside the accepted structures of Victorian society. By one misfortune or another, or by a series of misfortunes, they could lose husband or home or job or all three. And then, in the worst circumstances, they might face the grimmest prospect imaginable, of eking out an existence by selling themselves for sex.

This was not a new predicament for women. Prostitution had been rife since at least the sixteenth century in Edinburgh, at that time by far the largest Scottish burgh. The reason lay in the even more limited urban opportunities for poor girls in the pre-industrial era, and in the numbers of men having to spend time alone in the capital for this reason or that, whether trade at Leith or litigation in the Court of Session. Public acknowledgment of the problem came only in 1797, when the Edinburgh Magdalene Asylum was founded to take the girls off the streets and make honest women of them, usually as laundresses. Most ran away from employers they found unbearably conde-scending; they already knew of easier ways to earn a living.[61] The regular loss of about half the inmates before they completed their moral reformation seemed to make the managers of the asylum yet more priggish, as in this statement to donors of 1832:

> The pride, unsubdued tempers, long continued and therefore inveterate habits, the obstinacy and ingratitude of some under their care in your asylum, would frequently induce your committee, and the internal conductors, to abandon their posts altogether, were it not, that in the midst of their almost exhausted patience, they are cheered and animated by here and there a dawn of hope in the distant horizon.[62]

In fact, the sun of righteousness rose only dimly over the capital, if we can judge from the investigations of George Bell, a doctor and author of *Day and Night in the Wynds of Edinburgh* (1849). For him, a walk up the High Street on a Sunday evening was an approach to hell. The women always proved to be the worst: 'To see the mouth of a close choked up by a few of the corrupt female inhabitants thereof, all half drunk, and making the walls of the dismal access to their infernal homes shake with their hyena-like laughter and oath-impregnated voices of rage – to see this, I say, gives origin to a flood of gloomy reflections.' In a second tract, *Blackfriars Wynd Analysed* (1850), Bell tried to work out the cost of the alcohol they consumed to the 1,000 or so people living in this one thoroughfare running down from the High Street to the Cowgate. Assuming each drank four gallons of whisky a year (that works out at two modern drams a day, which seems a modest estimate), it would cost the wynd over £2,000 in all. Yet the average income per head there was £5, so £5,000 for the whole lot. Out of that, £3,000 would have to go on food and £650 on rent, not to speak of coal and clothing. Then how did the wynd subsist? The answer was begging or crime, that is to say, theft and prostitution. 'If we learned that they yield £2,000 per annum to the wynd, it would in no degree surprise us.' A black economy indeed.[63]

William Tait, another doctor, made his own study of *Magdalenism* (1842). He reckoned 800 prostitutes worked the city of Edinburgh. Among those treated for venereal disease, 4 per cent were under 15 (including children aged nine or ten), 66 per cent in the late teens and only 3 per cent over 30. While some lived 'privately', most were to be sought in 200 brothels, mainly in the Old Town, 50 in the High Street alone, but a few in the New Town too. Another 1,000 part-timers, 'sly prostitutes', sold themselves when they needed money or felt like it. They hired rooms in 'houses of assignation'. Why did they veer between virtue and vice? 'A very great number of the prostitutes confess that the desecration of the Sabbath ... was one of the principal causes of inducing them to go astray.' And how could you tell one who otherwise might just blend into the urban scene? 'All do not drink to excess – all do not lie – all do not steal – but almost all swear. It is one of the initiatory accomplishments of their profession, which the prostitutes early acquire; and they make use of it on all occasions.' There was demand as well as supply. It arose among 'lads who come from the country to learn businesses in town or to receive a college education'. Pornography was available, yet some still frequented brothels after starting a career: 'The young lawyer, physician and general student view this kind of relaxation as indispensable for their health', it being impossible before marriage to have sex with women of their own class. Heavens above, 'the pulpit is not even exempted from the inroads and consequences of these habits'.[64]

Isabella Bird, an intrepid lady who had led Sherpas across the Himalayas and rubbed noses with man-eating Hawaiians, went in 1869 on an expedition just as plucky through the closes of her native city. She found a roomful of whores, 12 foot square with ashes all over the floor and a bedstead, table and stool: 'A girl of about eighteen, very poorly dressed, was sitting on the stool; two others, older and very much undressed, were sitting on the floor, and the three were eating, in a most swinish fashion, out of a black pot containing fish.' It came back to Mrs Bird that she had 'shared a similar meal in similar primitive fashion in an Indian wigwam in Hudson's Bay Territory but the women who worshipped the Great Spirit were modest in their dress and manner and looked *human*, which these "Christian" young women did not'.[65]

While in Edinburgh the oldest profession dated probably from medieval times, in Glasgow it was a new spectacle for what had not long ago been a God-fearing, strictly regulated and rigidly orthodox Presbyterian burgh. Prostitution here could be counted a result of the industrial revolution, then, or rather of its social strains. A Magdalene asylum opened only in 1815.[66] It remained relentlessly active for the rest of the century, in the city beyond its walls too. The managers led a campaign to get the Glasgow Fair moved from its traditional site on the Green. It had for centuries been held there in the middle fortnight of July, formerly for the sale of livestock or hire of servants, now for amusement, with circus, concerts, plays – and prostitutes. One summer the asylum's aptly named Repressive Committee sent a delegation that found the site to be 'a prolific source of evil' and 'just one huge brothel'. The agitation against all this grew so clamant that in 1871 the corporation shifted the Fair further out to Camlachie.[67]

In Glasgow as in Edinburgh, the old core of the city turned into a den of vice once respectable citizens fled to salubrious suburbs to escape the deepening urban decay. The University of Glasgow followed in 1870 and left its beautiful old buildings, dating from the seventeenth century, to be knocked down and replaced by a goods yard. The principal, the Revd Thomas Barclay, gave as the main reason the problems of instructing the city's youth amid its worst slums. In particular, holding classes in the evening had become disagreeable or even dangerous when students needed to run the gauntlet of pestering prostitutes who hung round the gate of the college. Students from outside Glasgow often stayed in this part of town too, and might find themselves living on the same stair as fallen women.[68]

Glasgow's prostitution in its turn became the object of virtuous bourgeois investigations, here by men preferring to remain anonymous. One took the pen name of Shadow. He was an evangelical Christian who never shrank from pushing his way into the stews, to witness what was happening, to distribute tracts, to bring to light the shenanigans beneath the surface of a great commercial city and to call for public action so as to put things to rights. He sought to move his readers with the plight of pathetic women and children caught up in it all as helpless victims. Yet he could be brutally frank about things that shocked him:

> The smell, as we enter, is suffocating, made still more so by two scavengers carting away the filth from a receptacle within a couple of yards of the door. The room cannot be more than eight feet by ten, exclusive of two recesses for beds. In each of these are three unfortunate women, and on the floor are two others, with a man, apparently a protector – making nine persons in all sleeping in the apartment. The window shutters and door being closed, nothing but a small contracted chimney is left for ventilation.[69]

It is not too clear why anybody would want to have sex in such surroundings, but Shadow assured his readers there was plenty of it going on. He reckoned there were 1,800 prostitutes in Glasgow who provided a living also for 1,350 'bullies or fancy men' and for 450 'mistresses'. They were to be sought out in 450 brothels receiving an estimated 80 visits a week each, to yield a total of 36,000 acts of coition a year. Each one would cost the customer a shilling, but while he was at it his pockets and wallet would be routinely rifled of something like the same sum, after he had already spent double that on drink in order to arouse his libido, or not as the case may be. The total annual turnover of Glasgow's sex industry amounted to more than £500,000 (£48 million in today's money). Its practitioners were also its victims: each year 300 prostitutes died.[70]

Another investigator presented his findings in the manner of an official report, as *The Moral Statistics of Glasgow in 1863*. He reckoned the prostitutes in the city to number 2,500, a figure higher than Shadow's because 'sly harlots' were included, working part-time from lodgings or hired rooms and probably with an ordinary job too. They again supplemented their incomes by stealing from their customers: 'It is well known that scarcely one theft out of a hundred is reported to the police, the plundered victims being afraid to expose their folly.' Still the recorded rate of female crime in Glasgow was exceptionally high. In 1861 there had been 4,000 arrests of women for being disorderly, 8,000 for being drunk and disorderly, and 10,000 for 'prowling'. The worst result, this observer thought, lay in the corruption of the young. The 350 prostitutes who, by his reckoning, died every year were replaced by a supply of innocent girls lured from the country to be seduced and then put to work in the brothels.

As for the boys, 'how often in Glasgow . . . have we observed as many as four, or six mere lads, from 14 to 17 years of age, surrounding a prostitute and drinking in with loud laughter, and the kindled itching gusto of disastrously awakened lust, the frightfully obscene remarks which flowed so naturally from her putrid lips.' The solutions lay in policing and in evangelisation; though the author of the *Moral Statistics* conceded that practising Christians might also succumb to the whores' wiles. But somehow Scots had to learn to control their sexual urges – even or especially the adolescents, who should take warning at a diagnosis from the Glasgow Royal Asylum: 'We have been so thoroughly impressed with the conviction that masturbation is a more fruitful source of insanity than is generally supposed, that we resolved to investigate accurately the male cases admitted. We have assigned in nineteen cases masturbation as a cause of insanity . . . one-sixth of all the male admissions are cases of insanity the physical cause of which is masturbation.'[71]

Social reformers were not always so sanctimonious. In Aberdeen, the kindly Sheriff William Watson, founder of the city's industrial school, worried about the girls who during slumps 'were driven by necessity to prostitution. When trade revived, not a few continued to indulge in what the police called occasional prostitution, and gave birth to illegitimate children'. He discovered that in 1855, of 272 single mothers in Aberdeen, 101 had worked in factories and half were illiterate. For these, 'enforced idleness and the inadequate supply of the necessaries of life soon tell on their moral and physical state, and many of them are obliged to submit to prostitution in order to obtain food, shelter and clothing, which they could not otherwise procure . . . in bad times they and their children are brought to want, and to prevent starvation they send their children out to beg or steal for their support.' It was all, he concluded, the result of poverty rather than of sin: 'The mothers of illegitimate children who, when reduced to want from no fault of their own, resort to prostitution to earn a living, ought rather to be pitied than spurned.'[72]

Fellow-feeling came also from the young Robert Louis Stevenson, who escaped at every chance from his strict Calvinist home to the louche pleasures of Edinburgh:

> I love night in the city,
> The lighted streets and the swinging gait of harlots.[73]

The girls would call to him as he came along in his poseur's velvet coat: 'I have been all my days a dead hand at a harridan. I never saw one yet that could resist me.' Still, the elder Stevensons, while pious, were not prudes, the father being indeed a sponsor of the Magdalene Institute. Their son's own sexual initiation seems to have taken place in his teens and, we may guess, in a way that made him sensitive and generous towards the prostitutes, unlike certain of their other customers. He found in some of the girls an upright, direct, candid yet amiable quality that contrasted with the hypocrisy of bourgeois Edinburgh. Though he hated paying for sex and condemned the exploitation behind that, he found in the people of the bars and brothels a courage and generosity rising above their apparent degradation. When he insisted in verse, 'give me the publican and the harlot',[74] it was more than a pose.

In 1880, aged all of 31, Stevenson embarked on an autobiography but he left, as so often, only fragments of a work he had soon dropped:

And now, since I am upon this chapter, I must tell the story of Mary H. She was a robust, great-haunched, blue-eyed young woman, of admirable temper and, if you will let me say so of a prostitute, extraordinary modesty. Every now and again she would go to work; once, I remember, for some months in a factory down Leith Walk, from which I often met her returning; but when she was not upon the streets, she did not choose to be recognised. She was perfectly self-respecting. I had certainly small fatuity at this period; for it never occurred to me that she thought of me except in the way of business, though I now remember her attempts to waken my jealousy which, being very simple, I took at the time for gospel. Years and years after all this was over and gone, when I was walking sick and sorry and alone, I met Mary somewhat carefully dressed; and we recognised each other with a sort of joy that was, I daresay, a surprise to both. I spent three or four hours with her in a public-house parlour; she was going to emigrate in a few days to America; we had much to talk about; and she cried bitterly, and so did I. We found in that interview that we had been dear friends without knowing it; I can still hear her recalling the past in her sober, Scotch voice, and I can still feel her good honest loving hand as we said goodbye.[75]

PART IV
POLITICS

10

Despotism: 'The bad old school'

On hearing about the death of the second Viscount Melville, in July 1851, Henry Cockburn wrote: 'Is the great house of Arniston to end with him? It has been the greatest house in Scotland in the greatness which depends neither on rank nor on fortune, but on talent and public situation, for the last two centuries.'[1]

By 'the great house' Cockburn meant the Dundases of Arniston, their toponym coming from the estate in Midlothian where they had resided since the Reformation. They were indeed a talented and ambitious clan, long prominent in the public life of Scotland. Of the two centuries of its history Cockburn alluded to, they had for sixty years, straddling the eighteenth and nineteenth centuries, been its effective rulers. It was a remarkable achievement by a family that remained without, till near the end of the period, a noble title or, at any time during and after it, much money. They needed rather to rely, as Cockburn suggested, on sound good sense and strong political will to win and hold their positions of power in Scotland and then in Britain.

Their blood ran in Cockburn's own veins and he had been well acquainted with Henry Dundas, first Viscount Melville from 1801, at that climax of his career meriting the epithet of 'uncrowned king of Scotland'. He was also one of the most powerful men in the British Empire, in particular the far-sighted strategist who ran and soon won the naval war against Napoleon Bonaparte. Despite their political differences, the young Cockburn entertained a sneaking regard for this kinsman who did so much for his country. In return, Dundas had asked his country only to supply him with enough docile Scots MPs to advance and support his career at Westminster. With intense application and matchless skill he built up this faction till, after the general election of 1796, he controlled 43 of the 45 members from Scotland. Ever ready to listen to their importunities, he would yet stand no nonsense from them. It was in this sense that he set up what people called the Dundas despotism. Arguably he set up the whole modern tradition of Scottish political leadership that endures right down to our own day.[2]

Yet Melville lost his place at the heart of government in 1805 and then faced an impeachment, the last in British history, for his conduct of naval finances. He survived this, as did the Scottish political machine constructed by him. It survived also his death in 1811, to be taken straight over by his son, Robert Dundas, second Viscount Melville. It was the latter's passing that prompted Cockburn to write his eulogy, which went on:

> He deserved . . . unanimous public trust by plain manners, great industry, excellent temper, sound sense and singular fairness. Though bred in the bad old school of Scottish Toryism, and not a bad scholar in it, while that school was uppermost, his chief merit is that, as it went down, he neither got sulky nor desperate, but let his mind partake freely of the improvement of feeling which its decline implied. He stuck to his old politics, and his old political friends to the last, but not in their greater follies; and in candour and liberality became as good a Whig as a Tory can be.[3]

So far, this book has surveyed the economic transformation of Scotland after 1815, then a range of the social consequences. In the economy of the nineteenth century, the Scots people liberated themselves from the trammels of their past to create by the turn of the twentieth century a structure that suited them yet attained global importance, a unique achievement for such a small nation. It had endless implications for their society, forcing them in part to alter its inherited forms, in part to create new ones. They accomplished the task in different sectors with greater or lesser success, but more could not be expected of any people. Yet in politics they remained strangely unliberated, despite the enormous energy they devoted here, as elsewhere, to the realisation of their ideals. The next three chapters of the book will explore this odd phenomenon.

Scottish constitutional arrangements had by 1815 not altered since 1707. The Dundas despotism arose within them if not quite upon them, since the Treaty of Union had little to say about the practical detail of running Scotland as part of the United Kingdom. At the outset it was widely assumed a Scottish Secretary of State would keep a place in the British Cabinet, and a Scottish Privy Council would continue to supervise domestic affairs from Edinburgh, yet both vanished before long. The most senior Scottish post then surviving was that of the Lord Advocate, a legal official. On him, for want of anybody better, public business devolved. Soon he was having to deal with everything: not only to direct prosecutions in the central courts and to see to law and order over the rest of the country, but also to get elected to the Parliament at Westminster, to go and sit in the House of Commons, there to take charge of such Scottish business as came up (luckily for him, not a great deal of it). For most Lord Advocates, this amounted to as much politics as they would ever want to know about. Being lawyers, they nearly all saw the summit of their ambition as a place on the bench of judges in the Court of Session – to which, by a handy convention, they could appoint themselves. So, in political history, they have sunk without trace.[4]

Only Henry Dundas turned the post of Lord Advocate into the springboard for a Scottish, British and imperial career of the first order. In the later course of it, he inevitably left the land of his birth behind somewhat, yet it was always in his thoughts. Of all the Scottish leaders of the United Kingdom there have ever been, he was the one that kept the closest links with his country and took the warmest interest in its affairs. Though eternally overburdened in London, he seized every chance to return home, there to dole out jobs for the boys and to slaughter game. Compared to the vastness of the Empire this was a small place, with a burden of business so light as to be almost an agreeable diversion from greater affairs. Dundas served in London as Home Secretary, President of the Board of Control for India, Secretary of State for War and the Colonies and First Lord of the Admiralty. In all these positions he was right-hand man to his Prime Minister, William Pitt the Younger, with whom he shared days of hard labour and nights of hard drinking. As Home Secretary, to be sure, Dundas had direct responsibility for Scotland, but his other offices still gave him the power and influence to control the country informally, through a plentiful supply of military, naval and colonial patronage for distribution to his sharp-set countrymen. Any ambitious Scot needed to do no more than write to the great man; the National Archives of Scotland preserve volumes of their supplications. This carried on even after Dundas left the House of Commons. By now he had transformed the Union so as to give Scotland what it thought a due share of the benefits, especially the spoils of Empire. The English often bemoaned his favouritism to brother Scots, but that was what lured them into the imperial mission and into loyal service to a British state at war (unlike, for example, the Irish). A new British patriotism equalled, if it did not sometimes surpass, the older Scottish one. Dundas, combining the local and imperial in a unique manner, was the man most responsible for his nation's change of heart.[5]

At Henry Dundas's death in 1811, Robert Dundas stepped into his father's shoes though he never quite filled them. As the second Viscount Melville he had an assured seat at Westminster, but he was also a member of the Cabinet for 16 years – actually longer than the first Viscount. He offered his colleagues above all a safe pair of hands. He in his turn served faithfully as First Lord of the Admiralty, gained the confidence of his admirals and so succeeded without serious friction in running down the Royal Navy after the end of the French wars in 1815. He then kept it happy with technical improvements to warships and adventurous voyages to the Arctic or Australasia, in both of which quarters of the globe the explorers named islands after him. It was only in Scotland that he lacked his father's touch, probably because the necessary attention to local detail rather bored and irritated him. He did enough to maintain a wide electoral interest, yet the signs of its decay were already there when, during a ministerial crisis in London in 1827, he muddled his stance and found himself suddenly out of office. He got back briefly but by then had had enough of partisan politics. He made little effort to arrest the fall of the Scots Tories. The Whigs came in, passed the first Reform Act and at the general election of 1832 won the Scottish majority they were to hold (soon under the label of Liberals) for the rest of the century.[6]

If the Dundas despotism ended with a whimper rather than with a bang, that did less than justice to its achievements over six decades. Most Scots, contemplating the advance of their nation during this period, felt happy to count the blessings of the uniquely beneficent form of government bequeathed to them by the Union of 1707. It had given them peace and prosperity at home, security and commerce abroad. Meanwhile, it allowed them to dispense with the distraction of politics. Once the Jacobites vanished from the scene after 1745, there was nothing much to divide the nation. A Parliament no longer sat in Edinburgh, and British government seemed far away. The factious nobility was tamed by the need to seek favour in London. The bourgeoisie remained disfranchised, yet did not seem to care. The urban mob sometimes ventured forth, if driven by material grievance rather than political principle. On the land the peasantry remained pious and docile. Diehard Presbyterians might be roused by religious controversy, but this remained apolitical too. The Scottish

Enlightenment's revolutionary thought still left the intellectuals quiescent in public affairs. Where the ferment of thinking did flow over into the practical it was channelled with great energy into raising the standard of living through useful sciences.[7]

So there was little regret for the defunct Scottish state, with its anarchy and mayhem. Some of its political feuds had got wanly translated to Westminster, but there they became merely provincial and insignificant. London was on the whole content to leave well alone, and the Scots to look after themselves. Since the institutions shaping the lives of the people remained native, through them Scotland held on to a semi-independence. While their vices were at times more prominent than their virtues, they gave the nation a few benefits of full statehood without the tiresome responsibilities.[8]

Scottish politics therefore remained feasible, though in a limited form. The authorities in London believed, and so did the Scots, that it was to mutual advantage if as many as possible of the 16 peers and 45 MPs representing the country at Westminster should support the government. The peers were often the more easily recruited. The whole body of them elected those 16 representatives to the House of Lords, but they usually made their choice from the so-called King's list of official nominees. They produced a delegation so obsequious that some English peers talked of excluding it from their chamber. Occasional internal challenges to the King's list took shape, but the Scots nobility as a whole preferred to remain in postures of servility.[9]

For the election of the 45 MPs, Scotland had the narrowest franchise of any of the three kingdoms under the British crown. Up to 1832, voters in the counties never totalled more than 2,500, those in the burghs about 1,500. The sum of 4,000 compared with a national population of over 2 million by then. In relation to that, Scotland's share of the total membership of the House of Commons, with its 658 MPs, grossly underrepresented the country.[10]

To the Scottish counties 30 parliamentary seats were allocated. Eccentric rules for the suffrage, based on antique laws, restricted it to large landowners.[11] Precise application of the rules sometimes went awry, but in essence they enfranchised feudal superiors rather than proprietors in the conventional sense, a distinction important because the superiority could be sold separately from the land. A superior holding more than the minimum qualification might divide up his surplus so as to give a vote to others, such as his own friends and supporters, for their lifetimes. Or else the votes might be put on the open market and bought by social climbers from the towns, or by lawyers who traded and speculated in them. Blocs of votes would be constructed and deployed in obscure and vicious battles for control of the seat. The composition of the electorate in any county could become quite arbitrary. It was possible for the true landed interest to be submerged by all these fictitious or 'faggot' votes cast at the beck and call of one or two noblemen or of outsiders, especially the government. When a general election loomed, the preparatory skulduggery proved often more important than the actual poll. Only Ayrshire, with no stable majority available, saw a fierce struggle almost every time, but many counties had few contests and some none at all, since the decisive deals were on each occasion done in advance.

Imperious management was one weapon the government wielded to win loyalty from Scots voters, but more often it resorted to courting, cajoling and wheedling. Since the electorate of any county ranged in size from not many more than 200 in the most populous down to a handful in the smallest, seats could be lost by the desertion of just a few. The voters being nearly all by rank and education eligible for official patronage, they saw it as the duty of their MPs to obtain it for them. Patronage was yet sometimes a dangerous instrument, in that Scots could never get enough of it and some had to be disappointed. In reality, electoral interests might rise and fall because of or in spite of patronage. Such was political life in the Scottish counties.

As for the Scottish burghs, they had lost the position of a separate estate they once enjoyed in the old Parliament in Edinburgh. The eighteenth century saw their political importance continue to decline, though they all retained representation at Westminster. But since they numbered 66, some tiny, they were divided by the Treaty of Union into districts of four or five burghs, only the capital keeping a member to itself. This gave them 15 parliamentary seats altogether.

In these constituencies, so far from there being any popular franchise, not even the richest and most respected citizens could count on a vote. The MPs were chosen by the councils of the burghs in which, as variously defined by the sett (or constitution), membership had long been confined to certain interests, usually the old merchants' or craftsmen's guilds. Besides, each council possessed the legal power to elect its successor, and was naturally inclined to elect itself. In reality, then, only a minute fraction of the urban population enjoyed the franchise. Even Edinburgh had just 33 voting councillors, and the total sank as low as nine in the smallest burghs. Secrecy, irresponsibility, lack of real social standing induced in them a crass venality, which the government or other political interests were ever ready to satisfy. At the same time, the grouping of widely scattered burghs made them hard to manage. It was easy for each to be suborned by a different local landed interest, or by somebody more distant.

Still, a degree of independence was not wholly impossible at least for the biggest burghs. In the early decades of the Union, Edinburgh had been minded for the sake of its dignity as a capital to exercise a free choice in its parliamentary representation, and required tactful handling to be rendered safe. This spirit of independence, however tentative, was bludgeoned when it resulted – or so the British government claimed – in the Porteous Riot of 1736 and in the abject surrender of the city to the Jacobites in 1745. Edinburgh remained cowed after that and, at length, fell limply into the hands of the Dundas despotism (though the Dundases were, of course, local lairds). Glasgow underwent the reverse process, from lesser to greater independence. In the eighteenth century it earned such huge wealth that its plutocrats could not be kept out of politics. There was still the problem that the city shared its seat at Westminster with three small burghs nearby. But the victory in the general election of 1812 of Kirkman Finlay, one of its very richest merchants and the first native Glaswegian MP since 1741, showed political times were changing. When parliamentary reform arrived in 1832, the same elite remained in charge, merely changing its label from Tory to Whig.

Elsewhere the Scots burghs were either dominated by their own corrupt cliques, or else they got sucked into the larger political battles of surrounding counties. Even so, the Aberdeen Burghs managed in 1812 to elect the radical Joseph Hume, who was to win the reputation of Parliament's most boring member, though Robert Owen, who would have been even more boring, got nowhere with his efforts to find a niche in the Lanark Burghs. Atypical also were the Stirling Burghs, in the sense of being so venal that nobody could control them. One aspirant there informed Melville in 1820: 'The Stirling Burghs may be had at an easier rate than for many years past, but they are a sad set and I pity the man who has anything to do with them.'[12]

The legislative branch still admitted a variety of human types, then, but the executive government of Scotland was a preserve of lawyers; Henry Dundas had himself started his career in the courts, and served as Lord Advocate from 1775 to 1783. Lawyers were one of the groups that gained most out of the Union, under the separate judiciary retaining its prerogatives largely intact.

They formed the country's only large, trained, professional body (with the exception of the clergy, which kept out of politics). In Edinburgh there were hundreds of them, members of the Faculty of Advocates or Writers to the Signet, thronging the central courts primarily to service the interests of the nobility and landed gentry. This turned out to be convenient for the purposes of government too. Ideas for routine legislation could be sent as a matter of course to be mulled over at Parliament House in consultation with the parties concerned. If they agreed on the precise form of a Bill there was little trouble in getting it through at Westminster.

Legislation as such was rare, however. Strong prejudice existed against changing statutes at all without irrefutable reason, a view hallowed by constitutional tradition and explicitly embodied in the Treaty of Union's securities for national institutions and private law. William Dundas, Melville's cousin and MP for Edinburgh, gave voice to it in retort to a parliamentary proposal for reform of the burghs: 'The design which it openly manifests is to bear down the charters and extinguish the existing rights which have lasted for ages . . . After these articles of Union, so solemnly ratified, is England now to violate them? Is the richer country to turn upon the poorer? The stronger upon the weaker? I cannot believe that England would be guilty of such injustice.'[13] This Dundas was a purple-faced blustering blimp, who in preparation for his outburst might have put more alcohol into his veins than usual, yet it was true that Westminster's meddling in Scotland could be ignorant, heavy-handed and unpopular: better to pass no laws, then, than pseudo-English ones.

Anyway, Scottish affairs took up little time in London, so in practice Scots lawyers retained the initiative in codifying, interpreting, indeed reforming the law for the good of society. That did not necessarily entail legislation, for the Scottish institutional writers could make a better job of it.[14] Anyway, the output of legislation from Westminster had declined since 1707. Since at the Union the main English aim was to neutralise Scotland's capacity for independent initiative rather than to run Scottish affairs as such, parliamentary inactivity fulfilled the agenda. If Scots wanted political movement they could get it through their own public offices and institutions, still enjoying an authority confirmed rather than undermined by the treaty. All the same, after 1815 the Whigs started up a campaign of vilification against them as somehow uniquely despotic and oppressive. 'So far as we know,' spluttered Cockburn in a polemic against the prerogatives of the Lord Advocate, 'there is no one man armed with so great a power in any government professing to be free in Europe; and certainly there is no other within the sphere of the British constitution.' This was arrant nonsense, yet it helped to spread the idea that a potent landed minority was wielding great and unwarranted power over the rest of Scotland by its monopoly of public offices and institutions.[15]

And then the personnel of political administration, such as it was, consisted of law officers, the Lord Advocate and the subordinate Solicitor General. Though left a fair degree of discretion on the spot, they were responsible to a Minister in London, to the Home Secretary from 1782. Before long, their narrow formal powers got stretched, especially during the French wars when more civil together with some military organisation was necessary, and when sedition had to be suppressed. Charles Hope of Granton, Lord Advocate from 1801 to 1804, gave the House of Commons the classic exposition of the office in his time. Till 1707, he said, the work of ruling Scotland had been shared among five Ministers. Four had disappeared, leaving the Lord Advocate to discharge their functions alone. He now had 'the whole executive government of Scotland under his particular care'. Despite the Union it was still a different country: 'Its laws, its customs and its manners have undergone no change. In the application of general Acts much local explanation is required and therefore the Lord Advocate must frequently act on his on responsibility.'[16] While the authorities showed no desire to extend their powers far, the fact that the limits of legality were so indistinct could and did lead to arbitrary action by them.

This minimal political apparatus had a vital function as intermediary between the oligarchies in Scotland and the sources and resources of power in London, but its success depended not so much on its own mechanisms as on the qualities and connections of whoever operated them. During the first decades of the Union the task fell to a Secretary of State for Scotland whose office was, however, abolished in 1746 out of misguided political spite after the last Jacobite rebellion. Substitutes for it in the dominance of the ducal house of Argyll and then in the premiership of the Earl of Bute did not last. When he went out of office in 1763 he left just a void, acutely felt by Scots. They had no idea who to turn to in London and found nobody to speak for them there who was not himself prey to the clash of factions; London for its part neither knew nor cared who might prove its most able or faithful Scottish servants. The need was for one man to get a grip. That man would at length be found in Henry Dundas.

From then on it was the Dundases that defined the semi-independence of Scotland. They were not independent rulers, yet not mere local agents of British government either. With them sitting in the Cabinet in London, it could readily keep abreast of Scottish affairs so far as it needed to (not very far). In political terms, this made Scotland a partner of England, rather than a subaltern. The sign of it was that the English on the whole let the Scots do what they liked in their own country, so long as they posed no threat to British security. That was anyway a distant threat, and beyond their natural Caledonian canniness Scots had no need to feel defensive about it. In any case, caution by local ruling elites inside large composite states was hardly unique in the Europe of the Holy Alliance that emerged after the Napoleonic Wars. For example, the Hungarians still had their own diet ever on guard against Austrian efforts to centralise power in Vienna, while in the Czech lands all distinctive institutions were suppressed. Poland had been partitioned, and none of its three parts retained any autonomy. In Spain, Bourbon autocracy ruled, but the Catalan bourgeoisie, like its Scottish counterpart, liberated itself economically. Finland had entered into voluntary union with Russia in 1808 and so preserved its own institutions, as Scotland had done a century before. In all, the Scots' position was comparable in a variety of ways to that of several other small nations in a continent of great powers. Closer to home, the Scottish manager stood in his degree of independence far above the Governor General of Ireland, who was always British and primarily an agent of the central government in London.[17]

As successive managers of Scotland, the first and second Viscounts Melville had their different styles. The one could be brutal if thwarted, but for the other reconciliation was always the preferred option. Paradoxically, that made him less active as a reformer. The father, despite his conservative instincts, had been quite ready to reform when he deemed it expedient. The son preferred to let sleeping dogs lie. During his regime, remarkably little primary Scottish legislation was passed and virtually none by him. He almost boasted to his colleague, the Home Secretary: 'There is no part of the United Kingdom that has prospered more than North Britain for a century past, with the exception of a small mistake we made in 1745, and I have no relish for experimental changes by wholesale.'[18]

Under the second Viscount Melville, Scottish government therefore remained more or less synonymous with patronage. The English Lord Chancellor, Eldon, thought he handled it better than his father.[19] He kept separate in his papers his 'Scotch Appointments', memoranda of notes on the subject sent to HM Treasury. The only complete year for which the record survives is 1819, when he dealt with 48 cases. This implied, if the figure was typical of the current volume of such business, that it ran at about half the level dealt with annually in his father's time. The obvious reason lay not in any dereliction of duty on Melville's part but in the pruning of the Scottish official establishment undertaken by the government in London at the end of the French wars, as public economy grew imperative after a couple of decades of immense, inflationary spending. Even so, 48 annual appointments in a small country amounted in the long run to a powerful influence. That Melville assumed he had the effective authority to handle them came across in a note of 1818 to his Prime Minister, Lord Liverpool: 'I have acted towards you in regard to applications from Scotland very much in the same manner with those from the navy . . . and have stood between you and importunities from various quarters.'[20]

Melville's own interventions were indeed ubiquitous. In 1817 he recommended the Earl of Dalhousie as Governor of Canada. He was the channel of perennial efforts by sundry Scots nobles to be raised to the British peerage (so they could sit in the House of Lords by right rather than by election). The law officers asked for higher salaries through him. The construction of classical Edinburgh continued by his agency: Bills to build Calton Jail and to prohibit houses on the southern side of Princes Street passed on the nod from him, as did financial aid for the capital's observatory. At the request of the novelist John Galt, Melville solicited support among naval officers for the Caledonian Asylum. In 1819 he asked the Prime Minister for a grant to set up a ferry across the River Tay at Dundee, matching those already financed on the Firth of Forth and so completing a faster route to the north-east of Scotland. The next month he applied for money to repair buildings at the University of Aberdeen. That winter he seconded an appeal from the corporation of Glasgow for docks to be dug at the Broomielaw in order to provide work for unemployed weavers. Then he nominated William Pulteney Alison, Scotland's great pioneer of public health and reform of the Poor Law, for the chair of medical jurisprudence at the University of Edinburgh. The following spring he proposed the colourful John Wilson, known to the literary public by his pen name of Christopher North, for its chair of moral philosophy. And so on, and so on, and so on – there could be no doubt of Melville's omnipresence in Scottish patronage.[21]

There was one category of appointment with which Melville took special care, that of the sheriffs. His own grandfather had reformed the office in

1747, so no doubt he attached particular importance to it. In all sorts of matters, not just judicial, the sheriff represented central government in the Scottish counties. He sat as the local judge, called jurors to service, organised elections, ensured taxes were collected and maintained public order. These functions required independence. Melville declared himself 'decidedly averse to the nomination of a sheriff in Scotland on account of local interests or connections, or at local recommendations', because 'the sheriffs in Scotland, being judicial officers and in that respect unlike the sheriffs in England and Ireland, ought to be selected on professional grounds as advocates, and not merely as local patronage'. So, for example, he ruled that nobody related to or proposed by the Marquess of Stafford and the Countess of Sutherland should be appointed in their county, of which they were almost sole proprietors. The one general exception he admitted was that Highland sheriffs should be chosen from among those who knew Gaelic. In 1817, on a vacancy in Argyll, he insisted that the candidates should be 'constantly resident and accustomed to its people and language', deprecating the fact 'the Lord Advocate wishes that some Lowlander should be appointed'.[22]

Melville was similarly determined to maintain a high standard of patronage in the Church of Scotland, despite the 'very limited' influence he professed to enjoy. Here he, in fact, elaborated quite a detailed set of rules for the different cases coming before him. He regularised the procedures in a way his father had never bothered to do, though he always claimed to be merely following established administrative practice. For a living in the gift of the crown, the local MP conventionally nominated, but Melville would regard him only as a channel for the wishes of the heritors, whose recommendations he nearly always accepted. Certainly he would not foist anybody objectionable on them. Only if they disagreed was he prepared to judge for himself of the candidates' suitability, even then preferring to be guided by the choice of a resident majority. He explained why to the Duke of Buccleuch:

> Nobody knows better than yourself how necessary it is for the welfare and good order of a country parish in Scotland that the minister should if possible be on good terms with the heritors, as well as with the rest of the parishioners, and how injurious it would be, both to the state and to the interest of religion, if the reverse was generally to be the case. The crown and the heritors have the same object in view, and therefore as a general rule the former is safe in acceding to the recommendations of the latter.

If ever Melville did yield to different pressures, he told the Duke of Montrose, 'the crown would be a public nuisance and a most mischievous promoter of discontent in religious matters, instead of being, as I verily believe, the most conscientious and useful patron in Scotland'; this was important because the number of livings in its gift formed so large a proportion of the whole, about one in three. As for the rest of the lay patrons (landowners or burgh councils), he did not think it worthwhile to interfere with them, as 'in most cases it would be unsuccessful, and it is always an unwise and imprudent intermeddling in a person in my situation in Scotland'.[23] It followed that he saw no scope for the popular election of ministers according to the older Presbyterian tradition – 'an indecent proceeding as well as injurious to the public interest'. He noted with horror a case where a congregation tried to make its own choice regardless: 'Meetings had been held in the church which was extremely crowded on such occasions, and where long debates took place, as well as voting as to who should be minister.' He refused to accept the result, and asked the heritors to come instead to a private understanding. Yet in a dispute at Dunfermline, where no statutory rights were in question, he told the Lord Advocate not to appoint 'a person who though respectable as an individual might be extremely disagreeable to the parishioners'.[24]

Except for making sure his rules were kept, Melville showed little desire to control the Kirk's internal politics. Yet it was as well for him to offer tactful concessions to its rising faction of evangelicals. One of their aspirations lay in a programme of Church extension. The term meant building new places of worship to ensure adequate provision of clergy, and of the education and welfare they supervised, for the burgeoning population, especially in the towns. Here, too, there were obstacles. Most heritors declared themselves unwilling or unable to spend the necessary money. The Parliament at Westminster, when asked in 1819 and 1820, also refused to do so. The next year Melville called a conference of political and religious leaders to advise him. But the only general scheme of endowment they could agree was for the Highlands and islands, where places of worship had always been few and far between. It was decided to finance 30 new ones to be built there at a cost of £180,000, a sum met by parliamentary grant. Yet this merely glossed over the Kirk's deepest problems. They were to be found not in the north but in the central belt, where little extension took place before the later 1830s. So it proved impossible even for the Church, with its ready access to the secular authorities, to realise without great delay and difficulty its schemes of social improvement, limited and conservative as they were.[25]

The problem with Scottish patronage lay not in any mishandling by Melville but in the hostile attention it attracted from the Parliament at Westminster. Already in 1810, MPs had passed an Act 'for preventing excess and abuse in Scottish pensions' – a reaction, no doubt, to the great numbers of them doled out in Henry Dundas's heyday. The measure was designed to ensure that old Scots pensioners died off faster than new ones could be created, so that this head of expenditure would be reduced by the ravages of time to an acceptable level. No more than £300 was to be awarded to anybody, and the annual increase in the value of the list for the whole country would be limited to £800, till its total was cut from the current level of £36,000 to £25,000. Worse threatened to follow, for a select committee investigated sinecures in Scotland and found that £20,000 a year in salaries could easily be saved. If there were to be rewards in future for faithful Scots, they had to come cheap.[26]

Amid the post-war economic and financial crisis, ferocious cuts would anyway be made in expenditure of all kinds, while at Westminster backbenchers busied themselves digging up examples of waste. One by one, cherished but decrepit Scottish institutions were bound to topple under this pressure. An early and typical example came at the mint in Edinburgh, which dated from medieval times but had produced no coins since the Union; it was closed in 1817 at a saving of £1,200 a year. While Melville publicly asserted that the Scots 'have a fair right to expect that their great offices of state, as stipulated by the articles of union, shall be maintained', he also conceded that 'other offices, which are not of that national description, must be subject to the same economies as those in England'. Privately he admitted the 'great risk of being beat in detail, office after office' on the votes for money, unless MPs could be convinced it was well spent.[27]

By the end of Melville's rule he could do no more than despondently contemplate 'the many influential interests in Scotland who are pressing for the crumbs and remnants of the few offices which are now left at our disposal'.[28] He told an importunate Duchess of Atholl: 'When I state to your Grace that I shall not have any patronage, civil or military, for a twelvemonth to come, you will at once perceive that it would be improper for me at present to make any promises, or hold out any expectations of what may or may not be in my power to do next year.'[29] The resources of Scottish patronage, life's blood of the Dundas despotism, had drained away. Not even Melville's family was spared indignity. He rejected a niece's request on behalf of her husband: 'Any influence I may have in the disposal of offices is not to be exercised exclusively according to my private inclinations or for the benefit of my relations.'[30] Sir Walter Scott feared for the political effects – the gentry would stick by Melville, 'for they are needy, and desire advancements for their son, and appointments and so on. But this is a very hollow dependence, and those who sincerely hold ancient opinions are growing old.'[31] To him, Melville confessed in return: 'In the distribution of a sum so limited as the Scotch pension fund, what is given to one person must be withhold from another, who perhaps may be starving.'[32]

To rub salt in the wounds, some zealous English MPs talked as if the whole Scottish establishment consisted of sinecures (times have not changed). They took little care to discriminate in favour of posts serving a useful purpose. Melville complained that, as part of certain proposals for reform of the courts, 'it is rather hard that our criminal jurisprudence is to be surrendered to the stupidity of these reforming economists in the lower House'. His cousin Robert Dundas, Chief Baron of Exchequer, felt moved to protest over a measure tampering with his responsibilities: 'The nature of the offices and of the duties performed of them seems to have been entirely misunderstood by those who have framed this Bill that they are in many respects essentially and radically different from those of the same description in the Exchequer of England.'[33]

This latter comment pointed to a second pressure bearing on Scottish institutions, for compliance with English norms. In 1823 the whole boards of customs and excise, dating from the Union, were summarily eliminated in a move defended by Whigs on the ground that they had been nests of corruption. It was casually assumed their functions could be centralised in London. But Melville soon had to write to the Chancellor of the Exchequer: 'I have observed for some time past in your London revenue boards a strong propensity on the ground of contraction and consolidation to set aside laws and institutions in the North they don't understand, but without the aid of which they cannot in that part of the kingdom perform their duty to the public.' Services needed a certain minimum of staffing if they were to run at all. When in 1823 the job of Scottish deputy postmaster general got axed, Melville protested: 'Whatever may be the extent of the storm in the House of Commons, there will be a much louder one in Scotland if they are to be left without some superintending local authority to whom they can appeal on the daily concerns of that department.'[34]

The Whigs generating most of the penny-pinching proposals also often had the explicit purpose of anglicisation. Their allies among English MPs were moved in equal measure by ignorance of and antagonism to Scotland.

Ministers could sometimes be prevailed on to respond. For instance, the sole major legislative innovation during the early years of Melville's management came in the introduction of trial by jury in civil causes, copied from England, to supplement the normal Scottish practice of hearings before a judge sitting alone. The Whigs had long urged juries as a panacea for deficiencies in a legal system they considered harsh and tyrannical. But the measure muddied that system's logical division between criminal and civil jurisdiction, the first dealing with violations determined by the state (so that offenders had to have the security of a jury against its wrath), the second dealing with disputes between citizens (for resolution of which nothing more was needed than impartiality and learning in the law). Still, the proposal for civil juries had won support, had been considered and half-heartedly endorsed by a public inquiry and in 1815 was put into a Bill brought forward by Eldon.[35] He provided not for a general introduction of civil juries, as Whigs wished. It would be confined rather to a special court set up for an experimental period, presided over by commissioners, not judges, and empowered to decide only specified types of case referred there by a lord ordinary of the Court of Session. Melville still did not like it, arguing that on account of

> the preference justly due to our own system of law, secured to the people of Scotland by solemn compact at the Union, I think that any proposal to innovate upon our system should be received or adopted with great caution and only with a thorough persuasion that the scheme, whatever it may be, has something intrinsically better to recommend it than its novelty, or than a desire for experiment which might perhaps with more safety be left alone.[36]

Melville complained that the benefits predicted from earlier legal reforms had yet to materialise, and remained far from any success in one of their aims, the reduction of appeals to the House of Lords – which were rather multiplying. He felt angry at a provision for the court always to have on it one English lawyer, supposedly to keep the machinery in order. The Dundases at Westminster forced through an amendment that all appointments after the initial ones should be of Scotsmen. With that solace, the Bill passed. But the court, with its alien principles, would disappoint the hopes reposed in it. At the earliest opportunity, in 1830, it was merged into the Court of Session.[37]

The day-to-day maintenance of law and order Melville preferred to leave to his Lord Advocates, who spent more time on the spot in Scotland than he could. The man he inherited in this post was Alexander Campbell Colquhoun. The manager disliked but could not get rid of him till 1816, when Alexander Maconochie came in as a replacement. Maconochie obviously intended his parliamentary debut, early in the following year, to be an occasion to remember. He played the palace at Westminster with the assurance of one who knew he could make his audience's flesh creep. No nonsense of an innocuous maiden speech for him! Instead, promising to be a scourge of political radicals, he moved for a ban on their organisations in Scotland. At the climax he read out a secret oath that he said they were taking in Glasgow, calling for the establishment of democracy by violence if need be. His performance did make a great impression, and the House of Commons at once voted the repressive measures he asked for.[38] In fact, Maconochie was a fool.

With his new powers, Maconochie ordered the arrest of four radicals, though the evidence against them personally amounted to little. 'The circumstance of their having been engaged in a conspiracy to procure annual Parliaments and universal suffrage by physical force was deemed sufficient ground for charging them,' he uneasily explained. When they were tried, their Whig counsel suggested with some success that the whole business had been rigged. Public opinion swung behind the accused, and the jury was obviously reluctant to convict them. None received a sentence heavier than six months' imprisonment. Maconochie had had a case, not an open-and-shut case but a case all the same, which he mishandled and allowed to be pilloried as the product of *agents provocateurs*. He confessed himself 'mortified', and his effort to show a stern face to disaffection only backfired and damaged the government.[39] The last straw came in a different context, with his conduct at the General Assembly of the Church of Scotland in 1819. As Lord Granton described it to Melville, Maconochie on entering told a friend he was going to claim his privilege, without making clear what he meant. Approaching the throne, 'he then sat down and clapped on his hat – and this on the ground of the privilege or supposed privilege which the Lord Advocate has of pleading before the Court of Session with his hat on . . . He has made himself such a laughing stock that it really make me quite ashamed to have patronised him – and I am quite clear that he must cease to be Lord Advocate.'[40] This was what soon happened.

In Britain as a whole, meanwhile, the economic depression had deepened, bringing in England the demonstrations and riots culminating in the Peterloo

Massacre of August 1819. The Scottish authorities were on the alert too, and for once Melville took a personal interest in the practical maintenance of law and order – if only to conclude he faced no big problem. He wrote: 'Though I have no doubt that there are persons in Glasgow and the other manufacturing districts of the west of Scotland whose political views are as mischievous as any of those in Lancashire and elsewhere in England, and though it may be proper and necessary to take all due precaution to frustrate their designs . . . I have no apprehension of any general disturbance.' He remained sanguine even when trouble did break out in September. In January 1820 he could still say of it: 'I should hope it may be subdued without any violent excesses or any formidable attempt at insurrection. I have never felt any other alarm on the subject than what might arise from the country not being sufficiently alive to what was going on. It now appears to view the matter as it ought, and of course the great body of the nation are quite prepared to resist and put down the disaffected.'[41]

In February 1820 the Scottish authorities thought they might clinch the matter and exclude any chance of further trouble by arresting 27 agitators. They only produced the opposite effect (though this might have been part of the plan). On 1 April, posters appeared in the western towns signed by a committee for organising a provisional government. They called for a general strike and a popular revolt. Troops hurried to Glasgow, where skirmishes broke out in the streets on 5 April. The same day about 50 men set off from the city to seize the Carron ironworks. Soldiers met them near Falkirk in the so-called Battle of Bonnymuir. The military wounded a few and took them all prisoner: three would at length be hanged. If a small affair, it startled Scotland. Never before had this tranquil country emulated England with an actual armed rebellion of industrial workers.

Even so, the Scottish authorities kept cool. The new Lord Advocate was Sir William Rae, previously sheriff of Edinburgh, described by Granton as 'of conciliatory manner and frank and open temper', and by Melville as 'a most judicious adviser'. On hearing of the violence in the west Rae predicted 'this will end in nothing', despite 'the undue alarm which seems to pervade both the magistrates and the military commander in Glasgow'. He went there himself and remained unimpressed: 'Although we have had abundance of false alarms, all has continued quiet in Scotland . . . I am satisfied that the radical gentlemen are completely frightened, and that we shall have no opportunity of bestowing on them any of that description of chastisement which I came here in the hope of seeing inflicted.' He rebuked the corporation of the city for a lack of energy against disorder, yet for the most part he showed a good sense of public relations, tempered justice with mercy and struck shrewd plea bargains with radical prisoners and their counsel. His own forensic approach was rigorous by Scottish standards: 'I may notice it is an occurrence almost unprecedented in state trials that in the course of those now concluded not one juror has been challenged by the crown and not a single person offered as a witness who was either a spy, a *socius criminis* or liable to the most remote suspicion on any point of view.'[42]

The scale of the trouble was undeniably modest, and its significance lay rather in a more general effect on Scottish politics. The government had won this so-called Radical War, and the workers learned violence would neither intimidate it nor gain wider support. In that sense, proletarian radicalism had emerged only to isolate itself. Scott recalled the first impact of the French Revolution in Scotland during the 1790s, 'when the same ideas possessed a much more formidable class of people, being received by a large proportion of farmers, shopkeepers and others, possessed of substance'. The events three decades later rather made the workers recoil from all radical isolation, and fall back from the militancy that brought it about.[43]

This was, in fact, truer to Scottish traditions. The independent spirit of the people showed itself in their eagerness to better themselves through education and in their readiness to work out their own salvation in religious dissent. The old Presbyterian egalitarianism now came together with a new, more secular ideology of self-improvement, for which industrial society offered scope that rural Scotland could not. Moderation prevailed and endured among the majority of workers, who were neither crushed nor radicalised but did their best under an economic order that would bring them a real rise in living standards, if slowly and painfully. Common values never vanished in the emerging Victorian Scotland, and were still shared up and down the social scale. But the workers would have to wait longer to attain their political aims.

That order of things, while in the long run satisfactory to Scots, had for its immediate progress to get rid of a heap of inherited problems, not least the corrupt electoral apparatus. Yet here we find only limited interest in reform during the post-war period. That held true also of those members of the middle class who might realistically aspire to a vote. Cockburn eagerly chronicled their awakening political consciousness, and its expression in public meetings on anything from urban improvement to the abolition of slavery.[44] But it had no more momentous result before the unreformed parliamentary system began to collapse from within – and then in England, indeed in London, rather than in Scotland. The grand Tory coalition created in wartime by Pitt and Dundas dissolved into factions that steadily became incapable of working together. These were the circumstances in which, during the spring of 1827, Melville first lost office. Cockburn rejoiced at the end of 'the horrid system of being ruled by a native jobbing Scot'. He had to wait a little longer till Melville stepped down for good and the Dundas despotism finally expired. It happened in the autumn of 1830 as the Whigs formed a government after a quarter of a century in the wilderness. They at once introduced a Reform Bill. An unregenerate Parliament threw it out in the spring of 1831. The Whigs went straight to the country.[45]

Never, in the country, had there been such political excitement. A tactic of the Tories was to warn the Whigs they might soon find good reason to fear the Scots. 'If you unscotch us,' Scott had already warned, 'you will find us damned mischievous Englishmen.' Rae went round saying his country-men were not to be trusted with popular election, 'because they never could assemble without violence'. The Duke of Buccleuch claimed the people of Scotland were only interested in reform because they thought it would give them 'free whisky'. Even a Whig such as Cockburn, ever nervous of the masses, observed, 'The Scotch are bad mobbers. They are too serious at it; they never joke; and they throw stones.'[46]

On Glasgow's past record, big trouble might have been expected there and enormous popular demonstrations did take place. Yet they remained on the whole peaceful, and the city seemed rather intent on enjoying its last election under the old regime. Under that regime, the burghs composing each district took it in turn to be returning burgh, that is to say, to host the electors for the actual poll. This often offered a chance for it to ease in a favourite son. In Glasgow's district the returning burgh in 1831 was Dumbarton. It had its own candidate in Joseph Dixon, whose father was provost of the town and its leading manufacturer, engaged in making glass. In his commitment to reform Dixon did not differ from Kirkman Finlay, his older opponent – in fact, they were good friends, or had been. Now young Dixon saw his chance of a personal coup and seized it. It was vital for him to secure the vote of Rutherglen. He took its 14 burgesses by steamer down the River Clyde to Dumbarton, where they had a few fresheners before setting out in small boats to Luss while the hospitality grew more and more lavish. Next, with 'their wallets sae reamin' wi' a' kin's o' dainties', they mounted Highland ponies and were led to the top of Ben Lomond, where they 'subscribit a document read them', before being escorted back to the Dixons' mansion at Govanhill for more merriment. Dixon won the election. In the House of Commons, where he was nicknamed 'the glassblower', he made a mark by sporting its finest set of whiskers.[47]

Yet, next to scenes like these, trouble could also be found. In the same town of Dumbarton the county polled too. The victor this time was the Tory, Lord William Graham, son of the Duke of Montrose. While after the election he and his minders waited in the courthouse, a mob outside bayed for their blood and a squadron of cavalry had to be called down from the castle. Before it could arrive the Whig loser, John Campbell Colquhoun, gallantly arranged an escort of shipwrights to the quay for the Tories, where a rowing boat waited to take them out to a steamer moored in the Clyde. The mob followed throwing stones, forcing Graham to seek refuge in a house where he hid under bedclothes while rioters howled at the windows. An eyewitness said the 'mob would have killed . . . Graham if they had found him'. But at last he managed to get away in one piece.[48]

During the election for Lanarkshire, too, there were 'tumultuous and disorderly' scenes in the parish church of the county town where it took place. A rabble filled the gallery and, as the oaths were being administered, began to throw stones and even glasses at the Tory candidate, Charles Douglas, who was cut behind the ear. When he started to make a speech, he was drowned out by a 'perfectly indescribable' din. Again a chivalrous Whig opponent, John Maxwell, though he knew he was going to lose, tried to secure Douglas a fair hearing. As soon as the poll was over, the victor and his party rushed from the church by a side door, pelted with stones. Stones followed them down the street, smashing the windows of their carriages. The sheriff read the Riot Act and in the end had to summon a squadron of dragoons to clear the streets.[49]

In Roxburghshire the poll took place at Jedburgh, where once more the voters, all country gentlemen, had to make their way through hostile crowds of mill-workers to cast their votes. One of those gentlemen was Sir Walter Scott, who recorded that

> the mob were exceedingly vociferous and brutal . . . but the sheriff
> had two troops of dragoons at Ancrum bridge, and all went off
> quietly. The populace gathered in formidable numbers – a thousand
> from Hawick alone. They were most blackguard and abusive; the

day passed with much clamour and no mischief. Henry Scott was re-elected – for the last time, I suppose. *Troja fuit*. I left the burgh in the midst of abuse and the gentle hint of Burke Sir Walter. Much obliged to the bra' lads of Jedart. Upwards of 40 freeholders voted for Henry Scott, and only 14 [for] the puppy that opposed him.[50]

Sir Walter might make light of the matter in his journal, but many thought him deeply hurt by this evidence he had lost touch with his beloved Borderers. It added to the valedictory mood of his writings at the time. A year later he would be dead.

A few burghs had already turned into Whig strongholds, and here again the election offered a chance to celebrate a new order rather than confront an old one. In Fife, 'delegations from Falkland, Freuchie, Leslie, Markinch, Kettle, Colinsburgh, Leven, East and West Wemyss, Dysart, Linktown, Gallatown, Pathhead, Kirkcaldy and Kinghorn, marshalled four abreast, with bands of music and flags proclaiming loyalty, liberty without anarchy, reform' escorted their candidate, Robert Ferguson, to the town house of Kirkcaldy, where he got unanimously elected.[51] In the far north, the Whig standing for the burghs was James Loch, factor to the Marquess of Stafford and the Countess of Sutherland who, as advanced in their politics as in their economics, put him forward to champion reform. Even so the burgesses had forestalled them. The town council of Dingwall minuted that the Scottish representative system was 'defective and incongruous in the highest degree', because the royal burghs had come to be controlled by oligarchies whereas all householders 'who possess the wealth and constitute the respectable and intelligent part of such communities ought to have a direct influence in the election of their representative'. A public meeting at Tain resolved that, though Scotland had 'greatly increased its wealth and population since the Union', its electoral system, 'calculated to promote the interests of a very limited number of voters [was] altogether insufficient for affording a full and fair expression of the sentiments and wishes of the nation'. Loch promised the council here and in the other burghs of the district that he would vote for reform. He hoped he might be 'entitled to the confidence of any new constituency' – which indeed would return him as its MP till 1852.[52]

In the capital the Whigs put up as their candidate Francis Jeffrey, the former editor of the *Edinburgh Review* who had been serving as Lord Advocate in the new government and so was responsible for piloting the Scottish Reform Bill through the House of Commons. Meanwhile, he relished the challenge of fighting the Tories in a citadel of theirs where, even better, his opponent was another scion of the Dundases. Again with huge excitement in the crowd outside the City Chambers, the council voted 17 to 14 for Dundas. When the poll ended at four o'clock in the afternoon the lord provost, William Allan, foolishly walked 'down the middle of the High Street unguarded, through a great crowd of angry and disgusted people'. He was 'hustled and abused' and only saved himself from being thrown off the North Bridge by grabbing hold of one assailant and threatening to take him down too. Riots went on till midnight.[53]

Even before this general election of 1831, which produced as much of a Whig landslide as the unreformed system ever could, Melville had in effect thrown in the towel:

> If the English Bill should be rejected, it does not follow that some alteration may not be adopted with regard to the Scotch representative system . . . So far am I from thinking that the system in Scotland does not require amendment that I have been for several years endeavouring to carry measures for its improvement. I must protest, therefore, against being classed with those individuals who approve of the Scottish system in all its parts, though I am not inclined to go the length of the wild propositions which are so hastily advanced on every side.[54]

Yet the triumph of reform in 1832 should not obscure the fact that the method of running Scotland as it finally emerged from the Union had consisted in political management by a social elite acting on values of moderation and rationalism. So acting, it won wide freedom to govern Scotland. In a system taking political and cultural autonomy for granted, the country could resolve its own conflicts and resolve them in Scottish terms. Once Scotland reformed itself into greater homogeneity with the rest of the United Kingdom, this would become less possible.

Even such a shrill critic as Cockburn did not claim the Tories of the Dundas despotism had actually been unpopular: 'This party engrossed almost the whole wealth, and rank, and public office of the country, and at least three-fourths of the population.'[55] We should pause to recall the Whigs were no democrats anyway. Their philosopher, Dugald Stewart, wrote that the happiness of a people had more to do with the 'equity and expediency of the laws that are enacted' than with voting and participating in politics.[56] Of course, there were bound to be tensions between a ruling elite and the mass of the people not yet enfranchised (and not to be enfranchised, either, for another half-century, so that the tensions would continue). The virtue of the Dundas despotism certainly did not lie in its democracy either. It lay rather in the fact that Melville, while a member of the Cabinet in London, acted in Scotland through local agency. His regime retained an intimate involvement with the life of the nation over its whole territory: it used the 'safe and small', in the terms already employed to define a major thesis of this book. It is hard to imagine things would have been much different had the Union never taken place. The same could be said, then, for the welfare of the Scottish people.

11

Dominance:
'Out of the house of bondage'

George Gordon, fourth Earl of Aberdeen, spent the summer of 1852 in the peace and quiet of his home, Haddo House, a classical mansion more than a century old that he had extended and surrounded with beautiful policies. The earl loved pottering about there and at times like this, when he could take a rare break from politics, he regretted he did not have more money to spend on the estate. Beyond its walls a general election was going on but, as a peer, he had little need to involve himself with it. There was certainly no point in his bothering about Aberdeenshire. For this constituency a single candidate stood, his brother Admiral William Gordon, who had served as its MP ever since 1820; when he retired a couple of years later he would be succeeded by Aberdeen's eldest son, Lord Haddo. Here was a political Scotland left over from an earlier era. But the earl's idyll did not last long.[1]

The polls produced a hung Parliament – almost inevitably, in a political situation that had been confused ever since 1846 when the Conservative Prime Minister, Sir Robert Peel, repealed the Corn Laws and split his party. If any single faction could be said to have won in 1852, then it was the continuing Tories, now led by the 14th Earl of Derby, who returned with 310 seats out of 658 in the House of Commons. At the same time, it turned out a disaster for the rival camp of Peelites, coming back with no more than 60 after the loss of many stalwarts. In the previous Parliament they had held the balance between Tories and Whigs, but now that would no longer be so. The balance would instead be held, much more dangerously in most eyes, by radicals and by Irish members dedicated to dissolving the Union of 1801.[2]

Aberdeen, as Peelite leader in the House of Lords, would be a key to resolving this state of affairs, and to forming a coalition with any chance of lasting through the new Parliament. It was to him the Liberal leader, Lord John Russell, made the first approach once the result of the election became clear. Russell wrote saying the Peelites had three choices. They could remain aloof from the fray, as they had done in the last Parliament. Or they could come to an arrangement putting the Liberals in office while maintaining their own freedom of action. Or else the two parties could enter into a full coalition – which, however, the most radical Liberals might refuse to support. At any rate, the Liberal and Peelite leaders should concert their course of action once Parliament met.[3]

For himself, Aberdeen saw no great problem in acting with the Liberals, who agreed with the Peelites on free trade and frugal finance. So he felt happy to put Russell's suggestions to his closest colleagues. Most thought coalition the best option. The question then arose who should head it. One suggestion was Aberdeen himself. He did not at all like the idea. He was old, nearing 70, and ignorant of economics, since he had spent his whole career specialising in foreign affairs. But there were various possible parliamentary permutations and discussion of them continued up to the end of the year with no immediate prospect of a Peelite and Liberal coalition, or any other, being formed. It was doubtless this that prompted Benjamin Disraeli to tell the House of Commons: 'England does not love coalitions.'[4]

Disraeli was speaking, on 16 December 1852, as Chancellor of the Exchequer – for Derby, who had called the general election, remained undaunted by the lack of a Tory majority and had waited to meet the new Parliament. Disraeli at once brought in a bold budget seeking to compensate landlords for losses they had sustained through repeal of the Corn Laws. That night in December, he received a magisterial rebuke from William Gladstone – the first of many confrontations between these two great rivals of Victorian politics. During the subsequent divisions the government lost a vote, and resigned the next day. Now the formation of a different ministry could not be delayed. Aberdeen met Russell during a walk in Hyde Park. They agreed that Aberdeen as Prime Minister would have the better chance of constructing a workable coalition, and that Russell should serve under him. Aberdeen went to see Queen Victoria at Osborne House on the Isle of Wight. She asked him to form a government. By Christmas he had done so.[5]

❧

It was not to be an easy premiership. Aberdeen still had no absolute majority in the House of Commons, unless the Irish voted with him. His own Peelites were a small party yet, so Liberal MPs grumbled, they got the pick of the good jobs. Russell expected before long to take over as Prime Minister, and chafed at the bit. Meanwhile, in the Foreign Office, he lorded it over Aberdeen's own political base. A hallmark of the Liberals' international outlook was their hostility to Russia, as a tyranny that posed besides a threat to British interests in the Middle East. In that region the great powers' perennial rivalries all of a sudden came to a head in 1854 when the Crimean War broke out. The failures in British conduct of it need no rehearsal here. Aberdeen, a man of peace, was mortified. He took on himself all the blame for what had gone wrong and resigned in January 1855, after just over two years in office. He was the first Scottish Prime Minister since the calamitous Earl of Bute almost a century before. Though in his earlier career Aberdeen had achieved much for the United Kingdom, he did not improve on the Scottish record in its highest political office. Gladstone, who was devoted to him, thought fate had been cruel. When Aberdeen died five years later, his friends paid for a statue of him in Westminster Abbey inscribed with a wonderfully simple Greek epitaph: Δικαιοτατος, a very just man.[6]

Scotland showed greater love of coalitions than England did, and the path Aberdeen had taken through the political thickets reflected this. He started off in life as a protégé of Henry Dundas. Aberdeen was left an orphan at the age of seven and Dundas, with his wife Jane, more or less adopted him and his small brothers. This led to the earl's becoming a Scottish representative peer in 1805, as soon as he was old enough. A glittering career then opened before him. In 1812 he joined the Foreign Office and a year later was ambassador to Vienna. From 1828 onwards he served in every Tory Cabinet. Under Peel he was Foreign Secretary and remained loyal to him over the Corn Laws.[7]

After Peel's death in 1850, the way forward for his followers was obscure. Aberdeen kept them together, urging them to be true to their principles. He was the man that made them worth courting for a coalition. They entered the one in 1852 with heads held high. And in the event they added a vital component to the huge Liberal hegemony gathering together to rule Scotland through the rest of the Victorian era and beyond. The later Earls, then Marquesses, of Aberdeen became pillars of it, along with their ladies.[8]

The Peelites could comfortably take part in this process because the emerging Liberal consensus bore more than a passing resemblance to the

Tory consensus that had preceded it. Both aspired to represent the nation – at least the enfranchised part of the nation, but then many other Scots as well. The Liberal consensus was little interested in policy but stood for a general set of beliefs linked by a vague sense that all Scots were, or should be, or soon would be, free and equal. This amounted to something little more and little less vague than the earlier Tory consensus that all Scots were loyal Britons happy with the established order of things.

For example, a leading light of reformed Scotland was James Abercromby, son of a military hero, Sir Ralph Abercromby, who had fallen in his hour of triumph over the French at the Battle of Alexandria in 1801, creating such an aura of glory for his family that they were able to intermarry with the Dundases of Arniston. All the same, young James grew up not a Tory but a Whig, and was elected one of the MPs for Edinburgh in 1832. In 1835 he became Speaker of the House of Commons: here was a man at the heart of the new political establishment. On his retiral in 1839, he wrote:

> I think I see that times are coming in which my experience and caution would disqualify me from giving a cordial support to measures that might be proposed by those who think that liberal opinions are to be best advanced by violent changes. Those who entertain such views may judge more soundly or wisely than I do, but I think that in politics as in most other matters, it is never prudent to take a step in advance until you have made your ground firm and secure.[9]

These were sentiments surely indistinguishable from those of any but the most blimpish Tories; it is unlikely, for example, that Abercromby's kinsman, Lord Melville, would have disagreed with them during his progressive old age. The extent of such centrist sentiment might be gauged from what was written in the same tone 50 years later by an eminent lawyer, Alexander Taylor Innes, in a published collection of essays where various public figures explained why they were Liberals. The words he used were more partisan and nationalistic than Abercromby's, yet not so far from them in basic political outlook:

> I am a Liberal because I am a Scotchman. As a matter of personal constitution, the claim of the past, the authority of the present, and the sacred continuity of both, so press upon my imagination as almost to make me a Conservative. But in the history of my own country I find something deeper than the thin stream of its Conservative tradition. I find there in every age a passion for the

ideal, and a sense of the obligation of men who deal with public affairs to build upon nothing less than the principles of right.[10]

Whatever it was, the new consensus made the Liberal party totally dominant in Scotland. The nation was still not going to adapt to a two-party system on English lines. In that sense, after all the fuss of 1832, did reform really make so much difference?

The previous political unity in Scotland had been easy to achieve because it brought such tangible benefits, at home and overseas, as the Dundases doled out their loaves and fishes, paid for by the English. Not much about this redistributive mechanism of Scottish government changed after 1832, except that Whigs rather than Tories bore the basketfuls and that the basketfuls got smaller. But electoral competition still looked undesirable to Scotland, as distinguishing too absolutely between winners and losers. In the reformed system of the next half-century, only about half the burghs and a third of the counties ever saw a contest at a general election, most MPs being returned by the common consent of local bigwigs preferring to avoid the expense and fuss of the hustings. In 1832, 40,000 votes were cast in Scotland, from among 65,000 people now enfranchised. By 1852, the number of actual voters sank to 8,000, since most seats went uncontested: all but four of them, in fact, at the following elections of 1857 and 1859. Despite reform, this was in some ways still the same old system. In the counties, the practice of open polls consolidated the control of the landlords. In the districts of small burghs, too, their worthies looked to leadership from the surrounding countryside; the landed gentlemen they got elected would often be more interested in rural than in urban problems, this in a nation now predominantly industrial rather than agricultural. Many of Scotland's parliamentarians still bore surnames familiar in politics from before 1832 or even 1707.[11]

It was all rather hard to square with any notion that a total transformation of Scottish public life had taken place. In 1832 Henry Cockburn waxed euphoric: 'It is impossible to exaggerate the ecstasy of Scotland, where to be sure it is like liberty given to slaves: we are to be brought out of the house of bondage, out of the land of Egypt.'[12] He might have been slightly prejudiced because he, as Solicitor General, was the man that wrote the Scottish Reform Act (which for technical reasons had to be separate from the English Act). It gave Scotland eight more seats in the Commons for a total of 53, still a good way short of what the population merited. Edinburgh and Glasgow now had two seats each, Aberdeen, Dundee, Greenock, Paisley and Perth one each. Over the entire country the electorate increased sixteen-fold. In the burghs, the middle class – owners and tenants worth £10 a year – won the franchise. These new voters would also choose their MPs directly, so ending the practice of closed election in the town councils and the corruption that had gone with it. In the counties, the vote was given to landowners worth £10 and to tenants worth £50 a year, in other words, to all farmers of any substance. That did not destroy the authority of the great proprietors, since the land of Scotland was unequally divided and new voters proved neither numerous nor powerful enough to mount a challenge to the established rustic order. The political system still rested on property, not numbers.

A sign of it was that in the counties the manufacture of fictitious votes continued. This was Cockburn's fault, the result of his foolish contempt for feudal law and hence his sloppy drafting of the legislation. He has not escaped censure from historians, one pointing out that 'the main defects of the Act derive not just from trifling omissions but from actual ignorance of the law of Scotland'[13] – inexcusable in a man soon to be a judge. But there was another reason, probably more important. On starting his work, Cockburn gave away his general attitude to it with the exultant remark that 'we have got the £10 franchise and the other English things'.[14] The 'English things' were often what weighed with him. The reason he botched the qualifications in the counties was that he wanted to import into them the English concept of 'possession', which had no direct parallel in feudal law. Cockburn always preferred English solutions to Scottish problems if he could find them, egged on by intolerance of Scottish difference among the officials he was working with in London. So, for the particular case of agricultural tenants worth £50 a year, he wrote: 'It is settled for England and they are very desirous to have the scheme as much the same in the two countries as possible.' Matters turned nastier when he came to the registration of voters and faced 'a peremptory and inflexible resolution to make it conformable to what they have settled for England'. Later when amendments were forced on the floor of the House of Commons, even he deplored 'varying the qualifications in exact and servile imitation of the English Bill. The only questions asked as to these points were, How is it in our Bill? Why should it not be exactly the same in yours?'[15] What it all added up to in the end was that the reformed elections might be no better than the unreformed elections.

Still, the new voters' first trip to the polls in 1832 produced a big Whig majority in the Commons, decisively confirming Earl Grey's government in office.
In Scotland the victory turned out to be in proportion still greater than in
England: here Tories won only ten of the fifty-three seats. Francis Jeffrey,
carrying on as Lord Advocate, looked forward to making further laws in a
continuous programme of progressive legislation. He quickly introduced the
municipal reform of 1833, which had the effect of throwing the burgh councils open to popular election as well. It was a measure everybody in Scotland
welcomed, yet he felt amazed how hard he had to work at it. Cockburn wrote
of his overburdened friend: 'He was left to the mercies of every county, city,
parish, public body or person, who had an interest or a fancy to urge.'[16] In
general, the cause of progress was soon running into the sands.

To give a small example, one difficulty Jeffrey faced in municipal reform
was with those burgeoning towns, Greenock and Paisley, which had become
new parliamentary but not royal burghs. Desiring legal coherence, he wanted
to regularise their status yet felt unsure what to do. He wrote to the Prime
Minister, 'I took the liberty of inquiring what were the views of government as to the incorporation of similar places in England. And though your
Lordship then answered, that you did not believe the plan sufficiently matured
to be communicated, I must again state, that without some notion of the
constitution or privileges intended to be bestowed, it will be very difficult for
us to suggest anything useful, as to the analogous cases in Scotland.'[17] History
does not record a reply.

If conformity with England was a problem, it had become so because of
a peculiar attitude of Scots Whigs. Beyond the details of reform, they had
at the back of their minds a greater object they wished to promote, the yet
closer Union of Scotland with England. This was to them a fundamental
matter: they truly believed that the full effects of the Glorious or Bloodless
Revolution of 1688 still had to work themselves out north of the border. And
that revolution was in the first instance an English one; while revolutionary
events did take place at the same juncture in Scotland, they were a good deal
less glorious and far from bloodless. According to the English Whigs, their
victory then had established their country as a constitutional example to the
world, and this by dint of restoring its ancient liberties. According to the
Scots Whigs, their own nation had been struggling ever since to catch up. In
the debates on his Reform Bill, Jeffrey told the Commons: 'If we look back
to the career of glory which England ran during the reigns of the Tudors and
Stuarts, we find that England during those periods held a high rank among

nations for wealth and splendour, and even then was regarded by other nations as the country where the principles of liberty were best understood and practised.'[18] Despite the Union of 1707, the effects and the differences with Scotland were still to be observed at the present day – for instance, in 'the true sweet blooded simplicity of the old English aristocracy to which, I grieve to say, we have nothing parallel, and not much in the same rank that is not in harsh contrast, in Scotland'.[19]

Whigs would have had to concede that, by 1832, English politics also needed reform. Still, with this now accomplished, England was again a light among the nations, in particular a light to Scotland, setting a standard to its benighted northern neighbour that Scots could but gratefully emulate. Often, therefore, the right way to deal with any particular Scottish question was to see what the English would say or do about it. Here lay one clear difference from the outlook of the Dundas despotism, which had always avoided gratuitous anglicisation – especially if it arose from ignorance or negligence at Westminster of Scottish difference. For Scots Whigs this presented no problem.[20]

Still, it was soon found that reform in the legislature had not been enough, and that reform was needed in the executive branch of government too. There the Whigs sought to place Scotland on the same footing as England, without any separate political arrangements. Or, to put it another way, they wanted rid of the unofficial position of Scottish manager that had been filled by a Dundas for the last 60 years, the 'horrid jobbing Scot' of Cockburn's *Journal*. Whatever their sins, however, the Scottish managers at least always assured their country of a place in the British Cabinet. Now this would no longer be so. Out of office, Melville had already put his finger on the problem, pointing to

> the inconvenience frequently complained of by the natives of Scotland, particularly the members of Parliament, that there is no special officer or office in London for the transaction of business, parliamentary or otherwise, of that part of the kingdom, though in fact from the dissimilarity of our laws and institutions, such an establishment is even more necessary than a similar office for Ireland. It has hitherto devolved chiefly on the Lord Advocate, most improperly and inconveniently for the public service.[21]

The Whig government in London still had Scottish decisions to take. How? The Lord Advocate was a junior Minister, so needed to entrust his business in

Cabinet to one of two senior colleagues. The first was the Lord Chancellor of England, Henry, Lord Brougham, actually a Scotsman, a son of Edinburgh though one who had long ago left for London and shown no further interest in his homeland, unless it were hostile – 'his peremptory and impatient spirit, helped by his scorn and dislike to Scotland, will work us much evil,' Cockburn warned.[22] While it might have been feasible for Brougham to take over as Scottish manager, this would have made it hard to see in the new executive order anything much different from, or better than, the old one. Besides, Brougham showed no interest whatever in any such role and his colleagues in the Cabinet were not going to push him. In that case, there remained the English Home Secretary, Lord Melbourne, who indeed bore the formal constitutional responsibility for Scottish affairs. The Scots Whigs wanted him to exercise it. But he viewed communications from Scotland with languid indifference and was ready only with excuses for inaction. When Jeffrey tendered him advice, even if only on the technicalities of Scots law, Melbourne did not listen. Cockburn complained of 'the ignorance or indifference of government about matters purely Scotch'.[23] Discontent welled up among the Scots MPs too. It reached the point where Jeffrey and Cockburn arranged a meeting for them with Grey and Brougham (presumably there was no point in asking Melbourne). Cockburn wrote that the MPs 'testified so sturdily their discontent and indignation at the slighting way in which great Scotch interests were dealt with by the government, that I rather hope they bullied and sulked them into determination to fight the said Bills for them to the utmost of their power'.[24] The hope proved vain.

It had soon become clear, then, that on the executive side of Scottish government the new order was not working well. As early as the spring of 1833, Cockburn declared: 'I am more and more convinced every day, or rather hour, that Scotland can never be managed without some new and responsible person acting, no matter under what name, as Secretary, different from the Advocate, not only because no Lord Advocate can conduct everything, but because, even if he could, he ought not to be allowed or required to do so.'[25] That had been precisely Melville's point too. To Jeffrey himself Cockburn also confided it was

> necessary that some high person should be made Secretary for Scotland, and that it should be understood that the government is to support him. Nothing can be more shameful than that great measures such as burghs, patronage, etc, should be all left to swelter and flounder on as they may, according to the caprice of crazy

constituencies, or their crazier representatives, and that government does not feel its existence, character or comfort at all involved in the result, but leaves the Lord Advocate to be abused for everything, even for those things which they force him to do, or prevent his doing.[26]

These were all difficulties at Westminster. What difference did they make at home in Scotland? After reform, as before, the main contact most people had with the government came through writing in to apply for jobs or other favours. Scots Liberals, whose rapacity became notorious, now expected all the patronage previously reserved to Scots Tories to come their way. They importuned Jeffrey tirelessly. Yet this was his own fault. 'Let me have a list,' he had told Cockburn, 'of movable offices, held by Tories who have, either by overt acts, or by general and open declarations, taken part against the government, and I shall immediately take the sense of the government on the possibility of removing them.'[27] The list of movable offices must have gone down a long way. One Whig grandee, Lord Panmure, noted its results on the ground in his own Angus. It had been 'making ministers and schoolmasters politicians, the effect of which is already seen and felt', notably in radicalising the Church of Scotland.[28]

Melville had always done what he could to protect Scottish jobs, if never as much as he would have liked. Jeffrey seemed, on grounds of economy, quite happy to get rid of them. In 1831 the death was announced of the veteran Henry Mackenzie, who in his distant youth had won fame as a sentimental novelist (*The Man of Feeling*, 1771) but actually lived, like most novelists, off something else – in his case his salary as comptroller of taxes for Scotland. It was Jeffrey himself that wrote to the Prime Minister asking him to 'be pleased to direct that no new appointment . . . be made till farther communication is had with this quarter. I rather think it will be thought right to regulate and considerably reduce the expenses of this appointment.' Jeffrey was at that point MP for Perth, and he replied to one letter of recommendation from the provost: 'I am persuaded you would not wish me to give the sanction of an official recommendation to any person, merely because persons, to whom I am under great obligations [for their votes], are anxious for his success.' Soon afterwards, Jeffrey was asked to support a candidate for a professorial chair. He answered: 'It would obviously be improper for me to make myself the successive advocate to the government for every person who brought me a respectable recommendation – all that I can do is to forward any certificates or recommendations that are sent to me, with a request that they be favourably considered.' From the Dundas despotism these were changed days indeed.[29]

It was the same with patronage of the Church – a matter in which, as we saw in the last chapter, Melville had always been cautious and thoughtful. In October 1832, Jeffrey got a letter about a vacancy in the parish of Dalmellington in Ayrshire. He replied: 'I do not consider myself as at all responsible for the exercise of the crown's patronage of church livings, and have seldom any farther concern in it, than in transmitting to the proper quarter the applications that may be presented to me, as to the merit of the candidates or those by whom they may be recommended.' At the same time, 'I can by no means agree that this trust would be better, or more properly, fulfilled by systematically delegating the right of nomination to the resident heritors, and still less to any one individual who might happen to monopolise that character.'[30] In that case, given the Whigs' equal hostility to the popular election of ministers, who on earth was to make presentations? Cockburn wrote: 'I am against letting the people, in any sense, or any section of them, even heritors and elders, originate presentations. If they know that they are to nominate, they, probably moulded by the existing minister, will always begin, at a distance, preparing a candidate, and committing themselves in his favour, to the utter exclusion of better men.'[31] Apparently the Scottish authorities would forgo a power of presentation that the Scottish people were not to be allowed to assume. It hardly added up to a formula for the effective functioning of the Church of Scotland.

Jeffrey worked on the premise that the Lord Advocate's post was not an executive but an advisory one. When consulted by the sheriff of Stirlingshire on means of dealing with disturbances in his county, Jeffrey answered: 'I am aware indeed that I am also an officer of state, with certain, not very well defined, duties and privileges vested with some of the functions of a resident Secretary of State for Scotland.' But he wanted to get away from all this: 'It is the duty of the Lord Advocate I conceive to give advice, and to be ready to give it, and to consult with all the other authorities in the kingdom, and for that purpose to be constantly at headquarters, and accessible at all periods of general agitation.' To an enquiry from the Earl of Breadalbane, Jeffrey declared, 'My functions are limited to the humble tender of such advice when consulted or referred to by the distinguished persons with whom the decision exclusively rests.' Still, would they listen? Jeffrey also replied to an enquiry about Political Unions (which were radical associations), 'I am not directly in the confidence of his Majesty's Ministers, nor informed individually as to their particular sentiment on the subject of Political Unions.'[32]

Perhaps it was all a matter not so much of indifference as of frustration and boredom. Running a country turned out not so easy as writing reviews. Already in 1831, Cockburn had remarked of Jeffrey: 'I fear for him in Parliament – nearly sixty years of age, a bad trachea, inexperience and a great reputation are bad foundations for success in the House of Commons.'[33] And so it proved. In 1834 Jeffrey appointed himself to a vacancy in the Court of Session, and Cockburn soon followed. The political careers of the two leading reformers came to an end. They had not managed to solve the novel problems of Scottish government. Cockburn was later to say that it might be conducted 'by the Home Secretary, or an Under-secretary, or a Lord of the Treasury or anything else', but not by the Lord Advocate. He added: 'No sane man takes the position of Lord Advocate except to be well quit of it.'[34]

❦

Jeffrey's successor was John Archibald Murray, MP for Leith. A year or two as Lord Advocate robbed him, too, of a reformer's illusions and gave him instead an exact notion of things about Scottish politics that never changed: 'Scotchmen retain the character of being jobbers and not a day passes but there are one or more applications from Scotland for grants or allowances of public money in one shape or another.' He noted that the jobbery stood in direct contradiction to the Whig precept that they 'consider it their duty to resist expenditure of every sort great and small unless on clear and fixed principles and public economy is one of the greatest recommendations of any measure'. He did not really share this view himself, but saw how it set apart the political worlds of London and of Edinburgh: 'I'll grant that Edinburgh is so antiquated and provincial in its notions, and will not stoop to more modern opinion. In all money concerns they speak a different language from what is intelligible here [at Westminster].' The Solicitor General, John Cunningham, found to his amazement that the English would not sanction spending even for the sake of greater efficiency in Scotland: 'Murray has the feeling that he need propose nothing to the government which is to infer any present addition to the expense, whatever the alternate benefit and saving to the country may be.'[35] If it was any comfort, the English did not understand the Scots either. They thought, for example, 'that there would be no great difficulty in assimilating the laws of England and Scotland'. In one of Murray's exchanges with a jurist, 'I found he took the large and liberal view of taking whatever was

English if it was better than the Scotch but not imparting it when worse and he thought that English lawyers would agree to that which may be doubted.'[36]

Murray lasted as Lord Advocate till 1839 when Andrew Rutherfurd, the most brilliant advocate at the Scots bar, took over. He had already served as Solicitor General, but Cockburn all the same offered him this distillation of his acquired wisdom:

> A Lord Advocate generally walks over hot cinders, and sits on gunpowder. But this has of late been because he has not been duly supported by government, and government has failed to support him chiefly because he had not the command of the Scotch members. And you know how much these members have been averted from acting in concert in public matters not depending on mere party principles, by the manner of the Advocate not being calculated to bind them together.[37]

Good personal advice as it was to Rutherfurd, a man notorious for his harsh and overbearing manner, it revealed another novel political problem: individual Scots MPs were much harder to control. Under the Dundas despotism they had been perhaps too docile; one recommended the Lord Advocate should always be a tall man so they could easily follow him through the voting lobbies.[38] But in the reformed system there was a circular difficulty that the Lord Advocate's exclusion from the Cabinet made him less worth following and then he, not being followed, found it harder to command support from the Cabinet. Rutherfurd's own Solicitor General, James Ivory, pondered the problem: 'I cannot help thinking were you to assert your full place, as the representative of government in Scots matters – and this if I am not misinformed has only fallen into a sort of desuetude in later times – the government would be better served, and the country's interests better attended to.' The Cabinet was paying more heed to Ireland than to Scotland, and English Ministers might acquire the bad habit of interfering in the affairs of a second country to which they did not belong. That had to be resisted: 'What can they in the south know of Scots interests . . . compared to the Lord Advocate?' In the absence of anybody else, it fell to the Scots law officers to act 'if there is ever to be a remedy for many evils that have already accrued, and will be constantly recurring from the foreign interference of rash and meddling and eminently ignorant demagogues'.[39]

The Whigs' idea of having the Home Secretary run Scotland with advice from the Lord Advocate never really got anywhere. Most Home Secretaries were just not interested in Scotland and had far too many other things to attend to. Then the Lord Advocate, who actually needed to do all the donkey-work anyway, lacked the necessary authority. Till the eventual solution should be accepted, of setting up a Scottish Office in Whitehall under a Scottish Secretary, various intermediate expedients were tried – again, with little success.

One expedient was the appointment of an Undersecretary in the Home Office with special responsibility for Scottish affairs. When Lord John Russell became Home Secretary in 1835, he did just this and gave the job to Fox Maule, MP for Perthshire. Russell and Maule were friends, both being well-born chaps of radical outlook. Maule promised he 'would always advocate the interests of the poorer classes and do his best to redress their grievances'.[40] Unusually for those days he was also quite nationalistic, and somewhat unctuously declared he had not entered politics for himself: 'All I care for is mine already . . . an honest name among the Liberals in Scotland.' But he agreed the results of reform had so far been disappointing: 'Scotland must have more attention or she will turn restive.' Scotland was already turning restive in a religious sense, as the events leading to the Disruption of the Kirk unfolded. In his ecclesiastical appointments, Maule favoured evangelicals. That indicated an outlook he at length made explicit: 'We wish to abolish patronage and to render the Church more acceptable to all the people.' This was not an official policy, however, or a line Russell and other English Ministers could publicly endorse. After a contretemps, Maule declared simply, 'I fight for Scotland.' Such blunt patriotic sentiment tended to fluster the English – Russell warned Maule of his 'extreme views'.[41] Luckily they were both out of office by the time the great crisis of the Disruption did break in 1843. Maule's career would end after he became Secretary of State for War in 1855, just in time to carry the can for failures in the Crimean War that Lord Aberdeen had tried to take on himself. Meanwhile the concept of a Scottish Undersecretary at the Home Office was amounting to little. The concept would be resurrected in the 1880s, but then lead straight on to the foundation, as a separate department of state, of the Scottish Office.

A second idea was that the government should deal with Scotland not through the Home Office but through the Treasury. Two reasons could be adduced. First, the Scots' main interest in the Union lay in the money they could get out of it. Then there was the managerial reason that, in those days before a professional civil service, the daily work of the department came under the direction of junior lords of the Treasury, a title that survives today dignifying the government's whips. They were whips in Victorian times too, as well as dealing with electoral organisation in the country, but they also still retained their functions in the oversight of public spending. On either count, whether deciding on doles or rallying support for Whig governments from MPs supposedly elected to back them, there was plenty for a Scottish junior lord of the Treasury to do.[42]

For half a century after 1832 Scotland therefore always had a junior lord of the Treasury, bearing financial responsibilities but also working with the Lord Advocate and if necessary standing in for him at the House of Commons.[43] The first of these junior lords was Thomas Kennedy, MP for the Ayr Burghs. As a backbencher he had spent much of his time trying to make the Scots Poor Law even meaner than John Knox left it. Now in office he arranged, among other measures, for the eventual extinction of the Scottish Court of Exchequer in line with the Whig policy of pruning offices they judged inessential. He retired from Westminster with the rest of the older generation of reformers in 1834. Then he went off to work his charms on the Irish as paymaster general to their public services.[44]

Robert Steuart, MP for the Haddington Burghs, succeeded as the junior lord. He, too, was keen on public economy. But he assumed a more political role when he warned of rising hostility to the government in the Church of Scotland. Its leaders deplored how the Whigs pandered to urban radical dissenters for the sake of their votes. On the other hand, English Ministers tended to assume the Kirk was the proper Scottish body to consult on social policy, but Steuart put them right: 'This influence, be it great or small, would be made to operate against us politically, and . . . it would moreover be a needless sacrifice to a party in the state who at all points and on all occasions try to run us down and to lower us in the eyes of the people.' Especially powers of patronage, such as the appointment of schoolmasters, should not be entrusted to the Church. In this Steuart saw eye to eye with Maule at the Home Office.[45]

The Whigs lost power in London in 1841 then came back in 1846, now with William Gibson-Craig, an MP for Edinburgh, as the Scottish junior lord. Rutherfurd was once again Lord Advocate but the two never got on.[46] It was not the only reason why Gibson-Craig recommended moves 'greatly to increase the power and status of the Scotch Lord'. When he arrived at the Treasury, he found there was more Scottish business going on there than he had ever known about as a backbencher. Yet it was not handled in any co-ordinated fashion. So he went to the Chancellor of the Exchequer and said that 'if I was to be Scotch Lord of the Treasury, I must at least know what business was being done . . . If that was not conceded to me, I would not remain. I would not be Scotch Lord of the Treasury in name, and not in reality . . . All I asked was, that every Scotch paper that came to the Treasury should be laid on my desk before it was sent to any of the departments.' It did not prove easy to get the English clerks to change their ways: 'I had considerable difficulty in working that out, but I was quite determined about it; and after a short time I found all the papers from Scotland on my desk regularly.' The problem lay in the fact 'that former Scotch Lords had not got the Scotch business into a proper system, and they had let it slip through their hands'. Yet the Treasury remained the best place for it: 'Almost every species of business in the kingdom is brought into the Treasury, and there is therefore little Scotch business of much importance (except the legal) of which the Scotch Lord, being also an MP, may not be cognisant.'[47]

Then Lord Aberdeen, on becoming Prime Minister, wanted to curb Whig influence in Scotland. He was a kindly, tolerant man who, as he formed his government, wrote to Russell: 'Your Scotch Whigs are really too bad. I am unwilling to recognise the necessity of delivering Scotland into the hands of these violent and exclusive partisans, and I think they might be improved by seeing a gentleman of more liberal feelings introduced among them. If this Scotch spirit were to prevail no government could exist.'[48] Aberdeen had in mind a fellow Peelite as Scottish junior lord of the Treasury. He appointed Lord Elcho, the energetic and strong-minded MP for East Lothian, a scion of the aristocracy who defined its duty as improving the condition of the people. He had a good understanding with Rutherfurd's successor as Lord Advocate, James Moncrieff. Moncrieff, however, was to spend almost the whole of his official career on reforming Scottish education in the wake of the Disruption. It took him 20 years of hard graft against indifference at Westminster and obstruction in Scotland: the prime example of what had gone wrong with the reformed political system. Moncrieff heroically remained a conciliator, and there he saw eye to eye with Elcho. The junior lord meanwhile did everything else necessary to the government of Scotland. He had his whip's duties, to 'make a House, keep a House and cheer the Minister'. He also piloted legislation through: 'I carried in the House of Commons a Bill to do away with the religious test in our Scottish universities. I brought in a Births, Deaths and Marriages Registration Bill, going to France to study their registrations system there. I also brought in an Education Bill which was intended to extend our excellent parochial system in our towns.' For his part he thought his co-operation with Moncrieff had been exemplary: 'No change of system was required so long as the Lord Advocate and the Scottish Lord worked cordially together.'[49]

But this particular winning combination proved unique. A hallmark of reformed Scottish politics was its factiousness, another consequence of the lack of political management. But the factiousness remained confined within the Liberal party (so that the Tory opposition never profited). The Liberal party had to hold itself together not through personal relations among its factional leaders (which were usually bad), but rather through a more abstract high-mindedness, derived from the moral and religious convictions of a philosophical nation. With major issues turning so airy, minor issues came to the fore. Round these the factions locked themselves in bitter conflicts – and then the ramshackle mechanism of Scottish government could seize up altogether. The conflicts burst out in electoral rivalry too: there were more double parliamentary candidatures of men representing different strands of Liberalism than there were contests between Liberals and Conservatives. Scots still seemed happy so long as the party that had delivered reform stayed in power. They might be excused their complacency on the grounds that representative government was novel to them and the political interplay of men and ideas unfamiliar. But the comforting English notion of public business conducted by practical compromise remained alien. Scots stuck to their principles, spent all their energy on internecine strife and got nowhere on most matters. It was the penalty of a system with many factions but few elections: not exactly an advertisement for Scottish democracy.[50]

Liberal leaders did see the fault and tried to mend it. This was the brief given to W.P. Adam, the able young MP for Clackmannan and Kinross, when he became the Scottish junior lord of the Treasury in 1865. His main interest lay in organising the party in the country, so that it could fight elections as a united force. The Conservatives had grown moribund. Among their rump of seats some were still owed to fictitious voters, and Adam took action to get the electoral rolls in the counties purged. Of the 58,000 names on the existing registers, 21,000 were struck off. Then 14,000 were added, reflecting the fact that many entitled to vote had not bothered to enter their names because of the infrequency of contests. The new total of 51,000 was only about the same as in 1841, but more genuine – and, assuredly, more Liberal.[51]

Adam next set about regulating the quality and character of candidates. He sought to ensure the local associations chose men of broad enough appeal not to be challenged by unexpected rivals when the election was called. The

Liberals' infighting paraded their divisions and invited defeat even where they really had unassailable majorities: this was precisely what happened at the general election of 1874 in Glasgow, when one of its three seats was lost to a Tory. Adam took the view that Whig country gentlemen (much like himself) could best smooth things over, and, in fact, he kept radicals at bay for another two decades. On the same grounds, he also resisted the efforts by Joseph Chamberlain, himself a radical with his own base in Birmingham, to set up a central Liberal organisation for the whole United Kingdom. Adam retorted: 'We can manage our own business without his instructions.'[52] Yet again the net effect was to put distance between the sentiment of the country and its political representation. Adam demonstrated how useful a junior lord of the Treasury could be, but showed little interest in policy or law-making. So he did not solve the problems of Scottish government either.

Perhaps the time had come for a more thoroughgoing approach. This was the opinion of the Lord Advocate that Adam worked with, George Young, MP for the Wigtown Burghs. When he succeeded Moncrieff in 1869, he was intent above all on a fresh future for Scots law that would bring it much closer to, and at last into harmony with, English law. He had himself also qualified in England and was a bencher in an inn of court. He thought this would be 'useful in carrying out some legal reforms which I have in contemplation',[53] because he could readily work with English colleagues to produce a code or codes of law applicable across the whole United Kingdom. What he did not bruit abroad was that in the end he actually wished to abolish the Court of Session and transfer its business to London.[54]

Commercial law was the best place for Young to begin. Scottish capitalists wanted reform of it because its differences from English law were becoming irksome as the economies of the two nations started to grow together. Yet civil judgments handed down in the one could not be enforced in the other. A domiciled Scot was unable to sue in England, and the same held for a domiciled Englishman in Scotland. At this stage the preferred Scottish form of corporate organisation was the partnership (rather than the joint-stock company) and quite different laws regulated the partnership in England, so making it a legal nightmare for enterprises of this type to trade in both countries. Again, because of the difference in corporate structure, the law of bankruptcy was much stronger in England, in fact, the envy of Scots. Altogether, wide differences in the two sets of legal rules and methods rendered dealings in the common market of the United Kingdom excessively complex for Scots. This was a deregulating age: but would deregulation amount to anglicisation? The capitalists of Glasgow did not mind anyway, and they became Young's best allies. His real enemy was the inefficiency of procedures for Scottish legislation, so that his projected commercial reform remained fragmentary.[55]

Young's big achievement actually came in the quite different sphere of education. It fell to him at last to get through the Education Act (1872) for which Moncrieff had spent his entire parliamentary career working. This was not in origin an anglicising measure, but Young introduced some final changes that, at a minimum, offered the basis for a future anglicising project. Under this definitive legislation the Scottish Education Department was constituted as a committee of the Privy Council sitting in London, yet not directly responsible to the Parliament at Westminster or to the Scots MPs in it. In such a structure English influence on Scottish education could only grow (though in the event it would come to an abrupt end a mere dozen years later when, by public demand, the responsibility was transferred to the new Scottish Office).[56] A further reproach nowadays advanced against Young is that he made no effort to preserve Gaelic as a language of instruction in Highland schools, where many children arrived without any English. Gaelic provision by private pedagogues had been previously quite widespread, but Young's omission of it from the new public system brought it to an end. Indeed, soon there was positive discouragement of the use of Gaelic by pupils who had it: in the exclusively anglophone schools teachers began to punish pupils who did not conform. The effect was the loss of a whole social sphere to the language. It is odd, though, that this issue as such never cropped up in the parliamentary debates on the Act. The nearest anybody came was when Donald Cameron of Lochiel, MP for Inverness-shire and himself a Gael, managed to block a proposal that would have deprived the poorest crofters of a vote for the new school boards. He might have had in mind the pressure this could preserve in favour of Gaelic instruction; but that was as far as it went.[57]

In any case, Young found his broader anglicising programme overtaken by the effects of the second Scottish Reform Act of 1868 (to which, as Solicitor General, he had also contributed a good deal). Compared to the first Reform Act it represented for Scotland a clearer break with the oligarchy of the past. It made popular opinion a force not just through external pressure on the system but actually inside the system. Andrew Mitchell, a radical activist, wrote of the intermediate state of affairs: 'Our members are not our representatives. They do not share our opinions, they do not sympathise with our feelings. They do not respect our rights.'[58] Now all this would change. The prime reason was that the Act brought a big expansion of the urban electorate – in Glasgow, for example, from 18,000 to 47,000. The new voters came from the working class, who accounted for one-third of the roll before the Act but two-thirds now.[59] The respectable artisans at the core of Victorian Scotland at last arrived in strength on the political scene. Their aspirations could no longer be ignored, in education or in anything else.

The respectable artisans wanted collaboration rather than war with other classes. An obvious common cause was the better government of Scotland. The new MPs could claim a mandate for it. Gladstone was the first Prime Minister following the Act, and in 1869 he received a call from 40 of his Scots backbenchers – practically all of them – for the office of Scottish Secretary (abolished in 1746) to be resurrected. He did not want the expense of a new department of state, but was willing to concede a parliamentary inquiry. He appointed one chaired by the Earl of Camperdown who himself, under his courtesy title of Viscount Duncan, had been Scottish junior lord of the Treasury in 1855–58.

Several MPs who testified to Camperdown were radicals out to get the Lord Advocate, as a legal official who had lost touch with the people of Scotland. Edward Craufurd, MP for the Ayr Burghs, said: 'The present system of the Lord Advocate is objectionable, because the selection of the person to be appointed to the office is limited to one class – it is limited to the class of lawyers.' In future he should be no more than public prosecutor and legal adviser to the crown, and for Scotland there should be 'a department, with officers for the various sections of the department'. They could come under a 'Parliamentary Secretary for Scotland', who would have 'to undertake the responsible government of the country, and that alone would justify such an appointment'.[60] Duncan McLaren, one of the MPs for Edinburgh, was no less critical:

> There is a feeling among many who have no connection with Edinburgh, that Edinburgh and its lawyers rule everything, and there is a strong feeling of jealousy on the part of many. At present no man, let his talents be what they may, can ever be Minister for Scotland unless he becomes not merely a lawyer, but a successful lawyer, and gets to the head of his profession. Then he may retain office for a long term of years, thus stopping all promotion.

Probably these strictures were meant for, more than anybody else, Moncrieff, who had meanwhile left politics to become Lord Justice Clerk. Personal motives for them cannot be ruled out, but anyway he stoutly defended a system he had run under great difficulties, yet not without success. In his evidence to Camperdown he went back to the circumstances of 1832. There was no such thing as a Minister for Scotland except it were the Home Secretary, he said, to whom the Lord Advocate acted only as legal adviser. The criticism was therefore misdirected, and a remedy should be sought inside the Home Office rather than by attacking the law officers. Ingeniously playing a nationalist card, Moncrieff rejected the alternative of setting up a separate political structure for Scotland on the grounds that it would have to be based in London: 'In Scotland itself I believe the groundwork of opinion is favourable to the present system. It would certainly be unfavourable to anything that had a tendency to denationalise the conduct of Scottish business ... If it were once supposed that there was an intention to centralise Scottish administration in London, that which is a quite groundwork of feeling would probably become strongly developed.' The best thing would be to appoint a chief clerk under the Lord Advocate in London, 'to facilitate the conduct of Scottish affairs'. At the same time, Moncrieff recommended that 'the office of the Scotch Lord of the Treasury should be restored to the footing on which it stood formerly, when Sir William Gibson-Craig held it, and that he should conduct the Treasury business connected with Scotland.'[61]

Camperdown's report was far from radical. It did indeed propose the appointment of a Scottish Undersecretary at the Home Office, though it favoured the Lord Advocate retaining his full powers. It recommended further that the two of them should act as joint advisers to the Home Secretary, the former on political and the latter on legal questions. In addition, it asked the Home Secretary to pay closer attention to Scottish matters in future. This was actually a mixture of immobilism and wishful thinking, but in any case the government did not respond even to such modest proposals. Gladstone was unwilling to give Scotland priority of any kind. In 1872, confronted with a motion for the establishment of a select committee on Scottish affairs in the House of Commons, he said:

> I wish to remind the Scottish and Irish members of that part of the United Kingdom which has hardly been mentioned in the debate tonight – namely, that portion called England. Now I have not one word to say against the bringing forward of the grievances

of Scotland. But the grievances of Scotland are not more real to Scottish members than the grievances of England are real to English members. . . I should object to handing over under any circumstances to the representatives of one country the manipulation of measures brought before the House having reference to the interests of that country.[62]

It took another decade of drift before anything happened. Scotland had once been able to get by with its rudimentary, indeed shrinking, political apparatus. But the quantity of legislation was inexorably increasing, and separate Scots law meant some of it had to be Scottish legislation. Again, without a Scottish Minister, how and where could such business be done? Sir George Campbell, MP for Kirkcaldy, returning home from the governorship of Bengal, was amazed to find that

all the time which is usually given to Scotch business is in the small hours of the morning . . . The Scotch members are bound to sit up all hours of the night in order to watch Scotch Bills that do not come on . . . I am myself a man who has done a great deal of work in my day, and am willing to do a great deal still; but my health will not permit that I should be kept sitting up night after night until all the hours of the morning waiting in vain for Bills in which I am interested to come on. If justice is not done to the Scotch members in this respect, they are bound to take every constitutional means in their power to obtain it.

For instance, they might follow the disruptive tactics of the Irish MPs.[63]

Astoundingly, possible answers to the points at issue were meanwhile still being ruled out. The job of Scottish lord of the Treasury vanished because Gladstone, always keen on public economy, axed it in 1880. His Home Secretary, Sir William Harcourt, just did not want to run Scotland any more than his predecessors had done: 'Nobody but a Scotchman can manage Scotchmen.'[64] He would have been happy to lose Scottish business out of his department altogether. The Lord Advocate remained available, but in no better position to cope. Parliamentarians grew impatient. In 1881 Peter Maclagan, MP for West Lothian, put down a motion that the government should appoint a political Minister for Scotland as well as a legal one, and 33 others signed it.

It happened Gladstone was now being pressed on all this from another quarter, to which he could not so casually turn a blind eye.[65] Archibald Primrose, Earl of Rosebery, had been the brilliant orchestrator of the electoral campaign that in 1879 made Gladstone a Scots MP too, representing Midlothian (the seat he would hold till he retired in 1895). Rosebery was already himself being talked of as a future Prime Minister. He stepped into the debate over Scottish government and wrote to Gladstone with a warning that echoed Campbell's: 'If things go on as they are, you will have Scotland as well as Ireland on your hands.'[66] In the House of Lords the earl then spoke out publicly, during a debate where he condemned the present Scottish system for being as bad as the Dundas despotism or even the theocracy of John Knox: 'We in Scotland have been handed over to the legal rather than the spiritual arm . . . It really is a considerable disadvantage for the country to have its chief officer permanently excluded from the Cabinet.'[67] Rosebery's own ambitions bubbled beneath the surface of his show of public spirit. He now wanted to get straight into the Cabinet after spurning two junior jobs when Gladstone formed the government.

The Prime Minister thought this was a young man in a bit too much of a hurry. A chance to fob him off came with a vacancy in the post of Undersecretary at the Home Office in 1881. Harcourt, tired of wrestling with the complexities of the 'land of brown heath and shaggy wood',[68] and with a Lord Advocate in whom he had little confidence, wanted a deputy for Scottish business. Rosebery filled the bill. He accepted Gladstone's offer of the post, which they agreed should take Scotland as its main responsibility. The earl wrote: 'You are always devising some friendly plan for me and I fear you must often have thought me crotchety with regard to them . . . I am pleased and proud that I shall at last serve under you.'[69] Unwisely, Gladstone also hinted this might soon lead to greater things. Rosebery jumped to the conclusion that before long he would be representing Scotland in the Cabinet.

Meanwhile Rosebery proved quite unsuited to the subordinate performance of routine duties. He could work hard when he wanted to, but only if interested. Foreign and especially imperial affairs enthralled him, so he could not find in himself much enthusiasm for the detail of Scottish administration, however neglected it might previously have been. Defects in his working arrangements irked him too: 'People come to me on Scottish affairs and I have nowhere to receive them, except my country house seven miles from Edinburgh.' Gladstone entertained a genuine regard for this brilliant protégé, and owed him a real debt of gratitude for Midlothian. But a Prime Minister did not control his own diary. In December 1881, for example, he told Rosebery that 'it would be very difficult for me under the pressure of necessary business' to receive a deputation on the question of Scottish courts.[70] Besides, since the Undersecretary sat in the Lords, Scottish business in the Commons still had to be dealt with by the Lord Advocate, under the same handicaps as before. Hardly had Rosebery got into the job than he started hinting at resignation: 'The view taken in Scotland is that I have a considerable share in the responsibility and certainly wherever the Scottish halfpence may go, I shall get the Scottish kick. This is not an eventuality I am prepared to face, when I am of the opinion that the aggressive boot contains a toe of justice.'[71]

So things went on for a year, with the earl incessantly moaning though consoling himself that at least he could look forward to early promotion. But when Gladstone did finally stage a reshuffle in December 1882, there was nothing for Rosebery. At once he wrote to the Prime Minister to accuse him of breaking his word: without an assurance of promotion, 'I should never have connected myself with what I must regard as a very imperfect system of managing Scottish affairs or indeed have surrendered my liberty at all.' Now, 'I am compelled to view the situation in a new light.' He had only taken his job 'on the express terms that it would form the nucleus of a new office for the conduct of Scottish business which would soon be developed'. Therefore 'an acute crisis' threatened that could be resolved only by his own resignation or by an immediate new arrangement.[72]

Few Undersecretaries address Prime Ministers in such a manner. Rosebery and Gladstone were on a collision course – yet the earl had actually begun to get his way, just because most members of the Cabinet, too, assumed a man of such abilities and connections was bound before long to join their ranks. On 5 May 1883, they discussed fresh proposals for Scottish government. So keen were they to keep Rosebery on board that they accepted a scheme of reform for which they had no enthusiasm. The fifteenth Earl of Derby wrote up a summary of the session: 'The premier raised the question of Scotch administration, which led to a long debate. The Scotch, instigated by Rosebery, are asking for a Secretary of State or a Minister on the same footing as the Irish Secretary: there is no work for him to do and in the judgment of most English persons the proposal is a mistake but it seems that a certain amount of Scottish feeling, real or fictitious, has been got up on the subject.'[73]

Yet Rosebery refused to wait. On 31 May, during a debate in the Commons, several MPs complained that the Undersecretary at the Home Office should not be a peer. Rather than coming to Rosebery's defence, Harcourt made light of the matter. Given the increase in his department's workload, he said, it was 'inadequately represented not only in the House of Lords but also in the House of Commons', and the only reason for having a peer as his Undersecretary was to please the Scots. Rosebery took this personally and resigned, citing the tone of the debate in the lower house. The objection MPs had raised to 'the Under-secretaryship in the Home Department being held by a peer makes it impossible for me to hold that office', he snapped to Gladstone as he flounced off.[74]

Still, if Rosebery seemed most interested in himself, he did also represent the general and popular demand for reform of Scottish government. In January 1884, representatives of the political parties and of other public bodies held a rally in Edinburgh to promote that reform. So as to stress its non-partisan character they put a Tory peer, Lord Lothian, in the chair. In his opening address, he dwelt on the purely practical reasons for their all coming together: 'Gentlemen going up to London on public business do not know where to go, but are hunted from pillar to post. And when they wish to state their views they are received by that terrible person the permanent official who sees everything from an English point of view, who looks upon everything through English spectacles, and whose sole object in view is pounds, shillings and pence.'[75]

Slowly but surely, the Scots won their point. It helped that something needed done in Ireland anyway; it was then hard to meet with blank refusal the far from outrageous demands of a second nation which, unlike the first, was so loyal to Britain in general and to Liberalism in particular. Gladstone at last agreed to create the post of Secretary for Scotland. In the summer of 1885 it was Rosebery that introduced in the Lords the necessary legislation. A few weeks later the Liberal government fell amid the gathering crisis over Ireland. But Lord Salisbury's Tory caretaker government gave parliamentary time for the Scottish Bill, indeed left Rosebery in charge of it: quite a tribute to a political adversary. It received royal assent on 14 August 1885. Charles Gordon-Lennox, Duke of Richmond and Gordon, was appointed the first Secretary for Scotland.[76]

Salisbury had had trouble finding a suitable Conservative candidate for the job, and Richmond was not the first he approached. To him he wrote all the same in the friendliest terms: 'What are your feelings about the Secretaryship for Scotland? The work is not very heavy . . . but measured by the expectation of the people of Scotland it is approaching the Arch-angelic. We want a big man to float it – especially as there is so much sentiment about it. I think you seem pointed out by nature to be the man.'[77]

How could Richmond refuse? He replied with equally cordial courtesy: 'I am quite ready and willing to take the office of Secretary for Scotland if you would like me to do so and think that by doing so I can be useful to you. You know my opinion of the office, and that it is quite unnecessary, but the country and Parliament think otherwise – and the office has been created and someone must fill it. Under these circumstances I am quite ready to take it, and will do my best to make it a success (if that is possible!).'[78]

Salisbury breathed a huge sigh of relief: 'I really am very grateful to you for your kindness in taking the Scotch Office. It makes it a success at once, for the whole object of the move is to redress the wounded dignities of the Scotch people – or a section of them – who think that enough is not made of Scotland and your taking the office will make all the difference between the measure being a compliment to them, or a slight.'[79] And so, in a flurry of flowery compliments between this pair of high Victorian aristocrats, a new era of Scottish government opened. But it had in essence been the achievement of the Scots people and of their public representatives. Symbolic of the persistent disjunction between them and the political constitution under which they lived was that two figures so remote from them were the first to take charge of its practical dispositions.

12

Division:
'The masses against the classes'

On 15 August 1856, a baby boy was born to Mary Keir in a but-and-ben at the hamlet of Legbrannock, between Newhouse and Holytown in the heart of industrial Lanarkshire. The cottage still stands, extended and embellished, though not flattered by the warehouses full of industrial machinery that overlook it today. In the nineteenth century the landscape would have been a good deal bleaker, for this was the middle of a big coalfield. The miners' rows clustering close to the pitheads and winding gear, with the bings in the background, made even for those times a squalid spectacle.

Here, then, was where James Keir Hardie, pioneer of Scottish and British socialism, came into the world. His mother was a farmhand, a woman of strong will to whom he always remained devoted. She was religious as well, so we may wonder that she had an illegitimate child – though 'bundling', as the young folk termed it, was normal in a proletarian community and carried no special stigma there. When the girl's mother went to register the birth, she put down as the father William Aitken, a miner. But the bairn's parents evidently had no wish to set up home together. Two years later Mary Keir married David Hardie, a ship's carpenter, by whom she would have six more sons and two daughters. He was a typical boozing, not to say bundling Scotsman, tough and hard-working too. When he got home after a night out with the lads, he would taunt his wife about her bastard. No doubt it was this early experience that turned the adult Keir Hardie, as he always called himself, into a passionate advocate of temperance, as a matter of his own evangelical religion and of his desire to free the workers from their social shackles. He later wrote, 'I am of the unfortunate class who never knew what it was to be a child – in spirit, I mean. Even the memories of boyhood and young manhood are gloomy.'[1]

The family soon moved to Govan, where David Hardie hoped to find work in the shipyards; with a growing brood of children, he no longer wanted to go to sea. But his new employments offered little security, and it was young Jimmy that often had to be the breadwinner. He got his first job at a printer's, aged eight, then went into the brass-finishing shop of the Anchor shipping line, then to a boatyard as a rivet-heater, then to a baker's in Glasgow. There he worked 12½ hours a day. Once, with his father again unemployed and a baby brother dying at home, Hardie arrived late two mornings running. He was called out of the bakery into the living quarters: 'Round a great mahogany table sat the members of the family, with the father at the top. In front, there was a very wonderful-looking coffee boiler, in the great glass bowl of which the coffee was bubbling. The table was loaded with dainties.' In a mild tone of voice, his employer told him he was sacked. That night Mary Keir bore another child, in a household without fuel or food.[2]

The Hardies were just not making it in the big city. In 1867 they moved back to Newarthill in Lanarkshire, about a mile from where Jimmy had been born. He was sent down the pit as a trapper, that is to say, tending the traps that ventilated the mine. Explosions and rockfalls might occur without warning; once the boy trapping next to him was killed. The family moved again to Quarter, near Hamilton, and it was here, always at work down the pit, that he grew to manhood. Yet he showed a lively interest in the wider world. He went to night school to learn to read and write, and practised shorthand by scribbling the outlines on a blackened slate with the wire used to adjust the wick of his lamp. He got to love Robert Burns's poetry, though he also tackled more challenging texts, Thomas Carlyle's *Sartor Resartus* and John Ruskin's *Unto this Last*, both fierce critiques of modern commercial values.[3]

So far Hardie had been at best a nominal Christian but in 1877 he was born again and joined the Morisonians, a sect founded by the Revd James Morison of Kilmarnock.[4] It had no truck with anything socialistic; Morison once refused to put up Robert Owen at his manse on the grounds that, since he could do nothing for the visitor's soul, he would not do anything for his body either. The Morisonians also rejected the Calvinist doctrine of predestination, holding instead that heaven was open to all who repented and believed. In that sense their sect showed a democratic outlook, and it made a ready appeal to working people, especially in the west of Scotland, put off by the bourgeois character of conventional churches. Hardie was typical: self-taught, self-helping, afire with zeal to redeem humanity after his own conversion, though at this stage looking to personal salvation rather than to social reform. But later he would always say he first learned his socialism from the New Testament.[5]

At any rate, Hardie soon got involved in the labour movement. In 1878 he became agent in the district of Hamilton for the Lanarkshire Miners' Union, founded by Alexander MacDonald. A moderate leader, MacDonald recognised the weakness of the workers' position in the Victorian economy, so he advised them to avoid disputes. In evidence to a parliamentary committee he said they 'should endeavour to meet their employers as far as they can'. Seeing no way past the capitalist organisation of society, he thought winning political friends was the best means of getting legislation in his members' interests.[6] Hardie at first admired MacDonald (comparing him to Martin Luther), but in 1879 they quarrelled. Round Hamilton the miners' wages were being cut and Hardie, contrary to MacDonald's advice, led them out on strike. In fact, the stoppages continued, on and off, for a year. One became known as the 'tattie strike' because it took place during the potato harvest, and the miners lived from howking tatties for local farmers. But the strikes all failed, and Hardie had to leave the area. He carried with him the reputation of a fierce fighter for his members but also of a rash rabble-rouser as he moved, newly married, to Cumnock in Ayrshire.

Now Hardie needed to eke out a living for a family as well. He opened a small grocer's shop and also sold insurance. But more and more he lived off freelance journalism. Though self-taught, he proved to be one of nature's freelances. From 1882 he contributed as a regular columnist to the *Ardrossan and Saltcoats Herald* under the pen name of Trapper, recalling his job as a boy. His columns were often autobiographical but through them he developed his political and social outlook, evolutionary rather than revolutionary. Once, in rather purple prose, Hardie looked forward to a future 'when the war hatchet will be buried for ever, and when Capital and Labour shall meet together under a roof tree, to smoke the pipe of peace, and as the smoke slowly ascends it shall carry with it into oblivion all the feelings of discord that ever existed between those twin brothers whose best interests are inseparable'.[7] Ardrossan was a coaling port, so Hardie could expect of his readers some interest in the politics of the mines. He often wrote on this subject, setting his hopes for better conditions in the pits on the Liberal party, especially the more radical party that emerged after William Gladstone split it over Irish Home Rule in 1886. These years also saw growing militancy in the trade unions. Though it was a constitutional cause that led Gladstone to the left, the shift offered a chance for Scottish workers to assert their economic interests and make some political progress towards a democracy of self-respecting, self-improving citizens.

A return to the labour movement followed in August 1886 when Hardie took the job of secretary to a new Ayrshire Miners' Union, set up in parallel with unions in Lanarkshire, Fife and elsewhere. The manifesto he drafted struck a more radical note than before: 'Those who own land and capital are the masters of those who toil. Thus Capital, which ought to be the servant of Labour and which is created by Labour, has become the master of its creator'; the answer was to restore the original, natural order of things.[8] The Scottish miners' unions soon joined in a federation with a nominal membership of 25,000. Their main aim was an eight-hour day, with restriction of output – the 'wee darg' – to counter downward pressure on wages. But the federation collapsed within a year.

Still, Hardie's role in all this prompted him to think of going into politics. After the further extension of the suffrage in the third Reform Act of 1884, there was now a vote in the counties for many workers – and in the central belt of Scotland that often meant miners. During the spring of 1888, Stephen Mason, radical Liberal MP for Mid-Lanarkshire, resigned on grounds of ill health. At once the miners of Larkhall proposed Hardie in his place. With the wider franchise, parliamentary representation of the workers by the workers seemed feasible – and here was a chance to try the idea out. An assortment of progressive organisations supported it. The local Liberals, however, refused to adopt Hardie. He threw caution to the winds and stood on his own account, but his campaign did not go well. Even most miners in the constituency remained loyal to the Liberals. Hardie had a bad time at his public meetings, where he was truculent and provocative, attacking the clergy and the royal family, getting drawn into angry exchanges with hecklers. He polled 617 votes, 8 per cent of the total. So ended the first Labour candidacy in Scottish, indeed British, politics.[9]

With a single Labour candidate unable to get anywhere, the obvious way forward was to found a Labour party. A start might be made if the raggle-taggle from the political fringes that had supported Hardie in Mid-Lanarkshire could be persuaded to come together under one umbrella. They ranged from the Highland Land League, concerned first and foremost with crofters' rights, to a Labour Electoral Association in London to the First Socialist International. These and others sent delegates, 27 in all, to the meeting in Glasgow in May 1888 that set up the Scottish Labour Party. Its formal inauguration came in July with, as president, Robert Cunninghame Graham, MP for North-west Lanarkshire, as vice-presidents Gavin Clark, MP for Caithness, and John Murdoch, leader of the Highland Land League, and as secretary Hardie.[10] The policies it adopted were not especially socialist, rather a selection from the radical causes of the time: Home Rule for Scotland, the right of local communities to ban the sale of alcohol, above all land reform, even nationalisation of the land.

The Scottish Labour Party did not enjoy a long or successful run either. Just the routines of electoral organisation taxed it beyond its limits, and members seemed more intent on squabbling among themselves than on fighting their political foes. Efforts to persuade the Liberal party to adopt working-class candidates again foundered on the reluctance of the local associations. Before long Hardie decided he was never going to get anywhere in Scotland. In 1890 he put himself forward for the constituency of West Ham South in London. From his point of view it was a sensible move. The Scottish Labour Party would manage to nominate only three candidates for the general election of 1892, none with the slightest hope of victory. But, in West Ham South, Hardie did manage to draw together a wide range of support, including the Liberals of a working-class seat. He beat the incumbent Tory.[11]

The new Parliament met in August 1892. Hardie's constituents gave him a rousing send-off. They hired a two-horse brake to transport him from West Ham to Westminster, with a musician sitting on the box-seat and playing the Marseillaise on a cornet. Hardie had to alight when the police refused to let the cavalcade through the gates of the Houses of Parliament. Inside, what amazed people was the outfit he had chosen for this debut. In the words of an astonished journalist, he arrived in 'the ideal dress of a Labour member – yellow tweed trousers, serge jacket and vest, and soft tweed cap'. He bumped into Gladstone, who was stupefied. The contrast with the sartorial staidness of all others present could not have been starker. A second new Labour MP was John Burns. One fellow member said: 'Here is a Labour man dressed like a gentleman, but [pointing to Hardie] look at that bugger.'[12]

Hardie had arrived at Westminster yet also bidden his political farewell to Scotland. While he kept a home at Cumnock, he would never again be a candidate north of the border. His career now would be a British one. His first important move was to summon a national conference of the political and industrial sides of the labour movement to a conference at Bradford in 1893. It set up the Independent Labour Party, to which the Scottish Labour Party affiliated before dissolving itself; no native socialist body then remained in Scotland.[13]

The Independent Labour Party, if formally not a Scottish organisation, would be the standard-bearer of socialism in Scotland till after the Second World War. It attained this position despite the centralised structure of the party under a leadership located in London. For progress north of the border, it had to reach out to others. It sought allies among the trade unions, which were not strong in Scotland but did dispose of some money and organisation. They were also moderate in their politics, and a more radical impetus could only come from small socialist societies of intellectuals who had often learned more of the workers from Marxist texts than from personal experience. Their membership gave the Independent Labour Party cultural pretensions, especially in Scotland where higher education was not restricted to a narrow social elite. So here some sons of the proletariat got degrees too, and through them the party could gain access to the workers and a better appreciation of their needs. Still it remained fairly innocent of Marxism. On the contrary, it repudiated class war and preached a high-minded, rather sentimental sort of doctrine, often shot through with Christianity. It had little time for theoretical debate or industrial disputes, preferring to concentrate on practical good works, mainly in municipal government. It built up a reasonable strength in Scotland, with about 40 branches soon after its foundation, most round Glasgow and in practice autonomous of the national leadership in London. In this modest, earnest shape, Scottish socialism continued into the first decades of the twentieth century.[14]

Among the range of radical but respectable causes, Scottish Home Rule had perhaps the widest appeal – and to men of all classes, as well as to the minority of politically active women. 'Unionist nationalism' is the term that has been coined to define Scotland's sense of itself in the middle of the nineteenth century, and it seems just.[15] What it means is that, thanks to the terms of the Treaty of Union preserving Scottish civil society inside the United Kingdom, Scots enjoyed all the domestic autonomy they needed for the satisfaction of their national sentiments. Such sentiments therefore became consistent with the Union, which while indulging Scots in its institutional arrangements also offered them the opportunities in Britain and the Empire that a small nation could otherwise never hope for.

Yet we have seen in these pages that the history of Victorian Scotland was also a history of decay in the terms of the settlement of 1707. That followed from English indifference to Scottish interests, but also from the desire among Scots for modernisation, which often proceeded on English lines for want of any handier model. The desire could go the length of preference for straightforward assimilation to England as an end in itself (the position of certain Whigs), while on the other hand also starting to provoke some popular dissatisfaction with the Union as such. At any rate, by the end of the nineteenth century the façade of unionist nationalism was showing cracks.[16]

We need only think of the number of patriotic points at issue that have figured in this book. Foremost among them was the Disruption, even though the leaders of the Free Church in 1843 had taken care to avoid the impression they were engaged in any kind of nationalist struggle. The *Annals of the Disruption* tell how the Revd Walter Wood of Elie visited Langholm in Dumfriesshire in January 1843 as member of a mission, one of several, sent out by the General Assembly of the Church of Scotland on tours round the country to prepare faithful Presbyterians for an event which all now knew to be inevitable. Wood addressed a public meeting, and complained to it that at Westminster the voice of the Scots MPs was overborne by the English majority: 'I said, on the spur of the moment, that such injustice was enough to justify Scotland in demanding the repeal of the Union. With that, to my surprise, and somewhat to my consternation, the meeting rose as one man, waving hats and handkerchiefs and cheering again and again. No doubt the enthusiastic feelings of the people assisted our object, but I took care not to speak of repeal of the Union at subsequent meetings.'[17] Yet the Disruption was indeed in large part a constitutional dispute, concerning in particular the nation's religious establishment. In 1842 the fathers of the Free Church had drawn up a document, the Claim of Right, which set out their constitutional case. It rejected the English doctrine of the absolute sovereignty of Parliament. Instead, it sought to resurrect the Scottish constitutional theory, dating from the era of the Reformation, that the relationship between state and Church was a federal one, conceding to the latter a sovereignty of its own. Westminster took no notice whatever.

And why should it have done? In the secular sphere, after all, there was by now not even a shadow of a native constitutional tradition to draw on.[18] Since the Union the Scottish doctrine of a state with two equal and co-ordinate parts, secular along with religious, had been wholly overborne by the English doctrine of absolute parliamentary sovereignty. This was why the Scots Tories, though the least unionist party, could develop no coherent constitutional theory. Whigs often turned into assimilationists *tout court*. While, within the Liberal hegemony, they also faced resistance from radicals, these were people stressing the unity of the British peoples, the equality of the Scots with the English and their comradeship-in-arms in tearing down privilege. Such radicalism could not be characterised as merely Scottish or even merely British in outlook. A reformers' association reconstituted in Glasgow in 1858 declared its 'support of parliamentary reform and continental freedom'[19] – this with special reference to the current struggle for the unification of Italy. Everywhere the bugbear to radicals was central government, remote, ignorant and destructive of local individuality, in this sense offensive to the absolute rights and dignity of man. And radicals took their view whether the community in question was Scotland or Hungary or Armenia or Afghanistan. Nationalism in this guise could become rather abstract, however. A basic point about Scotland was that till 1832 it had enjoyed semi-independence, if with antiquated domestic political arrangements. On the reform of those arrangements the semi-independence was also swept away. Scots found it hard to disentangle the benefits of the first from the penalties of the second. One result was recurrent institutional crisis.

All the same, within a couple of decades Scotland saw the first identifiably nationalist agitation of modern times, under the aegis of the National Association for the Vindication of Scottish Rights. Established in 1853, it managed to drum up 3,000 subscriptions from the great and good. To inspirit the campaign it issued a statement setting out a list of grievances. The inaugural meeting, held in Edinburgh in November, drew an audience of 2,000, while a similar demonstration in Glasgow the next month attracted 5,000. The motions they passed called for various reforms, notably resurrection of the post of Scottish Secretary. But otherwise these gatherings were unsuccessful, and the association only kept going for about three years. A list of grievances proved not enough to overcome the differing political outlooks of the disparate membership, ranging from high Tories to rabid radicals. At bottom, they anyway all had an overwhelming attachment to a Union that guaranteed their material well-being. They sought no change in its basic structure, but rather equality for Scotland within it. In London, *The Times* ran a scornful leader remarking that the English were above nationalism and that 'the more Scotland has striven to be a nation, the more she has sunk to be a province'.[20] While the consensus of unionist nationalism had been scarcely disturbed, Scots still did not want it to turn their nation into a province. That process seemed, however, destined to continue.

A crux came in 1886, when the problems all at once burgeoned to become much bigger than Scotland. Gladstone's espousal of Irish Home Rule made a live issue of the re-emergent nationalism among the junior partners of the United Kingdom. It turned the Tories against this kind of nationalism, put the Whigs on the spot and stirred up once again the radicals' concern for consistency and equity: if Ireland was to have a Parliament, then Scotland should get one too – come to that, why not Wales? The Irish measure was anyway never popular outside Ireland (and there not in Ulster either). Leading Liberals, though not Gladstone himself, believed that for electoral reasons it needed to be toned down in tandem with some wider and less drastic plan. That, rather than a subterranean popular aspiration, created the concept of Home Rule all round, with the aim of some sort of Parliament for each of the nations of the British Isles.[21]

But this formed no part of Gladstone's own gamble in 1886: he saw Scotland had nothing like the grievances Ireland had, so he thought Scotland could wait. He would remain wary of, even hostile to, Home Rule all round. If the concept was to take shape, Scots needed to work at it for themselves. The Scottish Home Rule Association came into being with this purpose in the summer of 1886. By seeking through a quasi-federal system the basic reorganisation of the Union, it went further than the association of 1853, and so counts more properly as an ancestor of the nationalism of the twentieth century. Its chairman was John Stuart Blackie, professor of Latin at the University of Edinburgh, yet a man of far wider interests, champion of the crofters and campaigner for the chair of Celtic at his university, a kenspeckle character who strode about the capital clad in the tartan plaid of a Highland shepherd.[22] The association nominally transcended party but, though at first severe on Gladstone's policies and viewed with suspicion by his MPs, it soon felt able to make common cause with them. By 1888, Home Rulers could claim that 'at every important conference of Liberal Associations . . . a resolution had been unanimously passed in favour of Home Rule for Scotland'.[23] In that year it became the official policy of the Scottish Liberal Party.

Still the key still lay in Ireland rather than in Scotland. And Scots had never cared much about Home Rule for Ireland, though after centuries of close and often antagonistic contact they entertained strong feelings about the Irish. Anti-Catholic sentiment in Scotland was powerful, as was sympathy for the embattled Protestant minority across the water. Irish immigrants, in the face of such hostility, remained unassimilated, maintaining their own identity and institutions.[24] So Scottish attitudes did not provide receptive ground for Irish complaints. When in December 1885 the word got out that Gladstone, just re-elected to office, wanted now to do something about Irish Home Rule, it came as something of a shock in Scotland. It came as even more of a shock when he revealed the extent of his plans in the Bill he put before Parliament the following April. He had prepared them in secret, and they went much further than his previous remarks might have suggested. Bitter battles erupted everywhere among Scots Liberals. Within three months their party had split into a Gladstonian and a Unionist wing, the one following their leader, the other holding fast to the Union – the parliamentary Union of 1801, that is, between Great Britain and Ireland.

It turned out to be Scotland's major political event of the Victorian era. That it was in no way intrinsically Scottish showed the extent to which the Scots had already been integrated into the Union. Yet the event itself would weaken and in the long run tend towards dissolution of the Union. It produced such far-reaching consequences because it brought to a head a range of forces that had been building up all unsuspected in the interstices of Scottish society and in the imperfections of its political system.

The first of those consequences was a schism in Scottish Liberalism that went deep and proved permanent, cleaving in twain its wide and tranquil mainstream. The greater body of Liberals continued as the strongest force in Scottish politics, but a lesser body of Unionists divided off to follow its own deviant course. Relations between the two factions remained bad enough to forbid the reconciliation that many Liberals in principle long hoped for.

To state things in such broad terms is a necessary simplification, however, for the split between Liberals and Unionists turned out nothing if not complex. From the point of view of class, most Scots workers remained loyal to Gladstone and the Liberals. But the Protestant proletariat of the west of Scotland, which had suffered most from Irish immigration, swung to the Unionists and much of it stayed with them for decades afterwards. On different grounds, Gladstone was deserted by a large part of the middle class, businessmen, professionals and academics, to whom his new Irish policy meant the culmination of years of creeping radicalism. A great blow to him was the defection of the two leading newspapers, the *Glasgow Herald* and *The Scotsman*. He had been idolised in the Scottish press, but now had no organ of authority to speak for him. All these forces were strong in the cities and towns, so that Unionism became primarily an urban movement. The instinctive conservatism of the small burghs and counties expressed itself this time in fidelity to Liberalism. Religious allegiances further complicated the matter. Catholics of Irish descent supported Gladstone, though many were not voters. In reaction, the Unionist secession turned strongly Protestant. In Glasgow especially Unionism was able to recruit many migrant Ulstermen, as diverse in their urban roles as the scientist William Thomson, Lord Kelvin, or Sir Thomas Lipton, the retailer who made cheap tea available to the masses. On the other side of the fence and of the country, Rosebery, who had almost become the archetypal Whig, of noble blood, moderate opinion and imperialist sentiment, stayed loyal to Gladstone.[25]

Such untidiness clouded differences among the parties in the ensuing constitutional crisis: there was rather a delicate gradation of views about future relationships among the three kingdoms.[26] In fact, Liberal ideology would retain its force throughout Scottish society till 1914, disrupted but little corrupted. In philosophical terms there might still have been more to unite than to keep apart the two Liberal factions. Yet political divisions did come to correspond more closely to underlying social divisions. The class politics of the future had been germinated in Scotland.

For now, the schism brought the collapse of Gladstone's government when he failed to get a majority at the second reading of his Government of Ireland Bill. A general election followed in the summer of 1886. At the hustings no Liberal on either side advocated a permanent split. The candidates made much of Home Rule all round, with Unionists asserting any scheme would have to satisfy hopes on both sides of the North Channel and Gladstonians claiming a measure for Ireland was but the first step to one for Scotland. These similar lines of argument threatened the integrity of Gladstone's following. They may explain why so many incumbent Unionists retained their constituents' confidence. Their commitment to devolution also helped them in their insistence they were quite different from Conservatives. The anti-Gladstonian parties would later conclude an electoral pact, but meanwhile closer identification would often have been a handicap to the Liberal defectors.[27]

Given his rout elsewhere, Gladstone's performance in Scotland turned out not bad.[28] Overall at Westminster, Conservatives and Unionists emerged with a majority (though the latter did not join the government Lord Salisbury then formed). In Scotland as well, with its 72 MPs, the most striking result was the return of 27 Unionists, 17 of them Liberal Unionists rather than Conservatives. The parent Liberal party suffered the worst losses since 1832, if without losing its majority of seats. Forty-three constituencies returned Gladstonians, compared to 57 for the undivided Liberals at the general election of 1885. Scotland still mistrusted Conservatism, but a new body of floating voters made many more seats marginal. Despite the reservations, 1886 must count as a turning point in Scottish political history. Scotland cast off its pre-democratic structure, a sort of one-party state where individuals and cliques conducted public affairs, to become a country with a modern pluralistic system of organised collective interests.[29]

It was Unionism that created the pluralist system. In the very act of defecting from Liberalism, it transformed the Scottish opposition from a tiny, landed coterie to a political party containing some of the leading citizens, grounded on a popular base and espousing a patriotic, Protestant ideology. The Unionists were at this stage still distant from the Scottish Conservatives, the rustic relics of aristocratic power holding on to at best a dozen counties. In the House of Commons, the Unionists continued to sit on the same side as the Gladstonians, even while waging a war of words with them. It came as no surprise when a conference called in 1887 to arrange their reconciliation proved a flop.[30]

The confusion stretched from the House of Commons down to the political grassroots. Gladstone claimed this to be a struggle of 'the masses against the classes',[31] but the electoral sequel hardly bore that out. The seats the Unionists took in 1886, even in their stronghold of the west of Scotland, lacked any common social or economic profile. While Greenock, a shipbuilding town with a big Orange element, went Unionist, the Kilmarnock Burghs did not, though that district also included Port Glasgow, next door to Greenock and more Catholic in character. The same was true of other industrial towns along the River Clyde, Rutherglen and Dumbarton. Of the seven parliamentary seats Glasgow had after the third Reform Act – every single one of them Liberal at the election of 1885 – two now stood out as likely on paper to fall to the Unionists: College, with its big bourgeois element of academics, many of these, led by Kelvin, active against Gladstone; and then Bridgeton, with its sectarian Protestant proletariat. In fact, the Liberals held both seats, even as they lost similar ones at Central, St Rollox and Tradeston. Unionist victories across the rest of the country turned out if anything still more disparate. At their most disparate they drew together both Whigs aghast at Gladstone's drift to the left and radicals who thought his engineered constitutional crisis an unpardonable distraction from the real tasks of social reform.[32]

The Liberal schism and the political struggles it unleashed therefore cannot be explained by any series of socio-economic statistics. This was in the first instance a battle of ideas, if of somewhat messy ideas. On one side there stood the cosy, couthy, parochial Liberalism of old, on the other side the new Unionism defined by causes external, in particular the cause of imperial unity. Nebulous cause it might as yet be, but for many Scots one clear point was that Gladstone's notion of Irish Home Rule stood in contradiction to it. On all sorts of grounds they decided their national vocation lay in building and maintaining a British and imperial community of interest. In that context Home Rule all round might seem fair enough if it could ever be set up, along with the self-government of the Empire's white dominions. But Home Rule for Ireland by itself was a question of a different order, because the loyalty of the Irish could not be taken for granted: which side had they supported the last time Britain fought a continental war? The world was not becoming less dangerous, so the prospective autonomy of Ireland might well pose a threat to the security of the United Kingdom – quite apart from disrupting Ulster's links with Scotland and threatening the welfare of the province's Protestants, most of Scots descent. If all this entailed some hostility to the Irish, and in particular to the Irish Catholic immigrants who settled in Scotland, it was just too bad. Despite a lurking inconsistency, and certain unpleasant consequences of the sentiments evoked, we need not doubt their strength. They would last till the Empire came to an end.[33]

As the prospect of Liberal reconciliation faded, Unionists had to think how they could establish themselves as a permanent force in Scotland. To that end there was one thing to be learned from Ireland. Across the water law and order became ever harder to maintain (and deficient arrangements for the police had been among the main Unionist objections to Gladstone's Home Rule Bill). But law and order posed a question for Scots too. In urban Scotland crime had risen fast,[34] and many criminals were Irish. So it became easy for Unionists to suggest a parallel in social conditions on either side of the North Channel, then to draw the conclusion that both cases required action by a strong state against violence and robbery. This was a policy for the poor rather than for the rich, who could afford to pay for their own security. Just as the working class wanted a law-abiding Scotland, so it had an interest in a peaceful Ireland controlled by Great Britain.[35]

Here we see signs of a Unionist drift to the right. As yet greater, however, was the need still to appeal somehow to the nation's Liberal tradition and to stress the continuity of Unionism with it; otherwise the defectors would come across as mere Tory stooges. So they began to develop social concerns marking them out not only from Conservative reaction but also from Gladstonian *laissez-faire*. The concerns were geared rather to an argument that the Empire, the Union and Clydeside in particular depended on one another. In the west of Scotland skilled jobs sustained themselves by supplying heavy goods to the rest of Britain and by exports overseas of the products of advanced technology, especially in steel and shipbuilding. That line of argument was what won Unionist votes among the craftsmen of the big industrial complexes, the Parkhead Forge at Camlachie, the shipyards at Tradeston or the locomotive factories at St Rollox.[36]

This Unionist appeal did not stop at material interest, however, but also offered a chance to rethink how Scottish society might be managed. A practical example lay to hand in the paternalistic, not to say authoritarian, corporation of Glasgow. It was now taking symbolic shape in the City Chambers, an expression on a grand scale of civic wealth and pride, started in 1883 amid ceremonies including a march past by tradesmen and opened in 1888 by Queen Victoria herself. The corporation sitting within was drawn from the local mercantile and industrial elites. Individual members came and went, but the man who really ran Glasgow in this era was Sir James Marwick,[37] town clerk from 1873 to 1904. He 'held a unique place in the municipal, literary and social life of the city'[38] and felt especially keen to keep extending its boundaries so as to assure the financial base for its (or his) ambitions. He was also a Unionist.

Marwick often turned for advice to William Smart, professor of political economy at the University of Glasgow, who maintained his own political neutrality but as a general principle wanted to advance 'responsible' patterns of production and consumption. He was an intellectual innovator, introducing to Scotland the economics of both Alfred Marshall and the Austrian school, though for himself remaining a dirigiste with a nationalistic bias.[39] He believed in free markets, but with the aim for Glasgow of letting 'local bodies take toll of the larger incomes of the citizens, and sink them in permanent improvements and reconstruction of the common environment, clearing away the ugly debris left by the processes in which wealth is made, restoring sunlight and air and a clean atmosphere'.[40] Between them Smart and Marwick wielded both intellectual weight and practical clout for the policy of transferring Glasgow's public services into municipal ownership. So the values of the city's elites were transmuted into communal aspirations for all its citizens. A newspaper explained the political implications: 'It cannot be overlooked that Unionism evidently is more attractive to the Scottish people than Toryism ever was, and that many constituencies that had little favour for the one have given their support to the other . . . the old Tory spirit has given place to one which evinces more regard for the general welfare of the people.'[41]

Though primarily an urban movement, Unionism did not shy away from the most intractable Scottish social problems of all, those in the Highlands. The party secured an unexpected northward expansion when out of the blue it captured four of the region's seats at the general election of 1900. This happened in the middle of the Boer War in South Africa, where Highland regiments played a heroic part. Of doubtless more durable effect was the fact that the two great ducal houses of the region, Sutherland at one end and Argyll at the other, had both defected to Unionism. Perhaps this was a matter of their black reaction in things Irish, but in the Highlands they succeeded in giving a more progressive turn to public policy.[42]

During the Parliament that came to an end in 1900 the Unionists had for the first time gone to join the Conservatives on the government's benches in the House of Commons. In Highland policy this showed. True, it was the Liberals that had passed the Crofters' Act, opening a new era for its direct beneficiaries. Yet the Act remained (and remains to this day) unsatisfactory as a long-term solution for the whole region because it froze the way of life in the mould of 1886. Crofters had no incentive to better themselves on the land secured to them for, if they did anything else with it, they could lose their statutory privileges. And the Act offered nothing at all to that great majority of the population who happened not to be crofters: their sole way to improve their condition was to emigrate. The whole system added up to a formula for stagnation, and stagnation has down to this day been its result.[43]

Unionists sought to do something else. Argyll believed it would be best for crofters to be taken altogether out of their technical status as tenants and to become owner-occupiers. His own county contained some of the more fertile parts of the Highlands, and he knew these included thousands of acres which the many small estates would be glad to sell: 'If we could get a body of men to form a class of capitalists or actual freeholders the gains would be great [from] a measure which could provide facilities for the purchase of farms and the purchase of estates at low prices to be broken up'.[44] Actual public policy turned out less radical. In 1897 the government established the Congested Districts Board to acquire farms and estates for the enlargement of existing holdings and the creation of new ones. There were further projects such as the construction of the railway from Inverness to Kyle of Lochalsh. The Dukes of Sutherland meanwhile continued the programme of improvement they had inaugurated at the beginning of the century, with vast schemes to reclaim moor and bog for farming and with the completion of the railway from Inverness to Wick and Thurso. Not much came of all this, though at least on the eastern edge of Sutherland the population earlier cleared from the interior could now win a somewhat easier livelihood from the bigger crofts available here and from a range of supplementary employments.[45] The Unionists' policy in the Highlands turned out in the end little more successful than anybody else's policy, but they did mean well.

If with varying degrees of success, the Unionists altogether looked for a strategy of social reform that would put flesh on the bare bones of their commitment to the Union with Ireland. There was no other way, beyond the immediate crisis of 1886, to make a permanent appeal to Scots voters. And social improvements on the ground could be linked with airier aspirations to imperial unity in a policy of comprehensive reform for the United Kingdom. It all added up to a reconstructed form of Liberalism, in which the fierce, anarchic pursuit of personal rights was transmuted into co-operation for public welfare that might equally ensure them: out of it the system of Scottish government in the twentieth century was to grow.[46]

The Unionists then had one thing they wanted – clear blue water between themselves and the parent Liberal party. On the other hand, their shift tended to muddy the waters between them and the Conservatives. Finally Unionism became a bridge over which middle-class voters could pass from Liberalism to Conservatism without fouling their feet in blimpish reaction. That way forward appeared first in England, where relations between Unionists and Conservatives settled into harmonious co-operation quite soon after 1886. The path proved stonier in Scotland just because the Liberal tradition remained so much stronger, and a Tory alternative so much weaker. While in England the Conservatives absorbed the Unionists, in Scotland it was, at length, to be the other way round.[47]

The uneasy position of Scots Unionists persisted into the twentieth century. The question of their future was forced in the spring of 1912 after a formal merger of the English Unionists and the English Conservatives. Could the Scottish counterparts remain separate? They pondered the problem for seven months, then in December called special conferences in Edinburgh and Glasgow to make a decision. During this hiatus the ground for a Scottish merger was well prepared by George Younger, Tory MP for the Ayr Burghs. When the parties met, they had before them an identical resolution, 'that it is desirable that the present Central Conservative and Liberal Unionist organisations in Scotland should be united to form one consolidated Scottish Unionist organisation'. Younger urged them to pass it: 'It will tend to greater economy of administration, and I hope it will result in what we all earnestly desire, in sending into the wilderness at the earliest moment a party and a government of which most people are heartily sick' (this was a Liberal government). And pass it they did. At the meeting in Glasgow, the Unionist speaker James Cumming argued his party had not only 'carried on the principles of the true Liberal party, but we have brought our Conservative friends a good deal in our direction'. He added, 'The word Tory is all that remains of the old Tory, who revered things that existed simply because they existed, [and] is as dead as the dodo. Personally, I am a Unionist because I am a Liberal. Unionism means not only the union of Scotland, England and Ireland, but the union of all classes of the Empire, and also the union of all classes of the community in a homogenous whole.'[48] Indeed, from now till 1965, Unionist was to be the name the merged party normally went under.

Among Unionists some degree of Liberal identity evidently survived. It did so not least because since 1886 there had been a shift among a significant section of the continuing Liberals too. A new tendency emerged seeking to look beyond the sacred cows of local grievance that had forged the fiercest commitments of Victorian radicals. A new type of Scottish MP appeared as well. The leading younger members were Anglo-Scots, such as Robert Haldane and Ronald Munro Ferguson, or English carpetbaggers like Herbert Asquith and Augustine Birrell. The Cheviot Hills did not bound their horizons, they felt at home with the ruling circles in London and several would achieve great distinction. And to their mind Archibald Primrose, Earl of Rosebery, was the leader in waiting.[49]

Gladstone, after winning the general election of 1885, had appointed Rosebery his Foreign Secretary. Here was at last a job the earl relished. It secured his loyalty to the Prime Minister right through the crisis of 1886, but that ended with the Liberals out of office again. Rosebery developed various other interests, above all in the Empire. After he came back as Foreign Secretary under Gladstone in 1892, he pursued a forward imperial policy of which the most durable achievement was the annexation of Uganda. When Gladstone retired in 1894, Rosebery succeeded him as Prime Minister. He was the third Scot to fill the office, and turned out no better than the first two.[50]

The changeover took place during a three-year interlude of Liberal government between two extended periods of Conservative rule. Gladstone had tried a last time for Irish Home Rule but got nowhere. A fortiori Scottish Home Rule was off the agenda too, and the cause had little chance of flourishing under Rosebery. He had lost interest in it, though this did not hold true of the disciples gathering round him.[51] His cosmopolitan crony, Donald Mackay, Lord Reay, a former colonial governor and now junior Minister in his government, was elected rector of the University of St Andrews and at his installation said: 'If we had a Scottish Parliament sitting in Edinburgh, I have no doubt that the organisation of the universities would be the first number on its legislative programme. . . . This is not a matter of local importance. It concerns the greatness of the Empire. Development of more brain-power in Scotland means increased national efficiency and less danger from democratic ignorance.'[52] A big objection to Home Rule in 1886 had been that it would weaken the Empire, but on this novel reading it might rather contribute to imperial development by forming the foundation for some kind of unifying architecture to extend from the mother country over its far-flung colonies (the white ones). And it would put Scotland on a par with the other constituents of such an imperial federation. Here was a new kind of imperialism, a Liberal imperialism.[53]

It was imperialism with a domestic agenda too. Rosebery focused not just on the Empire but also on Britain's social and economic problems. To his mind these concerns were all connected because the United Kingdom could not maintain its international position unless able to compete with new and lusty industrial rivals, the United States and Germany, even Russia. The next goal of reform had to be what he termed 'national efficiency'. It may seem odd that, in order to promote this cause, Rosebery felt he needed to step down from the leadership of the Liberal party as soon as he lost his first general election. But he wanted some philosophic distance to develop his ideas. He set out to do so in high-minded disquisitions that sometimes seemed to retain only a tenuous relation with humdrum reality. Asquith's son Raymond wrote to the novelist and aspiring politician, John Buchan: 'Rosebery continues to prance on the moonbeam of efficiency and makes speeches on every street corner. But he might as well call it the Absolute at once for all the meaning it has to him or to anyone else. No one has the least idea what he wants to effect and beyond a mild bias in favour of good government and himself as premier, nothing can be gleaned from his speeches.'[54] Still, what he presumably did mean – an effective, powerful, managerial public sector guiding the nation's life – was to become a holy grail for many British governments in the twentieth century. Rosebery may be given the credit for first articulating the concept but, considering the record of his successors, is scarcely to be blamed for not getting much further with it.

Immediately obvious, on the other hand, was that a great many Liberals in the country would not like whatever it was Rosebery wanted to propose, if only because it appeared to differ little from the policies of the Unionists and Conservatives now in office together. One policy they pursued was imperial expansion. Its climax came in the Boer War waged against the Afrikaner republics of South Africa from 1899 to 1902. The Boers were sturdy God-fearing folk, Calvinists to boot; Scots radicals felt only horror at the effort to subjugate them. But Rosebery, and the Liberal imperialists round him, could not in all conscience disapprove of this British aggression.[55]

Here was a fine pickle for the man who had at length succeeded Rosebery in the Liberal leadership, Henry Campbell-Bannerman, MP for the Stirling Burghs, son of a lord provost of Glasgow and heir to a fortune from wholesale textiles. He was a moderate and a shrewd man, who saw it as his first duty to hold together a Liberal party that had already suffered one unhealed split, and now looked as if it might suffer another. In his attitude to the Boer War also he sought the middle course of maintaining a critical but neutral stance. The reward he reaped was to be attacked from every quarter for weakness and vacillation. During 1900 a series of embarrassing divisions in the Commons on various military issues demonstrated his lack of authority, as he persisted in abstention but failed to carry his party with him. By the time the Tories called a snap election at the end of the year, the Liberals were in the utmost confusion. In Scotland they lost the majority they had held ever since 1832, this time returning only 34 of the 72 MPs. Against one gain the Liberals suffered eight losses, four of them by candidates supporting the Boers. So it seemed clear the war had tipped the balance. Still, Campbell-Bannerman was a patient man too.[56]

Rosebery meanwhile decided that the time for philosophic distance was past, and that the hour had struck for his re-entry into the blood and dust of the political arena. He embarked on a fresh series of speeches round the country, more provocative this time in calling on the Liberal party to renew itself by facing up to the realities of imperial power. Meanwhile his supporters got to work at the grassroots of the party. Their aim was to take it over for him. This meant insinuating themselves into influential positions in the constituencies and then swinging the selection of Liberal imperialist candidates, at the same time co-ordinating their actions outside the official structures of the party: a tricky task, but Scotland was one place where there seemed to be some prospect of success. Here it was that Rosebery retained his greatest personal popularity. The imperialist city of Glasgow, with its bureaucratic but reforming corporation, showed how his principles of efficiency might be applied. He was weaker in the east of Scotland, but that region elected several of his friends to Westminster and from his home at Dalmeny he could exert an influence in the Lothians. Though he himself cared nothing for Home Rule, his followers were fond of holding before Scotland the promise of a special role within his dirigiste imperial framework.[57]

There were also underlying flaws in Rosebery's position, however. The great majority of Scots Liberals remained Gladstonian in outlook and just not open to his persuasions. For all the forward-looking nature of his thinking, real commitment to them was confined to an intellectual coterie. The problem troubled the earl little, as little as the accusations of rank treachery heard from fellow Liberals. He sought a transformation of attitudes, which he thought best achieved through the diffusion of his moral influence rather than by his direct political engagement. His manoeuvres never got much beyond the planning stage, however, for he disliked sordid politicking: he had, after all, never personally needed to stand for election to the Parliament at Westminster. He left the hard graft to lieutenants, himself withdrawing into long silences punctuated by the odd enigmatic and abstract enunciation of his views. But since he chose Scotland for his battleground, the factional struggle there assumed a special importance.[58]

Inside Scotland, though, Rosebery had also to face Campbell-Bannerman, a man much cannier than the earl gave him credit for. It was the Boer War that had caused most of the Liberal leader's problems, but in 1902 the war ended in a victory almost pyrrhic in the damage it did to Britain's international standing. He had early on sensed the turn of the tide. He restored consensus in his party not by condemning the war itself – which would have been too much for the Liberal imperialists – but the 'methods of barbarism' used to finish it, notably the concentration camps for Boer non-combatants.[59]

Once the war was over the government in London soon ran into domestic difficulties. The Liberals' lassitude began to lift as they scented power again. That put an end to internal strife. Before long Campbell-Bannerman felt able to claim: 'Everything I hear in Scotland is satisfactory . . . we have captured the local associations.'[60] From a position of growing strength, he did set out to conciliate Rosebery if he could. This only made the tetchy earl draw back into his shell. Relations deteriorated so far that Campbell-Bannerman demanded a firm statement on whether Rosebery still counted himself as a Liberal. The reply, in a letter to *The Times*, was couched in the usual ambiguous terms but did employ the phrase 'definite separation'.[61] The Liberal imperialist faction itself felt puzzled at Rosebery's deviousness. Munro Ferguson, MP for the Leith Burghs, who had been the earl's private secretary at one stage, wrote of his worry about 'a split between Rosebery and the rest of us – a finale which one always feels to be within the bounds of possibility but which we must try to avoid'.[62] In the event, Campbell-Bannerman was left all the scope he needed to reassert his authority.

Now came the turn of the Conservative government to tear itself apart in factional squabbles. The Prime Minister since 1902 had been Arthur Balfour (the fourth Scot to hold the highest office, and no better than the first three). He did have ambitions. In fact, he essayed a basic change of economic policy in the shape of tariff reform, that is to say, the end of the free trade that had been the official doctrine of the British state since 1846. Most Scots Tories felt happy with this, most Scots Unionists unhappy. Amid fierce disputes the government went to pieces, and Balfour resigned at the end of 1905. At the general election early in the new year the Liberals won an overwhelming majority. In Scotland they took 58 seats and 56 per cent of the votes. The Unionists, with 39 per cent, survived only in 12 constituencies. They suffered a spectacular reverse in Glasgow, where they had made a clean sweep in 1900; now it sent back four Liberal MPs, a Labour man and two Unionist free traders.[63]

Campbell-Bannerman became the fifth Scottish Prime Minister and, given a longer life, might have been the best. On the brink of power, he had won, in his unassuming way, a final victory over his imperialist critics. The two MPs most prominent among them in Scotland, Herbert Asquith and Richard Haldane, had earlier with the English member Sir Edward Grey formed the so-called Relugas compact, named after the lodge on the River Findhorn where they met on a fishing holiday and spent their evenings plotting. They resolved to refuse office under Campbell-Bannerman unless he agreed to go to the House of Lords, so leaving them and their faction pre-eminent in the House of Commons. The manoeuvre was too clever by half. Fortified by the king's commission, the leader could not be bullied. The compact dissolved as soon as he started offering jobs to the conspirators.[64]

Rosebery, with his chief allies reconciled to the Prime Minister, saw his influence plummet. His demise as a public figure of the first rank was marked by an extraordinary speech in June 1908, in which he took the side of the Lords in their resistance to the government's radical reforms. He chose Glasgow, of all places, to defend the dukes as a 'poor but honest class' and called that year's budget 'the end of all, the negation of faith, of family, of prosperity, or monarchy, of Empire'.[65] These inanities exposed him as an increasingly reactionary Whig and destroyed his popular following.

As long as Campbell-Bannerman lived, it could well be said the radicals had won the battle for the soul of the Scottish Liberal party. But he enjoyed office for only two years before his death in 1908. Even so, he left a legacy. In Scotland there was a visible continuity between his Liberal party and that of the middle and late Victorian era. Then, with the big battles for the suffrage won, the progressive bourgeoisie and the independent working class had come together to impose their ethical values and their political will on the effete aristocracy to one side of them, on the feckless, often Irish, urban underclass to the other. The winning combination in the middle was sure of what it believed in and across a range of public policy capable of effective reforms, though variably successful in achieving them. Some of their enthusiasms may be a bit hard to understand nowadays, such as the disestablishment of the Church of Scotland. Others, short Parliaments and reform of the hereditary House of Lords, would be only partly realised. For others again – 'one man, one vote', payment of MPs – fulfilment was just a matter of time. Certain particular items of legislation, such as land reform and local option for control of drink, seemed in 1906 well within the radical grasp. And soon there would once more be high hopes of Home

Rule, as part of a broader programme of federal reconstruction in the United Kingdom.[66]

◉

In 1906 Scots radicals at last felt they had their hands on the levers of power. Their local dominance was undisputed. And they could for the first time count on co-operation from central government, where Scotland was represented by nine MPs or peers in the Cabinet, under Campbell-Bannerman as Prime Minister and with, as Scottish Secretary, John Sinclair, MP for Angus, who had for years been his leader's closest confidant. It was one of the great reforming governments, not only fulfilling aspirations of the nineteenth century but also setting an agenda for the twentieth century. Scots Liberals did not quite conform to this character. True to their old principles, they regarded with suspicion all ideas for a more active policy of social welfare or for economic intervention. For no good reason, they did not attempt either to bring the lower classes into Parliament. In fact, their programme went no further than clearing up the unfinished business from the past.[67]

Land reform was the item that the radicals expected to bring the greatest social benefit.[68] Three-quarters of a century after the first Reform Act, the Scottish aristocracy remained powerful. True, it had lost political control except in a few rustic fastnesses, but it could still obstruct the will of the people. Visible proof of that lay in its ownership of vast tracts of land where tenants and labourers enjoyed few rights. The aim now was to curb this power. Every Liberal MP favoured it and had made land reform one of the big issues on the hustings. Sinclair said 'one need stands first: what Scotland wants is land for the Scots'.[69]

The policy had two aims. The first was to encourage smallholdings, which would be likely to erode the landlords' power, create a free peasantry and offer a better life to those in the cities who could not endure the overcrowding or risk of unemployment. The second aim was taxation of land values, with the purpose of placing a proper social burden on those regarded as owning the ultimate source of wealth. By the same token, the central government's capacity for raising taxes might be expanded to the point where a surplus could be created capable of being offset by cuts elsewhere or by spending on public works and welfare. Radicals also believed taxation would encourage economic development by forcing landlords to bring their property into profitable use in order to pay it. Land reform therefore appeared to be the answer to all sorts of problems, urban and social as well as agricultural.[70]

315

The plans were radical indeed. Sinclair's Small Landholders (Scotland) Bill really sought to extend the system of crofting from the Highlands to the whole country. It provided for the creation of new smallholdings, the enlargement of uneconomic ones, for security of tenure, fair rents and compensation for improvements. Despite wide public support for the Bill, furious opposition came from the Unionists and from Rosebery; it also went too far for some members of the government. Still, it passed the House of Commons with huge majorities in 1907 and 1908, only to be thrown out both times by the House of Lords.[71] Though the systems of land tenure on either side of the border were quite different, the Lords made so bold as to reject any principle in the Scottish legislation not to be found in an English Bill going through at the same time. So this soon passed into law, while Sinclair's measure was delayed for three years. When the more circumspect Asquith succeeded Campbell-Bannerman as Prime Minister in 1908, he even tried to drop the scheme for Scotland. The Scottish Secretary would not give up but was unable to get it through till 1912 in what became known as the Pentland Act, after the noble title he had meanwhile taken. It would never change Scotland as much as he hoped. Up to 1914 only 500 new holdings were created and fewer than 300 enlarged. Even a longer period of operation proved the demand for smallholdings had been overestimated, and in 1933 the policy was abandoned.[72]

Sinclair had more luck, though no more ultimate effect, with his ideas for land taxation. The essential basis was a general scheme of valuation. In 1907 Sinclair brought in a Bill to establish this. Again, the Lords wrecked it twice.[73] But because of its popularity the provisions were incorporated in David Lloyd George's controversial budget of 1909 and came into effect in 1911. Progress in their complex execution proved slow, however. Finally the First World War overtook it, and the Unionists exacted the sacrifice of Scottish land valuation in the jobbery that accompanied the formation of the all-party coalition in 1916. It was never reintroduced. The results of this long agitation over the land turned out nugatory, both in the political benefit they brought the Liberals and in their impact on Scottish society. The party failed to recognise that the biggest problems were now overwhelmingly urban and could not be tackled on the assumption of a common interest between city and countryside.

The second big item on the radicals' agenda was temperance. Given the lack of success for voluntary efforts to combat the demon drink, and the Scots' eternal love of it, a time seemed to have come to try official controls, so long as these could be given a democratic basis. For years a majority of the MPs had supported doing something or other, though without attempting to legislate. Still, the scenes on Scottish streets any Saturday night reminded them of the problem, and relentless propaganda by advocates of temperance had been altering the general climate of opinion. Once upon a time such people were dismissed as cranks, but now their views had attained almost the status of conventional wisdom. Campaigns for temperance satisfied the do-gooding instincts of the middle class yet also, and more to the point, met a response from workers willing to sign the pledge and commit themselves to abstinence. It still came as something of a surprise that the unfocused Liberal beneficence turned in 1913 into an Act of Parliament. This was a Scottish measure never imitated elsewhere in Britain, because it failed in its objects. It allowed local electorates to vote their areas dry, after which all public houses there were to be shut without compensation. But the polls could not be held till 1920, when only 14 parishes, 15 small burghs and 12 wards of burghs, including four in Glasgow, took the local option. Such meagre success destroyed the point of the exercise. It was no use having prohibition so limited in its coverage, which drinkers could get round just by crossing into a wet area. The country carried on boozing hard.[74]

The third big item on the radicals' agenda was Home Rule for Scotland. Since 1886 the concept had had a chequered history. Thirteen times the House of Commons considered motions in its favour, and on the last eight occasions approved them in principle. From the start – a motion put down by Gavin Clark in 1889 – the majority of Scots MPs supported it. Similar initiatives followed till in 1894 one of them managed to command a majority in the House as a whole. Yet this growing agitation inside the Liberal party coincided with a loss of interest among its leaders. The Cabinet, while acknowledging the defects in Scottish government and the desire of most MPs for reform, wanted above all to dispose of the matter with as little delay and trouble as possible. In the end it went no further than to set up a grand committee as a special channel for Scottish legislation in order to overcome the frequent delays to it on the floor of the House of Commons. The Liberals concluded then that they had done enough. For the lack of further action they found plausible excuses – till 1905 a long period of Unionist government and then the impossibility of getting controversial legislation through the House of Lords.[75]

In practice, Home Rule for Scotland could only be taken up again in conjunction with Home Rule for Ireland. It was therefore a matter of great delicacy, and no fit subject for hasty legislation. Campbell-Bannerman thought it might all be linked with a still more general scheme encompassing abolition of the House of Lords. He would have liked to establish unicameral legislatures for each of the four nations of the United Kingdom, subject in imperial matters to a further single elected chamber for the whole. But wariness about disturbing the settled state of Ireland, as well as the certain opposition of the Lords, meant such large schemes were postponed.[76]

Till 1912 Home Rule for Scotland made little headway. The Scots MPs set up a committee under Munro Ferguson to promote it, though the response even from their own government was cool. But then, with plans afoot for Ireland and the Lords no longer capable of obstruction, they managed to extract an undertaking from Asquith. Thomas McKinnon Wood, just appointed Scottish Secretary in succession to Sinclair, lent his support to a series of private member's bills. A fresh obstacle now arose in the form of reservations by English MPs. Their doubts centred on the problems likely to arise if there were to be a gradual move towards a general scheme of devolution for all four nations of the United Kingdom. England's size would unbalance the structure. In any case, it appeared superfluous to establish an English Parliament in addition to the imperial one. Winston Churchill was asked by the Cabinet to report on the problem. He proposed regional devolution within England. But this scheme looked too elaborate and gained support from nobody else.[77]

Without enthusiasm the government allowed itself to be persuaded by the Scots MPs that Home Rule for Scotland and Ireland should proceed more or less in step. When Asquith rose in the Commons to introduce his Government of Ireland Bill he told members it was but the start of a comprehensive policy of devolution. He kept his word. The Scottish Bill of 1913 provided for a Parliament of 140 members legislating for the existing responsibilities of the Scottish Office; in addition there would be a Scottish Privy Council and a Lord High Commissioner to represent the crown in Edinburgh. It passed second reading in the Commons in August 1914 but then, at the outbreak of war, had to be abandoned – somewhat to the government's relief.[78]

The radicals' victory in 1906 never fulfilled its promise. Land reform was carried but did not bring the expected effects: the decline of rural Scotland continued and urban problems remained untouched. Temperance reform, also carried, had yet to be enforced. Till the last moment, and then it was too late, Home Rule proved far too complex an affair. Meanwhile, English Liberals were accepting that domestic social conditions demanded a more active role of government and, in espousing the so-called New Liberalism, they, in fact, moved closer to the position Rosebery had once sought to propose.[79] The Scots at Westminster still did not like it. They were starting to look like some old-fashioned, fundamentalist sect – but also losing influence, and no more Scottish Liberals would lead the party or the country. The loss was not immediately felt because, unlike in the rest of the United Kingdom, these years proved to be politically tranquil for Scotland, reminiscent of the wide, peaceful stretches of the nineteenth century rather than of the turbulence that preceded and would immediately follow. In 1911 Buchan could still say of the Scots Liberal party:

> Its dogmas were so completely taken for granted that their presentation partook less of argument than of tribal incantation. Mr Gladstone had given it an aura of earnest morality so that its platforms were pulpits and its harangues had the weight of sermons. Its members seemed to assume that their opponents must be lacking either in morals or in mind. The Tories were the 'stupid' party. Liberals alone understood and sympathised with the poor; a working man who was not a Liberal was inaccessible to reason, or morally corrupt, or intimidated by laird or employer. I remember a lady summing up the attitude thus: 'Tories may think they are better born, but Liberals know they are born better'.[80]

During this final phase of politics in the long nineteenth century, Scots radicals did not remake themselves as a modernising force but remained a moralising, localising, levelling force. Of course they expressed popular ideals, drawn from the classless alliance of bourgeois enterprise and artisan respectability at the heart of Victorian Scotland. Once established in its political ascendancy by the Reform Acts, it had been invited to raise its sights, to map out a new future for Scotland in a wider, above all imperial world. Some novel loyalties did emerge, to be given expression by the remarkable succession of British and imperial statesmen that Scotland generated during this period. But Scotland never in the end transcended itself in Britain and the Empire. The core of the nation (and of a future nationalism) remained intact. This Scotland still preferred 'the safe and small'. By 1914 it at last seemed secure. The sequel would be cruel.[81]

Part V

CULTURE

13

Things:
'The light of truth and beauty'

On 9 November 1868, Edward, Prince of Wales, and his wife Princess Alexandra of Denmark arrived in Glasgow to lay the foundation stone for the new university.[1] It was to stand to the west of the city on Gilmorehill, one of the drumlins dotting the landscape there, that is to say, elevations formed from piles of debris dropped by retreating glaciers at the end of the last Ice Age. They often assumed the shape of a shallow cone, and on this particular drumlin 1,000 labourers had been employed for a year removing earth to flatten the top ready for the university's buildings to arise. As soon as the prince performed his own duty, the builders would be able to make a start.

The city of Glasgow had marked the royal visit with a holiday, and conferred its freedom on the prince and princess. They then drove out westwards cheered by huge crowds. About 20,000 people had gathered on Gilmorehill itself, a multitude 'so great as to be, to a certain extent, beyond control'. Stands erected for the occasion sagged under the weight of spectators crowding on to them; those who had paid for seats found many already taken by 'boys, servants, workmen about the place and so on'. Still, the actual ceremony went off without a hitch. The lord provost, Sir James Lumsden, one of the city's great merchants, gave a lunch for the royal couple. They left straight afterwards, though not without handing over 100 guineas as a contribution to the construction; later Queen Victoria would send £500. That evening the corporation of Glasgow held a civic banquet where the guest of honour was the principal of the university, the Revd Thomas Barclay, a Shetlander by birth whose long beard made him look, so his students said, like the Reformer John Knox.[2]

It would still be a couple of years before the first classes could be held amid the wide open vistas of Gilmorehill. Meanwhile the university needed to carry on regardless at its cramped original site in the High Street of Glasgow. The buildings here, 200 years old, were exquisite examples of native Scottish architecture that had developed, under the influence of the Auld Alliance, out of French styles adapted to a cold climate. But by now this quarter of the city, once picturesque and charming, was a slum. Rich people had abandoned it for salubrious residences on the surrounding drumlins, leaving only the poor behind them. The general council of the university minuted that it was 'one of the last places in the city which one would now propose for professors to reside in, or for students to frequent'. The site posed not only a moral but also an economic hazard, because 'owing to the progress of the city westwards, the present buildings are no longer conveniently situated for those classes of society in Glasgow which are most interested in the university'. The move to Gilmorehill would 'bring university education more generally within the reach of those citizens who are in the best condition and circumstances to avail themselves of it'.[3]

In 1870 the new building on Gilmorehill at last opened. Even yet it was not quite ready and would need another two years to its final completion. No matter, the moment had come for the move from the High Street. On 29 April that year's session closed and the students met in the common hall of the college to take their leave. On 29 July, the senate convened there for the last time. It would next day hand over possession to a railway company intent on clearing the site for a goods yard. The entire library was shifted to its new home without the loss of a single book. The removal men took more interest in the silver – a fine, antique collection built up over centuries, since it was the custom for graduates to donate a piece to their *alma mater*. Somehow, along the three miles from the High Street to Gilmorehill, this collection vanished except for one loving cup, two tassies and three candlesticks.[4]

❦

It was by contemporary standards a gigantic edifice waiting out on Gilmorehill to be filled with the academic paraphernalia. Its length of 540 feet, with tower and spire 100 feet high, made it the largest public structure erected in Britain since the completion of the new Houses of Parliament at Westminster ten years earlier. Like them it was built in Gothic style, putting a certain stamp on the urban environs. Even today, it dominates all views of the western side of Glasgow. We have got used to it now, but at the time many thought it an unhappy addition to the architecture of Scotland's biggest city.[5]

Vehement protests had arisen against the destruction of the college in the High Street. The reason for this act of vandalism was supposed to have been that in strict financial terms it would be difficult to do anything else. The university had not enough money to restore the original fabric, and the one way it could realise funds was to sell up and build on a new site. Still, the official excuse did not account for the course matters then took. The university had appointed a building committee that came to be dominated by Allen Thomson, professor of anatomy. He was a skilled chairman, but he also wished to make his number in academic circles in London (where he would soon move). In architectural terms he cultivated a special interest in the Gothic revival – itself all the rage in London, as we still see in the Houses of Parliament, Foreign Office and other novelties of the period. The architect of the Foreign Office was Giles Gilbert Scott. Thomson wanted him for the University of Glasgow too. Before any decision on a new design there was supposed to be a competition. Thomson sidestepped the prescribed pro-cedure and offered the commission straight to Scott. The architect would later explain his work in these terms: 'I adopted a style which I may call my own invention . . . It is simply a thirteenth-century or fourteenth-century secular style with the addition of certain Scottish features peculiar in that country to the sixteenth century, though in reality derived from the French style of the thirteenth and fourteenth century.'[6]

In Glasgow and elsewhere there were those who still thought the style alien and phoney. Of course, Scotland possessed Gothic buildings of its own, genuine ones dating from the Middle Ages. But nothing of note had been built in this style after Parliament House in Edinburgh during the 1630s. Architectural innovation went on, with native tradition developing in one of its aspects into the style now known as Scottish Baronial, which achieved a modern shape with Queen Victoria's rebuilding of Balmoral. Scottish architecture had also reflected the impress on the national culture of its phil-osophical concerns with individual and civic virtue. So the classical style or styles, recalling the country's intellectual debt to the ancient world, was what came to dominate prestigious new construction. This could be seen not only in the cities of Edinburgh and Glasgow and Aberdeen but also right round the country from Elgin to Kelso to Ayr, in great structures and in humble ones.[7]

The same was true of churches – for even Scottish religion had turned rational, at its higher levels anyway. Then by the Presbyterian way of thinking there could be nothing to associate religion with the Gothic style, as in the minds of the English architectural gurus of the age, John Ruskin, Augustus Pugin and Giles Gilbert Scott himself. They held the Gothic style to be uniquely Christian, indeed Catholic: Scott was born a Catholic, Pugin converted and Ruskin was tempted. Scots did not share this outlook. They had since the Reformation built kirks in various styles, the main requirement being the adaptation of historic types of structure to Presbyterian worship, focused on pulpit rather than altar. Examples existed from the sixteenth century at Burntisland, the seventeenth century in the Canongate, the eighteenth century at Inveraray.[8] By the turn of the nineteenth century Scots were putting up places of worship that followed the forms of Greek Revival too. For Scotland, especially Glasgow, this would continue longer than elsewhere with the work of Alexander 'Greek' Thomson at the three churches he built for his own United Presbyterian sect, in St Vincent Street, Caledonia Road and Queen's Park. Only the first remains intact; the second is a ruin and a German bomb destroyed the third in 1943.

Of course academic requirements are different from religious ones, but it comes as no surprise to find Greek Thomson incensed at what arose on Gilmorehill. He took it as an insult to the city's architects that an ancient Scottish university had turned its back on enlightened Scotland to ape the medievalism of Oxford and Cambridge. He unburdened himself in these terms to the Glasgow Architectural Society in a lecture 'On the Unsuitableness of Gothic Architecture to Modern Circumstances'. In particular, he dismissed the idea of the Gothic style being somehow uniquely Christian: 'This might have some weight in the Romish Church, but to Protestants of any sort, and more particularly Presbyterians, and still more particularly Presbyterian dissenters, the argument seems very absurd, for what has the philosophic Christianity of the Reformation to do with the sensuous ritual of the middle ages? The architecture, which was a consistent part of the latter, is diametrically opposed to the former.'[9] Lest he be suspected of Glaswegian parochialism, he went on to draw some comparisons with recent developments in the classical capital: 'Donaldson's Hospital in Edinburgh, of which great things were expected, fails to excite even a passing remark; while the High School, the fragments of the National Monument, Dugald Stewart's Monument, the Surgeons' Hall, and the Institution on the Mound, continue to illuminate their respective localities with the light of truth and beauty, giving to our northern metropolis an air of refinement which no other city in the kingdom possesses.' Thomson dismissed Scott's claim that he had employed a native style in Glasgow's new university: 'For all that remains of Scottish architecture in the new design, it might as well have been left out altogether.'[10] On the contrary, Scotland's architectural tradition had been betrayed, in predictable consequence of denying any local practitioner the chance to design one of the most important public buildings likely to be put up in Glasgow during the nineteenth century. Even if classicism was to be spurned – incredibly – as not learned and academic enough, it should have been possible to build something in the alternative Scottish Baronial style.

Generous words about Edinburgh do not often fall from Glaswegian lips, so it may be worth taking a closer look at what Thomson chose to commend there. The capital, while flourishing and expanding, had not changed its basic shape from when Sir Walter Scott knew and loved it as 'mine own romantic town'. The Old Town was romantic in the sense of being ancient and curious, if now decayed. The New Town had been at first a rational construction but before long came to look more romantic too, as it spread over the rugged, diverse terrain surrounding the city. Townscape continued to be deployed in landscape right through the nineteenth century, while Edinburgh pushed ever outwards from its historic core.[11]

Robert Adam had given Edinburgh its most distinguished classical architecture, though he died in 1792. But his greatest single achievement, Old College, carried on under construction till 1887 when it was at last crowned by its dome. His most ambitious urban composition, Charlotte Square, had been completed in 1820, setting an example to be exceeded only in grandeur, rather than elegance, by James Gillespie Graham's Moray Place, completed about 1836, and by William Playfair's comprehensive development of Calton Hill, not finished till 1860. Adam had handled small or flat sites; these two successors dealt besides in an inspired fashion with the demands of building across the heights and depths of a dramatic urban topography.[12]

By the middle of the nineteenth century the expansion of the New Town reached right down to the northern foot of its original site along the shallow ridge opposite the Castle, as far as Stockbridge and Canonmills, that is, to the Water of Leith – but had already crossed over to its further bank too. The city became romantic not only in Scott's sense of quaint urbanity but also in its novel blend with nature. Now houses could look out from among overhanging trees into sheer gorges – or else, where landscape itself did not do the work, surprise might lie in wait in the built environment as streets turned on to unexpected vistas. Who, seeing the initial regularity of the New Town, would ever suspect the roadfork-cum-precipice that terminates Queensferry Street, or the undulating Royal Circus that lurks round the corner from Howe Street? At this second spot the sightseer might otherwise carry straight on down the brae to enter a church (Playfair's vast St Stephen, Baroque and Greek at once) by its gallery! There was and is no end of epiphanies.[13]

In Glasgow the once palpable link between westward physical expansion and progressive stylistic fecundity has today been broken and fragmented by modern development. But in Edinburgh the progression is still there and plain to see. Playfair's oeuvre by itself bears witness to that. It starts in the east with the gaunt, spectral fragment of the Parthenon on Calton Hill, meant to crown the Athens of the North but showing in its unfinished state the fate of the city's purest classicism. It continues to the Royal Scottish Academy and Scottish National Gallery halfway along Princes Street, already exhibiting Victorian eclecticism within tasteful limits – except perhaps for the giant royal statue atop the academy's portico. Then far out to the west is the Donaldson's Hospital that Greek Thomson disliked, presumably for its profusion of Jacobean towers.[14]

Progression in Playfair's own work parallels progression in the general architectural history of the city. At the eastern end of the first New Town, Thistle Court contains its earliest buildings of 1768. Their Scottish plainness never got lost as the project marched west. On the contrary, this almost ran a risk of monotony, relieved only by a little vernacular eccentricity at the gables of cross-streets. Most houses were not, in fact, destined for a long life as residential property, but their impersonal amplitude, air of superior anonymity, lack of functional precision made them fit for other uses and prolonged their life even to the present. What they did offer was architectural harmony, sober at first but ready to be raised to a higher level altogether in the grace and dignity of Charlotte Square. By now, released from its original strict classicism, Edinburgh's style could wax sumptuous (and without the help of any phoney Gothic). So progression continued also in delightful diversity, majestic to intimate, regular to serpentine, right through the development of the second New Town.[15]

What might be called a third New Town then arose in the West End, laid out in the middle to late Victorian era. Its still classical formality was mixed with rich detail, the ensemble giving a strong sense of the prosperous security of the city at this period. The housing could outdo even the finest in the first New Town – for example, in the mansion on six storeys at Rothesay

Terrace built in 1883 by the Findlays of Aberlour, proprietors of *The Scotsman*, together with the rear outlook they also paid for, across a picturesque refurbishment of Dean Village. Round here antiquarianism came with modern conveniences: the large, superior tenement of 1906–07 at the opposite end of the terrace was served by Edinburgh's first private lift. From the back the proprietors could also view Thomas Telford's spectacular Dean Bridge (1829–31) by which the New Town crossed to the garden suburb beyond.[16]

Inaugurating a fourth stage of the westward progression, Palmerston Place is a Victorian residential street, where classicism, if still perceptible, has been overborne by more eclectic elements. Much of this area was constructed according to the designs of James Steel, who by the turn of the twentieth century became its richest citizen, and soon lord provost. Starting at Tollcross he erected whole suburbs: the extension of the West End beyond Palmerston Place, the working-class district of Dalry and all sorts of intermediate schemes, Comely Bank, Merchiston, Sciennes. In execution he was a feudal despot. A charter drawn up at his behest required that 'the whole of the fronts, as well as the ornamental parts, shall be of a style and quality of work to be approved of by the superiors', while actual walls were to be 'in stone from a quarry which in their opinion is suitable in colour and quality'. He not only served but also commanded – and sustained for a further term the architectural harmony of Edinburgh.[17]

Though the obvious progression is from the centre to the west, it is yet worth casting a glance to the east. Here the New Town descended by degrees into something still solid but less extraordinary, ending in lines of tenements that by the end of the century ran the length of Leith Walk. This then had something about it of a Parisian boulevard, at least one in the *faubourgs* – though in quality of housing it went downhill from stately at the top to scruffy at the bottom. Parallel yet different was Easter Road, the original route between the capital and its port of Leith. Even today – despite the modern fascias of the shops and the intrusion of motor traffic – it conveys the bustling impression of a Victorian working-class suburb with its thronged narrowness between high tenements. To reinforce the impression there stand, a stone's throw away, the colonies of London Road, with their own Artisan Bar.[18]

Tenements were Victorian Edinburgh's most common form of housing, invading or pressing on all but the most opulent suburbs. The biggest zone of them could be found on the opposite, southern side of the city beyond the open Meadows in Marchmont, Bruntsfield or Merchiston. The tone rather rose than fell with distance from the centre. The tenements, while respectable, gave way at length to a more usual sort of suburbia in the Grange. Its villas were often still classical in inspiration, if seldom so severe as in the first New Town, but could be tempted into variety. Bay windows grew popular here, to be imitated in other cities. They invited admiration of lilac and laburnum in the garden, while suiting Edinburgh's brief days of midwinter when more light was needed in the sitting room than a plain Georgian window flush with the façade could offer. Finally, workers' tenements teemed down Dalry, Gorgie and Slateford Roads too, in a close-built quarter criss-crossed by canals and railways. That squared the circle of the ancient urban core. Edinburgh's tenements were of stone, so they still stand and even today house about a third of the population. They are above all what make this a Scottish city (or indeed a European city, for Paris and Vienna have the same).[19]

In grander parts, classical austerity often conceals behind the sandstone frontage an opulent interior. Its acme at the turn of the nineteenth century came in plasterwork of exquisite virtuosity; by the turn of the twentieth century that translated into more lavish domesticity best seen in the work or influence of Robert Lorimer. He had started as a pupil of the architect William Burn, who built Edinburgh Academy and John Watson's Hospital (now the National Gallery of Modern Art) in classical style, then Dundas Castle and Lauriston Castle in Scottish Baronial. Lorimer's interests ranged wider and deeper to embrace craftsmanship in everything that could go into a building – stone, iron, wood, plaster, glass – or indeed in its plenishing – furniture, bedspreads, curtains and so on. His interiors survive in the New Town and West End, at Belgrave Crescent, Drummond Place, Heriot Row and Rothesay Terrace. He himself lived in Melville Street, where he altered a typical uniform terraced house with his own additions, a balcony and small-paned windows. He found ampler scope in spreading suburbs, especially at Colinton. Here he designed modern homes with a Scots accent in crowstep gables, stair-towers, harling and pantiles. Out in the Lothians, he helped to develop what are now resorts or commuter towns, Gullane and North Berwick.[20]

Wherever possible, Lorimer employed local artists and materials. His furniture he had made by the firm of Whytock & Reid, which traced its origins back to the eighteenth century and went out of business only in 2004. He collaborated best of all with two wood-carvers, Messrs W. and A. Clow. He was himself in his element in a carpenter's workshop: he loved the noise of plane and chisel, and drew inspiration from the slow emergence of form out of a shapeless block of wood. The Clow brothers had never met an architect so eager to exploit their skills, and for their part they set themselves to study and develop his ideas. Their stalls in his Thistle Chapel show how perfectly they came to understand his mind. His first biographer, Christopher Hussey, went to interview them after his death in 1929:

> I wish I could draw a lifelike portrait of the brothers Clow to whose genius in carving Lorimer owed so much. On the upper floors of a gaunt Edinburgh mansion one comes upon them out of a dark passage, surrounded by a garden of wooden flowers: two identical middle-aged men looking, in their long grey overalls, like Tweedledum and Tweedledee grown spare and kindly. To this day I do not know which is W and which is A for they have long since become a single personality and tend to speak antiphonally. To hear their memories of twenty-five years' work with Lorimer was like hearing the psalms read by a small congregation:
>
> W: No architect has given us such scope.
> A: We worked for him exclusively.
> Both: Aye, for 30 years we worked for nobody else.
>
> A: We met Sir Robert in 1892.
> W: He had been in practice a year.
> Both: He wanted someone to take an interest, ye see.
>
> W: At the same time he wanted to cultivate the crafts in Edinburgh.
> A: And give work to Edinburgh craftsmen for preference.
> Both: We took trouble.[21]

Here was how, at its most winning, Edinburgh's character evolved amid the massive Victorian securities of property and class – into not just architectural harmony but also harmony of city and people, and harmony with the land-scape in which both were cast.

Glasgow, too, was a European city in the way it housed its people. More lived in tenements here than anywhere else in Britain, and it would have been hard to find another type of structure sufficient to accommodate the supply of labour on the scale local industry needed. The tenements tended to follow a standard pattern: four storeys with eight flats on a common stair. They have won a bad reputation, not least from Scottish historians, but experts in urban studies are now starting to see their virtues, at least by comparison with any more recent alternative. In Glasgow they were soundly constructed in attractive red or honey-coloured sandstone (attractive, at least, till covered in soot), they seldom rose higher than the street in front was wide and they contained bigger rooms than council flats do. Those surviving the corporation's craze for demolition in the mid twentieth century appear desirable today; with modern plumbing installed, they are perfect for a more mobile population. Even at the time, they facilitated strategies for solving the problems of poverty among their swarming denizens. The tenements also helped to produce a harmony, sometimes almost monotony, in Glasgow's townscape that has since been lost.[22]

If the University of Glasgow lacked cultural confidence in the architectural choices it took, that could not be said of the Victorian city as a whole. Greek Thomson's work was central to it.[23] For this boomtown he designed every type of building, decorated by an encyclopaedic diversity of classical and pre-classical motifs. He laid out whole suburbs at Langside and Regent's Park, where he himself lived. He created grand terraces along the Great Western Road and gave them majestic interiors. He planned a huge tenement in Eglinton Street and lesser ones elsewhere. He built individual dwellings in the form of suburban villas, the Knowe at Pollokshields or Holmwood House at Cathcart, today run by the National Trust for Scotland as a memorial to the man and his work. This work reached its climax in his three United Presbyterian churches. They adapted a classical idiom to demanding sites, sloped or otherwise irregular. Out of the challenges there emerged not just Greek Revival but, more to the point, controlled compositions balancing diverse geometric masses. It was an achievement novel and modern, unlike anything else built in this era. The huge elongated dome at Queen's Park offered the most striking feature of all – a tragedy it has been lost. And while creating these extraordinary structures, Thomson felt happy to furnish an industrial city with the workaday edifices also necessary to it, offices and warehouses such as the Grosvenor Building, Grecian Buildings, Egyptian Halls and Buck's Head.[24]

Thomson was not a lonely genius but exerted a deep effect on his city. He showed it how to channel its wealth into modern architecture monumental in its Graecism yet lightened by exotic elements, Egyptian, Romanesque, Persian, Indian. The mixing of genres was what made him romantic as well as classical. At other hands the transition might have faltered and dissolved into a jumble of alien, eccentric and unreadable features. But he could accomplish with aplomb the abstracting shift from classical theme to romantic variation. And his whole oeuvre showed there might be historical inspiration even in the task of building for an industrial society – by erecting not mock temples and mausolea, and not only churches either, but also bourgeois villas, proletarian tenements and commercial premises.[25]

With so much of Victorian Glasgow gone,[26] it is hard to appreciate now how Thomson shaped the city in its heyday – including the influence he continued to exert after his death in 1876. It is best seen round Queen's Park, where his partner, Robert Turnbull, carried on working for a further quarter-century.[27] Though Glasgow underwent protean change, there remained a civic coherence, vigorous elegance and spontaneous order in its evolution, often swanky with swagger, even bombast. It all added up to more than the inchoate mass of similar industrial conurbations. The journal, *British Architect,* wrote of Thomson in 1888: 'The strong influence of his work is apparent in nearly all Glasgow architecture, giving to it – the city – a character unique among the large cities of this country.'[28] While he was trained in Glasgow and hardly ever left it, he saw himself as a European rather than Scottish architect. He was homebred but outward looking, just as he was classical but romantic. Inventive and theatrical, steeped in cosmopolitan history and inspired by evangelical religion, he brought exotic allure and cultural distinction to Victorian Glasgow's wet, grimy streets.[29]

Being also a European city, Glasgow could play its part in international developments.[30] Along with Barcelona, Hamburg, Paris, Prague, Riga or Vienna, it was a powerhouse of Art Nouveau – the reaction against the academic art of the age, inspired instead by natural forms and structures. Glasgow's own input, the Glasgow Style or Glasgow School, also arose from synthesis, of bourgeois enterprise and artisan respectability, of ostentatious sophistication and delicate naturalism. To other influences we must add a sense of this being an industrial community with aesthetic requirements of its own.

Glasgow felt proud of the engineering feats it paraded before the world at international exhibitions in 1888 and 1901, then at a Scottish national exhibition in 1911. The concept of craft here meant skill and precision, somewhat different from Edinburgh's blend of the vernacular and the manual. Both stood in contrast to England, where the leader of the arts and crafts movement, William Morris, called the Forth Bridge 'the supremest specimen of all ugliness'[31] – not a sentiment comprehensible in Scotland. Glasgow's wealth indeed arose from metallurgy, and Glasgow Style was pervaded by the possibilities of bending, puncturing, welding and moulding matter by art as well as by science. With its wealth now a century old, the city had the leisure and education for generous patronage. Yet, unlike the middle class of Edinburgh dominated by the learned professions, the equivalent Glaswegians were even yet a precarious and volatile bunch respecting lucre, not lineage or land. Economic structure determined cultural superstructure, and wealth needed to be shown off.[32]

To the foremost practitioner of Glasgow Style, Charles Rennie Mackintosh, the challenge was to clothe 'in grace and beauty the new forms and conditions that modern developments of life – social, commercial and religious – insist upon'.[33] Of humble origin, one of twelve children of a policeman at Townhead, he cultivated his aesthetic sensibilities at Glasgow's School of Art. The principal, Francis Newbery, took Mackintosh under his wing and sent him on a travelling scholarship (endowed by Greek Thomson) to study the art and architecture of Italy. After his return he exhibited his own watercolours in a student show. Its judge was the painter, James Guthrie; when told some drawings were by an architect, he turned to Newbery and said, 'This man ought to be an artist.'[34] Mackintosh would carry on painting right through his life and at the end return to it as his main preoccupation. He and his wife Margaret, with their in-laws, Herbert and Frances McNair, formed a clique known as The Four or, in jest, the Spook School, with reference to their use in various genres of mystifying symbolist motifs. A case in point was the posters Mackintosh drew for the *Scottish Musical Review*, quite shocking to the taste of the time. The magazine *The Studio* leaped to their defence but had to admit 'Mr Mackintosh's posters may be somewhat trying to the average person.'[35] Since it was hard to make a living as an artist, he went from college to join the architectural firm of Honeyman & Keppie. He had also learned, like many young Glaswegians, to drink and smoke too much. That did not stop him working: on the contrary, he would stay up all night at his firm's offices endlessly revising his plans, emptying a bottle of whisky as he did so.

Mackintosh could not be called a classical architect, though he had the inherent discipline of classicism. And while Glasgow Style was first of all something to be publicly flaunted, at Mackintosh's hands its most authentic expressions came in the private sphere. He left a fine example with the interior of his own house in Southpark Avenue at Hillhead, which he recast internally after moving there in 1906. Demolished in 1963 by the university, it was somewhat oddly reconstructed, though as accurately as possible, within the Hunterian Art Gallery.[36] We need to look outside the city for houses Mackintosh built entire. He found at Kilmacolm in Renfrewshire a patron, the merchant William Davidson, who in 1900 gave him his first chance to create both interior and exterior of a complete building, Windyhill. He and Margaret designed the furniture, fireplaces, panelling, glass, lighting, decoration, even the storage, where they brought their designers' skills to bear on built-in cupboards. Then in 1902 the publisher Walter Blackie commissioned from Mackintosh a new home overlooking Helensburgh down the River Clyde. On the outside Hill House was modernised Scottish Baronial, with harled bartizan and steep gable, reminding us how Mackintosh admired this style so different from his own – he had for it, he said, an 'instinctive affection'.[37] Yet on the inside all was Art Nouveau delicately enhanced by *Japonisme*. Attention to detail even extended to prescribing the colour of cut flowers the Blackies might place on a table in the living room, so as not to clash with the décor.

Almost as domestic were the tea rooms Mackintosh created for another generous patron, Catherine Cranston. They had become a Glaswegian institution, spots in a male-chauvinist city for women to be *entre soi* and live out, for an hour or two, a vision of modern urban chic. The Glasgow Art Club, for which Mackintosh signed off the drawings, offered some equivalent to the more aesthetic type (rather rare) of Glaswegian male. For real men of the city's hard school of journalism, he designed the old office of the *Glasgow Herald* in Mitchell Street with its dramatic water tower, then the printing works of the *Daily Record*, almost hidden off Hope Street between Renfield Lane and St Vincent Lane.[38]

Mackintosh got a different opportunity with his commission for a church at Queen's Cross – a small site by the junction of Garscube Road and Maryhill Road in a proletarian part of the city. There appeared nothing much avant-garde about the building from the outside. The congregation was of the Free Church, and wanted a plain place of worship. It consented to a dominating window that was Gothic, more or less, allowing Mackintosh the chance to work in a big floral motif. He could then do more of what he wanted with the pulpit, galleries and communion table, in discreet supplement to Presbyterian sobriety. The church with its distinctive massing more than holds its own in a row of tenements, especially now that today it is confronted with modern tat. There is in the elements profusion but no confusion: the faithful reflection of the interior in the exterior makes Mackintosh an heir of Greek Thomson.[39]

The rest of Mackintosh's legacy lay in educational buildings. He designed two schools, one the Martyrs' School at Townhead (in the street where he grew up), the other at Scotland Street in Govan. Local school boards had simple and obvious requirements for classrooms, a hall and so on, and the marvel is to see how he worked with them to flood the buildings with light, then to decorate them in Art Nouveau on doorways, ironwork and woodwork. Both need to be imagined in their original environment of close-packed tenements, all vanished today to leave the Martyrs' School on its own with an adjacent church and backdrop of recent New Brutalism – though at Scotland Street this perhaps even enhances the view of the school's glittering towers from the nearby motorway. The third example was Mackintosh's masterpiece, Glasgow School of Art on Garnethill. His firm won the contest to design it in 1897. It was built in two stages, the first in fluid Art Nouveau, the second in 1907–09 in purer geometric forms heralding the European movement of the Secession. The design is eclectic in a second and typical sense, for the straightforward, rational shape of the whole forms the setting for an infinity of internal adornment in timber, stone, iron, tiles, glass – at its finest in the library, with its air of a medieval scriptorium for all its unmistakable modernism.[40]

In 1913 Mackintosh tried to set up his own architectural practice. But this perfectionist insisted on controlling every project down to the tiniest detail, and found it hard to get work. In 1915 he and his wife left Glasgow for Suffolk, where he was briefly arrested as a German spy because local yokels could not place his thick accent.[41] Still prosperity eluded the couple, till in 1923 they abandoned architecture and moved to France to concentrate on painting. They stayed only two years before Mackintosh's worsening health forced a return to London. In 1928 he died at the age of 60 from cancer of the throat. He had had his hours of triumph, but the difference in his career from the careers of Robert Adam a century before, or of Alexander 'Greek' Thomson in a previous generation, was that the genius of Charles Rennie Mackintosh went largely unrecognised in his own nation in his own time.

Yet Mackintosh had put Scotland in the very forefront of the European architectural avant-garde. It was an extraordinary achievement in a nation with no state and hence no official patronage of this most public of arts: not that his work would have appealed much to politicians or civil servants. The achievement formed part of a vigorous development of the arts in general, not least of the painting in which Mackintosh was also an innovator.

In the age of the Enlightenment, painting had been a public art as well. It was reliant on patronage, if not from the state then from the aristocracy (a distinction anyway blurred in Scotland). Other countries possessed prestigious academies of art, often of royal foundation. But Scotland had to rest content with a modest drawing academy set up in 1760 by the trustees of the Board of Manufactures, an agency of the British government which in the early decades of the Union sought to inject some economic life into it. The prime purpose was to train craftsmen for the textile industry. It stood in Edinburgh at Picardy Place, this named after a colony of Huguenot weavers encouraged to settle here so they could teach sophisticated textile technique to doltish Scots. Soon the whole economy was anyway moving ahead under its own steam, and the trustees' academy could devote itself to more strictly artistic instruction. Many of the country's painters profited from it.[42]

Scottish artists had previously had an academy of their own called Italy. Scottish–Italian links remained strong through the eighteenth century because the exiled royal house of Stewart ended up in Rome. Henry, the Cardinal-Pretender, was a dilettante of art, and it was round his palace in the Piazza dei Santi Apostoli that Scottish painters visiting the country would gather and mix with the last of the Jacobites: since both groups tended to be penniless, each would hope the other was buying the drinks. These exchanges came to an end with the Napoleonic Wars, but they had done their job in enriching Scottish culture. Their influence lasted well into a new century.[43]

Among the beneficiaries was Alexander Nasmyth, a son of Edinburgh apprenticed to a coachbuilder who went to the trustees' academy as part of his training. He took to painting portraits and attracted the notice of a leading banker, Patrick Miller of Dalswinton, who at length offered Nasmyth a loan to go to Italy. Miller was also the patron of Robert Burns, and to this connection we owe Nasmyth's portrait of the handsome bard, the best known of the few extant. But it was with landscapes that Nasmyth made his name.[44] Enlightened visitors and natives alike regarded Scotland as an ugly (because unproductive) country. Landscapes got included in the decorative wall paintings of classical mansions, but as a rule they were idealised scenes of ancient Greece and Rome peopled with nymphs and shepherds. Nasmyth inaugurated a more naturalistic tradition. In Italy he travelled about copying works by old masters in the cities housing them, and for light relief painted his own scenes of the Roman *campagna*. If his mature landscapes of Scotland, most of the Highlands but some of the Lothians too, bathe in more sunshine than seems quite realistic, and if that points up greens dark enough for cypress (which yet cannot be cypress here in his chilly homeland), the Italian influence must be the reason.

Most painters need supplements to their income, and Nasmyth also practised as a landscaping consultant. He played a part in the layout of later stages of Edinburgh's New Town: for example, he designed St Bernard's Well by the Water of Leith, a circular Roman temple peering forth from the trees.[45] He laid out the grounds and advised on the siting of great Scottish houses, the Earl of Rosebery's Dalmeny and the Duke of Argyll's Inveraray. While on this second job, Nasmyth painted a big general view of the duke's project of improvement bringing out in his plan for castle, park and classical clachan its overall harmony with nature. But the idealism never overbore the realism, which Nasmyth perhaps owed more to his later study of Dutch and French painting. It became visible especially in his pictures of his hometown on the cusp of its transformation from medieval jumble to machine for rational living, *Edinburgh from Princes Street, with the Royal Institution under construction* and *Edinburgh from Calton Hill*.[46] Classical restraint was still there, but given a romantic twist – a refreshing blend of Nasmyth's own. Still, he saw himself as above all reproducing nature: 'The nearer you can get to it the better,' he said. When he died in 1840, David Wilkie wrote: 'He was the founder of the landscape painting school in Scotland, and by his taste and talent has for many years taken the lead in the patriotic aim of enriching his native land with the representations of her romantic scenery.'[47]

A second figure in this golden age of Scottish classical art was Henry Raeburn, who concentrated on people rather than places. Apprenticed as an orphan to a goldsmith, he started by painting miniatures on mourning rings and the like. He grew up a good-looking fellow with an easy turn of conversation and ready wit. They proved helpful in putting his later sitters at their ease, as they visibly were in his portraits. Meanwhile his manner won the heart of Ann, widow of Count Leslie, an Austrian mercenary general of Jacobite descent. Raeburn was commissioned to paint her portrait and ended up marrying her. This brought him the money he needed to go to Italy for two years, and the happy couple set off for Rome. The main thing he learned from the trip was always to paint from life.[48]

The Raeburns never had to starve in a garret; in fact, Henry became a landowner and developed the village of Stockbridge, his birthplace, into a suburb of Edinburgh, with the capital's finest small thoroughfare, Ann Street, named after his wife. From the start they moved in high society, the members of which were invited to sit at Raeburn's studio in George Street.

The first picture he painted on his return from Italy was of Robert Dundas, Lord President of the Court of Session: nothing like starting at the top. It shows the artist to be already a master of portraiture, and he continued to put Edinburgh's great and good on canvas till his death in 1823. If today we feel we know them better than Scots of any other age, we owe that to his vivid and revealing art. Theirs are compelling likenesses, created with a strong but never harsh realism. Arresting as general compositions with their dramatic treatment of light and shade, they still create a sense of intimacy between spectator and sitter. And Raeburn succeeds in showing his subjects in a moral, not just a physical sense; he paints their characters, not just their features.[49]

Raeburn produced more than 700 portraits. Perhaps nothing ever again quite equalled one of his early pictures, from 1792, of *Sir John and Lady Clerk of Penicuik* – an extraordinary celebration of mature intimacy. Many others among his best subjects are people who have lived long enough for experience to mark them, the women especially, Mrs James Campbell, Janet Dundas, Isabella McLeod, Mrs Robert Scott Moncrieff, Mrs Kenneth Murchison, Eleanor Urquhart. But practically all the great men of the late Enlightenment find a place in his oeuvre – and not only the great men either. His most popular portrait of all is *The Revd Robert Walker Skating on Duddingston Loch*. Highland chiefs come across splendidly too, for the ruder virtues to be perceived through the polite veneer put on for the capital – or is there some glimpse of foolish flummery in the expressions of Sir John Sinclair and Alasdair MacDonell of Glengarry? Doubtless in their vanity the chiefs saw these portraits as the equivalent in paint to what Sir Walter Scott committed to print in *Waverley* or *The Lady of the Lake*. Of him Raeburn did two portraits, the first of a youngster, a restless poetic genius tensed to burst on the world, the second of an older and wiser man, his humanity deepened by tribulation. This portrait was the last Raeburn ever finished; he died only days after doing so. Scott felt impressed by their encounter too: 'His manly stride backwards, as he went to contemplate his work at a proper distance, and, when resolved on the necessary point to be touched, his step forward, were magnificent. I see him in my mind's eye, with his hand under his chin, contemplating his picture, which position always brought me in mind of a figure of Jupiter.'[50] Robert Louis Stevenson would write that Raeburn could 'plunge at once through all the constraint and embarrassment of the sitter and present the face, clear, open and intelligent as at the most disengaged moments'.[51] If he is romantic, he is not sentimental. Nor does he reproach or satirise his subjects. Painter and sitter share standards and values. A classical Scottish culture is there for all to see.

In his novel *The Antiquary* (1816), Scott paid homage to a third artist: 'In the inside of the cottage was a scene which our Wilkie could have painted, with that exquisite feeling of nature that characterises his enchanting productions.' He wrote back with typical modesty to say that these words had placed him under 'a debt of obligation' as 'with an unseen hand in The Antiquary, you took me up, and claimed me, the humble painter of domestic sorrow, as your countryman'. But the closeness of what Scott did for Scotland in his writing to what Wilkie did for Scotland in his painting was palpable.[52]

Born in the Howe of Fife to the minister of Cults, David Wilkie went to the trustees' academy in Edinburgh but then moved on to London to gain wider experience. He emerged good at portraiture, if not as great as Raeburn. Even so his own study of Scott and family at Abbotsford, which he visited on his way home, was a masterpiece of homely restraint, understood in Scotland for its sympathetic insight into a private sphere but offensive in England for depicting a 'vulgar group' unworthy of an 'elegant poet'. Still, that unfriendly metropolitan reaction helped to confirm Wilkie in his role as a patriotic Scottish artist, and to point the way for him to develop his true genius in genre painting – the academic term for pictures of humble folk rich in the details of still life with pots, pans, nails in cracked walls and so on. With it he revived a style that, since the Dutch masters of the seventeenth century, had been largely absent from European art. It satisfies as composition yet makes a social statement, comic or moving. It might have lent itself to sentimental excess, but Wilkie avoids this. While his images are faithful they apply a light touch to human nature. *Pitlessie Fair*, depicting the village near his home where he first went to school, is the most famous, and he had completed that before he left for London. All Scottish life is there, including the scatology: a dog craps over Wilkie's signature in one corner of the canvas. In later examples, too, he ranges widely. *The Penny Wedding* or *Distraining for Rent*, showing the joys and the sorrows of peasant life, demonstrate the huge potential this artistic revival held for Wilkie and for Scottish art in general.[53]

Admiration for natural simplicity was something Wilkie shared with Scott (or indeed with Burns before him), and there was nothing naïve about it. Yet his admiration contained a different element from theirs. On the one hand it excluded any idea of the Highlands as representing primitive virtue. 'Scotland, the main portion of which is Lowland, has no more ado with the clan tartan than an Englishman with a Welshman's leek,' Wilkie said. He never went north of Fife and he painted no hills higher than those to be found between the Firths of Forth and Tay. On the other hand, and again unlike for Scott and Burns, Presbyterianism was central to Wilkie's concept of Scottishness. It seems to have been a fairly intellectual kind of Presbyterianism too, of the sort practised at St Andrews, only a few miles from Wilkie's birthplace, by the Revd Thomas Chalmers. Wilkie paid a visit to Rome in 1827, and while there he spoke at a dinner given him by a new generation of Scottish painters now resident in the city. He said: 'As artists the younger students should be aware that no art that is not intellectual can be worthy of Scotland.' Probably what he meant by this can be gleaned from his later statement that it had been 'left for painting, with all its undefinable powers over colour and form, over light and darkness, to represent the mysteries of a spiritual revelation. The art of painting seems made for the service of Christianity'.[54]

This was an entirely different side to Wilkie from his affection for a comic, couthy, carefree Scotland, and he made it a matter not just of philosophical words but also of artistic deeds. Calvinist Christianity came under attack in the 1830s during the prelude to the Disruption, and it was surely this that prompted him towards a further dimension of his art, in religious painting. In 1832 he finished *The Preaching of John Knox before the Lords of Congregation*, a portrayal of the first public act of the Scottish Reformation. A second similar project he never finished: *John Knox Administering the Sacrament in Calder House*, showing the institution of Holy Communion in the Reformed Kirk. He took immense trouble over the historical detail of these scenes, but then he also produced a further religious work purely of the imagination. *The Cotter's Saturday Night* is inspired by Burns's poem of the same name. In it the bard (despite being of the Devil's party) sets out what he could admire in Presbyterianism – including its patriotism, for the antepenultimate verse of the poem starts, 'From scenes like these, old Scotia's grandeur springs . . .'[55] To call this picture an example of genre painting sells its achievement short: it might have come from the hand of Rembrandt. The urge to create a modern revival of religious painting, as Rembrandt had done for his own time, took Wilkie in 1839–40 on a journey to Palestine, so that he would be able afterwards to paint images of the life of Jesus Christ with authentic backgrounds. Here his art went into a fourth stage different from his earlier sobriety and delicacy, to create a new style ablaze with colour and with delight at the exotic, in pictures of *The Turkish Letter Writer, Jews at the Wailing Wall, Mehmet Ali* (the Egyptian despot). All this promised much if Wilkie had been able to return home. But on the voyage back in 1841 he died, his consignment to the deep being immortalised in his friend J.M.W. Turner's *Peace – Burial at Sea.*[56]

Nasmyth, Raeburn, Wilkie – these three great classical artists of Scotland all live on today because they give us an authentic picture of the pre-industrial nation, without distortion or sentimentality: Nasmyth its landscapes, Raeburn its people, Wilkie its domestic scenes but also something of the life of the spirit beneath them.

By now the enhanced status of painting as a public art seemed, at least in certain quarters, to require a corresponding public institution. A body soon to become the Royal Institution, no less, had been founded in Edinburgh in 1819 for 'the encouragement of the fine arts in Scotland'. The great and good ran it, like other such bodies in Scotland. Not much time passed before the artists it was meant to benefit began to feel left out of it, especially in things that mattered to them: the selection of paintings for exhibitions and the level at which each was hung (which would affect sales). They suspected it was all a matter of social acceptability rather than of artistic merit. With Raeburn at their head, some seceded into a new outfit promptly dubbed the Scottish Academy. The two rival groups of artists continued to squabble for the next three decades. To a later age it is not always clear quite what the points at issue were, but they at length got resolved by a division of labour entailing the construction of two new public galleries, not just one, at the foot of the Mound. So it is that Edinburgh has a brace of such buildings where other capitals make do with a single example: the National Gallery of Scotland and the Royal Scottish Academy, both by Playfair, standing side by side though not (a relic of the feud?) in exact alignment. Today the former houses the collection of older paintings while the latter exhibits contemporary works.[57]

A pity that Scotland got round so late to establishing academies of art at this higher, rather than merely workaday, level. By the time it happened the corresponding institutions in other countries were starting to lose their lustre, in France especially. The academic system there meant that, to qualify themselves properly, young artists needed to spend four years of rigorous training, mainly in reproducing copies of older works in order to master the principles of perspective, contour, light, shade and so on. Then their tyrannical professors decided which of the copies should be publicly exhibited. All this no doubt perfected the artists' technique but it stifled their creativity. Scotland trailed well behind but was on the way to setting some such system up. In 1858 the Royal Academy took over the classes in drawing and painting from life hitherto run by the trustees' academy, which was now meant to content itself with merely elementary instruction (though in fact, in 1907, it turned into Edinburgh's College of Art).[58]

In France impressionism was the revolt against such a fuddy-duddy view of the artist as journeyman (rather than bearer of a divine spark). The revolt took shape in the *Salon des Refusés* of 1863, which really marked the beginning of modern art. Its most notorious exhibit was Manet's *Déjeuner sur l'Herbe*, depicting naked women as they lolled among fully clothed men in the open air while getting ready to have lunch, or something. Nothing that *osé* appeared in Scotland, but at least there was the entertainment of another spat between Edinburgh and Glasgow. While the capital's painters bickered among themselves about whose pictures should be accepted for exhibition (and how high they should be hung), artists from other parts of the country had little chance of a look in. Those in Glasgow grew so exasperated at being consistently ignored that they agreed among themselves to spurn the Royal Academy. These were the Glasgow Boys. Their city would not have a purpose-built public gallery of its own till Kelvingrove was erected in 1897–1901, again to a huge chorus of protest that an English architect got chosen over any Scot. Meanwhile there were the McLellan Galleries in Sauchiehall Street, put up by a rich merchant to house his own collection of paintings and bought by the corporation of Glasgow in 1856. At least the place did not lack hanging space.[59]

The Glasgow Boys anyway forged ahead painting in styles markedly different from the academic production Edinburgh had sunk into. While the Boys hardly added up to a distinct school by themselves, they did operate as a group in the sense of influencing and supporting one another. They were not only personal friends but also took working holidays together in the summer. They would fan out from Glasgow, usually to the Borders or indeed to the east of Scotland, where they seemed to find a greater wealth of scenes they wanted to paint. With them, formal portraits, ideal landscapes and historical scenes gave way to realism and naturalism, not limited by any requirement of decorum or dignity in the subjects. The Boys captured many facets of

Scotland never painted before, especially as they chose to work in the open air. And the people they painted were real people in real places, not models in galleries. Beyond that, the Boys opened themselves to the art of the rest of the world. They embraced change and they created masterpieces.[60]

Many of their paintings have become as familiar as the works of the preceding classical period. James Guthrie's large and sombre canvas of a *Funeral Service in the Highlands* sets a scene that would have been foreign to Lowlanders at the time and is no longer to be witnessed at all today, while his *Hind's Daughter* captures in a little girl at the menial task of harvesting cabbages a kind of self-confident dignity. W.Y. Macgregor's best-known work is his *Vegetable Stall*, but his townscapes repay attention: they make Crail or Melrose or Oban or Stirling look as if they were somewhere in *la France profonde. The Druids Bringing Home the Mistletoe*, by George Henry and E.A. Hornel, carry us far away in time, just as Arthur Melville's oriental and Mediterranean scenes carry us far away in space. Of all the Glasgow Boys, John Lavery comes closest to the French impressionists: the mood of *The Tennis Party* is summed up by an elegant young man in plus fours leaning on a fence and smoking his pipe, while sunlight dapples the lawn. Can this really be Newlands?[61]

Yet it is surprising that the potential pictorial drama of industrial Clydeside appeared to leave these painters cold. If they were the Glasgow Boys, where might we find their images of Glasgow? Their city allowed and impelled them to be what they were, rather than giving them subject matter to paint: this seems to be the only conceivable answer to the puzzle. It was indeed Glaswegian wealth that made their work possible. One or two actually had a merchant or a shipbuilder for a father, and so the means and confidence to pursue their artistic careers. For the rest, the local opulence created a market for paintings, and a discerning one. Captains of industry could move with their fortunes into not only this but also into the international market for art just as it began to develop. The shipping magnate Sir William Burrell became the most memorable example, after donating to the city of Glasgow his vast collection, including works by Cézanne, Degas and Rodin, now housed in the gallery named after him. Against such competition the Glasgow Boys were put on their mettle, but they amply rewarded the patronage that came their way.[62]

By contrast the earliest, and among the most striking, Scottish images of industry are from the hand of an artist in Edinburgh, member of a losing faction in the trustees' academy who therefore thought better to spend the rest of his career in Newcastle. William Bell Scott's *Iron and Coal* captures its era's ceaseless energy amid a bewildering rate of change, while yet focusing on the workers' comradeship in hard labour.[63] For any equivalent in Glasgow we need to look to a later generation than the Boys, one which at last found in the industrial life of the city not only drama and interest but even a kind of beauty. In the years before the First World War, the vigorous etchings of Muirhead Bone conveyed the awesome complexity of it all and the dwarfing of the individual in the vast productive hive that yet furnished matter for common achievement and pride. Bone, like Mackintosh, studied at Glasgow's School of Art and served an apprenticeship in an architectural office, but in his case his draughtsmanship became more or less the same as his etching. Much more than any Glasgow Boy he was the chronicler of the city. In him the austerity of black-and-white proved good not just for recording architecture but also for capturing the mood of a community defined by its labour.[64]

Yet it was colour, rather than black-and-white, that in the same pre-war period started to distinguish the nation's painting above all. The group that came to be known as the Scottish Colourists would usually have been found in Paris during the years before 1914 – they were young men still defining themselves as painters and perfecting their technique in the city where all the world's aspiring artists sought example and inspiration. Here art was ceasing to be earthbound, as it threw off the shackles of classicism or indeed of realism and naturalism. Painters instead explored and extended the inherent qualities of discrete elements of their art, and this is what the Scots did with colour. Why colour? Perhaps it was coming from such a cold, grey country that prompted them to concentrate on that, to subvert the classical use of tone and texture in portrait and landscape and to react into a blaze of brightness. This was disconcerting to contemporary taste, certainly at home in Scotland, and by no means a formula for instant popularity and success. All the same we can appreciate, a century later, how they renewed the art of their country and made their contribution to the continued autonomy of its figurative achievement.[65]

John Duncan Fergusson spoke up for the Colourists: 'Everyone in Scotland should refuse to have anything to do with black or dirty and dingy colours, and insist on clean colours in everything. I remember when I was young any colour was considered a sign of vulgarity. Greys and blacks were the only colours for people of taste and refinement . . . Well! let's forget it, and insist on things in Scotland being of colour that makes for and associates itself with light, hopefulness, health and happiness.'[66] His wife Margaret was the pioneer of modern dance in Scotland, and his exuberant canvas of *Les Eus* is a kind of testimony to them both. Francis Cadell was more restrained, though he came alive in his portraits of women.[67] Samuel Peploe also restrains himself, but on the brink of cubism, without ever quite taking the plunge.[68] As for the fourth member of the school, Leslie Hunter, he did the shrewd thing for a youngster in Paris by making the acquaintance of Alice Toklas and Gertrude Stein – though then they shocked him by introducing him to the painting of Matisse.[69]

Considering what Matisse was doing at the time with his *Portrait de Madame Matisse* or his *Nu Bleu, souvenir de Biskra,* let alone what Picasso was doing in his Blue Period and his Rose Period, the Scottish Colourists indeed remained a trifle tame.[70] But once they were home again after 1918, they showed that what they had learned in the paradisal, pre-war Paris might be transformed into a distinctive Scottish idiom. While they could be confident and vibrant in the use of strong colour, it was still a generally timid range of subjects they chose in comparison to their French and other Continental counterparts: insular landscapes, domestic interiors, fashionable models. And they never ventured into the seamy side of life, as the French impressionists had once been happy to do: no can-can, no absinthe here.

All the same, Colourists transformed the pictorial traditions of Scotland. Each in his own style, they redefined the qualities of light and colour in one medium and another. Alas, they could not in Scotland count on much of a sympathetic public to encourage them and buy their paintings: they had difficulty earning a living. Yet the Colourists made a promising start to the Scottish art of the twentieth century. They were the first Scots to see themselves as modern European painters. Just as important, their example of dedication and independence helped the succeeding generations in their own country to find a way forward in a new world of art without signposts but with journey possible in almost any direction.[71]

14

Words: 'Its own way of speaking and thinking'

On 27 January 1870, Prince Louis-Lucien Bonaparte, nephew of the late Emperor of the French, Napoleon I, offered lunch at his home, West Green in Middlesex, to the philologist, James Murray, exiled from Denholm in Roxburghshire and trying to scratch a living in London, initially as a clerk at the Chartered Bank of India (which was, of course, run by Scots). They were not quite such an ill-assorted pair as might appear at first glance.[1]

The prince had actually been born in England, where members of his family were interned in 1813 after the Royal Navy captured them while they sought to escape to America (having fallen foul of the emperor). Louis-Lucien never got to France till 1848, when he went there to support the revolution of his kinsman, soon to be Napoleon III. The prince did not wait that long, however. Though elected to the French Senate, he felt uncomfortable in public life. He returned to London, where he stayed for the rest of his days. He anyway moved in England's highest circles. Queen Victoria had him to dinner at Windsor Castle, and he counted William Gladstone as a friend. But his interest in statecraft remained minimal. What really fascinated him was linguistics, especially dialects and their history. He learned Basque and produced a classification of its dialects still accepted as valid today. He investigated the Celtic languages, especially the extinct Cornish. He showed no less interest in Lowland Scots, which within Great Britain was about as deviant as any vernacular could get from the aristocratic English of his own social milieu. Hence his invitation to Murray – whom he knew to be at work on a pioneering study, *The Dialect of the Southern Counties of Scotland.*[2]

Murray was self-taught too; at that time a philologist could not be anything else. He had been born in humble circumstances, the son of a draper. His only qualification for his future calling was a voracious intellectual appetite, which he needed to satisfy for himself because his parents could not even afford to school him above the elementary level. All the same he persevered and, according to a failed application of his for a job at the British Museum, he had a greater or lesser acquaintance with 22 languages.[3]

In Scotland only the extent of Murray's interest in language was unusual, not the fact of it. As the old Scots tongue started to vanish, patriots sought means to preserve it. A sign of that was John Jamieson's publication of his *Etymological Dictionary of the Scottish Language* in 1808, which opened up medieval sources so far hidden in manuscript from the public domain. Jamieson asserted Scots was just as good as any other mode of expression: 'I do not hesitate to call that the Scottish *language* which has generally been considered in no other light than as merely on a level with the different provincial dialects of the English. Without entering at present into the origin of the former, I am bold to affirm that it has as just a claim to the designation of a peculiar language as most of the other languages of Europe.'[4] This was a clarion call, yet of itself did not affect the way Jamieson's countrymen spoke. By the middle of the nineteenth century, Scots had been all but abandoned among the upper class in favour of a strangulated sort of English. Further down the social scale the Scottish accent grew stronger, but the grammar and vocabulary at this level did not by now much differ from standard English either. The old speech remained vigorous only among the lower orders.

On this and related subjects, Bonaparte and Murray had over their lunch plenty to talk about. The prince, an incessant chatterbox, was pushing a pet project of his own to print a volume of the Parable of the Sower from the New Testament in as many European languages and dialects as possible. Then laymen would be able to appreciate, from the rich agricultural vocabulary, the common origin of their own tongues back in the mists of time when the Continent's peoples had all been tillers of the soil speaking Proto-Indo-European. From Murray he wanted to get a Scots version in both its ordinary spelling, 'in which Scotchmen like to see Scotch written', then also in a script he had devised using phonetic symbols, for the interest of scientific philologists.[5]

We do not know quite what answer Murray gave Bonaparte but probably it was guarded. After some months he wrote saying he had found the agreed task impossible:

I know no rule, no standard whatever for the modern Scottish forms of speech. The spelling of Burns for example is *simply English*, partly disguised by the fact that he used a considerable percentage of *words not English*: these words unfortunately are such as can scarcely ever be pressed into service in the Gospel of Matthew, and the result is that when I try to write in Burns's orthography, my version looks scarcely different from the English, certainly not worth publishing as Scotch, inasmuch as it conveys almost no idea as to the *actual living thing* a Scotch dialect is, and its utter difference from English sounds . . . at present I feel that the work I have been trying to do is not worth the doing, and I would rather put it in the fire, than see anything of which I so fully disapproved issued under my name.[6]

This degree of scholarly scruple doubtless did nothing for Murray's friendly relations with the prince. But it would serve him well once he became, a decade later, editor of the *Oxford English Dictionary*.

If Bonaparte read Murray's study of Scottish dialects when it was published in 1873, he would have found out why his plan for the parable proved stillborn. In this work, which remains standard, Murray pointed out that the written language of Scotland 'became, by 1707, identical with that of England. Here and there a solitary archaic form survived a few years longer; thus *ane*, the article before a consonant, is found lingering till about 1720, but though in this and other respects the written language might present Scotticisms, it was no longer in any sense Scotch'.[7]

Murray insisted the spoken language had enjoyed a different history, however, for after the Union it underwent 'a brilliant revival as the vehicle of ballad and lyric poetry'. Later Sir Walter Scott and John Galt took up 'its copious use in prose works illustrative of Scottish life and character – a path which many successors have followed'. Even so, they did not employ the language in the same manner as the medieval makars, John Barbour, Robert Henryson or William Dunbar, and so were not of the same value as witnesses to the voice of the people. Instead the modern writers had invented their own linguistic conventions: 'To a greater or lesser extent they are all contaminated with the influence of the literary English – the language which their authors have been educated to write – whose rules of grammatical inflection and construction they impose upon their own Scotch, to the corruption of the vernacular idiom . . . *Scots wha hae wi' Wallace bled*, though composed of Scotch words, is not vernacular Scotch.' Rather it was cast in a novel literary Scots that 'looks like literary English with a good many apostrophes, a small percentage of words not to be found in the English dictionary, and about the same number of idiomatic phrases and grammatical constructions not recognised by the literary tongue.' *A Man's a Man for A' That* contained 115 different words, of which only 18 were not to be found in English, while *Auld Lang Syne* had 24 Scots words out of 80, and *Scots Wha Hae* a mere 9 out of 100.[8]

Here was a man who knew his ingans. Murray, together with his pupil William Craigie and their colleague John Wilson, formed the small but illustrious Scottish platoon in an army of European philologists. At length these together gave a fairly complete account of their languages' development from Indo-European roots to the forms of today. Scots was an example of what at the time might have seemed a special case but one that has turned much commoner since, a historic vernacular steadily yielding ground to a metropolitan standard. During the twentieth century that came to represent a typical linguistic situation in France, Germany, Italy, Spain and elsewhere.

While Wilson's main expertise lay in Indian vernaculars, he wrote in 1915 of the language he had grown up with at Dunning in Perthshire: 'There is no doubt that here, as elsewhere, the native dialect of the people is rapidly disappearing, and as each generation passes away, some of the good old pithy words and phrases pass away with it. Books and newspapers are teaching the people, even in remote villages, to think and speak in something like standard English. But the chief enemy of local dialects is the schoolmaster.'[9] Craigie, who crowned his career as professor of Anglo-Saxon at the University of Oxford, said in 1924 of the linguistic situation in his homeland a century earlier that 'there was no lack of good, and even great, Scottish writers who used the native language. The strain of poetry never died out, though only now and then attaining the level of the days of Burns, and really represents a remarkably widespread knowledge of the Lowland speech and a deep-rooted attachment to it.' In prose, too, Scots had made a comeback which would hardly have been conceivable in the eighteenth century, 'and its use in novels and tales, from those of Scott down to the modern short story in the magazine or newspaper, has had an immense effect in forcing upon the attention of the world at large the fact that Scotland still has its own way of speaking and thinking'.[10]

Pressures for Scots to conform to English had been at work even before the Enlightenment proposed the aim for a united Britain of a single linguistic standard. Deviation from it by region or class would then stand condemned, while uniformity and conformity could be upheld as desirable in themselves. The standard was, of course, to be the standard of London, the usage of its royal court or at least of its educated professional classes.[11] There were Scots willing to accept that their normal speech fell short of this standard. For them, manuals of instruction came out. One, *The Vulgarities of Speech Corrected* (1826), drew attention to the fact, for example, that 'throughout Scotland, it is nearly universal to sound "I" like "a" in "father", as "A did not intend to go" for "I did not intend to go"; and even the most careful speakers are apt to fall into this vulgarity.'[12] In that case, as in others, 200 years of correction have failed to make much difference.

We should indeed never underestimate the simultaneous resistance to or even resentment of these efforts to suppress Scots, and not only among the common people. Men of letters knew the language had a long historical pedigree and a fine cultural tradition. When Scott read a new edition of the memoirs of Sir James Melville, a diplomat before the Union of Crowns, he exclaimed: 'It is brave to see how he wags his Scots tongue and what a difference there is in the force and firmness of the language compared to the mincing English edition in which he has hitherto been known.'[13] And English had anyway not yet completely triumphed even at the upper levels of society. The crusty old Tory judges prided themselves on speaking Scots from the bench – so, in fact, did one Whig judge, among colleagues who more usually affected the mincing English. This story was told of John Clerk, Lord Eldin, a singular physical apparition, lame, ugly and one-eyed; it could be a shock when he opened his mouth too.

> One night he was interrupted in his studies by the rumbling entry of two Gilmerton carters. John turned up his grey eye, and as the men seemed inclined to hang about the door, he rose and hirpled up to them.
> 'My carts' broken,' said one.
> 'My horse dee'd last nicht,' said the other.
> 'And what have I to do with that, ye bitches?'
> 'You're my faither, sir,' said one, taking his front-lock in his hand and bowing.
> 'You're my faither, sir,' said the other, with the same sign.
> 'And wha was your mither?' inquired John.

'Twa mithers, sir,' replied the men at once.

'Twa mithers?' responded John.

'Ay, sir, we're cousins, and you're our faither, ye ken?'

John meditated grimly, and grinningly drew out his purse. 'Weel, there's five pounds; and never let me see your ugly mugs again.'

'If they're no bonnie, they're your ain,' returned one of the carters.

'Weel, ye bitch, that's worth another five pounds', and John, with a grin, handed him the money.[14]

At this social level it was otherwise the gentlewomen that remained more likely to speak Scots, because they had less chance to leave Scotland and allow their mother tongue to be corrupted. For this reason there still just about survived one prestigious form of the language, Court Scots, which was not in the least owed to anglicisation. Probably it had last been used in public when the future James VII was resident at Holyrood in 1679–81. Henry Cockburn recalled how during his childhood in the 1780s he had heard ancient ladies speaking it.[15] One might have been Mrs Baird of Newbyth, mother of David Baird, member of a group of young officers captured in India and chained together in pairs: 'Lord pity the chiel that's chained tae oor Davie,' she exclaimed when she heard. Another might have been Miss Johnstone of Westerhall, who had a cousin forced by penury to sell her furniture: 'But before the sale cam on, in God's gude providence, she just clinkit aff hersell.'[16] Perhaps the very last of these venerable dames was one who in 1879 died at Rothesay Place in Edinburgh, aged 85 – just such 'a genuine Scottish matron of the old school', Dame Margaret Sinclair of Dunbeath. She had been born in the Canongate in 1794 into a class even then vanishing, 'the clear-headed, stout-hearted yet reverent and gentle old Scottish ladies whom Lord Cockburn loved to portray'.[17] But while they were still around, there could be no difficulty in imagining how, without the Union of 1707, Court Scots might have developed a standard of its own, related to but different from standard English, just as American and British English are today.[18]

Murray insisted the Scots language imposed standards of correctness by no means the same as English standards, according to which they could therefore not be judged. For instance, he rejected the notion that a Scotticism such as 'Him and me set oot thegither' was incorrect. He pointed out how it represented in Scots exactly the same linguistic phenomenon as the disjunctive pronouns in French: 'There is a direct or proper nominative and a direct objective as well as an indirect case, used like the French *moi, toi, lui, eux* for both nominative and objective.'[19] He also gave an example of the usage of *mines* – still common enough today in colloquial Scots but normally condemned as a vulgar neologism formed by false analogy with the correct English forms of *yours, hers, ours, theirs.* Yet Murray writes of 'the form *meynes* . . . often heard in South Scottish vernacular – "Aa'll gi' ye yours, quhan ye bring mey meynes"'.[20] Nor was this merely spoken usage. Robert Louis Stevenson wrote in *Weir of Hermiston,* 'Mines is no to be mentioned wi' it.'[21] Equally the employment of the emphatic pronoun ending in *-self* or *-sell* as the independent subject of a sentence, not just in apposition to another pronoun, is regular for Sir Walter Scott, as in the *Heart of Midlothian:* 'Mysell am not clear to trinquet and traffic wi' courts of justice, as they are now constituted.'[22] Murray made many more detailed points in defence of a different yet valid Scots grammar. They were still not enough to halt the tendency to hypercorrection in the educational system and elsewhere – so that nowadays we are at a stage where not only will *Him and me* be rejected as the subject of a verb, but *You and I* will be accepted as its object. The decline of Scots is in the twenty-first century accompanied by the decline of English.[23]

But there existed another non-English language in Victorian Scotland, the Gaelic still spoken by a quarter of a million people at the turn of the twentieth century, one in five of them knowing nothing else. They were about to suffer a rapid fall in numbers, but 100 years earlier theirs had been a vigorous language too. In fact, the eighteenth century was the great age of a new Gaelic literature, just released from the shackles of Classical Gaelic and of the bards whose linguistic and literary tyranny had been sustained by the clan chiefs. As the clans collapsed, poets needed to please their equals rather than their superiors. They broke into a fervent lyrical chorus, in which the voices of Donnchadh Bàn, Rob Donn, Alasdair mac Mhaighstir Alasdair and Uilleam Ros stood out as the finest. The translation of the entire Bible into Gaelic, completed by 1801, was also a turning point, or should have been, because it gave the common people a motive to become literate. During the next half-century, the spread of Gaelic schools and of Gaelic newspapers, as well as of hymn books and of other devotional materials, showed literacy was on the increase. Still, only after the Disruption of 1843 did that moderate the long-standing hostility of the Church of Scotland to Gaelic, as a vernacular of Episcopalians and Catholics. The hostility had been reinforced by the British state's repressive measures against the Jacobites. Once this peril passed, Gaelic could win at least a little recognition and respect in the rest of the United Kingdom. That may have been what impelled James Macpherson to his publication of translations from the ancient Celtic epic of Ossian in 1762. But the row surrounding his exercise rather blunted its cultural effect. The linguistic situation, in fact, remained open till the Education Act of 1872 set out to seal the fate of Gaelic.[24]

The crucial change among actual speakers of Gaelic was a loss of confidence in their own language. 'Some young men,' wrote the disapproving minister of Gairloch in Wester Ross in 1836, 'consider they are doing a great service to the Gaelic, by interspersing their conversation with English words, and giving them a Gaelic termination and accent.'[25] By 1865 the Duke of Argyll's Royal Commission on Scottish education took evidence from a schoolmaster on Harris who said the families he worked among had no wish for Gaelic schools: 'I think Gaelic has become inefficient now. I would teach it in our [English] schools, but Gaelic schools the people won't have ... they much more quickly learn in English.'[26] English first replaced Gaelic at the upper levels of society or in situations where Gaels met non-Gaels, as in commerce. But it remained the normal language of the Church, the farms, the fisheries and every social gathering. Once an English linguistic minority established a foothold in any area, however, Gaelic could retreat quickly. At the end of the nineteenth century it was still spoken in Highland Aberdeenshire and Perthshire, though not for much longer. At that time Argyll had a big Gaelic-speaking majority, which within three decades shrank to a minority.[27] Highland education after 1872 took it as a principal purpose to turn Gaels into English-speakers. The eventual result was the drastic reduction of the Gaelic-speaking area, the use of English by Gaels for official or economic purposes even within that area, and so the impoverishment of the Gaelic tongue itself, losing old vocabulary or failing to acquire new vocabulary.

This linguistic background, of attrition in the native tongues of Scotland, also had an effect on the nation's literary activity. Nothing more will be said here of Gaelic, because after its golden age in the eighteenth century its literature fell into a decline not halted till the work of Sorley MacLean in the twentieth century. It was in the Scots language that the greater tension could be observed. The Lowland society using this vernacular underwent stupendous changes, for good and ill. Their literary expression did not live up to the scale or intensity of the experience. At the beginning of the period Scotland had an author universally acknowledged as great, together with two others who merit the same accolade but have less often received it, then near the end of the period a third great author. But in between there was little else.

Other nations nurturing great authors – England, France, Germany, Russia – faced no linguistic problem. Their languages were just there as a natural medium for expression of all the huge challenges their modernising societies needed to face, and the working out of those challenges in individual destinies. In Scotland things took another turn. Here, as the Orcadian poet Edwin Muir lamented when looking back from the 1930s, there had been a fatal disjunction of heart and head.[28] The language in which Scots couched their most personal and intimate thoughts was not the same as the language in which they conducted systematic thinking or addressed the public. Even if the two languages turned out on analysis to be in reality similar (as Murray had shown), they still left a feeling that they ought somehow to be different: that English would never be the language in which a Scotsman or Scotswoman could best express love or fear or hope or despair, but that Scots was no longer the language in which they could depict great events, cast profound thoughts or win an intellectual argument.

One achievement of Sir Walter Scott was that he found at least a provisional solution to this linguistic problem, without which a national literature might no longer have been possible. If not a wholly satisfactory solution, it worked for him and for many other Scottish authors. During the eighteenth century they had written in English, with the exception of subversive poets such as Allan Ramsay and Robert Burns. By the end of that era of Enlightenment, Scottish prose had become, well, prosy. It certainly needed enlivening for the genre Scott invented, the historical novel. The convention established by him, and almost universally followed since, was that while dialogue could go into Scots, narrative should go into English. It would prove a useful convention not only for historical novels but also for later realistic novels of contemporary life, because in their everyday circumstances the Scottish people continued to speak one language to family, friends and workmates, another to strangers, to authority and, not least, to God. The deity might originally have revealed himself in Hebrew or in Greek, but to Scots he first did so in English. They had to make of that what they would.[29]

This God exerted an effect not only on the form but also on the content of the national literature because, as expounded by John Calvin and the Scottish

Reformers, he had created a world radically divided between good and evil, with humanity on the evil side, *sauf un tout petit nombre*.[30] There are other pervasive qualities in Scottish literature not owed directly to God – a delight in the diminutive, a temptation to seek refuge in immaturity, an obsession with conflicts of father and son. But its most productive motif is the dichotomy between the beautiful seductions in the temporal lives of men and women and the terrible spiritual price to be paid for them.

Just as Scott solved his linguistic problem to his own satisfaction, so perhaps he thought he had solved this moral-cum-literary problem too. His answer lay in the temperance and moderation with which he imbued many of his heroes – though it tended to render them, alas, rather mediocre as characters. It can be said to Scott's credit that he sought to practise the same virtues in his own life. Often something deeper broke through, however. He never doubted the vanity of human desires or the transience of all earthly things, but he loved his country, its people, places and past, with a passion. He had a lucid, rational intellect all the same yoked to a wild, adventurous imagination. His novels sang the praises of robust common sense, while in real life he could be a fool, and notoriously so in matters of finance. He became a man of property and built himself a country house at Abbotsford, which he then proceeded to stuff with an amazing collection of vulgar knick-knacks. He found the rigours of Presbyterianism little to his taste and opted to be an Episcopalian, though more potent in him than any religious conviction was a brooding sense of supernatural mystery. If it also reinforced his own sense of the artist as a solitary being, he still sought company up and down the social scale from the high aristocracy to the humblest folk. He championed a holistic Scottish community surmounting distinctions of rank and wealth, and in this sense was a democrat; it did not stop him being also a Tory reverent when not subservient towards his feudal superiors and his sovereign. He remained a man of his time, sharing its views, its virtues and its vices. Scotland yet lived for him above all through its history, which he in turn wanted to make live again to his contemporaries; in fact, he continues to do that to readers far off in the future from him.[31]

Scott was in other words admirably suited to the historical novel. He composed the entire series on Scottish themes known collectively, after the first of them, as the Waverley Novels. They made him world famous, but his compatriots still admired him most for saying things about them nobody else had ever put into words. It counted for much in a country with a nationhood starting, even amid unexampled material prosperity, to look fragile, precarious and provisional. As the old Scotland faded away and a modern one struggled to be born, Scott's achievement in dealing with this disturbing duality looked all the more formidable.[32]

There is scarcely one of those novels that does not open with a formula echoing the subtitle of *Waverley* (1814) itself, *'Tis sixty years since*. In his introduction Sir Walter goes on to explain: 'Some favourable opportunities of contrast have been afforded me, by the state of society in the northern part of the island at the period of my history, and may serve at once to vary and illustrate the moral lesson.'[33] In other words, this is about, as much as anything, the movement of history, which will help to explain the actions of the characters and what the reader may understand from them.

Waverley, while it came first, was in many ways the culmination of the series, and it would be better in assessing the overall achievement to deal in advance with works treating of earlier periods, if published later. Scott's project of re-creating modern Scottish history in the novel first fully flowers when he comes to the struggles under King Charles II (1660–85) in the cause of the Covenant. The episode shows us the radical Calvinist vision of Scotland, but at its worst. By the Covenant the Scots had, in emulation of the ancient Israelites, pledged themselves to be a 'sworn nation of the Lord'. In Scotland as in Israel, holy zeal found one outlet in merciless savagery towards the enemies of Jehovah. This is the world of Scott's *Old Mortality* (1816), where the Covenanters rise up against a royal government that in reaction sets out to exterminate them. It is an insane world. The hero of the story, Henry Morton, remains a man of moderation but is unable to deal with the insanity all about him, where figures espousing every shade of extremism rage, fight and kill, each in his own sacred cause. And they drag one another down. Sir Walter puts his finger on a national vice: Scots, instead of uniting against their foes, would rather first fight out to the bitter end their own intestine quarrels. 'O remember, my brethren,' says Morton to the Covenanters, 'that the last and worst evil which God brought upon the people whom he had once chosen – the last and worst punishment of their blindness and hardness of heart, was the bloody dissension which rent asunder their city, even when the enemy were thundering at the gates!' That is where, in history, Scott sees Scotland's religion as having led. Morton no doubt speaks for his own creator when he says: 'Our resolutions, our passions, are like the waves of the sea, and without the aid of Him who formed the human breast, we cannot say to its tides, Thus far shall ye come and no further.'[34]

Readers may well turn with relief to *Rob Roy* (1817), which takes them three or four decades on into the aftermath of Scotland's Union with England (Sir Walter did not care in his novels to deal with the Union itself). Now a novel duality has been introduced into the nation. Half of it, the Highland half, remains barbaric. Here men, or indeed women, act towards one another in ways no civilised human being can condone. But already we have a different type of Scotsman, in some respects not as admirable as the heroes of the past yet in other respects much more so. The type is represented in Bailie Nicol Jarvie of Glasgow. He emerges as a richly comic creation, even something of an object of satire in the text. Obsessed with opportunities to make money in his now booming burgh, he justifies his worldliness through his contorted, not to say hypocritical Presbyterianism. Yet he is at heart a decent, admirable fellow who never finds killing other people heroic, least of all out of blind loyalty to some chieftain's command. When he witnesses an example of such brutality he makes his point at whatever risk to himself: 'I take up my protest against this deed, as a bloody and cruel murder – it is a cursed deed, and God will avenge it in his due way and time.' He does nothing else – he is not going to be a martyr for a new morality. But he carries overwhelming conviction. The calculating capitalist is in the right; the fearless fighters are in the wrong.[35]

The Heart of Midlothian (1818) carries us forward another couple of decades, to a point in the history of Edinburgh in particular when English power over the place has become palpable yet native defiance still flares up. This novel, too, starts out from a historicist formula: 'The times have changed in nothing more ... than the rapid conveyance of intelligence and communication betwixt one part of Scotland and another. It is not above twenty or thirty years ...'[36] Behind the action there again lies an acute sense of greater movement in the life of the nation, nowhere more literally and unforgettably than in the opening chapters. Scott here deploys true history, the history of the Captain John Porteous condemned in 1736 for having ordered his soldiers to fire on unruly onlookers, killing several, at an execution in the Grassmarket. Later, just as in punishment Porteous is about to be led to the same scaffold himself, a reprieve arrives for him post-haste from London. Scott creates an uneasy sense of foreboding as he describes the crowd of spectators breaking up, disappointed of a hanging. They ask, 'Is this to be borne – would our fathers have borne it? Are we not, like them, Scotsmen and burghers of Edinburgh?'[37]

Sir Walter is preparing us here for one of the greatest scenes in literature, when that night Porteous will be dragged from the Tolbooth and hanged high in revenge. The pause in the action is reinforced as the narrative zooms in on people climbing back up the West Bow into the city. We walk along with them. We hear their voices. Of course they speak Scots. One utters a sentence often quoted as summarising the political predicament of Scotland after the Union: 'I ken, when we had a king, and a chancellor, and parliament-men o' our ain, we could aye peeble them wi' stanes when they were na gude bairns – but naebody's nails can reach the length o' Lunnon.' Being ordinary folk, however, they waste little thought on the great issues of the time before returning to concerns of their own. Two are bores: Saddletree, a shopkeeper learned in the law, and Butler, a schoolmaster who keeps correcting his companion's Latin. They wrangle without listening to each other over obscure points of syntax and statute. Eavesdropping, the reader observes how Scott captures, for now softened into comedy, his countrymen's wilfulness.[38]

The Scots show another visage as, after darkness has fallen, a huge mob erupts with ugly fury into Edinburgh's streets. Sir Walter hated the mobs of his own time, yet his depiction of this one is sympathetic. Porteous's end appals us, as he is strung up and hacked at while he dangles, but he gets his just deserts. The people's rage cannot be condoned, though it can be understood. The cardinal virtue of justice is finally enjoined on all, whatever their station in life. Justice triumphs, first in a brutal and arbitrary way, then because the rulers of men see their way to temperance. One lesson Scott drew for his own time was that the Porteous Riot had been an episode 'unmingled with politics of Whig and Tory [which] must simply be regarded as a strong and powerful display of the cool, stern and resolved manner in which the Scottish, even of the lower classes, can concert and execute a vindictive purpose'.[39]

Next in the progression, *Waverley* itself deals with the Jacobite revolt of 1745. Like the real events it follows, it is a work of multiple significance. Those events meant a lot to Sir Walter, and he sought in his novel to explore or define their meanings. Steeped in Jacobite lore as he was, nobody could have been better equipped to write a story following the whole drama from Prince Charles Edward Stewart's raising of his standard at Glenfinnan to his escape through the heather after the catastrophe at the Battle of Culloden. Yet this is not what Scott does.[40]

The novel actually starts off in England. Its hero or anti-hero, Edward Waverley, is a young military officer from an old royalist family. He gets posted to Scotland. With a letter of introduction he visits a stubborn loyalist to the

House of Stewart, Baron Bradwardine, at the castle of Tully-Veolan, a dismal pile, an image of decay. In the character of Bradwardine, Jacobite futility comes across yet more clearly. His undying devotion to the cause is matched by his own punctilious, not to say pedantic, sense of honour. It renders him useless for any practical purpose. So the first we learn of Jacobitism is that it has lost all connection with reality.[41]

A second figure Waverley then meets, Fergus McIvor, is both like and unlike Bradwardine. McIvor represents more of what we expect from a Highland chief: he is brave, dauntless and ready to die for what he believes in (as he finally will). But we also learn he is a calculating man who might never have chosen this course unless urged on by a sly sister. It occurs to Waverley, and to us following his adventures, that people can become Jacobites as they might become Whigs – for their own gain. In making the point Sir Walter divests his Jacobites not just of their romance but also of their strangeness, perhaps especially to English readers. While Jacobites support a lost cause, they may also cherish the same ambitions as those on the winning side. This means, in more basic human terms than is provided by a long history of enmity, that the Union of England and Scotland can be successful – and in Scott's view it was, by his own time, successful. It had been right for both nations.[42]

Even now there was something left for Scott to say on the national history. *Redgauntlet* (1824) might be seen as, beside much else, the postscript to the Waverley Novels in its dealing with matters two decades after Culloden. Nobody can doubt Jacobitism is now dead – except for a few diehard Scots still clinging to the cause. A number of them lurk in a distant corner of the country by the shores of the Solway Firth, where the perilous shifting sands symbolise the dilemmas confronting them in the novel. Again, in its opening words, we are made aware how human affairs will inexorably move on even from the greatest historical crux. Sir Walter, or his narrator, remarks how Jacobitism has 'afforded a theme, perhaps the finest that could be selected, for fictitious composition, founded upon real or probable incident. This civil war, and its remarkable events, were remembered by the existing generation without any degree of the bitterness of spirit which seldom fails to attend internal dissension.'[43] Time has healed the wounds, then, so we can see Jacobitism in the round.

In *Redgauntlet* we see it in the round through a complex, compelling narrative constructed out of different views and strands. Since Scott himself felt torn between the deep emotions of Jacobitism and the cool intellect of the Enlightenment, he is able to breathe life into every one of his characters.

He, the genius at resolving paradox, does not now want to reconcile them, however. In fact, he refuses to let them be categorised glibly as right or wrong, good or evil, noble or base, reasonable or fanatical, of the past or of the present. Rather these qualities follow developments of their own embodied in the fates of the different figures: they may start off as one thing but finish up as the opposite. Of Redgauntlet himself we can see why he refuses to accept Jacobitism is finished when we, too, recall its basic nobility and the heroism of its followers in 1745. All the same, his stubborn intransigence threatens to render the sacrifice worthless, perhaps ridiculous – which is more painful even than treachery could be.[44]

Sir Walter gives us to understand this as he rounds off the book with a final twist; historical realism is not allowed the last word. Seeing that by this stage Prince Charles Edward Stewart has been found wanting too, General Campbell is right to tell Redgauntlet, 'It is now all over, and Jacobite will be henceforward no longer a party name.' Yet rather than arrest a traitor to the British crown, he lets Redgauntlet go. The old man responds in anguish: 'Then the cause is lost indeed.'[45] The book leaves us feeling that it is not always the best people who win, and that other things may be more important than success.

Overall, in the Waverley Novels, we have gained a broad view of humanity set amid the panorama of the modern history of a single nation. It had never had an easy history, rather one where contradictions led not to synthesis but to the constant peril of dissolution and ruin. Yet the nation has survived and now, all passion spent, can look forward to a less fraught future – perhaps.

Scott was in his time the greatest figure of Scottish literature, yet he did not stand alone. Here we can look at only two of his peers. Both men of their time too, they had much in common with him. John Galt was closer to the genial side of Scott, if with a narrower focus in the material he chose to write about – but for all that giving us, in thin disguise, real places and real changes in a real nation. He dealt above all with the west of Scotland, and was indeed a patriot of the region. It irked him that Edinburgh had won the epithet of Athens of the North and he tried to create a fashion for calling Glasgow the Venice of the North; somehow this never caught on.[46]

Galt's best book was *Annals of the Parish* (1821), the fictional autobiography of the minister, the Revd Micah Balwhidder, at the village of Dalmailing in Ayrshire for half a century. He writes its annals, his narrative of events year by year, in obvious expectation that the reader will take them at face value.

He is not the whole book, however. Galt shapes it so as to let the reader see things on a different, larger scale. The depiction of the minister is ironic, in other words, and through the irony we perceive underlying realities that escape him.[47]

Before our eyes Balwhidder turns from awkward novice into silver-haired patriarch, revealing himself along the way as kindly, sincere and generous yet also somewhat snobbish, timid and complacent. In the outside world it is an age of wars and revolutions, but only their distant echoes reach Dalmailing. Scotland here seems timeless, her people poor but hard-working, content with a communal life centred on the kirk. It is where Balwhidder has chosen to spend all his adult life, with only rare and disconcerting excursions to Glasgow or Edinburgh. He thinks his parish a refuge from change, yet he is wrong: he cannot stop change coming from outside, and it arises inside as well. The old laird, Lord Eglesham, is shot dead by a poacher and replaced by the upstart Mr Cayenne, arriving as a refugee from the American Revolution. He has salvaged enough to build a cotton-mill round which a settlement of weavers forms: a new social phenomenon, a harbinger of industrial society. Balwhidder notices the weavers stay away from the kirk and summons them to the manse to explain themselves. Out of respect they respond but the interview is awkward. He knows nothing of them, and at bottom is hardly interested. They run rings round him and dismiss his remonstrances as 'the light sayings of a vain man'. Not that he is stupid – on the contrary, as he proudly tells us, he mastered the principles of moral philosophy while at college in Glasgow during the 1750s (when Adam Smith was teaching there). But now we are in the 1790s and the weavers can educate themselves too; out of their meagre earnings they subscribe to a newspaper from London so they can follow the progress of the French Revolution. Balwhidder is not an otherworldly figure, yet his world progresses too fast for him to keep up. By the end he hardly even tries. He is an image of tension between the old and the new Scotland.[48]

The third great Scottish novelist of the age wrote a novel even greater than any of Scott's. He and James Hogg were friends. Both belonged to the Borders, and this common origin overcame any difference in their social status – between Sir Walter as a gentleman, if largely a self-made one, and Hogg as a man of the people, who had indeed remained illiterate till adulthood. That background would hardly be guessed from his best work, *The Private*

Memoirs and Confessions of a Justified Sinner (1824), a literary achievement of a high order. While it is little known outside Scotland, many think it the finest of all the nation's novels in the miraculous subtlety of its construction.[49]

The *Private Memoirs* was already underrated in its own time. On the one hand, its vernacular vigour struck the genteel as an insult to refined modern taste. And its unsparing interrogation of Presbyterianism made it, on the other hand, in the eyes of the devout no better than an infidel polemic. The combination proved enough to consign it to obscurity for more than a century. Then in 1947 a new edition was published with a glowing introduction by the French novelist André Gide, himself a French Protestant (and therefore Calvinist). Knowing almost nothing of Hogg, or of Scottish history and literature, Gide came to the work with an open mind. And he read it 'with a stupefaction and admiration that increased at every page . . . It is long since I can remember being so taken hold of, so voluptuously tormented by any book.' Later critics have followed this estimation of the novel. Now all appreciate its Gothic horror, its dissection of bigotry, its relentless satire of religious hypocrisy, its honest realism about criminals and prostitutes, its acute analysis of mental breakdown and schizophrenia. It is rich not only in content but also in form, in its echoes of romantic poetry, its exploitation of the *Doppelgänger* as literary device, its mixture of tragedy with comedy through ironies, symbols and puns.[50]

Hogg indeed concerns himself with religion here but at the service of art rather than of theology. The motor of the action is a Calvinist heresy, antinomianism, which states the elect of God cannot be damned even in committing the foulest crimes because they are predestined to salvation. The arid logic comes to life against a vivid interplay of character and incident, much of it set in Edinburgh shortly before the Union of 1707. The tension in the air is such that a walk up Salisbury Crags can produce hallucinations, while the Old Town forms a perfect backdrop to still deeper confusions of mind and sense. At one point, mobs of Whigs and Jacobites rush back and forth through closes and wynds, disappearing and reappearing, till two groups on the same side attack each other. They realise what they have done only when, bloody, battered and bruised, they come to be treated by the same surgeons. Such is the vanity of human perceptions and of human affairs in general: progress, whether personal or social, is not a matter of interest to Hogg.[51]

These three authors presented great themes of human life in literary forms, of language and content, unmistakably Scottish – at the same time fine enough to have constituted a literature that merits the epithet of classical. Just like the Scottish school of classical painting, however, it belonged to an age that was drawing to a close, 'the last purely Scotch age', as Cockburn called it.[52] In the following half-century Scotland was transformed by the industrial revolution and by the effects of widening contacts with the rest of Britain and with the Empire. This momentous process deserved a literary expression of its own, and in similar advancing societies it found one. But in Scotland, while Scottishness did persist in literature, the concern with great themes of human life vanished.

It was the era of the so-called kailyard, named after the Scots term for a cabbage-patch. Literature came during this period in the shape of undemanding stories about local, usually rustic matters, with a cast of predictable characters playing out parodies of the Scottish character, from which their rather repugnant virtues emerged invariably affirmed. A number of the authors were Presbyterian ministers, notably the Revd John Watson writing under the pseudonym of Ian Maclaren, secure in a wealthy expatriate charge in Liverpool, whence he produced in 1894 a volume of which the very title is redolent of the school, *Beside the Bonnie Brier Bush*. This and its other products were, despite their innocent air, carefully packaged and then heavily promoted by Sir William Robertson Nicholl, Gladstonian Liberal and former minister of the Free Church, latterly editor of the *British Weekly*. He viewed the kailyard as a force for 'tenderness, for purity, for a higher standard of life'.[53] No tension, then, no tragedy – and this in Scotland!

But let us for the time being pass over this ghastly literary phase to look at the last great author to whom Scotland gave birth in the nineteenth century, before returning to consider his place in the country's general cultural development. Robert Louis Stevenson was a precocious literary lion, after narrowly avoiding other avocations to which he might have been destined by his *haut bourgeois* family, as a builder of lighthouses or as an advocate in the Court of Session. Once embarked on the life of a writer, he was vindicated in his ambition by the extraordinary gifts he revealed. He became at once prolific, notably in personal essays which hit on a perfect blend of high polish and disarming candour, 'while aphorisms poured from his young mouth straight into the dictionary of quotations'.[54]

An early product was a piece that broke the Scottian rule of narrative in English, dialogue in Scots. *Thrawn Janet*, which appeared in a literary magazine in 1881, was couched entirely in Scots.[55] It is something less than 5,000 words long, and presented in the form of what the Germans call a *Rahmenerzählung*, a 'framework narrative' that has the effect of making unbelievable events, here supernatural, more credible because the author cedes his voice to an eyewitness. The reader may believe or not believe the eyewitness, but can still accept that the author is giving an accurate account. In content the story falls somewhere in between James Hogg's *Private Memoirs* and John Buchan's *Witch Wood* (1927). It is an achievement at least in the use of Scots but, like most of Stevenson's achievements in this phase of his career, it did not really lead anywhere. Where he felt the need in his later works, he continued to handle Scots dialogue deftly. But he never again tried to do more with the language. Meanwhile the literary world waited for his giddying promise to be otherwise fulfilled.

Stevenson was one of nature's freelances and produced hundreds of works of amazingly diverse character – as with most freelances, this was still seldom enough to ensure a steady flow of satisfactory income. And in the course of time his admirers began to feel a little disappointed in their hopes. He seemed busy enough, forever embarking on new projects and even making something of many. But when would the great works start to appear? Answer came there none. Instead there came only more works full of potential, yet hardly great.[56]

Among the finest boys' books ever written was *Treasure Island*, (1883) set in the West Indies (though the map of the island supplied in the text looks suspiciously like Scotland); it fairly bowls along in a series of wonderfully imagined episodes required by the fact it had originally to be written in instalments for a children's magazine. *Kidnapped* (1886) was in that respect much the same – and advertised as such, if this time set among Scottish landscapes. It is based on a famous Jacobite episode, the Appin murder of 1752, allowing oodles of romance to be mixed in with the realistic backgrounds. The same blend occurs in the two leading characters, the sober young Lowlander, David Balfour, and the volatile, charismatic Highlander, Allan Breck Stewart, though they differ in everything from temperament to politics. One way of looking at all this is in terms of the familiar Scottish dualism, here welling up from far beneath a fast-moving narrative. In this dawn of the modern Scotland, everybody has cause to lament the nation's disunity. Balfour wanders about one half of his country as an alien, not speaking the language, not sharing the people's allegiances, unable to interpret the semiology. Yet Stewart, despite his pride in being a Highland gentleman of long pedigree, has been turned by exile almost into a Frenchman. The vision of Scotland in the book is deeply unsettling: every Scot we meet is in some way embat-tled or threatened. This adventure could indeed only have been set during a traumatic, schismatic period in the history of the nation, standing at the start of a process that would break it up and divide it in both linguistic and cultural terms. Even so the book is no tragedy, and Stevenson not the Victor Hugo of *Les Misérables* or the Joseph Conrad of *Heart of Darkness*. We can see why *Kidnapped* was marketed as a children's story, though it is not quite even that.[57]

Still, Stevenson took a long step forward with *The Strange Case of Dr Jekyll and Mr Hyde* (1886). It is another fiction based on Scottish fact: the story from a century before of the double life of Deacon Brodie, by day a respect-able tradesman and civic dignitary, by night a burglar so clever as to put the wind up the whole city of Edinburgh. Stevenson transforms his material into something much more general and existential, a myth of modern man. Yet he cannot bring himself to set it in Edinburgh. Instead it is supposed to be set in London – the one unconvincing thing about it. Edinburgh still intrudes all the same. 'There is a square of ancient, handsome houses, now for the most part decayed from their high estate and let in flats and chambers to all sorts and conditions of men: map-engravers, architects, shady lawyers and the agents of obscure enterprises': obviously the rundown eastern end of the first New Town. At the time London's fogs were 'pea-soupers', descending and staying put for days on end, whereas Edinburgh had and still has fogs found nowhere else in the world, fogs which defy high winds and blow about rather than being dispersed. And what is the fog like in *Jekyll and Hyde*? 'The wind was continually charging and routing these embattled vapours . . . here it would be dark like the backend of evening; and there would be a glow of a rich, lurid brown, like the light of some strange conflagration; and here, for a moment, the fog would be quite broken up, and a haggard shaft of daylight would glance in between the swirling wreaths.' Is that London or Edinburgh? Or again, 'it was a wild, cold, seasonable night of March, with a pale moon, lying on her back as though the wind had tilted her, and flying wrack of the most diaphanous and lawny texture. The wind made talking difficult, and flecked the blood into the face.' It does not sound like an English moon or an English wind.[58] Still, such Scottish quibbles do not alter the fact of the book's huge success, which was international and continuing. Stevenson needed the money, and took no notice of his admirers' laments over his decline into mass popularity.

Then something finally clicked in *Weir of Hermiston* (1896), a novel of Edinburgh and in potential a great one, though in the event just a fragment. By the time Stevenson wrote it he had found refuge on Samoa, and the vast physical distance was evidently what he needed to write about Scotland so searchingly: in spirit, the author has never left the High Street of his home-town or the windswept braes of the Pentland Hills. It is the backdrop to a classic conflict between father and son, like that in his own family between the father who built lighthouses and the son who scribbled stories. Young Archie Weir's idealism and morality are arguably Stevenson's (underneath his poses), but it is the rough, crude, brutal Lord Hermiston that wins over the reader. His harshness hides an essential decency, whereas Archie's liberalism is vacu-ous: the father has durable values, the son only hopeful impulses. Hermiston's stoicism in the face of this flawed relationship is beautifully captured too: 'If he failed to gain his son's friendship, or even his son's toleration, on he went up the great bare staircase of his duty, uncheered and undepressed.'[59] The style of the work alone, pithy and sardonic, tells us how Stevenson relished giving life to these and to a further cast of convincing characters, all set in motion against a vivid social background. Yet it is still only a fragment of a novel, cut off from full development by the cerebral haemorrhage that had killed its author in 1894. If ever completed, it would doubtless have given Stevenson's admirers and critics alike the chance to forget his previous shortcomings in the uneven production of literary eccentricities. They might then at last have seen in the original and brilliant stylist, who at his best might bring to light the hidden depths of his age, a fulfilment of the original promise.

Scottish literature could barely afford such a loss, yet another lay in store. While Stevenson was seeking to live out a tropical idyll on Samoa, a young Scotsman unknown to him, George Douglas Brown, had embarked on his studies at Balliol College, Oxford. Brown got there not on account of any social privilege: in fact, he was the illegitimate son of a farmer from Ochiltree in Ayrshire and some Irish trollop. He made it to Oxford because he was so clever, and afterwards he went to London to start on the chancy business of freelance journalism. In the midst of these time-consuming and often dispiriting labours he suddenly produced an extraordinary novel, *The House with the Green Shutters* (1901). It was the sort of *succès de scandale* that might have launched a literary career, except there was to be no career: Brown died a premature death the same year.[60]

Brown starts like any author of the kailyard with a small town in the country where life seems safe and predictable, scarcely touched by modernity.[61] Here at Barbie (actually Ochiltree) there is a father, John Gourlay, proud and taciturn. There is a son, also John, insecure, neurotic and in the event unable to live up to the father's expectations. At home are a cowed wife and daughter who take refuge in novelettes or daydreaming. Outside they are all the object of spiteful comments and petty machinations from envious and idle villagers. Crisis comes with the arrival of a commercial competitor who proves hard for Gourlay to match. Instead he invests his hopes and his money in his son. Young John, however, is driven to drink by his inability to cope with life at university. Tension mounts and in the end he accidentally kills his father. It is a melodramatic story, remarkable for having really no pleasant characters at all. Even so it came across as the first truthful picture of Scottish provincial life since Galt's, and as a fuse lit to the falsities of the kailyard. Indeed all the familiar conventions get destabilised here, carted on to Brown's scene only to be upended. In place of make-believe we have savage parody, in place of hackneyed human relationships only grotesque and disturbing ones, in place of comforting social values others dealing destruction, in place of Christianity a lack of existential hope. There is nothing comforting here, only an utter lack of compromise.[62]

The book leaves us wanting to read more from the hand of a remarkable literary talent. Brown wrote to a friend from Balliol, the political scientist Ernest Barker, with a criticism of his own novel which is hard to fault: 'Well, I suppose you have read the Green Shutters by this time. 'Tis a brutal and bloody work; too sinister, I should think, for a man of your kindlier disposition. There is too much black for the white in it. Even so it is more complimentary to Scotland, I think, than the sentimental slop of Barrie, and Crockett, and Maclaren. It was antagonism to their method that made me embitter the blackness.'[63]

Yet perhaps the kailyard cannot be written off quite so easily.[64] It is worth noting that Stevenson had been on good terms with a couple of its authors, J.M. Barrie and S.R. Crockett. After receiving a collection of the latter's stories on Samoa, Stevenson wrote back about the delight he felt at 'being *drowned* in Scotland, they have refreshed me like a visit home'.[65] If they had been false to the nation, he was at least gentleman enough not to say so. Without making any great claims for the literary abilities of money-spinning Presbyterian ministers, we might see in their works some dim reflection of certain problems of the time: at least, say, the growing challenge to religion, the decline of rural Scotland, the questioning of traditional authority, the gradual atrophy of self-regulating communities. Stevenson had himself developed some of the repertoire. Behind both *The Master of Ballantrae* and *Thrawn Janet* there is a warped community of malicious gossips, or dour Calvinists turning into tormented zealots. In *Kidnapped* and *Catriona* there is quite a romantic picture of the Highlands, yet one undermined by the revelation of far from romantic double-dealing and cruelty. We can trace also certain connections from the kailyard to a successor literature that developed more modern variants on old themes, starting at *The House with the Green Shutters* itself. Brown's John Gourlay junior can, for example, be compared to the Eochan of George MacDougall Hay's *Gillespie* (1914), much more of a modern novel: both these youthful anti-heroes are alienated from family and community, uncertain of their identities and feeling their talents stifled under the limitations of their culture, society and country. Romantic history again yields to divided and hypocritical loyalties in Violet Jacob's *Flemington* (1911) and in some of the earlier fiction of John Buchan. The twentieth century that gave us, on television too, *Dr Finlay's Casebook* and *Para Handy* could hardly complain of the quality of Scottish culture it had inherited. Perhaps things will finally improve in the twenty-first century.

What precisely was it, then, that failed in the Scottish literature of the late Victorian era? Perhaps for structural reasons, in the nature of the literary market rather than the quality of the literary product, Scotland was already being suffocated by the imposition of British norms, another feature of the twenty-first century as well. It has been demonstrated that there was a huge body of fiction, published in serial form in provincial newspapers, dealing with realistic themes in Scottish life, especially urban life. But the very manner of the publication made this literature ephemeral, compared to the now well-established British mechanisms for production of the novel.[66]

At the same time, there can be no doubt about the genuine popularity of the kailyard. When Brown set out to overthrow it, his originality lay in unsettling an unspoken convention between novelist and reader that time should stand still while representative Scots interacted in finally reassuring situations. Yet the greatest writers of Scottish fiction, Scott, Hogg, Galt and Stevenson, did not give us a static Scotland, or one limited by any pandering to their readers. Rather they took fictions that they knew would challenge their readers, so these might out of the encounter change their ideas about their country.[67] It was a high standard for successors to live up to, and the general state of Scottish culture did not always favour it – then or now.

15

Thoughts: 'Still Scotch enough'

By 26 May 1881, the General Assembly of the Free Church of Scotland had got halfway through a fraught week. Overshadowing all its usual bureaucratic business of reports from committees and overtures for legislation was the need to take a final decision in the case of the Revd William Robertson Smith, professor of Hebrew at its theological college in Aberdeen, who that day stood before the ministers and elders arraigned of heresy. If this seemed to waft into William Playfair's Assembly Hall in Edinburgh a whiff of singed human flesh from three centuries back, it would have been all the more pungent for the fact that Robertson Smith stood at the very summit of Scottish scholarship. His country's most eminent theologian, he also enjoyed the highest reputation in Germany, Holland, Switzerland, the United States, in fact, everywhere that Reformed doctrines prevailed. Would it not be incredible for fundamentalist bigots to do down a man of such distinction? Here they all were approaching the end of a century when respect for scientific research and its acceptance into the general body of human knowledge had become guiding principles of Western civilisation. Yet in Scotland, so long a citadel of enlightened thinking, a vicious act of persecution was about to be carried out.[1]

For himself, Robertson Smith was already resigned to that. One way and another, his case had now been dragging on for four years. In 1880 it seemed to reach a conclusion favourable to him when he was acquitted on a charge of questioning the divine authority of the Book of Deuteronomy. He held that it had never been dictated by God to Moses but rather been compiled by various authors several centuries after the Jews' exodus from Egypt: its value lay in 'religious matters', not in the details of history. But Robertson Smith's enemies remained undeterred by losing that particular point. They were still out to get him, and they found a pretext when the *Encyclopaedia Britannica* afterwards published his article on 'Hebrew Language and Literature'. It started, as his previous writings had done, from the point of view of the 'higher criticism'. This rested on the idea that scholars should approach biblical texts as they approached any other kind of texts. When they did this with the Hebrew corpus, they at once found that the different books of the Bible, sometimes even competing voices within particular books, espoused various points of view. So these books had been edited, even doctored, and showed inconsistencies, if not errors, making them little different in this sense from many ancient writings. In his scholarly activity Robertson Smith therefore took it for granted, in principle and in practice, that Scripture was not inerrant in the traditional acceptation of the term. Divine revelation still lay within it, but might fail to emerge from a literal reading. Rather it would have to be teased out by rigorous scholarship.[2]

Alas for Robertson Smith, the inerrancy of Scripture remained unquestionable to many members of the Free Church. The Revd George Macaulay, a Highlander but minister in Edinburgh, led the pack. He was 'a typical Celt who combined great earnestness of conviction with very considerable powers of expression, and a deep sense of having a vocation'. He kept demanding of the General Assembly: 'Have we a Bible?'[3] – the implication being that if they let Robertson Smith get away with what he was saying there would soon be no scriptural authority left. The chink in the professor's armour was that the previous settlement of his case included a pledge from him always to take account of his Church's sensitivities before further publication – and in his article on Hebrew literature he had not done so. In fact, this article was now quite an old one because it had been held up in the press. Robertson Smith might have got it included in the earlier vindication of his writings, but neglected to. In any event, his enemies saw in all this bad faith and good reason for going at him all over again, now with a better chance of victory. He knew as much, but knew also that there were far greater matters at stake. He made this clear in his final address to the General Assembly:

In 1843 we left the state; we did not secede from the Church; we carried her with us. And there will be no secession from the Church now. There will be an adhesion to the principles of the Church, and there will be an open, frank declaration of that adhesion against any majority and any power. And, Moderator, my removal from the place which I now hold in this Church, painful as it is to me, and grieving as it is to me in my personal life, is a mere incident in the case before the Church itself. The case is only now beginning.

He was right that the General Assembly could not be about to pronounce the last word on the relation between science and theology. Meanwhile, however, a lesser but immediate crisis had to be faced:

> What all sound Free Churchmen will do is this. We will hold by the principles of the Church, by the freedom which Christ has given us and the constitution has secured for us. And we will endeavour, without dispeace or evil feeling, in every constitutional way, some as office-bearers, some as adherents of the Church, to make it plain, as we have done once and again before, that the people of the Free Church can pull it through any trouble which its leaders have got us into.[4]

To cheers from his supporters, Robertson Smith then walked out of the General Assembly and did not return. At the end of the debate it voted by 394 to 231 to depose him from his chair.

It was a long time since any Scottish Church had acted like this. Before the Union of 1707 religious dissent was persecuted in Scotland, and with rigour, but the ecclesiastical part of the treaty rested on an unspoken condition that such behaviour must stop. Here lay the reason for having two established churches in the new United Kingdom: at least in one European realm, slaughter in the name of God would now come to an end. Perhaps the Scots slightly regretted this, anyway more than the English did, and in the following decades the odd case still cropped up of academics being condemned for deficient doctrine by the universities that the Church of Scotland continued to control. But the Enlightenment substituted politeness for bigotry, and the professors' precise private convictions at length ceased to be much of an issue. Later the Disruption did reawaken sectarian strife, though the effect was to prompt the British state to step in and, in particular, to abolish religious tests for academic chairs.

Yet Scotland had always been a nation that overcame its divisions only with difficulty. During the era of Enlightenment it might have ceased for a period to be like this, at least in an intellectual sense. Edinburgh remained a capital of culture, where the cosy intimacy of everyday life encouraged thinkers from all backgrounds to mix and to enrich one another's knowledge and experience. The philosopher David Hume, the economist Adam Smith, the sociologist Adam Ferguson, the geologist James Hutton and the chemist Joseph Black, along with any number of legal and literary luminaries, felt perfectly at ease pursuing such agreeable activity at the city's clubs, taverns and dining tables. Their relations were close also with Glasgow, where both Black and Smith had taught, and where a continuous tradition in moral philosophy from Francis Hutcheson to John Millar ran right through the eighteenth century.[5] Thomas Reid formed part of it, as the successor to Smith in the university's chair of moral philosophy, but he came from Aberdeen and was the leading figure in that city's enlightened circles too.[6] All these men remained in close and (given one or two exceptions) friendly contact with one another. The cordiality was owed in large part to a common intellectual background – at the most basic level in the emphasis placed by Scottish education on moral philosophy, the sole compulsory subject for students of arts at the universities. Under its auspices they were trained from their youth up to react to and refine one another's ideas. In the end, despite the variety and difference among them, this intellectual cohesion made the Scottish Enlightenment an intelligible phenomenon, in its own time and in ours. To that extent, there was a unified national culture too.

During the nineteenth century the cohesion and unity weakened. It was, happily, seldom the case that they descended into acrimony and spite, as now in the example of William Robertson Smith. It was rather that the advance of the enlightened intellectual disciplines led each of them along paths gradually divergent, till the lawyer could no longer pronounce on philosophy, nor the minister have anything useful to say about chemistry. Scotland scarcely needed to reproach itself with this specialisation when the same phenomenon pervaded the entire Western world. It was just an aspect of complex modern civilisation that no one man, or even circle of men, might any longer encompass the full extent of human knowledge.[7]

Even so it represented a huge loss to Scotland, and one with unique consequences because of the nation's educational commitment to generalism and its consequent ability to see things in a comparative light. Nurtured by an alliance of Church and universities, the Scottish Enlightenment was different from others in Europe. In Paris and Berlin the intellectuals prided themselves on being sceptical in religion and progressive (if despotic) in politics. The Scots espoused polite religion yet still orthodox religion, with a number of the leading enlightened figures being themselves clergymen. And in politics they remained on the whole conservative – the French Revolution, itself a product of the Enlightenment, horrified most of them. In a small nation with no power over its own fate, public aims had to be modestly confined to the general virtue and happiness expected from a society intent on rational progress. The Scots were therefore reasonable without falling for elaborate constructions of rationality, unlike the Jacobins in France or the idealists in Prussia. The Scots put humane values first and took a rounded view of the past and the present.

In particular, their attitude produced what a later thinker, George Davie, called 'the accepted Scottish approach to the sciences'.[8] He meant by this that in Scotland pure science came adorned and extended by two other cultural values. It always possessed an experimental and technological basis, this strong enough to continue right through the nineteenth century. From, say, James Watt to William Thomson, Lord Kelvin, the connections were preserved rather than lost or dropped amid a growing division between pure and applied science. At the same time Scottish science had its own place in the nation's practice of a sort of humanistic democracy. The older Scottish values are hard to trace now that the tradition has all but vanished, but some idea of it was given by Herbert Grierson, a graduate of the University of Aberdeen who later went on to be a professor at Edinburgh, and the editor of Sir Walter Scott's letters. He described the classes of his youth, when Scottish higher education was still avowedly generalist in the old sense:

> The class was one which included, along with passmen of varying degrees of proficiency, the elite of the year of every kind of ability – classical, mathematical, philosophical and scientific . . . The effect for the student was an enormous volume of eager and generous emulation. The mathematical student contended for a good place in the Latin and Greek class; the classical student for a good place in mathematics and physics, both for distinction in philosophy and literature. Such a system was, one may suppose, simply an extension of the school, and so it was, but under new conditions of ever increasing freedom, self-determination and responsibility.[9]

It might have been a bit unfair of Davie to argue it was above all the encroachment of English scientific models, of a more narrowly inductive sort, that killed off this aspect of the Scottish intellect and thereby contributed to the weakening of the national culture. At any rate, by the end of the nineteenth century the battle to maintain the educational commitment to generalism was more or less lost.

One reason was that pure science had meanwhile not merely pushed out its boundaries but also ascended into a mathematical abstraction too advanced for laymen to follow. Kelvin pursued his first important work on the two laws of thermodynamics that he expounded in lectures to the Royal Society of Edinburgh in 1851–54. Yet he believed 'the life and soul of science is its practical application', and he had to his credit a range of inventions from the electric light to the submarine cable. In his later years he earned a fortune from his numerous patents.[10] Clerk Maxwell's theoretical contribution was of even greater importance, in his formulation of the equations governing electromagnetism that he published in 1873. He closed this work, *A Treatise on Electricity and Magnetism*, by saying he could 'scarcely avoid the inference that light consists in the transverse undulations of the same medium which is the cause of electric and magnetic phenomena'.[11] He suggested electromagnetic waves might be generated in a laboratory: eight years after his death in 1879 this proved indeed to be possible, so that the development of radio therefore originated with him. And all this paved the way for Albert Einstein's theory of relativity, establishing the equivalence of mass and energy. Einstein himself described Maxwell's research as 'the most profound and the most fruitful that physics had experienced since the time of Newton'.[12] It is admittedly harder to point to any direct influence of Maxwell's as great as Kelvin's on the ordinary lives of us lesser beings in the twenty-first century. But it may be worth mentioning that Maxwell developed colour photography, the first example being an image of a tartan ribbon that he exhibited in 1861. He also produced a theory of Saturn's rings, establishing by pure mathematical speculation that they consisted of dust rather than of solid matter; he was proved right when, in our own time, the first Voyager space probe reached the planet.[13]

Even leaving these two giants aside, Scottish scientific achievement continued into the twentieth century. After the Nobel prizes were instituted in 1901, Scotland did well at winning them and carried off four during the years up to the First World War, with a further two in the years after it for discoveries made before (compared to two in the entire second half of the twentieth century). Scots figured in the global scientific elite but their work here belonged to humanity, not just to Scotland.

By contrast, the Scottish philosophy that had underlain Scottish science preserved a more distinct character. It was one of a number of national schools of philosophy in Europe, some of which have kept going down to the present day. No Scottish school of philosophy now exists, even though it long appeared to be strong and thriving. David Hume, the greatest Scottish philosopher, had not really belonged to it, however. On the contrary, it came together out of opponents of his, shocked at the implications of his thought for Christianity in particular. They retorted with the philosophy of Common Sense.[14]

The label of Common Sense arose from the fact that its pioneers, Thomas Reid, Dugald Stewart and Sir William Hamilton, wanted to philosophise out of the ordinary thoughts of human beings – which after all even the greatest philosopher of paradox and scepticism had to make use of when not engaged in abstract speculation. In the process Stewart, Reid and Hamilton arrived at basic positions opposed to Hume's: that all human beings are intuitively sure they exist, that all see and feel objects external to themselves, and that they may then apprehend some first principles on which morality and religious beliefs can be founded. As Reid said, 'If there are certain principles, as I think there are, which the constitution of our nature leads us to believe, and which we are under a necessity to take for granted in the common concerns of life, without being able to give a reason for them – these are what we call the principles of common sense; and what is manifestly contrary to them, is what we call absurd.'[15] Given the Christian faith of these philosophers, it was convenient for them to be able to define scepticism as absurd, or so far contrary to ordinary experience that it had to be rejected. Alas, later generations did not agree, and for that reason among others ceased to find the philosophy of Common Sense of much further interest. Still, for a long stretch of the nineteenth century it dominated Scottish thought, as well as winning adherents in Europe and America. In France, Victor Cousin, who studied in Edinburgh, took back to Paris both a Scottish accent and an admiration for Scottish education that he applied to public policy in his own country: philosophy remains to this day a compulsory subject for the *baccalauréat*. In the United States, James McCosh, a minister of the Free Church, pursued an academic career and in 1868 became president of Princeton University, a Presbyterian foundation, whence he helped to set off the philosophical development of his new country.

At home in Scotland, intellectual hopes came to rest by the middle of the century on James Ferrier, professor of moral philosophy at St Andrews, who seemed ready to renew the Scottish tradition and to carry its work forward, initially by coming to terms with the German idealists. Born to a leading legal and literary family of Edinburgh, he appeared the obvious successor to the chair of moral philosophy at the capital's university when it fell vacant in 1850. Yet the town council, the patron of the chair, rejected Ferrier in favour of a nonentity backed by the Free Church, to which many of the councillors belonged. After this catastrophic break in its apostolic succession, Scottish philosophy lay helpless before the renegade onslaught of John Stuart Mill, son of the émigré James Mill who had gone to London and teamed up with the utilitarians round Jeremy Bentham. In 1863 the younger Mill published an *Examination of Hamilton*, tearing its subject, Sir William Hamilton, to pieces; his reputation was destroyed forever. In many ways this marked the end of any influence of Scottish philosophy outside Scotland.[16]

Scottish philosophy yet survived on its own turf. Probably the most original development came with the work of Alexander Bain at the University of Aberdeen who pioneered academic psychology in the light of Hume's account of the association of ideas. Otherwise, with German idealism now the centre of philosophical gravity in Europe, it was impossible for Scots to ignore it – reversing the situation of a century before when Immanuel Kant had been wakened from his 'dogmatic slumbers' by his reading of Hume. It was true that Scottish idealists, led by the brothers John and Edward Caird at the University of Glasgow, looked back to the sources of their own nation's philosophy even as they sought a place in this new international constellation. They and others found much Scottish material to rework in line with the fresh insights elsewhere. Ferrier wrote *Scottish Philosophy, the old and the new* (1856). James McCosh's book, *The Scottish Philosophy* (1875), was still concerned with Common Sense, including a chapter on Hume not as a member of that school but as the person it most sought to counter. Another contribution came from Andrew Seth in his *Scottish Philosophy, a comparison of the Scottish and German answers to Hume* (1885). Still, perhaps all this only went to show how Scottish philosophy was turning in on itself. At the same time there followed a change in the role of philosophy in the universities, from the preparation of citizens for public life to a narrower focus on a specifically philosophical following. On this criterion, by the end of the nineteenth century Scottish philosophy in the old sense was pretty much played out. Claims have been advanced on behalf of a string of further thinkers who till after the Second World War continued to hold chairs in the universities, where the native tradition was then finally swept aside by the linguistic philosophy of Oxbridge and to all intents and purposes became extinct. That could scarcely have happened if Scottish philosophy had shown greater vitality.[17]

Scotland also housed philosophers in the older and more generous sense of thinkers who by their originality and authority enriched wider society in a general way. Just as Scottish philosophy had picked on David Hume for an enemy in the eighteenth century, so it found in the nineteenth century a foe of its own in Thomas Carlyle. Carlyle was born in 1795 to poor, toiling peasants in Dumfriesshire, religious dissenters believing most of humanity doomed to hellfire. He left home aged fourteen and walked the 100 miles to Edinburgh to study with the aim of becoming a minister in their sect. They fretted that urban life might break his religious devotion. His mother wrote, 'Have you got through the Bible yet? If you have, read it again.' When he replied that he was delving into books, 'Italian, German and others,' of which she had never heard, he only upset her: 'I pray for a blessing on your learning . . . Do make religion your great study, Tom.' She sensed the doubts that at length caused him to abandon any idea of salvation coming through a particular Church.[18]

Yet Carlyle would always revere Calvinist Scotland: 'A country where the entire people is, or even once has been, laid hold of, filled to the heart with an infinite religious idea, "has made a step from which it cannot retrograde".' Thought, conscience, the sense that man is denizen of a Universe, creator of an Eternity, has penetrated to the simplest heart.' Scots had come to worship God through the intellect and not, like lesser breeds, through the senses or feelings: 'Thought, in such a country, may change its form, but cannot go out; the country has attained *majority*; thought, and a certain spiritual manhood, ready for all the work that man can do, endures there.' No wonder Carlyle even as a student mutinied against the form that thought took in the infidel aspect of the Enlightenment. In the classes at the university 'the young vacant mind was furnished with much talk about the Progress of the Species, Dark Ages, Prejudice and the like'. But this learning Carlyle found too self-satisfied in its liberal consensus and facile teleology. It could not nourish his spirit. On the contrary, it made the Enlightenment, the late Scottish Enlightenment at least, insufferable to him for its shallowness and complacency.[19]

In 1828 Carlyle returned in some disillusion to his roots at Craigenputtoch in Dumfriesshire, as the meagre income from his literary efforts made life in

Edinburgh too difficult. His rustic fastness turned out no better. In 1834 he took a more drastic step. He then became the first man of genius to decide that Scotland was too small, and that as a bright spirit of the next age only the larger life of London would do for him. Scots of any social or intellectual standing over the previous couple of centuries had all been to London, just as they had been to Paris or Rome, yet with the intention of coming back. Carlyle himself spent short spells in the English metropolis. But now he set a new trend: excepting brief visits home to Scotland, he was gone for good. Just before he left he descended for the last time on old friends in Edinburgh. He noted, 'The whole place impresses me as something village-like; after the roaring Life-floods of London, it looks all little, secluded, almost quiescent. But again it is very *clean*, and orderly in comparison; on the whole a desirable place. One thing village-like is the number of known faces I have met on the streets; all old friends, grown a little greyer in the whiskers.'[20] This gets rather patronising; in fact, London would never solve Carlyle's problems either. Yet he opened up and showed a Scottish way into exile for the sake of cultural fulfilment, a way that figures as diverse as William Robertson Smith, Robert Louis Stevenson and Charles Rennie Mackintosh were to follow.

Carlyle was probably right to think that only in the capital city of the United Kingdom and of a growing Empire could he extend himself on the more general level of thinking to which he had now moved. Still, he was nearing 40 years of age and, in order to make it in London, he had to make it quickly. Rather extraordinary was the fact he should have done so with his transcendental fable of *Sartor Resartus*, published in instalments in a review in 1833–34. Somehow, though, this bizarre tale of a misanthropic professor-narrator who discovers a need for revolution of the spirit struck a chord with the public in an age romantic and revolutionary, individualistic and enthusiastic.[21] Carlyle, despite his never less than challenging content and style, continued to exploit this market and serve as its guru.

While a witness of the industrial revolution, Carlyle cultivated a view of the world that was non-materialist, even spiritual in his own agnostic way. From today's perspective it is intriguing to note his esteem for the prophet Mahomet (his spelling), to whom he gave a special place in a book *On Heroes and Hero-Worship, and the heroic in history* (1841). Mahomet appears here under the heading of 'hero as prophet' and is praised for his role as an agent of reform in the saga of 'how one man single-handedly, could weld warring tribes and wandering Bedouins into a most powerful and civilized nation in less than two decades'. Above all, however, 'I like this Mahomet for his total freedom from cant ... no *dilettantism* in this Mahomet; it is a business of reprobation and salvation with him, of time an eternity'. He concludes that: 'the Great Man was always as lightning out of Heaven; the rest of men waited for him like fuel, and then they too would flame.'[22]

It is at the same time piquant to find Robert Burns defined as a hero too: surely no figure could ever been less Islamic. But, for Carlyle, 'the largest soul of all the British lands came among us in the shape of a hard-handed Scottish peasant ... This Burns appeared under every disadvantage, uninstructed, poor, born only to hard manual toil; and writing, when it came to that, in a rustic special dialect, known only to a small province of the country he lived in.' It seems superfluous to point out that Carlyle was thinking and writing not in any conventional terms, but according to his own scale of values: the hero represents a man who achieves fullness of being in whatever context he might find himself, regardless of contradictions. In fact, all heroes are flawed. Their heroism lies in their creative energy when confronted by difficulty, not in any moral perfection.[23]

Whether Carlyle regarded himself as a hero is unclear; to judge from his increasing frustration and grumpiness, even after he successfully established himself as a public intellectual, it may well be that in his heart of hearts he feared he might be a failure. Certainly there was a good deal of failure in the central relationship of his life, that with his wife Jane Welsh Carlyle. By the time he came, after her death, to write his *Reminiscences* (1881), it was clear he had loved her. The trouble lay in his inability to show this love during their lives together. Sex was the problem. After a courtship of five years they had got married in 1826, but puritanical inhibitions and romantic idealisations crept into bed along with the two innocents. Such evidence as there is suggests that, if able to express affection with whispers and embraces, neither of them got any physical satisfaction from the other, despite strenuous efforts during their first half-dozen years together. After barren decades, Jane's death in 1866 came without warning, while Thomas was away in Edinburgh to be installed as rector of the university, and it plunged him into despair.[24]

Carlyle's authorised biographer, J.A. Froude, believed the marriage had never been consummated. He got into a fearful row with the surviving kin over his publication of the couple's literary remains, included in the *Letters and Memorials of Jane Welsh Carlyle* (1883) and in the *Life of Carlyle* (1884). Froude had resolved to follow what he understood as his subject's own biographical principle of describing not only achievements and distinctions but also failures and faults. Many readers focused on the unhappy marriage then depicted, which soon came to figure in contemporary debates on sexual politics. This outraged those inclined to take issue with Froude such as the Scottish novelist and protagonist of the Free Church, Margaret Oliphant. Her review of the biography objected that this genre ought to be the 'art of moral portrait painting', whereas here there had been only the 'betrayal and exposure of the secret of a woman's weakness'.[25] As we shall see below, Victorian Scots thought and wrote more about sex than they get credit for nowadays.

One Scottish connection Carlyle had kept up so long as he could was with the Revd Thomas Chalmers, leader of the Disruption in 1843. In 1847 he wrote to Chalmers, by then within three months of his death, that we (he and Jane) 'are still Scotch enough to be very proud of you; still human enough to feel a true sympathy with you on all manner of things'. Carlyle went on to muse about the intellectual legacy of his homeland:

> It was, many years ago, my slow but at length clear practical conclusion, which I also rejoice to find intimated in this Paper [from Chalmers], that (for me, at least) the German transcendental Metaphysics had as it were swallowed and abolished the Scotch or French Sceptical; that the whole baleful *Universe of Cobwebs*, in which with blinded eyes, passionately searching thro' long years, I had nearly lost my life, was now *annihilated*; so that, by Heaven's unspeakable mercy, I could now look abroad with my own eyes over the *real Universe* once more, and *see!*

He had meanwhile come to the conclusion that all metaphysics and mental philosophy was a disease

> from which the healthy intellect of man seeks only, and must seek, to *escape*; – as accordingly we find, in all ancient healthy ages, men *have* used their intellect not for looking into *itself* (which I consider to be naturally *impossible*, and a mere morbid spasm), but to look out, as an *eye* should, over the Universe which is not we, and *there* to recognise innumerable things, and to believe, and do, – and *adore* withal, as in that case is a very universal and infallible result, among other blessed ones![26]

This was doubtless music to the ears of Chalmers, now having to cope with the unexpected consequences of a Disruption that had disrupted far more than the Church of Scotland. In fact, it was destroying the whole harmony and balance among Scotland's national institutions that underpinned the Enlightenment and many other national achievements. Beforehand, Chalmers's own life had exemplified this harmony and balance. He made of himself not only a philosophising minister but also an urban reformer, professor of theology, political economist, proficient mathematician and not least a scientific authority, certainly in his own eyes. He set out to prove as much with a book, *On the Power, Wisdom and Goodness of God, as manifested in the adaptation of external nature to the moral and intellectual constitution of man* (1833). Three years later he supplemented this with a work called simply *Natural Theology.*[27]

Natural theology had become an avowedly scientific branch of sacred learning, prompted by the decline all over Europe of the older sort of religious devotion that scarcely asked after rational justifications of the Christian faith. Now there were many doubters who, if they could not accept the letter of Holy Writ, might yet be pointed towards the confirmation of the existence of God to be found in his wonderful works, in other words, in nature. Chalmers did not believe the universe to be fully explicable by reason, so that some degree of revelation would always be necessary to understand it. But divine design permeated its structure, and science could make itself useful in demonstrating this. Chalmers wanted also to reassure fellow evangelicals that science need not be their enemy, as many feared, but on the contrary could strengthen the Christian view of the world. It might at least eliminate those misunderstandings of the Creation that gave reason for unbelief. For example, the idea, familiar today, of a vast universe was then new. Chalmers argued that the rational response to this phenomenon was that only God could have conceived of anything on this scale or have made of it a reality.[28]

When not thinking great thoughts, Chalmers spent much time on the politics of the Kirk and, in good Scottish fashion, building up a network of patronage. One beneficiary was Hugh Miller, destined to become the most famous of the amateur but eminent scientists of the Victorian era, exemplars of Scotland's democratic intellect. He had started out in life as a stonemason at the little burgh of Cromarty in Easter Ross, and it was his urge to write about what he unearthed in Highland quarries that launched him on his literary career. In 1840 Chalmers himself summoned Miller to Edinburgh to set up a newspaper, *The Witness,* intended to give evangelical opinions a hearing they otherwise lacked in the Scottish press. He kicked off his tenure of the editor's chair with a fascinating seven-part series of weekly articles entitled 'The Old Red Sandstone', telling readers about his earlier life breaking stones and what he had discovered in the course of it. This was a shrewd move: it hit on a rich vein of public interest and gave the paper a viable circulation from the start. The next year Miller republished the articles as a book that went through 26 editions and made his name far beyond Scotland. During his years of hewing rock he had painstakingly amassed a huge and tantalising collection of fossils. Poring over them, he sought to fit them into a coherent pattern. He saw how time, immense stretches of time, had been necessary for all the observable revolutions in nature to take place. This carried him into uncharted intellectual territory, at the time quite lacking in maps and names.[29]

But it was territory where Scots loved to venture. Geology was another science they had given the world. One of the luminaries of enlightened Edinburgh, James Hutton, merited his accolade of 'father of geology'. His life's work was to lay down the intellectual framework of the discipline, something he accomplished largely by looking at the rocks of his own geologically complex country. He did not publish much himself, but his labours were immortalised by his friend and pupil John Playfair, professor of natural philosophy at the University of Edinburgh, who brought out his own *Illustrations of the Huttonian Theory of the Earth* in 1802, five years after Hutton's death. According to the Huttonian theory, the Earth had existed for unknown aeons and over this time had been shaped by natural forces – in other words, not by a single act of Creation or by a catastrophe such as the Flood. This account the Scots defended against much abuse, not only from orthodox Christians but also from the scientific establishment in England. Miller recalled how 'the prejudices of the English mind' reacted 'with illiberal violence against the Huttonian doctrines. Infidelity and atheism were charged against their supporters, and had there been a Protestant Inquisition in England at that period of general political excitement, the geologists of the North would have been immured in its deepest dungeons.'[30]

Geological knowledge advanced all the same, and in 1830 Charles Lyell gave a definitive summation in the three volumes of his *Principles of Geology, an attempt to explain the former changes of the Earth's surface by reference to causes now in operation* – in its subtitle laying its Scottish principles right on the line. Lyell had grown up near Kirriemuir in Angus, and found his interest in the subject first awakened by the abrupt contrast between the rich farmlands of that county and the rugged Grampian Mountains rising immediately behind: the reason for the contrast was the Highland Fault running along in between. In later life Lyell became a close friend of Charles Darwin, who himself had studied at the University of Edinburgh in the 1820s. And Darwin did Lyell a favour when he set sail for five years round the world on the *Beagle* – the voyage that brought home to him the principle of natural selection and the theory of evolution. Lyell asked his colleague to collect geological as well as biological specimens, and Darwin recorded how the formations of rock he came to see 'through Lyell's eyes' made him, too, aware of the enormous expanses of time that must have been necessary for the formation of the Earth. Once he accepted this framework it became easier to conceive of the theory of evolution. On his return he set it forth in *The Origin of Species* (1859); Lyell might be given a little of the credit too.[31]

The intellectual atmosphere of Scotland, unlike that of certain other countries, was already receptive to a theory of evolution. An important part of the Scottish Enlightenment's intellectual apparatus had been the procedure of 'conjectural history'. It posited that humanity passed through successive stages of development, the features of which could be reconstructed, where direct evidence was wanting, from their survivals in later eras. The stadial structure in this argument could be readily transferred from society to nature. It was to be found, for example, in the writings of Robert Chambers, author and publisher (half of the house of W. & R. Chambers). He had himself produced a best-seller in his *Vestiges of the Natural History of Creation* (1844), which at the time he still thought better to bring out anonymously. This was because it removed God from history, except perhaps in the initial Creation, and assumed the universe had since run on under its own laws. Chambers portrayed the whole as an epic of progress – clouds of gas condensing into stars and planets, primeval soup giving rise to life, finally man ascending from the apes. This might seem to presage *The Origin of Species*, though it offered nothing as scientific as the principle of natural selection or the theory of evolution. During his travels Darwin had, for example, tarried on the Galapagos Islands to test his hypotheses by observations nobody else could have made; Chambers just cobbled together others' ideas to show to his own satisfaction how nature followed some force impelling it ever onwards and upwards. It was all book-learning, but he did have the gift of simple exposition. He passed on to his readers a range of knowledge that would otherwise have remained confined in learned tomes. This was what made him a risk to religious orthodoxy: philosophers of the Enlightenment might have agreed with him in substance, but their books had not been read by the masses.[32]

As fresh theories emerged, strict Presbyterians such as Chalmers refused to shift from the Mosaic account of the Creation. Yet it was a different matter for the no less devout Miller. The old red sandstone had impressed him, too, with the immeasurable age of the Earth. He also remained convinced, however, that there was a divine plan in nature. He set out his own blend of the traditional and the modern teachings in a polemical tract, *Footsteps of the Creator* (1849). He stressed how the cool empirical investigations of geologists established facts that could not just be written off by theologians. Yet Christians had no need to abandon their faith: the 'old, and as it has been proven, erroneous reading of the Mosaic account' was rightly giving way to the results of scientific research. These results equally revealed in nature an infinite yet interconnected complexity that redounded just as much to the glory of God. In his last book, *The Testimony of the Rocks* (1856), Miller returned to the task of harmonising the records of Genesis and of geology. He compared himself to the Christian geographers who had known the Church erred in maintaining the Earth was flat, or to the Christian astronomers who had known it erred in maintaining the Sun went round the Earth. His retort to theologians of the present day was to say they must be wrong again, for God's word did not lie and no ecclesiastical authority could outweigh scientific proof. Still, it may be doubted whether Miller truly believed he had reconciled geology and theology. In 1856, after a period of increasingly disturbed behaviour, he killed himself.[33]

Those many Scots who could no longer be bothered with literal readings of the Bible might readily accept the concept of evolution. In fact, it renewed the sources of Scottish intellectual enquiry. Right into the twentieth century, for example, it proved an inspiration to Patrick Geddes, another self-taught polymath. Geddes was professor of botany at University College, Dundee, from 1883 to 1920, though this fact gave little clue to the range of his interests. In an age of increasing specialisation, he spent much of his life in revolt against academic stuffiness. He would not sit exams on the grounds they stifled rather than encouraged real learning, yet on his own account he blithely undertook scientific research and publication. They were of a standard sufficient to win him his chair, if in a new institution carrying no conventional baggage but keen on fostering original work. Here Geddes became, among much else, a pioneer of modern sociology, especially in the study of urban form and development. He sought to represent it as a kind of evolution. He traced how cities grew out of their physical surroundings, producing cultures

that reflected but then also turned back on and transformed these environ-
ments. With the enhanced resources of industrial society and the choices it
gave, there really should be some planning of such processes. The task for the
planner was to foster fruitful development and avoid its opposite.[34]

Though Geddes held a chair in Dundee he preferred to stay in Edinburgh,
and here he set himself to practical endeavours in a patriotic spirit. Scorning
those Scots who compromised in hope of 'political honours from the other
side of the Tweed',[35] he wanted to restore to the capital some features that
had once contributed to its now slightly faded glory. In 1886 he bought a
tenement at James Court, long ago a select address but by this time, like the
rest of the Royal Mile, a slum. Here he embarked on a scheme of comprehensive improvement for this part of the Old Town and its intractable social
problems. One possible course of action would have been to knock down
the whole lot, but Geddes deplored any policy of sweeping clearance: it was
'one of the most disastrous and pernicious blunders in the chequered history
of sanitation', producing only 'dreary conventionality' rather than long-term
solutions. 'Unsparing to the old homes and to the neighbourhood life of the
area' and 'leaving fewer housing sites and these mostly narrower than before',
all it did was expel a population that would 'again, as usual, be driven to
create worse congestion in other quarters'.[36] Instead the existing urban fabric
should be preserved and transformed so as to provide once again desirable
residences for the bourgeoisie without driving out the proletariat. That would
restore the historic social mix in the heart of the capital. Today the upper end
of the High Street, especially Ramsay Gardens, is in its appearance largely
owed to Geddes, though not many of the working class still live roundabout.
Here Geddes also restored the Outlook Tower, once the home of the painter
Allan Ramsay, and installed a *camera obscura* to let visitors take in at a glance the
surrounding connections of landscape, architecture and people. In his later
life and work Geddes was to carry his regard for these organic connections to
many parts of the Empire, and his influence on concepts of urbanity persists
to this day.

So much for what might be called the sunnier side of evolution as it was
adopted into Scottish thinking. This being Scotland, a darker side had to be
there too. It was to be found, for example, in the writings of John McLennan,
an Invernesian of vigorous and combative intellect who pursued a successful
career at the Scots bar. He became at length parliamentary draftsman for

Scotland, that is to say, the official charged with writing the texts of Scottish Bills. A paid-up member of the northern kingdom's Liberal elite, therefore, he was also one of the last in the line of fine minds, stretching back two centuries, which had made the Faculty of Advocates an intellectual institution, rather than the closed professional cartel it was now turning into. He seems to have been a Gaelic speaker, and expertly handled the texts of Old Irish laws. It is in his ideas of law that we find McLennan's debt to the Enlightenment; he produced the big article on the subject in the latest edition of the *Encyclopaedia Britannica*. There he contended that the law of a civilised society might restrict the independence of individuals but it gave them liberty in the sense of security and justice: a savage could in a certain sense be free, but not as free as a law-abiding citizen of a modern society. This argument he owed to Adam Ferguson a century before.[37]

The law was a professional interest, but McLennan also had an amateur interest in prehistoric religion. It was amateur in the sense of Miller's interest in geology, for on this pet subject McLennan also went into print, with articles in the reviews that he then amplified in two books, *Primitive Marriage* (1875) and *Studies in Ancient History* (1876). He sought to trace the remote origins of social institutions for which documentary evidence was scarce or lacking. He had then to make use of a different kind of testimony, one quite as valid in his view. He looked instead for superstitions, customs or taboos that might represent survivals of early human society, with an original meaning forgotten but possibly recoverable by comparative method: here again was the enlightened procedure of conjectural history. He wrote: 'In the sciences of law and society, old means not old in chronology, but in the structure: that is most archaic which lies nearest to the beginning of human progress considered as a development, and that is most modern which is farthest removed from the beginning.'[38]

McLennan was especially intrigued by a practice in antiquity of marriage through collusive abduction – as in the Romans' Rape of the Sabine Women, an incident recounted by Livy and Plutarch that inspired many works of European art with its scope for depicting a crowd of semi-nude figures wrestling in passionate embraces. MacLennan found this was a common motif of legends all over the world, and wondered what had given rise to it. He concluded that primitive society must once have organised itself in hordes, recognising no kinship but indulging in promiscuous sex. They practised female infanticide too, so they needed to prey on each other for women. That laid down a custom of having sex with women outside the horde, of exogamy, which was in due course elevated into a religious principle. Over time, however, kinship did come to be recognised in its uterine form, that is, among children of the same mother regardless of the father, and a few Asiatic societies still preserved the practice. The whole showed how current conceptions of kinship had a matrilinear origin, evolution of which was connected with passage from primitive communism to the beginnings of private property, and so also to the origin of law.[39] McLennan was interested in a second social function of primitive religion, for which he coined the term totemism. From, among others, the Greek myths of gods turning themselves into bulls and swans, he concluded that the primitive hordes had worshipped animals round which they erected taboos.[40]

The interest in sex probably lost McLennan his bid in 1862 for the chair of public law at the University of Edinburgh, and perhaps did little for his advocate's private practice in the straitlaced capital. But it had two compensations. The first, a posthumous one, was the place he gained among the ancestors of modernist thought. More immediately his stock of spicy anecdotes assured him of an active social life, especially in the intellectual clubs that, then as now, formed a notable feature at the more raffish end of Edinburgh's social scene. In fact, he helped to found one such club, as reported by a certain member:

> I dined with Tait [professor of natural philosophy] yesterday, with Crum Brown [professor of chemistry] and McLennan, an advocate. There is a new talking club to be set up, and these two are to be members, as likewise Sir A. Grant [principal of the University of Edinburgh], Campbell Shairp [professor of humanity] and Tulloch [principal] of St Andrews, and a whole circle of literary and scientific men in or near Edinburgh, the object being to have one man at least well up in every subject. The selection is to be somewhat strict, so I was surprised when it was proposed last night to table my name.[41]

Well might he have been surprised, the twenty-year-old William Robertson Smith here writing home to his father in Aberdeenshire. It was indeed extraordinary for such a youngster to be invited into this exalted company. But though as yet a mere student at New College, Edinburgh, he had become the wonder of that institution for his amazing scholarly accomplishments. So now he met McLennan. The older man helped the younger one to get articles published in the reviews, not just in dry academic journals, receiving in return valuable information on ancient Semitic societies from an already acknowledged expert. The quirky lawyer and the avant-garde theologian became firm friends, indeed philosophical soulmates. Robertson Smith wrote to McLennan: 'I don't deny that traces of nature religion are to be found in the Old Testament; only the Old Testament religion did not, I hold, grow out of, but confronted and destroyed, these. That is a question for scientific inquiry which we may attack from our opposite points of view without cursing each other.'[42]

⚜

Robertson Smith's own researches would take him to German universities and to the Middle East on extensive tours. In writing up the results he also started from the enlightened Scottish assumption that history moved in stages. Not all of them made an appearance in the Bible, though survivals of them could be traced there – for example in the fact, evident from denunciations by the prophets, that there had been another type of Israelite cult apart from the worship of the true God. It was evidently a matter of superstition, magic and taboo stained by demonic, polluting and irrational elements, as in the revels Moses found going on round the Golden Calf when he brought the tablets of the law down from Mount Sinai. For Robertson Smith these were the lower forms of belief and morality only to be expected in lower stages of social and cultural development, as primitive peoples started to grasp the concept of deity. Among them the prophets were at first isolated and rejected figures, though proved right in the end. Not that the rituals and sacrifices then changed much: it was their new dedication to the true God that made the difference. Robertson Smith's first book, *The Prophets of Israel* (1882), traced this sanctification of savage rites as God revealed himself to man. Faltering steps in the progress towards higher forms of belief and morality at length culminated in the Christian revelation. Then the Old Testament gave way to the New Testament, and Christianity improved on Judaism, just as Presbyterianism would later improve on Roman Catholicism. Among Presbyterians themselves improvement could continue through returning to the Bible armed with advancing scholarly technique. Altogether, then, Christianity did not stand apart from history, and Christians could not, on the basis of Scripture, stand in judgment over history.[43]

From this point on Robertson Smith's development of an evolutionary, stadial theory became even more daring. If, as McLennan proposed, the horde had been the earliest stage of society, then the group (as opposed to the individual convert) was the basic religious unit. In antiquity, some common genetic origin might have linked the members of the group, but they felt more concerned to include within it their deities and the totemic animals from which they claimed to be descended. They performed the rites they thought necessary to sustain the order of things in their world, that is, to preserve the group and affirm their identity as its members. But what they really worshipped, Robertson Smith believed, was that order of things, their own society idealised and deified. They gave it religious sanction just because it seemed to their uninstructed minds natural and inevitable, therefore divinely ordained. In other words, the source of symbolic behaviour lay in the group. Beliefs had a social origin. This was the theory behind Smith's second important work, *Kinship and Marriage in Early Arabia* (1885).[44]

And totems played a vital part in all this. They had been present in Semitic religion from its early traces in the Old Testament down to the present day; after all, God's Chosen People were forbidden to eat pork. On the usual Victorian assumptions, totems figured only in the primitive cults of Africa and the Americas. But now it appeared they had been just as meaningful to the ancient peoples of the Middle East, the cradle of Western civilisation. Smith's greatest work, *The Religion of the Semites* (1889), analysed the many types of sacrifice mentioned in ancient records, biblical and non-biblical. In its highest form, at turning points of the year or in time of danger, members of the group killed their totemic animal, otherwise taboo to them, and devoured it as their brother-god.

Even in the religion of Jesus Christ, then, it would be possible to discern the survival of a primitive cult. Was it heresy to say so? Robertson Smith did not mean to subvert true religion – quite the reverse – but to show how it had revealed itself in the world, not apart from the world. The rites of true religion and false religion were in origin identical: the difference lay in the fact that the true rites led up to the culmination of history represented by the Messiah, while the false rites led down to error and delusion. Yet it is easy to see how others in the Free Church feared this might appear in a different light to those of weak or questioning faith or of none. Why should such people regard the culmination Smith found in Christ as symbolism separate from its prehistoric forms? Why should they not conclude that when Christians took communion they were working out a modern survival of totemic bloodletting? Why should they not see Christianity as just another product of error and delusion?[45]

A trial for heresy did not get rid of such disturbing questions. It caused Robertson Smith years of strain, obliged him to move out of Scotland and possibly hastened his early death, but it never prompted him to retract what he had written. The fanatical Calvinists who forced his prosecution if anything aroused distaste among Scots at large. In any event he persevered in his work. As well as becoming a fellow of Christ's College, Cambridge, he was appointed editor of the ninth edition of the *Encyclopaedia Britannica*, the 'scholars' encyclopaedia' – so called because it featured articles by a distinguished international range of authorities recruited by him. It was the first edition to incorporate the century's intellectual advances and set them before a broad public. So Robertson Smith's condemnation and exile neither limited his influence nor halted the evolution of his ideas.[46]

Another Scot at Cambridge was James Frazer, son of a Glaswegian pharmacist who would end up as professor of social anthropology. Robertson Smith never feared to make friends of infidels; he and Frazer in turn found they had much in common. The latter in his own studies regarded all religions, Christianity included, as stages in human progress from magic to rationality. He, too, was interested in cults, rites and myths. His tireless industry culminated in publication of the *The Golden Bough* (1890), a gigantic survey of them that to this day holds its place in scholarly esteem and in influence on the comparative study of religion. The work does rather sprawl, but one thing that comes clearly across is how, as between unreason and reason, man is dualistic: a Scottish thought, indeed. In a new century Frazer hoped for more progress from the one to the other than has, in fact, taken place, but he knew that, even while the human race progresses, it carries its past into its future. His famous example is the priest at Nemi, sacrificed every year in the sense of being killed by his successor, becoming by that fact a symbol of renewal: again the parallels with higher religions are unmistakable.[47] The symbolic cycle of life, death and rebirth that Frazer divined behind the myths of many peoples would captivate a generation of artists and poets, notably T.S. Eliot in *The Waste Land* (1922), as well as Ezra Pound, James Joyce, D.H. Lawrence and Joseph Conrad. The cultural influence has endured: Francis Ford Coppola's film, *Apocalypse Now* (1979), shows a copy of *The Golden Bough* in one of its final shots.

The contribution of Victorian Scots to the new human sciences of the modern age would leave many traces in many places. In Paris this influence stretched from the sociologist Émile Durkheim to the anthropologist Claude Lévi-Strauss, in Vienna from the psychologist Sigmund Freud to the philosopher Ludwig Wittgenstein. The creative exploits of the final phases of the Scottish Enlightenment therefore entered into the common fund of Western thinking.[48] But what did they do for Scotland?

In Scotland the followers of Robertson Smith were still being persecuted for heresy. For such a conservative, evangelical body, the Free Church produced a surprising number of progressive theologians, presumably just because it took the Bible so seriously. They proved to be also, however, tempting targets for its backwoodsmen. In 1889 Alexander Bruce, professor of apologetics and exegesis at the Church's college in Glasgow, published *The Kingdom of God*, which disputed the idea that Christ had regarded 'men, all or any of them, as predestined to damnation'. This naturally infuriated the Calvinist diehards. The whole matter went once more to the General Assembly. There, Bruce had been the chief supporter of Robertson Smith in 1881, but in his own case wiser counsels prevailed. The assembly held that the charge of heresy was based on a misunderstanding, though by his use of language Bruce had given some ground for the charges against him. With that mild rebuke, he was free to continue his distinguished scholarly career.[49]

The fanatics had this time failed to get their way, but they were far from finished yet. Robertson Smith, and Bruce after him, had got support from Marcus Dods, a minister in Glasgow who in 1889 was appointed professor of exegesis at New College, Edinburgh (of which he would one day become principal). But first he, too, needed to face a charge of heresy. Once the hardliners heard of his appointment they set about combing through his writings and found a sermon on *Inspiration* he had delivered and published in 1878. It said: 'No careful student of Scripture can well deny that there are inaccuracies in the Gospels and elsewhere – inaccuracies such as occur in ordinary writings through imperfect information or lapse of memory, sufficient entirely to explode the myth of infallibility.'[50] To Dods, as to Robertson Smith, the virtue of theology lay not in its immutability but in its capacity for development. And by now even their opponents were coming to accept that theologians might require a little latitude in their thinking. When Dods's trial for heresy came on at the General Assembly of 1890, it voted at once to drop the charge against him.

Yet the cry of heresy was heard right into the twentieth century. In 1902 the evangelicals turned on the Revd George Adam Smith, who had succeeded Robertson Smith in his chair at Aberdeen. The younger man like the older one went on exotic travels, and after roaming Palestine on a mule he produced a *Historical Geography of the Holy Land* (1884) showing the Bible still to be the best guide to it; so well had he come to know it that the Foreign Office appointed him an official adviser on its affairs during the First World War, when he was also Moderator of the General Assembly. Meanwhile he undertook an American tour in 1899, including a series of lectures at Yale

University that treated of such subjects as polytheism in ancient Israel, the relation of Genesis to Babylonian myth and the fanciful nature of the patriarchal narratives. When he got back to Scotland he found a charge of heresy waiting for him. But by this time the energy of the persecutors had flagged. When in 1902 the matter came to the General Assembly (now of the United Free Church), a large majority voted to take no action.[51]

A nation still trying heretics as the twentieth century dawned might expect its claims to modernity to be treated with some scepticism elsewhere. The appearance was, of course, wildly deceptive; as a matter of fact the Free Church had, through these rather painful acts of catharsis, put itself in the vanguard of liberal theology. It was in any case one of the most dynamic social and economic forces in Victorian Scotland. To that extent and in its own way, its energy and independence made it a good representative of the whole.

During the century from 1815 to 1914 Scotland made enormous material advances. They liberated wide sections of the nation from the shackles of history by smashing the outworn moulds of a traditional society. The new liberty was in principle for everybody without regard to origins, whether they were capitalists and entrepreneurs who now made fortunes, prosperous bourgeois who achieved security for themselves and their families, or hard-working artisans aspiring to a decent standard of living and greater opportunities for their children. Of course the practice could fall short of the principle. While here, as in all industrial countries, deep poverty persisted, this country was in national income per head almost certainly among the world's half-dozen leaders.[52] There can be no doubt about the economic and social achievements of Scotland in the nineteenth century.

In comparable countries, however, material advance created cultural confidence: this was certainly the case in big nations such as Germany or the United States, or indeed in small nations still in process of formation, such as Finland or the Czech lands. Scotland contrasted with this pattern. As it advanced into the twentieth century it sent out weak, uncertain, conflicting cultural signals – quite unlike the strong signals it had been sending out 100 years before. What had gone wrong with the culture during that time?

At the outset of the period Scotland had enjoyed a coherent culture, rapidly modernising but not yet a victim of the centrifugal forces of modernity. This was anyway a little country: the close connections among the intellectual elite made life cosy for them yet without any loss of integration with the rest of the people, for they stood at no great social distance either from the ruling class or from many ordinary hard-working, self-improving citizens. The Victorian age saw an end to this intimate, egalitarian sort of Scotland, for an immense number of reasons recounted in the successive chapters of this book. The nation, in becoming much more diverse, became much more divided too. It was then ill-equipped to resist influences that were provincialising it, as Scots seized the greater opportunities open to them in the United Kingdom and the Empire, and as all sorts of British authorities and social forces tightened their grip on Scotland. The culture, in the broadest sense, suffered the most from this. Not only did it become too weak to defend itself, but the Scots people also grew increasingly unsure if it was worth defending. Along with material success went, then, relative cultural failure: the stage was set for Scotland's twentieth century. The course of that century in turn saw the faltering of material success yet also a start to the reconstruction of the culture. It had been rich enough for enough of it, even now, to survive and offer some reward for the effort, so long as the people could recover a commitment to it: it seemed they could. That has helped Scotland to enter the twenty-first century in pursuit of a new destiny.

Epilogue:
'To perpetuate the tradition'

The history of Ceres, in the East Neuk of Fife, has been uneventful, but 24 June 1914, saw an occurrence of at least a little wider interest. At this time of year the village always held a celebration spread over two days, with a market on the first and a fair on the second. Then, among other diversions, the local lads would compete in athletic contests on the green – a charming spot surrounded by old houses with a burn running down the middle. The villagers carefully preserved these customs because they originated in a privilege granted to their ancestors six centuries before by King Robert Bruce after the Battle of Bannockburn. Even smaller though Ceres must have been then, it had yet sent 100 men to fight at his side against the English. By some strange chance every one of them returned unscathed, and this apparently miraculous outcome moved the generous hero-king to offer them a special reward. Hence the grant to their village of the fair, something that was otherwise essentially a burghal privilege and in normal circumstances the initial impetus to urban development.

But in 1914 Ceres remained much the same as it always had been. At least by then it housed its own brewery, so the people could celebrate any time they wanted. They were self-sufficient in other ways too. The village boasted ten dressmakers (one of whom also made straw bonnets), nine grocers, eight joiners, five cobblers, five tailors, a saddler, a wheelwright and a cooper. There had once been lime-kilns nearby and even some opencast mining, all now abandoned, though it was still possible for the villagers to ride out in a cart and hew coal for themselves at spots where the measures poked through the topsoil. Formerly a good many had earned a living as weavers, producing linen on handlooms. But that trade was almost dead and not much employment remained other than agricultural labour, with domestic drudgery for the wives. They might still entertain hopes of something better for their children. Ceres had boasted a resident schoolmaster since 1631, and in 1836 the heritors of the parish built a 'parochial academy' so handsome and solid that, much altered, it is still in use today. In that building, from the age of six to the age of fourteen, every child in Ceres could get an education. Here was an older Scotland little touched by the problems of the modern age.[1]

A literate population no doubt made it easier to keep the traditions of Ceres alive, and in 1914 somebody had the idea of a special event to mark out this particular 24 July. For the 600th anniversary of Bannockburn it was decided to erect a monument overlooking the green and dedicated to the men who had gone to fight for the freedom of their country. When it got unveiled on the big day, it turned out to be a most handsome monument too. It was nearly 20 feet high, a plain octagonal column of grey granite with a sculptured Gothic head consisting of a heraldic unicorn bearing a saltire shield, all set on a stepped base with the inscription: 'To commemorate the vindication of Scotland's independence on the field of Bannockburn 24th June 1314 – and to perpetuate the tradition of the part taken therein by the men of Ceres'.[2]

Was it only a local patriotism that stirred the watching villagers, or anything more? Scotland had now been integrating itself into the United Kingdom for two centuries. Many Scots were helping to run England in various capacities, while a fair number of Englishmen (such as the local MP, Herbert Asquith) had assimilated somewhat to life in Scotland. Yet the first decades of the twentieth century also saw a certain reaction against all this. A movement in favour of Home Rule won enough support to prompt the British government to introduce, that very year, a Bill giving Scotland back its own Parliament, with power to legislate for the modest range of functions already administered by the Scottish Office. Had this been achieved merely on an analogy with the much stronger demand for change in Ireland? Or were there still tenacious popular memories that could stir Scottish hearts with a desire to regain what the nation had lost in 1707? We cannot know: but perhaps the monument unveiled at Ceres on 24 June 1914 gives a clue.

Forty-one days later, the First World War broke out. One immediate political effect was the abandonment of Scottish Home Rule. There seemed now to be no doubt where the Scots' ultimate loyalties lay, not among the men of Ceres either. Though hailing from such a peaceful place, they were quite a warlike bunch. When a craze for military volunteering had swept Britain half a century before, prompted by a supposed threat of invasion from France, it found an eager response in Scotland, not least in Fife. The units of volunteers raised at that point kept going long afterwards. On the outbreak of the Second Boer War in 1899, 120 of the part-time soldiers from Ceres signed up for service in South Africa under a local laird, Sir John Gilmour, as colonel. Most were presumably farm-boys who would have loved their dashing blue serge uniforms and plumed helmets, at least till they found out what good targets these made for Boer sharpshooters. In the year they spent fighting, their casualties were heavy. But that seemed forgotten once they came home and donned their dress uniforms again for a final parade through the county town of Cupar.[3] A few years later, they joined with others in a territorial unit, the Fife and Forfarshire Yeomanry. When war returned in 1914, the men of Ceres stood ready as ever.

Now they were transformed a second time into the fourteenth battalion of the Black Watch. It was mustered at Blairgowrie in Perthshire on 12 August, then sent to various places in England for a period of training which, in the event, lasted a year: 'By this time a good many were thoroughly fed up with so long a spell of home service, fearing that the war would be over before we got out at all. And it was not till nearly the end of August that we got definite news that at last we were to receive the reward of all our hard training and see service overseas.'[4] They boarded ships for Gallipoli, which from the Allied point of view was to turn out one of the most inglorious episodes of the war. Withdrawn without having achieved anything, the fourteenth battalion moved on to Egypt and then to Palestine, where it took part in the capture of Jerusalem from the Turks in 1917. Not till the next year did the men of Ceres get to France, to be trained all over again for service in the trenches and to join in bringing about the final German collapse on the Western Front.

So, as these things went, the men of Ceres had not a bad war. They saw relatively little of the slaughter and privation endured for four years by their countrymen in France. There three great battles had taken place in which Scottish regiments played an especially prominent part. At Loos in the autumn of 1915, Scotland provided half the number of infantrymen sent into a massed attack, which came to nothing. Then in the offensive on the River Somme between July and November 1916 three wholly Scottish divisions participated, as well as Scottish battalions serving in other divisions: a total of 51 Scottish battalions of infantry, though they were never all in the front line at the same time. Finally the Battle of Arras in the spring of 1917 saw the deployment of 44 Scottish battalions plus seven Scottish-Canadian battalions, making it the largest concentration of Scots ever to have fought together. John Buchan estimated their presence at Arras to have been seven times greater than the entire army Bruce had led at Bannockburn in 1314.[5]

Then, on 11 November 1918, the war was over. Scotland lay far from the theatres of conflict and the sole attacks of note on its territory had come in attempts by German submarines to penetrate the naval base of Scapa Flow on Orkney. Otherwise only the uniforms on the streets and the lists of casualties brought the war home to Scotland. But those lists mounted alarmingly. Distant though the battlefields were, 148,000 Scots died on them.[6] It may not sound like so many compared to the 2 million Germans who were killed, or the 1.8 million Russians or the 1.4 million Frenchmen. But Scotland was a small country, and, in fact, the rate of casualties here exceeded that in any other Allied nation. It was proportionally more than the losses of Serbia and Turkey, countries that had been conquered and overrun. One big reason lay in the mind of the British commander-in-chief, General Douglas Haig, a son of Edinburgh who beyond all measure admired his own Scots soldiers and believed that, with their bravado and tenacity, they could win the war for him. This was why, in his relentless attempts to break through on the Western Front, he so often sent Scots over the top first. Not that they feared to go: they believed they could win the war too. So in high patriotic spirit, with no disaffection from the British state, Scotland fought a tragic and wasteful war to the end.

The peace also turned out tragic and wasteful, if in a different way. Survivors came back to a homeland bled of its Victorian vigour. There was no return to the halcyon days, only recurrent economic crisis rendering Scotland comparable to those European societies that under the same stresses suffered collapse and revolution. Industry shrank and famous companies vanished, into takeover or liquidation. Proud entrepreneurs and craftsmen either took their talents and skills elsewhere or swelled the shuffling, hopeless ranks of the unemployed. But there was no revolution. Instead, for the first time since the Union, the nation began to insulate itself from global progress and to seek refuge within a narrower British compass. It did not want to beat the world any more, asking only for subsidies from London. The war altogether cast a long shadow over Scotland's development, and changed the way the Scots saw themselves. The grand old Victorian ideals had dissolved. Scotland has never again found better ideals, though the time for that may be coming.

Chronology

(LA = Lord Advocate; PM = Prime Minister; SS = Scottish Secretary)

1815 Battle of Waterloo, end of Napoleonic Wars. Savings banks open in Glasgow and Aberdeen. Scottish Widows Fund founded. Magdalene Asylum founded, Glasgow.

1816 LA Alexander Maconochie. David Napier makes first marine engine on Clyde. Walter Scott, *The Antiquary.*

1817 Scott, *Rob Roy.*

1818 Gas lighting introduced in Glasgow. Scott, *Heart of Midlothian.*

1819 LA Sir William Rae. Jury court for civil causes set up. Select committee on state of Scots royal burghs. Thomas Chalmers becomes minister of St John's, Glasgow. Scott, *Ivanhoe.* Royal Institution founded, Edinburgh.

1820 Accession of King George IV. Radical War. Completion of Charlotte Square, and first New Town, Edinburgh.

1821 John Galt, *Annals of the Parish.* Official grant for 'parliamentary churches' in Highlands.

1822 King George IV visits Scotland.

1823 Charles Macintosh patents waterproof fabric. Edinburgh Assurance Company founded.

1824 Union Assurance Company founded. Scott, *Redgauntlet.* James Hogg, *Private Memoirs and Confessions of a Justified Sinner.*

1825 Standard Life Assurance Company founded.

1826 First Scottish railway, Monkland & Kirkintilloch, opens. Meg Dods, *Cook and Housewife's Manual*.

1827 Scottish political manager, Lord Melville, loses office. First Improvement Act for Edinburgh. Patrick Bell invents mechanical reaper.

1828 Alexander Baird begins to produce iron at Gartsherrie. William Burke and William Hare tried for murder.

1829 Muckle Spate in Strathspey.

1830 Accession of King William IV. LA Francis Jeffrey. Reform of Court of Session. Charles Lyell, *Principles of Geology*.

1831 Glasgow & Garnkirk railway opens, as does Innocent Railway, Dalkeith to Edinburgh.

1832 First Reform Act. Subsequent election results in huge Liberal victory. Mechanised jute production begins, Dundee. Dundee & Newtyle railway opens, first to carry passengers. Epidemic of Asiatic cholera.

1833 City of Edinburgh bankrupt. Municipal Corporations (Scotland) Act. Thomas Carlyle, *Sartor Resartus*. Thomas Chalmers, *On the Power, Wisdom and Goodness of God*.

1834 General Assembly of Kirk passes Veto Act. LA John Archibald Murray.

1835 Airdrie Savings Bank founded.

1836 Chalmers, *Natural Theology*.

1837 Accession of Queen Victoria. First iron ships built on Clyde. Cotton-spinners' strike in Glasgow defeated.

1838 Judgment of Court of Session in Auchterarder case. Walter Scrope, *The Art of Deerstalking*.

1839 LA Andrew Rutherfurd. James Young Simpson becomes professor of midwifery at Edinburgh. Eglinton Tournament.

1840 Royal Commission on mines. William Pulteney Alison, *Observations on the Management of the Poor in Scotland*. Thomas Carlyle, *Chartism*.

1841 Deep economic recession begins. Royal Commission on Anglo-Scottish railways. Tennant's Stalk erected, St Rollox, Glasgow. Carlyle, *On Heroes and Hero-Worship*. Hugh Miller, *The Old Red Sandstone*.

1842 First visit to Scotland by Queen Victoria and Prince Albert. Edinburgh & Glasgow railway opens. Wiliam Tait, *Magdalenism*.

1843 Disruption of Church of Scotland, formation of Free Church.

1844 Royal Commission on Poor Law. Stock exchanges founded in Edinburgh and Glasgow. Robert Chambers, *Vestiges of the Natural History of Creation*.

1845 New Scottish Poor Law. Banking (Scotland) Act. Railway mania. Compound marine engine patented, Glasgow.

1846 Repeal of Corn Laws. Start of Highland potato blight. New College, Edinburgh, opened. Thomas Cook begins Tartan Tours. William Thomson, later Lord Kelvin, becomes professor of natural philosophy at Glasgow, aged 22.

1847 Formation of the United Presbyterian Church. Thomas Guthrie founds ragged school in Edinburgh. Professor Simpson of Edinburgh inaugurates anaesthesia. Linoleum production begins, Kirkcaldy.

1848 Chartist disturbances in Glasgow.

1849 Court of Session rules against relief for able-bodied poor. George Bell, *Day and Night in the Wynds of Edinburgh*. Miller, *Footsteps of the Creator*.

1850 Camperdown Works, world's largest textile factory, built in Dundee. Robert Knox, *The Races of Men*.

1851 Professor Thomson of Glasgow expounds laws of thermodynamics.

1852 PM Lord Aberdeen. Queen Victoria buys Balmoral.

1853 Forbes Mackenzie Act on pubs' closing hours. Religious test abolished in Scottish universities. Queen Victoria anaesthetised for childbirth. Foundation of National Association for Vindication of Scottish Rights.

1854 Society of Accountants in Edinburgh founded.

1855 Institute of Accountants and Actuaries in Glasgow founded.

1856 Joint Stock Companies Act. Bankruptcy (Scotland) Act. Miller, *Testimony of the Rocks*.

1857 Police (Scotland) Act.

1858 Universities (Scotland) Act. Professor Thomson of Glasgow superintends laying of submarine cable across Atlantic Ocean.

1859 Water supply from Loch Katrine to Glasgow.

1860 Chambers's Encyclopaedia first published.

1861 White Horse whisky first produced.

1862 John Francis Campbell of Islay, *Popular Tales of the West Highlands*.

1863 Inverness connected to Perth by railway through Pass of Drumochter. Charles St John, *Wild Sports and Natural History of the Highlands*.

1864 Duke of Argyll's Royal Commission on Scottish education (report 1868).

1865 Macquorn Rankine invents screw propeller. Joseph Lister, professor of clinical surgery at Glasgow, inaugurates antisepsis. Queen Victoria, *Leaves from the Journal of our Life in the Highlands*.

1866 Improvement Act for Glasgow.

1867 Second Improvement Act for Edinburgh. Society of Accountants in Aberdeen founded. First women's suffrage society, Edinburgh.

1868 Second Reform Act (Scotland).

1869 LA George Young.

1870 University of Glasgow moves to Gilmorehill.

1871 Nobel Company founded, Glasgow. Napier shipbuilders liquidated.

1872 Education (Scotland) Act. Steel Company of Scotland founded. Colville ironworks opened, Motherwell. Rangers Football Club founded.

1873 James Clerk Maxwell, *Treatise on Electricity and Magnetism*. Scottish American Investment Trust founded. James Murray, *The Dialect of the Southern Counties of Scotland*.

1874 Railway reaches Wick and Thurso.

1875 George Hope evicted from Fenton Barns. John McLennan, *Primitive Marriage*.

1876 Appellate Jurisdiction Act. McLennan, *Studies in Ancient History.*

1877 Blantyre mining disaster.

1878 Tay Bridge opened (collapses next year). City of Glasgow Bank fails. Marcus Dods, *Revelation and Inspiration.*

1879 Midlothian campaign. Last important sailing ship, *Cutty Sark,* and first ocean-going vessel with steel hull, *Rotomahana,* launched at Dumbarton.

1880 Second Midlothian campaign.

1881 Highland Land League formed. William Robertson Smith deposed from chair. University College Dundee founded. Carlyle, *Reminiscences.*

1882 Battle of the Braes, Skye. Foundation of Celtic chair at University of Edinburgh. William Robertson Smith, *Prophets of Israel.*

1883 Robert Louis Stevenson, *Treasure Island.*

1884 Third Reform Act. Napier report on Highlands. Grand Central Hotel, Glasgow, completed. George Adam Smith, *Historical Geography of the Holy Land.*

1885 SS Duke of Richmond and Gordon. John Tulloch, *Movements of Religious Thought in the Nineteenth Century.* Robertson Smith, *Kinship and Marriage in Early Arabia.* Aberdeen art gallery founded.

1886 William Gladstone proposes Irish Home Rule. Liberal party splits with foundation of Liberal Unionist party. Scottish Home Rule Association formed. Crofters' Act. William Beardmore & Co founded. SS Lord Lothian. Stevenson, *Kidnapped, The Strange Case of Dr Jekyll and Mr Hyde.*

1887 Deer raid of Park, Lewis. Horse Shoe Bar, Glasgow, opens. Celtic football club founded.

1888 Scottish Liberal Party adopts Home Rule for Scotland. Keir Hardie stands at Mid-Lanarkshire by-election. Scottish Labour Party founded. International exhibition, Glasgow: City Chambers opened by Queen Victoria. Cable-hauled trams in Edinburgh.

1889 Universities (Scotland) Act. City Chambers in Glasgow completed. Robertson Smith, *Religion of the Semites.* Alexander Bruce, *Kingdom of God.*

1890 United Alkali Company formed, Glasgow. Forth Bridge opened. James Frazer, *The Golden Bough*.

1891 Scottish Orchestra founded.

1892 Universities opened to women.

1893 Independent Labour Party formed.

1894 PM Lord Rosebery. Alexander Cameron, *Reliquiae Celticae*. Ian Maclaren, *Beside the Bonnie Briar Bush*.

1895 SS Lord Balfour of Burleigh. North British Hotel, Edinbugh, completed.

1896 Coats Patons formed, Paisley. Royal Observatory opened on Blackford Hill, Edinburgh. William Sharp, *Lyra Celtica*. Robert Louis Stevenson, *Weir of Hermiston*.

1897 Congested Districts Board set up. Railway to Kyle of Lochalsh. Charles Rennie Mackintosh, Glasgow School of Art (to 1909).

1898 Electric trams in Glasgow.

1899 Albion Motor Car Co. founded, Glasgow.

1900 Liberals lose majority of Scots MPs. Formation of United Free Church. Plague in Glasgow. Alexander Carmichael, *Carmina Gadelica*.

1901 Accession of King Edward VII. George Douglas Brown, *House with the Green Shutters*. Railway to Mallaig. International exhibition, Glasgow.

1902 PM Arthur Balfour. Halford Mackinder, *Britain and the British Seas*.

1903 North British Locomotive Company formed. Caledonian Hotel, Edinburgh, completed.

1904 Catherine Cranston opens Willow Tea Room, Sauchiehall Street, Glasgow, designed by Mackintosh.

1905 PM Henry Campbell-Bannerman. SS John Sinclair. North British Hotel, Glasgow, completed. D.C. Thomson & Co founded, Dundee.

1906 Liberals regain large majority of Scots MPs. Turnberry Hotel completed.

1907 Discovery of Moine thrust belt, Sutherland, establishes existence of tectonic plates.

1908 PM Herbert Asquith.

1909 Royal Commission on Poor Law.

1910 Accession of King George V.

1911 Scottish national exhibition, Glasgow. Violet Jacob, *Flemington*.

1912 Pentland Act on land reform. Scottish Unionists and Scottish Conservatives merge. SS Thomas McKinnon Wood.

1913 Record shipbuilding tonnage launched on Clyde. Temperance Act.

1914 George MacDougall Hay, *Gillespie*. Home Rule Bill for Scotland reaches second reading. Outbreak of First World War.

Notes

Prologue: 'Scotland for ever'

1. A. Uffindell & M. Corum, *On the Fields of Glory* (London, 1996), 96.
2. R. North, *Regiments at Waterloo* (London, 1971), 14.
3. D. Howarth, *Waterloo, a near run thing* (London, 1972), 53.
4. J. Paget & D. Saunders, *Hougoumont, the key to victory at Waterloo* (Barnsley, 2001), 202.
5. North, *Regiments*, 81.
6. I. Fletcher, *Galloping at Everything, the British cavalry in the Peninsular War and at Waterloo* (Staplehurst, 1999), 200.

1 Agriculture: 'Fare ye well ye barnyards'

1. M. Brander, *Scottish Highlanders and their Regiments* (London, 1972), 122.
2. R.J. Adam (ed.), *Papers on Sutherland Estate Management* (Edinburgh, 1972), *passim*.
3. E. Sellar, *Recollections and Impressions* (Edinburgh & London, 1907), 1–10.
4. E. Richards, *The Highland Clearances* (Edinburgh, 2000), 139–41.
5. P. Robertson, *Report of the Trial of Patrick Sellar* (Edinburgh, 1816), 13.
6. T.H. Cook, *Science, Philosophy and Culture in the Early Edinburgh Review 1802–1829* (Ann Arbor, MI, 1976), 11; B. Fontana, *Rethinking the Politics of Commercial Society* (Cambridge, 1985), 3; C. Groffy, *Edinburgh Review 1802–1825, Formen der Spätaufklärung* (Heidelberg, 1981), 119.
7. *Edinburgh Review*, V (1804), 16.
8. E. Richards, *The Leviathan of Wealth* (London, 1973), 198.
9. J. Gifford, *The Buildings of Scotland: Highlands and Islands* (London, 1992), 554–94.
10. E. Richards, 'Patterns of Highland Discontent 1760–1860', in R. Quinault & J. Stevenson (eds), *Popular Protest and Public Order* (London, 1974), 88–91.
11. *Old Statistical Account*, XIII, 450 *et seq.*

12. *Communications to the Board of Agriculture on subjects relative to the husbandry and internal improvements of the county* (Aberdeenshire), VI (1812), 84 *et seq.*

13. *New Statistical Account*, XII, 317.

14. *The Journal of Sir Walter Scott*, ed. W.W.K. Anderson (Oxford, 1972), 290.

15. *New Statistical Account*, III, 80, 178, 462.

16. W. Cobbett, *Cobbett's Tour in Scotland, and in the four northern counties of England, in the autumn of 1832* (London, 1833), 203–4.

17. *Report of the Royal Commission on Labour,* Parliamentary Papers [hereinafter PP] 1893–94 XXXVII, part 2.

18. See above, note 7.

19. *Report of the Royal Commission on Agriculture*, PP 1881 XVII, Q40, 280.

20. A useful summary of the variety of experience in Scottish counties based on an analysis of the agricultural statistics for 1891 is in section ii.D of the *Miscellaneous Memoranda, Abstracts and Statistical Tables*, prepared for the Royal Commission on Labour PP 1893–94 XXXVII, part II.

21. E.H. Whetham, 'Prices and Production in Scottish Farming 1850–1870', *Scottish Journal of Political Economy*, IX (1962), 233–43.

22. There are places where it can still be traced, notably in Orkney and Shetland, see A. Fenton, *The Northern Isles* (Edinburgh, 1978), ch. 6.

23. *Report of the Royal Commission on Labour*, PP 1893 XXXVI, 13.

24. H.M. Briggs, *Modern Breeds of Cattle* (London & New York, 1980), 401.

25. M. Gray, 'Farm Workers in North East Scotland', in T.M. Devine (ed.), *Farm Servants and Labour in Lowland Scotland 1770–1914* (Edinburgh, 1984), 16.

26. Full text available at http://www.scottish-folk-music.com/lyrics/the-barn-yards-o-delgaty.htm.

27. G. Sprott, 'Lowland Country Life', in T.M. Devine & R. Finlay (eds), *Scotland in the Twentieth Century* (Edinburgh, 1996), 170.

28. C. Hope, *George Hope of Fenton Barns* (Edinburgh, 1881).

29. J. Wilson, 'Whether are large or small farms the most beneficial to the community', in *Journal of my Everyday Doings 1879–1881 and 1885–1892*, ed. P. Hillis (Edinburgh, 2008), 398–9.

30. *Return of Owners of Land, Scotland 1872–3,* PP 1874 LXXII, pt. 3.

31. *Memoirs of the Maxwells of Pollok* (Edinburgh, 1863), II, 119.

32. R. Leckie, *Grampian, a country in miniature* (Edinburgh, 1991), 81.

33. T. Speedy, *The Natural History of Sport in Scotland with Rod and Gun* (Edinburgh, 1920), 122.

34. J. Bryden & J.B.F. Houston, *Agricultural Change in the Scottish Highlands* (London, 1976), 140.

35. M.R.G. Fry, *Wild Scots, four hundred years of Highland history* (London, 2005), ch. 10.

36. C.S. Loch, 'Poor relief in Scotland: its statistics and development 1791–1891', *Journal of the Royal Statistical Society*, XLI (1892), 291.

37. *Report of the Commissioners of Inquiry into the Condition of the Crofters and Cottars in the Highlands and Island of Scotland* (Napier Commission), PP XXXII–XXXVI, evidence, appendix A, 68–72.

38. G. Campbell, 8th Duke of Argyll, *Reign of Law* (London, 1867); *Crofts and Farms in the Hebrides* (Edinburgh, 1883); *Scotland as it was and as it is* (Edinburgh, 1887); *Unseen Foundations of Society* (London, 1893).

39. J.S. Blackie, *Scottish Highlanders and the Land Laws* (London, 1885), introduction, 15, 129; W. Gillies, *Gaelic and Scotland – Alba agus a'Ghàilig* (Edinburgh, 1989), 9–39.

40. *Final Report of the Crofters' Commission*, 1913, xxvi.

41. J. Hunter, *The Making of the Crofting Community* (Edinburgh, 1976), 29, 46, 62, 74.

42. H. Barron (ed.), *Third Statistical Account: the county of Inverness* (Edinburgh, 1985), 485.

43. E.A. Cameron, *Land for the People? The British Government and the Scottish Highlands 1880–1925* (East Linton, 1996), 17.

44. J.G. Kellas, 'The Crofters' War 1882–1888', *History Today*, XII (1962), 281–8.

45. I.M.M. Macphail, 'The Skye Military Expedition of 1884–5', *Transactions of the Gaelic Society of Inverness*, XLVIII (1972–4), 62–94; National Archives of Scotland [hereinafter NAS], MacDonald Papers, GD 221/148/1, Ivory Papers, GD 1/36/1; Home Office Papers, HH22/4; Napier Commission, evidence, QQ9385, 9470–6, 9924.

46. The clearest account is in J.P. Day, *Public Administration in the Highlands and Islands of Scotland* (London, 1918), especially 187–92.

47. C.W.J. Withers, 'Destitution and Migration: labour mobility and relief from famine in Highland Scotland 1836–1850', *Journal of Historical Geography*, XIV (1998), 128–50.

48. D. MacDonald, *Lewis, a history of the island* (Edinburgh, 1978), 174.

49. Hunter, *Making*, 132–3

50. I.M.M. Macphail, *The Crofters' War* (Stornoway, 1989), 72.

51. A. Collier, *The Crofting Problem* (Cambridge, 1953), 133–41.

52. A.D. Hall, *A Pilgrimage of British Farming* (London, 1913), 137–41; see also C.M.M. Macdonald, *Whaur Extremes Meet* (Edinburgh, 2009), 57.

2 Industry: 'Blazing volcanoes'

1. I. Donnachie & G. Hewitt, *Historic New Lanark* (Edinburgh, 1993), 25.

2. T. Garnett, *Observations on a Tour to the Highlands and Part of the Western Isles* (London, 1800), II, 236.

3. *Life of Robert Owen Written by Himself* (London, 1857), viii–ix.

4. *Old Statistical Account,* XV, 41.

5. PP 1822, XX, 74; R. Southey, *Journey of a Tour in Scotland in 1819* (London, 1929), 259–65.

6. R. Owen, *A New View of Society* (London, 1816), 93–119.

7. A.K. Cairncross (ed.), *The Scottish Economy* (Cambridge, 1954), 77.

8. W.W. Rostow, *The World Economy* (Austin, TX, 1978), 33.

9. A.J. Durie, 'The Markets for Scottish Linen 1730–1775, *Scottish Historical Review,* LII (1973), 30–49; 'Imitation in Scottish Eighteenth-century Textiles: the drive to establish the manufacture of Osnaburg linen', *Journal of Design History,* VI (1993), 71–6.

10. A. Cooke, *The Rise and Fall of the Scottish Cotton Industry* (Manchester, 2009), 100 *et seq.*

11. Ibid., 87–91.

12. Ibid., 165.

13. J.G. Lockhart, *Memoirs of the Life of Sir Walter Scott* (Edinburgh, 1837), 149.

14. A. Slaven, *The Development of the West of Scotland 1750–1960* (London, 1975), 163–6; R.H. Campbell, *The Rise and Fall of Scottish Industry* (Edinburgh, 1980), 56–60.

15. *J. & P. Coats Limited . . . a brief outline of its early history to present date* (Cork, 1910), 21.

16. W.M. Walker, *Juteopolis, Dundee and its textile workers 1885–1923* (Edinburgh, 1979).

17. G. Gavin, D. Mechan & V. Seymour, *'The Queer-like Smell', the Kirkcaldy linoleum industry* (Kirkcaldy, 1992), 1–19.

18. C. Whatley, *The Scottish Salt Industry, an economic and social history* (Aberdeen, 1987).

19. F. Home, *Experiments on Bleaching,* including J. Ferguson, 'Experimental Essay on the Use of Leys and Sours in Bleaching' and J. Black, 'Explanation of the Effect of Lime upon Alkaline Salts' (Dublin, 1771).

20. J. Playfair, *Biographical Account of James Hutton* (Edinburgh, 1797).

21. R. Burns, *The Complete Poetical Works,* ed. J.A. Mackay (Darvel, 1993), 201.

22. B. Lenman, *Economic History of Modern Scotland* (London, 1977), 127, notes what he calls the 'lum-mania' of Scottish capitalists; the Port Dundas Townsend Chimney of 1859, at 454 feet even higher than Tennant's Stalk, was another example.

23. G. Dodd et al., *The Land We Live In* (London, 1847), II, 43.

24. R. Trotter (ed.), *Imperial Chemical Industries Ltd and its Founding Companies* (London, 1938), I, 20–3.

25. G. Macintosh, *Biographical memoir of the late Charles Macintosh of Campsie and Dunchattan* (Glasgow, 1847).

26. T. Hancock, *Personal narrative of the origin and progress of the caoutchouc or India-rubber manufacture in England* [*sic*] (London, 1857).

27. N. Crathorne et al., *Tennant's Stalk* (London, 1973), 55–98.

28. S.G. Checkland, *The Mines of Tharsis* (London, 1967); W.G. Nash, *Rio Tinto Mine, its history and romance* (London, 1904); M. Rodríguez Bayona, *La investigación de la actividad metalúrgica durante el III milenio A.N.E. en el suroeste de la Península Ibérica* (Oxford, 2008).

29. Trotter, *Imperial Chemical Industries*, 52–4; W.J. Reader, *Imperial Chemical Industries, a history* (Oxford, 1970), 24–5; J.M. Stopford, 'The Origins of British-based Multinational Manufacturing Enterprises', *Business History Review*, XLVIII (1974).

30. P.L. Payne, 'The Decline of the Scottish Heavy Industries', in R. Saville, *The Economic Development of Modern Scotland* (Edinburgh, 1985), 80.

31. *Royal Commission on Children's Employment* PP 1842 XVI, especially 449 *et seq*.

32. *Royal Commission on Labour*, PP 1893 XXXVII (1), 194.

33. *Report of the Commissioners appointed to inquire into the State of the Population in the Mining Districts*, PP 1844 XVI, 32.

34. *Report of the Commissioners appointed to inquire into the State of the Population in the Mining Districts*, PP 1848 XXV, 236.

35. J.A. Hassan, 'The landed estate, paternalism and the coal industry in Midlothian 1800–1880, *Scottish Historical Review*, LXIX (1980), 86–9.

36. E.D. Hyde, *Coalmining in Scotland* (Edinburgh, 1987), 13.

37. R.H. Campbell, *Carron Company* (Edinburgh, 1959).

38. A. McGeorge, *The Bairds of Gartsherrie* (Glasgow, 1875).

39. *Royal Commission on the Employment of Children in Mines*, PP XVI 1842, pt. 2, 81.

40. J. Napier, *Life of Robert Napier of West Shandon* (Edinburgh, 1904), 101; D.D. Napier, *Life of David Napier, engineer 1790–1869* (Glasgow, 1912), 93.

41. J.D. Marwick, *Glasgow: the water supply of the city from the earliest period, on record with notes on various developments of the city till the close of 1900* (Glasgow, 1901), 73–8.

42. H. Bessemer, *An Autobiography* (London, 1901), 176–80.

43. H.A. Brassert, *Report to Lord Weir of Cathcart on the Manufacture of Iron and Steel by William Baird & Co Ltd, David Colville & Sons Ltd, Jas. Dunlop & Co Ltd, Steel Company of Scotland Ltd, Stewarts & Lloyds Ltd* (London, 1929).

44. G.G. Endres, *British Aircraft Manufacturers since 1908* (London, 1995), 24.

45. P.L. Payne, *Colvilles and the Scottish Steel Industry* (Oxford, 1979).

46. R.H. Campbell, *The Rise and Fall of Scottish Industry 1707–1939*, (Edinburgh, 1980), 61 *et seq.*; J.R. Hume & M. Moss, *Clyde Shipbuilding* (London, 1975), 131–41.

47. H. Bell, *Observations on the Utility of Applying Steam Engines to Vessels* (Glasgow, 1813).

48. C.H. Wilson & W. Reader, *Men and Machines: a history of D. Napier & Son, Engineers, Ltd, 1808–1958* (London, 1958).

49. F.E. Hyde, *Cunard and the North Atlantic 1840–1973, a history of shipping and financial management* (London, 1975), 23.

50. In 1977 she ran on to rocks near Dunoon and in 2009 struck the pier there.

51. J. MacLehose, *Memoirs and Portraits of One Hundred Glasgow Men* (Glasgow, 1906), 118; R.H. Thurston, *A History of the Growth of the Steam Engine* (London, 1883), 97; W.J.M. Rankine, *A Memoir of John Elder, engineer and shipbuilder* (Glasgow, 1883), 29–30.

52. C.M. Castle, *Legacy of Fame, shipping and shipbuilding on the Clyde* (Erskine, 1990), 59.

53. P.L. Robertson, 'Shipping and Shipbuilding, the case of William Denny & Brothers', *Business History*, XVI (1974), 36–47.

54. C.E. Montague, introduction to M. Bone, *The Western Front* (London, 1917), a collection of prints and drawings.

55. A. Cobbing, *The Japanese Discovery of Victorian Britain* (London, 1998), 187.

56. H.H. Peebles, 'A Study in Failure: J. & G. Thomson and shipbuilding at Clydebank 1871–1890', *Scottish Historical Review*, LXIX (1990).

57. A. Carnegie, *A Rectorial Address delivered to the Students in the University of Aberdeen* (New York, 1912), 10.

58. B. Dunn, 'Success Themes in Scottish Family Enterprises', *Family Business Review*, VIII (1995), 17–28.

59. Ch. 11.

60. Mitchell Library, Glasgow, GC 920.04 BAI.

61. J.J. Jones, 'University Training for Commerce and Administration', *Proceedings of the Royal Philosophical Society of Glasgow*, XLIV (1913–14), 172.

62. M. Cooper, 'McGregor Gow and the Glen Line', *Journal of Transport History*, X (1989), 166 *et seq.*; D.W. Kim & A. Slaven, 'The Origins and Economic and Social Roles of Scottish Business Leaders', in T.M. Devine (ed.), *Scottish Elites* (Edinburgh, 1994), 153; R. Michie, *Money, Mania and Markets: investment company formation and the stock exchange in nineteenth-century Scotland* (Edinburgh, 1981), 155; P.L. Payne, *The Early Scottish Limited Companies 1856–1895, an historical and analytical survey* (Edinburgh, 1980).

63. H.R. Holst van der Schalk, *Kapitaal en Arbeid in Nederland* (Nijmegen, 1977), 239; J.-F. Bergier, *Histoire Économique de la Suisse* (Paris, 1984), 220; A. Lindbeck, *Swedish Economic Policy* (London, 1975), 33; F. Singleton, *Economy of Finland in the Twentieth Century* (Bradford, 1991), 91.

64. For the sequel, see C.M.M. Macdonald, *Whaur Extremes Meet, Scotland's twentieth century* (Edinburgh, 2009), ch. 2.

65. M. Hughes & J. Scott, *The Anatomy of Scottish Capital, Scottish companies and Scottish capital 1900–1979* (London & Montreal, 1980), 54.

3 Services: 'Many sensible men'

1. N. Ferguson, *Dundee and Newtyle Railway, including the Alyth and Blairgowrie branches* (Usk, 1995).
2. Quoted in D. Bremner, *The Industries of Scotland* (Edinburgh, 1869), 502.
3. C. Awdry, *Encyclopaedia of British Railway Companies* (Sparkford, 1990), 149.
4. R.P. Bradley, *Giants of Steam, the full story of the North British Locomotive Company* (Sparkford, 1995), 95.
5. C.H. Lee, *British Regional Employment Statistics 1841–1971* (Cambridge, 1979), series A, 38; A. K. Cairncross (ed.), *The Scottish Economy* (Cambridge, 1954), table 36.
6. C. Highet, *Scottish Locomotive History 1831–1923* (London, 1970), 120.
7. http://www.railbrit.co.uk/Edinburgh_and_Glasgow_Railway.
8. *Report and Resolutions of a Public Meeting, held at Glasgow, on Friday, March 20, 1846, in support of Sir Robert Peel's suggestions with reference to railways* (Glasgow, 1846), 13–14.
9. C.J.A. Robertson, *The Origins of the Scottish Railway System 1722–1844* (Edinburgh, 1983), 85.
10. J. Thomas, *The North British Railway* (Newton Abbot, 1969), I, 71.
11. Ibid., 124.
12. J. Prebble, *The High Girders: the story of the Tay Bridge disaster* (London, 1956).
13. W. McGonagall, *The Railway Bridge of the Silvery Tay* (London, 1972), 18.
14. M. Barclay-Harvey, *History of the Great North of Scotland Railway* (Shepperton, 1998).
15. C.D. Wilson, *Racing Trains* (Stroud, 1995), 81.
16. H.A. Vallance, *Highland Railway* (Newton Abbot, 1969).
17. J. Thomas, *The West Highland Railway* (Newton Abbot, 1965).
18. J. Gifford, C. McWilliam & D. Walker, *The Buildings of Scotland: Edinburgh* (London, 1984), 267–8, 285; M. Higgs, A. Riches, E. Williamson, *The Buildings of Scotland: Glasgow* (London, 1990), 176, 210.
19. P.L. Gordon, *Personal Memoirs and Reminiscences* (London, 1830), I, 62; E. Grant, *Memoirs of a Highland Lady* (Edinburgh, 1998), I, 207.
20. F.M. McNeill, *The Scots Kitchen* (London, 1929), 15–18.
21. Ibid., 82–3.
22. Quoted in Anon., *Charles Rennie Mackintosh* (Glasgow, 1987), 64.
23. W. Power, *Should Auld Acquaintance* (London, 1937), 186.
24. Ibid., 95–7; C. Brown & H. Whyte, *A Scottish Feast* (Glendaruel, 1996), 37.
25. I. Levitt & C, Smout, *The State of the Scottish Working Class in 1843* (Edinburgh, 1979), 137.
26. G.B. Wilson, *Alcohol and the Nation* (London, 1940), table 6.

27. An incomplete list: bevvied, birlin, bladdered, blazin, blitzed, blootered, bongoed, buzzin, charred, fleein, fu', gubbed, guttered, hammered, jaiked, moolered, muntit, mutted, ridiculous, rubbered, smashed, steamin or steamboats, stoated or stoatious, stoavin, troattered, wankered, wasted, wellied, wrecked.

28. J.J. Dunsimore, *Reminiscences of Glasgow (by an Englishman)* (Glasgow, 1874), 159.

29. Charles McHardy, evidence in *Report of the Royal Commission on Liquor Licensing Laws*, PP XXXVII 1898, 161.

30. R. Kenna & A.Mooney, *People's Palaces, Victorian and Edwardian pubs of Scotland* (Edinburgh, 1983); E. King, 'Popular Culture in Glasgow', in R. Cage (ed.), *The Working Class in Glasgow 1750–1914* (London, 1987), 153–62.

31. Higgs, Riches & Williamson, *Buildings of Scotland: Glasgow*, 224, 556, 600.

32. R.L. Stevenson, *Edinburgh: picturesque notes* (London, 1881), 44.

33. Quoted in J.E. Handley, *The Navvy in Scotland* (Cork, 1970), 335.

34. D. Wordsworth, *Recollections of a Tour Made in Scotland* (Edinburgh, 1894), 158.

35. J.G. Lockhart, *Memoirs of the Life of Sir Walter Scott*, (Edinburgh, 1837), III, 239.

36. Canto Third, II.

37. Canto Fourth, XII.

38. E. Swingleton, *Romantic Journey, the story of Thomas Cook and Victorian travel* (London, 1974), 104.

39. *Black's Picturesque Tourist of Scotland* (Edinburgh 1851), 14, 208, 332, 435.

40. PP 1872 IX, *Select Committee on Habitual Drunkards*, 110; Sale of Intoxicating Liquors on Sunday (Scotland) Act, 1882 c. 79.

41. S. G. Checkland, *Scottish Banking, a history 1695–1973* (Glasgow & London, 1975), pt.1 and table 9, 320.

42. Ibid., 183 *et seq.*

43. *Blackwood's Edinburgh Magazine*, XVI, 1844, 679.

44. Anon., 'The Royal Bank of Scotland and the London-Edinburgh Exchange Rate in the Eighteenth Century', *Three Banks Review*, XXXVIII (1958), 27 *et seq.*

45. K. Marx, *Grundrisse der Kritik der politischen Ökonomie* (Moscow, 1939), 125.

46. F.A. Hayek, *The Denationalisation of Money* (London, 1976), 101.

47. *Select Committee on Weavers' Petitions*, PP 1810–11 II, 4–10.

48. S. Smiles, *Thrift* (London, 1875), 398.

49. H. Duncan, *Essay on the Nature and Advantages of Parish Banks* (Edinburgh, 1816).

50. Checkland, *Scottish Banking,* 316–18.

51. *Returns relating to Depositors in Savings Banks in the United Kingdom*, no.1, PP 1866 LVII, 533.

52. M.R.G. Fry, *Banking Deregulation, the Scottish example* (Edinburgh, 1985).

53. Limited liability was available to the Scottish banks under legislation of 1862 but they had not availed themselves of it, believing it would reduce public confidence in them: Checkland, *Scottish Banking*, 480, but see also J. Carr, S. Glied & F. Mathewson, 'Unlimited Liability and Free Banking in Scotland', *Journal of Economic History* XLIX (1989), 975–6.

54. Checkland, *Scottish Banking*, 470–8.

55. Ibid., tables 17 & 20, 524 & 530.

56. M. Gaskin, *The Scottish Banks, a modern survey* (London, 1965), 33.

57. Ibid., pts. 5 & 6.

58. A. Rae, *The Other Walter Scott: the eighteen-twenties in Edinburgh, law, business, banking, insurance* (Edinburgh, 1985), passim.

59. M. Moss, *Standard Life 1825–2000* (Edinburgh & London, 2001), 54.

60. PP, *Papers relative to the Emigration to the North American Colonies*, XLVI (1854), 79.

61. T.A. Lee, *Shaping the Accountancy Profession* (London & New York, 1996), 176–7.

62. R. Michie, *Money, Mania and Markets: investment, company formation and the stock exchange in nineteenth-century Scotland* (Edinburgh, 1981), 101–3.

63. See above, 51.

64. Michie, *Mania,* 197–214, 257.

65. M.A. Simpson, 'The West End of Glasgow 1830–1914', in M.A. Simpson & T.H. Lloyd (eds), *Middle Class Housing in Britain* (Newton Abbot, 1977), 59.

66. R. Rodger, *The Transformation of Edinburgh* (Cambridge, 2001), 19–24, 142, 165–70.

67. This was the foundation of the fortunes of Ivory & Sime, which thus became one of the leading financial houses in Edinburgh: J. Newlands, *Put Not Your Trust in Money* (London, 1997), 71–87.

68. Rodger, *Transformation*, 36.

69. 'Scottish Capital Abroad', *Blackwood's Edinburgh Magazine*, CXXXVI (1884), 477.

70. C.H. Lee, 'Economic Progress: Wealth and Poverty', in T.M. Devine, C.H. Lee & G.C. Peden (eds), *The Transformation of Scotland* (Edinburgh, 2005), 139.

71. 'Scottish Investors in the Dumps', *The Statist*, XV, January 10, 1883, 37.

72. W.A. Thomas, *The Provincial Stock Exchanges* (London, 1973), 300–11; B.P. Lenman, *An Economic History of Modern Scotland* (London, 1977), 192; L.E. Davis & R.A. Huttenback, *Mammon and the Pursuit of Empire* (Cambridge, 1986), 214; C. Schmitz, 'Scottish Investors in Australian Mining 1870–1920', Scottish Records Association conference report, X, 1988; 'Patterns of Scottish Portfolio Investment 1860–1914', unpublished paper, 1993.

73. W.G. Stout, *Robert Fleming and the Dundee Merchants* (Dundee, 1999).

74. W. Menzies, *America as a Field for Investment* (Edinburgh & London, 1892), 21.

75. Newlands, *Put Not*, 90.

76. For the sequel, see C.M.M. Macdonald, *Whaur Extremes Meet, Scotland's twentieth century* (Edinburgh, 2009), 12–13.1977)

4 Class: 'Regularity and order'

1. Queen Victoria, *Leaves from the Journal of our Life in the Highlands* (London, 1865), 5.

2. J. Prebble, *The King's Jaunt, George IV in Scotland* (London, 1988).

3. Victoria, *Leaves*, 6.

4. Ibid., 7.

5. Ibid., 8.

6. Ibid., 66 *et seq*.

7. NAS, Melville Papers GD 51/5/749/40; Lady E. Grant of Rothiermurchus, *Memoirs of a Highland Lady*, (London, 1898) II, 166.

8. H. Heckmann, *Sachsen: historische Landeskunde Mitteldeutschlands* (Würzburg, 1985), 22.

9. Queen Victoria, *More Leaves from the Journal of our Life in the Highlands* (London, 1885), 136, 153.

10. *Leaves*, 147.

11. G.K. Chesterton, 'King Edward VII and Scotland', in *All Things Considered* (Beaconsfield, 1969), 95 *et seq*.

12. A. Baillie-Cochrane, Lord Lamington, *In the Days of the Dandies* (London, 1890), 81.

13. *Return of Owners of Land, Scotland 1872–3*, PP 1874 LXXII, pt. 3, 8.

14. J. Richardson, *The Eglinton Tournament of 1839* (London, 1843).

15. *Return of Owners of Land*, 1–3, 16.

16. PP 1874 LXXII, pt. 3, 5.

17. F.A. Walker, *The Buildings of Scotland: Argyll and Bute* (London, 2000), 607–12.

18. Liverpool Papers, British Library Additional Manuscripts 38296, f.56.

19. J. Pinder, 'Prophet not without honour: Lothian and the federal idea', *Round Table*, LXXII (1983), 207–20.

20. M.L. Melville, *The Story of the Lovat Scouts 1900–1980* (Edinburgh, 1981); M.P. Roth, 'Lord Dunmore VC', in *Historical Dictionary of War Journalism* (London, 1997), 103; I. Grimble, *The Sea Wolf* (London, 1978).

21. N. Barker, *Bibliotheca Lindesiana* (London, 1978).

22. J. Sinclair, Earl of Caithness, *Lectures on Popular and Scientific Subjects* (London, 1877).

23. *The Times*, 1 February 1900.

24. C. Smith and M. N. Wise, *Energy and Empire, a biographical study of Lord Kelvin* (Cambridge, 1989).

25. W. Thomson, Lord Kelvin, *Mathematical and Physical Papers,* 6 vols (Cambridge, 1882–1911).

26. S.P. Thompson, *The Life of William Thomson, Baron Kelvin of Largs* (New York, 1910).

27. D. Hamilton, 'The Scottish Enlightenment and Clinical Medicine', in A. Dow (ed.) *The Influence of Scottish Medicine* (Carnforth, 1986), 205 *et seq.*

28. R.E. Wright-St Clair, *Doctors Monro: a medical saga* (London, 1964).

29. R. Paterson, *Memorials of the Life of James Syme* (Edinburgh, 1874), 198–9.

30. G. Radick, *Edinburgh and Darwin's Expression of the Emotions* (Edinburgh, 2009).

31. R.B. Fisher, *Joseph Lister 1827–1912* (London, 1979), 136.

32. A.H.B. Masson, 'Dr Thomas Latta', *Book of the Old Edinburgh Club* (XXXIII), 1972, 143–9; E.D.W. Grieg, 'The treatment of cholera by intravenous saline injections, with particular reference to the contribution of Dr Thomas Latta of Leith (1832)', *Edinburgh Medical Journal*, LIII (1946), 256–63.

33. W.O. Priestley & H.O. Storer (eds), *The Obstetric Memoirs and Contributions of J.Y. Simpson* (Edinburgh, 1855–6).

34. J. Duns, *Memoir of Sir James Young Simpson* (Edinburgh, 1873).

35. Paterson, *Memorials*, 261–2; E.B. Simpson, *Sir James Young Simpson* (Edinburgh & London, 1896), 51, 63.

36. *Life of Sir Robert Christison, edited by his sons* (Edinburgh 1885–6).

37. H. Dingwall, *Physicians, Surgeons and Apothecaries* (East Linton, 1995), 38–9.

38. W.H. Fraser, *Conflict and Class, Scottish workers 1700–1838* (Edinburgh, 1988), 151–71.

39. A.B. Richmond, *Narrative of the Condition of the Manufacturing Population* (London, 1824), 54.

40. W.M. Roach, 'Radical Reform Movements in Scotland from 1815 to 1822', unpublished PhD thesis, University of Glasgow, 1970, 188.

41. Fraser, *Conflict and Class*, 96.

42. P.B. Ellis & S. Mac A'Ghobhain, *The Scottish Insurrection of 1820* (London, 1970).

43. Home Office Papers, NAS, RH 2/4/110/417.

44. *Report of the Select Committee into Combinations of Workmen*, PP III 1837–8, 30–40, evidence of Angus Campbell.

45. A. Alison, *Some Account of my Life and Writings* (Edinburgh, 1883), I, 389.

46. G. Robertson, *General Description of the Shire of Renfrew* (Glasgow, 1818), 57.

47. A. Dickson & W. Speirs, 'Changes in Class Structure in Paisley 1750–1845,

Scottish Historical Review, LXIX (1980–1), 68–71; T. Clarke & T. Dickson, 'Social Concern and Social Control in Nineteenth-century Scotland: Paisley 1841–1843', ibid, LXV (1986), 49–55.

48. W. Carlile, 'A Short Sketch of the Improved State of Paisley', *Scots Magazine*, July 1806, 17–18.

49. In 1883 a skilled tradesman on Clydeside might earn £200 a year, whereas an experienced clerk would be more likely to earn £80 a year. See H. Dyer, 'Technical Education, Glasgow and the west of Scotland', *Proceedings of the Philosophical Society of Glasgow*, XV (1883–4), 39.

50. See T.C. Smout, *A Century [sic] of the Scottish People 1830–1950* (London, 1986), 113–14, where he refuses to believe Scots workers earned good money, or T.M. Devine, *The Scottish Nation 1700–2000* (London, 1999), 264, who apparently thinks Scotland's industrial investment would have been better going into housing.

51. R. Dudley Baxter's analysis of *National Income of the United Kingdom*, published in 1867, identified the really rich in Scotland, with incomes of over £1,000 a year, as numbering 4,700, or a tiny elite of 0.3 per cent of 'productive persons' in the country. But he also thought a further 276,300 individuals by his measure could be included in the middle and professional class. In all, this group made up nearly one-fifth of 'productive persons'.

52. *Royal Commission on Children's Employment* PP XVI 1842, pt.2, 341, witness 276; pt.1, 449, witness 4.

53. L.W. McBride (ed.), *Reading Irish Histories: texts, contexts and memory in modern Ireland* (Dublin, 2003); N.C. Fleming & A. O'Day, *Ireland and Anglo-Irish Relations since 1800* (Aldershot, 2008).

54. *Fraser's Magazine*, LXXVIII (1868), 333–4.

5 Institution: 'I'm proud of my country'

1. T. Brown, *Annals of the Disruption* (Edinburgh, 1893), 103.

2. Ibid., 102.

3. S.J. Brown, *Thomas Chalmers and the Godly Commonwealth in Scotland* (Oxford, 1982), 303.

4. *Royal Commission on Religious Worship and Education, Scotland*, PP 1854 XIX, lix.

5. H. Cockburn, *Life of Lord Jeffrey* (Edinburgh, 1852), 431.

6. R. B. Sher, *Church and University in the Scottish Enlightenment* (Edinburgh, 1982).

7. S.J. Brown, *Chalmers*, 201–19.

8. Ibid., 363.

9. M.R.G. Fry, 'The Disruption and the Union', in S.J. Brown & M.R.G. Fry (eds), *Scotland in the Age of the Disruption* (Edinburgh, 1993), 31–43.

10. *Census of Attendance and Accommodation at Worship*, PP XXXIII 1852–3, Accounts and Papers.

11. For three of the cities, see M.R.G. Fry, *Edinburgh, a history of the city* (London, 2009), 292; R. H. Trainor, 'The elite', in W.H. Fraser & I. Maver, *Glasgow, II, 1830–1912* (Manchester, 1996), 244; P. Hillis, 'Religion', in W.H. Fraser & C.H. Lee, *Aberdeen 1800–2000, a new history* (East Linton, 2000), 353.

12. D. Watt (ed.), *The Christian Watt Papers* (Edinburgh, 1983), 24, 47.

13. A.H. Charteris, *Life of the Revd James Robertson* (Edinburgh, 1863).

14. D. Macleod, *Memoir of Norman Macleod* (Edinburgh, 1876).

15. M. Oliphant, *Memoir of the Life of John Tulloch* (Edinburgh, 1888).

16. G.C. Hutton, *The Case for Disestablishment in Scotland* (London, Edinburgh & Glasgow, 1878),

17. Ibid., 12–13; J. Tulloch, 'Disestablishment in Scotland', *Contemporary Review*, XLI (1882), 749–67; C.G. Brown, 'The Myth of the Established Church of Scotland', in J. Kirk (ed.), *The Scottish Churches and the Union Parliament 1707–1999* (Edinburgh, 2001), 48–74.

18. Quoted in P. Hillis, 'Presbyterianism and Social Class in Mid-nineteenth-century Glasgow: a study of nine churches', *Journal of Ecclesiastical History*, XXXII (1981), 54.

19. A.S. Matheson, *The Church and Social Problems* (Edinburgh, 1893), 14.

20. J. Bulloch & A.L. Drummond, *The Church in Victorian Scotland 1843–1874* (Edinburgh, 1975); S. Mechie, *The Church and Scottish Social Development 1780–1870* (Oxford, 1960).

21. G. Rosie, *Hugh Miller, outrage and order, a biography and selected writings* (Edinburgh, 1981).

22. J.S. Black & C.W. Chrystal, *The Life of William Robertson Smith* (London, 1912).

23. C.N. Johnston, 'Doctrinal Subscription in the Church of Scotland', *Juridical Review*, XVII (1910), 201–20.

24. D.M. Murray, *Rebuilding the Kirk: Presbyterian reunion in Scotland 1909–1929* (Edinburgh, 2000), 63–114.

25. I. Machin, 'Voluntaryism and Reunion 1874–1929', in N. MacDougall (ed.), *Church, Politics and Society: Scotland 1408–1929* (Edinburgh, 1983), 221–37.

26. G.E. Davie, *The Democratic Intellect, Scotland and her universities in the nineteenth century* (Edinburgh, 1961), 1.

27. Ibid., 10 *et seq.*

28. H. Cockburn, *Letters on the Affairs of Scotland*, (London, 1874), 137–8.

29. National Library of Scotland [hereinafter NLS], MS 10767/9, Janet Livingstone's advice to Revd W.G. Blaikie.

30. Black & Chrystal, *William Robertson Smith*, 39–41; *Chambers's Journal*, 4th series,

IX (1872), 279; W.R. Nicoll, 'The Homes of the Rural Students 1866–1870', *Aberdeen University Review*, I (1913–14), 36–41.

31. W. Elliot, 'The Scottish Heritage in Politics', in J.G.S. Murray et al. (eds), *A Scotsman's Heritage* (London, 1932), 53–65.

32. *Hansard*, 3rd series, CCIV, House of Commons, February 13, 1871, col. 215.

33. Davie, *Democratic Intellect*, 190, 289–90, 318–20.

34. R.D. Anderson, 'Brewster and the Reform of the Scottish Universities', in J.R.R. Christie & A.D. Morrison-Low (eds), *'Martyr of Science', Sir David Brewster 1781–1868* (Edinburgh, 1984), 31–2.

35. A. Thomson, *Ferrier of St Andrews* (Edinburgh, 1985).

36. Davie, *Democratic Intellect*, 282–93.

37. J. McDermid, 'Gender, National Identity and the Royal (Argyll) Commission of Inquiry into Scottish Education 1864–1867', *Journal of Educational Administration and History*, XXXVIII (2006), 249–262.

38. *Third Report of HM Commissioners appointed to Inquire into the Schools in Scotland: Burgh and Middle-class Schools*, PP XXIX 1867–8, I, 237.

39. R.D. Anderson, *Education and Opportunity in Victorian Scotland* (Oxford, 1983), 103–61.

40. *Report of the Royal Commission on Scientific Instruction and the Advancement of Science*, PP 1874 XXII, evidence, Q9512.

41. Davie, *Democratic Intellect*, 6–7, 78–80, 99–102.

42. *Third Report, Schools*, vii.

43. R.D. Anderson, 'Secondary Schools and Scottish Society in the Nineteenth Century', *Past and Present*, CIX (1985), 178.

44. *Fraser's Magazine*, new series, XIII (1876), 596.

45. *Endowed Schools and Hospitals (Scotland), first report of the Royal Commissioners*, PP 1873 XXVII, 337 *et seq.*

46. Ibid., 36–7, 524; *Endowed Schools and Hospitals (Scotland), third report of the Royal Commissioners*, appendix, PP 1875 XXIX, II, 354; T.J. Boyd, *Educational Hospital Reform, the scheme of the Edinburgh Merchant Company* (Edinburgh, 1871), 14; *Minutes of the Edinburgh Trades Council*, ed. I. MacDougall (Edinburgh, 1968), 356.

47. I owe these remarks on Glasgow to discussion with Colin Mackay, author of *Kelvinside Academy 1878–1978* (Glasgow, 1978), and wish to record my thanks to him.

48. R. Buchanan, *The Ten Years' Conflict* (Edinburgh, 1852), I, 289 *et seq.*; J. Bryce, *Ten Years of the Church of Scotland* (Edinburgh, 1850), I, 29–42.

49. Buchanan, *Conflict*, I, 398–491; II, 1–15; H. Watt, *Thomas Chalmers and the Disruption* (Edinburgh, 1943), 157 *et seq.*

50. H. Cockburn, *Journal* (Edinburgh, 1874), I, 308–9; C. Robertson, *Report of the Auchterarder Case* (Edinburgh, 1838), II, 2–3.

51. Ibid., 277.
52. W.E.K. Anderson (ed.), *The Journal of Sir Walter Scott* (Oxford, 1972), 604.
53. PP 1824 X.
54. Liverpool Papers, British Library Additional Manuscripts 38282, f. 326.
55. NAS, Melville Papers, 51/5/603/2, 537/3; *Parliamentary Debates*, new series, XI, col. 1428; XII, col. 711; N.T. Phillipson, 'The Scottish Whigs and the Reform of the Court of Session', unpublished PhD thesis, University of Cambridge 1967; Lord Cooper of Culross, 'The Central Courts after 1532', in Stair Society, *An Introduction to Scottish Legal History* (Edinburgh, 1958), 343; C.H. Paton, 'The Eighteenth Century and After', in Stair Society, *Introduction to Scottish Legal History*; T.B. Smith, *British Justice, the Scottish contribution* (London, 1961), 72–6; I.D. Willcock, 'The Origins and Development of the Jury in Scotland, *Stair Society*, XXIII (1966), 255–61; A. Murray, 'Administration and Law', in T.I. Rae (ed.), *The Union of 1707, its impact on Scotland* (Glasgow & London, 1974).
56. *Edinburgh Review*, XXXIX (1822), 363–76.
57. *Parliamentary History*, new series, VII, col. 1205.
58. N. Phillipson, 'Lawyers, Landowners and Civic Leadership of Post-Union Scotland', *Juridical Review*, 1976, 101–6; 'The Social Structure of the Faculty of Advocates 1661–1840, in A. Harding (ed.), *Law-making and Law-makers in British History* (London, 1980), 155–6.
59. Phillipson, 'Lawyers', 97–9.
60. Quoted in L. de la Torre, *The Heir of Douglas* (London, 1953), 186.
61. J.C. Watt, *John Inglis, Lord Justice-General of Scotland* (Edinburgh, 1893), 55.
62. R.L. Orr, *Lord Guthrie, a memoir* (London, 1923), 29.
63. A.T. Innes, *Report of Trustee Case in the Court of Session* (Edinburgh, 1878), 82. I am indebted to Professor Kenneth Reid for this reference.
64. A.D. Gibb, *Law from over the Border* (Edinburgh, 1955), 61.
65. C. Guthrie, 'Lord Young', *Juridical Review* (1907), 9.
66. Cockburn, *Jeffrey*, I, 327, II, 231.
67. This episode led to the development of the note exchange as a mechanism of control, preventing major bankruptcies till the end of the old Scottish banking system in 1845; see *supra* and NAS, Melville Papers, GD 51/5/167, Gordon of Invergordon Papers, GD 235/8/4/12; Public Record Office 30/8/157/2/208.
68. Quoted in T.M. Cooper, *Selected Papers* (Edinburgh, 1955), 49 *et seq.*
69. J.J. Brown, 'The Social, Political and Economic Influences of the Edinburgh Merchant Elite', unpublished PhD thesis, University of Edinburgh 1985, 111.
70. See C. Gross & C. Hall, *Select Cases concerning the Law Merchant 1239–1633* (Selden Society, 1908–32).

71. P.L. Payne, *The Early Scottish Limited Companies 1856–1895* (Edinburgh, 1980), 66.

72. For the industrial consequences, see above, 52.

73. *Session Cases 1915 (House of Lords)*, 65; *Juridical Review*, XXVI, 385.

74. J.F. Macqueen, *Reports of Scotch Appeals and Writs of Error* (Edinburgh, 1858), III, 265.

6 Region: 'Confidence and capacity'

1. R. Michie, *Money, Mania and Markets, investment, company formation and the stock exchange in nineteenth-century Scotland* (Edinburgh, 1981), 93–4.

2. *Aberdeen Herald*, 22 March 1845.

3. W.H. Fraser, 'Politics before 1918', in W.H. Fraser & C.H. Lee, *Aberdeen 1800–2000, a new history* (East Linton, 2000), 178.

4. See above, 15 *et seq.*

5. R.J. Morris, 'Urbanisation and Scotland', in W.H. Fraser & R.J. Morris, *People and Society in Scotland, II, 1830–1914* (Edinburgh, 1990), 73–102.

6. J.R. Coull, 'The Historical Geography of Aberdeen', *Scottish Geographical Magazine*, LXXIII (1963), 86–8.

7. Fraser & Lee, *Aberdeen 1800–2000*, 34, 91–2, 105–8, 158–9.

8. Ibid., 47, 75, 81–2.

9. C. Carter, *Alexander MacDonald 1837–1884, Aberdeen art collector* (Aberdeen, 1963), 5–8; I.M Harrower, *John Forbes White* (Edinburgh, 1918), 55–71.

10. D. Masson, *Memories of Two Cities, Edinburgh and Aberdeen* (Edinburgh, 1911), 193; J.G. Smith, 'The Growth of the City', in Fraser & Lee, *Aberdeen*, 25.

11. P.L. Payne, *Studies in Scottish Business History* (London, 1967), 519–29; D.S. Macmillan, 'The Transfer of Company Control from Scotland to London in the Nineteenth Century: the case of the Scottish Australian Company, 1853', *Business History*, XII (1970), 102–15.

12. G.S. Fraser, *A Stranger and Afraid, the autobiography of an intellectual* (Manchester, 1983), 37–8.

13. I.G.C. Hutchison, 'Elite Society', in Fraser & Lee, *Aberdeen 1800–2000*, 374.

14. *Report of the Select Committee on Petitions from the Royal Burghs of Scotland*, PP VI 1819, 21.

15. Ibid., 22–7.

16. Fraser, 'Politics', in Fraser & Lee, *Aberdeen 1800–2000*, 177–83.

17. A.A. MacLaren, *Religion and Social Class, the Disruption years in Aberdeen* (1974), 69–99, 218–20.

18. M. Angus, *Sheriff Watson of Aberdeen* (Aberdeen, 1913), 161.

19. PP 1842 XXVIII, *Sanitary Condition of the Labouring Population, local reports for Scotland*, 293.
20. Ibid., 294.
21. *Fifth Report, Aberdeen House of Industry and Refuge 1840–1841*, 5.
22. G. Morton, 'Identity out of Place', in T. Griffiths & G. Morton (eds), *A History of Everyday Life in Scotland 1800–1900* (Edinburgh, 2010), 266.
23. H. Cockburn, *Circuit Journeys* (Edinburgh, 1889), 210.
24. See above, 32–3.
25. E. Gauldie, *One Artful and Ambitious Individual: Alexander Riddoch 1745–1822* (Dundee, 1989).
26. J. Gifford, *Buildings of Scotland: Dundee and Angus* (London & New Haven, CT, 2012).
27. M. Watson, *Jute and Flax Mills In Dundee* (Tayport, 1990), 139.
28. B.P. Lenman, *Dundee and its Textile Industry 1850–1914* (Dundee, 1969), 83.
29. C.A. Whatley, 'The Making of Juteopolis – and how it was', in C.A. Whatley (ed.), *The Remaking of Juteopolis,* (Dundee, 1992), 12.
30. E. Gauldie, *The Dundee Textile Industry 1790–1885, from the papers of Peter Carmichael of Arthurstone* (Edinburgh, 1969), 16.
31. L.J. Murray, *A Zest for Life, the story of Alexander Keiller* (Swindon, 1999).
32. J. Grimond, *Memoirs* (London, 1979), 25.
33. A. Smith, D.B. Swinfen, C.A. Whatley, *The Life and Times of Dundee* (Edinburgh, 1993), 104.
34. D. Lennox, 'Working-Class Life in Dundee for Twenty-five Years 1878–1903', unpublished MS, Dundee University Library, MS 15/28, 213.
35. M.L. Walker & M. Wilson, 'Housing Conditions,' in Dundee Social Union, *Report on Housing and Industrial Conditions and Medical Inspection of School Children* (Dundee, 1905), 1, 3.29.
36. Ibid., 16, 7.
37. Ibid., 18, 21, 28.
38. A.M. Carstairs, *The Tayside Industrial Population 1911–1951* (Dundee, 1974), 33.
39. V. Wright, 'Juteopolis and After, woman and work in twentieth-century Dundee', in J. Tomlinson & C. Whatley, *Jute No More* (Dundee, 2011), 132–3.
40. Walker, 'Employment', 53.
41. C.T. Parsons, *Report on the Condition of Children . . . in Scotland*, PP 1910 Cmnd. 5075, III, 32–4.
42. Ibid., 48.
43. W. Sutherland, *Social Questions in Scotland* (Glasgow, 1910), 13.
44. R. D'Arcy Thompson, *D'Arcy Wentworth Thompson* (London, 1958), 69.
45. *Census of Scotland 1901*, PP 1904 CVIII.

46. I. Donnachie, *History of the Brewing Industry in Scotland* (Edinburgh, 1979), 148, 237–45.

47. H. Cockburn, *Letter to the Lord Provost on the Best Ways of Spoiling Edinburgh* (Edinburgh, 1849), 5.

48. H.D. Littlejohn, *Report on the Sanitary Condition of the City of Edinburgh* (Edinburgh, 1865), 19; F. McManus, 'Public Health Administration in Edinburgh 1833–1879', unpublished M. Litt. thesis, University of Edinburgh, 1984, 3–6; P.J. Smith, 'The Foul Burns of Edinburgh', *Scottish Geographical Magazine*, XCI (1975), 25 *et seq.*

49. H. Cockburn, *Memorials of his Time,* (Edinburgh, 1856), 86, 95.

50. E. Grant, *Memoirs of a Highland Lady* (Edinburgh, 1988), II, 103.

51. NAS, Melville Papers. GD 51/5/603/2, 612, 51/5/623. 51/5/749/2, 375.

52. J. Gifford, C. McWilliam & D. Walker, *Buildings of Scotland: Edinburgh* (London, 1984), 222–3.

53. J. Clark, *Life of James Begg* (Edinburgh, n.d.), 7.

54. W. Chambers, *The Lord Provost's Statement to the Town Council respecting Sanitary Improvements* (Edinburgh, 1865), 5–9; *City Improvements* (Edinburgh, 1866), 12–16.

55. C. Withers, 'The Demographic History of the City', in W.H. Fraser & I. Mavor (eds), *Glasgow, II, 1830–1912* (Manchester, 1996), ch. 4.

56. D.G. Barrie, *Police in the Age of Improvement, police development and the civic tradition in Scotland* (Cullompton, 2008), 157 *et seq.*

57. M. Mackay, *Sermon occasioned by the Lamented Death of the late Kirkman Finlay* (Glasgow, 1842); Anon., *Glasgow Reminiscences, memoir of the late James Ewing* (Glasgow,1854); M. Higg, A. Riches & E. Williamson, *The Buildings of Scotland: Glasgow* (London, 1990), 178.

58. W.H. Fraser, *Chartism in Scotland* (Pontypool, 2010), 132 *et seq.*

59. PP XXVIII 1842, 186–8, 190–1.

60. Ibid., 189.

61. Ibid., 165.

62. *Report of the Select Committee on Handloom Weavers' Petitions*, PP 1834 X, Q166. The lord provosts meant by the witness were Henry Monteith 1814–16 and 1818–20, and Robert Dalglish 1830–2.

63. *Tait's Edinburgh Magazine*, supplementary no. for 1834, 788.

64. *Glasgow Herald,* 10 October 1856.

65. C.M. Allan, 'The Genesis of British Urban Redevelopment with special reference to Glasgow', *Economic History Review*, XVIII (1965), 602 *et seq.*

66. *Royal Commission on the Housing of the Industrial Population of Scotland, Rural and Urban*, PP 1917–18 cmnd 8731, minutes of evidence, para. 794; *Reports from Assistant Commissioners on Handloom Weavers,* PP 1839 I, 93.

67. PP 1917–8 cmnd 8731, para 806.
68. G. Best, 'The Scottish Victorian City', *Victorian Studies*, XI (1968), 332 *et seq.*
69. W. Smart, 'The Municipal Industries of Glasgow', *Proceedings of the Philosophical Society of Glasgow*, XXXVI (1894–5), 36.
70. S.G. Checkland, *The Upas Tree, Glasgow 1875–1975* (Glasgow, 1976), 29.
71. E. Gauldie, *Cruel Habitations, a history of working-class housing* (London, 1974), 86.
72. A. Kay, *The Housing Problem in Glasgow* (Glasgow, 1902).
73. W. Smart, *The Housing Problem and the Municipality* (Glasgow, 1902), 19.
74. J.R. Russell, 'On the "Ticketed Houses" of Glasgow, with an interrogation of the facts for guidance towards the amelioration of the lives of the inhabitants', *Proceedings of the Philosophical Society of Glasgow*, XX (1888–9), 1–24.
75. W. Smart, *Economic Journal*, X (1900), 93–4.

7 Poverty: 'The worst of any'

1. PP XXVIII 1847, *Annual Report of the Board of Supervision 1845–1846,* app. C, no. 6, 39–40.
2. Ibid., 41.
3. *Extracts from the Records of the Burgh of Edinburgh*, eds. J.D. Marwick et al., (1869–), IV, 48.
4. R.A. Cage, *The Scottish Poor Law 1745–1845* (Edinburgh, 1981), ch. 1.
5. R. Mitchison, *The Old Poor Law in Scotland* (Edinburgh, 2000), ch. 7.
6. Cage, *Scottish Poor Law*, 5–9.
7. Mitchison, *Old Poor Law*, 28, 43, 47, 72, 83, 103.
8. *Poor Law Inquiry (Scotland)*, PP 1844 XXI, 241, 284, XXII, 441, 861.
9. *Faculty Decisions*, Dec. 29, 1821.
10. A.A. Cormack, *Poor Relief in Scotland* (Aberdeen, 1923), 84.
11. Edinburgh City Archives, minutes of the Edinburgh charity workhouse, 'Categories for admission', April 14, 1743.
12. Ch. 29.
13. M.R.G. Fry, *Edinburgh, a history of the city* (London, 2009), 244–5.
14. NLS, Lee Papers, MS 341, f.300.
15. PP 1842 XXVIII, *Sanitary Condition of the Labouring Population, local reports for Scotland*, 165
16. Ibid., 176.
17. E. Chadwick, *Report on the Sanitary Condition of the Labouring Population of Great Britain* (London, 1842), 99
18. S.J. Brown, *Thomas Chalmers and the Godly Commonwealth in Scotland* (Oxford, 1982), ch. 2.

19. 'Connexion between the Extension of the Church and the Extinction of Pauperism', *Edinburgh Review,* XXVIII, 1817, 24–5.

20. Brown, *Chalmers,* ch. 4.

21. Mitchison, *Old Poor Law,* is notable here.

22. See M. Blaug, 'The Myth of the Old Poor Law and in the Making of the New', *Journal of Economic History,* XXIII, 1963, 151–84; M.E. Rose, *The English Poor Law 1780–1930* (Newton Abbot, 1971); L.H. Lees, *The Solidarities of Strangers, the English Poor Laws and the people 1770–1848* (Cambridge, 1998).

23. The novels of James Kelman give graphic insights into this world – not that I expect Kelman would have agreed with Chalmers.

24. *New Statistical Account,* II, 220–1; W. Stark, *Considerations addressed to the Heritors and Kirk Sessions of Scotland . . . on certain Questions connected with the Administration of the Affairs of the Poor* (Edinburgh, 1826), 1, 15–19.

25. G.J.C. Duncan, *Memoir of the Revd Henry Duncan* (Edinburgh, 1848), 160.

26. H. Cockburn, *Letters on the Affairs of Scotland* (London, 1874), 35.

27. *Parliamentary Debates,* n.s., XIX, cols, 1034, 1369; R. Mitchison, 'The Making of the Old Scottish Poor Law', *Past and Present,* XLIII, 1974, 59; 'The Creation of the Disablement Rule in the Scottish Poor Law, in T.C. Smout (ed.), *The Search for Wealth and Stability* (London, 1979), 207; 'The Poor Law', in T.M. Devine & R. Mitchison, *People and Society in Scotland, I, 1760–1830,* 261–5; Cage, *Poor Law,* 119.

28. P. Shaw (ed.), *Cases decided in the Court of Session* (Edinburgh, 1828), VI, 738, *Watson v. Ancrum kirk session,* March 7, 1828.

29. W.H. Fraser & I. Maver, *Glasgow, II, 1832–1912* (Manchester, 1966), 433.

30. A. Alison, *Some Account of my Life and Writings* (Edinburgh, 1883), I, 458.

31. W.P. Alison, *Observations on the Management of the Poor in Scotland* (Edinburgh, 1840), 123.

32. *The Scotsman,* 26 September 1840.

33. T.C. Smout, 'The Strange Intervention of Edward Twistleton: Paisley in Depression 1841–1843', in T.C. Smout (ed.), *The Search for Wealth and Stability* (London, 1979), 226–37.

34. D. Murray, *Reminiscences of Sixty Years in the History of Paisley* (Paisley, 1855).

35. Public Record Office, Home Office Papers, 4 July 1842.

36. *Report from Her Majesty's Commissioners for Inquiring into the Poor Laws in Scotland,* PP 1844 XX, xiv.

37. NLS, Melville Papers, MS 642, f. 299.

38. H. Hunter (ed.), *Thomas Chalmers, problems of poverty* (London, 1912), 370.

39. *Annual Report of the Board of Supervision 1845–6,* PP XXVIII 1847, appendix C, no. 6.

40. 'Circular as to Poorhouses; February 2, 1850', in app, *Fifth Annual Report of the Board of Supervision* (Edinburgh, 1850).

41. R.P. Lamond, *The Scottish Poor Laws, their history, policy and operation* (Glasgow, 1892), 56–7.

42. *Glasgow Herald*, 7 & 8 August 1868, 15 & 16 September 1869.

43. The two cases were *Thomson v. Lindsay* and *M'William v. Maxwell Adams, Session Cases 1849*, nos. 131 & 132.

44. J.H. Treble, *Urban Poverty in Britain* (London, 1979), ch. 4.

45. Report by D.H.D. Littlehohn and Dr J.B. Russell on Glasgow City Poorhouse, 20 September 1897, Mitchell Library G362/5.

46. *Report of Committee appointed to Enquire into the Condition and Management of St Cuthbert's Poorhouse*, NAS, Board of Supervision minute book, Nov. 25, 1847, HH 23/2,

47. Board of Supervision minute book, 17 February 1870, HH 23/14; 7 February 1872, HH 23/15.

48. PP 1878–9, XXX, *Annual Report of the Board of Supervision 1878–1879*, app. A, no. 4, 11.

49. *Report of the Royal Commission on the Poor Law and Relief of Distress*, PP XXXVII 1909, minutes, VI, 881.

50. Ibid., 9; and *Report*, vol. 1 (majority report), 34.

51. M.A. Crowther, 'Poverty. Health and Welfare' in W.H. Fraser & R.J. Morris, *People and Society in Scotland, II, 1830–1914* (Edinburgh, 1990), 271.

52. *Statement by the Chairman of the Board of Supervision respecting the 'Bill for the further amendment and better administration of the laws relating to the relief of the poor in Scotland'*, HMSO 1872, 4.

53. L. Walsh, *Patrons, Poverty and Profit, organised charity in nineteenth-century Dundee* (Dundee, 2000), 14–15.

54. O. Checkland, *Philanthropy in Victorian Scotland* (Edinburgh, 1980), 208.

55. M. Bain et al., 'Why is mortality higher in Scotland than in England and Wales?', *British Medical Journal*, XXVII (2005), 199–204.

56. University of Glasgow Archives, National Health Service Greater Glasgow and Clyde Archives, GB 812 HB 3–4, 6, 8, 10–11, 13–14, 17, 22–3, 25, 36, 42, 44–5, 47–8, 50, 65, 73, 79, 81, 90; HH 66–7. See also O. Checkland & M. Lamb, *Health Care as History, the Glasgow case* (Aberdeen, 1982).

57. H. Kerr, 'Edinburgh', in A. Bosanquet (ed.), *Social Conditions in Provincial Towns* (London, 1912), 56–7.

58. NLS, Melville Papers, MS 642, f. 299; Ellice Papers, MS 15013, f. 161; T. Ferguson, *The Dawn of Scottish Social Welfare* (London, 1948), 194 *et seq.*; I. Levitt & T.C. Smout, *The State of the Scottish Working Class in 1843* (Edinburgh, 1979), 173–4.

59. *Report of the Royal Commission on the Poor Law and Relief of Distress*, PP XXXVIII 1909, 288 *et seq.*

60. Ibid., 82.

61. For the sequel, see C.M.M. Macdonald, *Whaur Extremes Meet* (Edinburgh, 2009), 136–40.

8 Race: 'Raising a pig'

1. Apparently he cannot be precise about the date, and thinks it might have been in 1845; C.J. Guthrie & D.K. Guthrie, *Memoir of Thomas Guthrie* (London, 1877), 441.

2. Ibid., 438.

3. J. Gifford, C. McWilliam & D. Walker, *The Buildings of Scotland: Edinburgh* (London, 1984), 192.

4. Guthrie & Guthrie, *Guthrie*, 447.

5. Gifford, McWilliam & Walker, *Buildings*, 317.

6. Guthrie & Guthrie, *Guthrie*, 687.

7. C. Prunier, *Anti-catholic Strategies in Nineteenth-century Scotland* (Frankfurt-am-Main & Oxford, 2004).

8. B. Collins, 'The Origins of Irish Immigration to Scotland in the Nineteenth and Twentieth Centuries', in T.M. Devine (ed.), *Irish Immigrants and Scottish Society in the Nineteenth and Twentieth Centuries* (Edinburgh, 1991), 1 *et seq.*

9. J.E. Handley, *The Irish in Modern Scotland* (Cork, 1943), 3–26.

10. Ibid., 27–41.

11. [J.R. McCulloch], 'Commercial Revulsions', *Edinburgh Review*, LXXXVII, 1826, 223–49.

12. *Glasgow Herald*, 11 June 1847.

13. J. Stark, *Report on the Mortality of Edinburgh and Leith* (Edinburgh, 1846–8), III, 128.

14. *Glasgow Evening Post*, 23 July 1831.

15. A.B. Campbell, *The Lanarkshire Miners, a social history of their trade unions 1775–1874* (Edinburgh, 1970), 183, 317–18; J.E. Handley, *The Irish in Modern Scotland* (Cork, 1947), 117 *et seq.*; E. MacFarland, *Protestants First, Orangeism in nineteenth-century Scotland* (Edinburgh, 1990), 64, 153; W.S. Marshall, *The Billy Boys, a concise history of Orangeism in Scotland* (Edinburgh, 1996), 34–7.

16. W. Matthews, 'The Egyptians in Scotland, the political history of a myth', *Viator*, I (1970), 289–306; John of Fordun, *Chronica Gentis Scotorum*, ed. W.F. Skene (Edinburgh, 1871); Andrew of Wyntoun, *The Orygynale Cronykil of Scotland*, ed. D. Laing (Edinburgh, 1872–9); M.J. Drexler, 'Attitudes to

Nationality in Scottish Historical Writing from Barbour to Bruce', unpublished PhD thesis, University of Edinburgh, 1979, 142–3.

17. C. Kidd, *Subverting Scotland's Past, Scottish Whig historians and the creation of an Anglo-British identity 1689–1830* (Cambridge, 1993), ch. 5.

18. H.R. Trevor-Roper, 'The Gaelic connection: the Highlands, Ireland and nationalism 1873–1922', in E. Hobsbawm, & T. Ranger (eds), *The Invention of Tradition* (Cambridge, 1993); S. Manning, 'Ossian, Scott and nineteenth-century Scottish literary nationalism', *Studies in Scottish Literature*, XVII (1972); D. McCrone, *Understanding Scotland, the sociology of a stateless nation* (London, 1992), ch. 7; J. Hunter, P. Scott, L. Paterson & A. Noble, 'Ossian and After, the politics of tartanry', *Bulletin of Scottish Politics*, II (1981).

19. J. Hunter, 'The Gaelic Connection: the Highlands, Ireland and nationalism 1873–1922', *Scottish Historical Review*, LIV (1975); R.J. Finlay, *Independent and Free, Scottish politics and the origins of the Scottish National Party 1918–1945* (Edinburgh, 1994), ch. 2.

20. P. Womack, *Improvement and Romance, constructing the myth of the Scottish Highlands* (Houndmills, 1989); J. Prebble, *The King's Jaunt: George IV in Scotland 1822* (London, 1988).

21. D. Hume, 'Of National Character', in *Essays, Moral, Political and Literary* (Edinburgh, 1753), I, xxi.1.

22. H. Home, Lord Kames, *Sketches on the History of Man* (Edinburgh, 1734).

23. Ch. 32.

24. Ch. 44.

25. *The Journal of Sir Walter Scott*, ed. W.E.K. Anderson (Oxford, 1972), 5–6.

26. O.D. Edwards, *Burke and Hare* (Edinburgh, 1984), ch. 6.

27. Ibid., ch. 8.

28. H.J.C. Grierson (ed.), *The Letters of Sir Walter Scott*, (London, 1932–7), XI, 108.

29. *Journal*, 574–7, 608.

30. I. Rae, *Knox the Anatomist* (Edinburgh & London, 1964), 50–104; S. Collinson, 'Robert Knox's Anatomy of Race', *History Today*, XL (1990), 44.

31. R. Knox, *The Races of Men* (London, 1850), 6.

32. C. Kidd, 'Teutonist ethnology and Scottish nationalist inhibition 1780–1880, *Scottish Historical Review*, LXXIV (1995), 45–68; 'Race, empire and the limits of nineteenth-century Scottish nationhood, *Historical Journal*, XLVI (2003), 873–92.

33. M.R.G. Fry, *Wild Scots, four hundred years of Highland history* (London, 2005), ch. 1.

34. Knox, *Races*, 212–3.

35. Ibid., 213–14.

36. Ibid., 58.

37. Ibid., 18.

38. Ibid., 13.

39. Ibid., 19.

40. Ibid., 15.

41. Ibid., 53–4.

42. Ibid., 41–3.

43. Knox, 27.

44. T. Carlyle, *Chartism* (London, 1840), 28–9.

45. *The Collected Letter of Thomas and Jane Carlyle,* ed. C.R. Sanders (London & Durham NC, 1970–), III, 191–4.

46. Carlyle, *Chartism*, 178–9.

47. Ibid., xix.

48. *The Times,* 3 May 1912.

49. H. Mackinder, *Britain and the British Seas* (London, 1906), v, preface to the second edition.

50. Ibid., 182–91.

51. H. MacDougall, *Racial Myth in English History* (Montreal & Hanover NH, 1984).

52. Plato, *The Laws*, XI; Aristotle, *Nicomachaean Ethics*, III. 7; Livy, *Ab Urbe Condita,* V. 36; Tacitus, *De Vita et Moribus Julii Agricolae*, §30.

53. J.S. Blackie, 'Scottish Nationality', in *Essays on Subjects of Moral and Social Interest* (Edinburgh, 1890), 173–4.

54. J.S. Blackie, *The Language and Literature of the Scottish Highlands* (Edinburgh, 1876), 23.

55. J. Hunter, 'The Gaelic Connection: the Highlands, Ireland and nationalism', *Scottish Historical Review*, LIV (1975); H. Hanham, *Scottish Nationalism* (Edinburgh, 1969), 40.

56. D. Mackinnon, *University of Edinburgh Celtic Chair, inaugural address* (Edinburgh, 1883), 7.

57. W. Sharp, *Lyra Celtica* (Edinburgh, 1896), li.

58. J.F. Campbell, *Popular Tales of the West Highlands*, 4 vols (Paisley, 1890), II, i.

59. Both in A. Lang, *The Orange Fairy Book* (London, 1906).

60. W.A. Craigie, 'Gaelic Words and Names in the Icelandic Sagas', *Zeitschrift für celtische Philologie,* I (1897), 439–54.

61. *Oxford Dictionary of National Biography*, eds. H.C.G. Matthew & B. Harrison (Oxford, 2004), XIII, 968.

62. M. Chapman, *The Gaelic Vision in Scottish Culture* (London, 1978), 81–7; E. Condry, 'Culture and Identity in the Scottish Highlands', unpublished D. Phil. Thesis, University of Oxford, 1980; P. Sims-Williams, 'The Visionary Celt, the construction of an ethnic preconception', *Cambridge Medieval Celtic*

Studies, XI (1986); V. Durkacz, *The Decline of the Celtic Languages* (Edinburgh, 1983), 201–2.

63. K.J. Obrátil (ed.), *Masarykova Cetinka* (Brno, 1920); A. Kowalczykowa, *Pilsudski i tradycja* (Chotomów, 1991).

64. For the sequel, see C.M.M. Macdonald, *Whaur Extremes Meet, Scotland's twentieth century* (Edinburgh, 2009), 279–80.

9 Sex: 'The walls of prejudice'

1. F. Chopin, *Letters,* ed. H. Opienski & E.L. Voynich (New York, 1988), 375.

2. Ibid., 376, 395.

3. Ibid., 383.

4. A.E. Bone, *Jane Wilhelmina Stirling 1804–1859* (Chipstead, 1980), 69 *et seq.*

5. For Scottish women in the twentieth century, see C.M.M. Macdonald, *Whaur Extremes Meet* (Edinburgh, 2009), 159–67.

6. E. Richards, *The Leviathan of Wealth* (London & Toronto, 1973), 7.

7. Ibid., 8.

8. R.J. Adam (ed.), *Papers on Sutherland Estate Management 1802–1816* (Edinburgh, 1972), 16, 26.

9. NAS, Sutherland Papers, GD 258/215, 593.

10. I. Carter, *Farm Life in North-east Scotland 1840–1914* (Edinburgh, 1979), 76–97; A. Blaikie, *Illegitimacy, Sex and Society, north-east Scotland 1750–1900* (Oxford, 1993), 52–8.

11. A. Blaikie, *Illegitimacy, Sex and Society*, 40.

12. W.W.J. Knox, *Lives of Scottish Women* (Edinburgh, 2006), 98–100.

13. C. Young, 'Middle-class Culture, Law and Gender Identity: married women's property legislation in Scotland 1850–1920', in A. Kidd & D. Nicholls (eds), *Gender, Civic Culture and Consumerism, middle-class identity in Britain 1800–1940* (Manchester, 1999), 138–42.

14. B. Griffin, 'Class, Gender and Liberalism in Parliament 1868–1882, the case of the Married Women's Property Acts', *Historical Journal,* XLVI (2005), 81.

15. *Cases decided in the Court of Session*, 1866–7, IV, *Smith v. Smith*, no. 61, 279–83.

16. *Cases decided in the Court of Session*, 1867–8, VI, *Chalmers v. Chalmers,* no. 97, 547–53.

17. *Cases decided in the Court of Session*, 1878–9, VI, *McDougall v. City of Glasgow Bank*, 1089–96.

18. *Cases decided in the Court of Session*, 1865–6, IV, *Dunlop v. Johnston*, 1867, no. 61, 279–83.

19. *Cases decided in the Court of Session*, 1874–5, II, *Menzies v. Murray,* no. 95, 520.

20. Ibid., 507.

21. *Cases decided in the Court of Session*, 1891–2, XIX, *Anderson v. Anderson's Trustee*, no. 4, 18–25.

22. W.P. Paterson & D. Watson, *Social Evils and Problems* (Edinburgh, 1918), 95–104.

23. S. Nenadic, 'The Small Family Firm in Victorian Britain', *Business History*, XXXV (1993), 86–114.

24. S. Nenadic, 'The Victorian Middle Classes', in W.H. Fraser & I. Maver (eds), *Glasgow, II, 1830–1912* (Manchester, 1996), 270–1; H. Corr, 'The Sexual Division of Labour in the Scottish Teaching Profession 1872–1914', in W.M. Humes & H.M Paterson (eds), *Scottish Culture and Scottish Education* (Edinburgh, 1983), 137–50.

25. R.G. Wilson, *Disillusionment or New Opportunities? The changing nature of work in offices, Glasgow 1880–1914* (Aldershot, 1998), 37.

26. Quoted in H. Corr, 'The Schoolgirl's Curriculum and the Ideology of the Home 1870–1914', in Anon., *Uncharted Lives, extracts from Scottish Womsn's Experiences 1850–1982* (Glasgow, 1983), 78.

27. E. King, *The Scottish Women's Suffrage Movement* (Glasgow, 1982), 10 *et seq.*

28. *The Scotsman*, 29 August 1913.

29. Lady F. Balfour, *Dr Elsie Inglis* (London, 1920).

30. S. Hamilton, 'The First Generation of University Women 1869–1930', in G. Donaldson (ed.), *Four Centuries, Edinburgh university life 1583–1983* (Edinburgh, 1983); L.R. Moore, 'The Aberdeen Ladies Educational Association 1877–1883', *Northern Scotland*, III, 1977.

31. *Blackwood's Edinburgh Magazine*, LXXV (1869), 782.

32. S. Jex-Blake, *Medical Women, a thesis and a history* (Edinburgh, 1886), 92.

33. G.M. Ritchie, 'The Medical Topography of Neilston', *Glasgow Medical Journal*, I (1828), 26.

34. PP 1843 LXI, *Accounts and Papers*, no. 27.

35. PP 1833 XX, *Factory Inquiry Commission, first report on the employment of children in factories*, 20.

36. E. Gordon, *Women and the Labour Movement in Scotland* (Oxford, 1991), 22.

37. R. Duncan, *Textiles and Toil, the factory system and the industrial working class in the early nineteenth century* (Aberdeen, 1985), 9.

38. PP XXXVII 1893, *Report of the Royal Commission on Labour*, I, 194.

39. B. Kay, *Odyssey, voices from Scotland's recent past* (Edinburgh, 1980), 38.

40. K. Durland, *Among the Fife Miners* (London, 1904), 116.

41. Ibid., 118.

42. I. Levitt & C. Smout, *The State of the Scottish Working Class in 1843* (Edinburgh, 1979), 78.

43. I.F. Grant, *Highland Folk Ways* (London, 1961), 168.

44. E. Gordon, 'Women's Spheres', in W.H. Fraser & R.J. Morris, *People and Society in Scotland, II, 1830–1914* (Edinburgh, 1990), 214.

45. PP 1890 XV *Return of the Rates of Wages in the Minor Textile Trades of the United Kingdom*, viii; PP 1887 VII, *Return of Wages 1830–1886*, 58, 310.

46. PP 1910 XL, *Royal Commission on the Poor Laws and Relief of Distress*, report on Scotland, appendix, vol. 6, minutes of evidence, 392.

47. W.H. Fraser & I. Maver, 'The Social Problems of the City', in W.H. Fraser & I. Maver (eds), *Glasgow. II, 1830–1912* (Manchester, 1996), 380.

48. L. Jamieson, 'Rural and Urban Women in Domestic Service', in E. Gordon & E. Breitenbach (eds), *The World is Ill Divided, women's work in Scotland in the nineteenth and early twentieth centuries* (Edinburgh, 1990), 137; Gordon, *Women and the Labour Movement*, 25, table 1.4,

49. L. Jamieson, 'Growing Up in Scotland in the 1900s', in *Uncharted Lives, extracts from Scottish women's experiences* (Glasgow, 1983), 27.

50. P. Horn, *The Rise and Fall of the Victorian Servant* (Stroud, 1996), 188.

51. *Census of Scotland 1871, 1881,* servants working in the county of Edinburgh, table ix; J. Merchant, 'The Maidservant and the Female Labour Market in Late Victorian and Edwardian Dundee', unpublished PhD thesis, University of Dundee (1998), 158–77.

52. NLS, broadside: 'Important Strike of the Maidservants of Edinburgh', March 9, 1840, LC 1268; J. Merchant, 'An Insurrection of Maids, domestic servants and the agitation of 1872', in B. Harris, L. Miskell & C.A. Whatley, *Victorian Dundee, image and realities* (East Linton, 2000), 104–21.

53. M.A. Simpson, 'The West End of Glasgow 1830–1914', in M.A. Simpson, & T.H. Lloyd, *Middle Class Housing in Britain* (Newton Abbot, 1977), 83; L. Davidoff, *Worlds Between, historical perspective on gender and class* (Oxford, 1995), 22.

54. J, Merchant, 'Insurrection', 107.

55. W. Walker, *Juteopolis, Dundee and its textile workers* (Edinburgh, 1979), 148.

56. C.A. Whatley, D.B. Swinfen & A. Smith, *The Life and Times of Dundee* (Edinburgh, 1993), 123.

57. Aberdeen Ladies' Union, *Annual Report*, 1891.

58. Gordon, *Women and the Labour Movement*, 20, 142.

59. D. Lennox, 'Working Class Life in Dundee for 25 Years 1878–1903', Dundee University Archives MS 15/28, 169.

60. W.H. Fraser, 'The Working Class', in Fraser & Maver, *Glasgow*, 323–4.

61. W. Creech, *Letters respecting the Mode of Living, Trade, Manners and Literature of Edinburgh in 1763 and the Present Period,* (Edinburgh, 1792), 18; *Report on the State of the Edinburgh Magdalene Asylum for 1806* (Edinburgh, 1806), 1–5.

62. *Report from the Directors of the Edinburgh Magdalene Asylum for 1830, 1831 and 1832* (Edinburgh, 1833), 20.

63. G. Bell, *Day and Night in the Wynds of Edinburgh* (Edinburgh, 1849), 23–6.

64. W. Tait, *Magdalenism* (Edinburgh, 1842), 5–9, 59, 193–6, 258.

65. I. Bird, *Notes on Old Edinburgh* (Edinburgh, 1869), 22.

66. S. Macgill, *A Sermon delivered at Glasgow . . . on the Opening of the Magdalene Asylum* (Glasgow, 1815).

67. L. Mahood, *The Magdalenes, prostitution in the nineteenth century* (London, 1990), 130–4.

68. J.R. Kellett, *Railways and Victorian Cities* (London, 1979), 217–18.

69. 'Shadow', *Midnight Scenes and Social Photographs* (Glasgow, 1858), 49.

70. Ibid., 126.

71. *The Moral Statistics of Glasgow in 1863* (Glasgow, 1864), 152–9.

72. W. Watson, *Pauperism, Vagrancy, Crime and Industrial Education in Aberdeenshire 1840–1875* (Aberdeen, 1877), 12–14.

73. R.L. Stevenson, *Collected Poems*, ed. J. Adam Smith (London, 1971), 82.

74. R.L. Stevenson, *New Poems,* ed. G. Hellman (London, 1918), 34.

75. NLS, Sir Graham Balfour Papers, MS 9897, f. 375.

10 Despotism: 'The bad old school'

1. H. Cockburn, *Journal* (Edinburgh 1874), I, 265.

2. M.R.G. Fry, *The Dundas Despotism* (Edinburgh, 1992), 201–4, 249–50.

3. Cockburn, *Journal*, I, 266.

4. Fry, *Dundas Despotism,* ch. 1.

5. Ibid., ch. 8.

6. Ibid., chs. 9 & 10.

7. Ibid., 382–4.

8. Ibid., 31.

9. Scottish Representative Peers Act 1707, 6 Ann c. 78.

10. D.R. Fisher, 'Scotland', in R.G. Thorne (ed.), *The House of Commons 1790–1820* (London, 1986), I, 70–99.

11. J. Fergusson, 'Making Interest in Scottish County Elections', *Scottish Historical Review,* XXVI, (1947), 119–33.

12. NAS, Melville Papers, GD 51/2/198/26/42.

13. *Parliamentary Debates*, new series, XV, col. 169.

14. See above, 127–8.

15. H. Cockburn, 'The Office of Lord Advocate in Scotland', *Edinburgh Review,* XXXIX (1821), 363–76; J. Innes, 'Legislating for Three Kingdoms: how the Westminster Parliament legislated for England, Scotland and Ireland 1707–1830', in J. Hoppit, *Parliaments, Nations and Identities in Britain and Ireland 1660–1850* (Manchester, 2002), 23 *et seq.*; J. Hoppit, 'The Landed Interest

and the National Interest', in Hoppit, *Parliaments, Nations and Identities*, 91 *et seq.*

16. *Parliamentary Debates*, II, 1804, cols. 797–803.

17. L. Paterson, *The Autonomy of Modern Scotland* (Edinburgh, 1994), ch. 5.

18. NAS, Home Office Papers RH 2/4/129/329.

19. British Library, Liverpool Papers, Add MSS 38269, f. 306; Peel Papers, Add MSS 40312, ff. 89–96; Boyle Papers, Kelburn, Ayrshire, 9/14/16, 9/31/2–7.

20. British Library, Liverpool Papers Add MSS 38276, f. 354.

21. British Library, Liverpool Papers Add MSS 38277, f. 243; NAS, Dalhousie Muniments GD 45/3/330; Melville Papers, GD 51/1/182, 5/479/1, 7, 129, 220; NLS, Melville Papers MS 9, f. 276; National Maritime Museum, MS 9441 MEL 103; R. Fulford & L. Strachey (eds), *The Grenville Memoirs 1814–1860* (London, 1938), I, 219; A. Youngson, *The Making of Classical Edinburgh* (Edinburgh, 1966), 88, 135; J.S. Gibson, *The Thistle and the Crown* (Edinburgh, 1985), 10.

22. NAS, Melville Papers, GD 51/5/749/2, 94, 102, 334; Home Office Papers RH 2/4/118/478.

23. NAS, Seaforth Muniments, GD 46/4/17/57/183; Melville Papers, GD 51/5/686/1, 2, 89, 120, 258, 457, 465.

24. NAS, Melville Papers, GD 51/5/684; NLS, Melville Papers, MS 9370, f. 3; British Library, Peel Papers, Add MSS 40317, f. 18.

25. NLS, Melville Papers, MS 11, f. 79; I.F. Maciver, 'The General Assembly of the Church, the State and Society in Scotland 1815–1843', unpublished M. Litt. Thesis, University of Edinburgh, 1977.

26. NAS, Melville Papers, GD 51/1/136/1; NLS, Melville Papers, MS 19301, f. 136; G. Rose, *Observations concerning the Public Expenditure and the Influence of the Crown* (London, 1810), 59.

27. NLS Melville Papers, MS 10, f. 13; J.P. Wood Papers, MS 3105, f. 69; NAS, Melville Papers, GD 51/17/74b, 2/437/10; Boyle Papers, Kelburn, Ayrshire 9/8/9 & 41, 9/24/17.

28. NAS, Melville Papers, GD 51/5/722.

29. Ibid., GD 51/17/17.

30. NLS, Trotter Papers MS 20269, 592.

31. NAS, Melville Papers, GD 51/17/77, 266; *Letters of Scott,* VIII, 469.

32. NLS, Letters to Scott, MS 1901, f. 179.

33. *Parliamentary Debates*, XXII, col. 1159; J. Laurie, 'Reminiscences of a Town Clerk', *Book of the Old Edinburgh Club*, XIV (1925), 265–6; *The Letters of Sir Walter Scott*, ed. H.J.C. Grierson (London, 1932), IV, 370.

34. British Library, Liverpool Papers, Add MSS 38296, f. 56; H. Cockburn, *Memorials of his Time* (Edinburgh, 1856), 454.

35. NAS, Melville Papers GD 51/5/496.

36. *Parliamentary Debates,* XXX, col. 585.

37. C.H. Paton, 'The Eighteenth Century and Later', in Stair Society, *An Introduction to Scottish Legal History* (Edinburgh, 1958), 54; T.B. Smith, *British Justice, the Scottish contribution* (London, 1961), 73 *et seq.*; A. Murray, 'Administration and Law', in T.I. Rae (ed.), *The Union of 1707, its impact on Scotland* (Glasgow & London, 1974), 51.

38. *Parliamentary Debates,* XXXV, col. 729; R.G. Thorne (ed.), *The House of Commons 1790–1820* (London, 1986), IV, 514; W.M. Roach, 'Radical Reform Movements in Scotland from 1815 to 1822', unpublished Ph.D. thesis, University of Glasgow (1970), 75.

39. NAS, Home Office Papers, RH 2/4/116/49, 117/268; Roach, 'Radical Reform Movements', 76, 80–1, 84–8, 118, 135.

40. NLS, Melville Papers, MS 10, ff. 160 *et seq.*

41. NLS, Melville Papers, MS 1054, f. 1073; NAS, Melville Papers, GD 51/2/609; Home Office Papers, RH 2/4/126/627.

42. NLS, Melville Papers, MS 10, f. 156; St Andrews University Library. MS 4712; NAS, Home Office Papers, RH 2/4/131/313. 135/163; M. Mackay, *Memoir of James Ewing* (Glasgow, 1866), 46; G.W.T. Omond, *The Lord Advocates of Scotland, from the close of the fifteenth century to the passing of the Reform Bill* (Edinburgh, 1883), 258–60; *Letters of Scott,* VI, 16.

43. *Letters of Scott,* V, 467.

44. Cockburn, *Memorials,* chs. 6 & 7.

45. Cockburn, *Journal,* 154–5.

46. Cockburn, *Memorials,* 465–7.

47. *Extracts from the Records of the Burgh of Glasgow,* ed. J.D. Marwick (Glasgow, 1881), XI, 421–2; H. Muir, *Reminiscences and Sketches . . . of Rutherglen* (Glasgow, 1890), 48–54.

48. J. Irving, *Book of Dumbartonshire* (Edinburgh, 1879), I, 332–3; Glasgow City Archives, Campbell of Succoth MSS, TD 219/11/54; Wellington Papers, University of Southampton Library, WP1/1185/19.

49. *Glasgow Herald,* 13, 16 May 1831.

50. Scott, *Journal,* 736–7; *Troja fuit* is an allusion to Virgil, *Aeneid,* II, 326, 'Troy has been', i.e. a glorious era is over. 'Burke Sir Walter' means suffocate him, deal with him in the same way as William Burke had dispatched his victims. The Whig 'puppy' was Sir William Eliott of Stobs.

51. *The Times,* 31 May 1831.

52. Brougham MSS, University College London, letter from J. Loch, Feb. 4, 1831; NAS, Sutherland Papers, GD 258/215, letter from J. Loch, March 16, 1831.

53. Cockburn, *Journal,* I, 14–15; G.W.T. Omond, *Arniston Memoirs* (Edinburgh, 1887), 351.

54. NLS, Melville Papers, MS 2, f. 175.

55. Cockburn, *Memorials,* 463.

56. D. Stewart, 'Account of the Life and Writings of Adam Smith', in A. Smith, *Essays on Philsophical Subjects,* eds. W.P.D. Wightman, J.C. Bryce & I.S. Ross (Oxford, 1980), 310.

11 Dominance: 'Out of the house of bondage'

1. M.E. Chamberlain, *Lord Aberdeen: a political biography* (London & New York, 1983), 81–8.

2. Ibid., 427.

3. Ibid., 428.

4. *Parliamentary Debates, House of Commons,* Dec. 16, 1852, col. 1666.

5. Chamberlain, *Aberdeen,* ch. 26.

6. Ibid., 531.

7. Ibid., 384–5.

8. I.G.C. Hutchison, *A Political History of Scotland 1832–1924* (Edinburgh, 1986), ch. 5.

9. NLS, Abercromby Papers, MS 24747, 9 May 1839.

10. A. Taylor Innes, 'Why I am a Liberal', in A. Reid (ed.), *Why I am a Liberal* (London, 1887), 160.

11. M. Dyer: *Men of Property and Intelligence, the Scottish electoral system prior to 1884* (Aberdeen, 1996), 56–9, 94–7, 143–53; *Capable Citizens and Improvident Democrats, the Scottish electoral system 1884–1929* (Aberdeen, 1996), 8–9.

12. H. Cockburn, *Journal* (Edinburgh, 1874), I, 5.

13. W. Ferguson, 'The Reform Act (Scotland) of 1832, intention and effect, *Scottish Historical Review,* XLV (1968), 113.

14. H. Cockburn, *Letters on the Affairs of Scotland* (Edinburgh, 1874), 400.

15. Advocates' MSS 9.1.8, Feb. 13, Feb. 28, June 30, Sept. 9, 1831.

16. H. Cockburn, *Life of Francis Jeffrey* (Edinburgh, 1852), 355.

17. NLS, Jeffrey Papers, MS 23220, 234–6.

18. NLS, Cockburn Papers, deposit 235, box 2, 20.

19. Advocates' MSS 9.1.8, Feb. 12, 1832.

20. M.R.G. Fry, *The Dundas Despotism* (Edinburgh, 1992), 382–4.

21. National Records of Scotland (hereinafter NRS), Melville Papers, GD 51/17/338.

22. Advocates' MSS 9.1.8, June 25, 1831.

23. Cockburn, *Journal*, I, 265; NLS, Cockburn Papers, deposit 235, box 1, March 6, 1831.

24. Advocates' MSS 9.1.10, Aug. 1, 1833.

25. Cockburn, *Letters*, 497.

26. NLS, Cockburn Papers, deposit 235, box 1, July 8, 1833.

27. Advocates' MSS 9.1.8, Nov. 7, 1831.

28. NLS, J.A. Murray Papers, MS 19736.

29. NLS, Jeffrey Papers, MS 23220, 24, 31, 49.

30. Ibid., 175.

31. NLS, Cockburn Papers, deposit 235, box 1, Feb. 25, 1833.

32. NLS, Jeffrey Papers, MS 23221, May 10, July 22 & Nov. 29, 1831.

33. Cockburn, *Journal,* I, 26.

34. Ibid., II, 294–5.

35. NLS, Abercromby Papers, MS 24753, Feb. 11, 1836.

36. NLS, Rutherfurd Papers, MS 9701, Feb. 28, 1837, April 6, 1853.

37. Ibid., MS 9687, May 3, 1839.

38. James Ferguson of Pitfour, MP for Aberdeenshire 1790–1820, see R.G. Thorne (ed.), *The House of Commons 1790–1820* (London, 1986), 645.

39. NLS, Rutherfurd Papers, MS 9694, July 2, 1840.

40. Sir G. Douglas & Sir G.D. Ramsay (eds), *The Panmure Papers* (London, 1908), 10–11.

41. NLS, Rutherfurd Papers, MS 9697, March 3, May 14, July 3, 1838, March 22, 1842; Douglas & Ramsay, *Panmure Papers*, 24.

42. A.C. Lowell, *Government of England* (London, 1908), I, xxv.

43. M.D. Young, 'A Man of no Common Stamp: Sir William Gibson Craig of Riccarton, Lord Clerk Register of Scotland 1862–1878', in H.L. MacQueen (ed.), *Stair Miscellany IV* (Edinburgh, 2004), 299.

44. NLS, Cockburn Papers, deposit 235, March 30, 1834.

45. NLS, Rutherfurd Papers, MS 9710, Jan. 5, 1838, and a letter of uncertain date, but 1838.

46. Ibid., MS 9689, Nov. 11, 1848.

47. PP XVIII 1870, *Report of the Commissioners appointed to inquire into Civil Departments, Scotland,* 47 *et seq.*, QQ 553, 558, 561; NRS 8/93/3.

48. G.P. Gooch (ed.), *The Later Correspondence of Lord John Russell* (London, 1925), II, 121–2.

49. F. Charteris, Earl of Wemyss and March, *Memories 1818–1912* (Edinburgh, 1912), 260–6.

50. M.R.G. Fry, *Patronage and Principle, a political history of modern Scotland* (Aberdeen, 1987), 74–5.

51. J. Brash, *Papers on Scottish Electoral Politics 1832–1854* (Edinburgh, 1974), xxxix–xl.
52. NLS, J.J. Reid Manuscripts, MS 19623, ff. 87–8.
53. NLS, Ellice Papers, f. 161.
54. G.W.T. Omond, *The Lord Advocates of Scotland 1834–1880* (London, 1914), 269–70.
55. Hutchison, *Political History*, 94–5.
56. Omond, *Lord Advocates,* 275–6.
57. *Hansard,* 3rd series, CCX, 6 June 1872, col. 1295. There is no further reference in *Hansard* that might be construed as bearing on the linguistic question. Possibly it was mentioned otherwise during proceedings in committee of which no record survives. But if these reflected the tenor of debates on the floor of the House of Commons, the main concern was with religious rather than linguistic contention.
58. A. Mitchell, *Political and Social Movements in Dalkeith* (Dalkeith, 1883), 73.
59. Hutchison, *Political History*, table 5.1, 132.
60. PP XVIII 1870, 15 *et seq.*, QQ 5, 6, 9, 55, 72.
61. Ibid., 52 *et seq.*, QQ 576, 583, 900.
62. *Hansard*, CCIX, col. 1879, 12 March 1872.
63. Ibid., CCXXXII, col. 930, 23 February 1877.
64. NLS, F.S. Oliver Papers, MS 24803 (no date).
65. The best account is in L. McKinstry, *Rosebery, statesman in turmoil* (London, 2005), ch. 4.
66. NLS, Rosebery Papers, MS 10077, Feb. 5, 1881.
67. *Hansard, House of Lords,* 13 June 1881.
68. Quoted in R. Crewe-Milnes, Marquess of Crewe, *Lord Rosebery* (London, 1931), 139.
69. British Library, Gladstone Papers, Add MS 44288, Aug. 1, 1881.
70. *Gladstone Diaries,* Dec. 11, 1882.
71. British Library, Gladstone Papers, Add MS 44288, May 18 & June 27, 1882.
72. Ibid., Dec. 6, 1882.
73. J. Vincent (ed.), *The Diaries of Edward Henry Stanley, 15th Earl of Derby* (Oxford, 2003), 351.
74. British Library, Gladstone Papers, Add MSS 44288, June 4, 1883.
75. *The Scotsman,* 17 January 1884.
76. D. Torrance, *The Scottish Secretaries* (Edinburgh, 2005), 5–12.
77. West Sussex Record Office, Goodwood MS 871, Aug. 7, 1885.
78. H.J. Hanham, 'The Creation of the Scottish Office 1881–1887', *Juridical Review*, X (1965), 229.
79. West Sussex Record Office, Goodwood MS 871, Aug. 13, 1885.

12 Division: 'The masses against the classes'

1. K.O. Morgan, *Keir Hardie, radical and socialist,* (London, 1975), 4.

2. Ibid., 5.

3. Ibid., 7–9.

4. W. Adamson, *The Life of the Revd James Morison* (London, 1898), 238.

5. F. Reid, 'Keir Hardie's Conversion to Socialism', in A. Briggs & J. Saville (eds), *Essays in Labour History 1886–1923* (London, 1972), 23: K.O. Morgan, 'The Merthyr of Keir Hardie', in G. Williams (ed.), *Merthyr Politics* (Cardiff, 1966), 67.

6. PP X 1873, *Select Committee on Coal,* Q4624.

7. *Ardrossan and Saltcoats Herald,* July 22, 1882.

8. NRS, Rules of the Ayrshire Miners' Federation, FS 7/3.

9. Morgan, *Hardie,* 23–31.

10. D. Lowe, *Souvenirs of Scottish Labour* (Glasgow, 1919).

11. J.G. Kellas, 'The Mid-Lanark By-Election (1888) and the Scottish Labour Party', *Parliamentary Affairs,* IV (1964), 325 *et seq.*

12. Morgan, *Keir Hardie,* 54–5.

13. H. Pelling, *The Origins of the Labour Party* (London, 1984), 45.

14. Lowe, *Souvenirs,* ch. 1; J. Paton, *Proletarian Pilgrimage* (London, 1935), 75 *et seq.*

15. G. Morton, *Unionist Nationalism, governing urban Scotland 1830–1860* (East Linton, 1999).

16. G. Morton, 'Scotland is Britain, the Union and unionist nationalism 1807–1907', *Journal of Scottish and Irish Studies,* I (2008), 127–41.

17. T. Brown (ed.), *Annals of the Disruption* (Edinburgh, 1876), 69.

18. C. Kidd, *Subverting Scotland's Past, Scottish Whig historians and the creation of an Anglo-British identity 1689–1830* (Cambridge, 1993), ch. 7.

19. H.J. Hanham, 'Mid-century Scottish Nationalism, romantic and radical', in R. Robson (ed.), *Ideas and Institutions of Victorian Britain* (London, 1967), 160.

20. *The Times,* 4 December 1856.

21. A.J. Jackson, *Home Rule, an Irish history* (London, 2003), 69 *et seq.*

22. S. Wallace, *John Stuart Blackie, Scottish scholar and patriot* (Edinburgh, 2006), 189.

23. Scottish Liberal Association MSS, Edinburgh University Library, Jan. 11, 1888.

24. J. Handley, *The Irish in Modern Scotland* (Cork, 1946), J. F. McCaffrey, 'The Irish Vote in Glasgow in the later Nineteenth Century', *Innes Review,* XXI (1970) and 'The Origins of Liberal Unionism in the West of Scotland, *Scottish Historical Review,* L (1971), W.M. Walker, 'Irish Immigrants in Scotland, their priests, politics and parochial life', *Historical Journal,* XV (1972).

25. McCaffrey, 'Origins', 47; D.C. Savage, 'Scottish Politics 1885–1886', *Scottish Historical Review,* XL (1961), 118–35.

26. I.G.C. Hutchison, *A Political History of Modern Scotland* (Edinburgh, 1986), 164–76.

27. I. McKean & A. McMillan, *State of the Union* (Oxford, 2005), ch. 4.

28. I. Hamilton-Gordon, Marchioness of Aberdeen, *Lord Tweedmouth 1849–1909, notes and recollections* (London, 1909), 42; G.M. Trevelyan, *Sir George Otto Trevelyan, a memoir* (London, 1932), 120.

29. R. Schroeder, *Max Weber, democracy and modernisation* (Basingstoke, 1998), 138.

30. W. Ferris, 'The Candidates of the Liberal Unionist Party', *Parliamentary History,* XXX (2011), 142–57.

31. W.E. Gladstone, *Speeches on the Irish Question,* (Edinburgh, 1886), 292.

32. McCaffrey, 'Origins', 71.

33. B. Porter, *Absent-minded Imperialists, Empire, society and culture in Britain* (Oxford, 2004), 225 *et seq.*

34. W.H. Fraser & I. Maver (eds), *Glasgow, II, 1830–1912* (Manchester, 1998), 386.

35. L. McIver, *Trade Unionism, an address to the electors* (Beaufort, 1891), 3–4. McIver was Unionist MP for Edinburgh South.

36. I. Cawood, *The Liberal Unionist Party, a history* (London, 2012), 181.

37. Marwick also edited and published volumes of extracts from the manuscript records of Glasgow. He had initiated the same project for Edinburgh where he served in an earlier phase of his career. He was an Orcadian by birth, and to that extent neutral as between the two cities. In any event Scottish historians, too, owe him an eternal debt of gratitude.

38. *Who's Who in Glasgow* (Glasgow, 1909), 142.

39. See Smart's evidence to the Royal Commission on the Poor Law, 1910 Cmnd 4978, minutes of evidence, VI, 127.

40. W. Smart, *Second Thoughts of an Economist* (London, 1916), 103.

41. *Falkirk Herald,* 27 July 1895, cited in Hutchison, *Political History,* 202–3.

42. For the background, see J.G. Kellas, 'The Crofters' War', *History Today,* XII (1962), 281–8; H.J. Hanham, 'The Problem of Highland Discontent', *Transactions of the Royal Historical Society,* 5th series, XIX (1969), 21–65; J. Hunter, 'The Politics of Highland Land Reform 1873–1895, *Scottish Historical Review,* LIII (1974), 45–68.

43. E. Richards, *Debating the Highland Clearances* (Edinburgh, 2007), 223.

44. Hatfield House MSS, 3M/E, June 27, 1895.

45. A. Tindley, 'Actual Pinching and Suffering, estate responses to poverty in Sutherland 1845–1886', *Scottish Historical Review,* XC (2011), 236–56.

46. Cawood, *Liberal Unionist Party,* 195.

47. E.H.H. Green, *The Crisis of Conservatism, the politics, economics and ideology of the British Conservative party 1880–1914* (London, 1996), 2006.

48. *The Scotsman,* 6 December 1912.

49. L. McKinstry, *Rosebery, statesman in turmoil* (London, 2005), ch. 14.

50. Ibid., ch. 10.

51. J. Kellas, 'The Liberal Party in Scotland 1876–1895', *Scottish Historical Review*, XLV (1965), 1–5.

52. *Rectorial Addresses given at the University of St Andrews*, ed. W. Knight (London, 1894), 202–3.

53. NLS, Rosebery Papers, MS 10001, ff. 31–2.

54. J. Joliffe, *Raymond Asquith, life and letters* (London, 1980), 156.

55. A.M. Davey, 'Scotland the Brave 1899–1902', *Journal of the South African Military History Society*, VI (1984), 26–40.

56. M.R.G. Fry, *Patronage and Principle, a political history of modern Scotland* (Aberdeen, 1987), 118.

57. McKinstry, *Rosebery*, ch. 15.

58. J. Kellas, *Modern Scotland* (London, 1968), 179–87.

59. J. Wilson, *CB, a life of Sir Henry Campbell-Bannerman* (London, 1973), 349.

60. Ibid., 356, 365.

61. Letter to *The Times*, 21 February 1902.

62. NRS, Novar Papers, March 27, 1903.

63. R.J.Q. Adams, *Balfour, the last grandee* (London, 2007), 240.

64. R.B. Haldane, *An Autobiography* (London, 1929), 158–9.

65. R.R. James, *Rosebery* (London, 1963), 465.

66. E. Biagini, *British Democracy and Irish Nationalism 1876–1906* (Cambridge, 2007), 220.

67. Wilson, *CB*, 497.

68. J. Brown, 'Scottish and English Land Legislation 1905–1911', *Scottish Historical Review*, XLVII (1968), 72–85.

69. M. Sinclair, *The Rt Hon John Sinclair, Lord Pentland, a memoir* (London, 1928), 67.

70. J. Scott, *The Law of Smallholdings in Scotland* (Edinburgh, 1933), 199.

71. *Hansard*, 4th series, II, cols. 165–89.

72. Fry, *Patronage and Principle*, 126.

73. *Hansard*, 4th series, CLXXXVI, cols. 1353–93.

74. *Brewers' Journal*, LVI (1921), 1.

75. Fry, *Patronage and Principle*, 127–8.

76. NLS, Haldane Papers, MS 5909, ff. 66–7.

77. J.A.M. Macdonald, 'The Constitutional Controversy and Federal Home Rule'. *Nineteenth Century*, LXX (1911), 33–43.

78. P. Jalland, 'United Kingdom Devolution 1910–1914, political panacea or tactical diversion?', *English Historical Review*, XCIV (1979), 757–85.

79. G.R. Searle, *The Quest for National Efficiency, a study in British social and economic thought* (Oxford, 1971), 95 *et seq.*

80. J. Buchan, *Memory Hold-the-Door* (London, 1940), 146.

81. For the political sequel, see C.M.M. Macdonald, *Whaur Extremes Meet, Scotland's twentieth century* (Edinburgh, 2009), pt. 3.

13 Things: 'The light of truth and beauty'

1. M. Moss, J.F. Munro & R.H. Trainor, *University, City and State, the University of Glasgow since 1870* (Edinburgh, 2000), 33 *et seq.*
2. *Glasgow Herald*, 10 November 1868.
3. Moss et al., *University*, 39.
4. University of Glasgow, *The Curious Diversity, Glasgow University on Gilmorehill, the first hundred years* (Glasgow, 1970), 21.
5. M. Higgs, A. Riches & E. Williamson, *The Buildings of Scotland: Glasgow* (London, 1990), 335.
6. University of Glasgow, *Curious Diversity*, 11.
7. M. Glendinning, R. MacInnes & A. MacKechnie, *A History of Scottish Architecture: from the Renaissance to the Present Day* (Edinburgh, 2002), 276–85.
8. D. Macgibbon & T. Ross, *The Ecclesiastical Architecture of Scotland* (Edinburgh 1897), III, 534–624.
9. G. Stamp (ed.), *The Light of Truth and Beauty, the lectures of Alexander 'Greek' Thomson, architect, 1817–1875* (Glasgow, 1999), 54.
10. Ibid., 78, 83.
11. M.R.G. Fry, *Edinburgh, a history of the city* (London, 2009), 308–9.
12. R, Graham, *Robert Adam, arbiter of elegance* (Edinburgh, 2009); J. Macaulay, *The architecture of James Gillespie Graham* (Edinburgh, 1977).
13. Glendinning, MacInnes & MacKechnie, *History of Scottish Architecture*, 120 *et seq.*
14. D. Gifford, C. McWilliam & D. Walker, *The Buildings of Scotland: Edinburgh,* (London, 1984), 282–3, 301, 367–8.
15. A.J. Youngson, *The Making of Classical Edinburgh 1750–1840* (Edinburgh, 1966).
16. Gifford, McWilliam & Walker, *Edinburgh,* 378–9.
17. R. Rodgers, *The Transformation of Edinburgh* (Cambridge, 2001), 270.
18. Gifford, McWilliam & Walker, *Edinburgh,* 448, 474–5, 562–3, 646
19. Fry, *Edinburgh,* 309.
20. P. Savage, *Lorimer and the Edinburgh Craft Designers* (Edinburgh, 1980); L.M. Shen, *A Comment on Tradition, Robert S. Lorimer's furniture design* (n.p, 1982); H. Richardson & G. Lord, *Lorimer and his Craftsmen* (Edinburgh, 1986).
21. C. Hussey, *The Work of Sir Robert Lorimer* (London, 1931), 106.
22. Higgs, Riches & Williamson, *Glasgow,* 48–51.
23. G. Stamp, 'A View from the Bay Window', in S. McKinstry & G. Stamp (eds), *'Greek' Thomson* (Edinburgh, 1994), 228.

24. R. McFadzean, *The Life and Work of Alexander Thomson* (London, 1979).

25. J. Summerson, 'On Discovering Greek Thomson', in McKinstry & Stamp, *'Greek' Thomson*, 3.

26. G. Stamp, 'A View from the Bay Window', 224.

27. Higgs, Riches & Williamson, *Glasgow*, 545–60.

28. *The British Architect*, XIX (1888), 222; J. McKean, 'Thomson's City', in S. McKinstry & G. Stamp (eds), *'Greek' Thomson*, 103–10.

29. *The British Architect*, XIX (1888), 238.

30. Hence the section devoted to Glasgow in the Musée d'Orsay, Paris; there is no equivalent in London.

31. T. Mackay, *The Life of Sir John Fowler, engineer* (London, 1900), 110.

32. J. Kinchin, 'Glasgow, the dark daughter of the north', in P. Greenhalgh (ed.), *Art Nouveau 1890–1914* (London, 2000), 311–15.

33. R.P. Robertson (ed.) *Charles Rennie Mackintosh, the architectural papers* (Glasgow, 1990), 222.

34. R. Billcliffe, *Mackintosh Watercolours* (London, 1978), 9.

35. Burrell Collection, PR.1977.13.ar.

36. Higgs, Riches & Williamson, *Glasgow*, 344.

37. C.R. Mackintosh, 'Scotch Baronial Architecture', paper to Glasgow Architectural Association, 1891, Hunterian Museum Archive, MS F(c).

38. Higgs, Riches & Williamson, *Glasgow*, 213, 228–30.

39. See http://www.mackintoshchurch.com.

40. H.J. Barnes & D.P. Bliss, *Glasgow School of Art and Charles Rennie Mackintosh* (Glasgow, 1988).

41. J. Cairney, *The Quest for Charles Rennie Mackintosh* (Edinburgh, 2004), 251.

42. A.J. Durie, 'The Markets for Scottish Linen 1730–1775', *Scottish Historical Review*, LII (1973), 30–49.

43. D. Angeli, *Storia romana di trent'anni 1770–1800* (Milan, 1931), 276 *et seq.*

44. I once had in my own possession a painting by Alexander Nasmyth of Melville Castle in Midlothian. It was of the old Melville Castle, dating from the sixteenth century, not the new Melville Castle, standing on the same site, built by James Playfair for Henry Dundas in 1787; which gives a *terminus ad quem* for the painting. Probably Dundas commissioned it to commemorate a historic building he was about to have demolished.

45. Gifford, McWilliam & Walker, *Edinburgh*, 404.

46. D. Macmillan, *Scottish Art 1460–2000* (Edinburgh & London, 2000), 190.

47. A. Cunningham, *Lives of the Most Eminent British Painters* (London, 1879–80), I, 459–89; II, 6.

48. W.R. Andrew, *Life of Sir Henry Raeburn* (London, 1896), ch. 1.

49. Ibid., 97–160.

50. *Journal of Sir Walter Scott*, ed. W.E.K. Anderson (Oxford, 1972), 286.

51. R.L. Stevenson, *Virginibus Puerisque* (London, 1881), 114.

52. W. Scott, *The Antiquary* (Edinburgh, 1816), ch. 31; Cunningham, *Lives,* II, 6.

53. Macmillan, *Scottish Art,* 176.

54. A. Cunningham, *The Life of Sir David Wilkie* (London, 1843), II, 184, 376–7; III, 503.

55. *Robert Burns, the complete poetical works,* ed. J.A. Mackay (Alloway, 1988), 320.

56. T.M. Kelley, 'J.M.W. Turner, Napoleonic Allegory and Romantic Allegory', *English Literary History,* LVIII (1991), 351–82.

57. E. Gordon, *The Making of the Royal Scottish Academy* Edinburgh, 1988), 9–14.

58. G. Harvey, *Notes on the Early History of the Royal Scottish Academy* (Edinburgh, 1873).

59. E. Gordon, *The Royal Scottish Academy 1826–1976* (Edinburgh, 1976), ch. 1.

60. R. Billcliffe, *The Glasgow Boys* (London, 2008).

61. Macmillan, *Scottish Art,* ch. 14.

62. R. Marks, *Burrell, portrait of a collector* (Glasgow, 1988).

63. W.B. Scott, *Autobiographical Notes,* ed. W. Minto (London, 1892).

64. M. Bone, *Muirhead Bone 1876–1953* (London & New York, 1984).

65. Fine Art Society, *The Scottish Colourists: Cadell, Hunter, Fergusson, Peploe* (London, 2000).

66. J.D. Fergusson, *Modern Scottish Painting* (Glasgow, 1943), introduction. The Fergusson Gallery in Perth is devoted to his art.

67. T. Hewlett, *Francis Cadell, the life and times of a Scottish Colourist* (London, 1988).

68. E. Cumming, F. Fowle & A. Strang, *S.J. Peploe* (London & New Haven, CT, 2012).

69. J.C. Mackenzie, *The Scottish Colourists: Hunter* (London, 2012), 3.

70. F. Gilot, *Matisse et Picasso, une amitié* (Paris, 1991).

71. For the sequel, see C.M.M. Macdonald, *Whaur Extremes Meet, Scotland's twentieth century* (Edinburgh, 2009), 301–4.

14 Words: 'Its own way of speaking and thinking'

NB Most of the novelists mentioned below have been published in so many editions that it might be rather inconvenient than convenient for the reader if I gave the exact page references of quotations. For *works of fiction only*, therefore, I make reference to the relevant chapter and nothing more.

1. K.M.E. Murray, *Caught in the Web of Words, James Murray and the Oxford English Dictionary* (New Haven, CT, 1977), 80.

2. G. Martineau, *Lucien Bonaparte, prince de Canino* (Paris, 1989).

3. Murray, *Web of Words,* 69–71.

4. J. Jamieson, *Etymological Dictionary of the Scottish Language* (Edinburgh, 1808), preface.

5. Murray, *Web of Words,* 81.

6. Ibid.

7. J.A.H. Murray, *The Dialect of the Southern Counties of Scotland* (London, 1873), 74.

8. Ibid., 75–6.

9. J. Wilson, *Lowland Scotch, as spoken in the lower Strathearn district of Perthshire* (Oxford, 1915), 13.

10. J. Buchan et al., *The Scots Tongue* (London, 1924), 8.

11. C. Jones, 'Phonology', in C. Jones (ed.), *The Edinburgh History of the Scots Language* (Edinburgh, 1997), 267.

12. *The Vulgarities of Speech Corrected, with elegant expressions for provincial and vulgar English, Scots and Irish* (London, 1826), 227.

13. *The Journal of Sir Walter Scott,* ed. W.E.K. Anderson (London, 1972), 325.

14. J. Heiton, *The Castes of Edinburgh* (Edinburgh, 1861), 57.

15. H. Cockburn, *Memorials of his Time* (Edinburgh, 1856), 57.

16. E. B. Ramsay, *Reminiscences of Scottish Life and Character* (Edinburgh, 1858), 48.

17. J. Grant, *Cassell's Old and New Edinburgh* (London, Paris & New York, 1883), III, 62.

18. *Vulgarities*, 273.

19. Murray, *Dialect*, 187.

20. Ibid., 192.

21. Ch. 5.

22. Ch. 26.

23. Especially in the writings of Prof. Thomas Devine.

24. C.W.J. Withers, *Gaelic in Scotland 1698–1981, the geographical history of a language* (Edinburgh, 1984), 97.

25. *New Statistical Account*, XIV, 95–6.

26. PP XVII 1865, *Reports from Commissioners, Education (Scotland),* 365.

27. Withers, *Gaelic in Scotland*, 99; N.C. Dorian, *Language Death, the life cycle of a Scottish Gaelic dialect* (Philadelphia, 1981), 39–40.

28. E. Muir, *Scott and Scotland* (London, 1936), 110.

29. G. Tulloch, *The Language of Sir Walter Scott* (London, 1980), ch. 8.

30. J. Calvin, *Institution de la religion chrestienne*, French edition (Paris, 1957–63), III, ch. 21, 'De l'élection éternelle : par laquelle Dieu en a prédestiné les uns à salut, et les autres à condamnation', 7.

31. John Buchan wrote a classic biography (London, 1932) and an excellent recent evocation is S. Kelly, *Scott-land, the man who invented a nation* (Edinburgh, 2010).

NOTES

32. C. McCracken-Fletcher, *Possible Scotlands, Walter Scott and the story of tomorrow* (Oxford, 2005), 120.
33. These are the concluding words of 'Chapter First, Introductory'.
34. Ch. 26.
35. Ch. 32.
36. Ch. 1, 'Being Introductory'.
37. Ch. 4.
38. Ibid.
39. Ch. 7.
40. P. Garside, 'Popular Fiction and National Tale, hidden origins in Scott's *Waverley*', *Nineteenth-century Literature*, XLVI (1991), 30–53.
41. M. Sankey & D. Szechi, 'Elite Culture and the Decline of Scottish Jacobitism 1716–1745', *Past and Present*, CLXXIII (2001), 90–128.
42. D. Daiches, 'Scott's Achievement as a Novelist', in *Literary Essays* (Edinburgh, 1966), 69–80.
43. Introduction.
44. J. Anderson, 'Sir Walter Scott as Historical Novelist', *Studies in Scottish Literature*, V (1967–8), 21–7.
45. Ch. 23.
46. J. Galt, *Literary Life and Miscellanies* (Edinburgh, 1834), 114.
47. H. Gibault, *John Galt, romancier écossais* (Grenoble, 1979), 91–114.
48. J. MacQueen, 'John Galt and the Analysis of Social History' in A.S. Bell (ed.), *Scott Bicentenary Essays* (Edinburgh, 1972), 172–86.
49. E. Batho, *The Ettrick Shepherd* (Cambridge, 1927).
50. A. Gide, 'Introduction' to Cresset Library edition of J. Hogg, *Private Memoirs and Confessions of a Justified Sinner* (London, 1947), ix.
51. S. Caporaletti, *Il diavolo come metafora, doppio e ambiguità formale nelle* Confessions of a Justified Sinner *di James Hogg* (Lecce, 1992).
52. Cockburn, *Memorials*, 52.
53. *British Weekly*, XII, January 1897.
54. C. Harman, *Robert Louis Stevenson, a biography* (London, 2005), xv.
55. *Cornhill Magazine*, XLIV (1881), 436–43.
56. Harman, *Stevenson*, 108–9, 153, 230–1, 238, 246, 434.
57. J. Calder, *Stevenson and Victorian Scotland* (Edinburgh, 1981).
58. R.L. Stevenson, *The Strange Case of Dr Jekyll and Mr Hyde*, (London, 1888), 20, 31, 51.
59. Ch. 2.
60. C. Lennox, *George Douglas Brown, a memoir* (London, 1903).
61. I. Campbell, *Kailyard* (Edinburgh, 1981), 12–16.
62. Ibid., 86–101.

63. Quoted, ibid, 7–8.

64. W. Donaldson, *The Language of the People, Scots prose from the Victorian revival* (Aberdeen, 1989), introduction.

65. B.A. Booth & E. Mehew (eds), *Letters of Robert Louis Stevenson* (London & New Haven, CT, 1994–5), VII, 352.

66. W. Donaldson, *Popular literature in Victorian Scotland, language, fiction and the press* (Aberdeen, 1986).

67. Campbell, *Kailyard,* 92, 113.

15 Thoughts: 'Still Scotch enough'

1. J.A. Black & G. Chrystal, *The Life of William Robertson Smith* (London, 1912), 438.

2. D.J.A. Clines, *On the Way to the Postmodern: Old Testament essays 1967–1998* (Sheffield, 1998), 23–45.

3. Black & Chrystal, *William Robertson Smith*, 201.

4. Ibid., 444–5.

5. A. Hook & R.B. Sher, *The Glasgow Enlightenment* (East Linton, 1995).

6. J. Carter & J.H. Pittock, *Aberdeen and the Enlightenment* (Aberdeen, 1987).

7. A.C. Chitnis, *The Scottish Enlightenment and Early Victorian English Society* (London, 1986).

8. G.E. Davie, *The Democratic Intellect, Scotland and her universities in the nineteenth century* (Edinburgh, 1961), 101.

9. J. Clarke (ed.), *The Problem of National Education* (London, 1919), 321.

10. C. Smith & M.N. Wise, *Energy and Empire, a biographical study of Lord Kelvin* (Cambridge, 1986).

11. J. Clerk Maxwell, *Treatise on Electricity and Magnetism* (Oxford, 1873), II, 450.

12. A. Einstein, 'Maxwell's Influence on the Evolution of the Idea of Physical Reality', in *James Clerk Maxwell, a commemorative volume* (Cambridge, 1931), 22–44.

13. M. Goldman, *The Demon in the Aether, the story of James Clerk Maxwell* (Edinburgh, 1983).

14. A. Broadie, *A History of Scottish Philosophy* (Edinburgh, 2009), 235–300.

15. T. Reid, *An Inquiry into the Human Mind on the Principles of Common Sense*, ed. D.R. Brookes (Edinburgh, 1997), 255.

16. A. Thomson, *Ferrier of St Andrews, an academic tragedy* (Edinburgh, 1985).

17. C. Craig, 'Beyond Reason: Hume, Seth, Macmurray and Scotland's Post-modernity', in E. Bell & G. Millar (eds), *Scotland in Theory, reflections on culture and literature* (Amsterdam, 2004), 249–83.

18. J.A. Froude, *Thomas Carlyle, a history of the first forty years of his life* (London, 1890), I, 65.

19. T. Carlyle, 'Sir Walter Scott', *London and Westminster Review,* XII, 1837, 42; Froude, *Carlyle,* I, 14–33, II, 95, 214.

20. *The Collected Letters of Thomas and John Carlyle,* ed. C.R. Sanders, VI (Durham NC, 1977), 291.

21. Not till 2000 was there a satisfactory annotated edition of *Sartor Resartus* (University of California, ed. R. Tarr & M. Engel).

22. T. Carlyle, *On Heroes, Hero-Worship and the Heroic in History* (London, 1869), 60.

23. Ibid., 301.

24. T. Carlyle, *Reminiscences* (London, 1881), 203–321.

25. *Contemporary Review,* XVII (1883), 746.

26. Carlyle, *Letters,* 20 February 1847.

27. S.J. Brown, *Thomas Chalmers and the Godly Commonwealth in Scotland* (Oxford, 1982).

28. Chalmers's work; *On the Power, Wisdom and Goodness of God* formed part of the Bridgewater Treatises; see J.M. Robson, 'The Fiat and Finger of God, the Bridgewater Treatises', in R.J. Helmstadter & B.V. Knightman (eds), *Victorian Faith in Crisis* (Stanford CA, 1990).

29. G. Rosie, *Hugh Miller, outrage and order* (Edinburgh, 1981)

30. H. Miller, *My Schools and Schoolmasters* (Edinburgh, 1874), 256.

31. R.S. Porter, 'Charles Lyell and the Principles of the History of Geology', *The British Journal for the History of Science,* XXXII (1976), 91–103.

32. J.A. Secord, *Victorian Sensation, the extraordinary publication, reception and secret authorship of* Vestiges of the Natural History of Creation (Chicago, 2001).

33. Rosie, *Miller,* 56.

34. V. Welter, *Biopolis, Patrick Geddes and the city of life* (London & Cambridge MA, 2002).

35. P. Geddes, *Scottish University, needs and aims* (Perth, 1890), 3.

36. H. Meller, *Patrick Geddes, social evolutionist and city planner* (London, 1993), 81–4.

37. H.G. Kippenberg, *Discovering Religious History in the Modern Age* (Oxford & Princeton, 2002), 72–3.

38. J. McLennan, *Studies in Ancient History* (London, 1876), xxx.

39. T.O. Beidelman, *William Robertson Smith and the Sociological Study of Religion* (Chicago, 1974), 18, 30–9.

40. J. McLennan, *Primitive Marriage* (Edinburgh, 1865), 6.

41. Black & Chrystal, *William Robertson Smith,* 116.

42. Ibid., 143–4.

43. Ibid., 53, 65–6.

44. W. Robertson Smith, *Kinship and Marriage in Early Arabia* (Cambridge, 1885), ch. 8.

45. Kippenberg, *Discovering Religious History,* 117–18.

46. Black & Chrystal, *William Robertson Smith*, 557–79.
47. R. Ackerman, *J.G. Frazer, his life and work* (Cambridge, 1983).
48. R.H. Lowie, *The History of Ethnographical Theory* (New York, 1997), 197–212; Beidelman, *William Robertson Smith*, 25, 42, 58–60; Davie, *Democratic Intellect*, 123.
49. A.B. Bruce, *With Open Face* (London, 1896).
50. M. Dods, *Revelation and Inspiration* (Glasgow, 1877), ch. 2.
51. Draft report by sub-committee anent the memorial on Prof. George Adam Smith's work *Modern Criticism and Preaching of the Old Testament,* United Free Church of Scotland, college committee, 1902.
52. PP XLVIII (1890–1), Financial relations (England, Scotland, Ireland).

Epilogue: 'To perpetuate the tradition'

1. http://www.fife.50megs.com/ceres-history.htm
2. J. Gifford, *Buildings of Scotland: Fife* (London, 1988), 123.
3. P. Mileham (ed.), *Clearly my Duty, the letters of Sir John Gilmour from the Boer War 1900–1901* (East Linton, 1996).
4. A.D. Ogilvie, *The Fife and Forfar Yeomanry* (London, 1921), 8.
5. J. Buchan, *History of the War* (Edinburgh & London, 1915–9), III, 452.
6. Estimates vary, but I use here the one given by T. Royle, *Flowers of the Forest, Scotland and the First World War* (Edinburgh, 2006), 359.

Index

453